Sewing & Knitting
A Reader's Digest step-by-step guide

Reader's Digest

Auckland · London · Montreal · New York · Sydney

Published in 1993 by Reader's Digest (Australia) Pty Ltd
26-32 Waterloo Street, Surry Hills, NSW 2010

National Library of Australia Cataloguing-in-Publication data:

Sewing & knitting.
    Includes index.
    ISBN 0 86438 398 3.
    1. Sewing.   2. Knitting.
646.2

The material in Part 1 of this book originally appeared in
Reader's Digest Complete Guide to Sewing, first published
in 1977, and the material in Part 2 appeared in Reader's Digest
Complete Guide to Needlecraft, first published in 1987.
Both parts have now been revised and brought up to date.

Revised edition created by Barbara Beckett Publishing
14 Hargrave Street, Paddington, NSW 2027

Contents

Necessities of sewing

Having the right tools for the job can make your sewing more successful and enjoyable. This chapter takes you through all the basic equipment, from pins and needles to sewing machines and overlocker machines. There are also sections on zippers, tapes and braids, fasteners and elastics. There is no need to spend a great deal on sewing aids initially. You will find described here the basic items required as well as the more specialised tools you may want to acquire as you become more versatile. A sewing machine can, however, represent a considerable investment, so this chapter explains how a machine works, which stitches and accessories are available to you, and what factors you should consider when choosing a machine. Overlocker machines are also described as they offer the advantage of quick and neat sewing. The chapter concludes with advice on how to organise your sewing area.

Sewing supplies

Measuring devices

The metric system of measurement has been used in sewing for some years now. Fabrics and trimmings are sold by the metre; commercial patterns give measurements in metric figures first, then in imperial figures (eventually, only metric measurements may be used). It is a simple, straightforward system to learn and use. **Make sure that all the measuring devices you buy and use are metric** and

you will find it easy to follow all the instructions given in this book.

The metric symbols are: mm = millimetre/s; cm = centimetre/s; m = metre/s.

Most of the measurements in this book are given in centimetres (cm). Very small measurements—less than one centimetre—are given in millimetres (mm). Very large measurements—for example,

lengths of fabric—are given in metres (m). **These are the only measurements you will ever need to use when sewing.**

Many measuring devices on sale now are marked in metric figures only, but some show both metric and imperial figures. Take care, when using any such dual-marked device, that you do not confuse inches and centimetres.

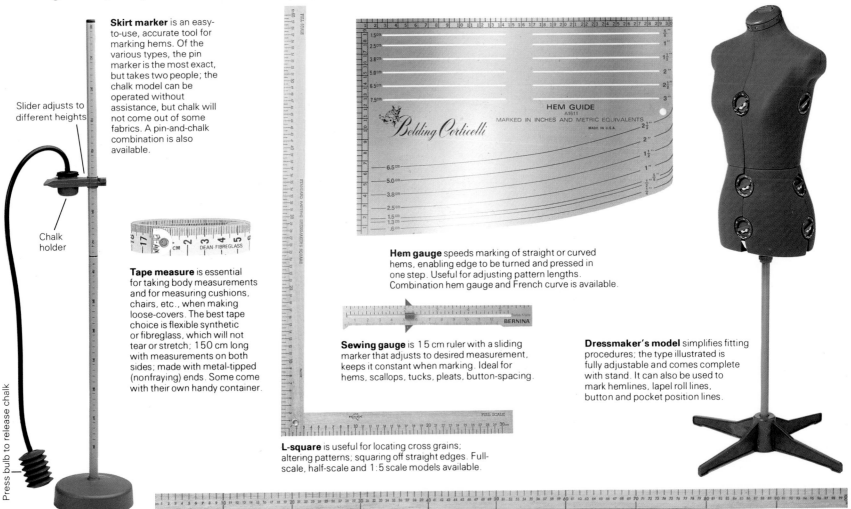

Skirt marker is an easy-to-use, accurate tool for marking hems. Of the various types, the pin marker is the most exact, but takes two people; the chalk model can be operated without assistance, but chalk will not come out of some fabrics. A pin-and-chalk combination is also available.

Slider adjusts to different heights

Chalk holder

Press bulb to release chalk

Tape measure is essential for taking body measurements and for measuring cushions, chairs, etc., when making loose-covers. The best tape choice is flexible synthetic or fibreglass, which will not tear or stretch; 150 cm long with measurements on both sides; made with metal-tipped (nonfraying) ends. Some come with their own handy container.

HEM GUIDE
A1611
MARKED IN INCHES AND METRIC EQUIVALENTS
Belding Corticelli

Hem gauge speeds marking of straight or curved hems, enabling edge to be turned and pressed in one step. Useful for adjusting pattern lengths. Combination hem gauge and French curve is available.

BERNINA

Sewing gauge is 15 cm ruler with a sliding marker that adjusts to desired measurement, keeps it constant when marking. Ideal for hems, scallops, tucks, pleats, button-spacing.

L-square is useful for locating cross grains; altering patterns; squaring off straight edges. Full-scale, half-scale and 1:5 scale models available.

Dressmaker's model simplifies fitting procedures; the type illustrated is fully adjustable and comes complete with stand. It can also be used to mark hemlines, lapel roll lines, button and pocket position lines.

Metric rule is the best device for taking long, straight measurements. Suitable for checking grainlines, marking hems, measuring windows for curtains.

Marking devices

Tailor's chalk wedges are ideal for construction markings and fitting alterations; come in several colours. One pack comes with holder and chalk sharpener; chalk can also be bought in separate packs.

Chalk in pencil form is used like any pencil; makes a thin, accurate line, fine for marking pleats, buttonholes and similar details. Chalk colours include white and pastel shades. A dressmaker's pencil may have a handy brush eraser attached.

Fabric marking pen can be used provided the marks wash away or fade with time. Check before using to make sure marks can be completely removed from the fabric.

Tracing wheel is used with dressmaker's carbon paper to transfer pattern markings to wrong side of fabric. Tracing wheels are suitable for most fabrics, but should be used with care on sheers and loosely woven fabrics.

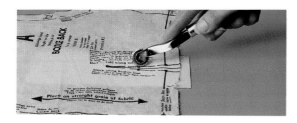

Dressmaker's carbon paper comes in packs containing several colours, including white. Test on a scrap of fabric before using to make sure that markings will not come through to right side of fabric when it is ironed.

Shears and scissors

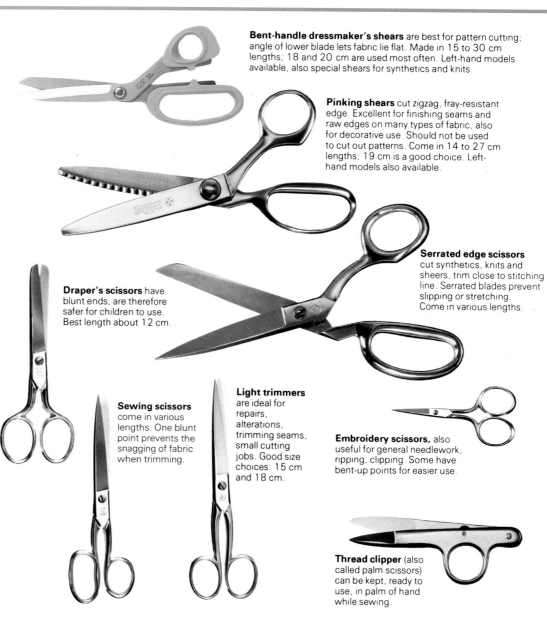

Bent-handle dressmaker's shears are best for pattern cutting; angle of lower blade lets fabric lie flat. Made in 15 to 30 cm lengths; 18 and 20 cm are used most often. Left-hand models available, also special shears for synthetics and knits.

Pinking shears cut zigzag, fray-resistant edge. Excellent for finishing seams and raw edges on many types of fabric, also for decorative use. Should not be used to cut out patterns. Come in 14 to 27 cm lengths; 19 cm is a good choice. Left-hand models also available.

Serrated edge scissors cut synthetics, knits and sheers, trim close to stitching line. Serrated blades prevent slipping or stretching. Come in various lengths.

Draper's scissors have blunt ends, are therefore safer for children to use. Best length about 12 cm.

Sewing scissors come in various lengths. One blunt point prevents the snagging of fabric when trimming.

Light trimmers are ideal for repairs, alterations, trimming seams, small cutting jobs. Good size choices: 15 cm and 18 cm.

Embroidery scissors, also useful for general needlework, ripping, clipping. Some have bent-up points for easier use.

Thread clipper (also called palm scissors) can be kept, ready to use, in palm of hand while sewing.

Sewing supplies

Thread

Thread for constructing a garment should be strong, durable and stretchy. There are three basic cotton threads: soft (untreated), glacé (polished) and mercerised (see explanation in chart below). Synthetic threads are usually made from polyester or nylon; core-spun thread is a mixture of cotton and synthetic fibre.

The best spun polyesters are suitable for any fabric. They do not fray, snap, shrink or rot, and have good stretchability. Polyester is strong, so the thread can be very fine; this means that it slips through the fabric easily and the stitches 'bed down' to create inconspicuous seams.

It is important to match needle and thread sizes. If the needle eye is too small, the thread will be damaged; if the needle eye is too large, the thread will not fill the needle punctures, leaving unsightly holes along the seam.

The chart below defines the most common thread types and gives recommendations for their use. Size numbers are given where they apply. The higher the number, the finer the thread; the median size is 50. Use thread one shade darker than the fabric; for a print or plaid, the dominant colour.

THREAD	FIBRES AND USAGE	THREAD	FIBRES AND USAGE
General purpose	**Polyester**: An all-purpose weight (approximately size 50), suitable for hand and machine sewing on most fabrics, but particularly recommended for woven synthetics, also for knits and other stretch fabrics of any fibre. Most polyester threads have a wax or silicone finish to help them slip through fabric with a minimum of friction. **Cotton**: A medium thickness (size 50) is available in a wide range of colours, including variegated shadings (other sizes made in black and white only although variegated cotton also comes in size 30). Used for machine and hand sewing on light and mediumweight cottons, rayons and linens. Cotton thread is usually mercerised, a finishing process that makes it smooth and lustrous, also helps it to take dye better. The lack of give in cotton thread makes it an unwise choice for knits or other stretchy fabrics, as the stitches tend to pop.	Button and carpet	**Polyester/cotton, linen**: Tough, thick thread made from a polyester core wrapped in cotton, or from linen. Used for hand-sewing jobs requiring super thread strength such as saddle-stitching, repairing carpets. Usually has a glazed finish to enable it to slip easily through heavy fabric.
		Buttonhole twist	**Silk**: Used for topstitching and hand-worked buttonholes, also for decorative hand sewing, including smocking, and for sewing on buttons. Size 40/3, available in a wide range of colours. May be difficult to find.
Soft machine cotton	**Cotton**: A loosely twisted thread, sizes 40 and 50, used for tacking. loose twist makes it easy to break for quick removal from the garment. Available only in white and black. Has no seam.	Elastic	**Nylon/cotton-wrapped rubber**: A thick, very stretchy thread used for shirring on sewing machine. Elastic thread is wound on bobbin only.
Heavy-duty	**Polyester**: Very strong thread, size 30. Comes in a wide range of colours Suitable for hand or machine sewing.	Embroidery	**Stranded cotton**: Six mercerised cotton thread strands twisted loosely together, made for decorative *hand* work. Strands can be separated for very fine work. Sold by the skein in a wide range of colours.
Nylon	**Nylon**: A strong, monofilament thread made in two transparent shades to blend in with light or dark-coloured fabrics. Used for hand and machine sewing of hems. Nylon thread has good elasticity, but it is very difficult to tie the ends off satisfactorily.		**Soft cotton**: Not mercerised; suitable for bold hand embroidery and tapestry work. Sold by the skein. **Mercerised cotton**: Special thread suitable for machine embroidery. Has different sizing: size 30 is medium fine and size 60 is very fine (suitable for pin tucking).
		Metallic	**Metallised synthetic**: Shiny silver or gold-coloured thread, used for decorative stitching by hand or machine.

Pins

Dressmaker's or silk pins come in 25 mm (standard) or 30 mm lengths; can be made from nickel-plated steel, brass, nickel-plated brass, stainless steel. Suitable for most types of fabric.
Lace pins Extra-fine 25 mm pins for delicate fabrics; nickel-plated brass or stainless steel.
Ball-point pins are made from nickel-plated brass or stainless steel. Used for knit fabrics to prevent piercing (and hence breaking) of yarn.
Coloured-head pins (glass- or plastic-headed marking pins) are long (30 mm), fine and easy to see and handle. Stainless steel or nickel-plated steel.
T-pins are convenient for heavy pile fabrics and loose knits; 25 to 50 mm.
Twist pins have plastic heads and a twisted stem; useful for holding loose-covers, etc., in place.
Plastic pins are clear plastic, used for hanging and pleating curtains and draperies.

Metals from which pins are made

Brass: soft metal; does not rust; usually nickel-plated*; retains sharp point for a long time.

Steel: sturdy metal; can rust; usually nickel-plated*; least expensive; can be picked up magnetically.

Stainless steel: strong metal; does not rust; retains sharp point; can be picked up magnetically.

*Nickel plating sometimes leaves a black mark on fabric.

Hand needles

Many different needles are made for hand sewing, each for a specific purpose. They vary according to eye shape (long or round), length (in proportion to eye), and point (sharp, blunt, ball-point or wedge). The chart below describes the basic types. Each embraces a range of sizes; the larger a number, the shorter and finer the needle. Examples are illustrated in comparable sizes to show the proportion from one type to another. For matching needle to job, consider the kind of work being done (some needles are named for their principal purpose, such as 'crewel'), fabric structure (knitted or woven), fabric weight and thread thickness. Generally, a needle should be fine enough to slip easily through fabric, yet heavy enough not to bend or break. Long-eyed needles are designed to accommodate thick thread or several strands. Whatever the type, always work with a clean, well-pointed needle.

GENERAL HAND SEWING

This group of hand needles is used for general-purpose sewing. Most of them are sharp needles and each has a size range sufficient to accommodate most weights of fabric.

Sharps (sizes 3–12) are the hand-sewing needles in most common use. They are medium length and have a round eye. Suitable for almost all fabric weights.

Straws or milliners (sizes 3–12) are longer than others, useful for tacking.

Betweens (sizes 3–10) are also known as quilting needles. Their shorter length enables them to take fine stitches in heavy fabric.

Ball-points (sizes 5–10) resemble sharps except for the point, which is rounded to penetrate between knit yarns.

Calyx-eyes (sizes 4–8) are like sharps but have a slot in place of an eye, for easy threading.

NEEDLECRAFT

This group of hand needles is used primarily for a variety of art and needlecraft purposes, such as embroidery, needlepoint, and decorative beading.

Crewels (sizes 3–12) are sharp, medium-length hand needles used primarily for embroidery work. The long eye allows several strands of embroidery cotton to be threaded at one time.

Chenilles or couching (sizes 18–24) are sharp and heavy for embroidering with yarn.

Beading needles (sizes 10–13) are thin and long for beading and sequin work.

Tapestry needles (sizes 18–24) are heavy and have blunt ends. Used mainly for tapestry work, they can also serve as a bodkin.

DARNING

These needles are used primarily for darning. They vary in length and diameter to accommodate most darning or mending jobs.

Cotton darners (sizes 1–9) are designed for darning with fine cotton or wool.

Double longs (sizes 1–9) are like cotton darners but longer and therefore able to span larger holes.

Knitters or wool needles (2 sizes) are long and heavy for sewing together knitted garment pieces.

HEAVY-DUTY SEWING

These hand needles are ideal for heavy sewing jobs. Both the glover and sailmaker types have wedge-shaped points that pierce leather and leatherlike fabrics in such a way that the holes resist tearing.

Glovers (sizes 3–8) are short, round-eye needles with triangular points that will pierce leather, vinyl or plastic without tearing them.

Sailmakers (sizes 14–17) are like glovers, but their triangular point extends up the shaft. Used on canvas and heavy leather.

Sack or packing needle has curved, wedge-shaped point, used for weaving, upholstery and sewing hessian.

Mattress or lampshade needles (sizes 4 to 8 cm) are used on upholstery, braided rugs, or lampshades—anywhere that a straight needle would be awkward.

Sewing aids

Of the many sewing aids made for home use, some are of course necessities, and some are very handy for general sewing—a needle threader and thimble, for example. Others, such as the loop turner, are needed only now and then for a special task, but are invaluable for that particular job. Then, too, there are the sewing aids, such as needle conditioners and scissor sharpeners, designed to keep equipment in good working order, and those meant to simplify the task of keeping a sewing area neat and tidy, such as pin cushions and magnetic pin holders.

A selection of such sewing aids is shown here; more are to be found on sewing counters, with new ones constantly being produced. When buying sewing tools and supplies, it is wise to begin with a few basic ones, purchasing more when the need arises.

In addition to these specialised sewing aids, you can also use some common household items for sewing jobs. A magnet will pick up stray steel pins and needles. A fine crochet hook is helpful when tying short thread ends or for pulling snags to the wrong side of a knit. Tissue paper is useful for making pattern adjustments and also facilitates sewing slippery or very soft fabrics. Tweezers deftly remove tiny thread ends, tailor's tacks, and tacking stitches. Clear tape is useful for guiding topstitching or holding pattern adjustments in place.

Wire is inserted into needle eye

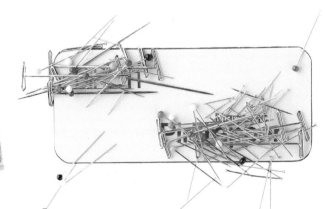

Seam ripper has sharp, curved edge for cutting seams open and a point for picking out threads. Can also be used for slashing machine-worked buttonholes. Use ripper carefully to avoid accidental cutting of fabric.

Needle threader eases threading of hand or machine needles.

An awl or stiletto is a small, sharp instrument used to make the round holes needed for eyelets or keyhole buttonholes. For safety, tool should have snug-fitting cover.

Beeswax is used to strengthen thread for hand sewing and to reduce tangling and knotting. To apply wax, slip the thread through the slots in the container.

Thimble protects middle finger during hand sewing. Comes in various sizes for a snug fit.

Pin trapper is a practical and safe magnetic plate on which to keep steel pins by you while you are sewing.

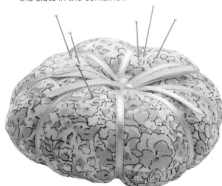

Pin cushion is a safe, handy place to store pins while keeping them accessible. Some have emery pack attached for cleaning pins and needles.

Bodkin is a tool shaped like a long, blunt needle and is used for threading elastic or cord through a casing. Can also be used to turn bias tubing. Bodkin types vary; some have an eye through which elastic or cord can be threaded, others a tweezer or safety pin closure.

Loop turner is a long, wirelike bodkin with a hook at one end for grasping fabric when turning bias tubing to the right side.

Pressing equipment

Pressing is important at every stage of sewing. A good steam iron and a firm, well-covered ironing board are essential; the pieces of equipment shown here are useful additions as they provide the surface areas necessary to press curved, small or hard-to-reach garment areas properly and easily.

Always follow these rules: (1) Press each seam before crossing with another. First press over seamline (to embed stitches) then press open. (2) Use a press cloth to prevent a shine on the fabric; dampen if more steam is needed. See-through press cloths are useful when using iron-on products. (3) Press with a gentle up-and-down motion. (4) Avoid pressing over pins. (5) To finger-press, run your thumb along the opened seamline.

A sleeve board clips onto the ironing board and provides a small flat surface on which seams and details of narrow garment sections such as sleeves and trouser legs can be easily pressed. Also helpful when pressing hard-to-reach areas such as necklines and sleeve caps. Below, sleeve is slipped over board, making its long seam easily accessible.

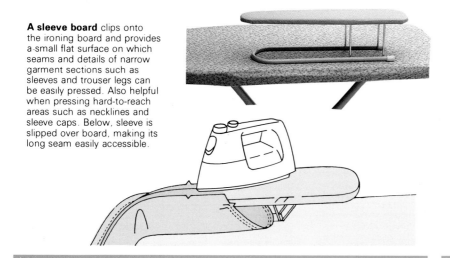

A tailor's ham has rounded surfaces for pressing shaped areas such as bust darts and curved seams; it is also used for moulding collars (as shown at right). To make one, draw a paper pattern about 5 cm larger all round than the face of an iron, in an egg shape. Use the pattern to cut two pieces of calico for lining, one piece of wool and one piece of cotton for outer fabric. Stitch lining and covering in one, with extra row of reinforcing stitches. Pack solidly with filling; use rice, split peas, or sawdust which can be obtained free from most timber yards.

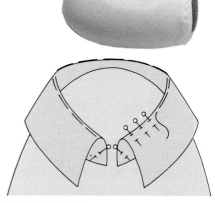

A press mitt, a padded glovelike cushion, is used as a pressing surface for small, curved garment areas; it is especially useful for pressing rounded sleeve caps. It is made with a scorch proof heat-reflecting surface on one side and cotton on the reverse, with a pocket to slip the hand into. Mitt can also be used over the end of a sleeve board.

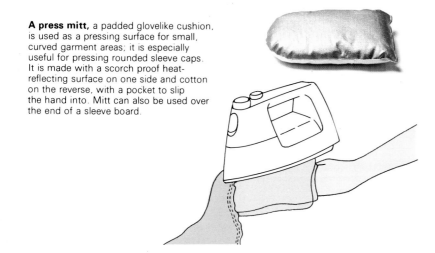

A seam roll is a firmly packed cylindrical cushion, used primarily for pressing long curved seams and seams in very narrow areas. To make one, draw a paper pattern 8 to 12 cm wide and at least 30 cm long; construction is as for tailor's ham, above. Seam roll can either be covered entirely with wool or have wool one side and cotton the other. Either kapok or sawdust would be suitable for padding; *do not* use foam.

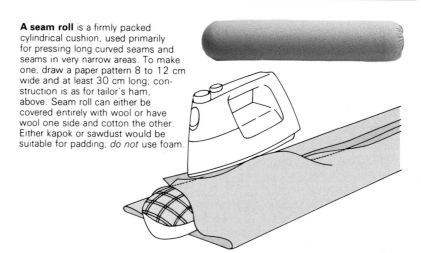

Sewing supplies

Zippers

At first glance it seems difficult to know which type of zipper to choose, but the first step—choice of *style*—narrows the field. The location and type of opening must be considered.

Zippers are made in three basic types: **conventional, open-end** and **invisible.** Along with an illustration of each, the chart gives a description of styles within each group.

The zipper weight should always be compatible with the fabric weight. A zipper's weight is determined by its tape and structure—ladder, chain or spiral. The ladder type, popularly used for skirts and dresses, is a continuous synthetic filament formed into teeth and edged with a poly-cotton tape. The chain consists of individual metal teeth attached to

Chain construction

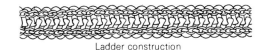

Ladder construction

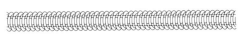

Spiral construction

a poly-cotton tape; the spiral, used for invisible zippers, is a continuous synthetic strand twisted into a coil and attached to a woven or knit synthetic tape. The ladder type, being lightweight and flexible, is ideal for light to mediumweight fabrics. The chain type is slightly more rigid, which can cause buckling on a lightweight fabric and is thus best used on medium to heavy fabrics.

Zipper length is usually stipulated on pattern envelopes. For loose-covers or other articles needing very long zippers, you can either use two, nose to nose, or ask your haberdashery supplier to order a special one.

CONVENTIONAL ZIPPER	STYLE	WEIGHT	STRUCTURE	LENGTH
Conventional zippers, whether metal, nylon or polyester, open at the top and are held together at the bottom. They come in a greater variety of styles than any other zipper type, each named for its most logical use. Some can be interchanged, however, if necessary. A skirt zipper, for instance, can be shortened (see Zippers) and used as a trouser zipper. Size ranges given represent the overall output of all major manufacturers, and can vary within any single brand. Also, size increases do not necessarily come in 1 cm increments; some styles increase in increments of 2 cm or more. Depending on the garment design, application may be by the centred, lapped, exposed or fly-front method (see Zippers).	Skirt / dress	Very light to medium	Metal, nylon or polyester	10–60 cm
	Trouser	Medium to heavy	Metal	13–25 cm
	Jean	Heavy	Metal	13, 15 and 18 cm

OPEN-END ZIPPER	STYLE	WEIGHT	STRUCTURE	LENGTH
Open-end zippers are made to open at both top and bottom, permitting the zipper opening to separate completely. Although used mainly on jackets, they can really be applied to any garment with a completely opened front. Open-end zippers are usually made of nylon. It is possible to get open-end zippers with fancy tabs. The heavyweight jacket, reversible and two-way open-end zippers are usually available on request through most good haberdashery counters, to whatever length required. A centred application is the method generally used.	Jacket and cardigan	Medium	Metal, nylon or polyester	20–60 cm
	Fancy tab	Medium	Nylon	30–60 cm
	Heavyweight jacket	Heavy	Metal	
	Reversible	Heavy	Metal	
	Two-way	Heavy	Metal or nylon	

INVISIBLE ZIPPER	STYLE	WEIGHT	STRUCTURE	LENGTH
Invisible zippers are the newest type of zipper. As the name implies, they are structured differently from other zippers and are applied in a special way so that they disappear into a seam. When properly applied, neither the stitching nor the zipper teeth or coil is visible on the outside of the garment. Invisible zippers are used principally in skirts and dresses but they can go, in general, wherever a conventional zipper might be used, except in a trouser placket. A special zipper foot or a conventional zipper foot may be used for the application of these zippers. The invisible zipper sizes are aggregates (see chart).	No distinction of styles	Light and medium	Metal, nylon or polyester	18–23 cm 30–35 cm 40–45 cm 50–55 cm

Buttons

Button buying involves both decorative and practical considerations. One overriding practical qualification: whether a button is washable or dry-cleanable. Buttons must be compatible with a

Sew-through buttons (4-hole and 2-hole)   Shank button

garment's care requirements. Though made in many shapes and materials, buttons are basically of two types—**shank** and **sew-through**. The shank button has a solid top, with a shank beneath to ac-

Button shell   Cloth cutout   Button back

commodate thicker fabrics and keep the button from pressing too hard against the buttonhole. *Covered* shank buttons can be purchased within limits, but can be made to suit almost any need with do-it-yourself kits like the one shown here.

The sew-through button has either two or four holes through which the button is sewn on. A thread shank can be added (see Attaching buttons).

Pin portion   Button

Jean buttons are not sewn onto the fabric. They consist of two separate parts, a pin portion and a button top, which are positioned on either side of the fabric and then hammered together. Buttonhole is then worked in the usual way. Jean buttons are suitable for jeans, overalls and work clothes, and can be useful time savers.

Snap fasteners

Prongs

Top snap   Bottom snap

Back plate   Button shell

Snap fasteners are two-part (socket and ball) fasteners with limited holding power. Sizes range from small (000) to large (10) in nickel, black-enamel or clear nylon.

No-sew snap fasteners are socket and ball fasteners that are not sewn to the garment but held in place by pronged rings. Holding power is good. Suitable for heavy fabrics.

Button press fasteners have four parts: two form a ball-and-socket fastener; one is the back plate; the last is a button shell (which can be covered with garment fabric). Components are positioned, then clamped to fabric.

Snap fastener tape comes with regular or no-sew snaps in three sizes. Permits multiple snap application at one time. Sold by the metre or in precut lengths.

Eyelets

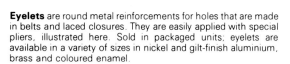

Eyelets are round metal reinforcements for holes that are made in belts and laced closures. They are easily applied with special pliers, illustrated here. Sold in packaged units; eyelets are available in a variety of sizes in nickel and gilt-finish aluminium, brass and coloured enamel.

Hooks and eyes

Hook and eye fasteners come with either straight eyes for lapped edges or loop eyes for meeting edges. Sizes from fine (0) to heavy (3) in nickel or black-enamel finish.

Covered hook and eye sets are usually large and suitable for coats, jackets, or garments made of deep pile fabric. Eyes are of the loop variety. Colours are mainly neutral.

Waistband hook and bar sets are extra sturdy, ideal for waistbands on skirts or pants. Special design keeps hook from slipping off the straight bar or eye. Available in nickel or black finish.

Hook and eye tape comes with medium hooks and eyes attached to cotton tape. Permits multiple hook and eye application at one time. Sold in neutral colours by the metre.

Hook and loop tape

Hook and loop tape fastener is composed of two tape strips, one with a looped nap and the other with a hooked nap. When pressed together, the surfaces grip and remain locked until pulled apart. Useful for children's clothing, detachable trims and loose-covers. Is available in sew-on, stick-on and iron-on forms.

Tapes and trimmings

Bias binding is a bias-cut fabric strip with folded edges, suitable for binding curved or straight edges, or for use as a casing. It is available in cotton, nainsook, nylon, poly-cotton and satin acetate in many colours. Width is generally 12 mm; there is an off-centre fold binding available which is 43 mm wide. Bias binding is sold in 3 and 6 metre packs, or by the metre.

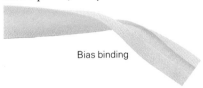

Bias binding

Seam binding is a straight, woven tape, used for finishing hem edges and staying seams in woven garments. An elastic lace is suitable for use as a hem finish on garments made from knit or other stretchy fabric.

Seam binding

Elastic lace

Cotton tape is a firmly woven, stable tape used mainly for staying and strengthening seams, especially in tailored jackets and coats. It is available in black and white, in widths of 6, 12, 20 and 25 mm.

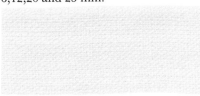

Cotton tape

Hem facing is basically a wide bias binding, with folded edges, available in 25 mm and 50 mm widths and a wide range of colours. It provides a neat finish to hems and helps to eliminate bulk in a hem made from a heavy fabric. Useful, too, when there is insufficient hem depth for a turned-up hem. Can also be used as a casing or a binding.

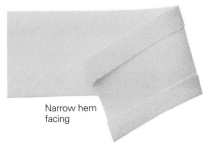

Narrow hem facing

Petersham ribbon is often used for finishing or staying waistlines. It comes in various ribbon widths and a wide range of colours. A special curved skirt petersham is available, 25 mm wide, in black and white only.

Petersham ribbon

Fold-over braid is folded slightly off-centre for easy application when binding or trimming an edge (wider side goes underneath to ensure that stitching catches it). Made of nylon in several colours. Sold by the metre.

Fold-over braid

Russia braid is a narrow, glossy braid used for trimming (stitch in the centre groove) and for making frog fastenings. It is available in several colours.

Russia braid

Scroll braid is a decorative 10 mm wide trim, used mainly on soft furnishings. A heavier type is wider. It can be appliquéd by hand or machine-stitched.

Scroll braid

Rick-rack braid is ideal for trimming garments, particularly children's. Made of polyester or cotton, it comes in three widths and a very wide range of colours, including some patterns. Two lengths of rick-rack can be entwined to form a dual-coloured trim.

Rick-rack braid

Cambric or eyelet lace, traditionally white, is a decorative trim with one finished edge; the unfinished edge must be enclosed in a garment seam or hem. When finished at both edges, it is called insertion lace; when dress width, it is called broderie anglaise.

Cambric or eyelet lace

Ribbon braid is a decorative trim with firm finished edges, available in many widths, in plain, satin or intricately patterned weave. Used to trim bed linen, curtains, blinds and children's wear.

Ribbon braid

Cable cord, sometimes called piping cord, is usually made of cotton and can be used wherever a cordlike filler is needed, for instance in corded buttonholes. As it is a decorative twine and comes in many bright colours, it can be used on its own as a fastening or inserted into bias tubing and used as a drawstring. It is usually sold by the metre in thicknesses ranging from approximately 2 to 12 mm.

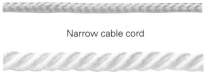

Narrow cable cord

Wide cable cord

Cording, or bias piping, is a decorative seam insertion, used on garments or home decorating items. One edge is welted, the other acts as a small seam allowance. It is made from a bias strip wrapped around a twisted cotton cord. Limited colour range.

Cording

Ribbings are knitted, stretchy, decorative bands, available in various widths and designs. The narrower ribbings are used as a quick finish and colour detail for neck and wrist edges; the wider ones, as waistline insets or edgings. You can also get packs of stretchy knitted cuffs for tracksuits and ski-wear. Ribbings vary in amount of stretch; use the knit gauge on page 69 to ensure that the stretch of the ribbing you want to use is suitable for the garment you are making. Usually sold by the metre.

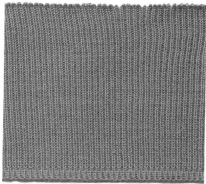

Ribbing

Belt kits containing iron-on interfacing, a buckle, prong and eyelets enable you to make covered belts to match the garment you are sewing. This type of kit is widely available.

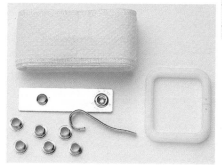

Cover-your-own belt kit

Waistband stiffenings give rigid stability to waistlines; select one to suit your need. The most frequently used insert for belts and waistbands is belting, a cardboardlike band with both edges folded and finished. Professional waistbanding, a non-roll, heatset stiffener, can be used in place of interfacing. Men's trouser waistbanding, an already assembled waistband which finishes the inside of men's trousers, is sometimes available from sewing suppliers. Petersham ribbon (see previous page) and sturdy elastic products like the one shown below are also used as waistband stiffenings.

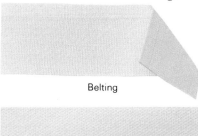

Belting

Professional waistbanding

Elastic waistbanding

Men's trouser waistbanding

Elastics

Most elastics are made from a rubber-core yarn covered with cotton, synthetic, or a blend of fibres. They may occur as a **single yarn** or as several yarns **braided** or **woven** together.

Single-yarn elastics can be used for hat bands, loop closings or as elastic thread for shirring; most elastics, however, fall into either the braided or the woven categories.

Braided elastics can be identified by the lengthwise, parallel ridges that give these elastics a stronger grip. Because of its structure, braid narrows when stretched, and is recommended

Braided elastic

Woven elastic

for casings rather than for stitching to the garment itself.

Woven elastics are usually softer; the woven construction enables them to maintain their original width when stretched. Wovens curl less than braided elastics, and so can be stitched to a garment more easily.

Elastics are made and sold for special purposes, such as pyjamas, lingerie, bra closures, etc. If you cannot find a particular type, look for an elastic with the features most suitable for the style and use of the garment. Consider construction (woven or braided), width, fibre content (especially important in swimwear, as rayon stretches when wet), gripping power and weight compatibility.

There are many new elastic products, such as wide, colourful woven designs that serve as waistbands for skirts or pants, and elasticated products for waistbands or belts.

Iron-on and fusible products

Iron-ons are adhesive-backed fabrics that are pressed onto the garment fabric rather than stitched. Some are available as interfacings (both non-woven and woven types); these are sold by the metre and in packaged quantities. Others come in the form of strips and patches for mending or adding strength to stress areas like knees or elbows; some are purely decorative. Iron-on pocket repair kits are available, and an iron-on heavy-duty tape suitable for canvas repair.

Iron-ons are generally recommended for use on fabrics that can withstand high iron temperatures (some require steam), but read the package instructions and always test carefully first.

There is a new powder which, when sprinkled onto a piece of fabric, forms an adhesive layer and enables another piece of fabric to be bonded to it. You can thus make your own iron-on patches and appliqués—but be sure to test the product first on any fabric you wish to use. The powder is not recommended for dry cleaning.

Fusibles are weblike bonding agents which, when melted between two layers of fabric, bind them together. Used properly, they will hold a hem, facing, trim or appliqué to a garment with no sewing. Fusible webs can also function as a lightweight interfacing between the garment and the facing. They are not intended to form part of a seam.

Fusible webs are sold by the metre, and also come in packaged pre-cut lengths and widths designed for specific areas, such as hems. They are recommended for all fabrics that can be *steam* pressed except sheers and a few synthetics. Check package instructions for recommendations, and test on a fabric scrap first. Follow instructions carefully when applying web.

Sewing machine

How a machine functions

With so much emphasis—in advertising especially—on the differences between sewing machine types and brands, it is easy to overlook the fact that all sewing machines are basically similar. All of the operating parts labelled on the photograph at the right are common to any average sewing machine that will do both straight and zigzag stitching.

A basic requirement of all machines is a precisely timed movement of needle and shuttle hook to manipulate a top thread and a bottom (bobbin) thread into a stitch (see below, right). Tension discs and thread guides, which every machine has, help to control the flow of these threads.

Another important working relationship in stitch formation is the interaction between the presser foot, needle and feed. While the presser foot is holding the fabric in place and the needle is going through the fabric into the bobbin area to form stitches, the feed is moving the fabric into position for each stitch.

The functions so far described are all that are required for any plain straight stitch. For the formation of zigzag and reverse feed stitches, those functions *plus* other devices are required. To form a zigzag stitch, the needle must be able to move from side to side. With reverse feed stitches, the needle moves from side to side, but it is the movement of the *feed* that distinguishes reverse feed from either straight or zigzag stitching. The feed moves the fabric in two directions, forwards and backwards, in forming the reverse feed stitch.

Capabilities such as these built into the machine, usually by cams or an electronic motor, but provision is always made for the user to activate them—most often by manipulation of stitch selectors and stitch length and width regulators.

Basic parts and controls

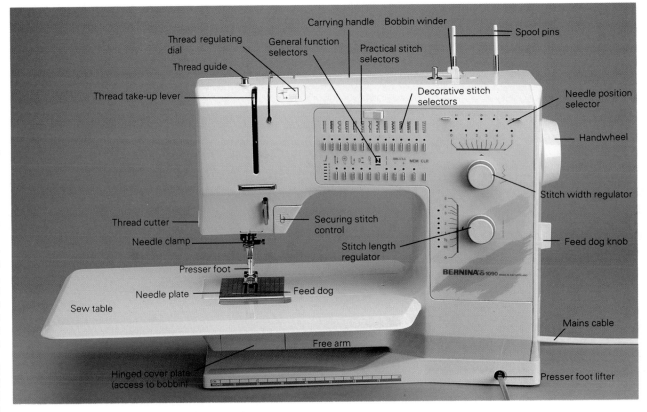

Timed sequence in stitch formation

1. Needle penetrates the fabric to bring top thread into bobbin area.

2. As needle rises, top thread forms a loop for shuttle hook to catch.

3. Shuttle hook carries thread loop around and under the bobbin case.

4. Loop slides off hook and bobbin case, goes around bobbin thread.

5. Threads are pulled up and are set into the fabric as a lockstitch.

Upper threading

Though the parts involved differ in location and appearance, the upper threading progression for any machine is basically the same. As illustrated at the right, thread is fed from the **spool** through the **tension discs,** then to the **take-up lever,** and finally down to the **needle.** The number of thread guides between these points will vary with the machine. The part that differs the most from one machine to another is the **tension assembly** (three types are shown below).

Before threading any machine, remember to do two things: (1) raise the presser foot—this will allow the thread to pass between the tension discs; (2) bring the take-up lever to its highest point so that the needle will not come unthreaded when the first stitch is started. On an electronic machine the take-up lever automatically stops at the highest point. For specific instructions regarding your machine, refer to its instruction book.

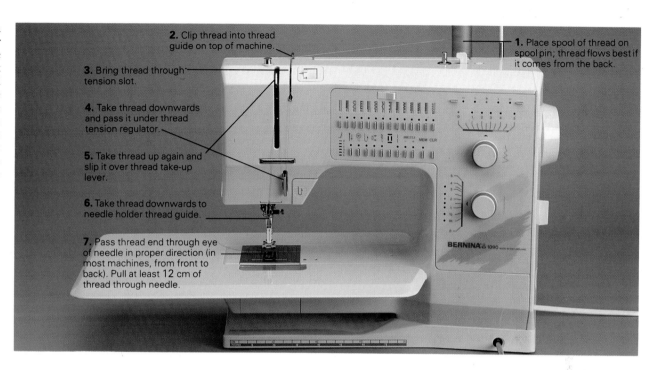

2. Clip thread into thread guide on top of machine.

3. Bring thread through tension slot.

4. Take thread downwards and pass it under thread tension regulator.

5. Take thread up again and slip it over thread take-up lever.

6. Take thread downwards to needle holder thread guide.

7. Pass thread end through eye of needle in proper direction (in most machines, from front to back). Pull at least 12 cm of thread through needle.

1. Place spool of thread on spool pin; thread flows best if it comes from the back.

Types of tension assembly

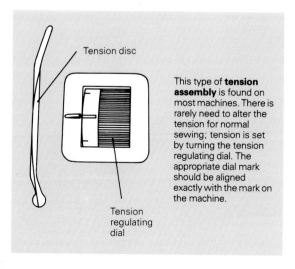

Tension disc

Tension regulating dial

This type of **tension assembly** is found on most machines. There is rarely need to alter the tension for normal sewing; tension is set by turning the tension regulating dial. The appropriate dial mark should be aligned exactly with the mark on the machine.

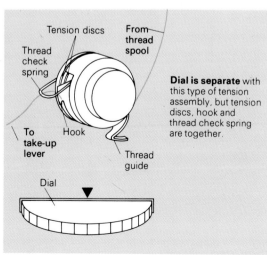

Tension discs

From thread spool

Thread check spring

To take-up lever

Hook

Thread guide

Dial

Dial is separate with this type of tension assembly, but tension discs, hook and thread check spring are together.

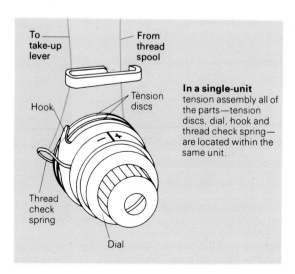

To take-up lever

From thread spool

Hook

Tension discs

Thread check spring

Dial

In a single-unit tension assembly all of the parts—tension discs, dial, hook and thread check spring—are located within the same unit.

Bobbin winding

The lower thread supply for any sewing machine is stored in the bobbin area, situated under the needle and needle plate and consisting of a small spool (the bobbin) and a case into which it fits. Both are precisely sized to fit each other and the machine.

To play its part in stitch formation, the bobbin must be filled with thread, a procedure that differs with the type

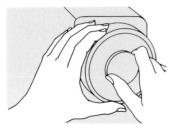

Disengaging needle

of sewing machine (see right). On most mechanical machines, the up and down action of the needle must be deactivated before the bobbin can be wound. This usually means loosening the release knob on the handwheel. **To disengage needle,** hold handwheel still and turn inner disc toward you.

The thread should be wound evenly onto the bobbin. If it is not, there may

Correct   Incorrect

be trouble in stitching, or unevenness in stitch tension. On some electronic machines a separate motor is used for bobbin winding. This eliminates the need to disengage the needle.

Methods of winding bobbins

With bobbin-winding mechanisms outside the machine (above and left), the needle is first disengaged. On the mechanical machine above, the thread feeds from the spool around the thread guide then onto the bobbin. This is the most usual winding mechanism.

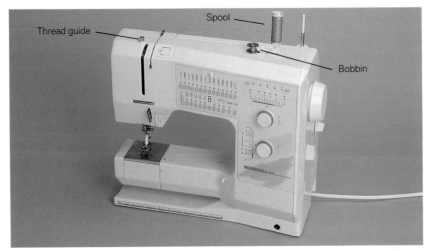

On some electronic machines, a separate motor is used for bobbin winding. As the photograph above shows, there is no inner disc on the handwheel since it is not necessary to disengage the needle before filling the bobbin with thread.

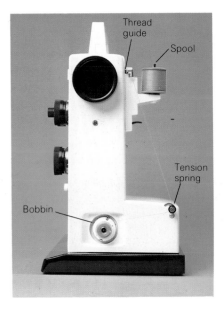

This bobbin is wound on side of machine. Thread goes from spool through thread guide and tension spring, then to bobbin.

Bobbin winding inside the machine. With upper portion of machine threaded, bobbin rotates and fills as needle goes up and down.

Types of bobbin

Bobbins are made to exact size and other specifications to conform to the requirements of particular sewing machines. Use only the type recommended by the manufacturer of your machine (non-sewing machine companies also make bobbins). Replace any bobbin that is worn, cracked or nicked; a damaged bobbin can cause sewing problems. A few extras are good to have on hand in any case.

Removable-case bobbins may be made of plastic or metal. Some of the metal ones have several holes in each of the sides.

Some drop-in bobbins are made of clear plastic, others are made of metal.

Special drop-in bobbins are made for machines that employ an inside-machine bobbin-winding mechanism. They are made of clear plastic; top part is sometimes larger than bottom part.

Bobbin removal

It is often necessary to remove a bobbin to either refill or replace it. Before removing a bobbin, bring needle and take-up lever to their highest positions, lift the presser foot and, if necessary, remove the fabric beneath it. Then open the cover plate to gain access to the bobbin area. The photographs below show the procedure for removing different bobbin types from their cases. Before removing any bobbin, it is best that the thread extending from the bobbin be cut short. This ensures that a minimum of thread will be pulled out from under the bobbin case tension spring.

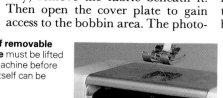

This type of removable bobbin case must be lifted out of the machine before the bobbin itself can be removed.

1. With thumb and index finger, take hold of the latch on the outside of the case.
2. Still holding latch, pull the bobbin case and bobbin out of the machine.

This type of removable bobbin case must also be lifted out of the machine before the bobbin can be removed, but in this case the left hand is used. With the index finger of the left hand, pull the bobbin case latch forward and remove the bobbin case.

With this type of removable bobbin case, simply pinch the case with your thumb and index finger to depress the latch and draw the case out of the machine. When you stop pinching the case the bobbin will come out.

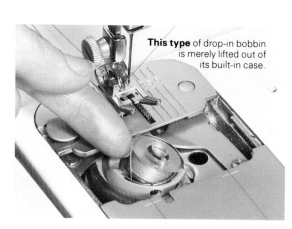

This type of drop-in bobbin is merely lifted out of its built-in case.

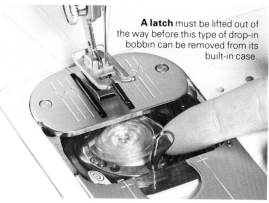

A latch must be lifted out of the way before this type of drop-in bobbin can be removed from its built-in case.

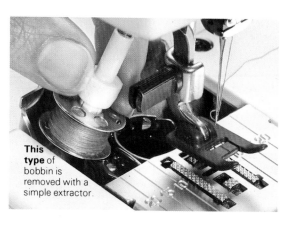

This type of bobbin is removed with a simple extractor.

Lower threading

Threading the lower portion of the machine involves feeding the bobbin thread out of the bobbin case correctly. The way this is done depends upon the bobbin case itself. There are basically only two types of bobbin case, built-in and removable, but within these types there are variations. Illustrated on these pages are examples of both types. Notice that built-in cases (this page) remain in the machine during threading and removable cases (opposite page) are taken out of the machine for threading.

For proper stitch formation, the flow of thread from the bobbin must be controlled. One way to control the flow is to force the thread to feed off the bobbin and through the slot opening of the case in a 'V' direction.

Another device, present on most bobbin cases, is the bobbin tension spring. Positioned over the slot opening of the bobbin case, this spring exerts pressure (tension) on the thread. The illustration below shows the direction the bobbin thread should take through the slot opening, under the tension spring. Some bobbin cases,

Tension spring

however, have neither a slot opening nor a tension spring; these employ other devices, such as a latch, to control the flow of bobbin thread.

The illustrations on these pages are meant to serve as a general guide for threading the lower portion of the machine. For more precise instructions for your machine, consult the manufacturer's instruction book.

Threading built-in bobbin cases

With this type of built-in bobbin case, make sure that when bobbin is placed in bobbin case, the holes in the bobbin are on top.

Exerting pressure on bobbin with your left index finger, bring the thread through the slot in the bobbin case.

Pull thread down as it comes out of the slot; you will hear a click as the thread draws around the tension spring.

With this type of built-in bobbin case, first drop bobbin into case so that the thread feeds in the same direction as the slot.

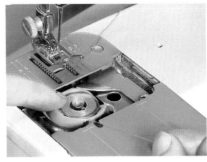

Exerting pressure on bobbin with one hand, grasp thread with the other hand and bring it to the opening of the slot.

Still exerting pressure on bobbin, pull the thread back and under bobbin tension spring. Release thread and let go of bobbin.

Case with latch but no threading points. With this type of bobbin case, you must first lift the latch up out of the way.

Then drop the bobbin into the case so that the thread is feeding off the bobbin toward the right-hand side of the latch.

Then push the latch down. The pressure that the latch exerts on the bobbin acts as a tension for the bobbin thread.

Threading a removable bobbin case

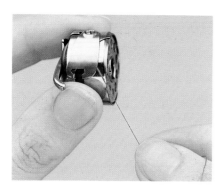

1. Hold case and bobbin with thread feeding off bobbin in same direction as slot in case.

2. Put bobbin in case; brace with finger. Grasp thread and bring to slot opening.

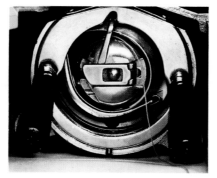

3. Bring thread down under tension spring. (Brace bobbin if necessary.)

4. Pull thread over and around end of bobbin tension spring. Case is now threaded.

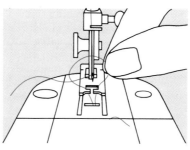

5. Grasp and pull out on the latch at the back of the bobbin case; bring case to machine.

6. Insert the case into the machine, then release the bobbin case latch.

Raising the bobbin thread

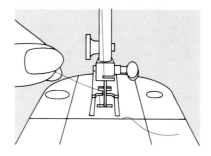

After the bobbin case has been threaded and, if necessary, inserted into the machine, close the bobbin cover plate and raise the bobbin thread as follows:

1. First, re-engage the needle by tightening the inner disc on the flywheel. Holding the top thread with your left hand, turn the flywheel with your right hand until the needle is all the way down in the bobbin area.

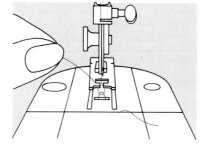

2. Still holding thread and rotating the flywheel, bring the needle up to its highest point. As the needle rises, a loop of bobbin thread will come up with it. Pull on the top thread to draw up more bobbin thread.

3. Release top thread, then pull on loop of bobbin thread to bring up free end of bobbin thread.

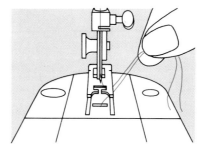

4. Pass both the top and bobbin threads under the presser foot and bring them back toward the right. The thread ends should be at least 12 cm long.

Needle sizes and types

It is essential to select a machine needle of the correct size and point type for the fabric and thread you are using. There are two systems in use for sizing machine needles; both ranges of needle are widely available. Most needles are marked in the metric system: size 60 is the finest needle (for very lightweight fabrics) and size 120 is the coarsest needle (for very heavyweight fabrics). In the 15 x 1 system, size 9 is the finest needle and size 19 is the coarsest needle. Sizes 70 to 90 (11 to 14) are the needles used most often for general sewing.

Needles also have different points, each designed for a particular type of fabric. The most commonly used are the sharp-point (for woven fabrics) and the ball-point (for knits and other stretchy fabrics); there are also extra fine-points (for twill, denim and heavy linen fabrics) and wedge-points (for leathers and vinyls).

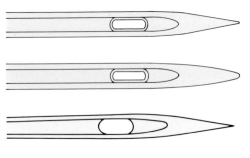

A normal (slightly rounded) sharp-point needle is recommended for all woven fabrics. Sizes range from 60 (9 in 15 x 1 system) to 120 (19 in 15 x 1 system).

A ball-point needle should be used on all knit and stretch fabrics. Sizes range from 60 to 120 (9 to 19), with the point rounded in proportion to the needle size.

An extra fine-point needle is designed for use on twill, workwear, heavy linen, denim and canvas. This comes in sizes 70 to 110. Pierces dense fabrics more easily.

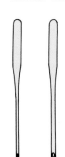

Machine needle sizes range, as a rule, from fine (size 60 or size 9) to coarse (size 120 or 19). When selecting a needle, remember that *the finer the weight of the fabric and thread being used, the finer the needle should be.*

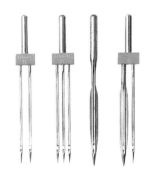

Twin and triple needles are used mainly for decorative stitching; **wing and twin wing** needles are used for hemstitching. All are available in limited size ranges. Consult your machine booklet for their use.

Needle insertion

Besides choosing a needle that is the correct size and type for the fabric, it is also important that the overall size and shape of the needle is correct for your sewing machine.

Needles can differ in length, in the size of the shank (and the position of the shank, a consideration with twin or triple needles), and in the position and size of the scarf. All of these aspects of needle conformation can be critical in stitch formation.

Machine needles within each sizing system are interchangeable but it is important to follow the recommendations of the machine manufacturer. Make sure you know which size your machine takes. Having chosen the proper needle, take care to insert it properly into the machine. The most universal method of needle insertion is explained below, but refer also to your machine instruction book. To remove a needle, reverse the insertion process.

Make frequent checks on the condition of the needle you are using; replace a blunt needle immediately.

Side and front views of a machine needle are illustrated here. The upper part of a needle is called the *shank;* the lower part is the *shaft.* One side of the shank is *flat,* the other *rounded.* On the same side as the rounded part of the shank is the *groove* of the needle. The *eye* of the needle is just above the *point.* The *scarf* is an indentation behind the eye.

Side and front needle diagram labels:
- Shank
- Flat side
- Round side
- Shaft
- Groove
- Scarf
- Eye
- Point

Side **Front**

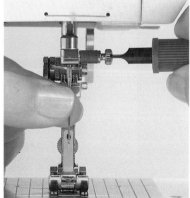

To insert a machine needle, first loosen the needle clamp screw. Then, with the flat side of the shank facing *away from* and the groove of the needle facing *toward* the last thread guide, push needle up into clamp as far as possible. Then tighten needle clamp screw using small screwdriver. This procedure is correct for most machines. Check the instruction book that accompanies your machine. To remove a needle, reverse the insertion process.

Needle faults

Many stitching problems are traceable to the needle. Listed below are the most common difficulties and remedies for them.

Needle is incorrectly inserted. If needle is not fully inserted into the needle clamp, or the groove is not positioned to the correct side, the result is usually skipped stitches or no stitches at all.
Solution: Carefully re-insert needle.

Needle is wrong size for machine or fabric. If wrong size for machine, stitch formation is affected. If too fine a size for the fabric, thread might fray; if too coarse, needle might damage fabric. With either too fine or too coarse a needle, the stitches might look unbalanced.
Solution: Select needle of the proper conformation and size, and insert.

Needle is damaged or dirty. If needle has a burr on the point, eye or groove, the thread might fray or break, or fabric might be damaged. A blunt needle can cause a thumping noise as it penetrates the fabric; it might also result in pulling on the fabric yarns or in skipped stitches. If the needle is bent, there might be skipped stitches, the fabric could be pulled to one side, or the needle might hit the needle plate and break. If the needle is dirty, it could cause skipped stitches.
Solution: Replace with a new needle.

Needle / thread / stitch length selection

The table at the right is a guide to the recommended needle, thread and stitch length combinations for most home sewing jobs. The selections are based on the following criteria:

Needle type relates to fabric structure—normal sharp-point for wovens; ball-point for knits; extra fine-point for twill, denim and heavy linen; wedge-point for leathers and vinyls.

Size of needle depends on the size of the fabric yarns—the finer the yarns, the finer the needle.

Thread type and size are chosen for compatibility with the fabric's structure and fibre content (see Threads). Note, however, that spun polyester is suitable for nearly all fabric types.

Stitch length for ordinary seaming depends on fabric *weight* (heaviness and density), *texture* and *structure*. Weight is the most important. As a rule, the heavier the fabric, the longer the stitch; the lighter the fabric, the shorter the stitch.

Within this rule, however, adjustments are made according to the other two characteristics, texture and structure. That is why the selection chart gives a *range* of stitch lengths for a specific fabric weight. Both velvet and crêpe, for example, are classified as mediumweight, soft fabrics, with a recommended stitch length range of 2 to 2.5 mm. Because the crêpe is less bulky, however, it needs a shorter stitch length than velvet.

A relatively long stitch is recommended for such fabrics as leathers and unbacked vinyls, because the structure of such fabrics makes them susceptible to ripping; the longer stitch length reduces this risk by spacing needle holes further apart.

Before starting any sewing project, it is wise to test and, if necessary, adjust the combination of needle, thread and stitch length.

Fabric	Needle	Thread	Stitch length (mm)
Woven artificial and natural fibres, such as linen, chiffon, batiste, organdie, wool, velvet	Normal sharp-point, (slightly rounded) needle 80	Polyester thread	1.5–2
Fine knitted fabrics, made from silk, synthetics, cotton and fine wool	Fine ball-point needle 70	Polyester thread	1.5–2.5
Heavier knitted fabrics in artificial or natural fibres	Medium ball-point needle 80–90	Polyester thread	2–2.5
Delicate or difficult stretch fabrics	Medium ball-point needle 80–90 or stretch needle 75	Polyester thread	1.5–2
Dense fabrics such as twill, workwear, heavy linen, canvas	Extra fine-point (cording) needle 80–90	Heavy duty polyester twist; linen thread Normal thread in bobbin	3–5
Leather, suede, calfskin, kid, pigskin, imitation leathers and suedes, plastics	Wedge-point (leather) needle 90–100	Heavy duty polyester twist; linen thread Normal thread in bobbin	2.5–5
Natural and polyester fabrics	Metalfil needle 80–100	Decorative, e.g. metallic threads	Check sewing machine manual
Natural and polyester fabrics	Cording needle 80–100	Ribbon floss; heavy lustrous rayon thread	Check sewing machine manual
Linen type fabric, fine batiste and other heirloom fabrics	Wing needle (hemstitch)	Very fine machine embroidery thread	2–3
Decorative fabrics, chiffon and organdie	Wing twin needle	Machine embroidery thread 50	2–2.5
Extremely fine fabrics	Twin needle 1.6 mm	Fine machine embroidery thread	1.5–2
Cotton fabrics	Twin needle 2 mm (most common)	Machine embroidery thread 30	1.5–2
Medium and heavyweight fabrics	Twin needle 2.5 mm	Machine embroidery thread 50–60	1.5–2
Stretch sewing fabrics	Twin needle 4 mm	Any thread	1.5–2
Extra heavy stretch fabrics	Twin needle 6 mm	Any thread	1.5–2
Decorative topstitching on any fabric	Triple needle	Any thread	Any length

Stitch length in straight stitching

All sewing machines provide a stitch length regulator that permits changes in stitch length for different sewing situations. For seaming, the stitch length is usually from 1.5 to 2.5 mm, depending on the fabric (see chart, p. 27). For temporary jobs such as tacking, or nonstructural details such as topstitching, the stitches can be longer. (Very short stitches, less than 1 mm long, are used mainly for satin stitching, a zigzag stitch. See pages 30–31 for length in zigzag stitching.)

Most machines also have a reverse control, a button or a lever, either as part of the stitch length regulator or separate from it. While this is activated, the machine sews in reverse at approximately the same stitch length as it did when stitching forward.

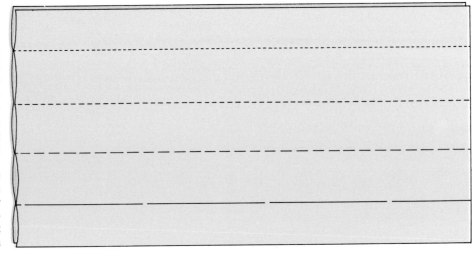

Short stitch length ranges from 1 mm to 1.5 mm. Mainly used for seaming lightweight fabrics.

Regular stitch length, ranging from 1.5 mm to 2.5 mm, is used most often for general sewing.

Tacking stitches range from 3 mm to 5 mm. Also used for easing, gathering and topstitching.

Longer tacking stitches, some as long as 5 cm, can be produced by some sewing machines.

Feed and stitch length

The major purpose of the feed is to move the fabric into position for each stitch. The distance that the feed moves the fabric is controlled by the stitch length regulator. When the regulator is set for a long stitch, the feed moves in a long rectangular path, advancing the fabric a considerable distance. When the control is set for a short stitch, the rectangular path of the feed is shorter, and the fabric is moved a shorter distance.

Stitch length regulators

The numbers on a stitch length regulator are usually based on the metric system. The numbers on the dial stand for the length of the stitch in millimetres: a dial set at 3 will produce a stitch 3 mm long. Some machines are still based on the imperial system, where the numerals stand for the number of stitches per inch. *Both, however, are measuring the same stitch:* if there are 10 stitches per inch, each stitch will be 2.5 mm long.

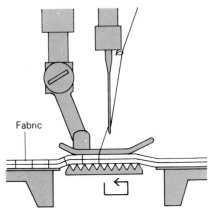

The larger the rectangular path of the feed, the longer the stitch will be.

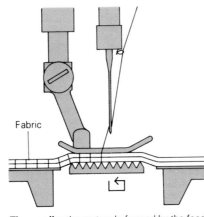

The smaller the rectangle formed by the feed, the shorter the stitch will be.

The metric system of measuring stitch length is used on this dial. The button in the centre of the dial is the reverse stitching control.

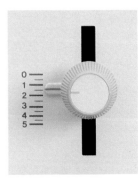

Both systems, stitches per inch and metric measurements, may be found on lever-type stitch length regulators. This one uses metric only.

A light beam or number system is used on some electronic machines to indicate stitch length. The reverse stitching control is not part of this dial.

Stitch tension

Every sewing machine has a tension control for the top thread; most machines also have one for the bobbin thread. These controls increase or decrease the pressure on the threads as they are fed through the machine.

Too much pressure results in too much tension and too little thread for the stitch; too little pressure produces too little tension and too much thread. In general, too little thread causes fabric puckering and strained, easily broken stitches; too much produces a limp, weak seam. When pressure is correct on both threads, a balanced amount of each thread is used, and the connecting link of each stitch is centred between fabric layers.

The link position is a good indicator of which thread tension is incorrect (see below). It can happen, however, that the link is in the right place, but either too much or too little of both threads has been used. To remedy this, adjust both tensions.

Test stitch tension before starting any sewing project. Use the same number and types of fabric layers as will be sewn, and the correct needle, thread and pressure for them.

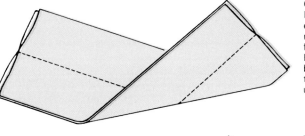

Correct tension: Link formed with each stitch will lie midway between fabric layers. Balanced amounts of both top and bobbin threads have been used for each stitch.

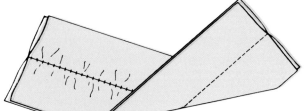

Top too tight: Links will fall toward top layer of fabric. This means that there is either too much tension on the top thread or too little on the bobbin thread.

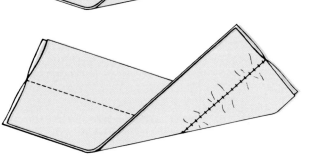

Top too loose: Links are toward bottom fabric layer. This indicates either that the top tension is too loose or there is too much tension on the bobbin thread.

Top thread tension

The tension regulating dial, situated on top of or close to the tension discs, bears numbers or symbols to indicate the amount of tension the dial is set for (see page 21). In the numbered system, five is the median number; symbols are plus or minus. Adjust this control with the machine threaded and presser foot down (when foot is up, tension discs are open).

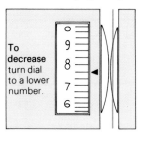

To decrease turn dial to a lower number.

When top tension is too tight, link in stitch will fall toward top layer of fabric. To bring link *down,* toward the centre of the fabric layers, *decrease* the top tension: Turn dial to a lower number (or into the minus range). This decreases the amount that the tension discs press against each other and the thread.

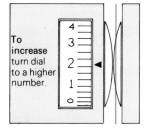

To increase turn dial to a higher number.

When top tension is too loose, the link will lie toward the bottom layer of fabric. To bring link *up,* toward the centre of the fabric layers, *increase* the top tension: Gradually turn control to a higher number (or into the plus range). This increases the amount that the tension discs press against each other and the thread.

Bobbin thread tension

If stitch tension and balance are not corrected by top tension adjustments, it may be necessary to adjust the bobbin thread tension. The bobbin thread tension control, if the machine has one, is a screw located on the tension spring of the bobbin case (see below). **Minute adjustments are usually all that is necessary.** Alter tension *after* case has been threaded.

Most built-in bobbin cases have an adjustable tension screw. Using a screwdriver, turn the screw *clockwise to increase* and *counterclockwise to decrease* the tension.

All removable bobbin cases have a tension screw. Like the screws in the built-in types, it is turned *clockwise to increase* and *counterclockwise to decrease* the tension.

Sewing machine

Zigzag stitching

Zigzag stitches are lockstitches with a side-to-side width (bight) as well as a stitch length. In mechanical machines, basic stitch formation is dictated mainly by a **stitch pattern cam;** maximum pattern width is established by the **stitch width regulator.** Stitch length is selected as for straight stitching (see p. 28), and is the same for both stitch types at the same setting, but occurs to the eye as a *distance between points* rather than an actual stitch measurement (see illustration, top right).

The cams built into the mechanical machine control stitch formation by means of indentations in their outer edges. A stitch pattern selector positions a fingerlike follower onto the appropriate cam. The follower, connected to the needle bar, tracks these indentations, moving the needle from side to side. The adjoining diagram illustrates the principle.

In most electronic machines, the zigzag stitch is programmed by a microcomputer which controls the movement of the stepping motor to direct the zigzag movement of the needles. The variable pattern widths are indicated by a light beam (LED) or a push-button number control (LCD).

Besides the controls mentioned, most machines have a **needle position selector,** which places stitches to the left or right of a normal (usually centre) position. This gives great flexibility and is helpful in constructing hand-guided buttonholes, sewing on buttons, and positioning stitches closer to or farther from an edge.

A zigzag stitch has more give than a straight stitch, and so is less subject to breakage. Stitches lie diagonally across the fabric so more thread is used, and the stress is not on a single line but is apportioned across a span. For any zigzag stitching, always use a zigzag foot and needle plate.

The diagram shows, in simplified form, the inner workings of a zigzag stitch mechanism in a mechanical machine. As the *cam* rotates, a fingerlike *follower,* connected to the needle bar, rides along the cam and tracks its indentations. As the follower moves in and out, the *needle bar* is moved from side to side. (At the same time, the needle bar is also moving up and down in time with the shuttle hook to form lockstitches between the top and bottom threads.)

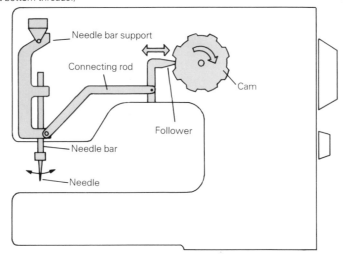

Needle bar support

Connecting rod

Cam

Follower

Needle bar

Needle

The diagram shows the inner workings of a zigzag stitch mechanism in an electronic machine. The zigzag stitch, programmed by a microcomputer, is controlled by the movement of the stepping motor.

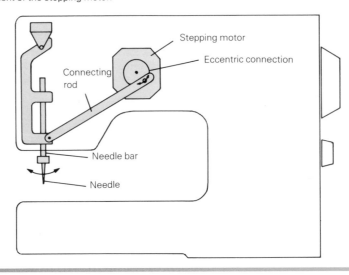

Stepping motor

Eccentric connection

Connecting rod

Needle bar

Needle

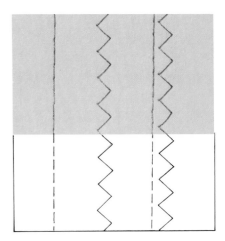

Stitch length is the vertical distance between needle penetrations. It is the same for straight or zigzag stitches at the same setting, but penetrations for zigzag are from side to side.

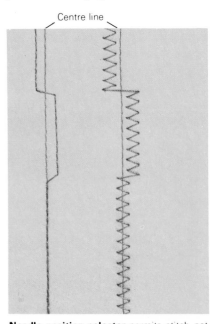

Centre line

Needle position selector permits stitch patterns to be placed to a side (or sides) other than normal. In the example, centre is normal position; stitches can go to left or right.

Length and width in zigzag stitching

A zigzag stitch can be varied in both length and width: *length* by the same stitch length regulator that controls straight-stitch length (see p. 28); *width* (how far the needle moves from side to side) by the stitch width regulator, with either symbols or numbers indicating the range. The higher the number, the wider the stitch; 'O' setting produces a straight stitch. The choice will depend on the fabric and the job. The stitch length rule for seaming (at a very narrow width setting) is usually the lighter the fabric, the shorter the stitch. For edge-finishing, a better stitch would be the multi-stitch zigzag (see page 32).

For decorative applications, stitch length and width is less crucial and can be set according to the desired effect.

Tension in zigzag stitching

The tension of a zigzag stitch can be adjusted just like that of a straight stitch (see p. 29). In a balanced zigzag stitch, the interlocking link of the top and bottom threads falls at the corner of each stitch and midway between the fabric layers. When the tension of the top and bottom threads is incorrect, the stitch tends to draw up the fabric, particularly one that is lightweight or spongy. The illustrations below show how to recognise and correct zigzag tension problems.

A zigzag stitch used in construction should be properly balanced. In decorative uses, the top tension can be loosened, or the eye of the bobbin case threaded, so that the link falls toward the bottom layer, making the resulting stitch pattern more rounded.

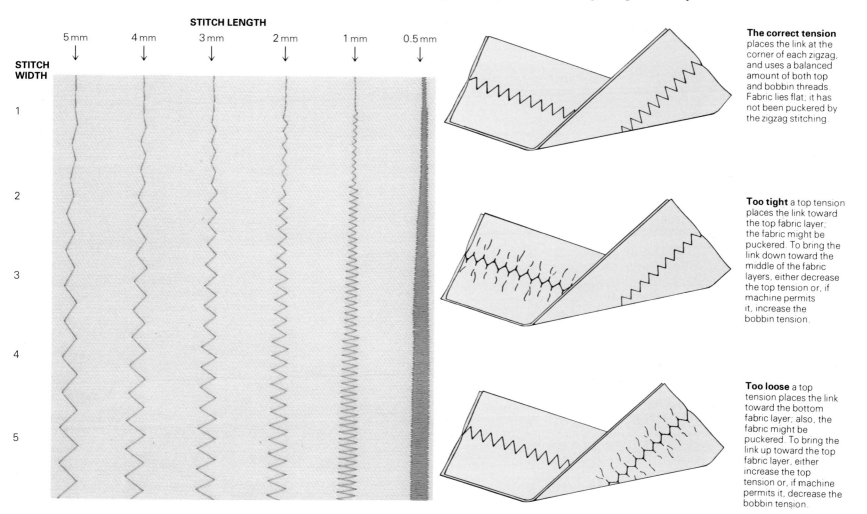

STITCH LENGTH

5 mm   4 mm   3 mm   2 mm   1 mm   0.5 mm

STITCH WIDTH: 1, 2, 3, 4, 5

The correct tension places the link at the corner of each zigzag, and uses a balanced amount of both top and bobbin threads. Fabric lies flat; it has not been puckered by the zigzag stitching.

Too tight a top tension places the link toward the top fabric layer; the fabric might be puckered. To bring the link down toward the middle of the fabric layers, either decrease the top tension or, if machine permits it, increase the bobbin tension.

Too loose a top tension places the link toward the bottom fabric layer; also, the fabric might be puckered. To bring the link up toward the top fabric layer, either increase the top tension or, if machine permits it, decrease the bobbin tension.

Sewing machine

Zigzag patterns that use straight stitches

In some of the patterns in this group, straight stitches are part of the design; an example is the blindstitch. Others, such as the multi-stitch zigzag, consist of straight stitches only, but in a zigzag configuration.

Length and width variations affect the practical uses of either type. For example, when the stitch length of the **blindstitch** is shortened, there are more zigzags to catch the fabric, an important consideration in hemming. When the stitch is widened, the zigzags extend farther from the straight stitches to cover a wider span; this helps when working with heavier fabrics.

The **multi-stitch zigzag,** combining zigzag placement with the frequent bights of straight stitches in series, offers great flexibility and fabric control. Set narrow, use it for edge-finishing fabrics that fray; at a wider width, for mending, attaching elastic, and stitching lapped and butted seams.

Decorative zigzag patterns

With decorative stitch patterns, it is useful to know whether one or both sides of the pattern are shaped. This helps in deciding which can be used for edgestitching or appliqué and how to place fabric under the foot.

Blindstitch consists of several straight stitches followed by one zigzag. An important fact about the blindstitch: the zigzag always falls to the left of the straight stitches, so the edge to which the zigzag should go must be to the left of the needle. Length and width can be varied to suit the job. Use longer and narrower (near right) for delicate fabrics, shorter and wider (second row) for heavier fabrics. Used for blind-hemming, seam finishing, double-stitched seams; decoratively, for shell-stitched edges (shown) and shell tucks.

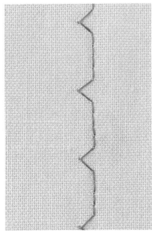

Blindstitch **pattern set** longer and narrower, shorter and wider;

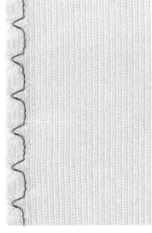

the blindstitch pattern shown as used for **blind-hemming** applica-tion; the blindstitch pattern used for a **shell-stitched** edge.

Both sides of most patterns are shaped. Patterns of this type are ideal as the centre motif in a decorative panel. If the stitch width is narrowed, the pattern can be placed to the left or right of the centre.

Multi-stitch zigzag is a series of straight stitches placed in a zigzag design. The longer, narrower version (near right) is excellent for edge-finishing fabrics that fray. Set shorter and wider (second row), the stitch is fine for mending. Pattern grows equally to the right and left of a centre line. For a faggoted seam (shown), the two edges should be an equal distance from the centre so that each stitch will catch an edge. The multi-stitch zigzag can also be used to reinforce edges.

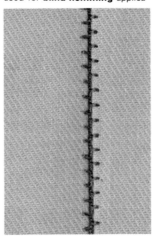

Multi-stitch **zigzag set** longer and narrower, shorter and wider;

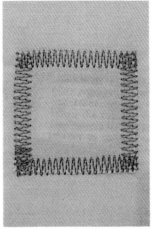

the multi-stitch zigzag as used in the stitching of a **faggoted seam;**

the multi-stitch zigzag used to **mend, darn or reinforce edges.**

A right-sided pattern is shaped on the right side and straight on the left. When such a pattern is being used for edgestitching, place fabric edge to the right of the needle. If the needle position is changed, stitch width must be reduced to fit within the narrower side-to-side limits.

A left-sided pattern is shaped on the left side and straight on the right. When such a pattern is being used to finish an edge, place the fabric edge to the left of the needle. If the needle position is changed, stitch width must be reduced to fit within the narrower side-to-side limits.

Using the plain zigzag stitch

As shown in the sample at the right, plain zigzag stitching can be both functional and decorative.

First, a plain *satin stitch* decoratively finishes a raw edge. In the second example, a *butted seam* is sewn with a zigzag stitch. The next two rows show *topstitching* with a zigzag—the first row is stitched with a single needle, the second row with a twin needle.

In the fifth example, machine *buttonholes* create finished openings for threading a ribbon. The ribbon is held in place by the zigzag stitches that are used to attach the *button*.

Next, a length of *cord* is secured to fabric with zigzag stitching. The row to its right shows how, by changing the *needle position*, stitch groups can be placed on either side of a centre. The final row is a *bound edge* finished with zigzag topstitching.

TOPSTITCHING

| Satin-stitched fabric edge | Zigzagged butted seam | Single needle | Twin needle | Buttonhole and button | Zigzag stitch over cord | Varying the needle position | Topstitched bound edge |

Using patterned zigzag stitches

Though patterned zigzag stitches are most often used decoratively, they can be functional as well. Several patterns are used in this way in the sample at the right. To finish a raw edge, instead of the plain zigzag in the sample above, the choice is a *solid scallop*. Next to the edge finish, a *full-ball* motif is top-stitched onto the fabric.

In the third pattern, the *needle position* alternates to place groups of stitches to the left and the right of a centre line. The next row in the sampler is a series of *arrowheads*.

The two rows that follow are examples of zigzag/straight stitch patterns, the first the *multi-stitch zigzag* used on a butted seam, the second a wavy motif that is topstitched onto the fabric with a *twin needle*.

In the last example, variable zigzag stitches are used as a decorative edge stitching along a *bound edge*.

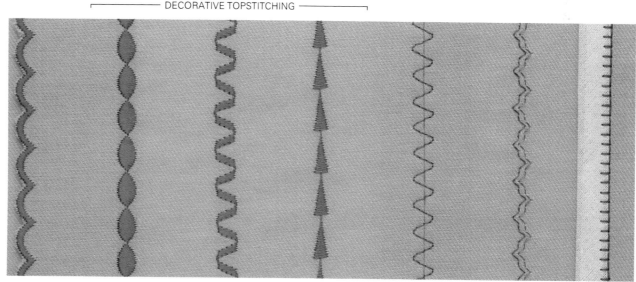

DECORATIVE TOPSTITCHING

| Solid scallop edge finish | Full ball | Alternating needle position | Arrowheads | Multi-stitch on butted seam | Twin needle topstitching | Topstitched bound edge |

33

Sewing machine

Practical stitching

Practical stitches are produced by coordinated motions of needle and feed—that is, while the needle is moving as for straight and zigzag stitches, the feed is automatically moving the fabric forward and backward according to the pattern's requirements.

Pattern formation, as with zigzag stitches, is controlled by built-in cams in mechanical machines or. by a stepping motor in electronic machines (p. 30). In some mechanical machines, the shape of one cam controls the needle action, the shape of another, the movement of the fabric by the feed. In electronic machines, a microcomputer is programmed to select stitches and a stepping motor then controls needle action and the movement of the fabric by the feed.

The forward and reverse movement of the fabric by the feed differs in some machines; it can be controlled by a separate cam or a separate stepping motor. The forward/back feed action results, with all *reverse* feed stitches, in several stitches being formed in the same place. For example, a typical reverse straight stitch consists of two stitches forward and one in reverse, or a total of three stitches.

In any stitching, reverse stitches tend not to be exactly the same length on various fabrics as those sewn in forward stitching. Where forward and reverse stitching are used in coordination, this tendency can cause pattern distortion. Some machines with reverse feed stitch capability are equipped with a pattern balance control, to help correct stitch differences.

Most practical stitches look best sewn at the length and width recommended by the machine manufacturer, but they can usually be modified. Consult your manual for machine settings on practical stitches. Straight and zigzag stitches used in a certain way can substitute for practical stitches. A reverse feed stitch might, for example, be somewhat heavy for a very soft, lightweight, stretchy fabric.

Functional practical stitches

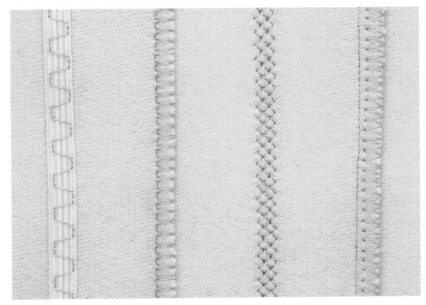

1. Universal stitch stretches to sew elastic without strain on fabric.

2. Overedge stitch is a supple stretch stitch best suited to single knit fabrics.

3. Honeycomb or **shirring stitch** set a recommended length and width.

4. Straight and zigzag stitches can be used as a substitute for practical stitches.

Using decorative practical stitches

As shown in the stitching sample at the right, practical stitches can be decorative as well as functional, and some patterns can be both.

The first row of stitches shows the *straight reverse* stitch, which is used for seaming. Next to that is a *rick-rack* stitch, used most often for topstitching, but also usable on a lapped seam.

The *featherstitch*, next, although topstitched onto this sample, is also ideal for use on a faggoted seam.

The two rows that follow are *reverse stitches* used for seams on woven and knit fabrics.

The last five rows are all *decorative topstitching* examples. The decorative effect is enhanced by the use of a twin needle and variegated thread.

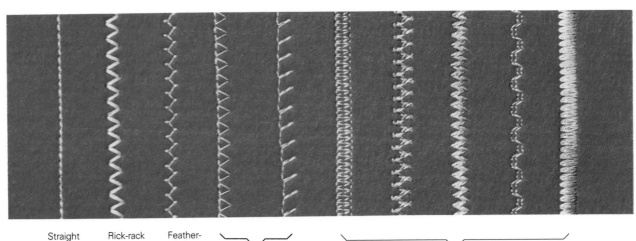

Straight reverse stitch   Rick-rack stitch   Feather-stitch   Reverse stitches   Decorative topstitching using variegated thread

What to look for in a machine

Buying a sewing machine can involve an outlay of several hundred dollars, so it is wise to take your time about choosing and make sure that you invest your money wisely.

Before you buy, decide what features you will require of a machine. If you will be using it only for plain sewing and mending, a **zigzag machine** might be all you need (a second-hand model will be easier to find as few are now being made). If you plan to do a lot of dressmaking and would like embroidery stitches, the more flexible **automatic machine** will suit your requirements better.

There are three types of sewing machine:
1. Zigzag. Can do straight stitching, zigzag, satin stitch and the stitches which can be made with satin stitch such as buttonholes and simple forms of embroidery.
2. Semi-automatic. Can do straight stitch, zigzag and satin stitch, plus a small range of useful stitches which will vary according to the make of machine. Examples would be automatic buttonhole, blind hemming and straight reverse stitch.
3. Fully automatic. Mechanical or electronic. Can do all that the above machines can plus a wide range of fancy stitches either with built-in cams or a stepping motor programmed by a microcomputer.

Flat bed, free arm and portable machines are available in all categories. Flat bed machines can be built into a cabinet.

If you want a machine with the widest possible range of uses, choose a free arm model. (All machines of this type can be converted to flat bed machines.) It will enable you to do tubular sewing, such as cuffs and pants, and to darn and patch knee and elbow areas without unpicking the side seams.

A number of feet are available to increase the range of jobs that a machine can be used for, including feet for hemming, darning, tacking, buttonholes and button sewing, braiding, pin tucking, cording and inserting zippers. There are also many attachments, among them ones designed to match plaids and checks easily and sew velvet without puckered seams, for ruffling and for making eyelets. A selection of feet and attachments is illustrated on the following pages.

Before making a final decision, have a test sew yourself on a few different models. Never accept a ready-made sample as it could have been made on another machine. Sew various types of fabric as it is important to know that your new machine can cope equally well with heavy and fine fabrics. Stitches should be reproduced consistently. Satin stitch is a good stitch to use to judge consistency of tension and stitch outline.

Take the bobbin out and replace it; try rewinding it. On some machine it is possible to wind the bobbin without unthreading the machine. Are the controls clearly marked and easy to use? How good is speed control at low speed? Is the machine noisy and does it vibrate? If there is too much vibration it can make work difficult to control. Is the light efficient and glare-free? An adjustable light or one situated above the needle is more effective than one on the cross-arm.

Machines vary considerably in weight (from 6 to 16 kilograms for some recent models) and this may affect your decision, particularly if you cannot leave your machine out.

There are other useful characteristics worth looking out for. Does the machine have a suppressor to prevent interference with television? Can the pressure on the presser foot be adjusted?

LEARNING TO USE YOUR MACHINE

Take full advantage of free lessons which are provided by the distributor. The number of free lessons dedends upon the machine you buy and the price you pay.

Although all machines should be straightforward to use after the initial period of familiarising yourself with the controls, remember that a demonstrator can often make the operation of the most sophisticated machine seem simple. The more complicated the machine the more lessons you are likely to need.

Make sure that you are given an instruction booklet to go with your machine.

GUARANTEES

The consumer is protected by warranties and conditions contained in government legislation and the vendor usually offers additional benefits. Most sewing machines have a twelve-month standard guarantee which will be honoured upon return of the machine to the place of purchase. The distributors do, however, reserve the right to charge you for repairs if damage has been caused to the machine by use other than in accordance with instructions provided in the manual.

Be sure to keep a record of your machine's serial number, model number and date of purchase.

AFTER SALES SERVICE

Availability of replacement parts during the lifetime of your machine is of vital importance and must be a major consideration when making your choice. Getting parts and service in metropolitan areas should not be difficult but problems may arise in country districts.

Most distributors have agents in large country towns who would carry a range of spare parts and do some servicing, but for a major service job your machine would, in most cases, have to be sent to the nearest fully equipped service depot or back to the area distributor.

If you do have a problem it would be as well to phone the agent or distributor first and explain what is wrong as they may be able to advise you on how to rectify it.

LOOKING AFTER YOUR SEWING MACHINE

Your machine should have an accessory box containing basic maintenance equipment such as an oil can, screwdrivers and a cleaning brush, along with various other items. Regular cleaning of the sliding parts in the bobbin area is essential so that lint and dust do not accumulate.

Oiling is the key to the smooth and silent operation of your machine. On some machines the oiling points are marked with red dots; it may be necessary to refer to the instruction booklet for their location on others. (One or two brands now available never need oiling.) Over-oiling of the motor is unwise; one or two drops twice a year should be sufficient.

When the machine is not in use cover it with an old sheet or piece of cotton to protect it from dust. Never cover it with plastic which will cause it to sweat and corrode.

Take particular care of the electric power cord and plug and have them repaired at the first sign of damage or wear.

Sewing machine

Machine feet

Shown below and opposite are various accessories designed to increase a sewing machine's versatility and efficiency. Most of them take the form of variations on the presser foot, but the group also includes special-purpose attachments and stitching guides and gauges.

The accessories illustrated here are a representative selection of those available. The names given to them may vary according to the make of machine. Also, some manufacturers may combine several features into one foot—for example, a buttonhole foot which can also be used for stitching over cord.

It should not be assumed that all the accessories shown are available for all machines, or that they are interchangeable from one machine to another. To find out which attachments are available for your machine, and how to use them, consult your machine instruction booklet.

When using any type of presser foot, it is important to know what stitch can be sewn with it. This depends upon the

Zigzag needle plate and foot

Straight stitch needle plate and foot

needle hole. If it is small and round, the foot can be used only for straight stitching; if the hole is wide, the foot can be used for straight and zigzag stitching. The same is true of needle plates, although the zigzag needle plate is used for most general sewing (the exception is very fine fabrics, where the fabric might be dragged into the wide needle hole).

Zigzag foot, or the all-purpose foot, is used primarily for plain zigzag stitching but can be used for straight stitching. Sometimes specially coated; made of metal or transparent plastic.

Zipper foot is used to stitch any seam with more bulk on one side than the other. Examples of such instances: zipper insertion, covering cord.

Invisible zipper foot is used only for insertion of invisible zippers; this foot fits all makes of machine. Bottom of foot has two channels through which zipper coils pass while zipper is being stitched.

Narrow hemmer or rolled hem foot allows a raw edge of fabric to be clean-finished. Foot automatically turns under fabric edge, which is then fed under the needle and stitched into place.

Straight stitch foot is the best one to use when doing single-needle stitching on very fine fabrics. It is a narrow foot; one toe is slimmer and shorter than the other.

Buttonhole foot is used when stitching machine-worked buttonholes. It may be of metal or transparent plastic. Guidelines are usually etched into foot to help with stitch placement.

Felling foot sews a flat-felled seam in two stages. In the first stage, the fold of the seam goes into the opening on the foot. In the second stage, the ridge of the seam goes into the opening.

Pin tucking foot, with the aid of a twin needle, will form small pin tucks. Foot comes in various widths with different numbers of grooves.

Cording foot has large groove underneath to sit over cord; another type sews with twin needle on either side of cord.

Embroidery foot is formed underneath to create a 'V' shape, permitting dense stitching to pass easily under the foot. Sometimes an open-toe foot is more useful.

Gathering foot gathers up a length of fabric as it is being stitched. Some gathering feet will gather one layer of fabric while stitching it to another flat piece of fabric.

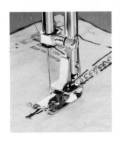
Tailor tacking foot is used to transfer markings from a paper pattern onto the fabric. Indicates seamlines or darts, with for example, tufts of thread.

Guides and gauges

Among the most useful supplements to the sewing machine are the gauges that help you to stitch a consistent distance from an edge or another line.

Another valuable aid is the blind-hemming guide. This is sometimes attached to a blind-hemming foot and sometimes to an all-purpose foot.

Other accessories

Other useful machine accessories are illustrated below. The range is very wide and this is a representative selection only. Accessories not illustrated here include a button sewing foot, a braiding foot, a circular sewing guide, an edgestitch foot and a chainstitch needle plate and attachment.

Seam gauge is attached to the machine bed, then adjusted to be a specific distance from needle.

Quilter guide-bar extends out from foot to fall along a guiding line.

Blind-hemming guide holds garment and hem edge in place for stitching.

Roller foot has grooved rollers which give better friction against plastics and synthetics. May be necessary to adjust presser foot pressure.

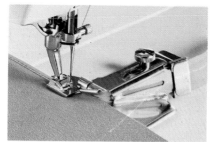

The binder positions the fabric and binding so that they can simultaneously be fed under the needle and stitched together.

Feed-related accessories

For proper stitching, fabric layers should move evenly together under the presser foot. Even feeding can be difficult, however, with some fabrics. To help with such feed problems, the feed control supplies auxiliary grasping action on the fabric, especially the top layer.

For some sewing jobs—for instance, darning, sewing on buttons and free-motion sewing—the action of the feed should be disengaged.

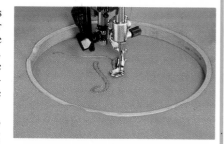

Embroidery hoop holds fabric taut for free-motion sewing. Feed must be disengaged.

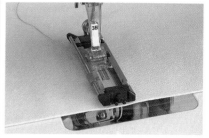

This buttonholer stitches buttonhole of the correct size for button in the attachment.

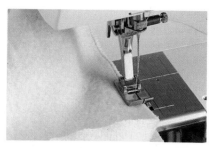

Bulky wool overlock foot has an open tunnel for braids, pearls or bulky knits to pass through.

Darning foot may need a special needle plate. Feed is disengaged; stitches can be any length and should be closely spaced.

Walking foot or **dual feed control** helps to match plaids, stripes or other patterns by feeding the two fabric layers evenly.

The ruffler attachment will quickly gather up a length of fabric. It is especially useful for home decorating projects.

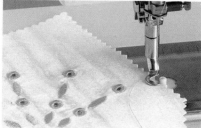

Eyelet embroidery attachment incorporates an awl, which pierces the fabric, and a small template for forming holes.

Overlocker machine (serger)

Types of overlocker machine

An overlocker machine (serger) does not replace a conventional sewing machine—it complements it. Overlocking is a quick way of finishing seam and hem edges as it cuts and neatens in one operation. It is also used to sew two fabrics together—cutting, seaming and oversewing in one operation.

There are various types of overlocker machine with different features. There is a three-thread overlocker, which seams knitted fabrics, finishes edges of woven fabrics and non-stress seams in woven garments. A four-thread overlocker, which can seam and finish most fabrics, integrates a three-thread overlock stitch with a mock safety stitch, producing a stronger seam. A five-thread overlocker machine has a three-thread overlock stitch and a separate two-thread chainstitch which is sewn simultaneously.

A very fine overlock stitch is used on fine fabric seams, such as for lingerie, and as a narrow finish for edges, such as hems, frill edges and table mats.

The main parts of an overlocker machine are shown above right. The model illustrated uses four threads and has four tension dials and two needles. By contrast, a three-thread machine has only one needle and three tension dials, while a five-thread model has two needles and another lower looper and tension dial.

There are many different makes of overlocker machine, but all are basically similar. One exception is in the type of needles used. Some machines use conventional sewing machine needles while others use industrial needles. Conventional sewing machine or industrial ball-point needles are also available for overlocker machines for use with knitted fabrics. Consult the manufacturer's instruction book for precise details on the appropriate needles for your machine.

Basic parts and controls

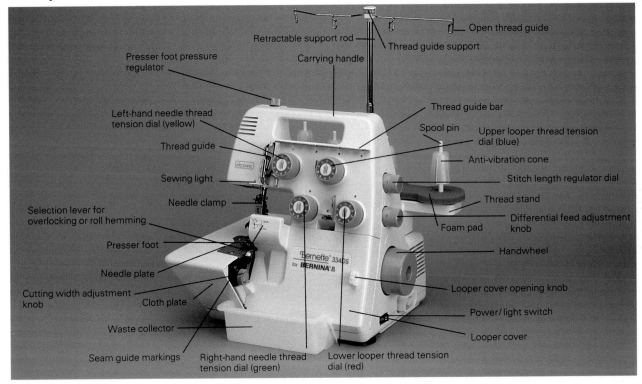

Open thread guide
Retractable support rod
Thread guide support
Presser foot pressure regulator
Carrying handle
Thread guide bar
Left-hand needle thread tension dial (yellow)
Spool pin
Upper looper thread tension dial (blue)
Thread guide
Anti-vibration cone
Sewing light
Stitch length regulator dial
Needle clamp
Thread stand
Selection lever for overlocking or roll hemming
Differential feed adjustment knob
Foam pad
Presser foot
Handwheel
Needle plate
Looper cover opening knob
Cutting width adjustment knob
Cloth plate
Power/light switch
Waste collector
Looper cover
Seam guide markings
Right-hand needle thread tension dial (green)
Lower looper thread tension dial (red)

Different stitch types

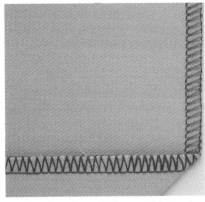

A three-thread overlocker machine makes threads lock at the seamline and the stitch looks alike front and back.

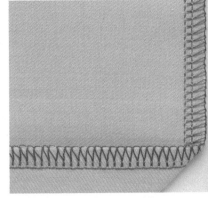

A four-thread overlocker machine uses two needles to make a three-thread overlock stitch and incorporates a safety stitch.

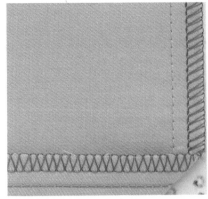

A five-thread overlocker machine has a three-thread overlock stitch and a separate two-thread chainstitch sewn simultaneously.

How the stitches are formed

The overlocker machine works with two knives—a moving upper knife and a stationary lower knife. Together they cut off frayed fabric edges to give a neat finish to seams. As the knives cut, a row of stitches oversews the edge.

The stitch formation is complex. The looper on an overlocker machine is like a moving arm which wraps the thread around the edges of the fabric, forming neat loops. The function of the needle thread or threads is simply to anchor the looper threads into the fabric. In contrast to a conventional sewing machine, where the needle zig-zags from side to side in order to over-sew, it is the backward and forward movement of the looper that guides the thread of an overlocker machine.

An overlock stitch is basically a loop formed by the looper and needle threads which in turn produces a chain. This is different from the conventional sewing machine stitch where the looper (bobbin) and needle thread form a lockstitch (see page 20).

The chain formed at the beginning and end of a seam only partly secures the stitching (chaining off). Hand-finishing is therefore advisable.

Types of tension assembly

The flow of thread from the spool to the fabric is controlled by tension knobs or dials. Tension dials are either on the outside (below left) or set into the machine (below right). The dials rotate to loosen or tighten. Most are either numbered or colour-coded. Small adjustments can change the stitch entirely.

Threading the overlocker machine

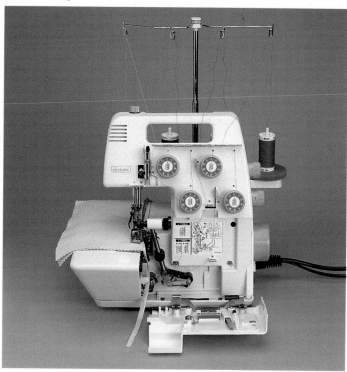

Thread the overlocker machine carefully and in the correct sequence. Practise, using different coloured threads, to see how the stitch is formed. Always use a double layer of fabric to check the stitch formation and thread tension properly.

Thread tension

Imperfect stitch formation can be corrected by adjusting the thread tension. A properly formed stitch is when the upper looper thread lies on the upper side of the fabric and the lower looper thread lies on the underside of the fabric. After threading an overlocker machine, sew a trial run to test the thread tension. To adjust the thread tension, turn the tension dials by only one number then make another test run. Consult the manufacturer's guide book for further information.

Stitch length and stitch width

The longer the stitch, the more likely it is that the seam will pull apart, especially on lightweight or loosely woven fabrics. It is best to use a longer stitch on heavier fabrics and a shorter stitch on lighter-weight fabrics. Stitch width should be wider on heavier fabrics, narrower on lighter-weight fabrics.

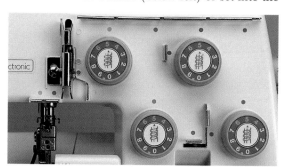

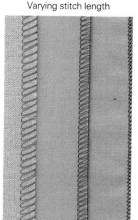

Varying stitch length

Varying stitch width

Using the overlocker machine

In the stitching sample at the right, the first row of stitches shows an *overlock edge*, which is used to oversew the edges of seams and hems on all types of fabric. Next to that is the *three-thread overlock seam*, which may be used for all knits, underwear and T-shirts. The example that follows is of a *five-thread overlock seam* where a three-thread overlock stitch is sewn simultaneously with a two-thread chainstitch.

The next row is known as *flatlocking*, that is when a flat seam has two layers of fabric joined with an overlock seam, then pulled apart until the seam lies flat. A variation is a *ladder stitch* using decorative thread.

A *rolled hem* on a three-thread machine, shown next, is for neatening hems, ruffles, scarves. A variation on a rolled hem is the *scalloped rolled edge* shown on the far right.

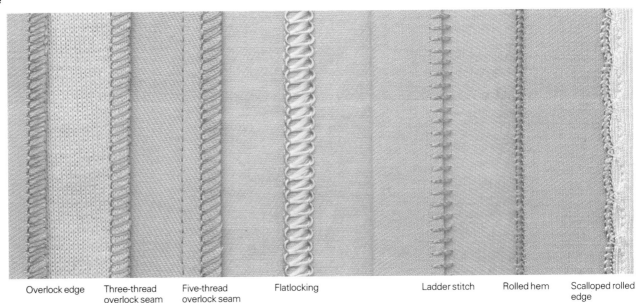

Overlock edge | Three-thread overlock seam | Five-thread overlock seam | Flatlocking | Ladder stitch | Rolled hem | Scalloped rolled edge

Overlocker machine feet and accessories

Various accessories are designed to increase the overlocker machine's versatility. With an elastic applicator foot, for example, elastic can be guided and tensioned automatically; the amount of stretch is determined by the pressure regulator. This is used on petticoats, lingerie, swimwear, aerobic wear and gymwear. The feet and accessories illustrated here are a representative selection of those available. The names given to them may vary according the make of the machine. To find out what attachments are available for your machine, consult your overlocker machine instruction book.

A blind-hem foot facilitates blind hemming and may be used to sew a hem on a T-shirt or a sweatshirt.

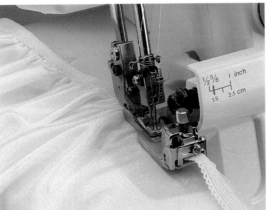

An elastic applicator foot stretches elastic as it is being overlocked onto a garment.

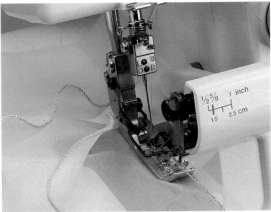

A cording foot is for decorative edging. For example, fishing line may be used to create a fluted edge on evening or bridal wear.

Providing the basic necessities

Although a fully equipped sewing area along the lines of the one illustrated below is something any home dressmaker would wish for, space and money are often limited and units such as those illustrated on page 42 might be a more suitable alternative. You might find a sturdy, spacious sewing box useful if your storage space is limited, and a box has the added advantage of being easily portable.

There are a variety of requirements that you should bear in mind when planning a sewing area. You will need a spacious table for cutting and handling fabric, and a table for your sewing machine and your overlocker machine. You will also need a good

chair without arms, pressing equipment, storage space and a full-length mirror. A dressmaker's model, while not essential, is extremely useful. Ideally the area where you will be working should be situated where there is good natural lighting plus generous artificial lighting to leave it shadow-free.

Inexpensive good quality whitewood furniture is widely available, and certain drawer, shelf and cupboard units could be used to form a sewing area best suited to your needs and the space available. Units from modular systems are made in many different finishes and would also be serviceable and attractive. If you plan to make a table, laminated particle-

board is particularly suitable. Make sure that the legs are well braced for sturdiness, especially if you plan to have a fold-back table. Metal legs, feet, brackets and other accessories can be bought from larger hardware stores.

Cutting and handling fabric calls for a surface about one metre by two metres, but when there is little space it may be necessary to reduce the table size or fold part of it. The height should be about 80 cm. Another way of calculating a convenient table height for standing work is to have it halfway between your waist and bust line. If a surface such as a dining table or bed has to be used, a cutting

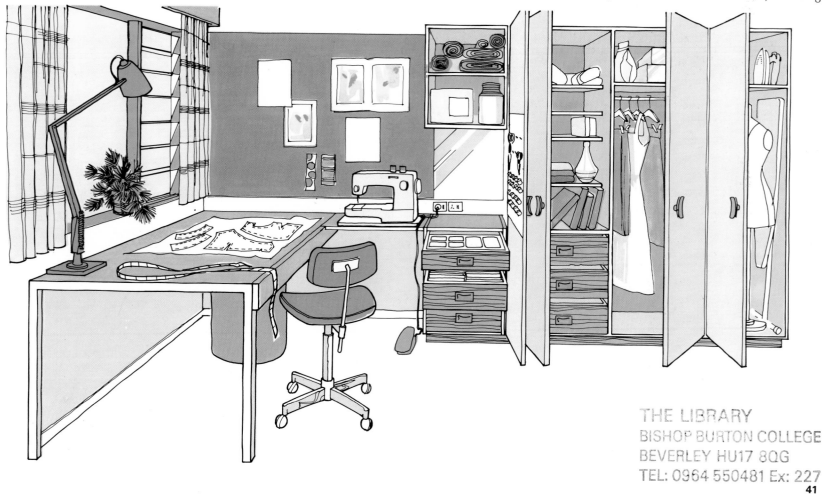

Providing the basic necessities (continued)

board is advisable. Besides providing efficiently for measuring, pinning and cutting, the board will protect the surface beneath.

The **sewing machine** and the **overlocker** should have a separate table about 70 cm high, although you may have to use your cutting table if there is little space. It is important that the table be sturdy; if it is unsteady it can be hard on the eyes and can even break the filament in the machine light globes. To avoid excessive lifting and carrying, store the machines as close as possible to the table.

Pressing equipment. Because pressing is important at every sewing stage it is best if the board, iron and special-purpose equipment are housed in or near the sewing area. This is usually a question of available space; sometimes a cupboard can be partitioned to take the board, and one of its shelves set aside for the other items.

This cupboard could also be used for the **dressmaker's model** and have a **full-length mirror** behind the door.

Specialised storage. The important considerations here are suitability and accessibility. Broad shelves or shallow drawers are best for fabrics. Inexpensive and practical drawers can be made from plastic-covered wire storage racks. Patterns stay in better shape and are easier to select if they are 'filed' on end, with pattern numbers on top. Threads require spool holders, the most convenient form being plastic trays that can be kept in a drawer or sewing box.

Cutting and other sharp tools should be stored so that blades or points are protected, and you can reach what you need without difficulty. Small items are much easier to find if they are stored in a partitioned drawer or tray.

A fairly generous waste bin is a necessity; plastic bins are conveniently lightweight, and are easily emptied as they do not snarl fabric scraps.

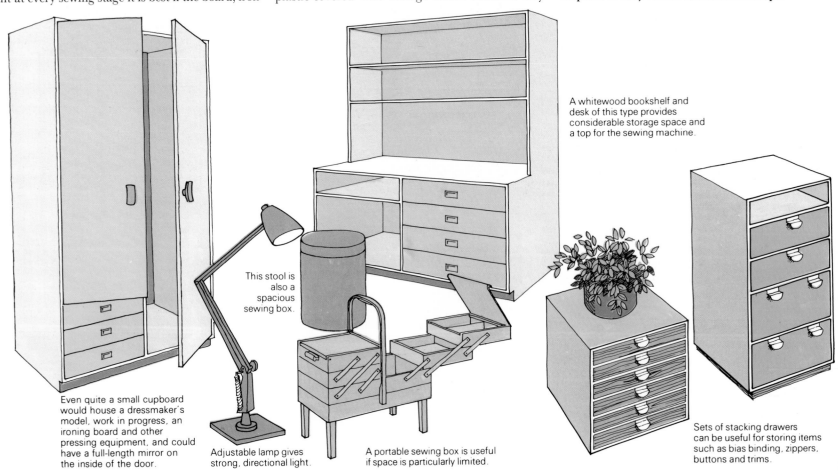

A whitewood bookshelf and desk of this type provides considerable storage space and a top for the sewing machine.

This stool is also a spacious sewing box.

Even quite a small cupboard would house a dressmaker's model, work in progress, an ironing board and other pressing equipment, and could have a full-length mirror on the inside of the door.

Adjustable lamp gives strong, directional light.

A portable sewing box is useful if space is particularly limited.

Sets of stacking drawers can be useful for storing items such as bias binding, zippers, buttons and trims.

Patterns, fabrics and cutting

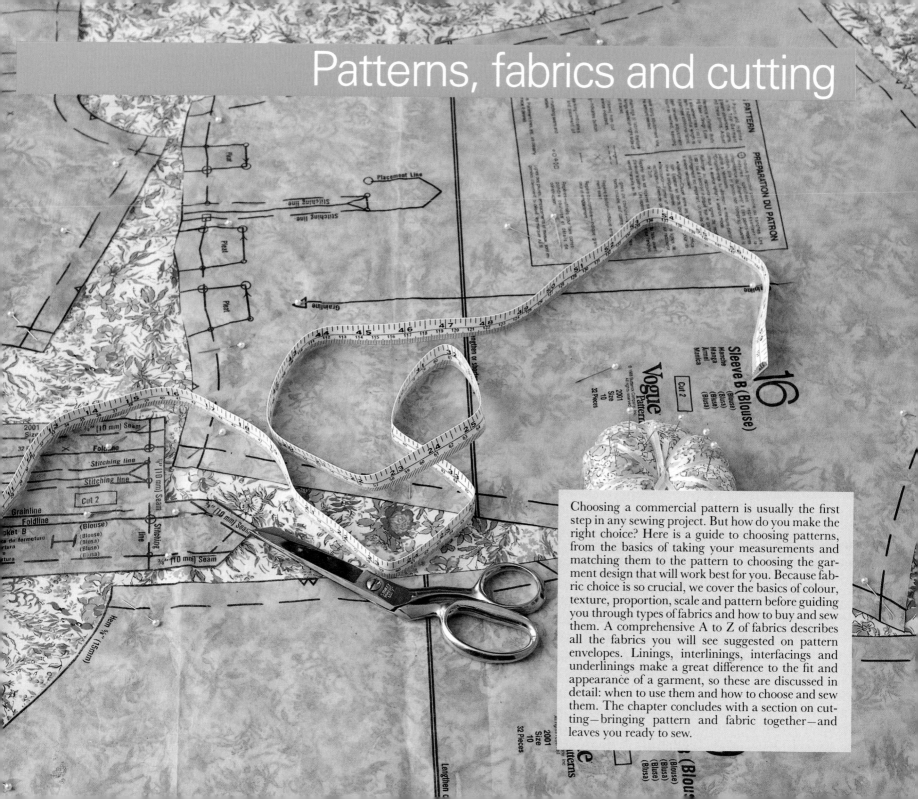

Choosing a commercial pattern is usually the first step in any sewing project. But how do you make the right choice? Here is a guide to choosing patterns, from the basics of taking your measurements and matching them to the pattern to choosing the garment design that will work best for you. Because fabric choice is so crucial, we cover the basics of colour, texture, proportion, scale and pattern before guiding you through types of fabrics and how to buy and sew them. A comprehensive A to Z of fabrics describes all the fabrics you will see suggested on pattern envelopes. Linings, interlinings, interfacings and underlinings make a great difference to the fit and appearance of a garment, so these are discussed in detail: when to use them and how to choose and sew them. The chapter concludes with a section on cutting—bringing pattern and fabric together—and leaves you ready to sew.

Pattern selection/size

Recognising your figure type

Female figures vary greatly in shape from person to person. There are, however, broad categories or **figure types** into which figures can be grouped. Commercial patterns are therefore sized not only for different measurements but also for figure types of varying proportions.

To decide which type most closely approximates your own figure, take your measurements accurately (see pages 46 and 47). Next, carefully appraise your silhouette, front and side, in a long mirror. (Wear undergarments or a body stocking for both procedures.) You will then be ready to compare your figure with the standard pattern types.

Overall height is one indicator of figure type, but length of legs, and sometimes of neck, can make it deceptive. Far more important are length of torso and location within it of waist and hip levels. The drawings at the right represent the standard pattern figure types; the labels indicate the total range of measurements spanned by each type for bust, waist, hips, back neck to waist and waist to hip. When comparing your figure with the standard types, take special notice of differences in back neck to waist length and waist to hip length.

Although figure types do not signify age groups, an age level may be implied and styles designed accordingly. It is best to stay within the size range of the figure type most like yours, but it is possible to choose from another and adjust the proportions (see Basic pattern alterations).

Metric measurements

Record your measurements in centimetres, since all measurements and instructions in this book are metric. Although most people are completely at ease with the metric system, you may still be hampered by a lingering affection for the old terms, particularly when referring to such familiar matters as height and body measurements. You will find it easier to appreciate metric figures, however, when you can see exactly how much they measure, and how much simpler they are to deal with than fractions of an inch, inches, feet and yards.

Above all, resist any temptation to convert the measurements given in this book into feet and inches. Such a conversion would serve no purpose, and could lead to confusion and mistakes.

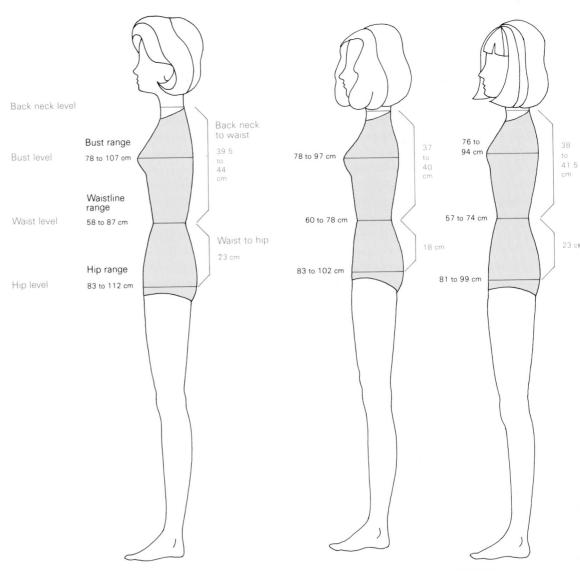

Back neck level

Bust level — Bust range 78 to 107 cm

Back neck to waist 39.5 to 44 cm

Waist level — Waistline range 58 to 87 cm

Waist to hip 23 cm

Hip level — Hip range 83 to 112 cm

78 to 97 cm — 37 to 40 cm

60 to 78 cm — 18 cm

83 to 102 cm

76 to 94 cm — 38 to 41.5 cm

57 to 74 cm — 23 cm

81 to 99 cm

MISSES'
About 1.65 to 1.68 m in height, well developed and proportioned. Taller, with longer back waist length, than all other figure types except Women's. Hip is measured at 23 cm below the waist. Statistically, this is considered to be the average figure.

MISS PETITE
About 1.57 to 1.60 m, with proportions similar to Misses', but shorter overall, with narrower shoulder. Hip measured 18 cm below waist.

JUNIOR
About 1.63 to 1.65 m, well developed, but shorter back waist length and higher bustline than Misses'. Hip is measured 23 cm below waist.

Size range charts (in centimetres)

MISSES'

Size	6	8	10	12	14	16	18	20
Bust	78	80	83	87	92	97	102	107
Waist	58	61	64	67	71	76	81	87
Hip	83	85	88	92	97	102	107	112
Back waist length	39.5	40	40.5	41.5	42	42.5	43	44

MISS PETITE

Size	6mp	8mp	10mp	12mp	14mp	16mp
Bust	78	80	83	87	92	97
Waist	60	62	65	69	73	78
Hip	83	85	88	92	97	102
Back waist length	37	37.5	38	39	39.5	40

JUNIOR

Size	5	7	9	11	13	15
Bust	76	79	81	85	89	94
Waist	57	60	62	65	69	74
Hip	81	84	87	90	94	99
Back waist length	38	39	39.5	40	40.5	41.5

JUNIOR PETITE

Size	3JP	5JP	7JP	9JP	11JP	13JP
Bust	78	79	81	84	87	89
Waist	57	58	61	64	66	69
Hip	80	81	84	87	89	92
Back waist length	35.5	36	37	37.5	38	39

YOUNG JUNIOR/TEEN

Size	5/6	7/8	9/10	11/12	13/14	15/16
Bust	71	74	78	81	85	89
Waist	56	58	61	64	66	69
Hip	79	81	85	89	93	97
Back waist length	34.5	35.5	37	38	39	40

HALF-SIZE

Size	10½	12½	14½	16½	18½	20½	22½	24½
Bust	84	89	94	99	104	109	114	119
Waist	69	74	79	84	89	96	102	108
Hip	89	94	99	104	109	116	122	128
Back waist length	38	39	39.5	40	40.5	40.5	41	41.5

WOMEN'S

Size	38	40	42	44	46	48	50
Bust	107	112	117	122	127	132	137
Waist	89	94	99	105	112	118	124
Hip	112	117	122	127	132	137	142
Back waist length	44	44	44.5	45	45	45.5	46

78 to 89 cm   35.5 to 39 cm

57 to 69 cm   18 cm

80 to 92 cm

71 to 89 cm   34.5 to 40 cm

56 to 69 cm   18 cm

79 to 97 cm

84 to 119 cm   38 to 41.5 cm

69 to 108 cm   18 cm

89 to 128 cm

107 to 137 cm   44 to 46 cm

89 to 124 cm   23 cm

112 to 142 cm

JUNIOR PETITE
About 1.52 to 1.55 m, with fully developed figure. Shorter than Junior but with similar proportions. Hip is measured 18 cm below the waist.

YOUNG JUNIOR/TEEN
About 1.55 to 1.60 m, a developing figure with small, high bust, waist larger in proportion to it. Hip is measured 18 cm below the waist.

HALF-SIZE
About 1.57 to 1.60 m, larger waist, shorter back waist length and narrower shoulder than Misses'. Hip is measured 18 cm below the waist.

WOMEN'S
About 1.65 to 1.68 m, similar to Misses' in height and proportions, but larger figure overall. Hip is measured 23 cm below the waist.

Pattern selection/size

Taking measurements

Measurements can be taken without assistance, but the task is easier when you have someone to help. For greatest accuracy, wear undergarments or a body stocking when measuring; use a tape measure that does not stretch. Before starting, tie a string around your middle and let it roll to the natural waistline. Take vertical measurements first, then those in the round. Pull the tape snug, but not too tight, always around the fullest part of each body area; be sure to keep the tape parallel to the floor. Record all measurements on a chart like the one on the opposite page. The dimensions listed there are sufficient for selecting pattern type and size. Other measurements may be needed for garment fitting and alterations (see Pattern alterations).

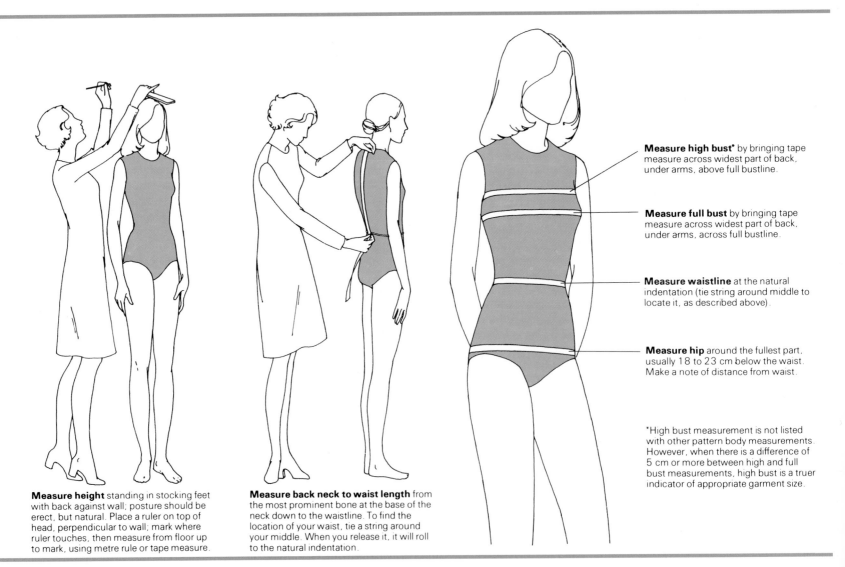

Measure high bust* by bringing tape measure across widest part of back, under arms, above full bustline.

Measure full bust by bringing tape measure across widest part of back, under arms, across full bustline.

Measure waistline at the natural indentation (tie string around middle to locate it, as described above).

Measure hip around the fullest part, usually 18 to 23 cm below the waist. Make a note of distance from waist.

*High bust measurement is not listed with other pattern body measurements. However, when there is a difference of 5 cm or more between high and full bust measurements, high bust is a truer indicator of appropriate garment size.

Measure height standing in stocking feet with back against wall; posture should be erect, but natural. Place a ruler on top of head, perpendicular to wall; mark where ruler touches, then measure from floor up to mark, using metre rule or tape measure.

Measure back neck to waist length from the most prominent bone at the base of the neck down to the waistline. To find the location of your waist, tie a string around your middle. When you release it, it will roll to the natural indentation.

Pattern size guidelines

After taking your measurements and deciding on the figure type most like your own (pp. 44–45), you are ready to choose a pattern size according to the guidelines below. If your measurements do not correspond exactly to any one size, consider all pertinent factors and choose the size that will require you to make the fewest major alterations.

Your pattern may, or it may not, be the same as your ready-to-wear size. It doesn't matter; ready-to-wear and pattern sizes do not necessarily have any relation to one another. Pattern sizes, however, *do* relate to each other—an important fact to remember. All commercial patterns are based on the same fundamental measurements, which makes sizing fairly consistent from brand to brand.

Where differences between pattern brands occur, they are usually in shaping—variations in shoulder slope, dart contours and position, armhole curve, sleeve cap shape and so on. These subtle differences often reflect fashion trends. They may also cause certain pattern brands to fit some people better than others, so shop around when buying patterns and try those of different makes; in time you will know which make suits your figure best. Fundamentally, however, the sizing is the same for all.

For the **first garment** you make, choose a simple pattern with few darts or seams. All pattern manufacturers include a range of simple-to-sew designs, with few pattern pieces, in their catalogue. These are aimed not only at the beginner but also at the woman who wants to run a garment up quickly without having to worry about intricate fitting details or trimmings. These ranges are particularly suited to building up a wardrobe of casual, loose-fitting garments.

Dress, blouse, coat and jacket sizes are selected according to the full bust measurement. If your waist and/or hips do not correspond to the waist or hip allowances for this size bust, the waist and hip areas in patterns are easily adjusted.

An exception to this selection rule is made when there is a difference of more than 5 centimetres between the high bust and full bust measurements (see previous page). Such a discrepancy indicates that the bust is full in relation to the body frame. Pattern sizes in such cases should be chosen according to the high bust measurement and the bust area should be adjusted (see Pattern alterations). Remember that

coat and jacket patterns already include an allowance for wearing over a dress or blouse, so buy according to your body measurements as usual and don't be tempted to buy a larger size.

Pattern size for skirts or pants is determined by the hip measurement, even if the hips are larger, proportionately, than the waist. It is easier to take in at the waist than let out at the hip.

If you choose a pattern that includes many types of garment—a blouse, skirt, jacket and pants, for instance—stay with your bust measurement.

Being one size on top and another on the bottom makes you one among many. Follow the recommendations above for pattern selection and adjust each pattern according to the instructions in the Pattern alterations chapter. If the difference is very great, it may be necessary to buy two sizes of the same pattern and use the appropriate pattern pieces from each. This can be expensive but will save a lot of time and ensure a better fit.

Some pattern manufacturers now recognise this problem and offer a range of styles that come in multi-size patterns. The ranges are, however, comparatively limited.

When measurements fall between sizes, such additional factors as bone structure, fabric and fit influence pattern selection. The smaller size may be better if you are small-boned, the larger if you are large-boned. Stretchy fabrics allow some size leeway, those with considerable give often permitting the smaller size choice. Determine the amount of stretch in a knit or other stretchy fabric you are intending to use (see page 69), and follow the recommendations on pattern envelopes.

Personal preference, too, may incline you toward a closer or looser fit—but don't forget that wearing ease is already built into each pattern. (See the chapter on Pattern alterations for an explanation of wearing ease.)

Finally, your choice of pattern size may sometimes be influenced by **style.** Because the Misses' figure type comes closest to the average in height and proportions (see comparison at right), this range offers the widest selection of designs. If you find that your taste and fashion preferences are not satisfied by the styles in your own group, consider choosing the Misses' size nearest your own and adjusting the pattern to fit you.

Measurement chart

When you have taken measurements and decided on a pattern size, a chart like the one below is well worth making. Keep it up to date by re-measuring every six months or so; changes may mean that you will need a different size. Enter your measurements in the first column, corresponding measurements for your pattern size in the adjoining column, differences (if any) in the third. Differences of 6 mm or more in length, 1 cm or more in circumference, indicate a need for pattern adjustments.

MEASUREMENT	YOURS	PATTERN	DIFFERENCE
Height			
Back neck to waist			
High bust			
Full bust			
Waistline			
Full hip			
FOR PATTERN SIZE:			

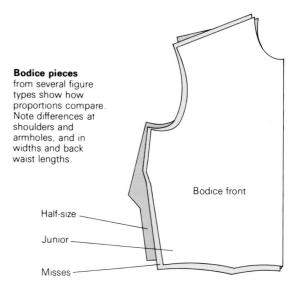

Bodice pieces from several figure types show how proportions compare. Note differences at shoulders and armholes, and in widths and back waist lengths.

Bodice front

Half-size

Junior

Misses

Pattern selection/style

Making design work for you

Combining style and fabric in a flattering fashion requires the artful use of four design elements—**line, detail, texture** and **colour.** While there is nothing mysterious about any of these, they each have the power to create illusion. By themselves or in combination, they can add to or diminish height, enlarge or reduce apparent figure size.

Examples of the ways each element works are given here and on pages 50–51. Once you understand what they do, you must decide how you want to use them. This requires a realistic analysis of height and figure type (as explained on page 44) and some careful thought about what features you want to emphasise or divert attention from. There are few rules in this regard, as the decisions are largely personal. For instance, if you are short, you might choose to emphasise your petiteness or aim for the illusion of greater height.

In general, *balance* is a desirable goal, and balance is achieved by minimising or counteracting anything excessive. For example, wide hips might be balanced by a wide shoulder area in the garment. There are two basic approaches to balance—formal, in which the two halves of a design are identical, and informal, where the areas are visually in equilibrium, but not the same. The vertical lines on the opposite page are examples of formal balance; the diagonals of informal.

An equally important goal is *harmony*—the aesthetically pleasing relationship of all the elements that go into a fashion. Harmony is mainly a matter of appropriateness—a sense of what things belong together, and to the situation. This might best be made clear by some negative examples. One might be the cluttered look of too many garment lines combined with a busy print. A heavy tweed, ideal for a tailored skirt or suit, is cumbersome and inappropriate in a softly draped, flowing design.

No matter how carefully you plan choices in relation to what you conceive to be your best and worst features, two other influences are bound to affect your decisions. One is current fashion; the other, your personal preferences. The trick is to play those influences together to your advantage.

Take colour and texture, for example. If this season's featured colour is unflattering to your figure, use it as an accent, preferably to call attention to one of your better features. If a popular colour clashes with your eye colour or skin tone, place it inside the garment as a lining. From the dominant trends in fashion, choose only those that you like and that suit you. Modify skirt width or length to your lines and liking; choose a less extreme version of a dress. Remember that what flatters is always more effective that what is simply new. When it comes to new styles, let this be your guide: think very carefully before buying a style sharply different from anything you've worn before.

If you find yourself confused by too many choices, scan your wardrobe for the garments you always feel good in, and for which you are often complimented. Stay within their limits of line, colour and texture—and you will never go wrong.

Silhouette (outside line)

The main lines of a garment are those that form its **silhouette,** or outside line. Basically, every silhouette is a variation of two familiar shapes—the rectangle and the triangle. (To see the shape more clearly, squint when you look at a garment.) Variations on these basic shapes are created largely by relative closeness of fit, which falls generally into four categories—*fitted, semi-fitted, slightly fitted* and *loosely fitted.* (The classification for a particular pattern is usually given on the envelope back.)

A fitted garment emphasises the figure's contours. The less fitted the shape, the less aware one is of the body and the more dominant the garment silhouette. The silhouette is dominant, too, when there are few seams or details to distract the eye, desirable if you wish to play up an interesting fabric. Fabric choice also affects silhouette: a crisp fabric, for instance, moulds garment shape; a soft one tends to outline, and thus emphasise, body shape. Fashion, too, has its influence on silhouette. Whole eras have been symbolised by a particular garment shape. Memorable examples are the bustle and the leg-of-mutton sleeve.

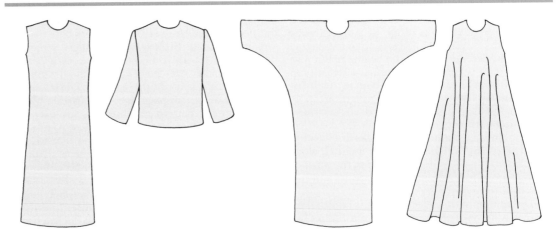

Rectangle is the basic silhouette when top and bottom are more or less equal in width. Narrow rectangle, left, is more slimming than wide or boxy one; box shape is excellent for diminishing height. Both shapes can be modified by seams, details and fabric choice.

Triangle is the basic silhouette when garment is wider at top or bottom. Width at top helps to balance a wide hipline, also diminishes height. Broad base at bottom counteracts wide shoulders or top-heavy figure. Exaggerated, either one creates drama by deliberate imbalance.

Structural lines (inside)

Lines within a design add another dimension to silhouette. Skilfully used, they create a pleasing illusion or diversion, and help to establish balance or good proportion for the figure.

Each kind of line—*horizontal, vertical, diagonal* and *curved*—has its own way of influencing a look (see examples below). At times, a line's placement may be more significant than its character, because our eyes tend to move in a habitual direction, formed by the reading pattern followed since childhood—left to right, and top to bottom. Thus, if vertical and horizontal lines exist equally in the same design, the eyes will be drawn first to the horizontal.

There are some general principles regarding use of line: (1) The longer, wider, or more repetitious a line, the greater its influence on the total design. (2) Folds (pleats, for example) create lines, but at the same time add bulk. (3) The more lines there are in a fabric design (for example, a print), the fewer lines there should be in the garment.

Details

Details such as sleeves, neckline, collar and pockets, though they are subordinate to the silhouette and seams, can have just as strong an influence, depending on their shape and location.

Among other things, they can be used to echo and reinforce a silhouette, as bell-shaped sleeves would do on a tent dress; to add interest to a plain garment; to alter a garment's mood from, say, dressy to casual; to call attention to a good feature, perhaps also away from a less attractive one, as a ruffle framing a pretty face might divert the eye from heavy hips.

Often a detail can create different impressions at the same time, as illustrated by the collars below. The one on the left makes the neck seem longer, while at the same time it adds width to the shoulder

Verticals usually create the illusion of height and slimness. However, when repeated at even intervals, they can cause the figure to appear both wider and shorter, because the eye is drawn alternately from side to side.

Horizontals tend to cut height, especially when used to divide a figure in half. One horizontal, however, used above or below the middle, makes a focal point of the smaller area, seeming to lengthen the longer one.

area and an impression of weight to the upper part of the body. The one on the right adds length to the face, but has little effect on height or neck length. Pockets at the hip always call attention to this area,

Diagonals may contribute to height or width, depending on their length and angle. A long diagonal creates a feeling of tallness. A short diagonal gives the impression of width and draws attention to the area in which it occurs.

Curves produce the same effects as straight lines of similar length and placement, but more subtly. The visual impact is softer, more graceful. A curve also adds roundness and a look of greater weight wherever it occurs on the figure.

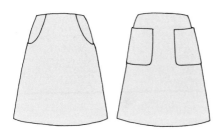

but the overall illusion varies with their size and placement. Whatever the intended purpose of details, do not overdo them; too many cause confusion and diminish the effectiveness of each one. Take care, too, that subsidiary features harmonise with the garment's silhouette and structural lines.

Colour and texture

Colour

Of the several elements that contribute to the overall effect of the garment you wear, colour is one of the most influential. In order to make the best use of colour, it is important to understand some of its properties and how you can use them.

We see colour when a surface reflects one of the colours of light. A green fabric, for example, is *reflecting* only green light and *absorbing* all the other colours that make up visible light. The word **hue** is used to describe the colour we see, and indicates where it is positioned in the spectrum. The **intensity** of a colour is its brightness or dullness, the **tone** (or value) describes how light or dark it is.

THE COLOUR WHEEL

The colour wheel is a convenient way of representing the relationship between colours. It is based on the spectrum or rainbow. All colours are derived from the three **primary** colours—red, yellow and blue—which are placed equidistant from each other on the colour wheel. When two primary colours are mixed in equal proportions they produce **secondary** colours, such as orange when yellow and red are combined, or violet when blue and red are mixed. Adjacent primary and secondary colours on the

wheel can be mixed to make **tertiary** colours, such as blue violet when blue and violet are combined. The diagrams below show the possible combinations.

Colours that occupy opposite positions on the wheel are known as **complementary** colours. Pairs of complementary colours include orange and blue, yellow and violet, and red and green. The diagram on the right shows the colour graduations produced by mixing different proportions of complementary colours, in this case red and green.

Black, white and grey are described as **neutrals** and are not colours. When a pure hue is mixed with white, it forms a tint; with black, a shade. Combined with white or black, a colour loses intensity and becomes either lighter or darker in tone, without a change in hue. A wide range of colour tones may be produced in this way within the one hue.

It is useful to know about the relationship between colours and to understand how different shades, tints and tones may be obtained. When we choose a colour scheme, however, we need to know more: how certain colours will interact, for instance, when placed side by side; and whether some kinds of colours will suit a particular garment design. The colour wheel can help here too.

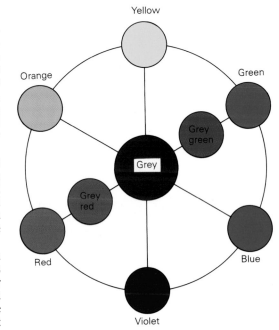

Complementary or opposite positions of colour.

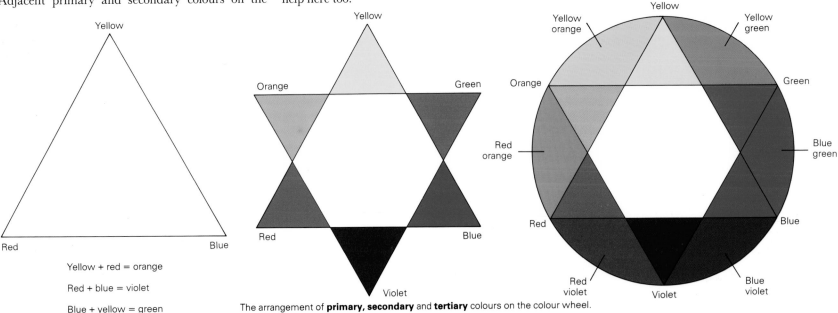

Yellow + red = orange

Red + blue = violet

Blue + yellow = green

The arrangement of **primary, secondary** and **tertiary** colours on the colour wheel.

The colour wheel

Red

Red violet

Red orange

Violet

Orange

Blue violet

Yellow orange

Blue

Yellow

Blue green

Yellow green

Green

The picture illustrates the transition between 100% red and 100% green. Mixing equal amounts of complementary colours produces grey. Adding more of its complement to a colour produces graduated mixtures known as intermediate tones.

Colour schemes

Combinations of colour, or colour schemes, can create a number of subtle optical illusions. A single colour by itself may appear to have certain qualities, but these can change greatly when it is seen with other colours.

Harmonious colour schemes are based on colours close to each other on the colour wheel, or on variations in one particular colour, known as a monochromatic colour scheme. Colours adjacent to each other on the colour wheel can soften and subdue each other.

Contrasting colour schemes are composed of colours far from each other on the colour wheel. When two opposite, or nearly opposite colours are used side by side, they enliven each other. A small amount of yellow as a feature collar or cuff will intensify the blue in a garment, 'pushing' the blue to appear stronger—more blue. The colour a person wears tends to emphasise the opposite colours in their complexion. You can prove this to yourself by draping a range of coloured fabrics against yourself.

Warm colours like reds, oranges and yellows will appear more prominent than cool colours such as blue, green and blue violet. The neutrals black and white can also provide contrast and emphasis.

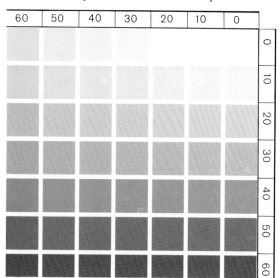

60	50	40	30	20	10	0	
							0
							10
							20
							30
							40
							50
							60

Colour and black selector chart used in choosing the varying tones of black and blue for Part 1 of this book.

51

Colour and texture

Selecting colour

We often do not know why we put certain colours together or why we like them. If we can learn to observe which colour schemes please us, and why, then we can expand our palette by experimenting with colour combinations we do not usually explore.

Colour choice is very personal. Essentially, we aim to enhance our features, such as skin, hair, eye and lip colour, to present an attractive appearance. There are several commercial schemes available for assessing an individual's colour characteristics and recommending categories of colour combinations they should wear. It is not difficult, however, to develop your own coordinated colour schemes.

The best way to gauge the effect of a particular colour on you is to drape a length of fabric over yourself and view it in a full length mirror, preferably in natural lighting. A colour that suits you should enliven your skin and eyes as well as complement your figure. Beginning with colours and combinations that you always feel good in, you could test many colours in this way—you will soon learn to appreciate the very great difference between what suits you and what does not.

If you discover that a colour you are attracted to does not create the effect you want, try a darker or brighter version, use less of it and/or combine it with other colours. A minor change in hue, tone or intensity can produce major changes in the overall effect, showing what a powerful tool colour is.

Using the colour wheel, you can experiment with softening strong colours or intensifying subtle ones to improve your natural colouring, figure shape and general attractiveness. It is important to experiment with the actual proportion of fabric you want to use against other fabrics you will be wearing. Shirt material can be draped against the top of your body above the skirt you are matching it with. Fabric for smaller features such as collars or pockets can be rolled up or folded to the approximate size to check the effect they will have.

The following illustrations provide some simple ways in which colour can be used to advantage in creating and modifying an overall colour scheme. Accessories such as shoes, handbag, scarf and even make-up should be considered as part of the total colour composition.

The **intensity** of a colour can be subdued by the addition of a paler tint.

A dark colour reduces apparent figure size; a light colour increases it.

Warm colours are more prominent than cool colours which appear to recede.

A colour in a print can be **highlighted** to draw it out.

Neutrals such as white and black can be used to add emphasis to colour schemes, whereas greys will soften them.

Harmonious colours, adjacent on the colour wheel, can soften each other.

Contrasting colours intensify each other. The colour here is made stronger by the presence of its opposite or complement.

Repetition of a colour emphasises both line and direction.

Colour can be used to **emphasise proportion** in a garment.

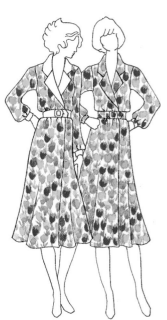

Colour can **accent** detailing features, such as pockets, collars and cuffs.

Colour and texture

Texture

The texture of a fabric appeals to the eyes (and even to the ears) as well as to the sense of touch. It offers enormous variety in **feel,** ranging from rough to smooth. It also affects the way light is reflected off its surface and hence can alter colour intensity. A roughly textured bouclé will look darker than a piece of cotton lawn dyed the same colour. Reflected light also affects apparent figure size: a dull finish appears to reduce size; a shiny fabric appears to increase it. Texture can even be heard—a good example is the characteristic swish of silk as it moves.

The degree of stiffness or softness and the weight and body of a fabric will influence the **drape,** that is, the way it hangs on the figure. Drape is an important factor in how well a particular fabric will move with the body and maintain the shape of a style.

Textured effects can be created in a garment by draping, shirring, ruching, quilting and stitching. Patterned fabric may provide an illusion of texture and the use of interfacings and linings will give textural properties to the shape of a garment. Variety in texture may be made a feature, but take care as heavily textured fabrics can be hard to match.

Bouclé or other rough textures are bulkier than most **smooth** ones and so make figures look heavier. A petite person must be especially careful when choosing a rough texture lest it be overwhelming.

A stiff fabric in an unbroken garment line will conceal the figure but make it seem larger. The same silhouette in **soft, clinging fabric** is figure-revealing. Neither extreme is flattering. Moderately soft or crisp textures are better choices.

Proportion and scale

The space divisions and their relationships within a design are termed **proportions.** These divisions may be defined by inner design lines (as illustrated on page 49), or result from the ways in which colour and texture are used (some examples are shown here). They always affect apparent height and figure size. While there are no hard and fast rules about proportion ratios, it is generally agreed that the more interesting ones are those that are uneven—two to three, three to five, and so on.

When proportions are in a harmonious relation to each other and to the figure, they are said to be in **scale.** In fashion terms, this means that small prints, stripes, plaids, and details (collars, pockets, etc.) suit a petite figure best, and larger elements a larger figure. The principle is simply that too great a contrast of sizes has a jarring effect because the larger components overwhelm the smaller ones.

Potential lack of proportion can be modified, however, by colour choices. A large print will not seem as large in subdued tones as the same motif would in vivid or contrasting colours.

A plaid may have various effects on a figure, depending on its space divisions and colour contrasts. In general, the wider the spaces between vertical bars, and/or the greater the colour contrast, the more enlarging the effect. To modify the impression of size, select a plaid made in muted colours and with minimal contrast.

A small print on a large figure, or **a large print** on a small one, creates too great a contrast to be pleasing. These results can be modified, however, by choosing subdued and subtle print tones instead of ones that contrast.

Developing your eye

Many designers use nature and art to inspire them in their colour and texture compositions. Their skills grow with experience, and with the deliberate training of their eye to perceive subtle colour and texture differences. Simply looking for small colour variations is one of the best ways to develop this ability. In nature, for instance, there are many shades of green to study. Awareness of texture can be developed in a similar manner. Use your sense of touch as well as your eyes to make fine distinctions between different textures, not only in fabrics but in many of the objects around you.

It is a good idea to study colour and texture combinations that attract you in clothing, fabric patterns, paintings, interior design and other forms of decorative art. In particular, you can look at what colours lie beside each other, whether they contrast or harmonise, and what overall effect is created.

Colours have been combined in the jumper photographed at the right to ensure that the complex details in the pattern are brought out but not exaggerated. The yellows create a unified effect, whereas the stronger shades of green, red and purple provide contrast and a vivid quality. Notice how often contrasting colours lie next to each other, increasing the richness of each without overwhelming the overall composition. A small amount of white gives a clear, fresh look to the neck, cuffs and waistband as well as accenting particular motifs.

Look closely at the work of experts in colour design, illustrated in magazines and books, or on display in museums. You can even base your colour schemes on their work. The advantage of analysing and working from an existing colour composition is that it gives you the experience of working with a balanced design and a good number of colours.

A striking summer outfit may be based on the main colours of a favourite painting, blended carefully with neutrals to achieve a harmonious effect. The subtle range of blues in the sea could inspire an outfit in pale blues where interest is achieved by flowing lines and good proportion, with the appropriate textural qualities.

The effect of scale, proportion, line and pattern are also important elements of design. As with colour and texture, you can train your eye to appreciate their contribution and in so doing increase your ability to create your own designs.

The colour combinations in the jumper and cushion covers were inspired by the painting, the flowers and the seashells.

55

Buying a pattern

How to use pattern catalogues

A pattern catalogue is a fashion directory where you can select the latest pattern designs, and also find information on suitable fabrics and accessories. Each catalogue is organised according to the pattern company's notion of its customers' needs, but all contain a wide variety of modern fashions. For women, these are grouped by style types, such as dresses, sportswear, or lingerie, and further classified by figure types. For example, Junior dresses may be in one section, Half-size dresses in another.

In addition, many catalogues contain sections for special categories, such as easy-to-make styles and designer fashions. Patterns for children, boys and men, for accessories, home furnishings and crafts (including toys and costumes) are in separate divisions, usually after the women's styles.

Specific information relating to each pattern is printed alongside the illustrations. Some of the facts are pertinent to pattern selection, such as the number of views to be found within the envelope. Also included are back views, fabric quantity requirements, notion needs and fabric recommendations.

The fabric recommendations are of special importance, particularly with regard to knits. 'Recommended for knits' means that knits as well as woven fabrics are suitable for the design. 'For knits only' means that wovens should not be used. Such a style has close fit and minimum shaping, relying on the stretchy fabric to mould to the figure. Other fabric limitations may be indicated, too, such as 'Not suitable for plaids or stripes'.

The newest fashions usually appear on the first few pages of the catalogue. These patterns were developed for the time period specified on the catalogue cover. They reflect trends for the coming season, not only in styles, but also in fabrics and accessories. The fabrics and accessories selected are thus current, available, and of course suitable for the fashions pictured.

A body measurement chart is located at the back of each catalogue. It includes measurements for all figure types and is a convenient reference, especially when you are sewing for someone else.

An index, usually on the last page, lists all the patterns in numerical order, and also the pages on which they appear. If you need to locate a certain pattern, and you know its number, the index is the fastest and easiest way to find it.

Catalogue tabs identify pattern types to be found within each section. The bulk of any book—about the opening two-thirds in most cases—is devoted to women's fashions, grouped by fashion images, figure types, and styles. Toward the back, you will find patterns for infants and children, men and boys. You will also find accessories for the home and craft projects at the back—the scope will depend upon the particular pattern company.

Pattern envelope front

The front of every pattern envelope bears the style number and illustrations of each fashion item and the variations on it that the envelope contains. Pattern price and size are usually included too. Before you buy, make sure that the style and size are the ones you have requested. Most stores will neither exchange nor give refunds for patterns.

Once you have decided on the view you prefer, the sketch or photo can guide you toward an appropriate fabric type. The fabric illustrated may be crisp or soft, printed or plain, depending on what best suits the fashion. If you are considering a plaid, stripe, or obvious diagonal, look for a view showing such a fabric being used. It's your best assurance that the fabric is suitable.

Special-feature notices appear on some envelope fronts, calling attention to one or more desirable or unusual characteristics of the pattern. They may say, for example, that the pattern is easy to construct, slimming, or created by a well-known designer. If it is 'For knits only', a knit gauge, for measuring knit stretchability, may appear on the front. (Some companies put it on the back.)

PATTERNS 000

MISSES' SIZE 12
BUST 87 cm

Pattern envelope front features a drawing, sometimes a photo, of each garment and any variations of it that the envelope contains. Illustrations can be used for guidance—garments are shown in fabrics chosen for their suitability to the design.

Buying extra fabric 70–71

Buying a pattern

Pattern envelope back

The envelope back supplies all the information needed at the outset of a sewing project. A typical envelope back is shown at the right, but the arrangement of the information may vary from pattern to pattern.

Look carefully at the envelope of each new pattern you buy; every part tells you something important about that particular design.

The most obvious feature, the fabric quantity block, lists exact amounts of fabric needed for each view and every size in that pattern's range. Space does not permit the inclusion of all fabric widths; if you plan to buy fabric in a width that is not included, consult the conversion chart below.

Note that although most patterns now give measurements in metric *and* imperial figures, they may eventually use metric figures only.

Fabric conversion chart

FABRIC WIDTHS

QUANTITY NEEDED

90 cm	115 cm	120 cm	135 cm	150 cm
1.6 m	1.3 m	1.2 m	1 m	0.9 m
1.8 m	1.5 m	1.4 m	1.3 m	1.2 m
2 m	1.6 m	1.5 m	1.4m	1.3 m
2.3 m	1.9 m	1.6 m	1.6 m	1.5 m
2.6 m	2.1 m	1.8 m	1.7 m	1.6 m
2.8 m	2.3 m	2.1 m	1.8 m	1.7 m
3.1 m	2.5 m	2.2 m	2.1 m	1.8 m
3.4 m	2.6 m	2.4 m	2.2 m	2.1m
3.9 m	2.9 m	2.5 m	2.4 m	2.2 m
4.1 m	3.1 m	2.8 m	2.5 m	2.4 m
4.4 m	3.3 m	3 m	2.7 m	2.5 m
4.6 m	3.6 m	3.1 m	2.9 m	2.7 m

Add additional 0.2 metre for: Large difference in fabric widths; one-directional fabrics; styles with sleeves cut in one with bodice.

Standard body measurements are given for reference.

The fabric quantity block gives exact amounts needed for each style, in several fabric widths. Amount is usually for material without nap; extra allowance must be made for 'with nap' fabric (see Fabrics).

Back views are line drawings that show construction details more clearly than sketches.

Finished garment measurements are useful for adjusting length (if necessary) and for comparing widths at lower edge of various garments.

Special advice concerns use or suitability of plaids, stripes, diagonals or napped fabrics.

Suggested fabrics are those the designer thinks most suited to the style.

Notions are the items, other than fabric, needed to complete the garment. Button sizes and number, zipper lengths, other closure requirements, trim and binding needs are given here.

BODY MEASUREMENTS								
Size	6	8	10	12	14	16	18	
Bust	30½	31½	32½	34	36	38	40	Ins.
Waist	23	24	25	26½	28	30	32	"
Hip	32½	33½	34½	36	38	40	42	"
Back waist length	15½	15¾	16	16¼	16½	16¾	17	"
SIZES	6	8	10	12	14	16	18	
Jacket								
44/45" ***	2¾	2¾	2¾	2¾	2⅞	2⅞	2⅞	Yds.
58/60" ***	1⅞	1⅞	2	2	2⅛	2⅛	2¼	"
Lining								
44/45" **	2⅛	2¼	2¼	2¼	2¼	2⅜	2⅜	"
Interfacing - 21" thru 25", 1 yd.								
Top								
44/45" ***	1⅝	1⅝	1⅝	1⅝	2	2	2⅛	Yds.
58/60" ***	1⅛	1¼	1¼	1¼	1¼	1¼	1¼	"
Interfacing - 21" thru 25", ¼ yd.								
Skirt								
44/45" ***	1⅝	1⅝	1⅝	1⅝	1⅝	1⅝	1⅝	Yds.
58/60" ***	⅞	⅞	⅞	⅞	1	1	1⅛	"
Shorts								
44/45" ***	1⅞	2	2	2	2	2	2¾	Yds.
58/60" ***	1½	1½	1½	1⅝	1⅝	1⅝	1¾	"
Interfacing - 21" thru 25", 1⅛ yds.								
FINISHED GARMENT MEASUREMENTS								
Back length from normal neckline								
Jacket	31	31¼	31½	31¾	32	32¼	32½	Ins.
Top	25½	25¾	26	26¼	26½	26¾	27	"
Back length from natural waistline								
Skirt	23½	23¾	24	24¼	24½	24¾	25	"
Measurement at bustline								
Jacket	41	42	43	44½	46½	48½	50½	"
Top	40	41	42	43½	45½	47½	49½	"
Measurement at hipline								
Skirt	36	37	38	39½	41½	43½	45½	"
Shorts	36½	37½	38½	40	42	44	46	"
Bottom width								
Skirt	35	36	37	38½	40½	42½	44½	"

****Without Nap ***With or Without Nap** - Use With Nap Yardages and layouts for pile or one-way design fabrics. Additional Fabric may be needed to match stripes or plaids.

SUGGESTED FABRICS: Jacket, Skirt, Shorts - Lightweight Linen • Cotton and Cotton Blends • Gabardine • Lightweight Wool and Wool Blends • Flannel • Wool Crepe; **Top, Skirt** - also Challis • Crepe de Chine • Soft Cottons; Jacket (Lining) - Lining Fabrics. **NOTE: All Garments** - Not Suitable For Diagonals.

NOTIONS: Thread, Belt; **Jacket** - Four ⅞" Buttons, ½" Thick Uncovered "Raglan" Style Shoulder Pads, or McCall's Ready Made Pads #10006; **Top** - Three ½" Buttons, ½" Thick Covered "Raglan" Style Shoulder Pads, or McCall's Ready Made Pads #10006; **Skirt** - 7" Zipper, One Hook and Eye; **Shorts** - 7" Zipper, Three ⅝" Buttons.

MESURES								
Taille	6	8	10	12	14	16	18	
Tour de poitrine	78	80	83	87	92	97	102	cm
Tour de taille	58	61	64	67	71	76	81	cm
Tour de hanches	83	85	88	92	97	102	107	cm
Longueur dos	39.5	40	40.5	41.5	42	42.5	43	cm
TAILLES	6	8	10	12	14	16	18	
Veste								
115cm***	2.50	2.50	2.50	2.50	2.60	2.60	2.60	m
150cm***	1.80	1.80	1.80	1.80	1.90	1.90	2.00	m
Doublure								
115cm**	2.00	2.00	2.00	2.00	2.00	2.20	2.20	m
Entoilage - 53 à 64cm, 1.00m								
Blouse								
115cm***	1.50	1.50	1.50	1.50	1.80	1.90	1.90	m
150cm***	1.10	1.10	1.10	1.10	1.10	1.10	1.10	m
Entoilage - 53 à 64cm, 0.20m								
Jupe								
115cm***	1.40	1.50	1.50	1.50	1.50	1.50	1.50	m
150cm***	0.80	0.80	0.80	0.80	0.90	0.90	1.00	m
Short								
115cm***	1.80	1.80	1.80	1.80	1.80	1.80	2.50	m
150cm***	1.40	1.40	1.40	1.40	1.40	1.50	1.60	m
Entoilage - 53 à 64cm, 1.10m								
MESURES DU VETEMENT FINI								
Longueur dos depuis encolure naturelle								
Veste	79	79	80	81	81	82	83	cm
Blouse	65	65	66	67	67	68	69	cm
Longueur dos depuis taille naturelle								
Jupe	60	60	61	62	62	63	64	cm
Mesure à la poitrine								
Veste	104	107	109	113	118	123	128	cm
Blouse	102	104	107	111	116	121	126	cm
Mesure aux hanches								
Jupe	91	94	97	100	105	111	116	cm
Short	93	95	98	102	107	112	117	cm
Largeur à l'ourlet								
Jupe	89	91	94	98	103	108	113	cm

****Sans Sens ***Avec ou Sans sens** - Utilisez le métrage à sens pour les tissus pelucheux et les imprimés à sens. Il faut davantage de tissu pour raccorder les rayures ou les écossais.

TISSUS CONSEILLES - Veste, jupe, short - Toile de lin fine • Coton et cotonnade • Gabardine • Laine et lainage fins • Flanelle • Crêpe de laine. **Blouse, jupe** - aussi Etamine • Crêpe de Chine • Coton souple. **Veste** (doublure) - tissus de doublure. **N.B. Tous vêtements** - Les diagonales ne conviennent pas.

MERCERIE - Fil, ceinture. **Veste** - 4 boutons de 22mm, épaulettes noncouvertes de 1.3cm d'épaisseur (pour manches raglan), ou les épaulettes toutes faites #10006 de McCall. **Blouse** - 3 boutons de 13mm, épaulettes recouvertes de 1.3cm d'épaisseur (pour manches raglan), ou les épaulettes toutes faites #10006 de McCall; **Jupe** - 1 glissière de 18cm, 1 agrafe. **Short** - 1 glissière de 18cm, 3 boutons de 16mm.

Using the pattern envelope back as a shopping guide

1. Read the section on suggested fabrics' to see what sort of fabrics are most suitable to the style. These are the fabrics recommended by the designer of the pattern.

2. Check for fabric cautions or restrictions to make sure that the fabric you have in mind is suitable.

3. Circle your size at the top of the fabric quantity block. Run your eye down the left side until you find the view and the fabric width you have chosen; then glance across from left to right until you reach the vertical column under your size. The number you find there is the amount of fabric that you will need to buy. If you have a special fabric in mind and the width it comes in is not included in the pattern envelope list, consult the conversion chart at the left for the approximate amount you will need to buy.

4. Look through the rest of the fabric quantity block for the interfacing, lining and trim requirements of your pattern, if any of these are needed.

5. Purchase all the bindings and fasteners specified for your view. Thread requirements are usually 1 small spool (91 metres) for a skirt, pair of pants or a simple top not requiring extensive seam finishing; 2 small spools or the equivalent (182 metres) for a dress, a coat or a suit.

The parts of a pattern

Inside the envelope

Contents of all pattern envelopes are basically the same. The key element is the **tissue pattern,** each piece identified by name and number, and by view when pieces differ for, say, Views A and B. Because garments are usually identical on right and left sides, most pattern pieces represent half a garment section and are placed on folded fabric. The **direction sheet,** which you should turn to first, is a guide to pattern pieces needed for each view, and to cutting and sewing. Of the varied assistance it gives, the most directly useful parts are shown below: (1) **pattern piece diagram,** for identifying the pieces required for each view; (2) **cutting guides,** arranged by view, fabric widths, and pattern sizes; (3) step-by-step **sewing instructions.** The pattern in the example below is for an imaginary dress. Views A and B differ in sleeve length (short for A, long for B) and skirt style (narrower for A).

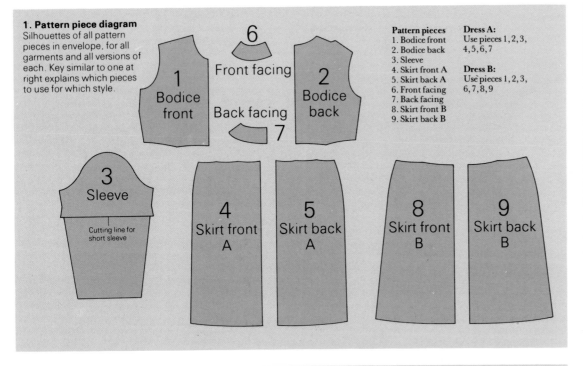

1. Pattern piece diagram
Silhouettes of all pattern pieces in envelope, for all garments and all versions of each. Key similar to one at right explains which pieces to use for which style.

Pattern pieces	Dress A:
1. Bodice front	Use pieces 1, 2, 3,
2. Bodice back	4, 5, 6, 7
3. Sleeve	
4. Skirt front A	**Dress B:**
5. Skirt back A	Use pieces 1, 2, 3,
6. Front facing	6, 7, 8, 9
7. Back facing	
8. Skirt front B	
9. Skirt back B	

6
Front facing

Back facing
7

1
Bodice front

2
Bodice back

3
Sleeve
Cutting line for short sleeve

4
Skirt front A

5
Skirt back A

8
Skirt front B

9
Skirt back B

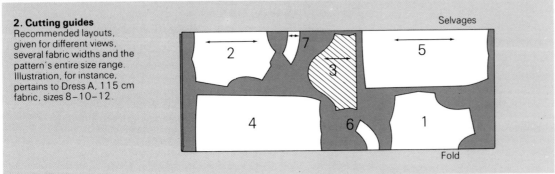

2. Cutting guides
Recommended layouts, given for different views, several fabric widths and the pattern's entire size range. Illustration, for instance, pertains to Dress A, 115 cm fabric, sizes 8–10–12.

Selvages

2   7   5

3

4   6   1

Fold

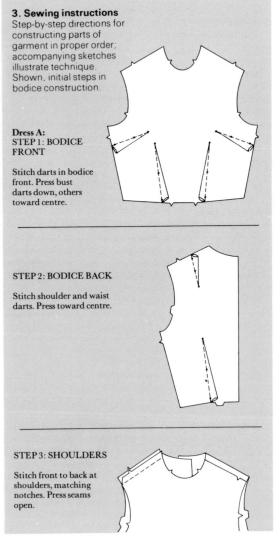

3. Sewing instructions
Step-by-step directions for constructing parts of garment in proper order; accompanying sketches illustrate technique. Shown, initial steps in bodice construction.

Dress A:
STEP 1: BODICE FRONT

Stitch darts in bodice front. Press bust darts down, others toward centre.

STEP 2: BODICE BACK

Stitch shoulder and waist darts. Press toward centre.

STEP 3: SHOULDERS

Stitch front to back at shoulders, matching notches. Press seams open.

The parts of a pattern

What pattern markings mean

Every pattern piece bears markings that together constitute a pattern 'sign language', indispensable to accuracy at every stage—layout and cutting, joining of sections, fitting and adjustment.

Note all symbols carefully; each has special significance. Some pertain to alteration. The double line in the bodice piece below, for example, tells you to 'lengthen or shorten here'. Other marks are used for matching related sections. Even piece numbers are important, signifying the order in which sections are to be constructed.

The markings defined below occur on most patterns. Less common ones—for buttonholes, pockets etc.—are explained in sections on those subjects.

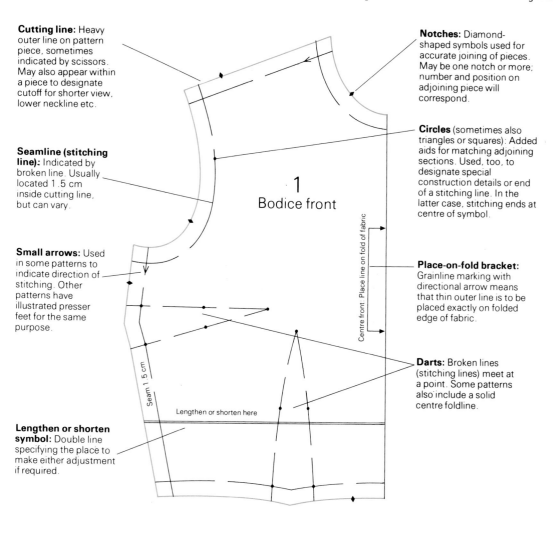

Cutting line: Heavy outer line on pattern piece, sometimes indicated by scissors. May also appear within a piece to designate cutoff for shorter view, lower neckline etc.

Seamline (stitching line): Indicated by broken line. Usually located 1.5 cm inside cutting line, but can vary.

Small arrows: Used in some patterns to indicate direction of stitching. Other patterns have illustrated presser feet for the same purpose.

Lengthen or shorten symbol: Double line specifying the place to make either adjustment if required.

1
Bodice front

Seam 1.5 cm

Lengthen or shorten here

Centre front. Place line on fold of fabric

Notches: Diamond-shaped symbols used for accurate joining of pieces. May be one notch or more; number and position on adjoining piece will correspond.

Circles (sometimes also triangles or squares): Added aids for matching adjoining sections. Used, too, to designate special construction details or end of a stitching line. In the latter case, stitching ends at centre of symbol.

Place-on-fold bracket: Grainline marking with directional arrow means that thin outer line is to be placed exactly on folded edge of fabric.

Darts: Broken lines (stitching lines) meet at a point. Some patterns also include a solid centre foldline.

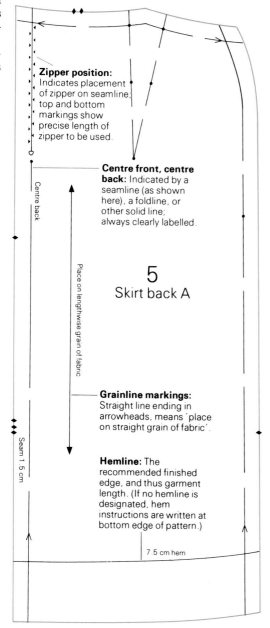

5
Skirt back A

Centre back

Place on lengthwise grain of fabric

Seam 1.5 cm

7.5 cm hem

Zipper position: Indicates placement of zipper on seamline; top and bottom markings show precise length of zipper to be used.

Centre front, centre back: Indicated by a seamline (as shown here), a foldline, or other solid line; always clearly labelled.

Grainline markings: Straight line ending in arrowheads, means 'place on straight grain of fabric'.

Hemline: The recommended finished edge, and thus garment length. (If no hemline is designated, hem instructions are written at bottom edge of pattern.)

Fabric fundamentals

Natural and artificial fibres

Fibres are the basic components of textile fabrics. Each has unique characteristics that it imparts to fabrics made from it. Although a fibre's character can be altered by yarn structure and by fabric construction and finish, the original characteristics are still evident in the resulting fabric and are central to its use and care.

Before this century, all fibres used for cloth were from natural sources. In recent years, a host of new, synthetic fibres has appeared, products of the chemistry laboratory. Whether a fibre is natural or artificial has some bearing on its general characteristics. A review and comparison of natural and artificial fibres begins below. Consult charts here and on the opposite page for the properties, uses and care of individual fibres.

Natural fibres have the irregularities and subtleties inherent in natural things. These qualities contribute to the beauty of natural fabrics. Absorbency and porosity are also common to natural fibres, making them responsive to changes in temperature and humidity and comfortable to wear in a variety of climatic conditions. Less desirable is the fact that natural fibres, especially cotton and linen, have limited resiliency, so that fabrics made with them tend to crease easily. This problem can be modified to a certain extent by crease-resistant finishes, but at some sacrifice to comfort.

Cotton, linen and wool occur as relatively short fibres (approximately 2 to 38 centimetres long) called *staples*. Before fabric can be constructed, the staples must be twisted (spun) into continuous strands called yarns (see p. 62). When fibres are sorted for spinning, the longer and shorter lengths are usually separated. The longer staples make high-quality yarns, identified as 'combed' for cottons,

'worsted' for wools. Fabrics made from these staples are supple and sleek and have a slight sheen. They are generally more expensive, but exceptionally durable.

Silk fibre is unreeled from the silkworm's cocoon into a long, continuous strand called a *filament*. The short strands left from this process are twisted together and used to produce rough-textured 'spun silk'.

Artificial is a term that refers to *all* fibres not found naturally. It covers both synthetic fibres (made entirely from chemicals such as petroleum) and fibres such as rayon and acetate which are made in the laboratory from cellulose, a natural product.

All **synthetic fibres** begin as chemical solutions; forced through tiny holes into a chemical bath or air chamber, these harden into long ropes of fibre, also called filaments. Unless they are further treated (texturised or spun), these filaments are smooth and slippery and so tend to unravel.

Synthetics are also highly resilient, and thus crease-resistant. On the other hand, almost all of them are low in porosity and absorbency, which makes them uncomfortable in hot or humid weather. Certain synthetics, nylon for one, are thermoplastic; that is, they can be moulded under carefully controlled conditions of heat and pressure, permitting the creation of interesting texture variations in the yarn or in the finished fabric.

One problem with synthetics, and artificial fibres in general, is the array of terms used to identify them. The chart on page 61 will allow you to distinguish between the **generic** name and the **trademark** names for each artificial fibre type.

In specially controlled conditions, it is now possible to form **microfibres,** which have the same chemical composition as other artificial fibres, but are finer than anything found in nature. Microfibres possess the strong points of synthetics (such as resistance to wrinkling and soiling) while bringing many improvements to fabric look and performance (such as soft draping, vivid colour and air permeability).

Fibre blends are combinations of two or more different fibres. Usually the fibre present in the highest percentage dominates the fabric, but a successful blend will exhibit the desirable qualities of all.

Natural fibres

Fibre and source	Characteristics	Typical fabrics and uses	Care
Cotton From seed pod of cotton plant	Strong; even when wet Absorbent Draws heat from body Tends to crease Good affinity for dyes Shrinks unless treated Deteriorated by mildew Weakened by sunlight	Versatile fabrics in many weights and textures Used for summer wear, season-spanning garments, work clothes *Examples: Corduroy, denim, poplin, terry, organdie, seersucker*	Most cottons can be laundered, colourfast ones in hot water, others in warm or cold water Tumble-dry at hot setting Chlorine bleach can be used if care instructions permit Iron while damp
Linen From flax plant	Strong Absorbent Draws heat from body Creases unless treated Poor affinity for dyes Some tendency to shrink and stretch Deteriorated by mildew	Fabrics usually have coarse texture and natural lustre Weave weights vary from very light to heavy Used for spring and summer wear; also many household items	Usually dry-cleaned to retain the crisp finish Can be washed if softness is preferred Usually shrinks when washed
Silk From cocoons of silkworms	Strong Absorbent Holds in body heat Crease resistant Good affinity for dyes, but may bleed Resists mildew, moths Weakened by sunlight and perspiration	Luxurious, lustrous fabrics in many weights Used for dresses, suits, blouses and linings *Examples: Brocade, chiffon, crêpe, satin, tweed, jersey*	Usually dry-cleaned If washable, usually done by hand in mild suds Avoid chlorine bleach Iron at low temperature setting
Wool From fleece of sheep	Relatively weak Exceptionally absorbent Holds in body heat Creases fall out Good affinity for dye Needs mothproofing Shrinks unless treated	Fabrics of many weights, textures, constructions Used for sweaters, dresses, suits and coats *Examples: Crêpe, flannel, fleece, gabardine, melton, tweed, jersey*	Usually dry-cleaned Many sweaters can be washed in tepid water and mild suds; do not wring Do not use chlorine bleach Some wools can be machine-washed; follow instructions

Artificial fibres

Fibre and trademarks*	Characteristics	Typical fabrics and uses	Care	Fibre and trademarks*	Characteristics	Typical fabrics and uses	Care
Acetate Chromspun[6]	Relatively weak Moderately absorbent Holds in body heat Tends to wrinkle Dyes well but subject to atmospheric fading Resists stretching, shrinking and moths Accumulates static electricity	Luxurious, silklike fabrics with deep lustre and excellent draping qualities Used for lingerie, dresses, blouses, linings *Examples: Brocade, crêpe, faille, satin, taffeta, lace, jersey, tricot*	Usually dry-cleaned If washable, can be done by hand or on gentle cycle of machine If tumble-dried, use low setting Iron all acetates at synthetic setting; they melt at high heat	**Nylon** Amilan[16] Perlon[1] Dorix[1] Antron[5] Cordura[5] Supplex[5]	Strong Low absorbency Holds in body heat Resists wrinkling, soil, mildew and moths Tends to pill Accumulates static electricity	Wide range of fabric textures and weights Often blended with other fibres Used for lingerie, linings, swimsuits, blouses and dresses *Examples: Fake fur, satin, jersey*	Can be washed by hand or machine in warm water, use gentle machine cycle Use fabric softener to reduce static electricity Tumble-dry or drip-dry Iron at low temperature
Acrylic Acrilan[13] Courtelle[2] Dralon[1] Exlan[17] Toraylon[16] Vonnel[12] Dolan[9]	Strong Low absorbency Holds in body heat Resists wrinkles, mildew, moths Good affinity for dyes Accumulates static electricity Tends to pull Heat-sensitive	Chiefly soft or fluffy fabrics, often with pile construction Often blended with other fibres Used for sweaters, dresses and outerwear *Examples: Fake fur, fleece, double knit*	Some acrylics can be dry-cleaned but laundering is usually recommended Can be machine-washed (warm), tumble-dried Use fabric softener to reduce static electricity No ironing needed if removed from drier promptly	**Olefin** Pylen[12]	Nonabsorbent Holds in body heat Difficult to dye Nonallergenic Heat-sensitive	Fabrics are usually bulky but lightweight, with a wool-like handle Used for outerwear, upholstery and filling for cushions	Machine-wash, lukewarm water; use fabric softener in final rinse Tumble-dry, lowest setting Iron at lowest temperature setting, or not at all
Elastane Dorlastan[1] Espa[17] Helanca[8] Lycra[5].	Strong Nonabsorbent Great elasticity Lightweight Light may yellow	Flexible, lightweight fabrics Often used with another fibre Used for swimwear, ski pants, foundations	Wash by hand, or by machine, gentle cycle Avoid chlorine bleach Drip-dry or tumble-dry Iron at low temperature	**Polyester** Coolmax[5] Dacron[5] Soluna[12] Teijin Tetoron[15] Thermax[5] Toray Tetoron[16] Toyobo Ester[17] Trevira CS[9] Trevira[9]	Strong Low absorbency Holds in body heat Resists wrinkling, stretching, shrinking, moths and mildew Retains heat-set pleats Accumulates static electricity	Wide variety of fabrics in many weights and constructions Used for dresses, suits, sportswear, lingerie, linings, curtains, thread, filling for cushions *Examples: Crêpe, double knit*	Most polyesters are washable in warm water by hand or machine Tumble-dry or drip-dry Use fabric softener to reduce static electricity May need little or no ironing; use moderate setting for touch-ups
HPPE Dyneema[4]	Strongest fibre known Cut and puncture resistant	Woven and knitted structures Used for gloves, sporting outfits, protective clothing	Dry-clean infrequently Brush and shake lightly to dislodge dirt and grit Avoid high temperatures	**PTFE** Gore-Tex[7]	Water-repellent but comfortable Excellent chemical, soil, stain resistance	A membranous fabric Used for skiwear, activewear, protective clothing	Dry-clean only
Metallic Glitrex[14] Lurex[3]	Weak Nonabsorbent Tarnished unless coated with plastic film Heat-sensitive	First made into yarns; these are usually coated with plastic, polyester or acetate film and made into glittery fabrics	Launder or dry-clean according to care instructions Do not use high temperature for either washing or ironing	**Rayon** Carille[2] Dorufil[9] Fibro[2] Tencel[2] Visil[11]	Relatively weak Absorbent Holds in body heat Good affinity for dyes Wrinkles, shrinks or stretches unless treated	Many fabric weights, textures silky to coarse Used for dresses, blouses, suits, linings, draperies *Examples: Butcher linen, matt jersey*	Many rayons must be dry-cleaned Some are washable in warm water, gentle machine cycle Chlorine bleach can be used Iron at moderate setting
Modacrylic Teklan[2]	Low absorbency Holds in body heat Resists wrinkles, moths, mildew Nonallergenic Very heat-sensitive Dries quickly Flame-resistant	Fabrics are chiefly deep-pile structures Used for coats, plush toys, carpets and wigs *Example: Fake fur*	Deep-pile coats should be dry-cleaned For washable fabrics, follow care instructions Avoid ironing; modacrylics melt at relatively low temperatures	**Triacetate** Arnel[10]	Relatively weak Resists wrinkling and shrinking Good affinity for dyes Retains heat-set pleats	Lightweight fabrics Used for sportswear and skirts where pleat retention is desirable *Examples: Sharkskin, tricot*	Hand or machine-wash in warm water Drip-dry pleated garments; tumble-dry other styles Ironing usually required

*These are the most common artificial fibres. Numbered names in fibre groups are registered trademarks of the following companies: [1]Bayer AG [2]Courtaulds Ltd [3]Dow Badische Company (USA) [4]DSM [5]E. I. Dupont de Nemours & Co. Inc. [6]Eastman Chemical Company (USA) [7]W. L. Gore & Associates [8]Heberlein Patent Corporation [9]Hoechst [10]Hoechst Celanese [11]Kemira Oy [12]Mitsubishi Rayon Company [13]Monsanto Company (USA) [14]Oike & Co. (Japan) [15]Teijin Ltd [16]Toray Industries Inc. [17]Toyobo Co.

Fabric fundamentals

The yarns that become fabrics

Yarns are continuous strands of fibres used in the making of woven and knit fabrics. There are two basic types, **spun** and **filament,** each with variations that give different characteristics to fabrics made from them.

A **spun yarn** is made by twisting together staples (short fibres). These can be products that occur naturally in this form, or synthetic filaments cut to short lengths.

The spinning process consists of several steps that are basically the same for all fibres, with a few variations for fibre type and desired end product. Natural staples are first cleaned and sorted into bunches of parallel fibres, deleting shorter staples—a process called *carding*. Sometimes the fibres are put through a second, more precise sorting called *combing*. In combing, the longest fibres are separated out and laid in parallel bunches; these then become the combed cotton or worsted wool yarns that are the basis of high quality fabrics.

The final spinning steps are *drawing* (pulling fibres lengthwise over each other) and *spinning* (twisting them together). The amount of twist affects fabric appearance and durability. A slack twist, for instance, is given to yarns intended for use in napped fabrics. A hard twist strengthens the yarn and produces smooth-surfaced fabrics, such as gabardine. When the yarn is over-twisted, it gnarls and curls, producing the lively effect seen in crêpe fabrics such as georgette.

A spun yarn variation is *ply yarn*— two or more single yarns twisted together. Another variation is *novelty yarn*. This can be either a single strand with varying amounts of twist, or ply yarn consisting of singles with different degrees of twist or different diameters. Examples are slub and bouclé. As a rule, novelty yarns are less durable than other types, because their uneven surfaces are subject to abrasion and snagging.

Filament yarn is the strand (several metres long) either extruded from the chemical solution from which synthetic fibres derive or unreeled from a silkworm's cocoon. It is characteristically smooth, fine and slippery. A single strand, or *monofilament*, is not generally used for fabrics. Two or more twisted together are *multifilaments*. Fabrics constructed with these are stronger and more opaque than fabrics made of monofilaments.

A filament variation is produced by *texturising*. In this process, a thermoplastic yarn is melted and heat-set to change its smooth surface to a coil, crimp or loop shape. Such treatment increases the surface area, giving the yarns greater resiliency, bulk, elasticity and absorbency. Stretch yarn is one result of texturising.

Many different ways of describing the thickness of a yarn are in use. In the best known yarn specification systems, **Denier** and **Yarn Tex,** the higher the count the thicker the yarn. Denier is the mass in grams of nine kilometres of yarn; Tex, the mass in grams of one kilometre of yarn.

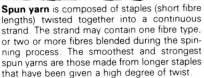

Spun yarn is composed of staples (short fibre lengths) twisted together into a continuous strand. The strand may contain one fibre type, or two or more fibres blended during the spinning process. The smoothest and strongest spun yarns are those made from longer staples that have been given a high degree of twist.

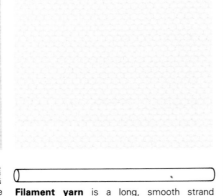

Filament yarn is a long, smooth strand unreeled from a silkworm's cocoon or extruded from a chemical solution (the source of synthetic fibres). It may take the form of a monofilament (single strand), multifilaments (two or more strands twisted together), or staples (cut lengths to be made into spun yarn).

Ply yarn consists of two or more spun yarns twisted together; the number of strands is usually indicated by the terms 2 ply, 3 ply, and so forth. When the combined yarns are different in thickness or degree of twist, the result is a novelty yarn, such as slub or bouclé.

Textured yarn is synthetic filament that has undergone special treatments to give its surface a coiled, crimped, curled or looped shape. Some textured yarns are the basis of woven stretch fabrics; others, of fabrics with qualities of softness or bulk closely resembling those of natural fibres.

Fabric structures

Woven fabric constructions

Woven fabrics are produced by the interlacing of yarns. *Warp* (lengthwise) yarns are wound onto a beam and tied to the loom so that they can be alternately raised and lowered by harnesses (movable frames). *Weft* (filling or crosswise) yarns, in precut lengths, are inserted at right-angles to the warp by gripper-like devices called 'rapiers', or by air or water jets. Weave structures can be varied by rearranging the pattern in which warp and weft are made to intersect.

There are three basic weaves, *plain, twill* and *satin*. Most other types are variations on these three, except for patterned weaves. These are complex structures that require special devices attached to the loom (see examples of patterned weaves, p. 64).

Every woven fabric has a ribbon-like or fringed edge, the **selvage,** running lengthwise along each side. Weft yarns should be at right-angles to the selvages (see Cutting). Though rough-textured fabrics can be interesting, those with smooth, tightly twisted yarns and a high thread count (number of yarns per square centimetre of fabric) are the most durable.

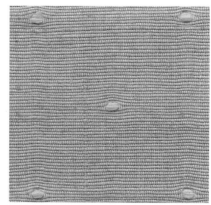

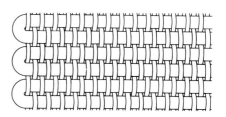

Rib weave: A variation of the plain weave in which the fine yarns are alternated with coarse yarns, or single with multiple yarns. The alternating thicknesses may be parallel. or at right-angles as shown above, producing a ridged or corded effect. Durability is limited because the yarns are exposed to friction.
Examples: Faille, ottoman, bengaline

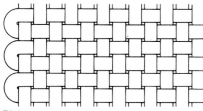

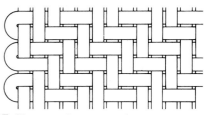

Plain weave: The simplest of the weave constructions, in which each filling yarn goes alternately over and under each warp yarn. Sturdiness varies with strength of the yarns and compactness of the weave structure. Plain weave is the basis for most prints.
Examples: Muslin, voile, challis, percale

Twill weave: A basic structure in which weft yarn passes over at least two, but not more than four, warp yarns. On each successive line, the weft moves one step to the right or left, forming a diagonal ridge; the steeper the ridge, the stronger the fabric. As a rule, twills are more durable than plain weaves.
Examples: Denim, gabardine, serge

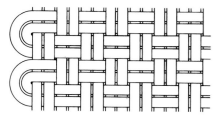

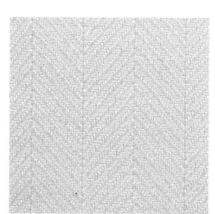

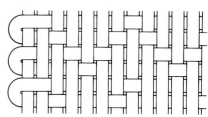

Basket weave: A variation of the plain weave in which paired or multiple yarns are used in the alternating pattern. The yarns are laid side by side without being twisted together. This makes the basket weave looser, less stable, often less durable than ordinary plain weaves.
Examples: Hopsacking, oxford shirting

Herringbone weave: A variation of the twill weave in which the diagonal ridges switch direction to form a zigzag pattern. The design is more pronounced when contrasting colours are used for the ridges.

Fabric structures

Woven fabric constructions

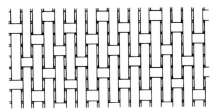

Satin weave: A basic structure in which a warp yarn passes over four to eight weft yarns in a staggered pattern similar to that of twill. Yarns exposed on the surface, called *floats*, give satin its characteristic sheen. **Sateen weave,** usually of cotton fibre, is a variation in which the floats are formed by weft yarns.
Examples: Peau de soie, crêpe-backed satin

Dobby weave: A patterned structure, usually geometric in form, produced by a special attachment (dobby) on a plain-weave loom. The dobby raises and lowers certain warp yarns so that warp and weft interlace in a constantly changing pattern. Most familiar is the diamond shape, shown here.
Example: Bird's-eye piqué

Pile weave: Here an extra filling or warp yarn is added to a basic plain or twill weave. By means of thick wires, the additional yarn is drawn into loops on the fabric surface. These loops can be cut as for plush, sheared as for velvet, or left in loop form as for terry cloth.
Examples: Corduroy, velours, fake fur

Jacquard weave: A patterned structure, more complex than the dobby. By means of a jacquard attachment, warp and weft yarns can be controlled individually to create an intricate design. Jacquard fabrics are usually expensive because of the elaborate loom preparation.
Examples: Damask, tapestry, brocade

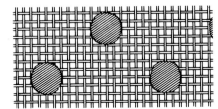

Swivel weave: To achieve this weave, an extra filling yarn is added to form a circle or other figure on the surface of a basic weave. Each swivel yarn is carried on the wrong side of the fabric from one design to the next, then cut when the fabric is completed.
Example: Dotted swiss

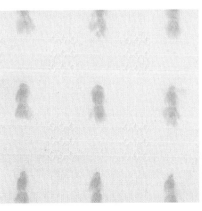

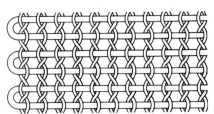

Leno weave (also called gauze weave): An open-mesh structure produced by a leno attachment on the loom. The leno continuously changes the position of the warp yarns so that they become twisted in a figure of eight fashion around the filling yarns.
Example: Marquisette

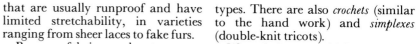

Fabric structures

Knit constructions

Knit fabrics are made up of a series of interlocking loops that result in a flexible construction. While all knits have stretch, they vary considerably in amount and direction of stretch. The factors that influence stretch are the yarn and the particular knit structure employed.

There are two basic knit structures, **weft** and **warp.** The first derives from age-old techniques of hand knitting. The second, a modern innovation, is the product of complex machines. Records show that the first knitting machine was invented in 1589. Today's advanced versions turn out a very wide range of fabrics from sheer lingerie knits to bulky sweater types, even piles and jacquard patterns.

Descriptions of knit variations are given at the right and on page 66. Relevant to them are the following terms: **knit stitch** is a basic link in which a loop is drawn through the *front* of the previous one; **purl stitch** is a basic link in which a loop is drawn through the *back* of the previous one. All knit variations are achieved by changing the arrangement of these two basic stitches. **Ribs** (wales) are lengthwise rows of loops; **courses** are crosswise rows. These are comparable to warp and weft in woven fabrics. **Gauge** denotes the number of stitches per centimetre. Usually, the higher the number, the finer the fabric.

Knit fabrics may be tubular or flat. Some flat types have perforated lengthwise edges comparable to the selvages in woven fabrics.

Complex stitches and special finishes can sometimes obscure a knit structure, making it difficult to tell whether a fabric is knitted or woven. To settle the question, pull a thread from one crosswise end. If loops show, the fabric is a knit; if a fringe appears, the fabric is woven.

Warp knits

Warp knit fabric is constructed with many yarns that form loops simultaneously in the lengthwise (warp) direction. Each yarn is controlled by its own needle, and interlocked with neighbouring yarns in zigzag fashion. This interlocking produces fabrics that are usually runproof and have limited stretchability, in varieties ranging from sheer laces to fake furs.

Because of their complex structures, warp knits are produced only by machine. *Tricot* and *raschel* (shown below) are the most widely produced types. There are also *crochets* (similar to the hand work) and *simplexes* (double-knit tricots).

Warp knits are widely available, and comparatively low in cost—the machines used can produce several square metres of fabric per minute.

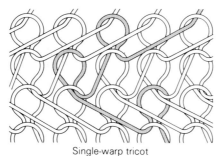

Single-warp tricot

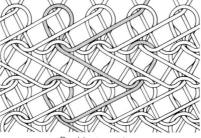

Double-warp tricot

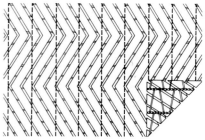

Typical raschel knit

Tricot knit: Fine ribs on the face, flat herringbone courses on the back. Can be single, double or triple-warp construction. Technical differences are not discernible to the eye, but they do affect performance. Double and triple-warp tricots are runproof; single-warp is not. Tricots are usually made from fine cotton or synthetic yarn. They have a soft, draping quality and are suitable for linings, casual wear, lingerie and dresses.

Raschel knit: A wide range of fabrics from fine nets to piles. The most typical raschel pattern has an open, lacy structure, with alternating thick and thin yarns. Any yarn type is suitable, including metallic and glass.

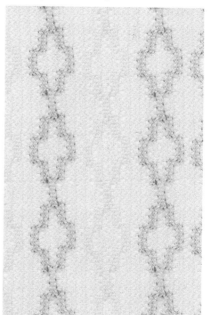

Fabric structures

Weft knits

Weft knit fabric is constructed when the yarn is made to form continuous rows of loops in the horizontal (weft) direction. Basically, the machine stitches are exactly like those done by hand, and fabric characteristics are similar. This means that the stretch is greater in width than in length, and that a broken loop will release others in a vertical row, causing a run.

There are two distinct weft knit categories—*single* and *double*. Single knits have a moderate to great amount of stretch. Though very comfortable to wear, they may eventually sag in stress areas, such as seat or knees. Also, their edges tend to curl, creating difficulties in cutting and stitching. Double knits have body and stability similar to those of a weave.

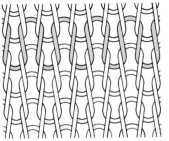 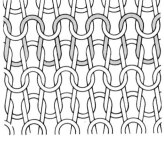 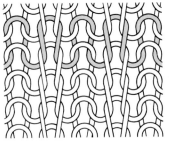  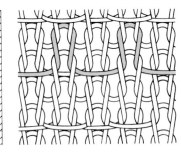

Plain jersey knit: A single construction in which all loops are pulled to the back of the fabric. The face is smooth, and it exhibits lengthwise vertical rows (wales); on the reverse side, there are horizontal rows of half-circles, characteristic of the purl stitch. Plain knits stretch more in width than in length.

Purl knit: A single construction in which loops are pulled in alternate rows to the front and back of the knit, causing a purl stitch to appear on both sides of the fabric. Purl knits have nearly the same amount of stretch in both the lengthwise and the crosswise directions; this makes them ideal for infants' and children's wear.

Rib knit: A single construction, with rows of plain and purl knit arranged so that the face and the reverse sides are identical. Rib knits have expansive stretch and strong recovery in the crosswise direction, which makes them especially suitable for cuffs and waistbands.

Patterned knits: Complex variations on the basic plain and purl knits. A cable knit is a typical example of a patterned knit.

Double knit: Produced by two yarn-and-needle sets working simultaneously. Double knits have firm body and limited stretch capacity. Depending on the design, the face and back may be alike or differ. Some complex double knits resemble the woven dobby and jacquard patterns (see page 64).

Fabric structures

Other fabric constructions

There are several fabric constructions or processes that cannot be classified as knit or woven. These fabrics have many household uses and are also finding a growing number of industrial applications. Each type has a significance worth noting.

Felting, possibly the oldest method of producing fabric, has wide applications for accessories and household articles. Netting and braiding are also very old techniques and are used in lacemaking. Fusing, bonding and laminating use adhesives to interlock short fibres or glue fabrics together.

For appliqué or cut work on fine fabrics, extruded PVA films provide a firm base which may be removed later by dissolving in water. Sheets of films are sold by large haberdashery stores.

 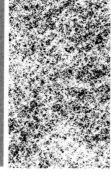

Felting is a process in which moisture, heat and pressure are applied to short fibres, interlocking them in a matted layer. Wool is the primary fibre in felt fabric because it tends naturally to mat. Felts do not unravel, can be cut or blocked to any shape. They do, however, shrink when dampened and they tear easily.

Netting is a fabric construction in which the yarns are held together by knots at each point where they intersect. This open-mesh structure can be varied to produce fabrics as heavy as fish net and as delicate as the mesh portion of a sheer lace. Today, many net fabrics are made on tricot knit machines.

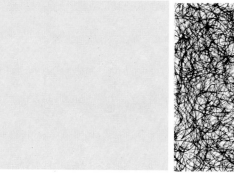 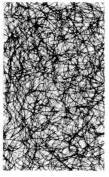

Fusing is similar to felting except that it employs a bonding agent to hold the fibres (usually cotton or rayon) together. The product can be a nonwoven fabric of the type used for interfacing (see p. 88) or a web, which is itself a fusible bonding agent (see Fusible products).

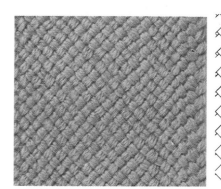

Braiding is a fabric construction in which three or more yarns from a single source are interlaced diagonally and lengthwise (just as in braiding hair). There are two forms, *flat* and *tubular*. Both yield a fabric that is narrow and flexible. Braiding is used primarily for garment trims, cords and elastics.

Bonding is a process by which two or more fabrics are joined with an adhesive. The combination usually is a knit or loosely woven fabric backed by a lightweight lining. If one layer is a vinyl or foam, the product is called a **laminate.** All self-lined fabrics offer the advantages of dimensional stability, opaqueness, and body.

Malimo is a fabric construction in which weft yarns are laid over warp yarns, then joined by a third yarn of interlocking chain stitches. The basic technique can be varied to produce an extremely wide range of fabrics, with uses ranging from coats and other clothing to curtains and upholstery.

Fabric finishes

Types and purposes

Fabrics are given a variety of treatments—before, during or after construction—designed to alter their performance and final appearance. Familiarity with these finishes will help you to select fabrics that meet your needs. To simplify classification these finishes are divided here into **functional** (affecting fabric behaviour) and **decorative** (affecting a fabric's look or feel). The divisions, however, are not always so clear-cut. Napping, for instance, alters texture and adds warmth as well.

Functional finishes make a fabric more versatile or better suited to a particular need. Often, a single finish imparts more than one quality. Some side effects are desirable, others less so. Preshrinking, for example, makes a weave more compact and therefore more durable; a water-repellent finish tends to ward off stains and dirt as well as moisture. Treatment for crease resistance, on the other hand, makes cotton less inclined to wrinkle, but also less cool and comfortable.

Decorative finishes make fabric a pleasure to see and feel. Those described at the right are in wide commercial use. Not listed are hand techniques and those less frequently used by the fabric industry. Permanence, a major consideration with colour and texture, depends largely on the quality of the dye or technique used (see opposite page for ways to test quality). Commercial factors are influential, too. Fibre and yarn dyeing, for instance, are usually more permanent than piece dyeing, but less practical for meeting changing fashion needs.

The lasting potential of finishes is based on a garment's normal life expectancy. To get maximum benefit from all finishes, find out as much as possible about a fabric before buying it, and care for it properly.

Functional finishes—what to expect

Anti-bacterial: Resists many types of bacteria, including those in perspiration.

Anti-static: Does not accumulate static electricity, therefore does not cling.

Crease-resistant: Resists and recovers from creases caused by normal wear.

Flame resistant / flame retardant: Does not actively support a flame once its source has been removed. (Few textile fabrics can be made 100% fireproof.) Always make sure that you buy fabric with this type of finish if you intend to make clothes for children, especially nightdresses and pyjamas.

Mercerised (cottons and linens): Has greater strength and lustre and better affinity for dye.

Mothproof: Resists attacks by moths.

Permanent press / durable press: Sheds creases from normal wear; requires no ironing when washed and dried according to care instructions; retains heat-set creases or pleats. Has low abrasion resistance and should be laundered wrong side out for best results.

Preshrunk: Will not shrink more than the percentage indicated (usually 1% to 2%) if care instructions are followed.

Soil release (for permanent press fabrics): Permits removal of oil-based stains.

Stain resistant/spot resistant: Resists water-based and/or oil-based stains. This finish can be applied with an aerosol product.

Stiffened (permanent): Retains crisp finish through many washings (fibre structure has been permanently altered with chemicals).

Stiffened (temporary): Has body and crispness that may be lost in laundering but can be restored by adding starch (fabric has been sized, i.e., starched, to retain these attributes to time of purchase).

Stretch resistant/sag resistant (knit fabrics): Maintains original dimensions through normal wear and many washings.

Wash-and-wear (also called *easy care* and *minimum care*): Requires little or no ironing after washing; resists and recovers from creases caused by normal wear. Follow care instructions carefully. This fabric should not be twisted when it is washed; chlorine bleach may cause yellowing.

Waterproof: Is totally impervious to water under any and all conditions; the pores of the fabric are completely closed.

Water-repellent: Fabric with this type of finish will resist absorption and penetration of water, but remains porous.

Decorative finishing processes

COLOUR

Bleaching: All natural colour and staining are removed if the cloth is to be finished white; also necessary before dyeing or printing.

Fibre (stock) dyeing: Natural fibres are dyed before spinning into yarn or matting into felt. A thorough and relatively permanent process.

Solution (dope) dyeing: Synthetic fibres are dyed in the liquid form before extrusion into filaments. Generally the most colourfast of the colour treatments.

Yarn (skein) dyeing: Spools or skeins of yarn are immersed in a dye bath, permitting dye to penetrate to the core of the yarn. Permits the use of different colours to create a design such as a plaid or check. Gingham, for example, is a yarn-dyed fabric.

Piece dyeing: Fabric is dyed after construction. One common method is to unroll fabric, pass it through a trough containing dye solution, then re-roll it at the other end. The largest percentage of fabric by far is dyed this way because it allows for greater flexibility in manufacturing. Colour is relatively fast if dyes used are those most suitable for the fibre.

Cross dyeing: There are three methods of cross dyeing: (1) Fabric is constructed with a combination of dyed and undyed yarns, then piece-dyed. (2) Fabric is constructed with undyed yarns of two different fibres, then piece-dyed in two different dye solutions, each with an affinity for one fibre. (3) Same as method 2, but with two different dyes combined in a single dye bath. Many unusual effects—for example, frosty and iridescent—can be obtained with cross dyeing.

PRINTING

Roller printing: Design is transferred to fabric by means of engraved copper cylinders, a different roller for each colour. Fast and relatively inexpensive—thousands of metres per hour can be printed.

Screen printing: The dye is forced through screens with an impermeable coating on all areas not part of the design; a different screen is used for each colour. Slower than roller printing but permits larger designs and brighter colours. Can be used successfully for knits.

Transfer printing: Design is first printed on paper, then transferred to fabric by means of heat under pressure. Quality of result is comparable to that of roller or screen printing, yet cost is about half. Can be used for knits.

Parchmentising (or **acid-etching**): Fabric is 'printed' with chemicals which actually dissolve one of the fibres used in construction. Usual result is a raised motif on a sheer ground.

Discharge printing: Fabric is first dyed, then roller-printed with a chemical that bleaches out the design.

Duplex printing: Fabric is roller-printed on both sides, producing woven design effect.

Flocking: Fabric is roller-printed with an adhesive, then cut fibres are applied to the surface, resulting in textured pattern.

Resist printing: Resist paste (impervious to dye) is roller-printed on fabric. Fabric is next piece-dyed, then the paste is removed, leaving light pattern on darker ground.

Warp printing: Warp yarns are roller-printed before weaving, then interlaced with plain weft yarns; design is usually mottled.

TEXTURE

Calendering: A pressing process in which the fabric is passed between heavy rollers to make it smooth and glossy. Conditions of heat, speed and pressure can be varied to achieve different effects.

Ciréing: Calendering variation in which wax or other sheen-producing substance is applied to fabric before contact with heated rollers. Final surface is very glossy.

Embossing: Calendering variation in which engraved and heated rollers form a raised design. Can be used for any fibre except wool; effect is permanent when the fibre is a thermoplastic, such as nylon, or when fabric has been treated with chemical resins.

Glazing: Calendering variation in which starch, glue or shellac is applied to fabric before passing it over hot steel rollers moving faster than the fabric. Chintz is a glazed fabric.

Moiréing: Calendering variation in which two layers of fabric (usually rib weave of silk, acetate or rayon) are passed over ridged rollers. Moisture, heat and intense pressure create wavy bars that reflect light in differing ways. To preserve water wave effect, iron only with care.

Napping: A process in which the fabric surface is brushed to raise the fibre ends (yarn must be spun). The resulting texture is compact, soft and warm. Fleece and flannel are examples of napped fabrics.

Plisséing: A treatment with caustic soda solution for cotton-based fabrics that shrinks fabric areas where it is applied, at the same time causing dry areas to pucker. The result is a crinkled surface that may or may not be permanent.

Shopping for fabrics

Basic buying considerations

A successfully chosen garment fabric will complement the pattern design, flatter the wearer, perform according to expectations and be of good quality for the money.

To determine a fabric's **suitability for a pattern,** check the pattern envelope. Illustrations on the front show fabrics appropriate for the design; the envelope back lists suggested fabrics chosen by the designer.

To find out whether a fabric is **becoming to you,** drape at least 2 metres of the material over yourself in front of a full-length mirror. In this way you can see the precise effect of colour and texture on your skin tone and figure. (For guidance in the use of both colour and texture, see Patterns.)

To predict a fabric's **probable behaviour,** you must know its content and finishes, also how much it will shrink and exactly how it should be cared for. Find out as much as you can at the time of purchase and follow any washing directions carefully.

To **recognise quality,** or lack of it, you must become aware of the characteristics that signify excellence and those that disguise inferiority. The distinguishing features are often small and subtle, and detectable only to an experienced eye. There are some more obvious criteria, however, that can be used to advantage by novice and experienced shopper alike:

1. Weave should be firm. You can test this by scratching the surface; if the threads shift easily, the garment seams may be inclined to slip or develop holes around the stitching.

2. Weave should be uniform. Hold it up to the light and check for any unusually thick or thin areas. A fabric that has them would not wear evenly. The light test will also show up any weak spots or imperfections.

3. Filler yarns should meet selvages at right angles. Yarns at an oblique angle mean fabric is off-grain (see Cutting for test and remedy).

4. Dye colour should be even and look fresh. If there is a creaseline, check whether colour has rubbed off there.

This could indicate poor dye quality, and will pose problems when cutting.

5. Print colour should be even, with no white (undyed) spots showing through them, except in areas that are clearly meant to be white.

6. A print that is geometric or otherwise symmetrical should meet the selvages at a right angle. An irregular print cannot be corrected.

7. No powdery dust should appear when fabric is rubbed between the fingers. Visible powder is an indication of too much sizing, a frequent device for concealing poor quality.

8. Fabric should shed creases after crushing. If it does not, the garment will always look rumpled.

Special buying considerations

Extra thought must be given to the purchase of certain fabrics because of special or unusual qualities. A review of this group begins here and continues to page 71.

Knits vary in stretchability. Just how much a knit stretches crosswise should be determined before you buy it. If the pattern you have chosen is marked 'for knits only', it will probably supply a gauge like the one below, but only for one of the three stretch categories—slight, moderate or super. The gauge helps you to tell whether a particular knit will suit the pattern style. This is how the gauge works. Holding a 10 cm crosswise section of your knit against the gauge, stretch gently from the 10 cm mark to the outer limit of the ruler. If the fabric stretches comfortably to the designated point, or even beyond it, the knit has enough stretch for the pattern.

Notice, after stretching, whether the fabric returns to its original dimensions. A knit that does not recover completely may sag or stretch out of shape during wear.

Leather and suede are usually sold by the square metre instead of the linear metre. (Suede is the same kind of skin as leather, finished on the flesh side rather than the hair side.) You must therefore calculate the quantity you require before buying.

Here is a conversion method, using 4 metres of 115 cm fabric as the example: (1) Calculate the number of square metres in 1 metre of the fabric width called for; in 1 metre of 115 cm fabric, the example chosen, there are 1.15 square metres. (2) Multiply this number by the required length of fabric; in this case, 1.15 times 4, or a total of 4.6 square metres. (3) To this total, add an extra 15% for piecing and wastage; 4.6 times 0.15 is 0.69; adding this amount to 4.6 gives 5.29. You need 5.3 square metres.

You should also consider the size of the usable portions of each skin. If possible, compare these with the largest pattern pieces, taking into account any holes or irregular edges. You might need to piece the leather or divide large pattern pieces into smaller sections.

Here are some approximate needs: a waistcoat, 2 skins; an A-line skirt, 4 skins; a short jacket, 5 skins.

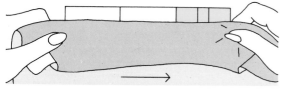

To use knit gauge, fold over a crosswise edge of the knit about 5 cm. With left hand, brace knit against left edge of gauge. With right hand, take hold of knit at the 10 cm mark and gently stretch it to the mark it reaches comfortably.

	5 cm	10 cm	12 cm	13 cm	15 cm
10 cm width of fabric			SLIGHT STRETCH		
10 cm width of fabric			MODERATE STRETCH		
10 cm width of fabric			SUPER STRETCH		

Fabric quantity requirements

The construction or design of some fabrics imposes special quantity requirements. Such special needs may be specified on the pattern envelope; if they are not, you will have to do the calculating yourself. Examples of such fabrics are shown below and on the opposite page. Some fabrics could fall into more than one category. A large-scale print, for instance, might also be a one-way design. Consider all aspects when calculating quantity. When **matching or design placement** is a factor, the length of one *repeat* should be added for each metre of fabric called for. (A repeat is the

Matching

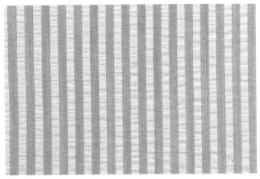

Plaids (multiple bands crossing at right angles; the repeat is a 4-sided area in which the design is complete): Require lengthwise centring and crosswise matching. Size of the repeat determines how much extra fabric is needed for matching. You will need still more fabric for uneven plaids because they require a one-way layout. These necessities apply also to geometric designs (a check, for example) where repeat is larger than 6 mm.

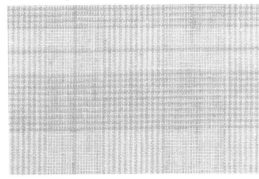

Stripes (parallel bands of colour in one direction only): Matching requirements depend on the direction of the lines and the pattern style. Extra fabric may be needed for horizontal (crosswise) stripes, or to match stripes in a chevron design (for details, see Cutting). No extra fabric is required for lengthwise stripes that will be used vertically.

Diagonals (lines that are woven or printed at an oblique angle to selvage): Matching may or may not be possible, depending on the angle of the pattern seams. As a rule, extra fabric is needed only if the stripes are broad, or printed or woven in a variety of colours

Special design placement

Large-scale prints (motifs 8 cm or more wide or deep): Design must be balanced and motifs carefully placed on the figure (for details, see Cutting). Extra allowance must be made for matching if design is geometric (for example, checked or diamond). Additional fabric is needed if design is one-way.

Border print (marginal design along one selvage): No extra fabric is needed if the border is used vertically. Less than the specified amount may suffice if border is used horizontally (see Cutting). Choose a pattern that has a border-print view on the envelope, or calculate quantity by making a trial layout, aligning pattern pieces with the crosswise grain. (Note: border prints with pattern across *width* rather than along selvage are also available. These have repeating panels, usually about one metre apart.)

Lace (an openwork structure featuring flower or other motif on a net ground): A unique fabric because it has no grainline, making layout possibilities (and quantity needs) flexible. Thought must be given to placing motifs attractively on the figure, to matching them where possible, to laying them in one direction if necessary. Some laces have a scalloped edge that can be used at garment edges, such as sleeve or skirt hem, neckline or front opening, eliminating the need for hem allowances and facings.

area covered by one complete motif of the design.) For example, if 4 metres are required, and the repeat measures 5 cm, buy 4.2 metres of the fabric.

If a **one-way layout** is necessary the required quantity depends on the shape of the pattern pieces. If top and bottom widths are approximately the same, no extra fabric should be necessary. When the top and bottom widths differ considerably (such as in a widely flared skirt), a reasonable allowance is an extra 0.2 of a metre for each metre of fabric specified. A more accurate approach, however, is a trial layout (see Cutting for procedure).

One-way layout

One-way design (printed or woven motifs not the same in both lengthwise directions; flower and paisley patterns are often one-way): Check pattern envelope for napped fabric quantities or estimate amount needed, using the above criteria.

Napped fabric (the surface of a plain or twill weave, or plain knit, has been brushed to create a soft, fuzzy texture; typical example is flannel): Pattern pieces must be laid in one direction, usually with the nap running down.

Short-pile fabric (downy-textured surface less than 3 mm deep, usually made by shearing pile yarns, as in velveteen): Cut with the nap running up for the richest colour, with nap running down for a frosty effect.

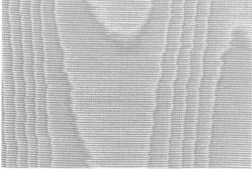

Moiré, satin or iridescent (slick, shiny surface reflects light differently in each of the lengthwise directions): Can be cut in either direction, depending on the effect desired.

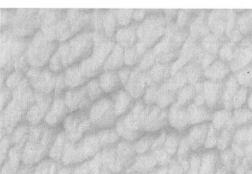

Deep-pile fabric (downy-textured surface more than 3 mm deep, formed by extra warp or filling yarn, or by a special knit structure; plush and fake fur are examples): Almost always cut with the nap running down.

Certain knits (may have jacquard or other patterned design that is one-way, or character of surface may cause it to reflect light in differing ways): Inspect fabric closely. If uncertain about its needs or limitations, buy quantity given for nap, use a one-way layout to be safe.

Fabrics A to Z

Although many types of textile fibre have been in use for thousands of years, since the early years of this century technology has been constantly adding to the range. Artificial fibres have brought great variety to the textile industry and have added many desirable qualities which are unobtainable in natural fibres. Frequently the blending of natural and artificial fibres achieves the best in both performance and aesthetic appeal.

Of the natural fibres, the most commonly used today are cotton, flax, wool and silk. The apparent multiplicity of fibre and fabric names in the artificial range is due to competition between different fibre producing companies. There is an equal diversity of wool and cotton yarns and fabrics, but they are not promoted in the same way. For further information on the different types and properties of natural and artificial fibres see pages 60 and 61.

Fabric names are derived from a variety of sources. The name can refer to the fibre from which the fabric is made, the method of weaving or finishing, the part of the world in which the fabric originated, its traditional use, or even a skin or animal it may resemble (for instance, *chenille* is the French word for caterpillar). The following list is by no means exhaustive but includes a selection of fabrics in common use; a number of others that are rare or no longer obtainable have been included for general and historical interest.

Acetates *see* pages 60–61
Acrylics *see* pages 60–61

Aida cloth Basket weave construction, often of polyester and cotton, with untwisted yarns laid into the weave. Embroidery.

Alpaca Lighweight, lustrous soft wool or wool blend, made from the fleece of the South American alpaca. Llama fleece is often used as a substitute. Now rare and expensive. Suits, trousers, jackets.
Angora Woven or knit fabric of extremely soft hair, now taken generally from the angora rab-bit but sometimes from the angora goat (the latter is usually called mohair). Coats, dresses.
Astrakhan Heavy woven fabric with tight curly pile imitating pelt from unborn or very young lambs. Now difficult to find. Formal wear.
Baize Light, thick felt, usually bright green. Can be used to line drawers, and for pads under vases to protect polished furniture.
Barathea Fine fabric with broken rib pattern and pebbly surface, originally wool or silk, now of various fibres. Men's and women's suits.
Batik A method of dyeing from Idonesia, in which the parts of the fabric not being coloured are covered with wax. Term now also refers to the cloth so dyed; it is sometimes incorrectly used to describe traditional Indonesian batik designs not printed by the batik method. Often comes as border print fabric. Blouses, dresses.
Batiste Lightweight, fine, sometimes sheer fabric of wool, cotton or man-made fibre in plain weave. Blouses, lingerie, linings, handkerchiefs.
Beaver cloth A soft-finished fabric of wool with thick nap designed to resemble beaver fur. Coats, hats, skirts.

Bedford cord Stout woven fabric with ribbing down the grain, made from a variety of fibres. Dresses, slacks, coats, upholstery.

Bengaline Now rare. Strong, lightweight fabric usually of silk and cotton, or silk and wool, with crosswise rib. Dresses.

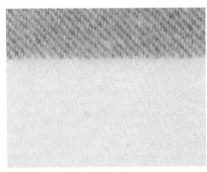

Blanket cloth Heavyweight overcoating, often napped with plaid design, mainly of wool.
Blister *see* **Cloqué**
Bombazine Twilled or corded fabric of cotton and worsted, or silk and worsted. Traditionally black for mourning clothing, it is now available in other colours too.
Botany twill Generic term for the finest grades of wool and worsted yarns. Name derives from Botany Bay, Australia.
Bouclé (pronounced *booclay*) Wool or wool blend fabric of looped or knotted yarn, giving

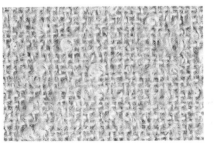

a nubby surface. Yarn itself is also called bouclé. Women's tailoring.
Broadcloth Fine lustrous cotton fabric of poplin type, used for men's shirts. Woollen broadcloth is a fine, twill fabric, generally dyed dark colours, used for men's suits.
Brocade Rich jacquard weave fabric with an all-over interwoven design. True brocades are woven but the term is now also used for knits with a similar look. A tarnish-proof gold thread is sometimes included in the weave. Formal and evening clothing, upholstery.

Broderie anglaise Eyelet embroidery on cotton, generally white on white but obtainable in plain colours and prints. Available in dress widths for blouses, dresses in narrower widths, for trimming, it is sometimes called 'broderie', 'cambric lace' or 'eyelet lace'.
Buckram A stiff open weave fabric—a form of cheesecloth with a glued finish. Used mainly for hat shaping, belt stiffening and interfacing.
Burlap *see* **Hessian**
Calico Generic name for lightweight, plain weave cotton with a smooth surface. Now frequently made with small print designs. Often used to make up a fitting shell before cutting an expensive fabric.

Cambric Fine cotton fabric with a slightly glossy surface. Once used for women's caps, handkerchiefs and underclothing but now more often used for upholstery and book binding.

Cambric lace *see* **Broderie anglaise**

Camel hair Lightweight coating fabric, usually in twill weave. Name derives from the use of the extremely soft inner coat of the camel. Today it is usually blended with other fibres such as wool, and is classified for labelling as wool. The term can also refer to the colour, a yellowish tan. Men's coats, women's tailoring.

Campbell twill (also known as **Mayo twill**) Broken twill used extensively in the finer woollen and worsted trade. Suits.

Candlewick Coarse folded yarn, usually 100% cotton, used in craft of candlewicking. Name for soft, thick yarn which is pulled through a base fabric and then cut to form tufts. The term also describes fabric made by this method. Bedspreads and dressing gowns.

Canvas Heavy, strong, plain weave fabric usually made from cotton but sometimes from artificial fibres or blends. Blinds, chair seats. See also **Hair canvas.**

Casement cloth This term is usually limited to open weave curtain fabrics, but is also applied to sheer curtaining fabrics in general.

Cashmere A luxury fibre, knitted or woven. Originally hair from the downy undercoat of the Asiatic goat; now includes similar quality hair obtained through selective breeding of Aus-

tralian, New Zealand and Scottish feral goats. It is usually blended with sheep's wool or artificial fibres to increase wearing ability and to lower cost. Tailored clothing.

Cavalry twill Strong, twill weave cloth traditionally used for riding breeches and uniforms. Raincoats, skirts, pants.

Challis (pronounced *shallee*) Light, supple, plain weave fabric of wool, rayon, cotton or

blends. Traditionally printed on dark background with floral or paisley design. Dresses.

Chambray (pronounced *shom-bray*) Traditionally a plain weave cotton but now usually

made from polyester/viscose or other artificial fibres. Usually made with a coloured warp and a white filler. Is available in plain colours, stripes and checks and can resemble denim, although lighter in weight. Work clothes, sportswear, pyjamas and shirts.

Chamois (pronounced *shammy*) Soft, pliable yellow-coloured leather, usually with a slightly napped surface, named after the chamois goat from which the skin is obtained. Other animal skins may be substituted and synthetic imitations are also available. Shirts, vests.

Chanel tweed This term is loosely used for any tweed made from bulky yarns, thick and thin with many slubs. Popularised by the French designer Coco Chanel. Suits, coats.

Cheesecloth Plain, loosely woven fabric, usually of cotton, sometimes used for fashion clothing and interlinings, but more often for

curtains, flag buntings and polishing cloths. Formerly used in cheese making.

Chenille (pronounced *sheneel*) Name comes from the French word for caterpillar. Soft yarn, with pile protruding on all sides, generally made from wool blends. Rugs, bedspreads, dressing gowns.

Cheviot Rough surfaced, heavily napped fabric resembling serge, originally made from the wool of the Cheviot sheep. Coats.

Chiffon Originally made from silk but today generally made from artificial fibres. Very lightweight, soft, sheer fabric, printed or plain, noted for its draping ability. Formal wear.

China silk Lightweight, inexpensive silk used for linings and scarves. Synonymous with **jap silk** or **jappe.** Has been almost completely replaced by artificial fibres.

Chiné French name refers to the Chinese origin of the procedure in which the warp threads of a fabric are printed then woven to produce a shadowy effect. Dresses.

Chino Trade name for a type of medium-weight, twill weave cotton with a slight sheen. Sportswear.

Chintz Closely woven, plain weave fabric printed with figures and birds but most often

flowers. Usually has a glazed finish. Soft furnishings, curtains.

Cloqué (pronounced *clock-ay*) Any fabric with an embossed design. Knitted cloqué is a rib-based weft knit structure the surface of which exhibits a characteristic blister effect. Swimwear, gymwear, dresses, tops.

Clydella Trade name for 81% cotton/19% wool fabric of plain weave, printed or plain. Children's wear, dresses and blouses.

Corduroy Name possibly derives from the French *corde du roi.* 'king's cord'. Cotton weft pile fabric woven or shorn to produce ribs in the direction of the warp. It is available in various widths of rib and in both printed and plain colours. Uncut cord has all-over nap. Children's clothing, jackets, coats, slacks.

Cotton Named after the plant from which it is obtained. There are many qualities of cotton fabric depending on the staple length and fitness of the fibre used. Names like Sea Island and Egyptian refer to the quality of the fabric. The range of fabrics cotton is made into includes every known woven and knitted structure, and every weight from the flimsiest muslin and lace to the heaviest canvas and blankets. Cotton is very often blended with other fibres to maximise its advantageous properties (strength, moisture absorbency for summer wear, warmth for winter wear) while minimising its disadvantages (inelasticity, creasing).

Crash Coarse, rough-surfaced linen, cotton or rayon fabric generally used for bookbinding but occasionally for clothing and curtains.

Crêpe (pronounced *crape*) Name applies to fabrics with a dull crinkled surface. Traditionally woven, but now produced in knits. Satin backed crêpe is a double-sided fabric, with satin finish on one side and crêpe on the other. Embossed crêpe is also available. Blouses, dresses.

Crêpe de chine (pronounced *crape de sheen*) Fabric produced in plain weave by twisting silk in both directions of the weave. Now usually made from artificial fibres. Formal wear, blouses.

Crêpon (pronounced *crape-on*) Similar to crêpe but thicker and firmer, with lengthwise texture sometimes patterned with jacquard designs. Babies' dresses.

Cretonne Mediumweight unglazed fabric, usually cotton, made in a variety of weaves and finishes. Generally printed with bright floral patterns. Curtains.

Damask Name derives from the fact that damask was originally brought to Damascus by Marco Polo. Firm, reversible fabric of jacquard weave, similar to **brocade.** Home furnishings, tablecloths.

Denim Strong, twill weave fabric traditionally made with coloured warp (usually blue) and white filler. The name is often given to brushed (knit and plain) cloths which resemble it. Work clothes, jeans, jackets, skirts, soft furnishings.

Dimity Fairly sheer, lightweight fabric made traditionally from cotton but now also from artificial fibres. Often has fine lengthwise cords, stripes, checks or very small printed patterns. Dresses, curtains.

Doeskin Now usually the skin of a white sheep, but the name is also used for fabrics made from wool or artificial fibres that have a soft, usually napped finish with a 'kid glove' feel. Dresses, women's jackets, vests.

Dotted Swiss Traditional Swiss fabric is a fine, sheer fabric of almost any fibre. Dotted Swiss refers to this fabric with small dots woven in, flocked or sometimes printed. Bridesmaids' dresses, children's formal wear.

Double knit Knitted fabric with both sides identical, except when patterned. Has excellent body and good recovery. Tops, skirts, jackets.

Double piqué Knit fabric with a rib structure. Collared T-shirts.

Drill Strong, twill weave cotton similar to denim, often dyed khaki. Work clothes, small boys' pants.

Duck Heavy, tightly woven fabric of cotton or linen available in plain or ribbed weaves in various weights. The terms 'duck' and 'canvas' are now synonymous. Aprons, artists' canvas.

Duffel cloth Thick, heavily napped coating fabric, usually tan or green. Generally made up into short coats referred to as duffel coats.

Dupion Also called 'douppioni', 'dupioni'. Slubbed fabric made from fibre formed by two silk worms which have spun their cocoons together. It is now uncommon and expensive, but imitations are woven from artificial fibres. Formal wear, suits.

Eyelet *see* **Broderie anglaise**

Faille (pronounced *fale*) Closely woven fabric made from silk, cotton, wool or artificial fibres, with a light, flat crosswise rib. Evening and formal wear.

Fake fur *see* **Fun fur**

Feathers Feathers from cocks, marabous and ostriches are available in a wide range of colours either sewn onto a 12 mm tape or with the quills overlocked onto string. Available by the metre, the strips can be used to trim coats and formal wear, or to cover the entire surface of an evening jacket or stole.

Felt A nonwoven fabric composed of wool, fur or hair fibres which have been meshed together by heat, moisture and mechanical action. Available by the metre or in small squares for toy making.

Flannel Plain or twill weave fabric of soft (sometimes brushed) wool or cotton. Suits.

Flannelette Napped cotton in plain weave, sometimes blended with artificial fibres, made in prints and plain colours. Children's wear.

Foulard Lightweight, plain or twill weave fabric usually of rayon or silk. Ties, cravats, scarves.

Frieze thick, heavy fabric with rough surface of cut or uncut loops. Made from cotton or artificial fibres. Upholstery.

Fun fur Fabric, usually acrylic, made to resemble real animal fur. Term is synonymous with **fake fur.** Available by the metre and in strips for trimming.

Gabardine Strong, clear finished, medium to heavyweight twill weave fabric made from many different fibres or fibre blends. Raincoats, sportswear, slacks.

Galatea Strong, twill weave cotton fabric. Work clothes, small boys' pants.

Gauze Open weave, sheer fabric made from many different fibres. Bandages, curtains.

Georgette Similar to but heavier than **chiffon.** Made from crêpe yarns and has a dull texture. Blouses, evening wear.

Gingham Plain weave fabric formerly of cotton but now often made from blends of artificial fibres. Made by dyeing yarns then weaving them in checked or striped patterns. The checks (which come in a variety of sizes) make an excellent base for cross-stitch work. Dresses, blouses, children's clothing.

Granite cloth Usually worsted or linen, a hard but lightweight cloth finished with a grainy surface. Now uncommon. Men's suits.

Grenadine Loosely woven, leno weave fabric with a clipped dobby design. Curtains, summer dresses, skirts.

Grosgrain *see* **Petersham**

Habutae (pronounced *hab-u-tie*) Lightweight, soft fabric with a gloss finish, formerly made from silk, now from artificial fibres. Linings.

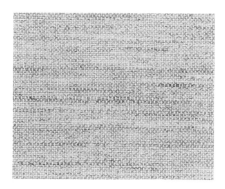

Hair canvas Sometimes called 'haircloth' or 'haircord'. Plain weave fabric characterised by fine rib lines in the warp direction created by alternate coarse and fine ends. Made from natural and artificial fibres combined with animal hair, usually goat or horse. Upholstery, interfacing.

Headcloth Inexpensive, coarsely woven fabric, generally of cotton. Children's clothing; also used as a base for embroidery.

Hessian Coarse, heavy fabric made from jute, hemp or cotton. Synonymous with **burlap**. Curtains, wall coverings, upholstery.

Holland Firm, plain weave fabric with glazed finish, originally of linen, now often made from cotton. Window blinds, furniture coverings.

Homespun Rough-surfaced, loosely spun fabric of wool, jute, linen or cotton. Today the term may refer to fabrics made of almost any fibre in imitation of the hand-made look.

Honan silk Synonymous with **pongee**. Traditionally a fine, crisp, hand-woven wild silk fabric with occasional lustrous and thick-thin threads. Formerly always tan coloured but now often dyed. Linings, dresses.

Hopsacking Named after the sacks used for hop-gathering. Coarse fabric with rough surface made from cotton, linen or rayon. (Hopsack is also the term used for a variation of plain weave.) Upholstery, some fashion items.

Houndstooth check Small combination of twill weave and colour pattern formed in warp and weft. Suits, trousers, sports jackets.

Huckaback Also called 'huck'. Term refers to a weave of cotton, linen or artificial fibres principally used for hand or dish-towels. With its pattern of small squares it makes an excellent base for embroidery.

Interlock A fine gauge knit formerly used only for underwear but now used for outer garments. Edges should be finished or reinforced to prevent runs. Plain colours.

Jap silk *see* **China silk**

Jacquard An intricate patterned weave or knit, often with a raised surface. Damask cloths, jackets. See page 64.

Jersey Generic term for any plain knitted fabric. Available in plain colours, stripes and prints. See weft knits, page 66.

Jute A natural fibre from the jute plant, used for making burlap, twine rug backing, trimmings and belts. It is also popular for macramé—knotted thread work.

Kapok Fluffy fibre from the pods of the kapok tree, used to fill pillows, cushions, toys and seam rolls. Now largely replaced by artificial fillings, polyurethane foam, polyester fibrefill.

Kersey A closely woven lustrous, compact fabric of wool or cotton, diagonally twilled or ribbed, with a fine nap. Made in plain colours. Work clothes and uniforms.

Lace Fabric or trimming with floral or scroll design differing from embroidery in that it is formed without a base fabric. Lace is now produced by machine; *needlepoint lace* is worked with a needle either on a core of fabric or built up entirely of looped or buttonhole stitches; *bobbin lace* is woven or plaited, each

thread being wound on a bobbin, and characteristically has a cloth-like background with a fancy filling and net-like surround. Laces are made from a variety of fibres; some are washable, others require very careful treatment. Laces are available in a wide range of colours, although white and ecru predominate. With one exception, noted below, laces come in dress and trimming widths. The principal types are:

Alençon (pronounced *al-on-son*) A design outlined with heavy thread (often silk) on a sheer net surround. Named after the French town of the same name. A luxury lace.

All-over A regularly repeating pattern with no surrounding net and no edging scallops.

Chantilly (pronounced *shan-tilly*) An elaborate design on a fine mesh surround finished with scallops at both edges. Popular for bridal wear.

Cluny A fairly heavy, rugged lace, generally of cotton, often with guipure designs but less expensive than guipure. It has no surround; the pattern sections are fixed in place by interlacing thread bars.

Guipure (pronounced *gee-poor*) The pattern is embroidered on a fabric which is later dissolved, leaving the motifs intact, joined by bars of thread. The motifs can be cut away and appliquiéd as a trimming on blouses, dresses and tablecloths. The lace is thick and the designs stand up in relief.

Insertion lace Trimming lace with two straight, finished edges.

Needlerun lace Embroidered design superimposed on net.

Ribbon lace Created by stitching ribbons (usually rayon-based) in floral pattern to a net background. Requires great care in handling. Women's evening wear, bridal wear.

Raschel Made on a raschel knitting machine, often imitating Chantilly designs. Its popularity owes much to its lower cost.

Valenciennes Also called 'Val' and 'Vals'. Available in trimming widths only. A flat bobbin lace worked with one thread forming both design and background.

Lambswool Very soft wool from a sheep up to seven months old. It is unusual to find it woven. Often blended, it is generally made into sweaters and cardigans.

Lamé (pronounded *lah-may*) Any woven or knitted fabric which has a metallic yarn combined with it to give either pattern or background a glittery effect. Can also be fabric embroidered with metallic thread. Evening and formal wear.

Lawn Sheer, lightweight, plain weave fabric of cotton or artificial fibre. Available in plain colours and printed designs. Children's clothing, summer dresses.

Leather There are a number of leathers suitable for making into coats, jackets and skirts,

but as many skins are imported their availability can be restricted from time to time. It is usually necessary to buy complete skins or hides as companies find it difficult to sell remnants. The principal types of leather are:

Garment suede split Available in fashion colours, the most popular choice for home

sewing as it can look effective without the finer details of tailoring. It can be printed.

Modelling hide Heavyweight, and popular for bags, belts and wallets. This leather is usually dyed by the modeller.

Full grain garment leather Locally produced. This is one of the more commonly used hides. Available in fashion colours. Usually sold in whole skins but occasionally in smaller pieces.

Lambswool Generally used for trimming (5-6 cm fibres), and for making babies' rugs.

Kidskin Finest quality skin and versatile in use. Available in various colours.

Deerskin Another fine quality leather.

Pigskin This skin is available in natural colours.

Sheep nappa (lambskin) and *kip (calfskin)* are available in a variety of colours.

Leatherette Imitation leather available by the metre in a number of finishes such as suede and chamois. Tailored coats, jackets.

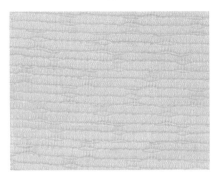

Leno Fabric produced by leno attachment on loom (see Woven fabric constructions, page 63), giving a lacy effect. Is strong and stable. Summer dresses, curtains.

Linen One of the world's oldest fabrics, made from fibres from the stalks of the flax plant.

Now generally combined with artificial fibres to improve crease resistance and washability. A very strong, absorbent, smooth, crisp fabric. Available in various strengths of weave. Bleached or natural (ecru) linen is a popular base for embroidery. Tailored suits, dresses.

Linsey-woolsey A coarse, uncomfortable fabric made in the eighteenth century by weaving wool and linen together.

Loden cloth Wind and water-resistant cloth, similar to duffel cloth, made from wool or artificial fibres. Coats.

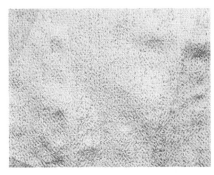

Lurex Trade mark owned by Dow Badische Company for a metallic thread, but sometimes refers to fabric woven through with this thread.

Madras muslin Cotton gauze fabric with an extra weft yarn that is bound into the gauze texture in the figured parts and cut away elsewhere. Traditionally, in bright plaid designs. Shirts, dresses.

Marocain Wool, cotton or silk dress crêpe with a crosswise rib. No longer available. Evening and formal wear.

Marquisette Lightweight, leno weave fabric of silk or artificial fibres, generally used for curtains and mosquito netting.

Matelassé (pronounced *mat-uh-lass-ay*) Luxurious, often jacquard weave fabric with raised design giving a puckered, quilted effect. Sometimes woven through with metallic thread. Evening wear, upholstery.

Melton Sometimes called 'melton cloth'. Very closely woven, twill weave, napped fabric similar to **broadcloth** but less expensive. Wind-resistant. Now usually made from artificial fibres. Uniforms, coats, snow suits, under collars in tailored jackets.

Milanese Low quality woven cotton fabric. Also a warp knit fabric with diagonal design. Many uses. Lingerie, curtains.

Mogador Plain weave fabric similar to **faille**, made from silk or artificial fibres, usually striped. No longer available. Sportswear, ties.

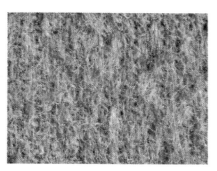

Mohair Lustrous, lightweight, silky fabric made from the hair of the angora goat. Now usually combined with other fibres. Suits, coats.

Moleskin Thick, heavy cotton fabric napped and shorn to produce a suede-like finish. Tends to shrink, but is very hard-wearing. Pants, work clothing.

Molleton Reversible cotton fabric, napped on both sides, usually brightly printed. Used mainly for dressing gowns.

Moss crêpe Crêpe woven with a mossy texture, giving a spongy handle. Can be made from any fibre, including polyester. Available in plain colours and prints. Blouses, dresses.

Mousseline de soie (pronounced *moos-uh-leen de swah*) Silk muslin, *de soie* meaning 'of silk'. A similar fabric produced from artificial fibres is called 'mousseline'. Mousseline de soie is the crisper of the two, and is lightweight, sheer and similar to **chiffon** in appearance. Available in plain colours and prints. Blouses, evening dresses.

Muslin Fine, gauzy, inexpensive soft cotton of plain weave, made in various weights. Now often made from a blend of cotton and artificial fibres. True Indian muslin, however, is

often woven with gold or silver thread and is an expensive luxury. Muslin fluctuates in popularity as a dress or shirt fabric. It can also be used, like calico, to make up a fitting shell before cutting an expensive fabric.

Nainsook Name comes from the Indian words for 'eye' and 'pleasure'. A soft, plain weave cotton made from mercerised yarns, it is suitable for babies' clothing and lingerie. Artificial fibres have largely superseded its use in dress widths, but nainsook is used to make fine quality bias binding.

Net Open fabric, knotted in geometrically-shaped holes, usually hexagonal. It is made in several weights and can be made from a variety of fibres. Silk or nylon net, popular for bridal and ballroom dancing wear, is called **tulle**. Curtains, mosquito nets.

Ninon Sheer, lightweight fabric in plain or novelty open weave, once made from silk but now generally from nylon. Curtains, dresses.

Nylon A generic term for an artificial fibre, and no longer a trade name. Pure nylon fabrics are durable but non-absorbent, which sometimes makes them uncomfortable to wear, especially

in warm weather. Nylon is often blended with other fibres such as cotton, wool, rayon and acetate to make fabrics with greater absorbency. The durability of other fibres can be increased by blending them with nylon. For further information, see page 61.

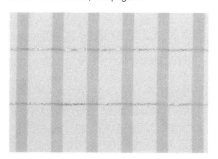

Organdie A fine, semi-sheer, lightweight, loose weave of cotton or artificial fibres. Curtains, blouses, evening wear.

Organza Sheer, crisp silk organdie with a sheen and of very fine weave. Formerly popular for bridal and evening wear. Expensive.

Osnaburg Coarse, strong, plain weave cotton, used mainly for bags and industrial purposes.

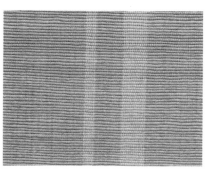

Ottoman Heavy fabric with crosswise ribs of varying widths, originally made with a silk warp and wool weft. Once popular for evening clothes, now used for coats, suits, academic gowns and upholstery.

Oxford cloth Wool fabric of basket weave with coloured (generally very dark grey) warp and white filling thread. Men's suits. The term 'Oxford' also refers to a shirting fabric of plain or basket weave.

Panama Lightweight, usually wool worsted fabric of basket weave, popular for summer suiting before it was largely replaced by artificial fibre fabrics.

Peau de soie (pronounced *po de swah*) Name is French, meaning 'skin of silk'. A heavy, smooth, satin weave fabric with a dull sheen. Now generally made from artificial fibres, including polyester. Wedding dresses, evening wear.

Percale Fine, lightweight, plain weave fabric with a smooth finish, now usually made from a blend of cotton and artificial fibres. Printed or plain. Sheets.

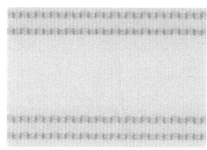

'Petersham Heavily ribbed fabric made with silk or rayon warp over round, firm cotton cords

Usually only available in ribbon widths in a wide range of colours. Ribbons, waistbands.

Piqué Cotton or cotton blend fabric woven with small, raised, geometrically shaped patterns on a loom with a dobby attachment. Plain or printed. Sportswear.

Plaited knit Knit fabric incorporating two yarns, the thicker yarn usually on the face, the thinner, plaited yarn (often lycra) inside or at the back of the structure. This imparts great stretch and resilience. Swimwear, gymwear, hosiery.

Plush Thick, deep, warp pile fabric made from silk, wool, mohair or rayon. The pile is longer and more open than that of velvet. Used for coats, rugs and upholstery.

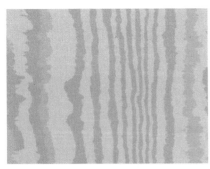

Polished cotton Also called 'satin cotton'. Cotton fabric which has had a sheen applied in the finishing process. It is less shiny than glazed cotton. Dresses, soft furnishings.

Pongee Plain weave, lightweight silk fabric with a slight slub effect. The terms **Honan** and pongee are today interchangeable. Fabric manufacturers tend to use the term pongee to describe a wide range of fabrics made from artificial fibres that resemble it in appearance or weight. Blouses, dresses.

Poodle cloth Heavy, looped fabric once made from wool, now often from artificial fibres. It is meant to resemble the coat of a French poodle. Coats, jackets.

Poplin Tightly woven, hard-wearing fabric with a fine horizontal rib, usually of cotton but also

cotton/artificial fibre blends, or made from silk. Summer dresses, children's clothing.

Poult taffeta Heavy, stiff-ribbed tafetta. Plain colours or shot (glimmering with the two colours used in the weave). Now rare.

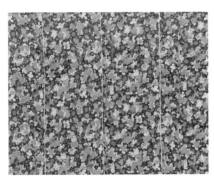

Quilting The effect is obtained by stitching by hand or machine (or welding by sonic vibrations) two or more layers of fabric together in geometrical patterns, with padding between. The padding makes the fabric warm, and quilted cotton and nylon are popular decorative fabrics for dressing gowns, vests, upholstery and bedcovers. The term does not refer to pintucked denim.

Ratine Rough, nubby fabric, loosely woven in plain weave from a yarn produced by twisting a thick and a thin fibre under uneven tension. A somewhat old-fashioned fabric. Between-season dresses.

Raw silk Silk fibre before processing. The term is sometimes incorrectly used for wild silk.

Rayon Generic name for fabrics produced from the first artificial fibre, which used to be called 'artificial silk'. It is inexpensive, soft, comfortable (having good moisture absorbency) and dyes well, but is weakened by exposure to sunlight and because of its low wet strength may shrink or stretch unless treated. Blouses, dresses, linings, curtains. The main types are:

Viscose rayon Made by the most common method. Not strong, especially when wet.

Polynosic rayon Made by a more recently developed process than viscose rayon. It is less likely to shrink or stretch.

Cuprammonium rayon Made by a process that allows very fine filament fibres to be formed, giving a finer, softer fabric than viscose rayon.

Sailcloth Generic name for fabrics used for making sails. Term, when used for dressmaking fabrics, refers to a firmly woven canvas-style fabric now made from artificial fibres as well as cotton. Children's clothing, dresses.

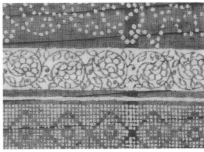

Sari The term refers to a length of cloth, usually 2.5 to 4.5 metres long, traditionally worn by women in India and Pakistan. It is elaborately swathed around the body. Sari cloth nearly always has a border design and is sometimes made from extremely fine silk with border designs in gold or silver thread.

Sateen Variation of satin weave. Fabrics made from cotton or artificial fibres. It is woven in such a way that it resembles satin. Strong, lustrous and lightweight. Blouses, dresses.

Satin The term refers to a weave, used for cotton, silk and artificial fibres. There are many styles of satin fabric, including: *antique satin,*

reversible with a lustrous surface on one side and a slubbed effect on the other; *crêpe-backed satin,* also reversible; *duchesse satin,* a luxurious, heavy and expensive fabric, often used for wedding dresses; *slipper satin,* often cotton-backed, strong and also expensive.

Scrim An open, plain weave mesh fabric usually made from cotton, but also from nylon and other artificial fibres. Printed or plain colours. Curtains; also used as bunting.

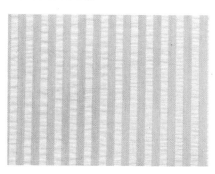

Seersucker Lightweight fabric made of cotton or artificial fibres with puckered look achieved in the weaving process. Made in many different qualities, and in plain colours, stripes, plaids and prints. The effect is now imitated in knit fabrics. Blouses, summer dresses, tablecloths.

Serge Twill weave, smooth fabric formerly made from wool but now made also from artificial fibres. It is becoming difficult to find. Uniforms, coats.

Shantung Plain weave fabric with slubs in the yarn producing slightly rough, nubbed surface. Originally made from silk, now generally from artificial fibres or blends. Formal wear.

Sharkskin Heavyweight, semi-crisp, hard finish fabric with a slight sheen. Now generally made from acetate or triacetate and used for tennis

dresses because of its stark whiteness and suitability for permanent pleating. It can also be found in colours, used for suiting.

Shot silk Silk woven with the warp and weft in differing colours so that the fabric appears to change colour at different angles. The effect can also be produced using other fibres. Evening and formal wear.

Silk A natural fibre, discovered by a Chinese princess 5,000 years ago, obtained by unwinding the cocoons of the silk-worm larvae. Silk fabrics give warmth without weight, but are cool in summer; are strong but have a delicate appearance; have high resistance to creasing and generally have a sheen. Silks are luxury

fabrics, although not always particularly expensive, and are in many cases being replaced by artificial fibre fabrics which retain the names previously applied only to natural silk fabrics, e.g. China silk, Honan silk, pongee, shantung, crêpe de Chine, surah. When silk is blended with other fibres it is usually in order to reduce its price. Occasionally silk is blended with another fibre to achieve a particular effect, but such fabrics are uncommon.

Strawcloth A fairly strong common fabric. Summer dresses, children's clothing.

Suede cloth Woven or knitted fabric of cotton, wool, artificial fibres or blends, usually napped, and shorn to resemble suede. Examples: **Ultra suede** and butter-suede. Tailored clothes.

Surah Soft twilled silk fabric with a sheen, often imitated with artifical fibres. Ties, dresses.

Sweater knit A knit fabric resembling hand-knitting. Sold by the metre, it can be cut and sewn to give the appearance of a hand-knitted garment. Example: **Jersey**.

Swiss cotton Lightweight, crisp, fine quality cotton, dotted, figured or in plain colours. Summer dresses.

Taffeta Crisp, plain weave silk fabric with shiny surface and a great deal of scroop (rustle).

Available in a variety of weights and often reproduced using artificial fibres such as acetate. Formal wear, linings.

Tarlatan Transparent, loosely woven, open-mesh, cotton cheesecloth fabric, given a dressing to stiffen it. Mainly used, layer upon layer, for theatrical costumes.

Tartan Wool, twill weave fabric in plaid designs, each design belonging to a Scottish clan. Most clans simply have one tartan, though where this is brightly coloured a low-key pattern in dark greens called a hunting tartan is used for everyday outdoor wear. In addition, some clans have dress tartans for more formal wear. For a tartan to be authentic it has to be approved by the Lord Lyon King of Arms, who is responsible for all heraldic matters in Scotland, but there are many imitation tartans available.

Terry cloth Cotton fabric with loop pile on one side, noted for its ability to absorb moisture. *Terry towelling* has the uncut loop pile on both

sides. A jacquard can create a patterned raised pile. Reverse colour patterns are also possible. Used mainly as towels but also for clothing such as beach coats. *Stretch towelling* is available and used for such things as car seat covers and babies' crawling suits.

Thai cotton Mediumweight cotton woven in Thailand, with slight slub. Brilliant colours, usually with characteristic print designs. Summer dresses, blouses.

Thai silk Fabric always of silk, made in Thailand, with slight slub and in iridescent colours. In plain colours (sometimes shot), woven checks, and

characteristic print designs. A luxury fabric. Dresses, shirts and blouses, cushion covers.

Three thread fleecy Knit fabric where the face appears as a rib stitch and the back is brushed to give a fleecy finish. Valued for warmth and softness. Sweatshirts or sloppy joes, tracksuits.
Ticking Very strong woven fabric, usually dark brown or black stripes on white, but also in jacquard and dobby weave. Generally used as covering for pillows and mattresses, but is sometimes popular for dresses.
Toile de Jouy (pronounced *twahl de zhoo-ee*) Cotton or artificial fibre fabric with a sheen, printed with a pictorial design. Usually used in soft furnishing, but also for dresses.
Tricot Fine, sheer, single knit with vertical ribs (wales) on the front and crosswise ribs on the back. Highly run-resistant. Very little lengthwise stretch. Used as a backing on bonded knits and can be used to line jersey dresses. *Lingerie tricot* is very lightweight.
Tulle *see* **Net**

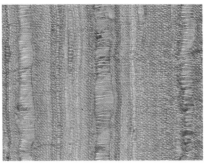

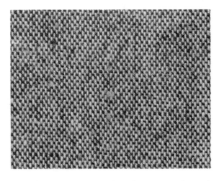

Tussore Also called 'tussah'. Silk fabric woven from silk of uncultivated silkworms, slightly coarser and stronger than that of domestic silkworms. It is naturally fawn. The term is also used for fabrics designed to imitate its irregular, heavy, crisp appearance. Formal wear.
Tweed Woven fabric with a somewhat hairy surface, characterised by coloured slubs of yarn. It is firm, hard-wearing and warm. Some tweeds are pure wool; others are of wool blends or other fibre combinations. Some well-known tweed types are:
Donegal Woven by hand in County Donegal in Ireland. Can now mean any tweed with thick, coloured slubs.
Harris Hand-woven from yarns spun by machine on the Outer Hebrides islands of Scotland. Very warm and tough.
Irish Distinguished by a white warp and a coloured filling. (Donegal is an Irish tweed.)
Ultra suede Also called 'Ecsaine suede'. Trade name for washable imitation suede made from cotton. It has no nap and can be cut in any direction. It is flammable and expensive, but easily washable and available in a wide range of colours. Jackets, pants, skirts, coats.

Union cloth Strictly the name for a fabric made from two or more fibres. Its primary use was for underwear, such as combinations, and it is now uncommon.
Velour Also called 'velours'. Woven or knitted fabric with a thick short pile. Has the lustrous look of velvet or velveteen, and is often dyed in deep, rich colours. Knit velour is suitable for men's and women's tops.

Velvet Silk or imitation silk fabric with short cut pile giving soft texture and lustrous, rich appearance. Skirts, evening wear, tailored clothing, curtains, upholstery. Some common types of velvet are:
Ciselé Satin weave fabric with a pattern of velvet on a sheer ground. Similar fabrics are made by flocking.
Crushed Pile is pressed flat in one or several directions to give a shimmering appearance.
Embossed has certain areas pressed flat.
Panne Pile is flattened in one direction to give a lustrous sheen. Is available with printed designs as well as in plain colours, and is both stretchable and washable.
Uncut Pile is left in loop form.
Nacré Woven with backing of one colour and pile of another, giving an iridescent appearance.
Velveteen Cotton or artificial fibre fabric produced in the same way as corduroy but with short cut pile covering the entire surface. Skirts, dresses, pants, children's clothing.
Vicuña Cloth made from the reddish-brown wool of the vicuña, a llama-like animal found only in Peru. It is particularly soft, light and lustrous and is the most expensive wool fabric. Nearly every country in the world has banned the sale of this cloth in order to protect the vicuña, which is threatened with extinction.
Vinyl In connection with dressmaking and soft furnishing, the term refers to a strong, woven or knit fabric coated with the plastic polyvinyl chloride, commonly called PVC. This gives a waterproof, slightly tacky surface, smooth or slightly textured. Raincoats, chair coverings.
Viyella Trade name for lightweight, plain weave fabric, 45% cotton, 55% wool, preshrunk and washable, made with printed designs or in plain colours. Dresses, blouses, children's clothing.
Voile (pronounced *voyl*) Plain weave, crisp, lightweight, sheer fabric of cotton or cotton blends, made with printed designs or in plain colours. Summer wear, curtains.
Whipcord Strong, heavyweight cotton, wool or artificial fibre fabric with bold twill weave. Uniforms, riding clothes.
Winceyette Very finely woven, soft, hard-wearing cotton fabric with fluffy surface, similar to flannelette. A good fabric for children's clothing, but extremely dangerous if not treated as it is highly flammable.
Wool The fibre obtained from the fleece of domesticated sheep; all other animal fibres are traded as hair or fur. Woollen fabrics are soft, warm and resilient. Fabrics labelled 'pure new

wool' in Australia contain a minimum of 95% wool; in New Zealand the terms 'all wool' and 'pure wool' are applied to fabrics containing at least 80% sheep wool, with the rest entirely of other animal hair or fur.
Worsted Type of wool yarn and fabric. Worsted fabrics are made from wool fibres which have been combed (to eliminate impurities) and carded. Worsted fabrics have a clear, smooth surface, while woollen cloths, which are only carded, are soft and some are almost felt-like. Worsteds are harder wearing and usually more expensive than woollens. Used mainly for tailored clothing.
Zephyr Fine cloth in plain weave, often with stripes on a white ground and coarse threads woven in at intervals. Dresses, blouses. Also a fine, soft low-twist yarn for hand-knitting, originally of wool but now usually acrylic.

Fabric patterns

Checks Any small regular pattern of squares which is woven or knitted into or printed onto a fabric. Examples:

Broken check A pattern in which the checks are irregular, not forming perfect squares.

Houndstooth check A small check pattern in plain weave or twill fabrics, regular in colour.

Pin check A check pattern in which the squares are extremely small.

Overcheck A design in which one check is woven or printed over others.

Tattersall check An overcheck pattern in two colours, usually on a white but sometimes on a coloured ground. These checks were named after Richard Tattersall who used the pattern on horse blankets.

Dots A circular design, woven, knitted or printed, usually positioned in a regular pattern on the fabric. Size usually determines the name of the dots. Examples:

Aspirin dots Dots the size of aspirin tablets, also called 'polka dots'.

Coin dots Dots the size of coins.

Pin dots Extremely small dots.

Liberty prints Traditionally printed on lawn or on a blend of wool and cotton. The name refers to designs created by Liberty's, a London-based store, founded in 1875. Prints are often in muted tones and feature floral, art nouveau and other stylised patterns.

Paisley A design derived from the cone design on woven Indian fabrics and shawls. The design was later adapted for printing, the woven shawls proving too expensive to produce.

Paisley, in Scotland, developed a large industry producing Indian-derived shawls which are now known as paisley shawls.

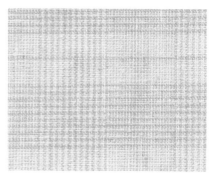

Plaids Originally the term used for the length of fabric in a tartan design worn as the traditional highland dress in Scotland, but it is now used to refer to any pattern of multiple stripes which cross at right-angles forming rectangles. Examples:

Balanced plaid Also called 'even plaid'. A plaid in which the stripes are arranged evenly on both the cross and length of the grain.

Bias plaid A plaid design which forms a diamond pattern, not rectangles, with the intersection of its lines. *Argyle plaid* is an example of a bias plaid.

Blanket plaid A brightly coloured plaid, usually woven into or printed onto a napped fabric such as that used for blankets.

Unbalanced plaid Also called 'uneven plaid'. A plaid in which the arrangement of the stripes is different on the crosswise and lengthwise grain of the fabric. When making a garment with this type of plaid, special care must be taken to match the design (see page 103).

Stripes Bands of woven, knitted or printed coloured yarns on a plain ground. Stripes are usually in multiples, are narrow or wide in alternat-

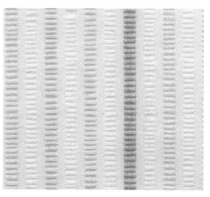

ing colours or multi-coloured patterns. Stripes on seersucker fabric create textured bands which may or may not be coloured.

Balanced stripes A pattern of stripes in which the same colours and widths are used on both sides of the centre.

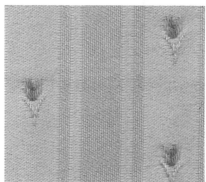

Blazer stripes A type of vividly coloured stripe used for jackets which became known as blazers because of their extremely bright colours. The stripes are usually at least 4 centimetres wide.

Pin stripes Very narrow stripes in any colour. When white they are often called 'chalk stripes'. Popular for suiting.

Roman stripes Narrow multi-coloured stripes which cover the entire surface of the fabric. They can range from extremely vivid colours to the most muted shades.

Fabrics in use

Special stitching and pressing needs

Because of their structure or finish, some fabrics call for special handling in stitching and pressing. A knowledge of these unusual requirements will help you to make sound fabric choices, especially when extra time or skill will be involved. You should consider, for instance, whether or not you have the time to finish seams in a sheer garment, or the experience to handle a delicate brocade.

Awareness of special fabric characteristics can also guide you in establishing fabric/pattern relationships. Easing possibilities are limited in permanent press fabric, for example, making it a poor choice for a style with very full set-in sleeves.

Each fabric here and on the opposite page represents a group. Your selection could belong to more than one; an example is panne velvet with a stretch knit structure. Also, some judgement must always be made as to whether a fabric has all the characteristics of its category. Most crêpes, for instance, are slippery, but not all. Any special techniques mentioned here are explained elsewhere in the book—see cross references above.

Crêpe
Stitching: Stitch length and tension must be adjusted carefully to avoid puckering, usually to longer stitch and lessened tension. Most crêpes have a tendency to slip and stretch. Tissue strips next to feed dog will solve the first problem; stabilising of certain areas, such as shoulder and neckline, may be necessary to remedy the second.
Pressing: Steam causes some crêpes to shrink or pucker; a fabric scrap should be tested first. A light touch is necessary to avoid overpressing.

Taffeta (brocade, satin)
Stitching: Can be stitched only once; removed stitches will leave holes. Should be handled as little as possible, because it creases and soils easily. Does not ease well.
Pressing: May waterspot; use a *dry* iron at low temperature setting. Tip of iron should be used for opening seams, a press cloth and light touch for other areas; folded edges should not be flattened. Covering ironing board with thick pad or towel helps to prevent flattening.

Sheers
Stitching: Inner construction of sheers must be neat because it shows through to the right side. Typically, French or other enclosed seam types are used. Soft sheers, such as chiffon, are inclined to slip or shift during stitching: they require tissue strips between fabric and feed dog.
Pressing: Soft sheers should be handled just like crêpe. Crisp sheers rarely require any unusual pressing techniques.

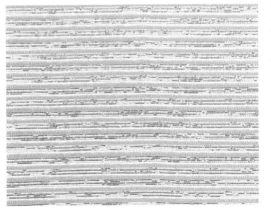

Metallic fabric
Stitching: Can be stitched only once; removed stitches will leave holes. Metallic threads may be cut by stitching; use fine needle and change it often. Garment may have to be lined to the edge to prevent scratching skin. Does not ease well.
Pressing: Same requirements as brocade. Steam may tarnish metallic yarns. Fullness of ease cannot be pressed out.

Lace
Stitching: Seams must be neatly finished as for sheers, or the fabric should be underlined to conceal them. Seams can be made nearly invisible by the appliqué method, and edges can be finished this way.
Pressing: The same as for sheers; take care to avoid snagging.

Fabrics in use

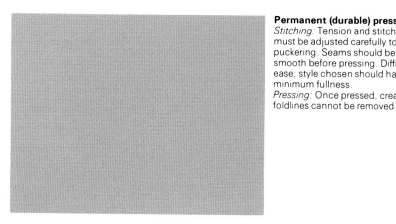

Permanent (durable) press
Stitching: Tension and stitch length must be adjusted carefully to avoid puckering. Seams should be smooth before pressing. Difficult to ease; style chosen should have minimum fullness.
Pressing: Once pressed, crease and foldlines cannot be removed.

Stretch knit
Stitching: To prevent seams from 'popping', stretch must be introduced by means of special stitches or techniques. In areas where stretch is undesirable (as at shoulders), seams must be stabilised with tape. For knits that curl at the edges, overedge or overlock seams may be necessary. Use ball-point needles; other types may cause holes.
Pressing: May be stretched or distorted unless handled lightly. Seam allowances may leave marks on right side; to prevent this, place strips of paper under them when pressing.

Velvet
Stitching: Can be stitched only once; removed stitches may leave holes. Should be stitched with fine needle, preferably in direction of nap
Pressing: It is extremely difficult to press velvet successfully. This is the one time you can break the rule about always pressing seams as you go; the less handling of velvet the better. The best way to deal with the problem is to hang a velvet garment in a steam-filled bathroom for about half an hour. Open the window and let the fabric dry out completely before you handle it again.

Leather
Stitching: Can be stitched only once; removed stitches will leave holes. Wedge-point needles should be used—they penetrate leather neatly and minimise tearing. Use a specially coated presser foot to prevent leather from sticking.
Pressing: Seams should be pressed open, using fingers or dry iron set at low temperature, or flattened with a mallet. Adhesive may be needed to hold the seam allowances flat.

Deep pile
Stitching: Stitch length and tension should be adjusted carefully; usually pressure is increased. Seams should be stitched in the direction of the pile; bulk is removed by trimming pile from the seam allowances (see Seams). Does not ease well.
Pressing: Must always be pressed from the wrong side with minimum pressure to avoid flattening pile. Tip of iron or fingers can be used to press the seams open.

Double-faced fabric
Stitching: To take advantage of the reversible quality, garment sections are usually joined with flat-felled seams. Garment edges are finished, as a rule, with fold-over braid or a similar trim.
Pressing: A heavy-duty press cloth is needed to flatten seams.

Underlying fabrics

Fabric types and selection

The underlying fabrics of a garment can be considered tools with which to build a better garment. Each of them —underlining, interfacing, interlining and lining—has a specific function that influences the garment's finished appearance. This part of the book deals with the purpose, selection and application of each of these fabrics.

While all of the fabric types listed may not be used in a particular garment, the order of application is always underlining first, interfacing next, then interlining, and finally lining.

Underlining is mainly intended to support and reinforce the garment fabric and the overall design. It also reinforces the seams. An additional benefit of underlining is that it will give a degree of opaqueness to the garment fabric. This keeps the inner construction details and stitching from showing through to the outside.

Interfacing is also used to support the garment fabric and design. But, since it is usually a sturdier fabric than is used for underlining, its effect on the garment fabric is more apparent and definite. An interfacing can be applied to the entire garment but is usually applied only to parts.

Interlining is applied to a garment to supply warmth during wear.

Lining serves to give a neat finish to the inside of a garment and also contributes to the ease of putting the garment on and taking it off.

When considering which of the underlying fabrics are advisable or necessary for the garment you are constructing, it is much easier to decide about a lining or interlining than about underlining and interfacing. Linings and interlinings are, in effect, extras added to a garment for comfort and, in the case of linings, to conceal the inside of a garment. Neither of these helps in any way, however, to build in or maintain the shape of the garment. Underlining and interfacing do that.

There are two determining factors with underlining or interfacing: how much shape or body is intended by the garment design, and how much support is needed in order for the garment fabric to achieve that design. Generally speaking, the more structured and detailed a design is, the greater its need for an underlining and interfacing. The weight of the garment fabric is another factor to consider. The lighter in weight or softer the fabric is, the more support it needs.

You should not, however, oversupport or undersupport any garment fabric in an attempt to achieve a certain garment design. Instead, choose another garment fabric more appro-

	Purpose	Where used	Types	Selection criteria
Underlining	Give support and body to garment fabric and design. Reinforce seams and other construction details. Give opaqueness to garment fabric to hide the inner construction. Inhibit stretching, especially in areas of stress. Act as a buffer layer on which to catch hems, tack facings and interfacings, fasten other inner stitching	The entire garment or just sections	Fabrics sold as underlinings—can be light to medium in weight, with a soft, medium or crisp finish. Other fabrics, such as China silk, organdie, organza, muslin, batiste, lightweight tricot (for knits)	Should be relatively stable and lightweight. Colour and care should be compatible with garment. Finish (e.g., soft, crisp) should be appropriate for desired effect
Interfacing	Support, shape and stabilise areas, edges and details of the garment. Reinforce and prevent stretching	Entire sections such as collars, cuffs, flaps. Garment areas such as the front, hem, neck, armholes, lapels, vents	Woven or nonwoven interfacings with or without iron-on properties—can be light, medium or heavy in weight	Should give support and body without overpowering the garment fabric. Care and weight should be compatible with rest of garment. Iron-on interfacings, especially firmer grades, tend to add some rigidity to fabric
Interlining	Provide warmth	The body of a jacket or coat, sometimes the sleeves	Lightweight, warm fabrics such as flannel, flannelette, felt, lightweight blanket fabric, brushed cotton	Light in weight. Will provide warmth. Not too bulky. Care requirements should be compatible with rest of garment
Lining	Cover interior construction details. Allow garment to slide on and off easily	Coats, jackets, dresses, skirts and pants, in their entirety or just partially	Lightweight fabrics such as fine rayon, silk, satin, sateen, crêpe, batiste, taffeta, blouse fabrics, georgette	Should be smooth, opaque, durable. Weight, colour and care should be compatible with the rest of garment. An anti-static finish is desirable

Garment fabric

Underlining. Applied before interfacing, interlining, lining.

Interfacing. Applied after underlining, but before interlining or lining.

Interlining. Applied after underlining and interfacing, but before lining.

Lining. Applied last, as the finishing touch.

Garment to which all four underlying fabrics could be applied has been chosen to show relation of these fabrics to one another and the order of their application. Regardless of number used, all fabrics should be draped together over your hand to see their combined effect.

priate to the needs of that particular design. A certain amount of judgment must always be exercised in the selection of a garment fabric to carry out a specific design. Some fabrics, even supported by both an appropriate underlining and interfacing, will still be too lightweight to sustain a very structured design. For certain designs, on the other hand, some fabrics may be too heavy.

When using any combination of fabrics, always drape them over your hand to see their combined effect.

Underlining

Underlining is a lightweight fabric that is applied to the wrong side of the garment fabric primarily to give additional strength, support and durability to the garment. Underlining also helps to maintain the shape of the garment and to reinforce its seams. Usually it will make the garment fabric opaque so that the inner construction details and stitching cannot be seen on the outside of the garment.

Underlining fabrics are made from various fibres, finished in several different handles (soft, medium and crisp), and available in a wide range of colours. There are also other fabrics, such as organza, tricot and lightweight blouse and lining fabrics, that are not classified as underlinings but can serve the same purposes.

Underlinings are applied by two different methods; these are illustrated and explained on pages 86–87. Depending on the desired effect, either the entire garment or just some of its sections can be underlined. As illustrated on the right, a fitted dress, which usually needs support and shaping in all of its sections, is most often completely underlined. The sheer blouse, however, needs the opaqueness given by an underlining for its bodice, but its soft full sleeves are more effective if left unhampered.

Occasionally, underlining may be applied only to certain areas of a garment section—for instance, the seat of a skirt or the knees of a pair of pants—to reinforce the parts that take the greatest strain.

When deciding which underlining fabric is suitable, look for one that matches the garment fabric in *care requirements,* not necessarily fibre content. Since the main purpose of an underlining is to support and strengthen the garment fabric, make sure that the underlining gives no

more than the garment fabric. Use a woven underlining with a woven garment fabric and cut out both on the same grain. Knits are not usually underlined but they can be if this is desired. A woven underlining cut on the straight grain will restrict the give of the knit; a woven underlining cut on the bias will allow the knit some give. To maintain most or all of the knit's give, use a lightweight tricot as an underlining and cut it out in the same direction as the knit fabric.

Choose a soft underlining if you want to maintain the softness of the garment fabric; a crisp underlining to give the garment fabric some crispness. Some garment designs may require more than one type of underlining. For example, a garment might need a crisp underlining to support its

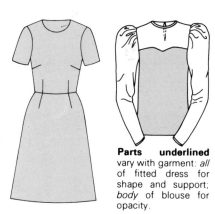

Parts underlined vary with garment: *all* of fitted dress for shape and support; *body* of blouse for opacity.

A-line skirt but require a soft underlining for its more fluid bodice.

As for the colour of the underlining, choose one that will not show through enough to change the colour impression of the garment fabric. As a final selection test, drape together all fabrics to be used to see if they will function well together and complement the garment design.

Underlying fabrics

Methods of underlining

There are two methods of underlining a garment. In the first, the two fabric layers (underlining fabric and garment fabric) are always treated as though they were one layer. In the other method, the two fabrics are handled separately up to the construction of darts and are then handled as one.

With either method, it is necessary to reposition the underlining in relation to the face fabric before garment sections are seamed. The reason is that a garment, on the body, is cylindrical; the underlining, because it will lie

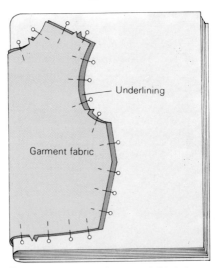

To reposition underlining, tack fabric layers together down centre or one edge. Wrap fabrics around a thick magazine with underlining next to magazine. Smooth out fabrics; pin together, as they fall, along the edges.

closer to the body, must be made into a slightly smaller cylinder than the one formed by the outer fabric. After repositioning, the excess underlining is trimmed. New underlining seamlines must be marked (use sewing gauge and chalk) to align with garment fabric seamlines.

Method 1: Treating two layers as one

Of the two underlining methods, the technique shown and described below, in which garment and underlining fabrics are treated as one through-out, is used more often. When it is used the underlining layer will reinforce all construction details, including darts, and will prevent them from showing through to the outside of the garment. Since the underlining will be uppermost during all construction steps, only that layer need be marked.

1. Cut out entire garment from the garment fabric. It is not necessary to transfer pattern markings to garment fabric; the underlining fabric will be marked and it will be uppermost during garment construction.

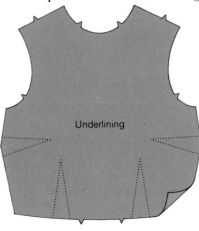

2. Remove pattern pieces from garment fabric sections. Decide which garment sections will be underlined and pin those pattern pieces to the underlining fabric. Cut out; transfer all pattern markings to the *right* side.

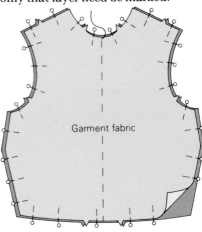

3. Wrong sides facing, centre garment fabric over underlining. Tack fabrics together—down centre of wide sections, along one edge of narrow pieces. Align tacking with spine of magazine and reposition underlining (see left).

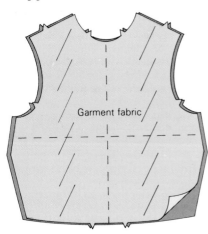

4. Remove fabric layers from magazine. With garment fabric uppermost, tack across centre, then diagonal-tack a few rows within section. Remove pins; trim underlining at edges; mark new seamlines to match those on face fabric.

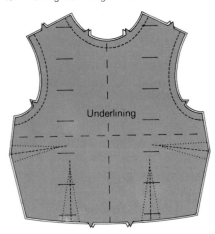

5. With underlining fabric uppermost, stay-stitch, where necessary, through both fabric layers. Machine-tack, through both fabrics, down centre of each dart, starting 2 to 3 stitches beyond point of each dart.

6. Fold each dart along its centre. Match, pin, tack and stitch each dart; remove hand tacking and the machine tacking that extends beyond dart points. Press each dart flat, then in the proper direction (see Darts).

Interlining

Interlining is a special type of underlying fabric whose main purpose is to insulate a garment, usually a coat or jacket, so that it will keep the wearer warm. To do this, an interlining must have some insulating property built into it, as a napped fabric has.

Interlinings should be lightweight but not thick; they should not add undue bulk or dimension to a garment. The most familiar interlining choices are flannel, flannelette and brushed cotton. Other fabrics can serve the same purposes; among them are felt, some pyjama and nightwear fabrics and thin blanket fabrics. Then there are the fabrics sold and handled as linings that also work as interlinings. Examples are quilted, insulated and fleece-backed linings.

An interlining's care requirements should match those of the rest of the garment, although interlined garments are best dry-cleaned. Choose a colour that will not show through to the outside of the garment.

Make sure, when you plan to interline, that there is adequate wearing ease to accommodate the added thickness; keep this ease in mind while fitting the garment. Because of the ease problem, sleeves are not usually interlined; they can be if ease is sufficient. Use the lining pattern pieces to cut out the interlining.

There are two methods of interlining. The first is to **apply the interlining to the lining,** in a way similar to the underlining method on page 86, then apply lining to garment.

The other method is to **apply interlining to garment** and then line the garment. See page 92 for basic lining methods.

Applying interlining to lining

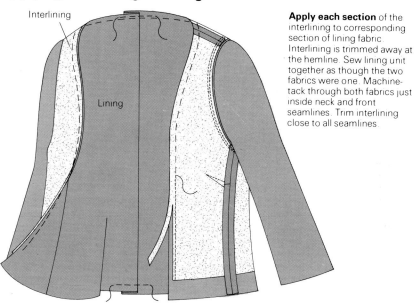

Apply each section of the interlining to corresponding section of lining fabric. Interlining is trimmed away at the hemline. Sew lining unit together as though the two fabrics were one. Machine-tack through both fabrics just inside neck and front seamlines. Trim interlining close to all seamlines.

Applying interlining to garment

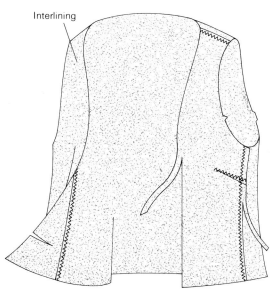

1. Stitch the interlining sections together, lapping seams and darts (see p. 88). Trim away the interlining along the lower edge to a depth that is equal to twice the width of the garment's hem. Trim away the neck and front seam allowances.

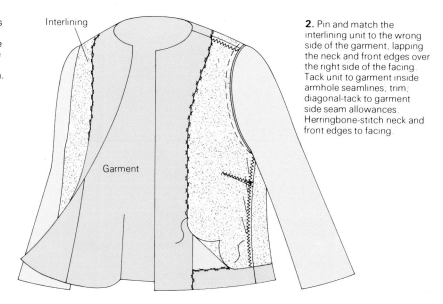

2. Pin and match the interlining unit to the wrong side of the garment, lapping the neck and front edges over the right side of the facing. Tack unit to garment inside armhole seamlines; trim; diagonal-tack to garment side seam allowances. Herringbone-stitch neck and front edges to facing.

Preparing fabrics for cutting

Preparing woven fabrics for cutting

Proper fabric preparation is an essential preliminary to cutting. It is helpful, before undertaking this procedure, to understand the basic facts of fabric structure. In weaving, fixed or *warp* yarns are interlaced at right angles by filler or *weft* yarns. A firmly woven strip, called the *selvage*, is formed along each lengthwise edge of the finished fabric. Grains indicate yarn direction—*lengthwise*, that of the warp; *crosswise*, that of the weft. Any diagonal intersecting these two grainlines is *bias*.

Each grain has different characteristics that affect the way a garment drapes. Lengthwise grain, for instance, has very little give or stretch. In most garments, the lengthwise grain runs vertically (that is, from shoulder to hemline). Crosswise grain has more give and thus drapes differently, giving a fuller look to a garment. As a rule, crosswise grain is used vertically only to achieve a certain design effect, as in border print placement (see Unusual prints, p. 104). Bias stretches the most. A bias-cut garment usually drapes softly. It also tends to be unstable at the hemline.

Straightening fabric ends. This first step must be taken with every fabric so that it can be folded evenly, also checked for grain alignment. Three methods are shown at right; each is suitable for different kinds of fabric. *Tearing* is the fastest, but appropriate only for firmly woven fabrics; other types may snag or stretch. *Drawing a thread* is slower, but the most suitable for loosely woven, soft or stretchy fabrics. *Cutting on a prominent line* is a quick,

simple method for any fabric that has a strong woven linear design.

Checking fabric alignment comes next. During manufacture, the fabric may have been pulled *off-grain*, so that grainlines are no longer at perfect right angles. A garment made with such fabric will not hang correctly, so re-alignment must be done before cutting (see opposite page). Bear in mind that not every off-grain fabric can be corrected, especially those that have water repellent or durable press finish, or a bonded backing.

Preshrinking is advisable if shrinkage possibilities are unknown, if two or more different fabrics are being used for a washable garment, or if maximum shrinkage is expected to be more than one percent. To preshrink washable fabric, launder and dry it, using the same methods to be used for the garment (follow fabric care instructions).

To preshrink drycleanable fabric, (1) dampen fabric (see first re-aligning step opposite); (2) lay on flat surface to dry (do *not* hang it up); (3) press lightly on wrong side. *One caution:* This process may cause some fabrics to waterspot or become matted. It is wise to test a scrap first. If both shrinking and grain adjustment are necessary, preshrink first, then re-align grain.

Press fabric that is wrinkled or has a creaseline, testing to see if the crease can be removed. If it cannot, or a faded streak shows up along the fold, this area must be avoided in layout and cutting (see Folding fabrics, p. 99).

Straightening ends

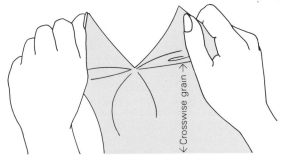

Tearing is suitable for firmly woven fabrics. First make a snip in one selvage; grasp the fabric firmly and rip across to opposite selvage. If the strip runs off to nothing on the way across, repeat, snipping selvage farther from end.

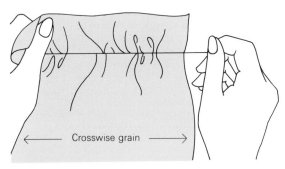

A drawn thread is better for soft, stretchy or loose weaves. Snip selvage; grasp one or two crosswise threads and pull gently, alternately sliding thread and pushing fabric until you reach other selvage. Cut along pulled thread.

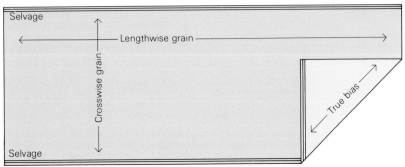

Woven fabric: Basically two sets of yarns, *warp* and *weft*, interlaced at right angles.

Selvage is formed along each lengthwise edge. **Lengthwise grain** parallels selvage; **crosswise grain** is perpendicular to it. **Bias** is any diagonal that intersects these grains; **true bias** is at a 45° angle to any straight edge when grains are perpendicular.

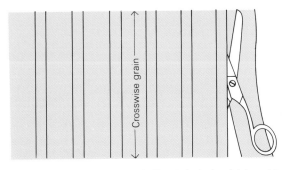

Cutting on a prominent fabric line is limited to fabrics with a *woven* stripe, plaid, check or other linear design. For *printed* designs of this type, use first or second methods (tearing or drawn thread), whichever is appropriate.

Preparing fabrics for cutting

Re-aligning grain

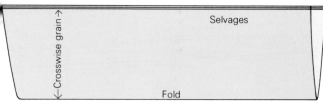

After straightening ends, fold fabric lengthwise, bringing selvages together and matching crosswise ends. If fabric edges fail to align on three sides (as shown), or if edges align but corners do not form right angles, fabric is skewed or *off-grain* and must be re-aligned before cutting.

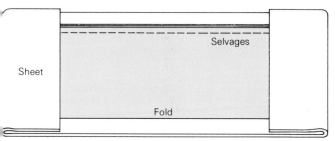

Dampening fabric is first step in re-aligning it. This relaxes finish, making fabric more pliable. Fold fabric lengthwise, matching selvages and ends; tack edges together. Enclose in a damp sheet (as shown) and leave several hours; or moisten fabric itself, using sponge or spray bottle. Test a small area; if water damages fabric, omit this step.

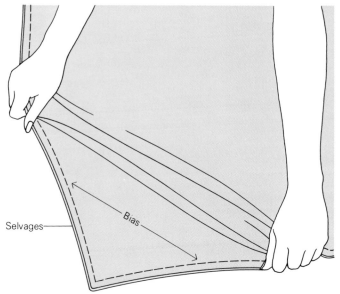

Next, fabric is stretched on the bias. This is usually sufficient to put it back in proper shape. Pull gently, but firmly, until fabric is smooth and all corners form right angles (easier to accomplish if two people work together). Use caution; too much stretching can cause further distortion. Lay fabric on a flat surface to dry, then press if necessary.

An off-grain print makes fabric seem crooked even if grainlines are true. This cannot be corrected. Avoid such fabrics by carefully examining print before purchase.

Preparing knits for cutting

Knits are structured differently from wovens but prepared for cutting in much the same way, except for straightening of ends. Since there are no selvages, and threads cannot be pulled, you must rely on your eye to tell whether a knit is even. If the design is boldly structured, cut along a prominent line; otherwise follow the procedures below.

Knit fabrics come in two forms, *flat* and *tubular*.

Some flat knits have perforated lengthwise edges which are comparable to the selvages on wovens. These should not be used, however, as a guide for aligning fabric; they are not dependably straight.

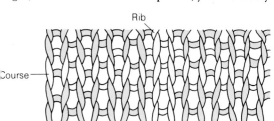

Knit fabric is formed by interlocking loops of yarn called *ribs*, which can be compared to the lengthwise grain in woven fabrics. The rows of loops at right angles to ribs, called *courses*, are comparable to crosswise grain of woven.

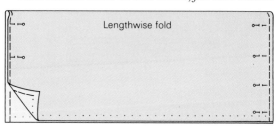

To straighten ends of a flat knit, tack with contrasting thread along one course at each end of fabric. Fold fabric in half lengthwise; align markings and pin together. (For alternative method, see Folding knits for cutting, p. 99.)

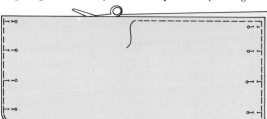

Straighten ends of a tubular knit same as flat knit, then cut open along one rib. If edges curl, press lightly, then tack together. Only exception is a narrow tube (usually 45 cm wide); this is used as is, without lengthwise seams.

Preparing fabrics for cutting

Handling pattern pieces

1. Assemble all pieces needed for your view.

2. Return to the envelope any pattern pieces that are not needed; they could cause confusion.

3. Cut apart small pieces, such as facings and pockets, if printed on one sheet of tissue.

4. *Do not trim* extra tissue margin that surrounds cutting lines; this is useful for alterations.

5. Determine how many times each piece is to be cut (such information is on the tissue itself).

6. Press pattern pieces with warm iron, if exceptionally wrinkled; otherwise smooth with hands.

7. Alter pattern, if necessary (see Pattern alterations). Make certain that any alterations made are visible on both sides of the pattern tissue.

8. Check overall garment length; change if desired.

9. Consider possible style changes. You may wish to reposition or eliminate pockets, create a more convenient opening, eliminate or add a seam (see Cutting basic design changes, p. 105). All such remodelling must be decided upon before cutting.

Identifying right side of fabric

Right side or *face* of fabric should be identified before cutting. Often it is obvious, but sometimes careful examination is needed to tell right side from wrong. One means of identification is the way fabric is folded—cottons and linens are folded right side out, wools wrong side out. If fabric is rolled on a tube, face is to the inside.

Here are some additional clues. **Smooth fabrics** are shinier or softer on the right side. **Textured fabrics** are more distinctly so on the face; for example, slubs may be more outstanding, a twill (diagonal weave) better defined. Such fabrics often have small irregularities, such as extra thick nubs, on the wrong side. **Fancy weaves,** such as brocade, are smoother on the right side, floats usually loose and uneven on the back. **Printed designs** are sharper on the right side, more blurred on the back. The **selvage** is smoother on the right side. Some knits roll toward the right side when stretched crosswise.

The fabric face is generally more resistant to dirt and abrasion but you can use the wrong side if you prefer its look. When there is no visible difference between sides, make one the wrong side and mark it with chalk to avoid confusion.

Selecting pattern layout

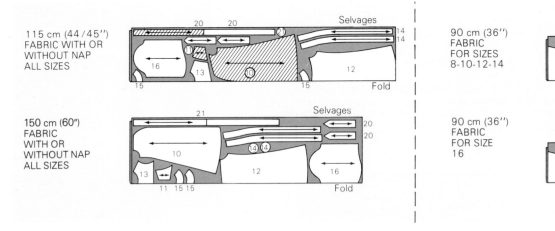

115 cm (44/45″) FABRIC WITH OR WITHOUT NAP ALL SIZES

150 cm (60″) FABRIC WITH OR WITHOUT NAP ALL SIZES

90 cm (36″) FABRIC FOR SIZES 8-10-12-14

90 cm (36″) FABRIC FOR SIZE 16

To find correct pattern layout, look for view that corresponds to your choice, then for fabric width and size that match yours. Circle this view so that you won't confuse it with other views as you work. If there is no layout for your fabric width, or if you are combining views, a trial layout may be necessary (see Trial layout, p. 105, for procedure).

How to interpret cutting guides

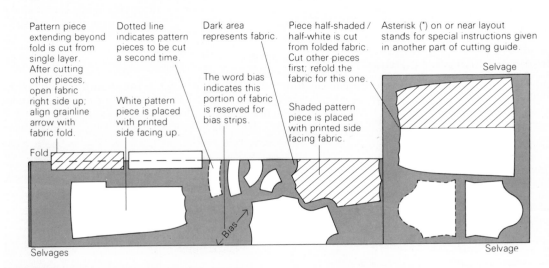

Pattern piece extending beyond fold is cut from single layer. After cutting other pieces, open fabric right side up; align grainline arrow with fabric fold.

Dotted line indicates pattern pieces to be cut a second time.

White pattern piece is placed with printed side facing up.

Dark area represents fabric.

The word bias indicates this portion of fabric is reserved for bias strips.

Piece half-shaded / half-white is cut from folded fabric. Cut other pieces first; refold the fabric for this one.

Shaded pattern piece is placed with printed side facing fabric.

Asterisk (*) on or near layout stands for special instructions given in another part of cutting guide.

Cutting layout above is representative of types to be found in any pattern guide sheet. To make the drawing more informative, all possible variations are included; the average actual layout is usually much simpler. Every pattern company provides, in its instruction sheets, a key to the use of its particular layouts. Consult this before proceeding.

Folding fabrics for cutting

The first step in following a cutting layout is to determine how the fabric should be folded, if at all. Precision is vital here. Where selvages meet, they should match exactly. (Shifting of slippery or soft fabric can be prevented by pinning selvages together every few centimetres.)

If the material was folded at the time of purchase, make sure the foldline is accurate and re-press it if necessary. Also test to see if the fold can be removed —a permanent crease must be avoided in cutting. (A double lengthwise fold, far right, is one way around the problem.) When no fold is indicated, lay fabric right side up.

Fold *right sides* together when the layout calls for partial lengthwise fold. Fold *wrong sides* together when you are working with napped fabrics, designs to be matched, prints with large motifs, non-symmetrical designs and fabric to be marked with carbon paper (see Marking methods, p. 106).

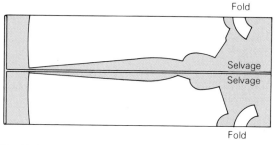

Partial lengthwise fold: Made on lengthwise grain with one selvage placed a measured distance from fold, balance of fabric is single layer. Width of double portion is determined by widest pattern piece to go in this space. Care must be taken to maintain uniform distance from selvage to fold.

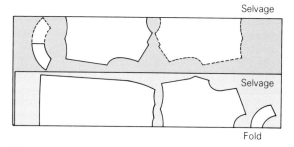

Double lengthwise fold: Two folds, both lengthwise, with selvages usually meeting at centre. Substitute for standard lengthwise fold when creaseline cannot be removed; also when both front and back pieces are to be cut on fold. Keep distance consistent from each fold to selvage.

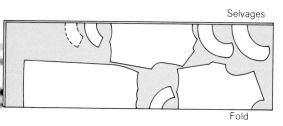

Standard lengthwise fold: Made on lengthwise grain with selvages matching along one edge (the way fabric often comes from the bolt). The fold most often encountered in layout guides, it is convenient and easy to manage.

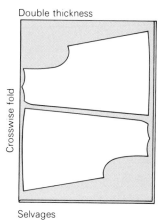

Crosswise fold: Made on crosswise grain with selvages matching along two edges. Generally used when the lengthwise fold would be wasteful of fabric, or to accommodate any unusually wide pattern pieces. *Not* to be used for napped or other one-way fabrics (see Cutting directional fabrics, page 102).

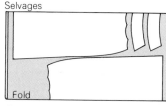

Combined folds: Fabric is folded two different ways for same layout. Most often consists of one lengthwise and one crosswise fold, though any combination is possible. Usual procedure is to lay out pattern pieces for one portion, then cut off remaining fabric and re-fold. Before dividing fabric, measure second part to make sure there is enough length.

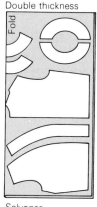

Folding a knit

There are two ways to fold knit accurately. You can either match the crosswise tacking used for straightening ends (see Preparing knits for cutting, p. 97) or mark a lengthwise rib, as at right.

Should the knit be too fine for either method, fold it as evenly as you can, making sure ribs are not twisted along foldline. If the fabric already has a crease, check it for accuracy; re-press if necessary; also make sure the crease can be removed. Special care must be taken with a knit fold—it acts as a guide for straight grain when the pattern is pinned.

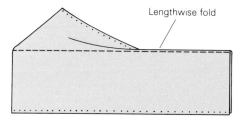

Before folding knit lengthwise, tack along one rib near centre of fabric, using contrasting thread; fold on tacked line. If knit has perforated edges, these need not match.

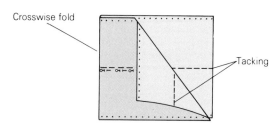

When folding knit crosswise, tack first as for lengthwise fold, then fold fabric, aligning the tacking marks. Pin along tacked line through both layers of fabric.

Basic cutting

Pinning the pattern to the fabric

For pinning pattern to fabric, the general order is *left to right* and *fold to selvages*. For each pattern piece, pin fold or grainline arrow first, then corners, and finally edges, smoothing pattern as you pin. *Place pieces as close together as possible,* overlapping tissue margins where necessary.

Each layout is designed to use fabric economically. Even small changes may result in the pieces not fitting into the space apportioned to them. The efficient way to place pins is diagonally at corners and perpendicular to edges, with points toward and inside cutting lines. (On delicate fabrics, and leather and vinyl, in which pins could leave holes, pin within seam allowances.)

Use only enough pins to secure foldlines, grainline arrows, corners, and notches—too many pins can distort fabric, making it difficult to cut accurately. A few more than usual, however, may be needed for slippery or soft fabrics. A firm hand on the pattern while cutting should give adequate fabric control. Do not allow fabric to hang off the edge of the cutting surface. If it is not large enough to accommodate all fabric at once, lay out and pin one portion at a time, carefully folding up the rest.

Before starting to cut, lay out *all* illustrated pieces, then re-check your placements. Cutting is a crucial step, not to be done in haste. If underlining, lining or interfacing are to be cut using garment pattern pieces, cut garment first; remove pattern and re-pin to each underlying fabric.

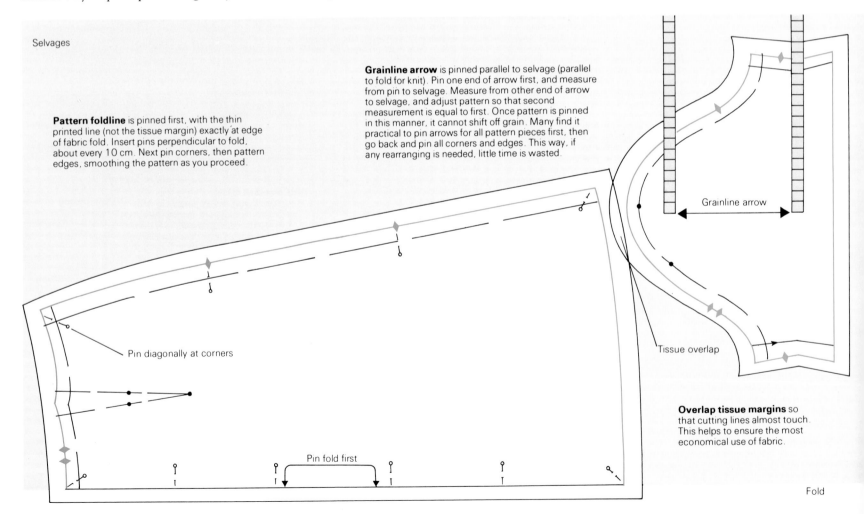

Selvages

Grainline arrow is pinned parallel to selvage (parallel to fold for knit). Pin one end of arrow first, and measure from pin to selvage. Measure from other end of arrow to selvage, and adjust pattern so that second measurement is equal to first. Once pattern is pinned in this manner, it cannot shift off grain. Many find it practical to pin arrows for all pattern pieces first, then go back and pin all corners and edges. This way, if any rearranging is needed, little time is wasted.

Pattern foldline is pinned first, with the thin printed line (not the tissue margin) exactly at edge of fabric fold. Insert pins perpendicular to fold, about every 10 cm. Next pin corners, then pattern edges, smoothing the pattern as you proceed.

Grainline arrow

Pin diagonally at corners

Tissue overlap

Overlap tissue margins so that cutting lines almost touch. This helps to ensure the most economical use of fabric.

Pin fold first

Fold

Cutting

For accurate results when cutting, always keep the fabric flat on the cutting surface, and use the proper shears and techniques as described below.

Bent-handle dressmaker's shears help to keep the fabric flat. They are available in three blade types—*plain, serrated* and *pinking*. Use only the first two types for cutting out a garment. Plain and serrated blades can be used interchangeably, but note that serrated blades are specially designed to grip knits and slippery fabrics. Pinking shears should be used *only* for seam finishing; they do not produce precise enough edges for cutting out.

Make sure that the blades of any scissors you use are sharp; dull blades will chew the fabric. Have the scissors sharpened professionally whenever they need it. *Never* cut paper with your dressmaker's scissors, and try to avoid accidentally cutting onto pins as this burrs the blade edges.

If the scissor action is stiff, adjust the blade screw slightly or apply a greaseless lubricant.

Special cutting tips

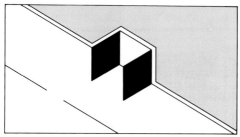

Cut double or triple notches as single units, snipping straight across from point to point—simpler and more convenient than cutting each one individually.

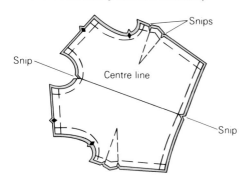

Identify garment centre lines with small snip (3 mm) into each seam allowance at top and bottom edges; do same for any adjoining piece, such as collar. Snips are useful, too, for identifying dart lines, especially when pin/chalk marking method is used (see p. 106).

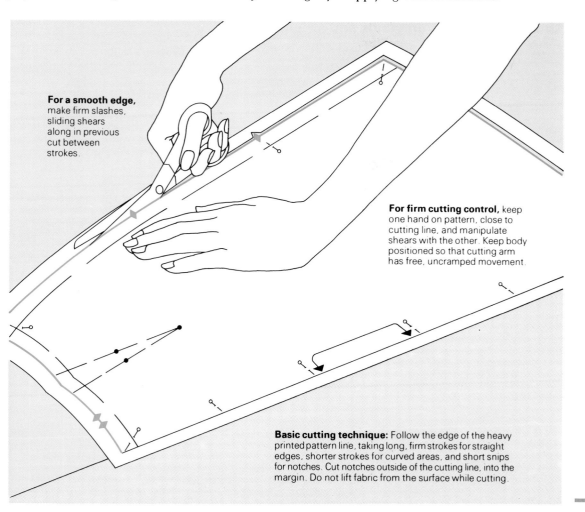

For a smooth edge, make firm slashes, sliding shears along in previous cut between strokes.

For firm cutting control, keep one hand on pattern, close to cutting line, and manipulate shears with the other. Keep body positioned so that cutting arm has free, uncramped movement.

Basic cutting technique: Follow the edge of the heavy printed pattern line, taking long, firm strokes for straight edges, shorter strokes for curved areas, and short snips for notches. Cut notches outside of the cutting line, into the margin. Do not lift fabric from the surface while cutting.

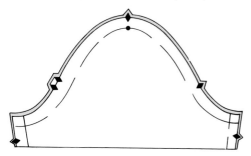

Identify top of sleeve cap by cutting a notch just above large circle on the pattern. Such a notch is easier to see when setting in the sleeve.

Cutting special fabrics

Pattern selection and layout

Certain fabrics involve special considerations in pattern selection and layout. Guidelines for the handling of such fabrics begin here and continue to page 104. A fabric can fall into one of the problem categories, or more than one. A plaid, for example, might also be a directional fabric.

Directional fabrics are so called because they must be laid in one direction for cutting; they are described as 'with nap' on pattern envelope and guide sheet. Included in this category are truly napped fabrics (with pile or brushed surfaces); designs that do not reverse (one-way designs); and surfaces that reflect light in varying ways (shaded). Satins and iridescents are examples of the last.

To determine if a fabric is a directional type, fold it crosswise, right sides together, then fold back a part of the top layer along one selvage. If the opposing layers do not look exactly the same, the fabric is a 'nap' for cutting purposes.

To test a napped fabric (one with pile or brushed surface) for direction, run a hand over it. It will feel smooth with the nap running down and rough with the nap running up.

When deciding which direction to use, consider the following: *short naps* (such as corduroy or velvet) can be cut with nap running up for rich colour tone or down for frosty effect. The same is true of *shaded* fabrics. *Long piles* or shags should be cut with nap running down for better appearance and wear. *One-way designs* are cut according to the natural bent of the design, or the effect desired.

Because all pattern pieces must be laid in one direction (see illustration, top right), a crosswise fold cannot be used. If such a fold is indicated, fold fabric as specified, with wrong sides together; cut along foldline and, keeping wrong sides together, turn the top layer so nap faces in the same direction as it does on the layer beneath.

Plaids, most stripes, and other geometrics are, for the most part, the same for cutting purposes. What differences occur are due to proportions within the design (see details opposite). These fabrics are usually more effective and easier to handle in a simple style. A good pattern choice is one that shows a plaid or stripe view on the envelope. *Avoid* any pattern designated 'not suitable for plaids or stripes'; stay away, too, from princess seams and long horizontal darts.

Directional fabrics

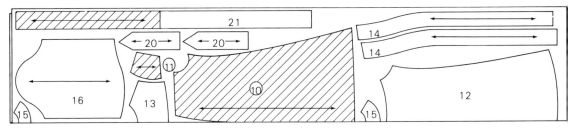

Typical layout for directional fabric

Laying out pattern on plaids and stripes

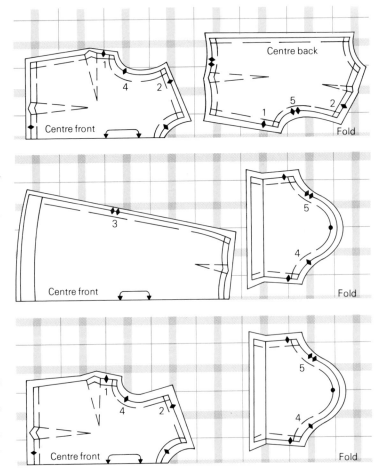

Centring is the first consideration when laying pattern on plaid, stripe, or comparable geometric design. Decide which lengthwise bar or space is to be at garment centre. Fold fabric exactly in half at this point for pattern piece that is to be cut on a fold; for other sections, align point with the centre seamline (or centre line for piece with extended facing). Centres must be consistent for bodice and skirt, sleeve and collar—all major garment sections.

Placement of dominant crosswise bars is the second consideration when planning a layout in plaid or crosswise stripes. As a rule, the dominant stripes should be placed directly on, or as close as possible to, the garment edges, such as hemline and sleeve edge. (Exceptions are A-line or other flared shapes. In these cases, place the least dominant colour section at hem edge so the curved hemline will be less conspicuous.) Avoid dominant stripes, too, at the waist and across the full part of bust or hip.

Crosswise matching of major garment sections is accomplished by placing corresponding notches on identical crossbars (lines that will be horizontal). To match sleeve and garment front, for example, place front armhole notches of both sleeve and garment on the same crossbars. *Do all matching at seamlines— not at cutting lines.* It may or may not be possible to match such diagonals as darts, shoulder seams and pants inseams. This depends on angle of stitch line and particular fabric design.

Even and uneven plaids

A plaid is a design of woven or printed colour bars that intersect at right-angles. The arrangement of these bars may be even or uneven, as illustrated at right; which it is should be determined before fabric is purchased because this affects pattern choice as well as layout necessities.

A four-sided area in which the colour bars form one complete design is called a *repeat*. To tell whether a plaid is even or uneven, fold a repeat in half, first lengthwise, then crosswise. A plaid is *even* when colour bars and intervening spaces are identical in each direction; it is *uneven* if they fail to match in one or both directions.

Stripes may also be even or uneven; each type is handled by the same methods as a corresponding plaid. The exception is a diagonal stripe, discussed on page 104.

Even plaids, either square or rectangular, are the easiest to work with, though a rectangular plaid is somewhat more difficult to match where seaming is on the bias. An even plaid is suitable for a garment with a centre opening or centre seams, also for one cut on the bias (see Chevron, p. 104).

Uneven plaids require extra thought and care in layout planning and have fewer style possibilities. **When plaid is uneven crosswise,** pattern pieces must be laid in one direction, like napped fabrics. **When plaid is uneven lengthwise,** the repeats do not have a centre from which the design can be balanced out in both directions, and so the design goes around the body in one direction only. A type of balance can be established, however, by placing a dominant vertical bar or block at centre front and back. *Avoid* designs with centre seams or kimono or raglan sleeves.

An exception can be made to these precautions when a plaid fabric that is uneven lengthwise is reversible. In this case, the pattern should have centre seams, or they must be created (see Design changes, p. 105). Plan the layout so that the design reverses itself to each side of the centre seams. This is accomplished by cutting each garment section twice, with printed side of pattern facing up, and using wrong side of fabric for half the garment.

When plaid is uneven in both directions, the same considerations apply as for plaids that are uneven lengthwise, plus the need to lay all pattern pieces in one direction as for napped fabrics.

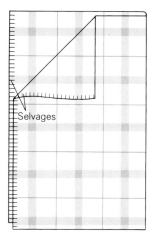
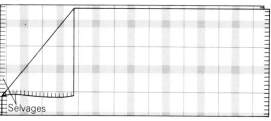

An even plaid matches both lengthwise and crosswise when folded through the centre of a repeat. An *even square plaid*, left, also forms a mirror image if folded diagonally through the centre of one design. An *even rectangular plaid*, shown below, is even, but not identical, both lengthwise and crosswise.

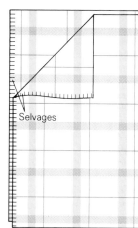
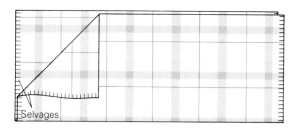

An uneven plaid may not match in one or both directions. When plaid is *uneven lengthwise*, left, a repeat folded in half crosswise matches; folded lengthwise it does not. With plaid that is *uneven crosswise*, as below, repeat forms a mirror image when folded in half lengthwise; does not when folded crosswise. Plaid that is *uneven in both directions* (not shown) does not match folded either way—lengthwise or crosswise.

Cutting plaids

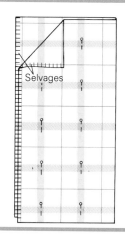
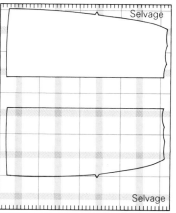

With fabric folded: Identical intersecting bars of the repeats should be pinned, through both fabric layers, every few centimetres. This technique lessens the risk of the layers slipping and thus not matching.

With a single layer, cutting is more accurate than with folded fabric but it takes more time. With fabric right side up, pin and cut each pattern piece once. To cut second piece, remove pattern and lay garment section right side down against remaining fabric; match bars lengthwise and crosswise; pin. For pattern piece to be cut on a fold, use method for folded plaid.

Cutting special fabrics

Diagonals

Of the woven diagonals (twill weaves), some have barely perceptible ribs, as typified by gabardines; ribs of others are bold, as in the example below.

The first type is handled like any plain weave. The latter group, which also includes diagonally printed stripes, requires careful pattern selection. *Avoid* any pattern designated 'not suitable for obvious diagonal fabrics', and designs with centre seams, long diagonal darts, gored skirt sections, collar cut on fold, or a V-neckline.

An exception to the above limitations can be made for an obvious diagonal fabric that is reversible. Here the wrong side of the fabric is used for half the garment; diagonals are then balanced in *chevron* or V-shaped seams. Chevrons can also be created by cutting a plaid, stripe, or other geometric on the bias. To work this way, a design must be even lengthwise (see test below).

Diagonals should be cut from a single layer—each pattern piece pinned once with printed side up, once with printed side down. *Exception* is a chevron of reversible fabric. Here all garment sections are cut with pattern pieces face up and half of the *fabric* sections reversed for the left side.

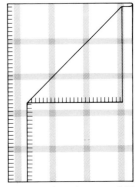
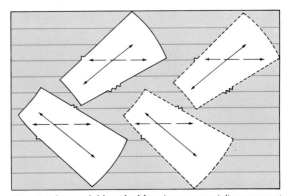
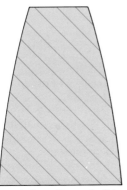
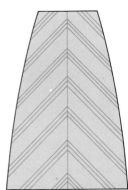

A woven diagonal may form an obvious 'stripe' on the bias. Such fabric requires careful pattern selection.

To test for chevron, fold fabric lengthwise; turn a corner back diagonally through centre of repeat.

To cut stripe or plaid on the bias, draw new grainline arrows at 45° angle to original ones (unless already provided). Cut each garment section individually, following centring and matching principles on pages 102 and 103.

An obvious diagonal will be most successful in a pattern design that involves few seams or structural details.

The typical chevron shape is a 'V' pointing up at centre, down at sides. Chevron above is a stripe cut on the bias.

Unusual prints

Fabric with a large motif requires careful placement, and sometimes matching, of the design. A precise motif, such as a diamond, must be centred and matched just like a plaid. A random one, paisley for instance, need not be matched, but should be balanced. Whatever the design, seams and intricate details should be as few as possible.

To decide on placement, drape fabric over your figure before a full-length mirror and try various approaches. If the garment has centre seams, motifs might be placed opposite one another an equal distance from the centre. As a rule, though, the asymmetrical balance illustrated at the right is more pleasing. In any case, do not place motifs directly on the full part of bustline or buttocks. Another point to remember: a large scale print is often a one-way design, in which case pattern pieces must be laid out as for directional fabrics (see p. 102).

Border print fabric with a marginal design running lengthwise along one edge can be used in two ways. One is to run the border vertically, placing it to each side of centre front and/or centre back seams. The other, more usual way is to place the border at the garment hem, as shown at right. For the latter, major garment sections are cut on the crosswise grain (with new grainline arrows drawn perpendicular to the original ones).

If the garment being cut this way has no waistline seam, its entire length must fit on the fabric width, leaving little or no hem allowance. One solution is to place hemline at the selvage, omitting hem altogether. Or you can leave a small allowance at the selvage for stitching on a hem facing (mandatory if there is printing on selvage). *Avoid* A-line or gored skirts for horizontal border; it cannot be matched on bias-cut seams.

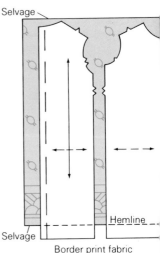

Fabric with large motif

Border print fabric

Special cutting techniques

Professional tips

Listed below are supplements to basic pinning and cutting techniques; ideas based on experience.

1. To keep fabric from slipping, and also protect the cutting surface, cover cutting area with felt or a folded sheet. A useful alternative is a cutting board (a sewing aid available at haberdashery counters). Fabric can be pinned directly to it to prevent slipping.
2. For better control and more comfortable cutting, have cutting surface accessible from at least three sides. If this is impossible, separate pattern sections so that you can turn pieces around if necessary.
3. For bulky fabrics, which are often difficult to pin, delicate fabrics or leathers and vinyls that could be marred by pins, consider pin substitutes such as upholstery weights or masking tape.
4. Heavy or bulky fabric can be cut more accurately if you cut through one layer at a time.
5. When cutting from a single layer, cut each pattern piece once with printed side up, once printed side down, to obtain right and left sides for garment.

6. A very thin or slippery fabric, such as chiffon or light-weight knit, will shift less if you pin it to lunch paper (the same paper can be used later to facilitate stitching). Such fabrics are also easier to cut with serrated scissors, which grip the fabric.
7. For fewer seams to finish, place the edge of any pattern piece that corresponds to the straight grain, directly on a selvage. If selvage is tight and tends to pull, clip into it every few centimetres.
8. Use each pattern piece the correct number of times. Such items as cuffs often require more than two pieces.
9. Keep shears sharp by cutting nothing but fabric with them (paper dulls the blades).
10. Sharpen slightly dull scissors by cutting through fine sandpaper. Take very dull ones to a professional.
11. Save fabric scraps left from cutting; they are often usable for small items, such as buttonhole patches, and for testing stitches and pressing techniques.

Trial layout

Should you need to establish a layout not provided in the cutting guides, the simplest approach is to choose the one closest to your requirements and follow it closely, making changes as needed. At first, pin only foldlines or grainline arrows, so that pieces can be shifted with minimal re-pinning.

If none of the layouts even approximates your needs, proceed as follows: fold fabric with standard lengthwise fold (see p. 99). Without pinning, lay out all pattern pieces, first the major garment sections, then smaller pieces. Experiment with various pattern arrangements and, if necessary, different fabric folds, until everything fits satisfactorily; then pin all pattern pieces.

To determine how much fabric you will need of a width not specified on the pattern envelope, simply fold a bed sheet to the desired width and proceed as above. When you are satisfied with the layout, measure the sheet area used.

Cutting basic design changes

Some characteristic of a fabric, such as its bulk or design, may suggest a change in basic pattern style. For example, a coat of heavy fabric would have sharper edges without facing seams. Or you might want to change some pattern feature, such as the location of an opening.

As a rule, seams that are added or eliminated should correspond to the fabric straight grain; if they do not, garment grainlines may be altered. Remember that a change in one section can affect the treatment of an adjoining one. Make sure that all garment sections affected are altered.

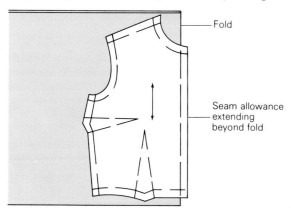

Eliminate a seam by placing pattern seamline on fabric fold. Such a change is recommended when fabric will be more attractive with fewer seams (for example, a plaid or large print). Method is applicable only to seams that coincide with straight grain. If zipper opening is eliminated by this step, decide where to re-locate it before proceeding.

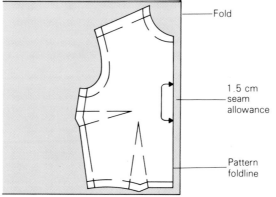

Create a seam by adding a 1.5 cm seam allowance to the pattern foldline. This technique can be used to provide a more convenient opening, or to balance an uneven plaid or obvious diagonal when fabric is reversible. The new seam must fall on the straight grain. Pattern piece need not be cut near fabric foldline, but if it is, the fold must be slit.

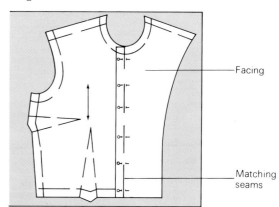

Eliminate a facing seam by pinning garment and facing patterns together with seamlines matching; both seams must coincide with straight grain. This produces an extended facing, as shown above, which is recommended for bulky fabric. A seam that joins two facing pieces can be eliminated in the same way (such a seam need not be on the straight grain).

Marking the cut pieces

Marking methods

Marking—the transfer of significant pattern notations to fabric—is done after cutting and before removing pattern. The symbols selected for transfer are those that make clear *how* and *where* garment sections are shaped and joined and details are placed. Usually included are dart, tuck, gathering and pleat lines, large dots and squares, centre front and back locations, buttonhole and other detail placements. It is helpful to mark seamlines that are intricately shaped; *all* seamlines, if you are inexperienced. When garment is to be underlined, usually only the underlining is marked.

Common marking methods and their typical uses are discussed below. You must decide which is most suitable for each situation. In general, any device can be used provided that it makes a precise, clear mark without disfiguring the fabric. *Always test a small fabric swatch* to make sure marks show up clearly and can be removed later.

The dressmaker's carbon paper and wheel method is fast and works best on plain, opaque fabrics. It is less satisfactory for multicoloured fabrics, and not recommended for sheers, because marking shows through to the right side. It is preferred to

other methods for its convenience, but the wheel can rip tissue, thus limiting the reusability of a pattern, and may damage the threads of the fabric if used too heavily. While tracing, keep a piece of cardboard under the fabric to prevent marring the work surface beneath, or use a cutting board.

With fabric folded wrong sides together, both layers can be marked at once, using double-faced paper or two sheets back to back. With fabric right sides together, layers are marked one at a time.

Tailor's chalk is also a quick marking device. Only dots are registered, but these can be connected with the chalk and a ruler after the pattern is removed. Remember that the chalk rubs off some fabrics easily, so try to sew up the garment as soon as possible after it has been marked.

below. Both are made by hand. A third version, **machine tailor's tacks,** shown and described in the Machine stitch section, is particularly useful for multiple markings, such as pleat lines. If many tacks must be made on one garment, it is helpful to use a different colour thread for each pattern symbol—one for darts, another for seamlines, etc.

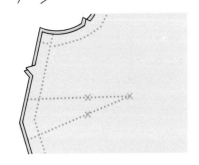

To trace marks, place waxed side of dressmaker's carbon paper against *wrong side* of fabric. (It may be necessary to move a few pins.) Trace markings with wheel, taking short firm strokes; use ruler as guide for straight lines.

Traced marks should be precise, in a colour that contrasts, but not drastically, with fabric. Use cross hatches (X's) to indicate pattern dots. Individual dots can also be recorded, using dull pencil or stick.

Chalk marking: First push pin through each symbol and both fabric layers, forcing pinheads through tissue. Remove pattern. Make chalk dot at each pin, on wrong side of each fabric layer.

For seamlines, remove pattern; set sewing gauge pointer for 1.5 cm. Then, sliding gauge along cut edge of fabric, make short lines 1.5 cm from cut edge, spacing them 2 to 5 cm apart.

Tailor's tacks take the most time and effort of all the marking methods. They are indispensable, however, for sheer or delicate fabrics, also for spongy or multicoloured types on which neither carbon paper nor chalk will make a sufficiently distinct mark. The two basic tack types are shown

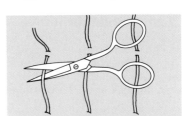

Tailor's tacks: Used to transfer individual markings to doubled fabric. When completed, tacks are cut apart between the fabric layers. (See page 148 for detailed instructions.)

Simplified tailor's tacks: Uneven tacking used to mark single fabric layer. Very useful for marking fold, centre and pleat lines. (See p. 147 for instructions.)

Thread-marking is a practical way to transfer markings, such as pocket placement symbols, which must show on the right side. Markings are transferred with carbon paper, then re-traced with hand or machine tacking, depending on the fabric.

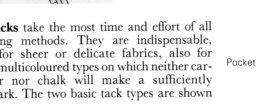

Centre front — Facing

Pocket — Foldline

Thread-marking: With carbon paper and wheel, trace symbol onto wrong side of garment section. Remove pattern; then go over marking with uneven tacking or straight-stitch machine tacking. Use a contrasting thread colour.

Being able to make clothing that will fit perfectly is one of the biggest advantages of sewing for yourself and your family. This chapter gives you all the secrets of achieving the perfect fit. This means first getting to know your figure, taking careful measurements, and choosing the pattern that's right for you. A three-step method is all that is needed to bring a commercial pattern closer to your own body measurements. Altering patterns for length and width, for the placement of darts, and for smooth shoulders, necklines, armholes and sleeves are all covered in detail. And for the advanced sewer, there are clear instructions for making a fitting shell and your own block pattern to simplify alterations on every pattern you might use in the future. You will soon be able not only to alter patterns for size, but also to change them to suit the whims of fashion.

Fitting

Fitting methods

Made as they are for millions of people, patterns naturally have their limitations. The chances are that a pattern will fit you well in some places and less well in others. The trick in making clothes that fit is learning where you and the pattern part company. Once you learn what the differences are, the pattern alterations are, in fact, simple.

To help you know what type of alterations you need and the complexity you can expect with each, we have grouped the alterations into two types.

The first group is **basic pattern alterations.** These are the alterations that are concerned primarily with bringing the paper pattern measurements closer to your own. To make them, you work with some of your own body measurements plus the measurements printed on the back of the pattern envelope, and in some cases, actual measurements of the printed pattern. This group of alterations includes basic length and width changes as well as positioning of darts. Instructions begin on p.112.

Advanced pattern alterations, the second group, are made with the aid of a *fitting shell*. A fitting shell is made from a basic pattern, in an inexpensive test fabric, such as calico, for the express purpose of checking the specifics of fit: location of grainlines, darts and seams; drape of the garment; sleeve fit, etc. Completed shell adjustments are recorded on a *block pattern*, which is used with each new pattern, making it easy to locate areas requiring alteration. Instructions for advanced pattern alteration begin on page 123.

Preliminary pattern alterations are not the only means to a good fit, however. There are other helpful tests and adjustment methods to use as you sew. The **try-on session,** midway through construction, is a useful technique for making simple adjustments before you have finished sewing (pp. 130–131). A **test garment** can make a very practical contribution, and we explain how to use such a trial run to best advantage (p. 132).

As you gain experience with fitting, you will find that it becomes second nature. You will also learn which steps, if any, you wish to take for individual garments—some garments are worth the trouble, some may not be. Be selective in this decision, though. Even if it is not a special garment, it may not really be wise to skip fitting steps on something you will wear constantly.

Getting to know your figure

If your pattern selection meant compromising on a measurement or two, as it usually does, you will need to alter the pattern accordingly. Before you think about pattern alterations, however, consider how well you know your figure.

You should know your own figure well enough to analyse its relation to a standard pattern figure. To help you, we show below the ways people and patterns can differ: in proportion, in contours, in posture and in symmetry. If you haven't already done so, now is the time to make an honest appraisal of your figure. The better you know your own body, the easier it will be to achieve the desired fit.

It can be difficult to be honest about our own shortcomings. It is often easier to see what is right than what is wrong. Remember also that your figure is not a fixed thing: the process of maturing tends to change the human form.

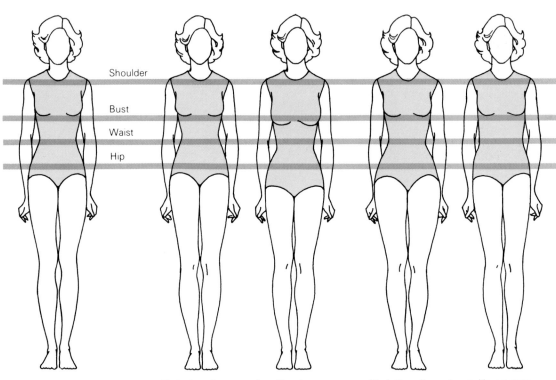

Standard pattern figure: The figure for which any pattern is sized is an imaginary one. It has perfect posture, symmetrical features, and unvarying proportions and contours. Your own figure is almost sure to differ in some way from this ideal standard.

Variations in proportion: Your key features—bust, waist, hips—may fall higher or lower along your height than those of the pattern's standard. Hem lengths are also a question of personal proportions, whatever the current fashion. Altering a pattern to suit your proportions is a simple process of taking measurements and adjusting lengths and widths.

Variations in contours: Your curves, bulges and hollows may not only differ from the pattern's standard, but also change with time. Weight gained or lost, physical maturing, foundation garments (or their absence) all affect contours. Fitting a pattern to your personal contours may call for adjusting the darts and curved seams that shape a garment to the figure.

What is good fit?

There are several ways to ensure objectivity during self-appraisal. A good start is taking accurate, if unflattering, figure measurements. They can provide the basis for comparison with patterns, as recommended on page 113. The fitting shell (page 123) also points out areas in need of attention.

Another way to recognise potential fitting problems is to trade a fit analysis with a friend, or make it a mother/daughter project. If you are working alone, try to cultivate detachment during the figure checking process by blotting out your face in your mind's eye as you study your reflection in the mirror. This focuses your attention on the details of the fit, rather than on the overall impression, and seems to make honesty easier to achieve.

Another approach is to critically examine photographs of yourself wearing home-sewn garments, covering the face as you study.

The goal of any pattern alteration is to make the pattern fit better, but before you alter, you must decide what you *mean* by good fit. In making this judgment, there are four main factors to consider: **appearance, comfort, design** and **fabric.**

For a good **appearance,** all darts and seams must fall in the proper places, as shown below. Your garment should have a smooth look. The other factors to consider are covered on the following pages.

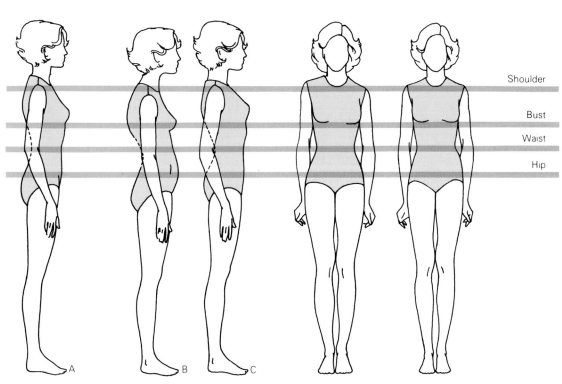

	Shoulder
	Bust
	Waist
	Hip

Variations in posture: Standard posture is shown in A; B and C are two common variations that cause fitting problems. Test your posture by standing against a wall. If shoulders, shoulder blades and hips touch, your posture is standard (A). When just the shoulder blades touch (B), there's a tendency to slump and be round-shouldered. When just the shoulders touch (C), the posture is super-erect and square-shouldered. Pattern alterations at shoulder seams, bodice back and abdomen are usually needed with the B or C postures.

Variations in symmetry: Almost everyone's left side is different from their right. When a figure is noticeably asymmetrical, garments hang differently, or wrinkle more, on one side than the other. Of the uneven figure features that lead to fitting problems, these are the most common: one shoulder is higher or slopes more than the other; one hip is higher than the other; one side of the waist curves more than the other. In order to achieve a good fit, seams and darts in the affected areas may have to be adjusted.

Shoulder seams rest smoothly on the shoulder tops, point toward and end at shoulder joint.

Sleeves hang straight to the elbow, then bend toward the front, as the arm does when relaxed.

All vertical seams look straight from beginning to end, are not wavy along their length.

The hem is even and hangs parallel with the floor.

Darts taper toward and stop short of fullest part of area they shape.

Waist seam rests at the natural waist (if this is the style); fits closely without binding

Fitting

What is good fit? (continued)

As explained on the previous page, **appearance** is one of the important factors to consider when you are judging garment fit. The garment should have a smooth look, with no pulls or wrinkles, no sagging or baggy areas. The other main considerations are **comfort, design** and **fabric.**

Comfort is, of course, extremely important. The most attractive garment in your wardrobe will hang there forever unless it feels good when you wear it. Of course, some garments are less comfortable than others yet still get worn, and people tend to take more notice of current fashion trends than of the practical aspects of clothing; but it is common sense to make sure that you can sit, bend, walk and reach in any garment without straining its seams or feeling restricted. The main contributor to comfort is *wearing ease*, explained fully on page 113.

The **design** of a garment may be based on either a close fit, as illustrated below, or a loose fit, as shown on the opposite page. It is important to bear in mind the look the designer was aiming for when you fit individual garments. The photographs and illustrations in the pattern catalogue and on the pattern envelope you choose can be valuable guides in this respect.

In addition, certain features of a garment indicate close fit: a silhouette that defines the form

CLOSE-FITTING DESIGNS tend to stay fairly near the figure, sometimes hugging it more in certain areas. With styles of this sort, it is important not to overfit; this can result in strained seams and wrinkles. A trim fit usually flatters a slender figure, a looser fit is kinder to a figure that is fuller.

The presence of a waist seam signals a comparatively snug fit, wherever it falls on the garment. This could be at the natural waistline (centre), as is most usual; above it, as in an Empire style (right); or below it on the hipline (left), as is the case in blouson tops or two-piece garments.

Darts and curved seams shape fashions close to the body, as in the dresses above. Both silhouettes conform similarly to the body; waist seam in one makes fit even closer.

Shaped inserts are often cut with no seams or darts; shaping is built into pattern.

and, within it, such details as a waist seam; darts and curved seams; shaped inserts, and occasionally bias-cut sections.

A *loose* fit is often signalled by such design devices as a silhouette that camouflages the details of the figure beneath; within the silhouette, fullness controlled softly by gathers, shirring, release tucks or unpressed pleats rather than by darts and fitted seams. Bear in mind that some parts of a garment may be close-fitting and other parts soft and loose. The classic shirtdress, made with a gathered or pleated skirt, is an example. Even on loose-fitting garments, some parts of the garment may be fitted to the body, as is the waistband on a full, gathered skirt, or the shoulder seam on a smock.

Fabric is crucial to good fit—recommendations on the pattern envelope are to be taken seriously. Styles for 'stretch knits only' are relying on some give in the fabric. Those calling for thick fabrics are usually designed a bit larger to accommodate the bulk; the same style in a thinner fabric would probably be too big.

When fabric types are interchangeable—soft or crisp, for example—remember that the style will look different according to which you use. Also note the clinging tendency of some fabrics; these define body shape even if a garment is loose-fitting.

LOOSE-FITTING GARMENTS

may be designed to have a sweep of fullness, as are the cape, caftan and tent dress; or with softening influences— blouson top, full sleeve, dirndl skirt, shirred yoke. Larger figures might need to add to all but the fullest designs to achieve the intended draping.

Gathers and release tucks both control fullness, each in a distinctive way. Gathers soften an entire area; release tucks change from close control to fluid fullness.

Unpressed pleats are like release tucks; they fit at the top, then fall into soft folds.

A-line silhouettes can be used to create either a dramatic or a restrained impression of fullness. They are a favourite design device for giving a graceful line to a skirt or dress.

Pullover dresses tapered towards the hemline give a loose fit without fullness.

Basic pattern alterations

The three-step method

Most of the corrections needed to bring patterns closer to individual body measurements can be done right on the pattern. What follows is an easy three-step method for making these basic alterations. If you need further alterations, use this method as the starting point for later construction of a fitting shell (see p. 123).

The first step is **taking key figure measurements.** Some of these are additional to the measurements taken to determine pattern size. For this procedure you will need a tape measure, some string to mark the waist, and a friend to help. The second step is **comparing your measurements with the pattern's** to find the places that need alteration. The final step is **making the alterations.** Those covered on pages 114 to 122 are the most frequent, involving changes in length and width.

This method assumes selection of blouse and dress patterns according to bust measurement, a basis that works well for most women. When it does, bust alterations will usually be a matter of simply repositioning darts. If, however, the bust is disproportionately large in comparison with the other standard body measurements, or if bra cup is a size C or larger, you may find it easier to stay with the pattern size that accords with your other measurements and enlarge the bust area (see p. 117 for this alteration). The bodice should fit satisfactorily in the back and chest and the shoulder area. The high bust measurement (see pages 46–47) is often a clue to situations where this size choice will be appropriate.

Pants patterns should be chosen by hip measurement and waistline and length altered if necessary.

An important factor to keep in mind when doing pattern alterations is the need to keep the design lines intact. For example, if you measure less than the pattern and have to alter, don't take away too much or the style could be lost. It is generally better to allow yourself too much fabric than too little, because it is easier to take in than it is to add on. You can also lose style lines by adding too much, particularly if a garment is intricately seamed.

If you discover that you need a great many pattern alterations, it would seem sensible to question the accuracy of the size you have chosen. Perhaps another size, or a comparable size in another figure type, will fit with fewer alterations.

One: Taking key measurements

Careful and honest measuring is essential. For the most reliable results, stand naturally and wear your customary type of undergarments. If you recently took some of the measurements described below in the course of selecting your pattern size, note them again (no need to re-measure). You may want to record your measurements for future reference. If you do, don't forget to check them every six months or so, or if you gain or lose weight, to see if there have been any significant changes.

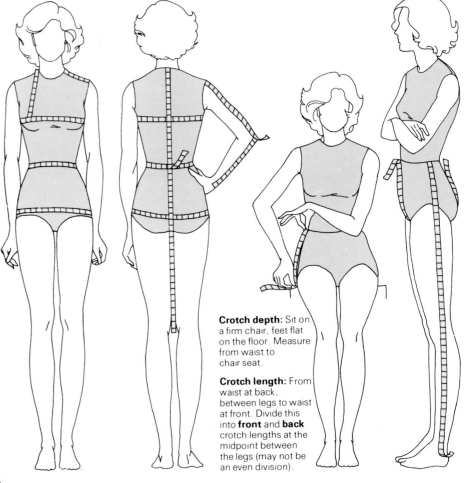

Shoulder length: From base of neck (shrug shoulders to find this) to the shoulder edge.

Apex of bust: From base of neck to point of bust.

Bust: Measure across widest part of back, under arms, across full bustline. Note distance across front, side seam to side seam.

Waist: Mark waist by tying a string snugly around your middle; it will roll to the natural waist. Take measurement at the string marker.

Hips: Keeping tape measure parallel to the floor, measure around fullest part (18 to 23 cm below waist).

Back waist length: From prominent bone at base of neck, centre back, to the natural waist.

Sleeve length: With hand on hip, from the shoulder joint to the wrist bone. For **elbow dart placement,** note length from shoulder to elbow.

Finished length: For *dresses,* measure from base of neck at centre back to the hem. For *skirts,* subtract back waist length from finished dress length. For *blouses,* use back waist length plus a tuck-in allowance.

Crotch depth: Sit on a firm chair, feet flat on the floor. Measure from waist to chair seat.

Crotch length: From waist at back, between legs to waist at front. Divide this into **front** and **back** crotch lengths at the midpoint between the legs (may not be an even division).

Finished length (pants): Measure from waist to hem, at the side of the leg. May be more or less than pattern, depending on curve of hips.

Two: Comparing measurements

To decide when and where you need pattern alterations, you must compare your personal figure measurements with the corresponding measurements on the pattern. In some cases you will measure the pattern itself; in others, the relevant measurements will appear on the pattern envelope. Take into consideration what you learned in your figure analysis (pp. 108–109). This, combined with your measurements, and an idea of the kind of fit you wish to achieve, will show you where to alter.

Remember that your measurements are not supposed to exactly match those of the paper pattern. No garment can or should fit as closely as the tape measure, for you need enough room in any garment to sit, walk, reach and bend. The chart below gives the *least* amounts a pattern should measure over and above your figure in six crucial places.

This extra amount is called **wearing ease,** which should be distinguished from design ease. Design ease is the designed-in fullness that will cause some styles to measure considerably larger, overall or in particular areas, than your figure plus the applicable minimums given in the chart. You cannot know how much design ease has been included in a pattern, but you will be sure of keeping it, and therefore of retaining the style lines of the garment, if you take care to include wearing ease in your alterations. There are exceptions to the wearing ease estimates below: a pattern designed for stretchy knit will provide less wearing ease; strapless garments will also be given less; larger figures may need more than the suggested minimum for a truly comfortable fit.

Fill in your own measurements on the chart and use them when altering the paper pattern. When comparing your measurements with those on the back of the pattern envelope, make no allowance for wearing ease.

MEASUREMENT	YOURS	PLUS EASE: AT LEAST	TOTAL	PATTERN MEASURE	CHANGE + −
Bust		7 cm			
Waist		2 cm			
Hip		5 cm			
Crotch depth		1 cm			
Front crotch length		1 cm			
Back crotch length		2.5 cm			

Compare **bust, waist, hip** and **back waist length** measurements given on the pattern envelope with your own (without any allowance for wearing ease).

Measure the pattern's **shoulder seam** and compare it with your **shoulder length.** The two should match closely. For a dropped shoulder seam or yoke, measure pattern at shoulder markings. If the neckline is set below the neck base, the pattern will specify by how much; add this amount to the shoulder seam before making the length comparison.

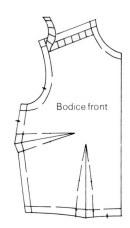

Bodice front

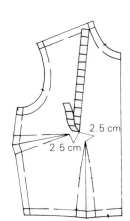

2.5 cm
2.5 cm

To check **bust dart placement,** measure pattern from neck seam (where it meets shoulder seam) toward the dart point to determine where pattern locates apex of bust. Then, using your body measurement, compare actual apex of bust to location on pattern. Bust darts should point toward the apex of your bust but end 2.5 cm from it. If the neckline is set below the neck base, the pattern will tell you by how much; add this amount when measuring.

To compare **sleeve lengths,** measure the pattern down the centre. (On fitted sleeves, this will not be a straight line.) For **elbow dart placement,** note how far from the shoulder the darts occur. This will tell you whether to alter sleeve length above or below darts, or both. The elbow dart points to the elbow when it is bent. If there are two, the elbow goes between; if three, the centre one points to the elbow. If there is a cuff, allow for its finished width when comparing. Extra length must be allowed, too, for a very full sleeve.

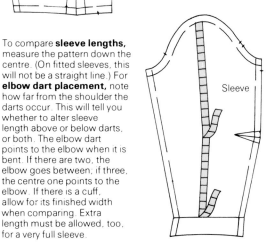

Sleeve

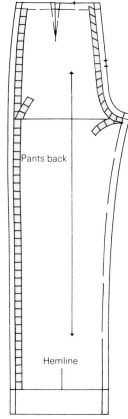

Pants back

Hemline

If the garment's **finished length** is given on the pattern envelope, use it for comparison with the length you need or want. If it is not given, measure all patterns except pants patterns at centre back, pants pattern along side seam, to determine pattern's finished length.

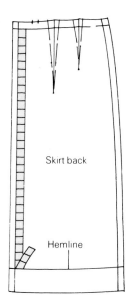

Skirt back

Hemline

To find **crotch depth** of a pants pattern, draw a line (if there is none on pattern) at right angles to the grain from the side seam to the crotch point at the inseam. Do this on front and back pattern pieces. Measure from the waist seam to this line, along the side seam, for pattern crotch depth.

For **front and back crotch lengths,** measure the crotch seam on the pattern and compare result with your measurements. (The pattern should be longer for a comfortable fit.) Stand the tape measure on edge to measure accurately around curves of pattern.

Basic pattern alterations

Three: Making the alterations

When you have compared your figure measurements with those of the pattern, as described on the preceding page, and decided where and how much you will need to alter, you are ready to make the basic pattern alterations. The steps for specific individual alterations are described in detail on the following pages.

To ensure accuracy in any of these alterations, follow these basic principles whenever you work with pattern pieces:

1. Press the paper pattern pieces with a warm, dry iron to remove creases before making any alterations on the pattern.

2. All pattern pieces must be flat when any alteration is completed. Sometimes a pattern piece must be cut and spread; this can cause bubbles. The bubbles must be pressed flat before the pattern is laid onto the fabric for cutting.

3. Pin the alterations in first, check them with a tape measure or ruler for accuracy, then tape the change in place.

4. If it is necessary to add length or width, use tissue or tracing paper to accomplish the increase.

5. Take any necessary tucks **half** the depth of the required change. Remember that the total amount that is removed by a tuck will always be twice the depth of that tuck.

6. When an alteration interrupts a cutting or stitching line, draw a new line on the pattern that is tapered gradually and smoothly into the original line. This will keep your alteration from being obvious in the finished garment.

When several alterations will have to be made, the *length* alterations should always come first. This is the only way to make certain that any width alterations you may later make will be at the correct place on the pattern. Length alterations should be attended to in the following order: above the waist, below the waist or overall length, sleeves.

Your next area of attention should be *dart placement.* When you are satisfied that your darts are pointing in the proper direction and are the correct length, you are ready to move on to any *width* adjustments that are needed. Width adjustments should be made first at the bust, then at the waist, then at the hip.

Other specialised alterations take place after all basic length and width changes have been made.

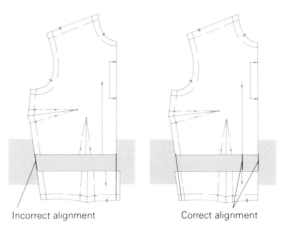

Incorrect alignment   Correct alignment

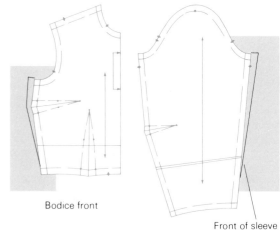

Bodice front

Front of sleeve

Grainlines and 'place on the fold' lines must be straight when any alteration is completed. Note grainline indication on original pattern piece and take care to preserve it on the altered piece. To redraw a 'place on the fold' line, align a ruler with the intersection of seamline and foldline at top and bottom of pattern piece; draw a new line.

Be alert to the chain effect of an alteration. Quite often, an alteration in one pattern piece calls for a corresponding alteration elsewhere, or for a matching alteration on pieces that join the changed one, so that seams will match. This is very important at the armhole. If you add to the side seam of a bodice, be aware of the effect on the sleeve seam.

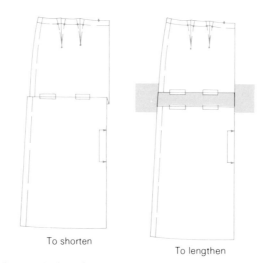

To shorten

To lengthen

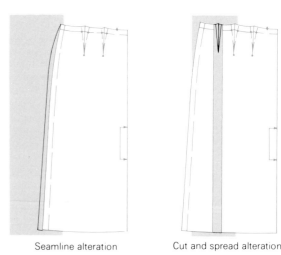

Seamline alteration   Cut and spread alteration

For length alterations, use the printed line labelled 'lengthen or shorten here' for any length alterations required in the body of the garment. Skirts and pants can be altered at both the alteration line and the lower edge if a large amount is being added or removed. Apportioning the alteration in this way retains the original garment shape.

For width alterations, remember that you can usually add or subtract up to 5 cm at seams. Divide the required change by the number of seams and add or subtract the resulting figure at each seam. If more than 5 cm is to be altered, a technique known as 'cutting and spreading' puts the enlargement or reduction exactly where it is needed.

Length alterations (increasing)

DRESSES AND SKIRTS

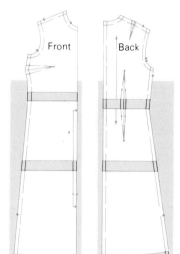

Fitted: When altering back waist length, alter bodice front to match. To keep skirt shape, cut and spread at alteration line. More length may be added at lower edge if needed.

A-line: Add length above waist mark at centre back to alter the waist length; below the waist mark to alter the finished length. Make the same alterations front and back.

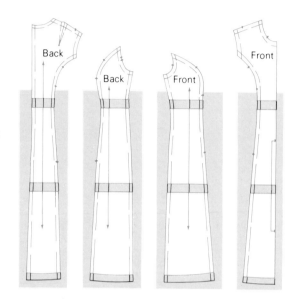

Princess: Add length above the waist mark at centre back to alter the back waist length; below the waist to alter the finished length. Alter all the panels to match. If no additional length is needed at centre front, taper to nothing from side seams to centre front.

SLEEVES

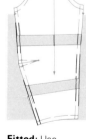
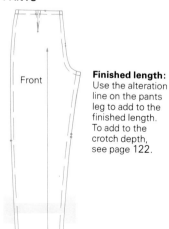

Raglan: Use both alteration lines if two are given to keep sleeve shape. Spread half amount at each line.

Fitted: Use measurement for elbow dart placement to determine length to add at each alteration line.

Kimono: Because this sleeve is not fitted, only one alteration line is needed. Add all the required length there.

PANTS

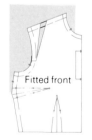

Finished length: Use the alteration line on the pants leg to add to the finished length. To add to the crotch depth, see page 122.

SHOULDER

Seam: Cut pattern from midway on shoulder seam to armhole seamline; spread as needed.

Yoke: Cut through yoke pattern and spread. Alter bodice so that seams are same length.

Basic pattern alterations

Length alterations (decreasing)

DRESSES AND SKIRTS

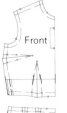

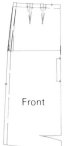

Fitted: When altering the back waist length, alter the bodice front to match. To keep shape of skirt, remove excess length with a tuck at the alteration line. Additional length may be taken from lower edge if needed.

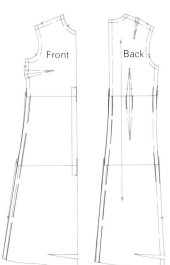

A-line: Alter above the waist mark at centre back to shorten the waist length; below the waist mark to shorten the finished length. Make the same alterations on front and back.

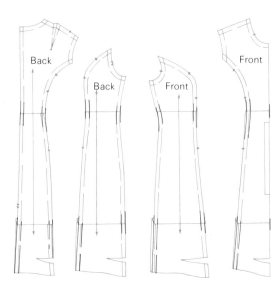

Princess: Alter above the waist mark at centre back to shorten the back waist length; below the waist mark to shorten the finished length. Make the same alterations on all panels.

SLEEVES

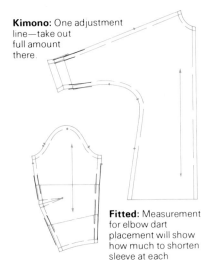

Kimono: One adjustment line—take out full amount there.

Raglan: Shorten half of the amount needed at each alteration line if two lines are provided.

Fitted: Measurement for elbow dart placement will show how much to shorten sleeve at each adjustment line.

PANTS

Finished length: To alter the finished length, use alteration line on pants leg. To shorten the crotch depth, see page 122.

SHOULDER

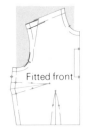

Seam: Cut pattern from midway on shoulder seam down to armhole seamline; lap edges to take out required amount.

Yoke: Cut through yoke pattern piece and lap edges as shown. Alter bodice patterns so that seams are same length.

Raising bust darts

To raise bust darts slightly, mark the location of the new dart point above the original. Draw new dart stitching lines to new point, tapering them into the original stitching lines.

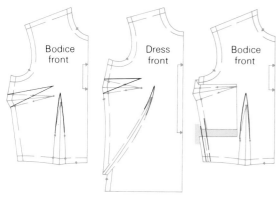

An alternative method, especially useful when an entire dart must be raised by a large amount, is to cut an 'L' below and beside the dart as shown at right above. Take a tuck above the dart deep enough to raise it to the desired location.

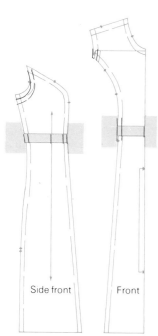

For princess styles, raise the most curved portion of the centre front pattern piece by taking a tuck about halfway down armhole seam. To keep waist length equal to that of back pattern pieces, cut front pieces above the waist; spread apart by the amount bust section was raised. The underarm notches at the side seam will no longer match. You must lower seamline and cutting line at underarm by the amount removed in the tuck; taper into original lines.

Lowering bust darts

To lower bust darts slightly, mark the location of the new dart point below the original. Draw new dart stitching lines to new point, tapering them into the original stitching lines.

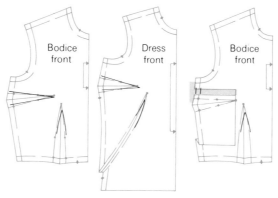

An alternative method, especially useful when the entire dart must be lowered by a large amount, is to cut an 'L' above and beside the dart as shown at the right above. Take a tuck below the dart deep enough to lower it to the desired place.

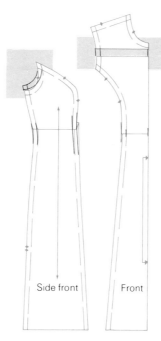

For princess styles, lower the fullest part by cutting the centre front pattern piece about halfway down the armhole seam. Spread pattern the required amount. To keep the waist length equal to that of back pattern pieces, take a tuck in the altered front pattern pieces; the amount taken out by the tuck should equal amount that pattern was spread. Underarm notches at the side seam will no longer match. You must raise seamline and cutting line at underarm to equal the amount spread; taper into original lines.

Enlarging the bust area

Additions of up to 5 cm can be made at the side seams. Apportion the amount equally and taper to nothing at armhole and waistline. For larger additions, cut and spread as explained below.

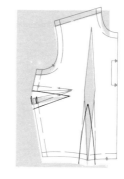

Fitted: Cut pattern from waist to shoulder seam, cutting along foldline of waist dart and through mark for bust apex. Also cut side bust dart on foldline to within 3 mm of bust point. Spread the vertical cut at the bust point by half the amount needed. (Do not spread at waist or shoulder.) This will open up the underarm cut, making bust dart deeper. Locate dart point within cuts. Redraw darts, tapering into original stitching lines.

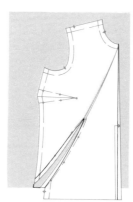

French dart: Draw a line extending foldline of dart to centre front. Cut on this line and spread pattern apart half the total amount needed. Keep neck edge on original centre front. Locate dart point and redraw darts, tapering into original stitching lines. Redraw centre front line.

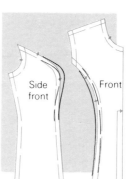

Princess seam: Up to 5 cm can be added this way; remember that an additional 5 cm can be added, if necessary, at side seams. Divide total centimetres to be added by 4 to determine how much to add to each seam. Mark new stitching and cutting lines outside the old ones at fullest part of curve. Redraw lines, tapering them into original cutting and stitching lines at armhole and waistline.

Basic pattern alterations

Width alterations: increasing the waist

In general, to increase the waist you add a quarter of the total amount to each of the side seams, front and back. To make sure that you do not distort side seams when adding large amounts, distribute some of the increase over any darts or seams that cross the waistline. (Note exception for circular skirt.)

PANTS

When increasing the waist by a large amount, add to front and back crotch seams, as well as side seams. Taper to nothing at curve of crotch seam.

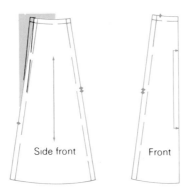

WAISTBAND

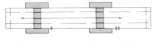

Enlarge a waistband (of pants or skirt) by the same amount and in the same places that the garment was enlarged. This is usually at the side seam marks. Cut and spread the pattern the amount needed.

DRESSES

Bodice

Waistline

Skirt

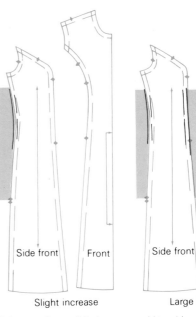

Side front   Front   Side front   Front

Slight increase   Large increase

Fitted: Add same amount to bodice and skirt at waist

A-line: Add at the waist only; taper into seamline.

Princess: For a slight increase, add to side seams on side front and back panels only. For large increases, apportion the increase over all the seams.

SKIRTS

Gored: Slight increases are made at the side seams only; there is no change on the centre front and back panels. To make a large increase, apportion the increase over all of the seams.

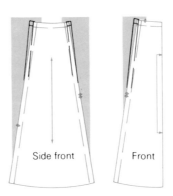

Side front   Front   Side front   Front

Slight increase   Large increase

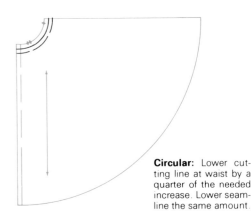

Circular: Lower cutting line at waist by a quarter of the needed increase. Lower seamline the same amount.

Width alterations: decreasing the waist

Generally speaking, to decrease at the waist you take away a quarter of the total reduction at each of the side seams, front and back. If the decrease is larger, distribute some of it over any darts or seams that cross the waistline. (Note the exception for a circular skirt.)

PANTS

When decreasing the waist of pants by a large amount, alter front and back crotch seams. Note: Taper smoothly into original cutting line.

WAISTBAND

Decrease a waistband (of pants or skirt) by the same amount and in the same places that the garment was decreased. This is usually at the side seam marks. Tuck out amount to be reduced.

DRESSES

Bodice

Skirt

Fitted: Take away same amount on both bodice and skirt waist.

Waistline

A-line: Make reduction at waist only; taper into seamline.

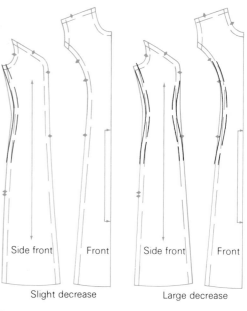

Side front · Front · Side front · Front

Slight decrease · Large decrease

Princess: For a slight decrease, reduce the side seams on the side front and back panels only. For a large decrease, apportion the reduction over all of the seams.

SKIRTS

Gored: Slight decreases are made at the side seams only; there is no change on the centre front and back panels. For a large decrease, apportion the reduction over all of the seams.

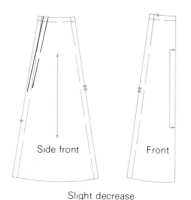

Side front · Front

Slight decrease

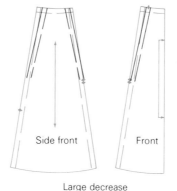

Side front · Front

Large decrease

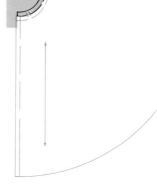

Circular: Raise cutting line at waist by a quarter of the needed reduction. Raise seamline the same amount.

Basic pattern alterations

Width alterations: increasing the hipline

To add **5 centimetres or less** to the hipline, enlarge pattern at side seams; add a quarter of the total amount needed at each side seam, front and back. To add **more than 5 centimetres,** distribute it more evenly over the garment with the 'cut and spread' methods shown on this page.

PANTS

If hip measurement is followed when pants patterns are purchased, only a slight alteration should be necessary. Add to the hipline at side seams, tapering to the original cutting line at waist and thigh.

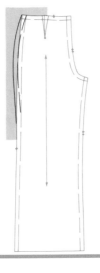

DRESSES

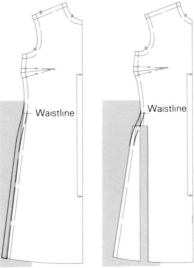

5 cm or less   More than 5 cm

A-line: Up to 5 cm, add at side seams. More than 5 cm, slash pattern parallel to grainline; spread ¼ of amount needed, front and back.

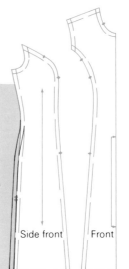

5 cm or less   More than 5cm

Princess: To add 5 cm or less, increase at the side seams, making no change on the front and back panels. To add more than 5 cm, apportion the increase over all of the seams.

SKIRTS

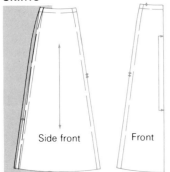

5 cm or less

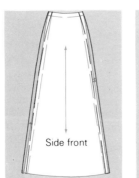

More than 5 cm

Gored: To add 5 cm or less, increase the pattern at the side seams, making no change on front and back panels. When adding more than 5 cm, apportion the increase equally over all of the seams. Taper to nothing at the waistline.

5 cm or less   More than 5 cm

Fitted: More than 5 cm, cut parallel to grain; spread ¼ of amount needed, front and back. Add waist dart.

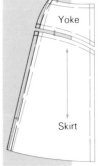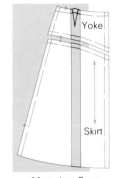

5cm or less   More than 5 cm

Yoked: For more than 5 cm, cut both patterns parallel to grainline; spread a quarter of amount needed, front and back. Add dart at waist.

Width alterations: decreasing the hipline

In most cases, to decrease at the hipline, you take away a quarter of the total reduction at each of the side seams, front and back. The new cutting lines taper from waist to hem. It is usually not wise to try to remove more than 2.5 centimetres unless there are many seams, because style lines would be lost.

PANTS

If the hip measurement is followed when pants patterns are purchased, only a slight alteration should be needed. Decrease the hipline at the side seams, front and back, tapering into the original cutting line at the waistline.

DRESSES

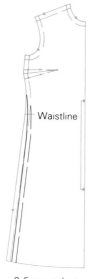
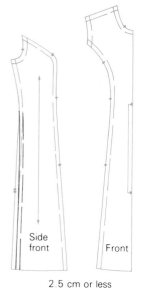
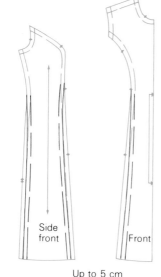

2.5 cm or less
A-line: Decrease only at hipline; taper into the original waistline.

2.5 cm or less   Up to 5 cm
Princess: To reduce the hipline 2.5 cm or less, alter at the side seams, making no change on the front and back panels. To take away up to 5 cm, apportion the decrease over all of the seams.

SKIRTS

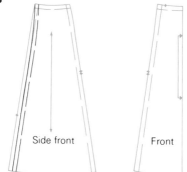
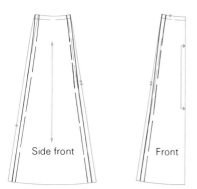

2.5 cm or less   Up to 5 cm   Up to 5 cm   Up to 5 cm

Gored: To reduce the hipline by 2.5 cm or less, alter at the side seams only; make no changes on the front and back panels. To reduce the hipline up to but not more than 5 cm, apportion the reduction over all of the garment seams.

Fitted: The hipline can be decreased up to 5 cm by taking away at the side seams.

Yoked: Decrease the hipline up to 5 cm on both the yoke and the skirt at side seams.

Adjusting the pants crotch seam

Good fit in pants depends primarily on how the torso portion is fitted—the legs usually need attention only if you wish to restyle the shape. (See page 112 on taking body measurements.) **Width** alterations for waist and hip have been discussed in the preceding pages. The other two measurements that are vital to good torso fit are **crotch depth** and **crotch length.** One or both may need altering.

The **crotch depth** is the measurement of the distance from your waist to the bottom of your hips, taken when you are sitting. This measurement indicates whether any adjustments are needed in the area between your waist and the top of your legs. Consequently, any alterations to the crotch depth will affect both crotch seam and side seam.

The **crotch length** is the actual length of the crotch seam, taken between the legs, from waist at centre front to waist at centre back. This measurement takes into account any extreme stomach or hip contours, and it affects only the crotch seam—not the side seam. It is important to apportion the total crotch length into what is needed at the front and at the back. For example, if you have just a protruding stomach, you would want all the additional length at the front where it is needed, not half at the front and half at the back.

The crotch length can be altered at the crotch point, which is at the intersection of the crotch seam and the inseam, or it can be altered along the crotch seam itself.

When the length is altered at the **crotch point,** an additional change occurs—either an increase or a decrease in the width of the pants leg at the top of the thigh, depending on whether the crotch seam is lengthened or shortened. In most instances, this is an advantage.

Use the **crotch seam** method of altering the crotch length if only stomach or bottom is a problem. This method adds or takes away fullness exactly where it is needed at the front or back. It is possible to alter at both the point and along the seam for very rounded or flat stomach or bottom.

When both crotch depth and crotch length alterations are needed, **alter the crotch depth first.** A crotch depth alteration will change the crotch length. It is necessary to re-measure the pattern's crotch seam before determining how much (if any) additional altering the crotch length will need.

Altering crotch depth

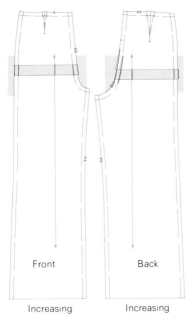

Front   Back

Increasing   Increasing

Front   Back

Decreasing   Decreasing

To increase: Cut the pattern on the 'lengthen or shorten here' line and spread full amount needed. Alter pants front and back alike.

To decrease: Take a tuck on the 'lengthen or shorten' line. Make the tuck half as deep as the total amount needed. Alter pants front and back alike.

Altering crotch length

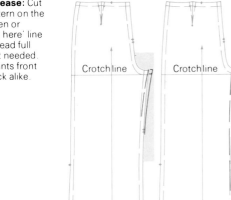

Crotchline   Crotchline

Front   Front

Increasing   Decreasing

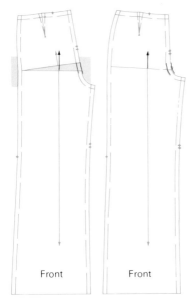

Front   Front

Increasing   Decreasing

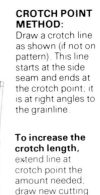

CROTCH POINT METHOD:
Draw a crotch line as shown (if not on pattern). This line starts at the side seam and ends at the crotch point; it is at right angles to the grainline.

To increase the crotch length, extend line at crotch point the amount needed; draw new cutting lines at inseam and crotch.

To decrease the crotch length, shorten line at crotch point as needed; draw new cutting lines at inseam and crotch.

CROTCH SEAM METHOD:
Cut and spread to add length; take a tuck to decrease length.

To increase the crotch length, cut the pattern on alteration line to (not through) the side seam. Spread as needed, tapering toward side seam.

To decrease the crotch length, fold the pattern on the alteration line to take away the amount needed at the crotch seam. Taper the fold so that no change is made in the side seam.

Advanced pattern alterations

Fitting shell and block pattern

If you need more than the basic pattern alterations, or if you want additional knowledge of fitting techniques, you will want to make a fitting shell and block pattern. A **fitting shell** is made from a basic pattern—it may be a dress, pants, or just a bodice—sewn in inexpensive fabric and used exclusively for solving fitting problems. After the shell has been altered to fit you perfectly, all the adjustments you have made are transferred to the shell's paper pattern. The adjusted shell pattern then becomes your **block pattern.**

This method takes some time and patience, but your block pattern can save considerable time and trouble whenever you sew. By using it with each new style you make, you can check for potential fitting problems before cutting the garment out of the fabric, avoiding an expensive waste of fabric and time. To make a fitting shell and block pattern, you will need the following supplies:

Pattern: The classic fitting shell is a closely fitted sheath. Most pattern companies offer just such a style for use in fitting. The purpose of such a dress is not to actually wear it, but to use it to fit body areas as closely as possible. The block pattern that you develop from it can be used to alter virtually every pattern you sew. If your fitting problems occur in the bust or shoulder area only, use just the bodice for your shell.

Another possibility is to make the shell from your favourite pattern—the one that you sew again and again—and use your block pattern for this style. If you want a pants shell, choose a straight-leg style with a waistband and darts. Once the waist and hips have been fitted, the shell can be used with any pants style, no matter how full or narrow the legs.

Fabric and notions: A fitting shell is often called a 'calico', this being the traditional fabric for this use. You may prefer another fabric. Gingham is good and the woven checks help to keep grainlines straight. An old sheet will do, or fabric leftovers, so long as they are firmly woven and of medium weight. Of course, you must be sure your fabric is grain-perfect.

In addition, you will need any zippers called for by your pattern and, if your shell is a skirt or pants, some petersham ribbon to use as a firm, non-stretchy trial waistband. A tracing wheel and dressmaker's carbon paper are also necessary.

How to make the shell

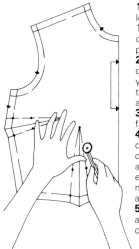

1. Make any basic alterations for length and width (see pp. 114–122) to take care of major changes and bring pattern into proportion with your figure.
2. Lay out the pattern, omitting details like facings, collars, etc., if you are using a pattern other than the classic shell. Keep grainlines accurate.
3. Cut out the pattern, saving fabric scraps for later use.
4. Transfer all stitching lines for darts and seams to fabric, using dressmaker's carbon paper and a tracing wheel. This makes it easier to keep track of any adjustments in your shell, and aids in altering the block pattern as well.
5. Mark centre front on bodice and skirt with hand tacking in a contrasting thread colour.

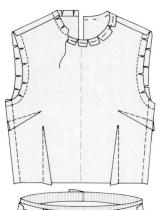

6. Sew the shell together, following the pattern instructions; use a long machine stitch for easy removal (a chain stitch, if available, is ideal). For the dress shell, eliminate the sleeves for the first fitting—put them in after shoulders have been adjusted. Omit waistband from pants or skirt—use a length of petersham instead.
7. Staystitch armholes and neckline on stitching line; clip seam allowances and press to wrong side.
8. Tack all of the hems in place.

Judging the fit

Wearing shoes and the appropriate underclothes, try on your shell, right side out. Be very critical about the fit; this is the time to settle all fitting problems, however troublesome they might be.

Track down the cause of every wrinkle and see to the adjustment that makes it disappear. Remember, too, to give your shell the comfort test: sit, reach, bend and walk to find out whether there are any strained seams and if so, where they occur. Be sure to study your own back view as well (another person is helpful here) and try to think objectively about the way the shell fits your figure.

To adjust the shell, first locate your fitting problems among those shown on the pages that follow. The solutions include explanations of how to adjust the shell as well as how to transfer the adjustment to the block pattern.

Resolve *all* your fitting problems on the shell before putting *any* on the block pattern. This may take more than one fitting session and require taking out and restitching darts and seams. If this seems time-consuming, remember it will save you many hours in future sewing.

Fit your shell from the top down, because a single adjustment on top might solve the problems below. Keep a record of all the adjustments you make.

Advanced pattern alterations

Neckline adjustments

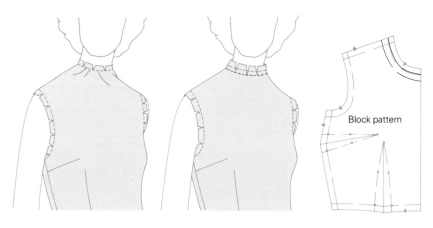

The neckline binds.
Solution: Lower the seamline to the neck base; clip the seam allowance until neckline feels comfortable.
Alteration: Draw cutting and stitching lines in new lowered position on the bodice front and back. Alter the neckline facings to match.

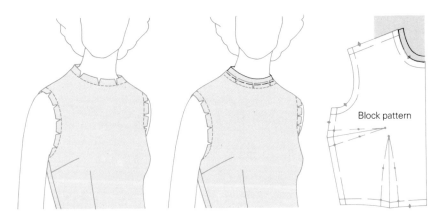

The neckline gapes.
Solution: Raise the seamline to the neck base with a self-fabric bias strip.
Alteration: Draw cutting and stitching lines in new raised position on the bodice front and back. Alter the neckline facings to match.

Shoulder adjustments

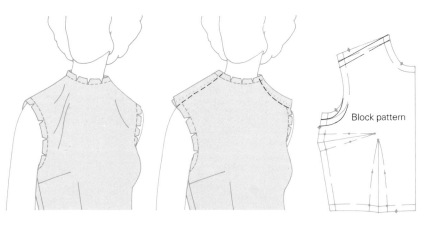

Shell wrinkles above the bust dart at the armhole and below the shoulder at the back. This occurs when shoulders slope more than pattern; one shoulder may slope more than the other.
Solution: Open up the shoulder seam; take out excess fabric by stitching seam deeper. Taper to original seamline at neckline. Redraw armhole to keep its shape.
Alteration: Draw new cutting and stitching lines for shoulder seams and armholes, lowering armhole at underarm by an amount equal to that removed at shoulder.

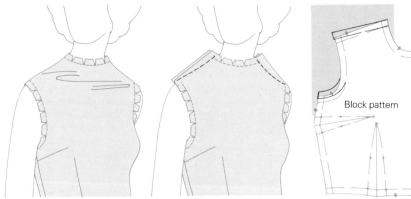

Shell feels tight and wrinkles across the shoulders at front and back. This occurs when shoulders slope less than pattern.
Solution: Release the shoulder seams and restitch a narrower shoulder seam to gain additional space. Taper to original seamline at neckline. Redraw the armhole to keep its original shape.
Alteration: Draw new cutting and stitching lines for shoulder seams and armholes, raising armhole at underarm by an amount equal to that added at shoulder.

Bust adjustments

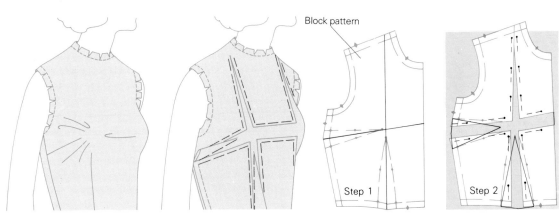

Block pattern

Step 1

Step 2

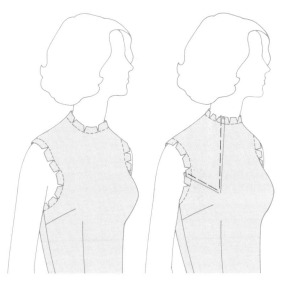

Bodice too tight across bustline. Shell wrinkles under dart and the grain may be pulled up in front.
Solution: Release the bust darts, then cut the fabric through the centre of each dart to the centre front and to the shoulder, respectively, crossing the apex of the bust. Spread each cut until bodice fits smoothly, filling in open spaces with scraps. Restitch darts, using original stitching lines.

Alteration: On lines drawn through the centres of the bust darts, cut the pattern and spread it the amount needed for one side—half the total amount. Locate original point of dart within each slash and redraw dart stitching lines, starting at original stitching line at base. Restore grainline and 'place on fold' line.

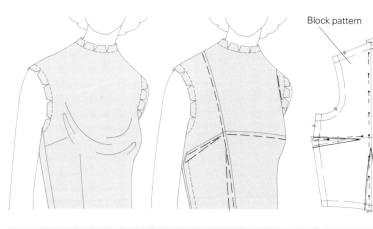

Block pattern

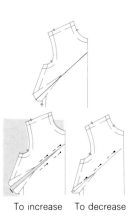

To increase   To decrease

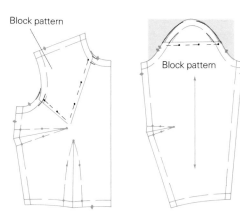

Block pattern

Block pattern

Bodice is too loose across bust. Shell caves in at bust.
Solution: Release the bust darts, then fold out excess fullness, picking up through the centre of each dart. Tack folds in place, then restitch darts.
Alteration: Extend foldlines of darts to shoulder and centre front; fold pattern on these lines until amount needed for one side—half the total amount—is removed. Locate original point of dart, and redraw dart stitching lines, starting at original stitching line at base. Darts become shallower.

French dart alteration:
On a line drawn through the centre of the bust dart, cut and spread (or fold out) ½ total amount needed. Keep neck edge on original centre front.

Armholes and/or neckline gape because of full bust.
Solution: Remove excess fabric by folding out fullness from gaping area to bust point as shown above. (Since this makes the armholes smaller, you will need to remove extra ease in the sleeve cap by taking a tuck a quarter as deep as the alteration dart at the armhole.)
Alteration: Cut pattern from armhole and/or neckline to bust point, and lap the cut edges to remove excess. (Remove excess ease from the sleeve cap with a tuck, as shown.)

125

Advanced pattern alterations

Shoulder and back adjustments

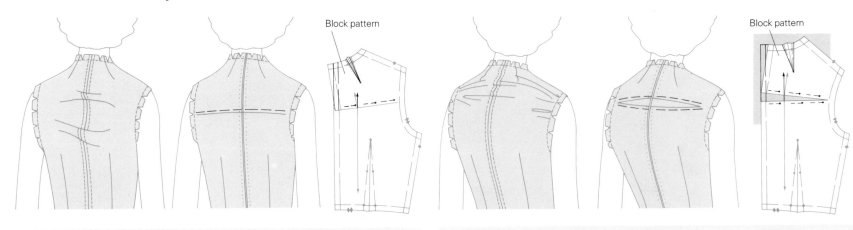

Shell wrinkles across shoulder blades because posture is very erect.
Solution: Tack a tuck across the shoulder blades, tapering to nothing at the armholes. (Note: This requires removal and subsequent replacement of the zipper.) Also, let out the neckline or shoulder darts, making them shorter if necessary.
Alteration: Take an identical tuck in back bodice pattern. Straighten the centre back cutting line and make the neckline dart shallower (or omit it) to compensate for the amount taken away when straightening the centre back line.

Shell pulls across the shoulders from slumping posture (round shoulders).
Solution: Cut shell across the back where it is strained; do not cut through armhole. Spread slash open until back fits smoothly; fill in with fabric scraps. (Note: This procedure requires removal and subsequent replacement of the zipper.)
Alteration: Cut and spread the pattern same as the shell. Straighten the centre back cutting line and deepen the neckline dart (or create one) to compensate for the amount added when straightening the centre back line.

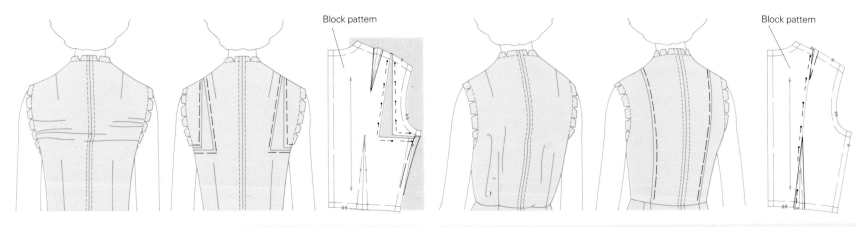

Bodice is too tight at armholes. Seamline may be strained to breaking point.
Solution: Relieve the strain by cutting an 'L' from the side seam (do not cut through the armhole seam) to the shoulder seam. Spread slash open until back fits smoothly; fill in with fabric scraps.
Alteration: Cut and spread pattern the same as shell. Deepen shoulder dart to remove any excess in shoulder seam. Redraw side seam, tapering from new position at underarm to original position at waistline. Add same amount to sleeve seams.

Bodice is too loose across back. Shoulder and waist are too big across the back.
Solution: Remove excess fabric by tacking a continuous waist-to-shoulder dart.
Alteration: Take a tuck from waist to shoulder, incorporating waist and shoulder darts. This is called a *fitting tuck* (it will not appear on a final garment). Because waist and shoulder darts must be retained in the pattern for fitting body contours, restore the darts lost in the fitting tuck to their original position, making them shallower, if necessary, so that waist and shoulder seams will match.

Armhole adjustments

Sleeve adjustments

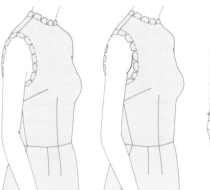
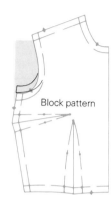
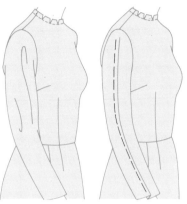
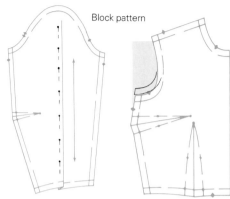

Block pattern

Block pattern

Take horizontal tuck across sleeve cap ¼ as deep as total taken from fitting shell.

Armholes are too low.
Solution: Raise the underarm curve by tacking in place a self-fabric bias strip.
Alteration: Draw new cutting and stitching lines to raise the underarm curve on front and back bodice patterns. Curve on sleeve at underarm must be raised by the same amount so that sleeve can be easily set into armhole.

Sleeves are too loose.
Solution: Take a tuck down the top of the sleeve to remove the excess, tucking the entire length if the whole sleeve is too big. If it is only the upper arm that is too large, taper tuck to nothing at the elbow.

Alteration: If you have taken in the sleeve along its entire length, take a tuck down the centre of the pattern, keeping it parallel to the grainline. The tuck will remove some ease from the sleeve cap, so you must alter the armhole by raising the underarm curve (the notches on sleeve and armhole will no longer match). If only the upper arm needed adjustment, see the drawing at the far right above. Underarm curve must be raised in this situation as well.

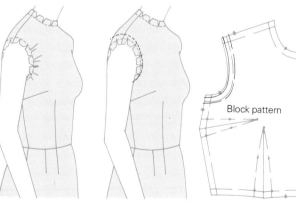
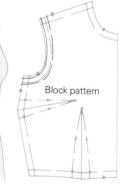

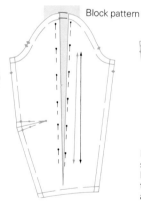

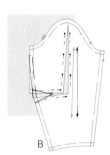

Block pattern

Block pattern

A

B

Full upper arm: Slash as shown above (A) and spread the same amount as shell.
Large elbow: Slash through dart, then up toward sleeve cap, and spread amount needed as shown above (B); redraw seam and dart.

Armholes are too high.
Solution: Relieve the strain by clipping into the seam allowance; mark a new stitching line for the armhole seam.
Alteration: Draw new cutting and stitching lines to lower the underarm curve on front and back bodice patterns. Curve on sleeve at underarm must be lowered by the same amount so that sleeve can be easily set into armhole.

Sleeves are too tight.
Solution: Slash shell down centre of sleeve to wrist, then spread until sleeve fits smoothly. Fill in with fabric scraps. You may enlarge the entire sleeve, just the upper arm, or the elbow (see the drawing at the right).

Alteration: If entire length of sleeve needs enlarging, cut the sleeve pattern down the centre to the wrist, parallel to grainline, and spread to add the needed width. This adds to the sleeve cap; to compensate, alter the armhole on front and back bodice patterns by lowering the underarm curve. The notches on sleeve and armhole will no longer match. An alteration to the armhole is required for a large upper arm alteration, but not for the elbow alteration.

Advanced pattern alterations

Skirt or pants front adjustments

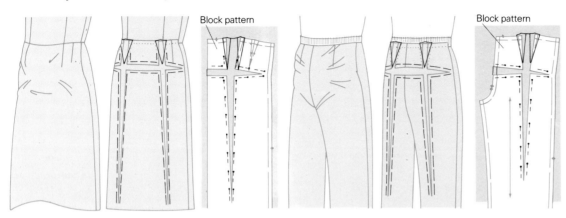

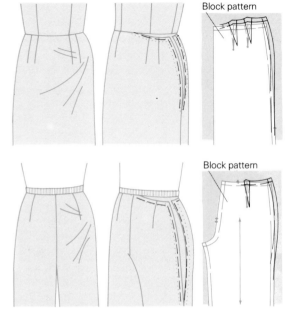

Skirt/pants side seam adjustments

Shell is too tight across abdomen. Strain may cause skirt hem to pull up, pants to wrinkle at crotch.
Solution: Release the darts nearest centre front. Enlarge the area over the abdomen and make the darts deeper by cutting through the centre of the released waistline darts to within 2.5 cm of the hem edge (or to knee on pants). Cut again from side seam to side seam just below the dart points. Spread cuts the amount needed, keeping the centre front line straight; fill in the spaces with fabric scraps. Pin the darts back in, using the original stitching lines. (Darts will be much deeper; if they are very deep, make two darts instead of one.)
Alteration: Carefully transfer the changes to the block pattern by cutting and spreading it to match shell.

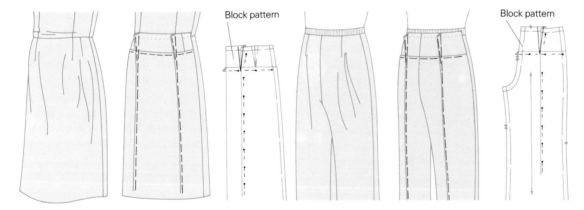

Shell caves in at abdomen. If abdomen is very flat, the skirt may droop in front; pants may wrinkle.
Solution: Release darts nearest to centre front. Reduce the fabric over the abdomen and make the darts shallower by taking a tuck through the centre of the dart that tapers to within 2.5 cm of hem edge (or to knee on pants). Take another tuck from side seam to side seam, just below dart points. When satisfied that enough excess has been removed, tack the tucks in place and pin the darts back in (if they were not eliminated in tuck), using original stitching lines. Darts will be shallower.
Alteration: Carefully transfer changes by tucking pattern to match shell. Taper horizontal tuck to nothing at side seams. Redraw darts, using original stitch lines.

Shell pulls on one side of the body because one hip is higher or larger than the other.
Solution: For a slight adjustment, let out the waist and side seams and fit the darts to the figure contours. Do this at front and back. For a major adjustment, cut and spread the shell across the hipline as shown below. Do this in addition to the dart and seam adjustments described for slight adjustment.
Alteration: Transfer the shell changes by drawing new cutting and stitching lines. Label the alteration as for right or left side. For a major alteration, make a separate pattern piece for the affected side.

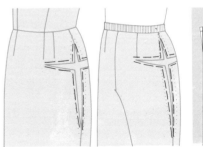
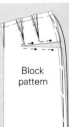

Skirt or pants back adjustments

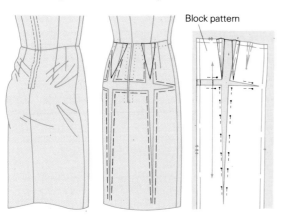

Block pattern

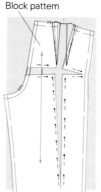

Block pattern

Pants legs adjustments

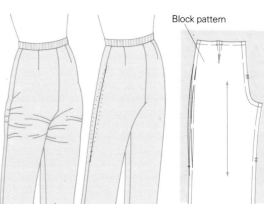

Block pattern

Shell is too tight at back only. Skirt may be wrinkled below the waist; pants wrinkle at the crotch.
Solution: Release the darts nearest centre back. Enlarge the area over the buttocks and make the darts deeper by cutting through the centre of the released waistline darts to within 2.5 cm of the hem edge (or to knee on pants). Cut again from side seam to side seam just below the dart

points. Spread cuts the amount needed, keeping centre back line straight, and fill in the spaces with fabric scraps. Pin the darts back in, using the original stitching lines. (Darts will be much deeper; if they are very deep, make two darts instead of one.)
Alteration: Carefully transfer changes to the block pattern by cutting and spreading it to match shell.

Pants legs are too tight at thigh.
Solution: Let out side seams until shell fits smoothly; taper addition to nothing at hip and knee.
Alteration: Transfer the changes made in the shell by drawing new cutting and stitching lines on the pants back and front patterns. Divide the increase equally between front and back side seams.

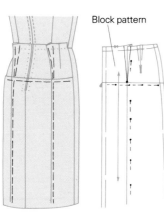

Block pattern

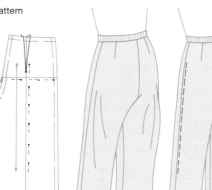

Block pattern

Block pattern

Shell is too loose at back only. Skirt will collapse in the back and the hem may droop. Pants are inclined to wrinkle from sagging at the crotch.
Solution: Release darts nearest centre back. Reduce the amount of fabric over the buttocks and make the darts shallower by taking a tuck through centre of dart that tapers to within 2.5 cm of hem edge (or to knee on pants). Take

another tuck from side seam to side seam, just below dart points. Tack tucks in place and pin darts back in (if not eliminated in the tuck) using original stitching lines. Darts will be much shallower.
Alteration: Carefully transfer the changes by tucking pattern to match shell. Taper horizontal tuck to nothing at side seams. Redraw darts.

Pants legs are too loose at thigh.
Solution: Take in side seams until shell fits smoothly; taper reduction to nothing at hips and knee.
Alteration: Transfer the changes made in the shell by drawing new cutting and stitching lines on the pants back and front patterns. Divide the reduction equally between front and back side seams.

129

Advanced pattern alterations

How to use the block pattern

When the shell has been adjusted to solve all fitting problems to your satisfaction, you are ready to transfer the adjustments to the pattern pieces from which the shell was made. The adjusted pieces are your block pattern. For future reference, note on the block pattern each amount you have added or taken away. When adding to pattern, use tissue or tracing paper and transparent tape.

Label any asymmetrical pattern alterations for the right or the left side. Later, you can cut out on the line for the larger side and, with dressmaker's carbon paper and tracing wheel, mark the differing stitching lines for each side. If this is impractical, as it will be when, for instance, one hip is much higher than the other, make separate patterns for right and left sides and cut out the pattern pieces from single layers of fabric.

Back your altered block pattern with non-woven, iron-on interfacing; this will make it durable. Keep your fitting shell and try it on from time to time. If you find you need to make new adjustments because of figure changes, you can easily alter your block pattern.

To use the block pattern with other patterns, follow this two-step suggestion. First place the block pattern under related pieces of the new pattern and check for **length** adjustments. Align the new pattern with the block pattern at shoulders or underarm if a bodice or a dress, at waistline if a skirt or pants. Make all the needed length adjustments. Then put the new pattern over the block pattern again and match up the waistlines.

Check for **width** adjustments at bust, waist and hip. Also make sure that **darts** are correctly positioned. Other specialised alterations, such as high hip, gaping neckline or armhole, should be noted at this time.

The basic fitting sheath, although it consists of a separate bodice and straight skirt, can be used to check the fit of almost any style of garment. For example, if you want to test the fit of a dress that has no waistline seam, lap the waist seamlines of the block bodice and skirt (keeping a straight line at centre front), then lay the new pattern on top of the block pattern. If your new pattern has a shoulder yoke, lap the seamlines of the bodice and yoke and pin in place; then slip block pattern underneath and see where alterations will be needed.

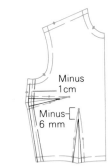

Minus 1cm

Minus 6 mm

Plus 1cm

6mm 6 mm

Right side

Skirt front

Note on block pattern the amount added or taken away by each of your alterations as close to the alteration as possible. This will be useful for future reference and will avoid any possible confusion about the nature and extent of individual alterations.

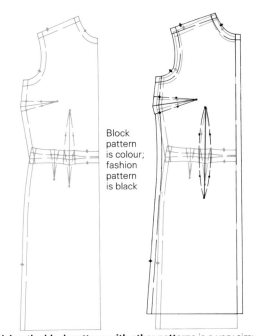

Block pattern is colour; fashion pattern is black

Using the block pattern with other patterns is a very simple procedure. Simply slip block pattern piece underneath the appropriate piece from new pattern; match up centre fronts or centre backs and other key points. You will be able to see clearly where the new pattern requires alteration.

The try-on fitting

It is wise to try on any garment as soon as the major seams have been stitched. Some fine adjustments can only be seen when fabric and pattern meet. This is a good time, too, to make minor seam and dart adjustments that may still be needed.

Schedule a try-on fitting when back and front have been joined at sides and shoulders, and underlining and interfacing are in place. Staystitch armholes and necklines to prevent stretching; expect these openings to be snug because of extended seam allowances. Pin up hems. Lap and pin openings.

Try on pants and skirts before the waistband is attached. Staystitch at waist to prevent stretching.

To get a clear and accurate picture of fit, wear appropriate shoes and undergarments. Remember also to try your garment on right side out.

Machine-tack sections together for this fitting; it will be easier to make changes. If your fabric is too delicate for machine stitching, pin-tack instead, placing the pins several centimetres apart on the right side along the stitching lines.

If you are using a different fabric from those recommended on the pattern envelope, you may have to take in or let out some seams. Work from the shoulders down, adjusting darts, if necessary, along the way. Pin in place all patch pockets, flaps etc., to check positioning.

You can pin-tack or machine-tack for this fitting if there is a possibility of many changes. Pinning is better for a delicate fabric.

Sit, stand, walk, bend and reach— take every relevant position in your garment to thoroughly test its fit.

Adjusting after the try-on fitting

Problem: A stand-up collar is too high.
Solution: Adjust the collar, not the neckline. If the collar is shaped, restitch a deeper seam along the top edge. If collar is a folded bias band, take deeper seam at neckline edge of collar only.

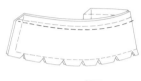

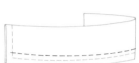

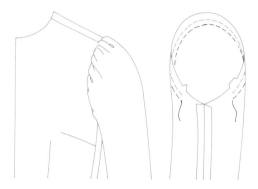

Problem: Too much ease in sleeve cap; material ripples.
Solution: Remove sleeve from garment; smooth out cap. Easestitch 5 mm from seamline, within cap area (sleeve cap seam allowance now measures 2 cm). Retack sleeve to armhole, aligning new ease line with armhole seam and maintaining 1.5 cm seam allowance between underarm notches.

Problem: A stretchy knit garment ends up too big around the middle.
Solution: Take in side seams for a closer (but not too close) fit. Remember to deepen seam allowance on sleeve underarm seams so that sleeve and bodice armholes will match.

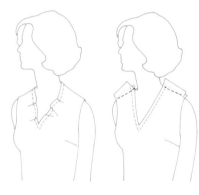

Problem: A low U-shaped or V-shaped neckline gapes.
Solution: Lift bodice front at shoulder near neck to remove excess fabric between bust apex and shoulder. Taper adjustment to nothing at the armhole. Alter the neckline facing to match.

Problem: Wrinkling on either side of darts.
Solution: Darts may be too straight to conform to your figure. Restitch darts, curving them slightly inward. Taper carefully to points. Darts may need shortening.

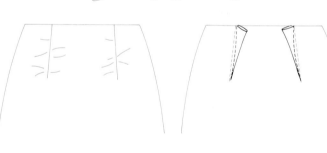

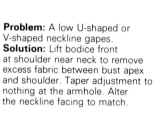

Problem: Front opening, or lapped edge on wrap skirt, sags slightly.
Solution: First try re-pinning the hem. If unevenness is extreme, or if it is back fold that sags, try correcting by raising waist seamline in sagging areas until hem is even. A third possibility: support the sagging edge with concealed snap fasteners (especially if fabric must be matched crosswise).

Problem: Fabric bulges or sags below the dart.
Solution: Darts are probably too short. Restitch to a longer length, maintaining the original width. Sometimes this problem arises when dart has not been tapered smoothly to point in stitching. Restitch.

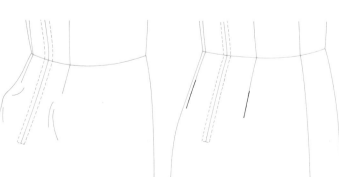

Advanced pattern alterations

When to make a test garment

If you approach a new sewing project with any uncertainty, it can be well worth the time it takes to make up the pattern you have chosen in a cheaper fabric than the one you plan to use. This test garment can prevent expensive mistakes and disappointments in the actual garment.

Several considerations may suggest the advisability of a test garment. Perhaps the **fabric** is an expensive or unusual one, such as a beaded knit or bridal lace. Or it may require special treatment during sewing. Leathers and vinyls, for example, show pin and needle marks, which makes it impossible to fit them after cutting. Still another difficulty may be the design—a large-scale or border print, or an intricate plaid. By pencilling the motif onto a test fabric, you can determine design placement before cutting the real fabric.

Sometimes the **pattern** is the problem. It may be a more intricate style than you are accustomed to, or a silhouette you have never worn. A test garment lets you practise new or complicated techniques in advance, check the suitability of the style to your figure, and make sure of the accuracy of any pattern alterations you have made.

Choose a test fabric as close as possible in weight and draping properties to your final fabric—except if the garment is to be underlined. When this is the case, construct your mock-up of underlining fabric, make your adjustments in it, then take it apart for use as a sewing guide.

On test garments, you can eliminate facings, collars and pockets, and, if you are fairly sure of their fit, the sleeves. If you like the garment in the substitute fabric, you can finish it later.

An intricate style can pose problems of many kinds. In this hypothetical dress design, not only do the parts go together in an unusual way, but welt seaming is featured throughout. A test garment would give advance practice in all steps, avoiding costly mistakes in cutting and sewing actual fabric.

Fashion trends often incorporate design variations, such as this draped collar. Those who shy away from such patterns because they seem too advanced should welcome the idea of test garments.

Unusual applications can deviate significantly from standard techniques, as in this pleated skirt. Your test fabric in such a situation should fold, hang, and otherwise perform as much like the final fabric as possible.

Top-quality fabrics ensure the effectiveness of garments with simple lines. You can feel more confident cutting into such luxurious material if you have solved all fit problems beforehand on an inexpensive fabric.

Large-scale prints call for very careful placement if they are to be striking in the way the designer intended, and flattering to the wearer. When the motif must also be matched, as it is here, a test garment is almost indispensable.

Basic construction techniques

A good understanding of basic construction techniques will help you achieve a truly professional finish in your sewing. This chapter covers all the hand and machine stitches you will need, with clear diagrams and step-by-step instructions, from knotting a thread to ending off. The best ways to sew seams, and finish them neatly, are also covered in detail, followed by a discussion on darts, those essentials in shaping garments. And then there are all the ways of creating and controlling fullness in clothing: tucks, pleats, gathering, shirring and smocking. All of them, as well as ruffles, which complete the chapter, are also decorative features of clothing, and knowing how to sew them will open up the full range of fashion styles to you.

Hand sewing

Hand sewing tips

Though precise recommendations vary from one procedure to another, there are general principles that apply to hand sewing of any kind.

Threading tips: Cut thread at an angle, using sharp scissors. Never break or bite thread—this frays the end, making it difficult to push it through the eye of the needle.

To thread a needle, hold the needle in the left hand and the thread end in the right between thumb and index finger. Pass thread end through the needle eye and, with the same motion, transfer the needle to right thumb and index finger. Then, with left hand, draw thread end out from the eye about one-third of the way down the remaining thread supply.

Hand-sew with a comparatively short thread. For permanent stitching, use a working length of 45 to 60 cm; for tacking, the thread can be longer. (Working length is from needle eye to knot.) Except for buttons, snap fasteners and hooks and eyes, you will seldom need a double thread.

Needle choice: Select a hand needle that is suitable for the thread and fabric, and comfortable for you. A fine needle is best: short for short, single stitches, such as padding stitches; longer for long or multiple stitches such as tacking.

Thread colour and type: For tacking and thread-marking, use white or a light-coloured thread that contrasts with the fabric. Dark thread can leave marks on a light-coloured fabric. For permanent hand stitching, thread can match or contrast as you prefer.

Polyester thread is the easiest to use for hand sewing, and is especially good for tacking because it will not leave an impression after pressing. Cotton threads and cotton/synthetic threads are acceptable. Silk twist is used for buttonholes and buttons, and also for some decorative hand sewing.

Twisting and knotting can be a problem in hand sewing—with any thread, but particularly with those that are made entirely, or partly, of synthetic fibres. To keep the problem to a minimum, use a short length of thread, and do not pull tightly on it.

It is also helpful to thread the needle with the end cut from the spool and to wax the thread before starting to sew. When twisting does occur, allow the thread to untwist itself in this way: first let the thread dangle, with the needle end down, then slide your fingers gently down the thread.

Securing stitching at beginning and end

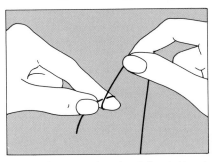

To tie a knot in a thread end, first hold end between thumb and index finger while bringing supply thread over and around finger.

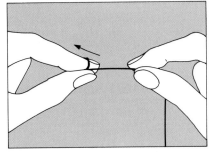

Holding supply thread taut, slide index finger along thumb toward palm. This will cause the thread end to twist into the loop.

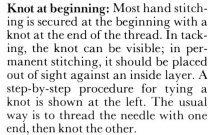

Knot at beginning: Most hand stitching is secured at the beginning with a knot at the end of the thread. In tacking, the knot can be visible; in permanent stitching, it should be placed out of sight against an inside layer. A step-by-step procedure for tying a knot is shown at the left. The usual way is to thread the needle with one end, then knot the other.

Backstitching can also be used to secure the beginning as well as the end of a row of stitches. Sometimes it is even preferable to a knot, especially in garment areas where a knot could leave an indentation after pressing. A typical instance is in tailoring, where a thread knot within a section that has been padstitched would show on the right side of the garment.

The shorter the backstitch, the more secure it will be. In general, use a short backstitch to secure permanent stitches and a long backstitch to secure those that will be removed, such as tacking. For a very secure finish, use a backstitch in combination with a loop, as shown below.

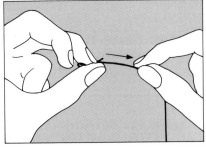

Slide index finger farther back into palm so that the loop will slide off finger. Hold open loop between tip of index finger and thumb.

Bring middle finger down to rest on and hold the open loop. Pull on supply thread to make loop smaller and form the knot.

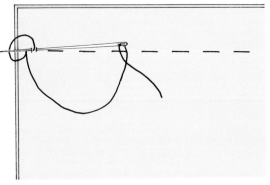

To secure thread at the end of a row of stitching, bring needle and thread to the underside. Take one small stitch behind thread, catching only a single yarn of the fabric. Pull needle and thread through, leaving a small thread loop. Take another short backstitch in the same place, but pass needle and thread through loop of first stitch. Pull both stitches close to fabric; cut thread.

ARROWHEAD TACK   **see Tacks** (construction)

BACKSTITCH

One of the strongest and most versatile of the hand stitches, the backstitch serves to secure hand stitching and repair seams; it is also used for hand-understitching, topstitching and hand-picking zippers. Though there are several variations, each is formed by inserting needle behind point where thread emerges from previous stitch. **The beginning or end** of a row of hand stitching can be secured with a backstitch. Fasten permanent stitching with a short backstitch; use a long backstitch to secure stitches that will be removed. A more secure finish combines the backstitch with a loop through which the stitch is fastened.

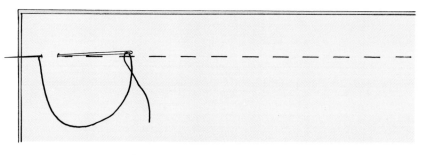

As a beginning or end in hand stitching: Bring needle and thread to underside. Insert needle through all fabric layers a stitch length *behind* and bring it up just at *back* of point where thread emerges. Pull thread through.

For a more secure finish, take a very short backstitch just behind the point where the thread emerges, but leave a thread loop by not pulling the stitch taut. Take another small backstitch on top of the first; bring the needle and thread out through the loop. Pull both stitches taut and then cut thread.

Even backstitch is the strongest of the backstitches. The stitches look much like machine stitching, as they are even in length with very little space between them. This stitch is used mainly to make and repair seams.

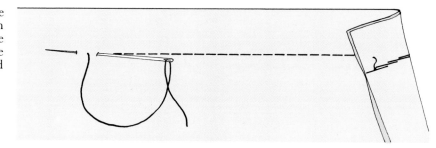

Even backstitch: Bring needle and thread to upper side. Insert needle through all fabric layers approximately 2–4 mm (*half* a stitch length) behind the point where the thread emerges, and bring needle and thread out the *same* distance in front of that point. Continue inserting and bringing up needle and thread half a stitch length behind and in front of the thread from the previous stitch. From top side, finished stitches look similar to straight machine stitching.

Half-backstitch is similar to the even backstitch except that the length of stitches and spaces between them are equal. Although not as strong as the even backstitch, this stitch can also be used to repair a seam.

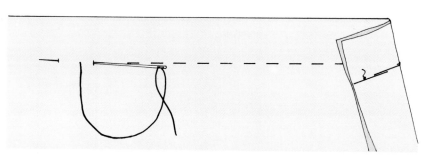

Half-backstitch: Similar to even backstitch except that, instead of finished stitches meeting on top side, there is a space between them equal to the length of the stitches. Needle is inserted through all fabric layers approximately 2 mm behind the point where the thread emerges, but is brought out *twice* this distance (4 mm) in front of that point.

Glossary of hand stitches

BACKSTITCH (continued)

Prickstitch is a much more decorative backstitch than the even or the half-backstitch. Seen from the top side, the stitches are very short, with long spaces between them. This stitch is mainly used to hand-pick a zipper.

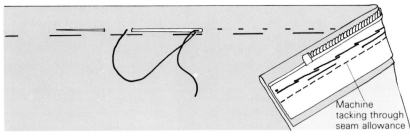

Machine tacking through seam allowance

Prickstitch: Similar to half-backstitch except that the needle is inserted through all fabric layers *just a few fabric threads* behind and then brought up approximately 3 to 6 mm in front of the point where thread emerges. Finished stitches on the top side are very short, with 3 to 6 mm space between them.

Pickstitch can look like any of the backstitches; the only difference is that the stitch is not taken through to the underlayer of fabric. Primarily a decorative backstitch, it is ideal for topstitching and hand-under-stitching, where only the top part of the stitch should be seen.

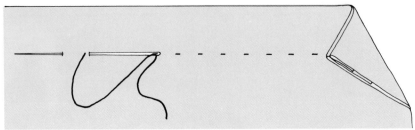

Pickstitch: Any of the backstitches but *made without catching underlayer* of fabric. When the underlayer is not caught underpart of stitch becomes invisible.

BAR TACK

see Tacks (construction)

BLANKET STITCH
Traditionally an embroidery stitch, the blanket stitch can also be used in garment construction. It often serves, as in the illustration, to cover fabric edges decoratively. Another use is in construction details. A bar tack is formed, for example, by working the stitch over threads.

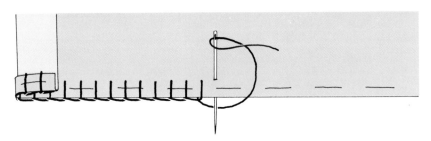

Blanket stitch: Work from left to right, with the point of the needle and the edge of the work toward you. The edge of the fabric can be folded under or left raw. Secure thread and bring out below edge. For the first and each succeeding stitch, insert needle through fabric from right side and bring out at edge. Keeping thread from previous stitch *under* point of needle, draw needle and thread through, forming stitch over edge. Stitch size and spacing can be the same or varied.

BUTTONHOLE STITCH
A 'covering' stitch used as a decorative finish and in the making of hand-worked buttonholes.

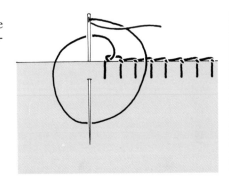
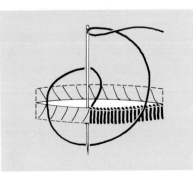

Buttonhole stitch: Work from right to left, with point of needle toward you but edge of fabric away from you. Fasten thread and bring out above the edge. For first and each succeeding stitch, loop thread from previous stitch to left, then down to right. Insert needle from underside, keeping looped thread *under* both *point and eye* of needle. Pull needle out through fabric, then *away* from you to place the purl of the stitch on the fabric's edge. Stitch depth and spacing can be large or small depending on fabric and circumstance.
For hand-worked buttonholes: Follow basic directions for buttonhole stitch, making stitches 3 mm deep with no space between.

CATCHSTITCH

see Tacking stitches

CHAIN

A thread chain can serve as a belt carrier, thread eye or button loop, or as an alternative to the French tack. It can be as long as needed. The chain may be fastened to lie flat against the garment, or given a looped shape by making the chain longer than the distance between the markings that indicate its beginning and end.

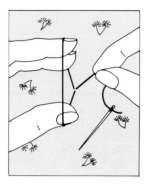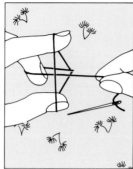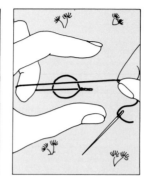

Thread chain: Mark on garment where chain begins and will be fastened. At the first mark take a small stitch and draw thread through, leaving a 10 to 12 cm loop. Hold loop open with thumb and first two fingers of left hand; hold supply thread with right thumb and index finger (1). Reach through and grasp supply thread with second finger of left hand to start new loop (2). As you pull new loop through, the first loop will slide off other fingers and become smaller as it is drawn down to fabric (3). Position new loop as in 1; continue chaining to desired length. To secure, slip needle through last loop and fasten.

CHAINSTITCH

A continuous series of looped stitches that form a chain. Can be used decoratively, as illustrated at right, on clothing, linens, lingerie. Takes a more functional form in the thread chain shown and described above.

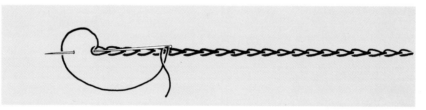

Chainstitch: Work from right to left. Fasten thread and bring up to right side. For each stitch, loop thread up and around; insert needle just behind where thread emerges and bring it up, over the looped thread, a stitch length in front of that point. Pull thread through, to the left, to form looped stitch.

CROSS STITCH

Horizontal stitches, taken parallel to each other, whose floats cross in the centre to form X's. Can be used decoratively or constructively, either in a series, as shown at the right, or as a single cross stitch.

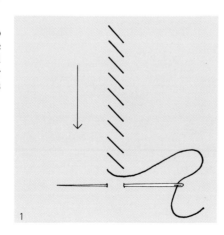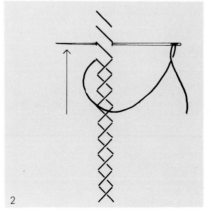

1

2

Cross stitch: Working from top to bottom (1) with needle pointing left, make row of small horizontal stitches spaced as far apart as they are long. Pull the thread firmly but not taut. This produces diagonal floats between stitches. When the row is finished, *reverse direction,* working stitches from bottom to top (2), still with needle pointing left. Thread floats should cross in the middle, forming X's.

CROSS-STITCH TACKING

see Tacking stitches

Glossary of hand stitches

DIAGONAL TACKING   see Tacking stitches

EVEN BACKSTITCH   see Backstitch

EVEN SLIPSTITCH   see Slipstitch

EVEN TACKING   see Tacking stitches

FAGGOTING STITCH

A decorative stitch used to join two fabric sections, leaving a space in between. As a rule, faggoting should be used only in those areas where there will be little strain, such as yoke sections or bands near the bottom of a skirt or sleeve. The fabric edges must be folded back accurately to maintain the position of the original seamline, which, after faggoting, should be at the centre of the space between the folded edges.

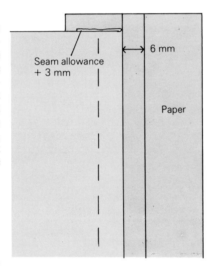
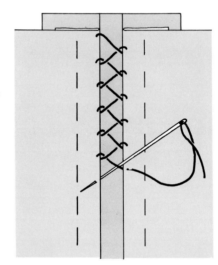

Faggoting stitch: On paper, draw parallel lines to represent width of opening between folded-back fabric edges (usually 6 mm). Fold each seamline back by half this measurement, then pin and tack each edge to paper along parallel lines. Fasten thread and bring up through one folded edge. Carry thread diagonally across opening and insert needle up through opposite fold; pull thread through. Pass needle *under* thread, diagonally across opening, and up through opposite fold. Continue in this way along entire opening, spacing stitches evenly. When finished, remove paper and press seam.

FEATHERSTITCH

Primarily decorative, featherstitch is made up of a series of stitches taken on alternate sides of a given line.

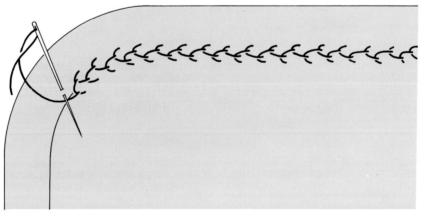

Featherstitch: Mark the line the stitching is to follow on right side of fabric. Fasten thread on underside of stitch line and bring up to right side of fabric. For first and each succeeding stitch, pass needle and thread diagonally *across* line to *opposite* side. Holding thread in place, and with needle pointing down and diagonally toward line, take a small stitch above thread, bringing point of needle out *on top* of thread. Draw on stitch until thread under it curves slightly. Continue making stitches on opposite sides of line, keeping stitch length, spacing, and needle slant the same.

FRENCH TACK   see **Tacks** (construction)

HALF-BACKSTITCH   see **Backstitch**

HEAVY-DUTY TACKING   see **Tacking stitches**

HEMMING STITCHES
Used to secure a hem to a garment. Depending on the situation, the choice will be either a *flat* or *blind* hemming technique.

HEMMING STITCHES, FLAT
These stitches pass over the hem edge to the garment.

Slant hemming Quickest, but least durable because so much thread is exposed and subject to abrasion.

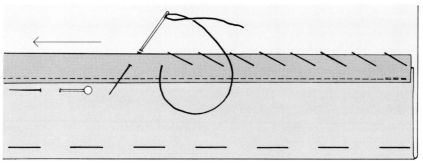

Slant hemming: Fasten thread on wrong side of hem, bringing needle and thread through hem edge. Working from right to left, take first and each succeeding stitch approximately 6 to 10 mm to the left, catching only one thread of the garment fabric and bringing the needle up through edge of hem. This method produces long, slanting floats between stitches.

Vertical hemming A durable and stable method best suited to hems whose edges are finished with woven or stretch-lace seam binding. Very little thread is exposed, reducing the risk of fraying and breaking.

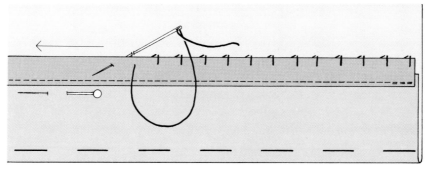

Vertical hemming: Stitches are worked from right to left. Fasten thread from wrong side of hem and bring needle and thread through hem edge. Directly *opposite* this point and beside the hem edge, begin first and each succeeding stitch by catching only one thread of garment fabric. Then direct the needle down diagonally to go through the hem edge approximately 6 to 10 mm to the left. Short, vertical floats will appear between the stitches.

Slip hemming A durable and almost invisible method suitable for a folded hem edge. The stitches (actually uneven slipstitches) are slipped through the fold of the hem edge, minimising the possibility of the thread fraying or breaking.

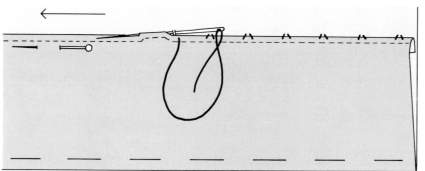

Slip hemming: Stitches are worked from right to left. Fasten thread, bringing needle and thread out through fold of hem. Opposite, in the *garment,* take a small stitch, catching only a few threads. Opposite that stitch, in the *hem* edge, insert needle and slip through fold for about 6 mm. Continue alternating the stitches in this fashion.

Glossary of hand stitches

HEMMING STITCHES, FLAT (continued)

Herringbone stitch is a strong hemming stitch particularly well suited to a stitched-and-pinked hem edge. Take special note of the direction for working and of the position of the needle. Notice, too, that with each stitch, the thread crosses over itself.

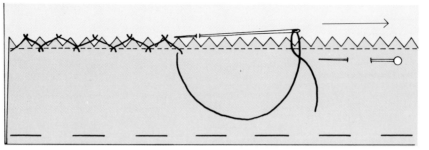

Herringbone stitch: Stitches are worked from left to right with needle pointing left. Fasten thread from wrong side of hem and bring needle and thread through hem edge. Take a very small stitch in the garment fabric directly above the hem edge and approximately 6 to 10 mm to the right. Take the next stitch 6 to 10 mm to the right in the hem. Continue to alternate stitches, spacing them evenly. Take special care to keep the stitches small when catching the garment fabric.

HEMMING STITCHES, BLIND

These stitches are taken *inside*, between the hem and the garment. In the finished hem, no stitches are visible and the edge of the hem does not press into the garment.

Blind-hemming stitch is a quick and easy stitch that can be used on any blind hem.

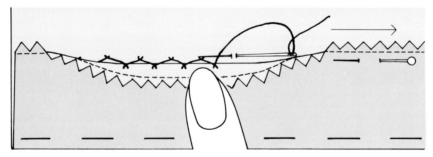

Blind-hemming stitch: Work from right to left with needle pointing left. Fold back the hem edge; fasten thread inside it. Take a very small stitch approximately 6 mm to the left in the garment; take the next stitch 6 mm to the left in the hem. Continue to alternate stitches from garment to hem, spacing them approximately 6 mm apart. Take care to keep stitches small, especially those taken on garment.

Blind herringbone stitch is the same stitch as the herringbone stitch used for flat hemming except that it is done between the hem and the garment. This stitch is a bit more stable and secure than the blind-hemming stitch, and is particularly good for heavy fabrics.

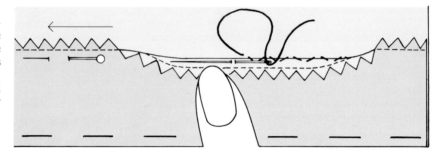

Blind herringbone stitch: Work from left to right with needle pointing left. Fold back hem edge and fasten thread inside it. Take a very small stitch about 6 mm to the right in the garment; take the next stitch 6 mm to the right in the hem edge. Continue to alternate stitches from garment to hem, spacing them approximately 6 mm apart. Keep stitches small, especially when stitching on the garment fabric.

HEMSTITCHING

This is an ornamental hem finish, traditionally used for linens and handkerchiefs. Hem edge is folded under and tacked in place, then several threads are pulled from the fabric directly above this edge. Number drawn depends on fabric's coarseness, but space they leave should be 3 to 6 mm. Every stitch must group an equal number of lengthwise threads.

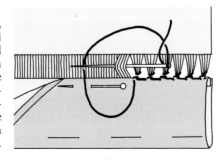
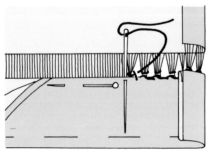

Hemstitching: Working on wrong side and from right to left, fasten thread; pull up through folded hem edge. Slide needle under several lengthwise threads; loop thread to left *under* point of needle (1). Pull thread through to left and draw it down firmly near the hem edge. Then take a stitch through garment and hem edge catching only a few fabric threads (2). Repeat until edge is finished. Keep the number of lengthwise yarns the same in each group.

HEMSTITCHING (continued)

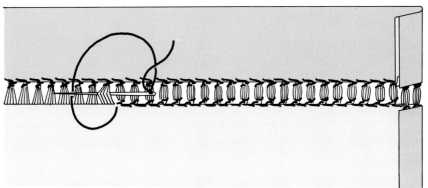

Double hemstitching: When one edge has been finished as described on the previous page, turn work and make duplicate stitches along the opposite edge of the drawn threads. Take care to retain the thread groups that were established on the first edge.

HERRINGBONE STITCH

see Hemming stitches (flat)

HERRINGBONE STITCH (blind)

see Hemming stitches (blind)

HERRINGBONE-STITCH TACKING

see Tacking stitches

OVERCAST STITCH

This is the customary hand stitch for finishing the raw edges of fabric to prevent them from fraying. In general, the more the fabric frays, the deeper and closer together the overcast stitches should be.

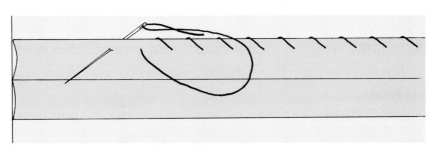

Overcast stitch: Working from either direction, take diagonal stitches over the edge, spacing them an even distance apart at a uniform depth.

OVERHAND STITCH

These tiny, even stitches are used to topsew two finished edges as, for example, when attaching lace edging or ribbon to a garment.

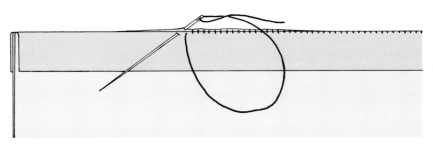

Overhand stitch: Insert needle diagonally from the back edge through to the front edge, picking up only one or two threads each time. The needle is inserted *directly behind* thread from previous stitch and is brought out a *stitch length away*. Keep the stitches uniform in their size and spacing.

Glossary of hand stitches

PADDING STITCHES

Padding stitches are used, primarily in tailoring, to attach interfacing to the outer fabric. When the stitches are made *short* and close together, they are also helping to form and control shape in certain garment sections, such as a collar or lapel. *Longer* padding stitches are used just to hold interfacing in place; they are like diagonal tacking except that they are permanent and stitches are shorter.

Chevron padding stitches are formed by making each row of stitches in the opposite direction from the preceding one; that is, work from top to bottom on one row, then, without turning fabric, work next row bottom to top.

Parallel padding stitches are formed by making each row of stitches in the same direction.

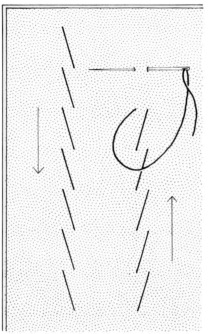

Chevron

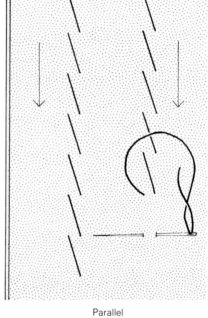

Parallel

Chevron padding stitches: Working from top to bottom, make a row of short, even stitches from right to left, placing them parallel to each other and the same distance apart. Without turning the fabric, make the next row of stitches the same way except work them from bottom to top. Keep alternating the direction of the rows to produce the chevron effect.

Parallel padding stitches: These stitches are made the same way as the chevron padding stitches except that all rows are worked in the same direction.

PICKSTITCH

see **Backstitch**

PRICKSTITCH

see **Backstitch**

RUNNING STITCH

A very short, even stitch used for fine seaming, tucking, mending, gathering, and other such delicate sewing. The running stitch is like even tacking except that the stitches are smaller and usually permanent.

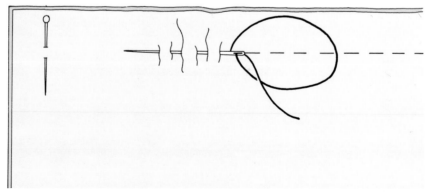

Running stitch: Working from right to left, weave the point of the needle in and out of the fabric several times before pulling the thread through. Keep stitches and the spaces between them small and even.

SADDLE STITCH

This is a variation of the running stitch, but the stitches and spaces between them are longer, generally 6 to 10 mm. Used primarily for hand topstitching and welting, and intended to be a strong accent, the saddle stitch is usually done with buttonhole twist, embroidery thread or tightly twisted yarn, often in a contrasting colour.

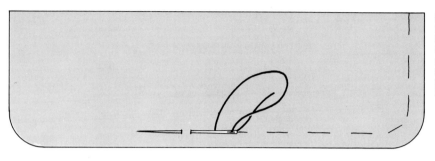

Saddle stitch: Fasten thread and bring the needle and thread through to right side of fabric. Working from right to left, take a stitch 6 to 10 mm long, leave a space the same length, then take another stitch. Continue taking stitches in this way, making them equal in length and in intervening space.

SIMPLIFIED TAILOR'S TACKS

see Tacks (marking)

SLANT HEMMING

see Hemming stitches (flat)

SLIP HEMMING

see Hemming stitches (flat)

SLIP TACKING

see Tacking stitches

SLIPSTITCH

This is an almost invisible stitch formed by slipping the thread under a fold of fabric. It can be used to join two folded edges, or one folded edge to a flat surface.

Even slipstitch is used to join two folded edges. It is a fast and easy way to mend a seam from the right side, especially one that would be difficult to reach from the inside.

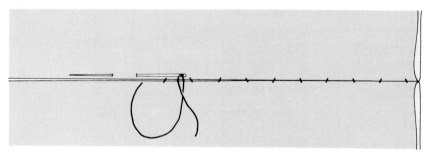

Even slipstitch: Work from right to left. Fasten thread and bring needle and thread out through one folded edge. For the first and each succeeding stitch, slip needle through fold of opposite edge for about 6 mm; bring needle out and draw the thread through. Continue to slip the needle and thread through the opposing folded edges.

Uneven slipstitch, also known as slip hemming, is used to join a folded edge to a flat surface. Besides being a flat hemming stitch, it is useful for attaching patch pockets, trims, and coat and jacket linings, as well as for securing the edges of a facing to zipper tapes.

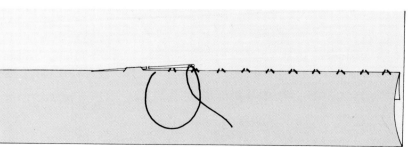

Uneven slipstitch: Work from right to left. Fasten thread and bring needle and thread out through the folded edge. Opposite, in the *garment,* take a small stitch, catching only a few threads of the garment fabric. Opposite this stitch, in the *folded edge,* insert needle and slip it through the fold for about 6 mm, then bring the needle out and draw the thread through. Continue alternating stitches from garment to fold.

Glossary of hand stitches

TACKING STITCHES

Hand tacking (or basting) is used to temporarily hold together two or more fabric layers during both fitting and construction.

Even tacking is used on smooth fabrics and in areas that require close control, such as curved seams, seams with ease, and set-in sleeves.

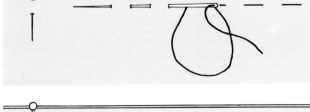

Even tacking: Short (about 6 mm) temporary stitches, taken the *same distance* apart. Working from right to left, take several evenly spaced stitches onto the needle before pulling it through.

Uneven tacking is used for general tacking, for edges that require less control during permanent stitching and for marking (marking stitches can be long and spaced far apart).

Uneven tacking: Like even tacking, these are short temporary stitches, about 6 mm long, but taken 2 or 3 cm apart.

Diagonal tacking consists of horizontal stitches taken parallel to each other and producing diagonal floats in between. It is used to hold or control fabric layers within an area during construction and pressing. Short stitches, taken close together, give more control than do longer stitches taken farther apart. The *short* diagonal tacking is used to hold seam edges flat during stitching or pressing; the *long* diagonal tacking, for such steps as holding underlining to garment fabric during construction.

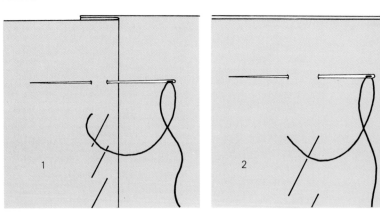

Diagonal tacking: Small stitches, taken parallel to each other, producing diagonal floats in between. When making the stitches, the needle points from right to left. For greater control, take short stitches (1), spaced close together. Where less control is needed, stitches can be longer (2), with more space in between them.

Slip tacking is a temporary, uneven slipstitch that permits precise matching of plaids, stripes, and some large prints at seamlines. It is also a practical way to tack intricately curved sections, or to make fitting adjustments from right side.

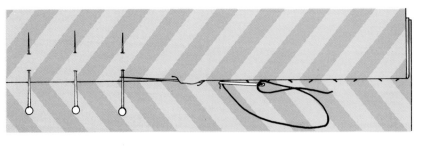

Slip tacking: Crease and turn under one edge along its seamline. With right sides up, lay the folded edge in position along the seamline of the corresponding garment piece, matching the fabric design; pin. Working from right to left and using stitches 6 mm in length, take a stitch through the lower garment section, then take the next stitch through fold of upper edge. Continue to alternate stitches in this way, removing pins as you go.

TACKING STITCHES (continued)

Blanket-stitch tacking is formed between two garment sections as, for example, a facing and a garment front. The blanket stitch is used, but differently from the way it is used to cover an edge. In tacking applications, it catches and joins *two* fabric layers and there is *more space* (about 2 to 5 cm) between the stitches.

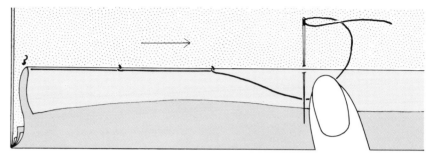

Blanket-stitch tacking: Work from left to right, with facing folded back and needle pointing toward you. Fasten thread in facing. Two to five centimetres to right, with needle passing over supply end of thread, take a small vertical stitch in interfacing or underlining, then through facing. Draw needle and thread through. Repeat at 2 to 5 cm intervals, allowing a slight slack between stitches.

Herringbone-stitch tacking is similar to blind hemming using a herringbone stitch. When used to tack, the stitches are more widely spaced, approximately 1 to 2 cm, and they are used to hold such garment sections as a facing to a front section.

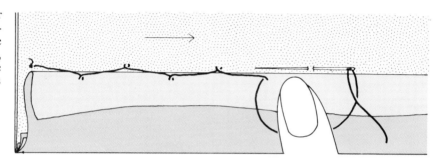

Herringbone-stitch tacking: Work from left to right, with facing folded back and needle pointing left. Fasten thread in facing. Two to five centimetres to right, take a small stitch in the interfacing or underlining. Pull needle and thread through. Take the next short stitch 1 to 2 cm to the right in the facing. Repeat sequence, allowing a slight slack between stitches.

Heavy-duty tacking is a very sturdy stitch that is used for joining areas of a heavy garment.

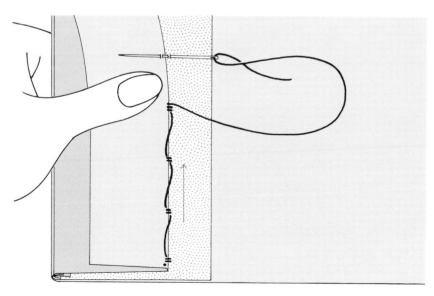

Heavy-duty tacking: Work from bottom to top, with the facing folded back and the needle pointing from right to left. Fasten thread in facing. Take a short stitch, catching only a few threads of interfacing or underlining and then facing. Draw needle and thread through; take one or two more stitches above first. Do not pull thread taut. Make the next and each succeeding set of stitches 2 to 5 cm above the set just completed.

TACKING STITCHES (continued)

Catchstitch is used for tacking together sections of lightweight garments. It is like the blind-hemming stitch except that the stitches are spaced farther apart.

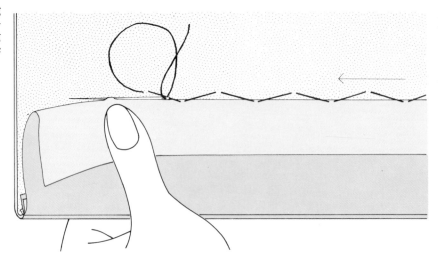

Catchstitch: Work from right to left, with facing folded back. Fasten thread in facing. Take one short horizontal stitch 1 cm ahead in the interfacing or underlining; then, 1 to 2 cm ahead of this stitch, take another short horizontal stitch in facing. Pull needle and thread through and repeat. Do *not* pull thread taut.

Cross-stitch tacking is used to tack folds in place, such as those found at the shoulder or centre back of a jacket or coat lining. Both decorative and functional, such tacking provides a degree of flexibility not possible with machine stitching.
Single cross-stitch tack is used in such areas as a facing edge, where only one spot needs to be tacked. Usually stitched several times.

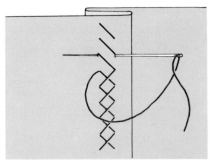

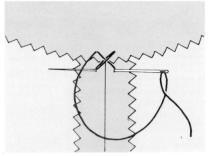

Cross-stitch tacking: Pin fold in position; tack in place with a series of cross stitches.
Single cross-stitch tack: Make a cross stitch over edge to be tacked (here a neck facing edge at shoulder seam), then make two or three more cross stitches, in the same place, over the first. (For basic cross stitch, see p. 137.)

TACKS
Certain hand stitches done during construction or for marking.
TACKS, CONSTRUCTION
Stitches used to join areas that must be held together without a seam, or as a reinforcement at points of strain.
Arrowhead tack is a triangular reinforcement tack stitched from the right side at such points of strain as the ends of a pocket.

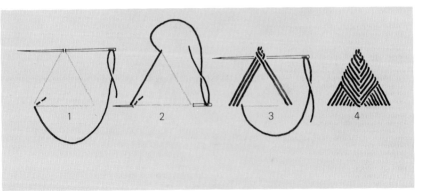

Arrowhead tack: Using chalk or thread, mark triangular arrowhead shape on right side of garment. Take two small running stitches *within* triangle and bring needle and thread out at lower left corner. At upper corner, take a small stitch from right to left (1). Draw thread through and insert needle at right corner, bringing it out at left corner barely *inside* previous thread (2). Draw thread through and repeat, using marked lines as guides and placing threads side by side until triangle is filled (3) and (4).

TACKS, CONSTRUCTION (continued)

Bar tack is a straight reinforcement tack used at such points of strain as the ends of a hand-worked buttonhole or the corners of a pocket.

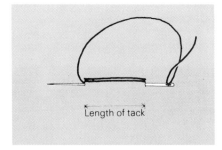

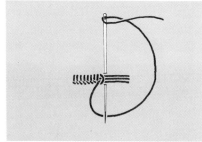

Bar tack: Fasten thread and bring needle and thread through to right side. Take two or three long stitches (the length that the bar tack is to be) in the same place. Catching the fabric underneath, work enough closely spaced blanket stitches around the thread to cover it. (For basic blanket stitch, see p. 136.)

French tack is made similarly to the bar tack. It is used to link two separate garment sections, such as the bottom edge of a coat to the bottom edge of its lining, while still allowing a certain amount of independent movement to the two sections that are linked.

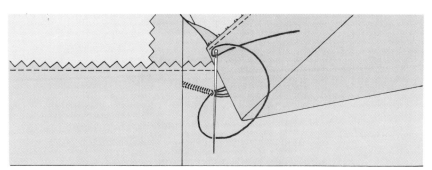

French tack: Take a small stitch through top of garment hem edge, then another small stitch directly opposite in the lining, leaving a 2 to 5 cm slack in the thread between stitches. Take similar stitches several times in the same places. Then work closely spaced blanket stitches over the threads. (For basic blanket stitch, see p. 136.)

TACKS, MARKING

Marking tacks are used to transfer construction details and matching points from the pattern to cut fabric sections. As alternatives to chalk or dressmaker's carbon paper, they can be more time-consuming, but in certain situations, marking tacks are necessary (see Marking methods).

Simplified tailor's tacks are basically uneven tacking stitches. They are best confined, as a general rule, to marking single layers of fabric; they are especially well suited to such markings as fold or centre lines.

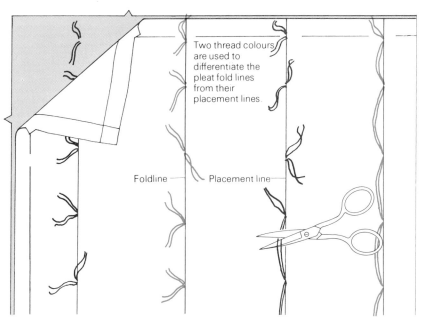

Two thread colours are used to differentiate the pleat fold lines from their placement lines.

Foldline — Placement line

Simplified tailor's tacks: Using a long length of double, unknotted thread, take a small stitch on pattern line through pattern and fabric. Pull needle and thread through, leaving a 3 cm thread end. Take similar stitches about every 5 to 8 cm, leaving thread slack in between. Cut threads at centre points between stitches and gently lift pattern off fabric, taking care *not* to pull out thread markings.

Glossary of hand stitches

TACKS, MARKING (continued)

Tailor's tacks are used to transfer individual pattern symbols, such as dots, to double layers of fabric.

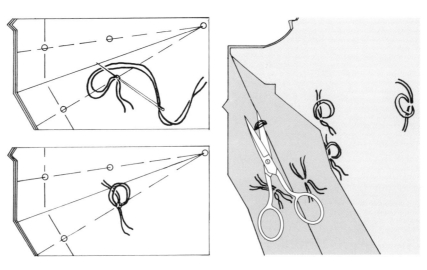

Tailor's tacks: With sharp end of needle, slit the pattern across the symbol to be marked. Using a long length of double, unknotted thread, take a small stitch through pattern and both layers of fabric at this point. Draw needle and thread through, leaving a 3 cm end. Take another stitch at the same point, leaving a 3 to 5 cm loop. Cut thread, leaving second 3 cm end. When all symbols have been marked in this way, lift pattern off fabric carefully to avoid pulling out thread markings. Gently separate the fabric layers to the limits of the thread loops, then cut the threads.

THREAD CHAIN   see Chain

TOPSTITCHING   see Backstitch, Saddle stitch

UNDERSTITCHING   see Backstitch

UNEVEN SLIPSTITCH   see Slipstitch

UNEVEN TACKING   see Tacking stitches

VERTICAL HEMMING   see Hemming stitches (flat)

WHIPSTITCH
This is a variation of the overhand stitch, the main difference being the angle at which the needle is held. Though generally used to topsew two finished edges, it can also hold a raw edge neatly against a flat surface.

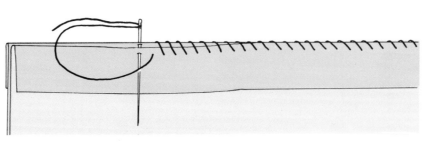

Whipstitch: Insert needle at rightangle and close to the edge, picking up only a few threads. Slanted floats will be produced between the tiny stitches. Space between stitches can be short or long, depending on the circumstances.

Machine facsimiles of hand stitches

ARROWHEAD TACK　　　**see Tacks** (construction)

BACKSTITCH

Used to secure the beginning and end of a row of machine stitching. Backstitching eliminates the need to tie thread ends, but it should not be used to secure stitching in such areas as the tapered end of a dart because reversing the stitching direction can sometimes distort the fabric.

Tying thread ends is another way of securing threads at the ends of a row of machine stitching. Although not as strong as backstitching, it is a neater finishing technique and is especially useful in securing such decorative work as topstitching.

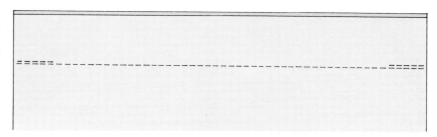

Backstitch: Made by utilising the reverse stitching mechanism, the backstitch can be produced by any machine. Position these stitches on top of, or just inside, those that form the seam. Avoid backstitching beyond the cut edge; this can result in fabric being pulled down into the needle-plate hole.

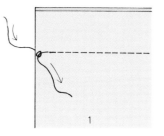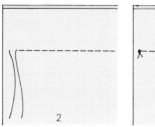

1　　2　　3

To tie thread ends, you must first bring the lower thread through to the other side of the fabric. Pull on upper thread to start lower thread (1), then pull it through completely (2). Tie threads together, using a square knot; trim away excess thread ends (3).

BAR TACK　　　**see Tacks** (construction)

BASTING　　　**see Tacking stitch**

BLIND-HEMMING STITCH

Referred to as the blindstitch, this zigzag stitch pattern is used primarily for blind hemming by machine (see Hems). It can also be used to stitch seams and to finish seams (see Seams).

How the fabric is folded for blind hemming differs according to the type of fabric used. The method shown on this page is used primarily for woollens, stretch fabrics, jerseys and other fabrics that do not fray. There is no need to fold under the hem edge; the hem allowance is left flat before being folded back for stitching. See next page for the folding method to use for all other fabrics.

Blind-hemming stitch (blindstitch): The stitch pattern usually consists of 4 to 6 straight stitches followed by 1 zigzag. Some machines form a blindstitch consisting of several *narrow* zigzag stitches followed by 1 *wider* zigzag. This stitch is suitable for stretch fabrics.

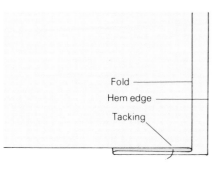

Fold
Hem edge
Tacking

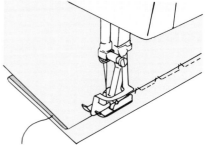

To blind-hem knits and fabrics that do not fray, first fold up hem allowance and hand-tack in position 1 cm below hem edge. With wrong side up, fold hem allowance under and position beneath foot with fold slightly to the left of the centre of the foot and the hem edge to the right of foot. Stitch so that the large zigzag stitch bites into the fold. Stitch length and width, and the positioning of the garment, should be tested before hem is stitched.

149

Machine facsimiles of hand stitches

BLIND-HEMMING STITCH (continued)

To blind-hem fabrics that fray, it is necessary to fold under the hem edge before stitching, as shown.

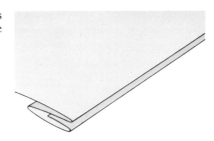

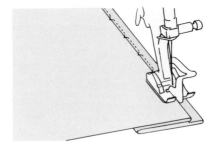

To blind-hem fabrics that fray, fold up hem allowance then fold under the hem edge as shown. This ensures that the raw edge of the hem is enclosed within the hem allowance. Stitch as explained on previous page.

The blindstitch can also be used to produce the effect of hand-prickstitching in a machine zipper application (see Zippers).

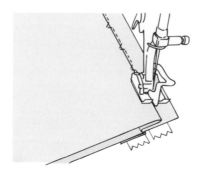

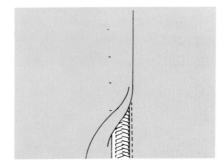

A prickstitch effect on a zipper placket is achieved by using the blindstitch in place of topstitching in the last step of a zipper application. Fold zipper placket under, letting one seam allowance extend. Using zipper foot positioned to the right of the needle, place placket under foot with fold toward the left. Stitch, placing the straight stitches on the seam allowance and letting zigzag catch the fold. It is best that seam allowance be wider than normal (about 2 cm) and zigzag stitch as narrow as possible. Test before applying to garment.

BUTTONHOLE STITCH

Machine stitching of buttonholes, whether automatic or manual, generally requires the use of a zigzag stitch. All machine-made buttonholes have two straight sides, and bar tacks are formed at each end.

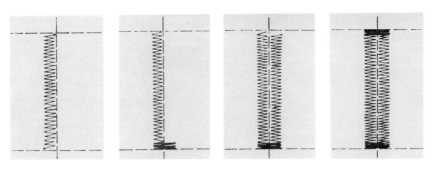

Machine-worked buttonholes are made with a zigzag stitch. Differences in how a buttonhole is formed lie in the mechanism by which buttonhole is produced and which steps are automatic. (See Machine-worked buttonholes.)

CHAINSTITCH

A series of interlocking stitches made from a single thread (needle thread), the chainstitch can be used for seaming and also as a thread chain for belt carriers and French tacks. When used to stitch on fabric, it looks like ordinary straight stitching from the top side and a series of interlocking loops on the underside. Unless

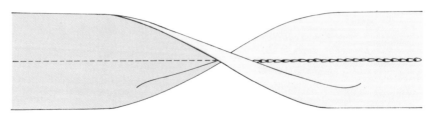

Chainstitch: This stitch is available on some modern machines. It is achieved through fitting a chainstitch needle plate. The upper thread twists around the empty bobbin case and the bobbin thread is not used.

CHAINSTITCH (continued)

secured, the stitches can easily be removed by pulling on the thread end. Because of this characteristic, the chainstitch can also be used as a temporary seaming stitch.

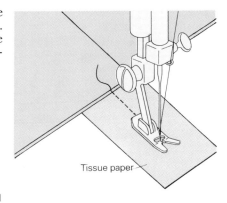

Tissue paper

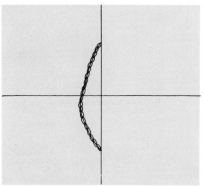

A thread chain is the most common use of the machine chainstitch. Start the chain on the garment, then stitch off the garment to the length required. (Sometimes an underlay of tissue paper is required when stitching off the garment.) Cut thread. To fasten, bring cut thread end through the last loop; remove paper and fasten end to garment by hand.

FAGGOTING STITCH

This is a stitch that is used for decorative joining of garment sections, leaving a space between the edges. The fabric edges must be folded back and positioned accurately to ensure that the original seamline, after faggoting, falls at the centre of the space between the edges. Suitable for faggoting: any stitch pattern that stitches equal distances to the right and left of the centre of the foot. Faggoting should not be applied to garment areas that must withstand strain during wear.

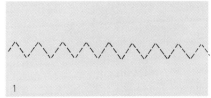

1

2

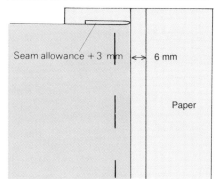

Seam allowance + 3 mm ← 6 mm →

Paper

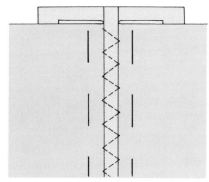

Faggoting stitches: Two stitch patterns that are well suited to faggoting are the multistitch zigzag (1) and the featherstitch (2). These stitches are built into many machines.

Faggoting: First test to determine stitch length and width. On paper, draw two parallel lines to represent the width of the stitch (this will also be width of space between the two folded edges). Fold back each seamline by half this width, then pin and tack each edge to paper along lines. Centre the opening under presser foot and stitch, being sure to catch each folded edge in stitching. (When you have done this stitch a few times, you may find that you no longer need to use the paper underlay).

FEATHERSTITCH

A decorative as well as functional practical stitch that can be used for faggoting, embroidery or quilting. Featherstitch, when set at the 0 stitch width, may also be used for the straight reverse stitch.

Featherstitch: A practical stitch that may be either built into the machine or produced by the insertion of a separate stitch pattern cam. Stitch length and width usually adjustable.

FRENCH TACK

see Tacks (construction)

Machine facsimiles of hand stitches

HEMSTITCHING

Decorative hemming process which is characterised by drawn threads or by a pattern created in the fabric through the use of a wing needle. Fully automatic machines have built-in hemstitching capabilities, others can produce hemstitching through the insertion of special cams.

If your machine fits neither of these categories, you can simulate the effect by drawing threads out of the fabric and zigzag stitching on either side (as shown at right), or by using a wing needle and zigzag stitch.

Best fabrics for hemstitching with a wing needle are very fine fabrics such as organza and lawn; for drawn-thread work, coarser fabrics such as linen and cotton are ideal.

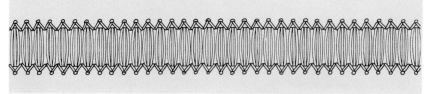

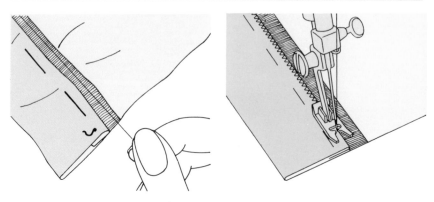

Hemstitching: This hemstitch can be produced by any zigzag machine by drawing out threads and finishing the edges with a zigzag stitch.

To hemstitch, first fold up hem allowance, then fold under hem edge and tack in place. Draw out threads of fabric above hem edge. Zigzag along both edges of the drawn-thread section, catching the folded-up hem and the drawn threads in the stitching.

Other decorative hemstitching can be produced by using a wing needle which makes large holes in the fabric. Some machines are capable of producing hemstitches such as the point de Paris stitch, Turkish hemstitch and Venetian hemstitch.

OVERCAST STITCH

Zigzag and other overedging stitches that will form stitches over the edge of the fabric can be used as overcast stitches. The most basic applications are formation of narrow seams and finishing of seams.

Overcast stitch: Basically the zigzag stitch, but can be any machine stitch that will form stitches over the edge of the fabric. Stitch length and width can range in size from short and narrow to long and wide. Position fabric so stitches will form over the edge, or stitch and then trim away excess fabric.

OVERHAND STITCH

see Overcast stitch

OVERLOCK STITCH

A series of stitches used to neaten seams and edges of fabrics. This over-edge stitch is not available on a sewing machine, but is made by an overlocker machine which trims the fabric edge, using two blades, and machine stitches in the same operation.

Overlock stitch: The looper on an overlocker machine moves to wrap thread around the fabric edge, forming neat loops which the needle thread anchors into the fabric. Three-, four- or five-thread machines can use multi-coloured threads for a decorative effect.

PADDING STITCHES
Stitches used to hold interfacing to such garment parts as under collar and lapel of a tailored garment. Machine padding stitches show on outside of sections they are applied to.

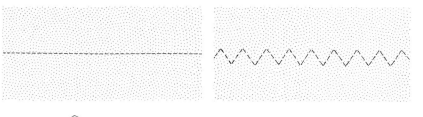

Padding stitches: Either plain straight stitch or multi-stitch zigzag stitch can be used for machine padding.

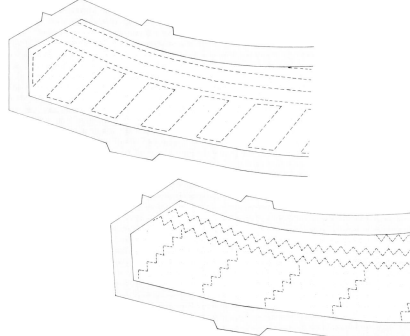

The straight stitch is available on all types of sewing machine.

The multi-stitch zigzag is included in many sewing machines.

PRICKSTITCH

see Blind-hemming stitch

TACKING STITCH
Machine tacking is a long straight stitch used to hold fabric layers together during fitting or permanent machine stitching. The longer tacking stitches can sometimes be used as a marking device. Machine tacking or marking should not be used, however, on fabrics that will be damaged by the piercing of the needle.

Tacking stitches: These are produced by setting the straight stitch at the longest available stitch length. On most machines the longest length available for plain tacking is 4 or 5 mm.

A longer tacking stitch is available on some more elaborate machines.

Machine facsimiles of hand stitches

TACKS, CONSTRUCTION

Arrowhead tack. A decorative triangular tack used to reinforce small areas of strain.

Bar tack. A straight tack used for reinforcement at such small areas of strain as the ends of a pocket.

Arrowhead tack: This tack is basically an individual unit of the arrowhead stitch pattern. The stitch pattern may be built into the machine or require use of a separate stitch-pattern cam.

Bar tack: This type of tack can be made with a wide zigzag stitch set at a very fine stitch length (1); or a medium-width zigzag set at a fine stitch length (2).

French tack. Free-swinging tack used to hold together two separate garment sections while allowing each to move independently of the other.

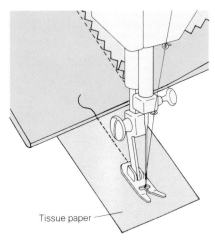

Tissue paper

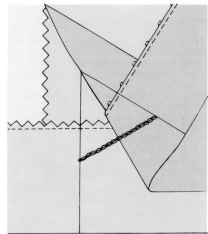

French tack: This tack is made with the chainstitch. A chainstitch capability is available on machines equipped with special fittings that permit the needle thread alone to make the entire stitch. Start the chain on one garment edge, then chainstitch off the garment to the desired length. It is recommended that an underlay of tissue paper be used when stitching off the garment. To secure stitches, cut thread and bring through last loop; remove paper and hand-fasten the free end of the chain to the other garment edge. An overlocker machine (serger) that has a rolled hem setting may also be used to make a thread chain. Fasten the chain to the garment by hand.

TACKS, MARKING

Tailor's tacks. These stitches, like the hand-made tailor's tacks that they derive from, are used to transfer pattern markings to fabric sections.

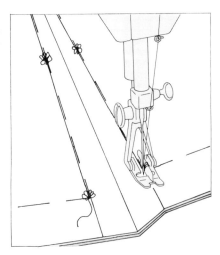

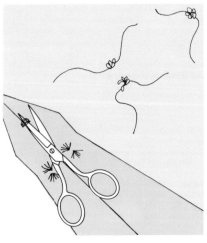

Tailor's tacks: Basically a wide zigzag stitch, this tack also relies on a special machine foot with a raised bar that allows the stitches to be held in an upright position. Very little tension is used. To tack, set machine for a very fine stitch length, or drop feed altogether. Stitch several times in the same place, then slide tack backwards off the bar of the foot. To remove paper pattern, cut top thread between tacks. Gently pull the fabric sections apart to limit of thread loops and cut threads.

THREAD CHAIN　　　　see Chainstitch

TOPSTITCHING
Machine stitches done from the right side of garment for decorative or functional reasons, sometimes both.

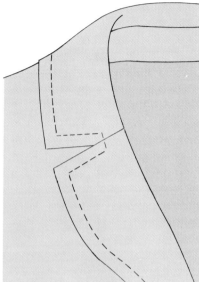

Topstitching: Most often it is the plain straight stitch, set at a longer-than-usual stitch length, that is used for topstitching, but in some situations a zigzag can be appropriate. It is sometimes advisable to tighten the top tension. The thread can be ordinary sewing thread or a heavier thread, such as silk buttonhole twist. A double thickness of regular thread can also be used in the needle. Thread colour can match or contrast, according to effect desired.

UNDERSTITCHING
A line of straight stitching applied along certain seamlines, such as neckline facing seams, to keep facing and seam allowances lying flat in a particular direction.

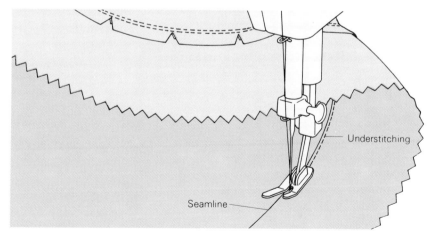

Understitching: This technique uses the straight stitch. The stitching is done from the right side, close to the seamline, and through all fabric layers and seam allowances. The seam allowances are first trimmed, graded, and clipped or notched, then pressed to the side where the understitching will be placed.

Understitching

Seamline

WHIPSTITCH　　　　see Overcast stitch

Directional stitching

Directional stitching is the technique of stitching a seam or staystitching a seamline in a particular direction. Its purpose is to support the grain and to prevent the fabric from changing shape or dimension in the seam area. The need for directional stitching arises especially with curved or angled edges, or when constructing garments from loosely woven or dimensionally unstable fabrics.

Stitching should be done with the grain whenever possible. An easy way to determine the correct stitching direction is to run your finger along the cut fabric edge. The direction in which the lengthwise and crosswise fabric yarns are pushed together is **with the grain.** The direction in which they are pushed apart is **against the grain.**

In general, if you stitch from the wider part of the garment to the narrower, you will be stitching with the grain. On edges where the direction of the grain changes, for example a long shaped seam, stitching should be done in the direction that stays longest with the grain. Illustrations at right show typical examples of grain direction on various garment sections. Also, stitching direction is sometimes indicated on the pattern seamline.

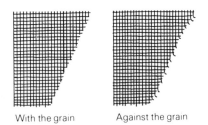

With the grain   Against the grain

Necklines are treated somewhat differently from the usual because the grain, over an entire neck edge, changes direction several times. It is advisable to staystitch each neck edge in two stages, according to the changes of grain direction peculiar to each. When seaming these edges, however, it is inconvenient—and unnecessary—to change stitching direction to follow the grain, especially if edges have been staystitched. Proper pressure and stitch tension will help to enhance the total effect of directional stitching.

The exception to the principles of directional stitching occurs with pile fabric. It is more important to stitch in the direction of the pile than that of the grain. For example, a skirt cut with the pile running down should be stitched accordingly, from waist to hemline.

Staystitching is a row of directional stitching, placed just inside certain seamlines, to prevent them from stretching out of shape during handling and garment construction. It also helps to support the grain at the seamline. The most important seamlines to staystitch are those that are curved or angled, as at a neckline or armhole. When working with a loosely woven or very stretchy fabric, it is advisable to staystitch all seamlines.

Staystitching is done immediately after removing the pattern from the cut fabric sections, and before any handling, such as pinning, tacking or fitting. It is done through a single layer of fabric, using a regular stitch length and matching thread, usually 1 cm from the cut edge. (On placket seamlines, place staystitching 6 mm from cut edge.) Stitch with the grain whenever possible and change direction whenever necessary.

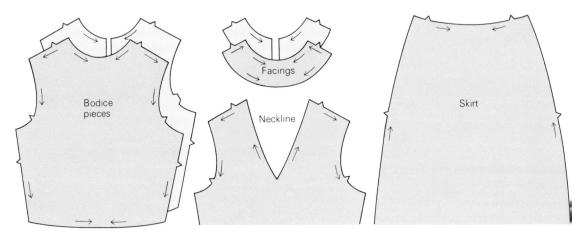

Facings

Bodice pieces

Neckline

Skirt

Staystitching for knits

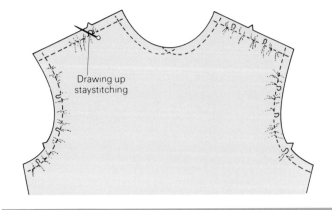

Drawing up staystitching

Staystitching for a knit is just as important as for a woven fabric, even though there is no grain direction. The principal purpose is to prevent stretching. After staystitching, lay pattern on top of each fabric section to see if it is the correct size and shape. If knit has stretched slightly, pull staystitching up gently with a pin at 5 cm intervals until fabric shape matches pattern. If knit has been pulled in too much, clip staystitching in a few places.

Forming a seam

The seam is the basic structural element of any garment and so must be formed with care. The machine should be adjusted correctly to the fabric for stitch length, tension and pressure. Thread should be properly matched to fabric. Most often, right sides of fabric are placed together; however, in some instances wrong sides are together. Although 1.5 cm (15 mm) is the standard seam width, always check your pattern for required width in special seaming situations. Seams should be backstitched at the beginning and end for reinforcement.

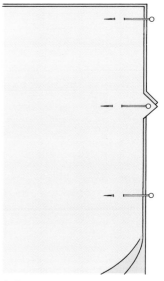
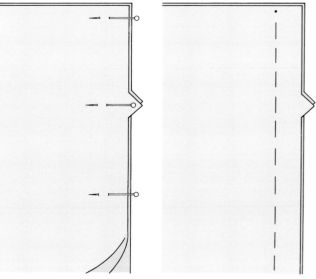
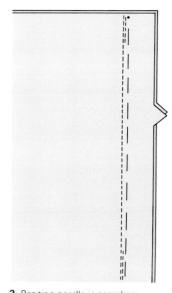
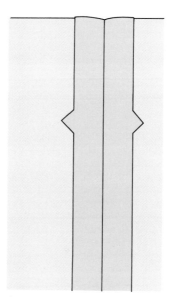

1. Pin seam at regular intervals, matching notches and other markings along seamline. Place pins perpendicular to seamline with tips just beyond seamline and heads toward seam edge.

2. Hand-tack close to the seamline, removing pins as you tack. As your skill increases, it may not always be necessary to hand-tack; with many simple seams, pinning and machining will be sufficient.

3. Position needle in seamline 1 cm from end; lower presser foot. Backstitch to end, then stitch forward on seamline, close to but not through the tacking. Backstitch 1 cm at end. If seam was pinned only, remove pins as you stitch. Clip threads close to stitching.

4. Remove tacking stitches. Unless instructions specify another pressing method, seams are first pressed flat in the same direction as they were stitched, then pressed open. Some seams may need clipping or notching before being pressed open.

Keeping seams straight

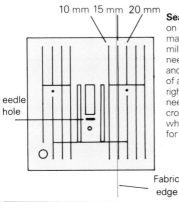

Seam guidelines are etched on the needle plate of many machines. These lines indicate millimetres (on some machines, needle plates are numbered and may be marked in eighths of an inch) and extend to the right, left, back and front of the needle. There may also be crosslines on the slide plate, which act as pivoting guides for stitching corners.

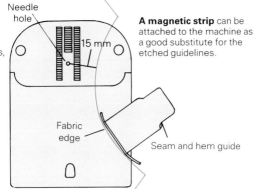

A magnetic strip can be attached to the machine as a good substitute for the etched guidelines.

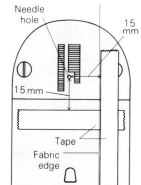

Masking or adhesive tape, placed at a distance of 15 mm from the needle hole, will provide the necessary guidance on a machine that has neither etched guidelines nor a separate gauge.

Seams

Plain seams

A straight seam is the one that occurs most often. In a well-made straight seam, the stitching is exactly the same distance from the seam edge the entire length of the seam. In most cases, a plain straight stitch is used. For stretchy fabrics, however, a tiny zigzag or special machine stretch stitch may be used.

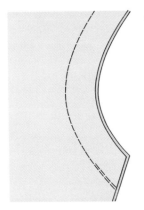

A curved seam requires careful guiding as it passes under the needle so that the entire seamline will be the same even distance from the edge. To achieve better control, use a shorter stitch length (2 mm) and slower machine speed.

A cornered seam needs reinforcement at the angle to strengthen it. This is done by using small stitches (1 to 1.5 mm) for 2 cm on either side of the corner. It is important to pivot with accuracy (see top right). When cornered seams are enclosed, as in a collar, the corners should be blunted so that a better point results when the collar is turned.

How to make cornered seams

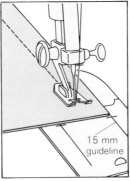 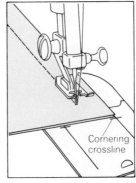 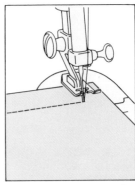 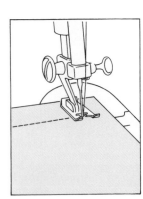

To stitch a cornered seam, line up edge of fabric with 15 mm guideline on needle plate. Stitch seam toward

corner, stopping with needle in fabric when edge reaches cornering crosslines on slide plate. Raise presser foot.

Pivot fabric on the needle, bringing the bottom edge of fabric in line with the 15 mm guideline on machine.

Lower foot and stitch in the new direction, keeping edge of fabric even with the 15 mm guideline.

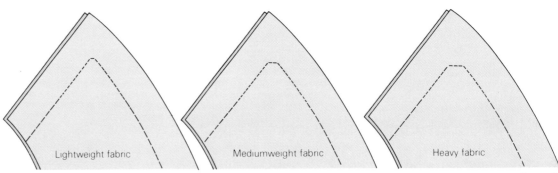

Lightweight fabric | Mediumweight fabric | Heavy fabric

Blunting the corner is the best way to achieve a well-formed point on an enclosed seam in, for example, a collar, cuff, or lapel. Take one stitch diagonally across the corner of a fine fabric, two on a medium one, three on heavy or bulky fabric.

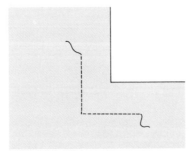 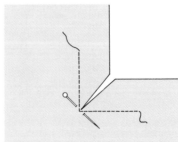 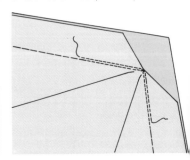

To join an inward corner with an outward corner or straight edge, first reinforce inward angle, stitching just inside seamline 2 cm on either side of corner.

Insert a pin diagonally across the point where stitching forms the angle. Clip exactly to this point, being careful not to cut past the stitches.

Spread the clipped section to fit the other edge; pin in position. Then, with clipped side up, stitch on the seamline, pivoting at the corner.

Additional seam techniques

You may need to take additional steps, other than pressing, with some seams if they are to look smooth and professional. Whether the steps are necessary or not depends upon the location and shape of the seam. The range of supplementary procedures is shown below. In some situations, one extra step will suffice; in others, however, it will take several—or even, as in the case of a faced neckline seam, *all* of them—to make a seam lie flat.

When more than one technique is involved, this is the appropriate progression: (1) trim, (2) grade, (3) clip or notch, (4) understitch.

A good pair of small sharp scissors is indispensable for most of these processes.

Fabric that does not fray can be trimmed closer than one that does. Keep clipping or notching to a minimum on loosely woven fabric. The thicker the fabric, the greater the need to reduce bulk.

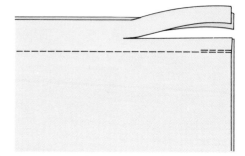

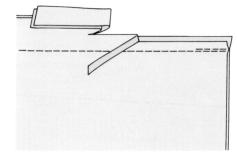

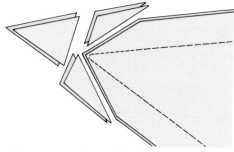

Trimming means cutting away some of the seam allowance. It is done when the full width of the seam allowances would interfere with fit (as in an armhole) or with further construction (as in a French seam). It is the preliminary step to grading (see the next drawing); seams are first trimmed to half their width before grading.

Grading (also called blending, layering or bevelling) is the cutting of seam allowances to different widths, with the seam allowance that will fall nearest the garment side cut the widest. It is recommended that seams be graded when they form an edge or are enclosed. The result is a seam that lies flat without causing a bulky ridge.

To trim a corner of an enclosed seam, first trim the seam allowances across the point close to the stitching, then taper them on either side. The more elongated the point, the farther back the seam allowance should be trimmed, so that when point is turned, there is no danger of seam allowances overlapping and causing bulk.

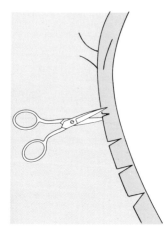

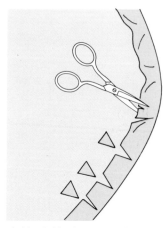

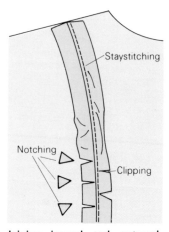

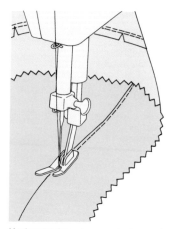

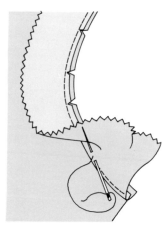

Clipping and notching are used on curved seams to allow them to lie smooth. *Clips are slits* cut into the seam allowance of convex, or *outward*, curves that permit the edges to spread. (With either technique, hold scissor points just short of seamline to avoid cutting past the stitching.) *Notches are wedges* cut from seam allowance of concave, or *inward*, curves; space opened by removal of fabric lets edge draw in. When clips and notches face one another, as in a princess seam (see next sketch), they should be staggered to avoid weakening seam.

Joining inward and outward curves: This is handled in a special way. First staystitch outward curve and clip seam allowance to stitching. With clipped edge on top, stitch seam. Notch inward curve to make seam lie smooth. Press seam open over tailor's ham.

Understitching keeps a facing and its seamline from rolling to garment right side; it is done after seam allowances have been trimmed and graded, then clipped or notched. Working from the right side, stitch through facing and seam allowances, staying close to seamline.

Hand understitching is desirable on a fine fabric or when machine stitching could distort a tailored shape. Use hand pickstitch; stitch through facing and seam allowances, as with machine understitching. Advisable on tailored collar as fabric control is more precise.

159

Seams

Seam finishes

A seam finish is any technique used to make a seam edge look neater and/or keep it from fraying. Though not essential to completion of the garment, it can add measurably to its life. Less tangibly, finished seams are a trim professional touch, in which you can take pardonable pride.

Three considerations determine the seam finish decision: (1) The type and weight of fabric. Does it fray excessively, a little, or not at all?

(2) The amount and kind of wear—and care—the garment will receive. If a garment is worn often, then tossed into the washing machine, the seams need a durable finish. On the other hand, if the style is a passing fad, or will be worn infrequently, you may elect not to finish the seam edges.

(3) Whether or not seams will be seen. An unlined jacket warrants the more elaborate bias-binding finish. A lined garment requires no finishing at all, unless the fabric frays a great deal.

Plain straight seams are finished after they have been pressed open. Plain curved or cornered seams are seam-finished right after stitching, next clipped or notched, then pressed open.

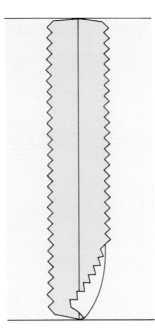

Pinked: Cut along edge of seam allowance with pinking shears. For best results, do not fully open shears or close all the way to the points. If fabric is crisp and lightweight, it is possible to trim two edges at once, before pressing seam open. Otherwise do one edge at a time. Pinking is attractive, but will not of itself prevent fraying.

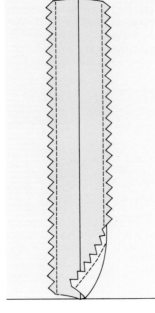

Stitched-and-pinked: Using a short stitch, place a line of stitching 6 mm from edge of seam allowance, then pink edge. This finish can be used where pinking is desired, and it will minimise fraying.

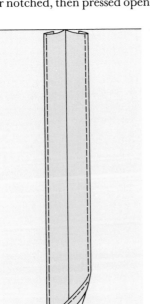

Turned-and-stitched (also called clean-finished): Turn under edge of seam allowance 3 mm (6 mm if fabric frays easily); press. Stitch along edge of fold. It may be helpful, on difficult fabrics or curved edges, to place a row of stitching at the 3 or 6 mm foldline to help turn edge under. This is a neat, tailored finish for lightweight to mediumweight fabrics, and is suitable for an unlined jacket.

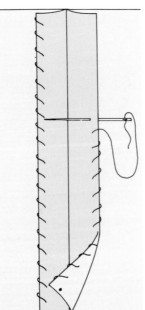

Hand-overcast: Using single thread, make overcast stitches at edge of each seam allowance slightly more than 3 mm in depth and spaced 6 mm apart. Do not pull thread too tight. Use this method when a machine finish is impractical or a hand finish is preferred.

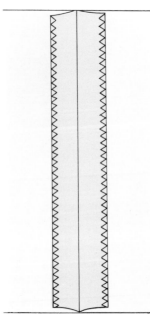

Zigzagged: Trim seam allowance. Set stitch for medium width and short (about 1.5 mm) length. Stitch on edge of seam allowance. This is one of the quickest and most effective ways to finish a fabric that frays. If fabric is lightweight and frays very easily, turn the seam allowance edge under after trimming and zigzag over the turned edge. A zigzagged finish *can* be used on a knit, but care must be taken not to stretch the seam edge or it will ripple.

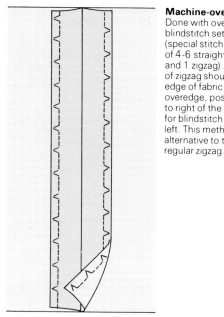

Machine-overedged:
Done with overedge or blindstitch setting (special stitch pattern of 4–6 straight stitches and 1 zigzag). Point of zigzag should fall on edge of fabric. If using overedge, position fabric to right of the needle; for blindstitch, to the left. This method is an alternative to the regular zigzag.

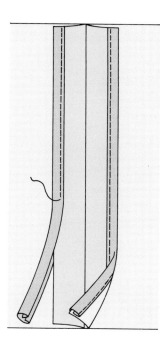

Bias-bound: Trim notches from seam edge; wrap bias binding around it. (Use ready-made binding, or cut your own from lining or underlining fabric.) Stitch close to edge of top fold, catching underneath fold in stitching. Bias binding is especially good for finishing seams in an unlined jacket or coat.

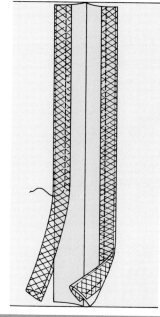

Net-bound: Cut 2 cm-wide strips of nylon net or tulle; fold in half lengthwise, slightly off centre. Trim notches from seam edge and wrap net around edge with wider side underneath. From top, edgestitch narrow half of binding, catching wider side underneath in the stitching. This is an inconspicuous and appropriate finish for delicate fabrics, such as velvet or chiffon.

Overlocker (serger) finish:
A three-, four- or five-thread overlocker machine (serger) can be used to neaten seams on all fabrics. An overlocker trims the edge of the fabric, and it stitches by looping threads to neatly encase the edge of the fabric, all in one operation.

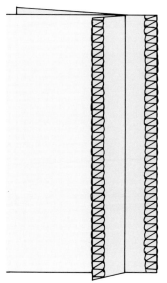

In knitted fabrics the neatening of edges reduces the curl on seam allowances. Seams are also sewn and oversewn with overlock (serger) stitch. In loosely woven fabrics, such as brocade, linen and towelling, overlocking reduces the tendency to fray.

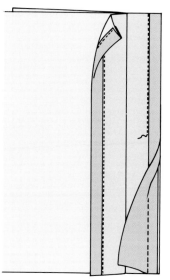

Hong Kong: An alternative to the bias bound finish, this is especially suitable for heavy fabrics. Proceed as follows. Cut 4 cm wide bias strips from lightweight fabric that matches garment fabric, or use purchased bias binding and press it open. With right sides together, stitch bias strip to seam allowance, 6 mm from edge. Then turn bias over the edge to the underside and press. From the right side, stitch in the crevice of the first stitching. Trim the unfinished edge of the bias.

Seams

Self-enclosed seams

Self-enclosed seams are those in which all seam allowances are contained within the finished seam, thus avoiding the necessity of a separate seam finish. They are especially appropriate for visible seams, which occur with sheer fabrics and in unlined jackets. Also, they are ideally suited to garments that will receive rugged wear or much laundering. Proper trimming and pressing are important steps if the resulting seams are to be sharp and flat rather than lumpy and uneven.

Precise stitching is essential, too. See Topstitching of seams (page 164) for helpful suggestions.

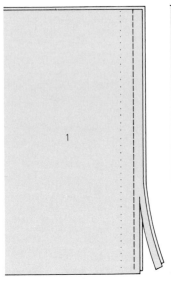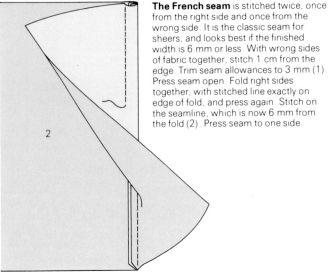

The French seam is stitched twice, once from the right side and once from the wrong side. It is the classic seam for sheers, and looks best if the finished width is 6 mm or less. With wrong sides of fabric together, stitch 1 cm from the edge. Trim seam allowances to 3 mm (1). Press seam open. Fold right sides together, with stitched line exactly on edge of fold, and press again. Stitch on the seamline, which is now 6 mm from the fold (2). Press seam to one side.

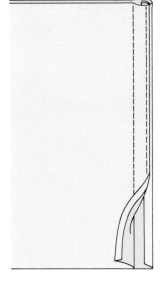

The mock French seam can be used in place of the French seam, especially on curves where a French seam is difficult to execute. With right sides of fabric together, stitch on the seamline. Trim seam allowances to 1.2 cm. Turn in the seam edges 6 mm and press, matching folds along the edge. Stitch these folded edges together. Press seam to one side.

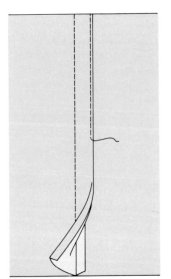

The flat-felled seam is very sturdy, and so is often used for sports clothing and children's wear. Since it is formed on the right side, it is also decorative, and care must be taken to keep widths uniform, within a seam and from one seam to another. With wrong sides of fabric together, stitch on the seamline. Press seam open, then to one side. Trim the inner seam allowance to 3 mm. Press under the edge of outer seam allowance 6 mm. Stitch this folded edge to the garment. Be careful to press like seams in the same direction (e.g., both shoulder seams to the front). A felling foot or jeans foot is available for some machines. This foot rolls the fabric under as it stitches.

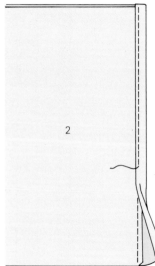

The self-bound seam works best on lightweight fabrics that do not fray easily. Stitch a plain seam. Trim one seam allowance to 3 mm. Turn under the edge of the other seam allowance 3 mm and press (1). Turn and press again, bringing the folded edge to the seamline, so that the trimmed edge is now enclosed. Stitch close to fold as shown in (2), as near as possible to first line of stitching.

Cord 18
Zigzag stitching 30–33
Overhand stitch 141
Running stitch 142

Shell tucks

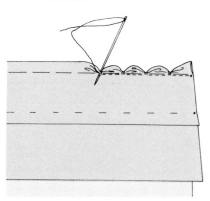

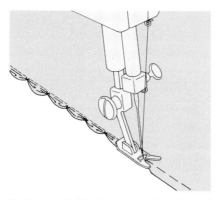

To form a shell tuck by hand, tack, then sew a narrow tuck. Use a running stitch, but every 1 cm take a few overhand stitches in place to scallop tuck. Or machine-stitch tuck; then do overhand stitches, passing thread through tuck between scallops.

To form a shell tuck by machine, first tack a 3 mm tuck. Set machine for the blindstitch. Place tuck under foot with fold to left of needle so that the zigzag stitch will form over the fold and scallop the tuck. Test first for proper stitch length, width and tension.

Corded tucks

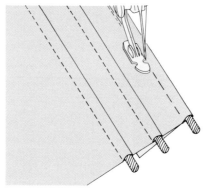

To make a corded, or piped, tuck, fold the tuck, positioning cord inside along the fold. Tack. Using a zipper foot, stitch close to cord. Test this procedure before tucking garment to make sure that the size of the cord is right for the width of the tuck.

Cross tucks

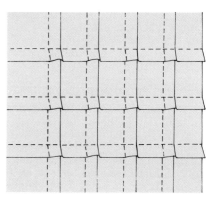

To form cross tucks, first stitch all the lengthwise tucks and press them in one direction. Then form the second, or crossing, set of tucks at right angles to the first, taking care to keep the first set of tucks facing downward as you stitch. Press carefully.

Adding tucks to plain garments

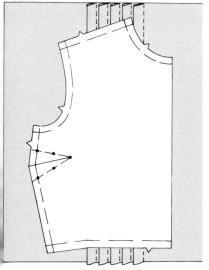

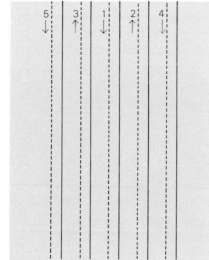

Tucks can be added to any plain garment *before it is cut.* Tuck fabric first, then strategically position pattern over tucks and cut out section. Required extra fabric width is equal to twice the width of a tuck times the total number of tucks being added to the garment piece.

Stitch the tucks in the order shown above. Start in the *centre* of the piece of fabric and stitch the first tuck downwards on the lengthwise grain. Alternate stitching direction for rest of tucks as shown. This way, the fabric does not ripple and tucks will be straight.

Dart or released tucks

Dart tucks, sometimes also called released tucks, are used to control fullness and then release it at a desired point, such as the bust or hips. They can be formed on the inside or outside of the garment; fullness can be released at either or both ends. Sometimes the tuck is stitched across the bottom. Dart tucks may be stitched on the straight grain, or, in some instances, the stitching lines may be curved to build in a certain amount of shaping. Care must be taken, especially when stitching lines are curved, to match them accurately. Reinforce the stitches by tying threads or backstitching. Press carefully to avoid creasing folds.

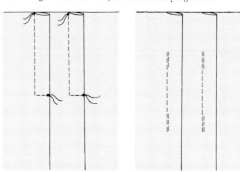

Pleats

How pleats are formed

Pleats are folds in fabric that provide controlled fullness. Pleating may occur as a single pleat, as a cluster, or around an entire garment section. Basically, each pleat is folded along a specified line, generally called the **foldline,** and the fold aligned with another line, the **placement** line (see illustrations at right). Patterns will vary as to what these lines are actually called and how or whether they appear on the pattern.

Most pleats are formed by folding a continuous piece of fabric onto itself. The exception is a pleat with a separate underlay stitched at the back. Pleats can be folded in several different styles (see below), the most common being the **knife pleat, box pleat, and inverted pleat. A pleat with an underlay** is always an inverted pleat. Such variations as **accordion** and **sunray pleats** are difficult to achieve at home and are best done by a commercial pleater.

Pleat folds can be soft or sharp, depending on how they are pressed, but any pleat will hang better if it is folded on the straight grain, at least from the hipline down.

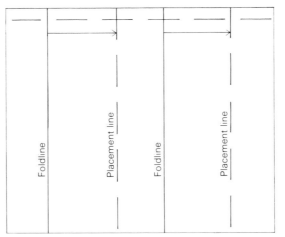

Though pattern markings vary, each pleat requires a foldline and a placement line or other marking to which it is brought. Arrows showing folding direction may also appear. Sections to be pleated are usually cut as a single layer.

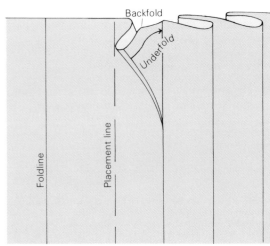

Each pleat is folded along its foldline, then brought over to align with its placement line. The folded section between fold and placement lines is called the pleat **underfold**; its fold is referred to as the **backfold** of the pleat.

Types of pleat

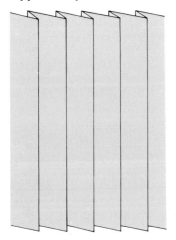

Knife pleats have one foldline and one placement line; all the folds are turned in the same direction. Some garments may have one cluster facing one way and another facing the opposite way.

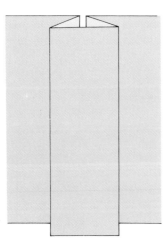

Box pleats have two foldlines and two placement lines; the two folds of each pleat are turned away from one another. The backfolds in box pleats are facing and may meet, but it is not necessary.

Inverted pleats have two foldlines and a common placement line. The two folds of each pleat are turned toward each other and in this case they must meet. The backfolds face away from each other.

Pleat with separate underlay: An inverted pleat in appearance, but constructed with a separate underlay that forms underside of pleat. In place of usual two backfolds, there are two seams.

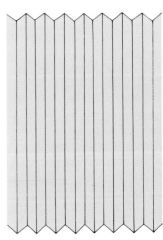

Accordion pleats are very narrow pleats of uniform width resembling the bellows of an accordion. Front folds stand slightly away from the body, giving flared effect. Best done by a commercial pleater.

Fabric considerations

Almost any type of fabric can be pleated provided that the right pleating techniques and finishes are employed. These are some of the considerations to bear in mind when choosing a fabric for pleating.

Pleat folds may be either soft or sharp. The fabric best suited for sharply folded pleats is one that will crease easily, is smooth and crisp, light to medium in weight, and firmly woven. Gabardine is a typical example. The fabric can be made of almost any fibre. Some synthetics, such as the acrylics, will resist creasing enough to make pleating difficult, but not impossible. Knitted fabrics, too, are generally difficult to crease, especially the heavier, bulkier knits.

Consider, too, whether the garment will be laundered or dry-cleaned. Either cleaning process can remove sharp pleats, but when a garment is professionally dry-cleaned it is automatically re-pressed in the process. Laundering at home will necessitate re-forming and pressing the pleats yourself each time the garment is washed. This should not discourage use of a fabric you like; if each fold is **edgestitched** (see p. 183), the folds will stay in shape and in place through any type of cleaning. **Topstitching** can be used to keep pleats in position in the hip-to-waist area (see pp. 182–183).

Another possibility is to have the fabric, or the finished garment, professionally pleated. Commercial pleaters can apply a finish that makes pleats truly permanent. Elaborate pleats, such as accordion pleats, can only be made successfully by a professional pleater. Consult pleaters in your locality for the types of pleats they offer, the cost, and the amount and type of fabric required. Also check whether or not the fabric will need to be prepared in any way.

For soft, unpressed pleats, almost any fabric is suitable. The best choices are those that are fluid and will fall into graceful folds. Any material that cannot be sharply pleated is a likely candidate for soft pleats. With thick, spongy fabrics, soft pleats are usually the only possibility.

To be sure a fabric will pleat as you want it to, it is wise to make several test pleats before pleating the garment. It is often worth testing edgestitching or topstitching as well, to see whether these techniques will help. If you find that the pleats do not hang properly, consult page 187.

Pleat size and fabric weight should also be co-ordinated. Lightweight fabrics usually pleat well into any size and type of pleat. Heavier fabrics should generally be limited to pleats that are not too deep and have ample space between them.

Pleats hang better and hold their shape longer if they are folded on the straight, preferably length-wise grain, at least from the hip down. If the garment is shaped to fit the body from the hip up, it will be impossible to maintain the straight grain in this area. Before cutting the garment out, be sure to position the fabric on grain. Take special care to square the grain of a woven stripe or plaid so that the fabric's horizontal lines will square with its vertical lines after the pleats are formed. If the fabric is a printed stripe or plaid, be sure that it is printed on grain; if it is even slightly out of true, do not use the fabric for pleating.

When marking pleat lines, it is sometimes better to use the pattern just to locate these lines and then, with the pattern removed, thread-mark the lines, following the grain with your eye.

An exception to the use of the lengthwise grain would be a fabric with a border print along one selvage. To achieve the desired effect, it may have to be positioned on the crosswise grain. It might also be possible to pleat a plaid on the crosswise grain, which could reduce the fabric requirements.

Underlinings are generally not recommended for a pleated garment, especially if it is being pleated all around. This is because it is extremely difficult to keep the fabric layers together along all of the folds. If an underlining should be necessary, carefully match and tack it to the fashion fabric along all of the pleat lines before folding. It will be a further help if all of the folds are edgestitched after the pleats have been formed. If there are only one or two pleats in the entire garment, edgestitching may be unnecessary.

A pleated garment may be lined, but the lining itself should not be pleated and should in no way interfere with the movement of the pleats. To retain the desired swing, the lining can be a half lining, that is, one that extends to just below the fullest part of the hips. It can also be a full-length lining, extending to garment hem, but with side seams left open far enough up to allow movement.

If there is no pattern piece for the lining, you can make it yourself in two ways. With one method, you first pleat the pattern and then cut out the lining from the pleated-down pattern, following the shape of its outer edge. The other way is to use a plain A-line skirt pattern to cut out the lining. Bottom edge can be hemmed or seam-finished. The turned-and-stitched finish (see Seam finishes) is usually sufficient for a lining.

Pleat finishes

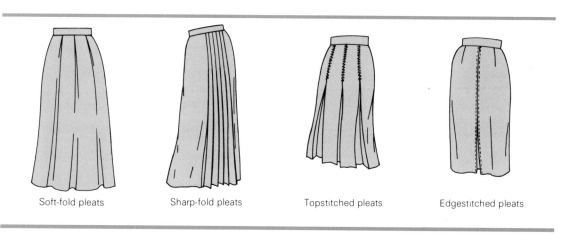

Soft-fold pleats   Sharp-fold pleats   Topstitched pleats   Edgestitched pleats

Pleats

Pleating methods

Pleats can be formed from either the right side or the wrong side of the fabric. The method will depend on the fabric, the type of pleat being formed, and the pattern being used. If the fabric has a definite motif that must be followed in order to achieve a particular effect, it is best to mark and form the pleats from the right side. If the pleat is a type that is to be stitched on the inside from the hip to the waist, it will be easier to mark and form the pleats from the wrong side.

Some patterns may also have certain seaming requirements that will make it necessary to match and stitch the pleats from the wrong side. This will be the case, for example, when you are constructing a pleat with a separate underlay.

In pressing pleats, use a press cloth whenever possible. If soft pleats are desired, press lightly if at all; if pleats will be sharp, use steam to help set the creases. If you want sharper pleats, dampen press cloth, press, then allow pleats to dry thoroughly before moving them. To help maintain folds during further construction, do not remove the tacking stitches holding pleats until necessary.

Pleats formed from the right side

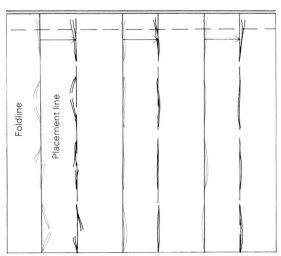

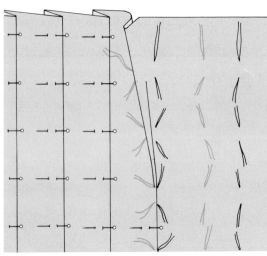

1. With pattern pinned to right side of fabric, mark each fold and placement line with simplified tailor's tacks. Use one thread colour for foldlines, another for placement lines. Take small stitches every 7 cm, leaving thread loose between them. Before removing pattern, clip thread between stitches.

2. Remove pattern carefully to avoid pulling out thread markings. Working from right side, fold fabric along a foldline; bring fold to its placement line. Pin pleat through all thicknesses in the direction it will be worn. Do the same for each pleat, removing thread markings as you pin.

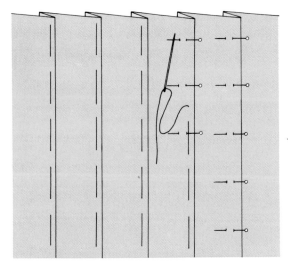

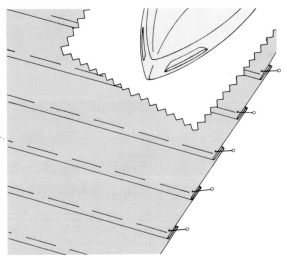

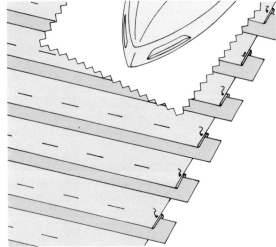

3. Tack each pleat close to the foldline through all thicknesses. Remove pins as you tack. Tack with spun polyester thread; it leaves the fewest indentations in the fabric after pressing. This tacking should be retained as far into further garment construction as possible.

4. With fabric right side up, position a group of pleats over ironing board. (Support rest of garment during pressing.) Using a press cloth, press each pleat. For soft pleats, press lightly; for extra sharp pleats, dampen the press cloth and let pleats dry before moving them.

5. With garment wrong side up, press pleats again, using press cloth. If backfolds leave ridges during pressing, remove them by first gently pressing beneath each fold; then insert strips of heavy paper beneath folds and press again. Ridges can also be pressed out from the right side.

Pleats formed from the wrong side

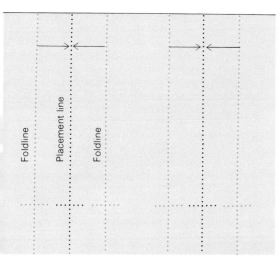

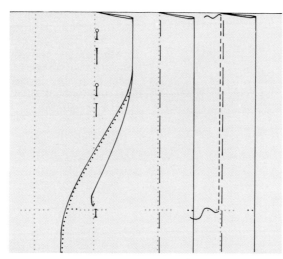

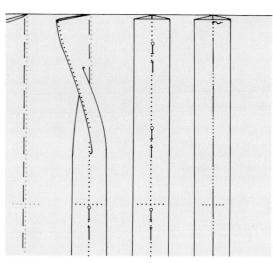

1. Before removing pattern, mark, on the wrong side of fabric, all foldlines and placement lines. Choose a method of marking that will show on but not mar the fabric (carbon paper is illustrated). Use one colour (thread or carbon paper) to mark foldlines; another to mark placement lines.

2. Working from wrong side, if *knife* or *box* pleats, bring together and match each foldline to its placement line; if *inverted* pleats (shown), bring together and match each set of foldlines. Pin and tack through both thicknesses. If pleats will be stitched, as from hip to waist, do this now.

3. Position *inverted* pleats in the direction they are to be worn. This is done by spreading open the underfold of each pleat and aligning placement line to matched foldlines. Pin, then tack in place with spun polyester thread, through all thicknesses for the entire length of each pleat.

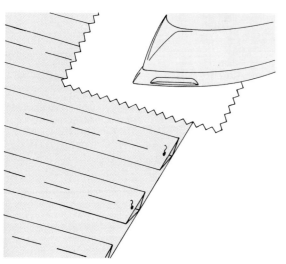

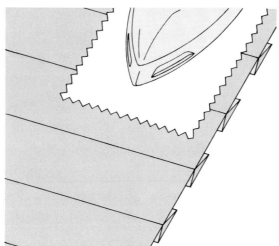

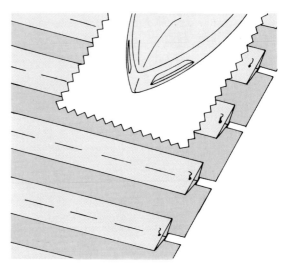

4. With wrong side up, using a press cloth, press all of the pleats in the direction they will be worn. When they are *knife* pleats, all of the backfolds should be turned in one direction; the backfolds of *box* pleats will be facing each other; *inverted* pleats are pressed as shown above.

5. Turn garment to right side and, using a press cloth, press again. Be sure that all the pleats are facing in the direction that they will be worn. The tacking that is holding the pleats in position should be left in place as long as possible during the rest of garment construction.

6. To remove ridges that may have been formed by the backfolds, turn garment to wrong side and press again, but using these techniques: first press gently under each fold; then insert strips of heavy paper under the folds and press again. These procedures can also be used on right side.

181

Pleats

Pleat with separate underlay

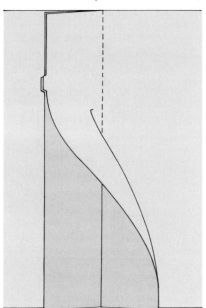

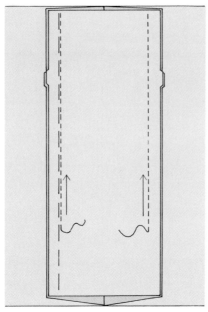

1. To form a pleat with a separate underlay, first bring together and match foldlines. Tack. If the foldlines are to be partially stitched together, do this step next; then remove tacking from stitched area only. Press pleat extensions open along foldlines.

2. With right sides together, position pleat underlay over the pleat extensions, matching markings; tack along each seam. Beginning 15 cm up from the hem edge, stitch each side of the pleat underlay to each pleat extension. Remove tacking and press seam flat as stitched.

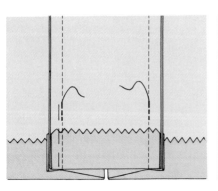

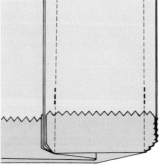

3. Remove tacking holding foldlines together. Hem skirt and pleat extensions separately from underlay. After hemming, match, retack, and stitch the unstitched part of the underlay to the pleat extensions. Stitch from hem edge up to previous stitching.

4. Press seams flat as stitched. Finish seam allowances of underlay and extension so their edges will not show beyond hem edge: first trim diagonally across the corners of all seam allowances; then whipstitch together each set of seam allowances within the hem area.

Topstitching and edgestitching pleats

Topstitching and edgestitching are two valuable techniques for helping pleats to lie and hang as they should. **Topstitching,** though primarily decorative, serves also to hold pleats in place in the hip-to-waist area. It is done through all thicknesses of the pleat. **Edgestitching** is applied along the fold of a pleat both to maintain the fold and to give it a sharper crease. It is done after the hem is completed.

When using either of these techniques, stitch from the bottom of the garment up toward the top. When applying both techniques to the same pleat, edgestitch first.

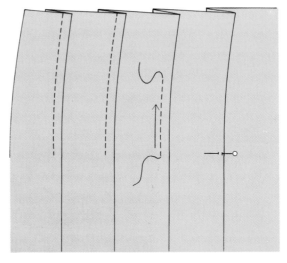

To topstitch knife pleats in the hip-to-waist area, first pin-mark each pleat at the point where the topstitching will begin. Then, with the garment right side up, stitch through all thicknesses, along the fold, from the pin to the top of pleat. Bring thread ends to underside and tie.

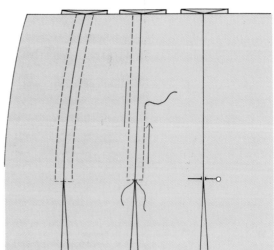

Topstitch inverted pleats on both sides of the matched foldlines. Pin-mark each pleat where the topstitching will begin. With garment right side up, insert needle between foldlines at marked point. Take two or three stitches across the pleat, pivot, then stitch along foldline to waist. Beginning again at the mark, stitch across pleat in opposite direction, pivot, then stitch to the waist. Bring all threads through to the underside and tie.

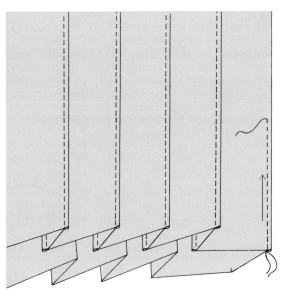

To edgestitch pleat folds, extend the pleat and stitch, through the two thicknesses, as close to the fold as possible. Stitch from the finished hem edge up. Bring thread ends through to underside and tie. Both folds can be edgestitched, as shown, or just outer or inner folds if that is more suitable.

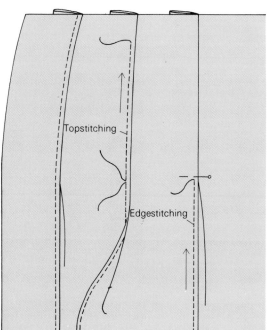

To edgestitch *and* topstitch: Folds are first edgestitched up to the point where the topstitching will begin. If pleat has already been stitched together in the hip-to-waist area, remove a few stitches so that the edgestitching can extend to exact hip point where the topstitching will begin. Starting at that point precisely, topstitch from hip to waist through all thicknesses. Bring all thread ends to underside and tie.

Staying pleats

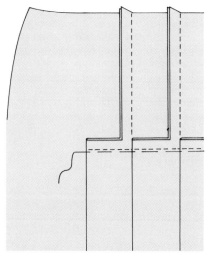

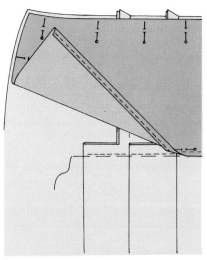

Separate stay can be added to give support to stitched-down pleats in which top part of underfold has been eliminated by pattern piece. Seam each pleat down, then across underfold; tack in wearing direction.

Cut stay as wide as garment part and deep as area to be stayed plus seam allowances; turn-and-stitch lower edge. Tack in place at top; slipstitch lower edge to tops of underfolds (other edges will be caught in seams).

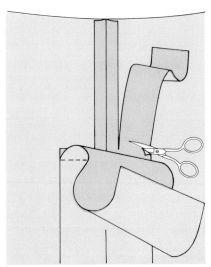

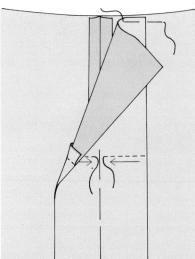

Self-stay can be formed on a stitched-down inverted pleat. First stitch down pleat. Then, in two steps, stitch across both sides of underfold. Slit along backfolds to stitching; trim fabric behind to 1.5 cm from stitching, as shown.

Bring the top of the trimmed underfold back up to top edge of garment. Carefully align this self-stay with the rest of the pleat and tack it in place along top. This top edge will be caught into the seam.

183

Pleats

Hemming pleated garments

Depending upon the type of pleats, the hem in a pleated garment is sewn sometimes before and sometimes after pleats are formed.

Hemming before pleating is easier, but it is appropriate only when the pleats are all-around and straight, or when the top portion does not require seaming or extensive fitting. If shortening is necessary after hemming, garments pleated as described can be raised from the top without distorting the pleats. The amount that can be *added* after

hemming is very limited: only half the width of the top seam allowance is available for the purpose.

Hemming after pleating is the more common order of procedure and is necessary when there is only a single pleat or cluster; when the pleat is formed with a separate underlay; or, when, on an all-round-pleated garment, the pleats are seamed or fitted at the top. Sometimes, especially with heavier fabrics, it may be helpful to press in the pleat folds to within 20 cm of the hem edge, complete the hem,

then press in the pleat folds the rest of the way.

Seams within a hem are treated in different ways according to where the seam is—that is, whether at a flat part or at the backfold of the pleat—and whether the seam is stitched before or after hemming (see below). Most seams are stitched before hemming, but, in some cases, such as a garment that is hemmed before pleating, or a pleat formed with a separate underlay, there will be one or two seams to be stitched after hemming.

Handling seam allowances in hem area

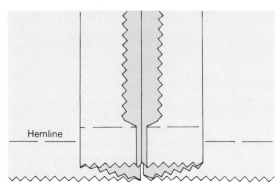

A seam that is at a flat part of the pleat is first pressed open and then trimmed to half its width from the hem edge to the hemline. This is a grading technique that will eliminate unnecessary bulk from the hem in this area.

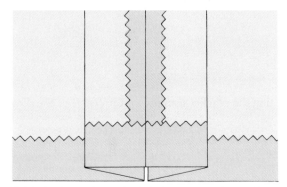

Finish the hem edge and stitch the hem in place, using a method that is suitable for the fabric (see Hemming). When turning up hem, make certain that seamlines are matched and seam allowances are in the pressed-open position.

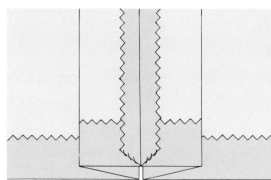

If this seam is stitched after hemming, it is treated differently. First press seam open, then trim diagonally across each corner at the bottom of the seam allowances. Whipstitch these trimmed edges flat to the hem.

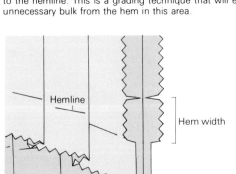

A seam that is at the backfold of a pleat is also first pressed open and trimmed to half width from hem edge to hemline. Then, so that seam allowances can turn in different directions, clip into them a hem width above hemline.

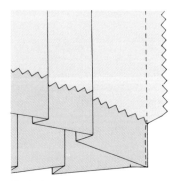

Finish the hem edge and stitch hem in place, using a suitable hemming method. To keep backfold creased, edgestitch close to the fold, from the hemline up, to meet the seam at the point where it was clipped. Secure thread ends.

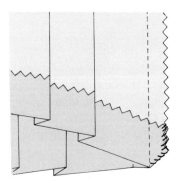

If this seam is stitched after hemming, first press seam flat as stitched. Then trim diagonally across both corners at bottom of seam allowances. Whipstitch together the trimmed edges, then rest of hem area seam allowances.

Estimating amount of fabric needed

Fabric needs for an all-around-pleated plaid skirt depend mainly on **width of fabric, desired skirt length,** and **hip measurement.** Fabric width and hip measurement are simple, but skirt length takes some calculating. It is the *finished length* plus *top seam and hem allowances.* You will probably need two to three lengths for one skirt. To each extra length, you must add a full horizontal motif to allow for matching. Based on the premise that the unpleated circumference should be about two and one-half to three times the hip measurement, minimum requirements are *two* lengths of 140-cm-wide fabric and *three* of 90 or 115 cm wide fabric. For 92 cm hips, for example, 270 cm would be roughly sufficient. To achieve it, you would have to join *two* skirt lengths of 140 cm or *three* of 90 or 115 cm fabric. Larger hips might require another whole length, though all of it might not be used.

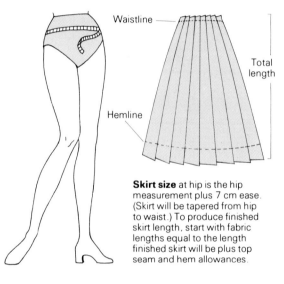

Skirt size at hip is the hip measurement plus 7 cm ease. (Skirt will be tapered from hip to waist.) To produce finished skirt length, start with fabric lengths equal to the length finished skirt will be plus top seam and hem allowances.

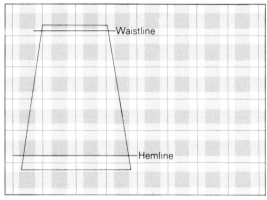

Plan each skirt length so that the hemline is located, on each length, at the same dominant horizontal motif or stripe. When cutting out additional lengths, be sure to include an additional horizontal motif to allow for matching all the lengths horizontally to the first length.

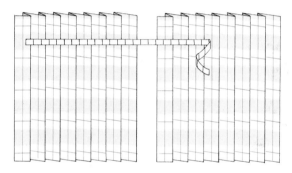

Cut lengths to match horizontally *and* repeat vertical progression exactly; slip-tack lengths together. Locate seams, especially placket seam, at centre of underfold for inverted or box pleats (zipper, centred or invisible); at backfold for knife pleats (special lapped application, p. 185).

Single or cluster pleats

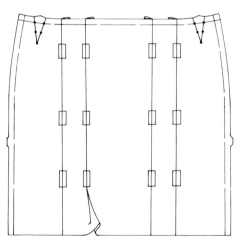

For a single pleat or cluster, use the pattern, as follows: First pleat pattern, pinning or taping each pleat along its entire length. Then pleat fabric according to its lines, conforming as closely as possible to type, size, and number of pleats in pattern.

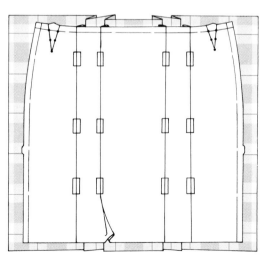

Position pleated portion of pattern over the pleated fabric (the two should be the same, or very nearly the same, in area). Pin the pattern to the fabric, then cut out the garment piece along the outside cutting lines.

Gathering

Gathering explained

Gathering is the process of drawing a given amount of fabric into a predetermined, smaller area, along one or several stitching lines, to create soft, even folds. Fabric is usually gathered to one-half or one-third the original width; the effect may be soft and drapey or crisp and billowy, depending on the fabric. Gathering most often occurs in a garment at waistline, cuffs, or yoke, or as ruffles. Gathering is done after construction seams have been stitched, seam-finished, and pressed. Because gathers fall best on the lengthwise grain, the rows of stitching should run *across* the grain.

Stitch length for gathering is longer and tension is looser than usual; it is advisable to test both on a scrap of your fabric first. Suitable stitch lengths vary from 2 mm to 4 mm, shorter for sheer or light fabrics and longer for thick, heavy materials. The shorter the stitch length, the more control you have over the gathers, no matter what the fabric.

In gathering, it is the bobbin thread that is pulled, and a looser upper tension makes it easier to slide the fabric along the thread. For heavy fabrics or extensive gathering, use an extra-strength thread in the bobbin.

How to gather fabric

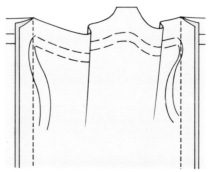

1. Working on the *right* side of the fabric, stitch two parallel rows in seam allowance, one a thread width above seamline, the other 6 mm higher. Leave long thread ends. Break stitching at seams, as illustrated; it is difficult to gather through two thicknesses.

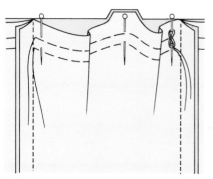

2. Pin the stitched edge to the corresponding straight edge, right sides together, matching notches, centre lines, and seams. Anchor bobbin threads (now facing you) at one end by twisting in a figure 8 around pins. Excess material is now ready to gather.

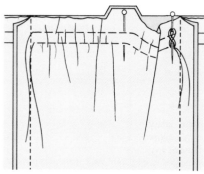

3. Gently pull on the bobbin threads while, with the other hand, you slide the fabric along the thread to create uniform gathers. When this first gathered section fits the adjoining edge, secure the thread ends by winding them in a tight figure 8 around a pin.

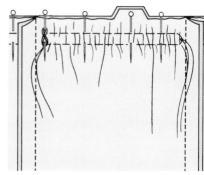

4. To draw up the ungathered portion, untie the bobbin threads and repeat the process from the other end. When the entire gathered edge matches the straight edge, fasten the thread end. Adjust gathers uniformly and pin at frequent intervals to hold folds in place.

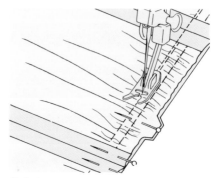

5. Before seaming gathered section, be sure machine is set to stitch length suitable to fabric and tension is balanced. With gathered side up, stitch seam on seamline, holding fabric on either side of needle so that gathers will not be stitched into little pleats.

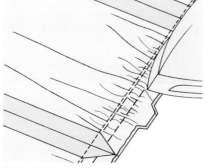

6. Trim any seam allowances, such as side seams, which are caught into the gathered seam. Press seam as stitched, in the seam allowances, using just the tip of the iron. Seam-finish the edge with a zigzag or overedge stitch, *or* apply a stay (opposite page).

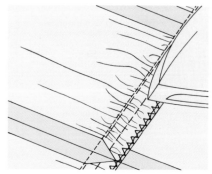

7. Open garment section out flat and press seam as it should go in finished garment—toward bodice if a waistline seam, toward shoulder if a yoke seam, toward wrist if a cuff. Again, work with just the tip of the iron, pressing flat parts only, taking care not to crease folds.

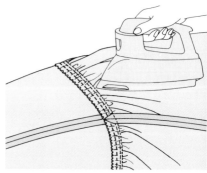

8. Press the gathers by working the point of the iron into the gathers toward the seam. Press from the wrong side of the fabric, lifting the iron as you reach the seam. Do not press *across* the gathers; this will flatten and cause them to go limp.

Gathering

Corded gathers

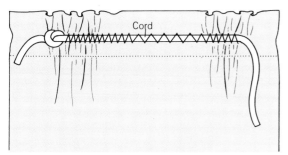

Zigzag stitching over a thin, strong cord is useful when a long strip or a bulky fabric is to be gathered. Place cord 6 mm above seamline; use widest zigzag stitch over cord to hold it in place. Pull on cord to form gathers.

Gathering by hand

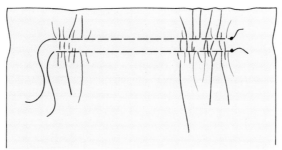

Hand stitching can replace machine stitching for gathering small areas or very delicate fabrics. Using small, even running stitches, hand-sew at least two rows for best control. To gather gently pull unknotted ends of threads.

Gathering by machine

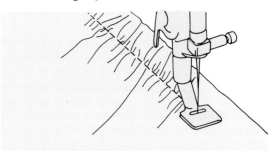

A gathering foot automatically gathers with each stitch machine takes. The longer the stitch, the more closely the fabric will be gathered. Determine amount of fabric needed by measuring a sample before and after gathering.

Staying a gathered seam

A gathered seam often needs a stay to prevent stretching or fraying, to reinforce or to add comfort, and to give a professional look to the inside. Stay can be woven seam binding, cotton tape, or narrow petersham ribbon. With gathered edge of seam up, place stay on seam allowances so that one edge is right next to permanent stitching.

Straight-stitch close to lower edge, through all thicknesses. Trim seam allowances even with the top edge of the stay. If fabric frays readily, zigzag-stitch seam allowances to the stay. Press seam and stay in correct direction (Step 7, opposite page).

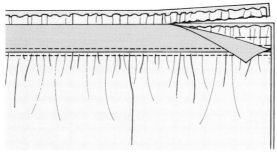

Do not trim seam to be stayed until tape is stitched on.

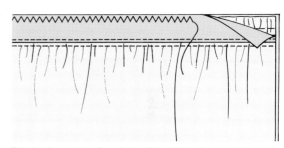

Stitch along top edge of stay if the fabric frays easily.

Joining one gathered edge to another

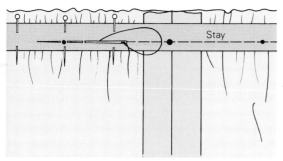

1. Cut a stay to match length finished seam is to be. Transfer pattern markings to stay and pin to wrong side of one section, matching markings. Gather section and tack to tape.

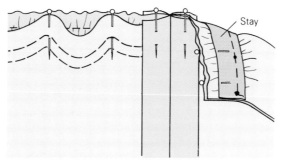

2. Pin ungathered section to section gathered in Step 1, right sides together, matching all markings. Gather second section to fit first one, and tack in place.

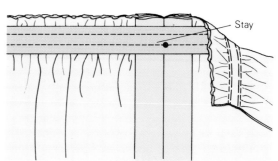

3. Stitch through all layers, including stay tape, on seamline. Stitch a second row 6 mm into seam allowances. Press seam allowances in one direction with stay uppermost.

191

Shirring

Shirring explained

Shirring is formed with multiple rows of gathering and is primarily a decorative way of controlling fullness. In contrast to gathering, in which fullness is controlled within a seam, the fullness in shirring is controlled over a comparatively wide span.

Lightweight fabrics are the most appropriate for shirring; they may be either crisp or soft. Voiles, batistes, crepes and jerseys are excellent choices. No-iron fabrics are good because it is difficult to press shirring without flattening it.

Your pattern should specify the areas to be shirred; these can range from a small part, such as a

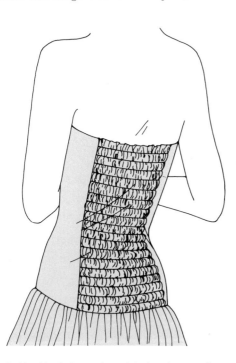

A shirred back gives a dramatic look and an easy fit.

cuff, to an entire garment section, such as a bodice. Rows of shirring must be straight, parallel, and equidistant. They may be as close together as 6 mm or as far apart as 2 or 3 cm, depending on personal preference and pattern specifications. Width to be shirred is determined by the pattern.

How to shirr fabric

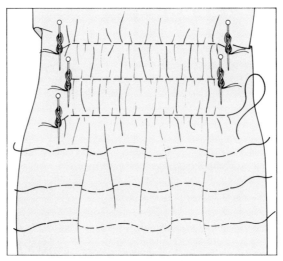

1. Stitch repeated rows of gathering stitches over section to be shirred, spacing rows an equal distance apart. Gather each row separately by pulling on bobbin thread. Measure first row when it is shirred and make sure that all subsequent rows are gathered to the same length.

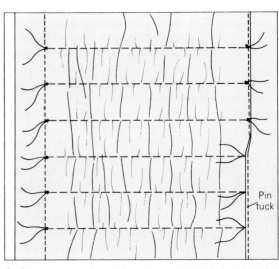

2. Secure rows, after all have been gathered, by tying the thread ends on each row; then place a line of machine stitching across the ends of all rows. **If ends of shirred area will not be stitched into a seam,** enclose the thread ends in a small pin tuck to hold them securely.

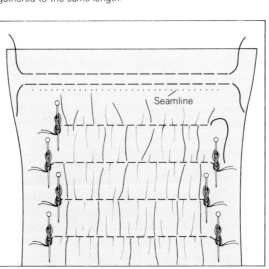

Seamline

If shirring is to be joined to a flat piece, first place gathering stitches in seam allowance, one row just inside seamline and a second 6 mm above. Stitch rows for shirring, and shirr to desired width. Gather and attach seam as specified in basic procedure for gathering (p. 190).

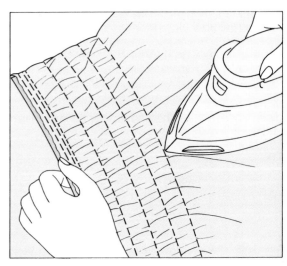

3. The fullness produced by shirring should be pressed with great care; if it is not, the weight of the iron will flatten the folds and ruin the intended effect. Press on the wrong side, into the fullness, with just the point of the iron. Do not press into the shirred area itself.

Staying a shirred area

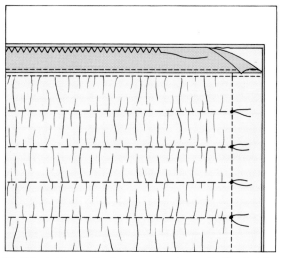

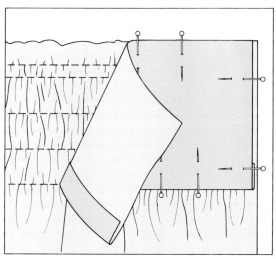

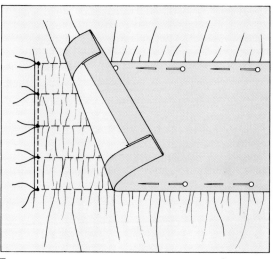

To stay a seam only, the procedure is exactly like that for a gathered seam (p. 191). Position stay tape over shirred side of untrimmed seam allowance, keeping edge just next to seamline. Stitch lower edge of tape; trim seam allowances even with top edge, then zigzag through all layers.

To stay a seam and a section, cut stay fabric the same width and 1 cm deeper than shirred section. Pin stay to wrong side of shirred area, turning under lower edge and keeping seam edges even; tack. Stitch stay into seams when garment sections are joined; secure lower edge to last row of gathering.

To stay a shirred section, cut a strip of self-fabric 2 cm wider and deeper than shirring. Turn in raw edges 1 cm on all sides; pin in place to the wrong side of shirred area. Hand-sew the stay in place with small, invisible stitches. A stay will protect the shirred area from strain.

Elasticised shirring

This stretchy, flexible form of shirring hugs the body neatly, yet expands and contracts comfortably with body movements. It is easily done by using elastic thread in the bobbin and regular thread in the needle. Wind the elastic thread on the bobbin, stretching it slightly, until the bobbin is almost full.

Set the machine to a 4 mm stitch length, and test the results on a scrap of your fabric. Adjust stitch length and tension if necessary. Sometimes, to get the desired fullness, the bobbin (elastic) thread must be pulled after stitching as in gathering.

Mark the rows of shirring on the right side of the garment. (Or, after marking the first row, you can use the quilter guide-bar to space the other rows.) As you sew, hold the fabric taut and flat by stretching the fabric in previous rows to its original size. To secure ends, draw the needle thread through to the underside and tie. Run a line of machine stitching across all the knots or hold them with a narrow pin tuck at each end of the shirred section.

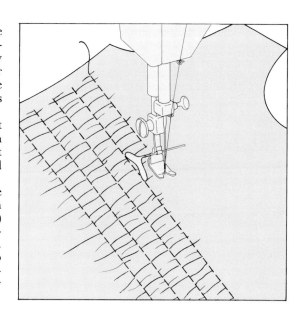

Shirring with cord

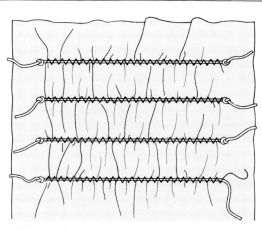

This technique is essentially gathering with cord (see p. 191) but in multiple rows. Cord is placed directly on shirred lines; ends are secured by knotting.

193

Smocking

Smocking explained

Smocking consists of fabric folds decoratively stitched together at regular intervals to create a patterned effect. The folds may be pulled in as the stitching is done, or the fabric may be first gathered into folds and then smocked (see **Gauging,** below). A smocking pleater machine can also be used to gather the fabric before smocking. Lightweight and crisp fabrics are best, but almost any fabric can be smocked. You will need two and one-half to three times the desired finished width; patterns specify fabric required.

Smocking is done before the garment is constructed. Popular areas for smocking are yokes, bodices, pockets, sleeves and waistlines. Smocking is based on a grid of evenly spaced dots (see **Stitching guide,** below); stitch variety is achieved by joining dots at differing points. If a fabric like gingham is being used, its pattern can serve as a guide in place of the grid.

A decorative thread, such as six-strand embroidery cotton or silk buttonhole twist, is best for smocking; the colours can be chosen to match or complement the fabric. It will take long crewel needles to reach the span required by some of the stitch patterns. Smocking can be simulated by means of the decorative stitches provided by modern sewing machines.

Typical use of smocking shows decorative effect.

Stitching guide

The stitching guide or pattern may be purchased as an iron-on transfer, or you can make your own dot pattern with a very hard-leaded pencil. Rows of dots should align with the fabric grain.

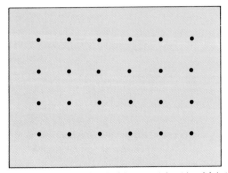

Mark the dots to guide stitching on *right* side of fabric.

Gauging (advance gathering)

Taking small stitches under dots, as shown, tack along each row. Leave one end loose; draw up two rows at a time to desired width. Dots will appear at tops of folds to indicate smocking stitch points.

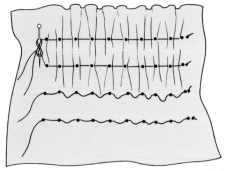

Smock at dots; when finished, remove gathering stitches.

Cable stitch

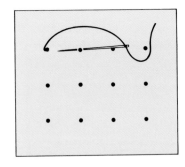

Bring the needle up from underside at first dot. Keeping thread *above* needle, take a short stitch through fabric under the second dot and draw fabric up.

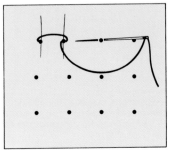

Keeping thread *below* needle, take a short stitch under third dot. Draw up fabric. To keep folds even, always pull thread at right angle to stitch.

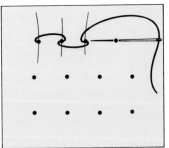

On fourth dot, keep thread *above* needle. Alternate in this way until the row is finished. Try to keep folds even when drawing up stitch.

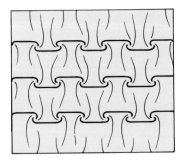

Repeat the identical procedure for each subsequent row, alternating thread above and below needle in matching pattern dots. This will make rows exact duplicates, as this pattern requires.

Smocking

Honeycomb stitch

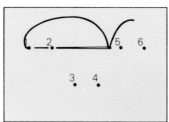

Work from left to right with needle pointing left. Bring the needle out at 1, then take a small stitch at 2 and another at 1; pull thread taut.

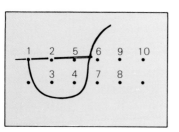

Re-insert needle at dot 2 and bring it out at dot 3 in row below (two rows are worked together for this design). Thread will be underneath the fold.

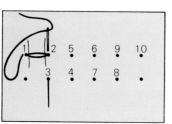

Repeat first stitch procedure by taking a small stitch at dot 4 and another at dot 3. Pull the thread taut. Then re-insert the needle next to dot 4.

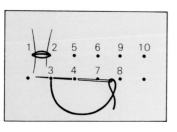

Pass the needle up from dot 4 to dot 5 in the upper row, and continue to repeat pattern until the whole row is done. End stitching in the bottom row.

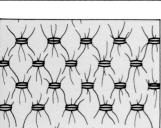

This stitch produces long floats on wrong side. A stay will prevent snagging of the floats during wear. Apply the stay the same as for a shirred section.

Wave stitch

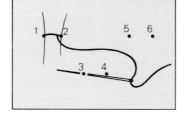

Bring the needle up from the underside at dot 1. Keeping thread *above* the needle take a stitch at dot 2. Pull thread tight to complete stitch.

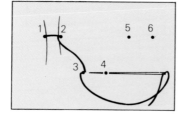

Take next stitch at dot 3 in second row (in this design, two rows are worked together); draw the thread through.

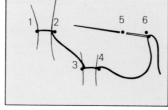

Keeping the thread *below* needle, take a stitch under dot 4 and draw stitches together by pulling thread up. The thread emerges from inside the stitch.

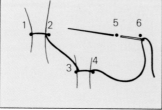

Return to first row by taking complete stitch at dot 5. Keep thread *above* needle when picking up dot 6. Draw stitches together. Continue to end of that row.

Repeat for all pairs of rows, with thread *above* the needle on upper rows and *below* needle on lower rows.

Smocked effect by machine

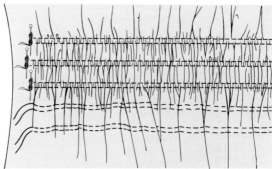

1. Place rows of gathering stitches in groups of two 6 mm apart. Repeat paired rows as required by size of smocked area, spacing them 2 cm apart. Gather each group.

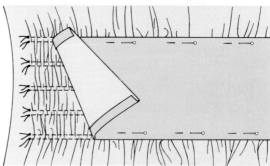

2. Cut an underlay 2 cm wider than the shirred area; fold under *long* raw edges 1 cm and pin or tack to wrong side. Test decorative machine stitches for maximum width of 6 mm.

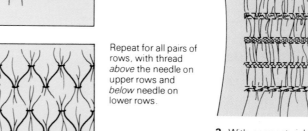

3. With garment right side up, place decorative stitching between the 6 mm rows of shirring. Striking effects can be created using different patterns and thread colours.

Ruffles

Types of ruffle

A ruffle is a strip of fabric cut or handled in such a way as to produce fullness. Though primarily decorative, ruffles may also serve a practical purpose, such as lengthening a garment.

Ruffles are of two types, **straight** and **circular,** which differ in the way they are cut. The straight ruffle is cut as a *strip* of fabric; the circular ruffle is cut from a *circle*. With the straight ruffle, both edges are the same length and the fullness is produced

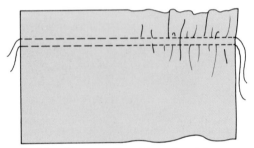

Straight ruffles are gathered to produce fullness.

through gathering or pleating. For the circular ruffle, a small circle is cut from the centre of a larger one and the inner edge forced to lie flat, producing fullness on the outer, longer edge. Soft, lightweight

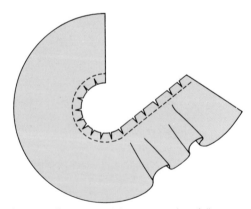

Circular ruffles are specially cut to produce fullness.

fabrics ruffle best. A general rule for deciding the proper relation between ruffle width and fullness: the wider the ruffle (or the sheerer the fabric) the fuller the ruffle should be.

Straight ruffles

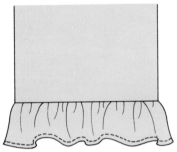 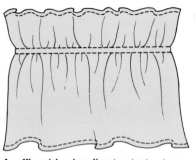 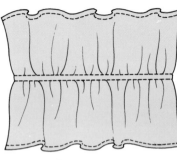

A plain ruffle has one finished edge (usually a small hem); the other edge is gathered to size and then sewn into a seam or onto another unfinished edge.

A ruffle with a heading has both edges finished or hemmed. It is gathered at a specified distance from the top edge to give a gracefully balanced proportion.

A double ruffle is gathered in the centre, halfway between the two finished edges. It is then topstitched through the centre to the garment section.

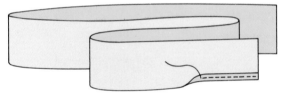 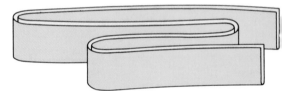

Single-layer ruffles are made from one layer of fabric and the edges finished with either a narrow machine or a hand-rolled hem. The edges can also be finished with decorative stitching, if appropriate to design of finished garment.

A self-faced ruffle is a single layer of fabric folded back on itself. It is used when both sides of a ruffle will be visible, or to give added body to sheer or flimsy fabrics. It creates a luxurious appearance wherever it is used.

Determining length

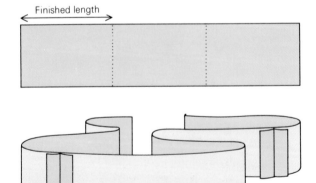

Finished length

To determine length of fabric needed for a ruffle, allow about three times the finished length for a fully gathered ruffle, twice the length for a ruffle that is slightly gathered. Straight ruffles are usually cut on either the crosswise or the bias grain.

Piecing of fabric strips is frequently necessary to achieve required length. Seam strips with right sides together, making sure sections match in pattern and direction of grain. On ruffles for sheer curtains, strips can be cut along the selvage to get maximum length without piecing and to avoid the necessity of hemming.

Ruffles

Single-layer straight ruffles

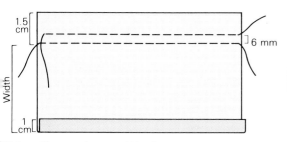

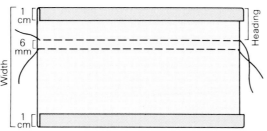

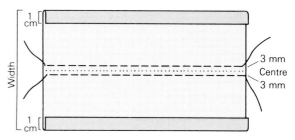

Plain ruffles can be any width. Cut strip to desired finished width plus 2.5 cm. This allows for 1.5 cm seam allowance and 1 cm hem. Make hem first (see Hemming, below). Then place two rows of gathering stitches, 6 mm apart, inside seam allowance. Pull bobbin threads to gather to desired length.

Ruffles with headings require a fabric strip 2 cm wider (for hems) than the finished width. Make a 1 cm hem on each edge (see Hemming, below). Determine width of heading; place first gathering row that distance from one edge. The second row is placed 6 mm below. Gather to size.

Double ruffles require strips 2 cm wider than ruffle is to be. Make a 1 cm hem on each edge (see Hemming, below). Place gathering rows at the centre of the strip, one 3 mm below and the other 3 mm above the centre line. Stitch so bobbin thread is on right side of ruffle; this makes gathering easier to do.

Hemming single-layer ruffles

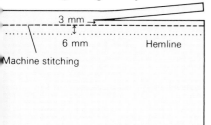

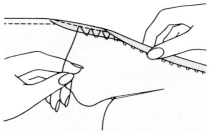

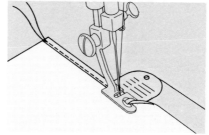

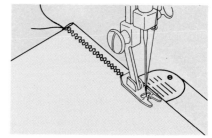

To hem edge by hand, first machine-stitch 6 mm above marked hemline. Trim hem allowance to 3 mm. Fold hem to wrong side, turning just far enough so that the stitch line shows.

Working right to left, take small stitch through fold; then, 3 mm below and beyond that stitch, catch a few threads of ruffle. Pull thread to roll hem to wrong side.

Machine hems can be made to look very much like hand-rolled hems with the help of a hemmer foot attachment. Check machine instruction book for specific directions.

Decorative machine stitching can be placed on a turned-back hem edge to both hold and finish it, or it can be applied along a raw, un-turned edge using overlocker machine (serger).

Self-faced ruffles

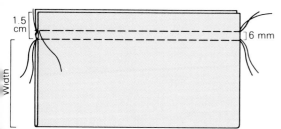

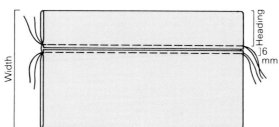

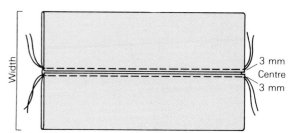

Plain ruffles to be self-faced require a double width of fabric folded in half, wrong sides together. Cut strip twice as wide as ruffle is to be, plus 3 cm (1.5 cm seam allowance on each layer). After folding strip, stitch gathering rows and pull threads as for single-layer type.

Ruffles with headings require a fabric strip double the intended width. Fold fabric wrong sides together, so edges meet on underside at desired depth of heading. Pin the edges. Then, where edges meet, sew two rows of gathering stitches, 6 mm apart, each holding a raw edge in place.

Double ruffles that are to be self-faced require strips exactly twice the desired finished width. Fold fabric, wrong sides together, so edges meet at centre line. Pin. Stitch gathering rows 6 mm apart (3 mm from each edge). Have bobbin thread on right side; it aids gathering.

197

Ruffles

Stitching a plain ruffle into a seam

To sew a ruffle into a seam, first hem or face the ruffle strip; next pin the ungathered strip to one garment section; then gather the ruffle to fit and permanently stitch it in place. The adjoining garment section is sewn on over the ruffle.

Special care must be taken with the ruffle seam allowance so that its extra fullness does not cause bulk in the completed seam. The seam allowance should be pressed flat before the second garment section is attached; after attaching, the seam should be carefully graded, clipped, and notched.

The finished seam should be pressed so that the seam allowance of the ruffle is not pressed back onto the ruffle, where it would distort the hang of the ruffle. It would also necessitate extra pressing, which could flatten out the fullness.

Stitching a ruffle to curves or corners

Ruffles must frequently be sewn into curved seams or sharp corners, a situation that occurs often in collars. In such cases, the ungathered ruffle must be pinned to the garment piece with extra fullness provided at the curve or corner. This allows for the greater distance the ruffle's outer edge must span.

After stitching, the fullness within the seam allowance should be carefully graded and notched out.

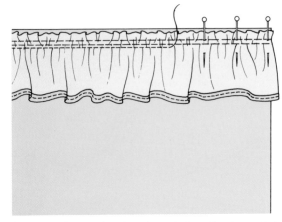

1. Pin-mark the prepared ruffle strip and the garment edge to which it will be joined into an equal number of parts. Right sides together, match and pin ruffle to garment at markings. Gather ruffle to fit edge, distributing fullness evenly.

2. When ruffle is gathered to size and pinned in place, stitch it to garment section on seamline. Stitch with ruffle up, and, as you stitch, hold work in such a way that the gathers are not sewn into little pleats.

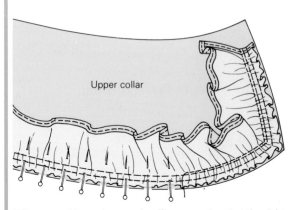

When attaching a hemmed ruffle, remember that the right side of the ruffle must show on the completed garment. If the garment piece is a collar, have right side of ruffle against right side of upper collar as you stitch.

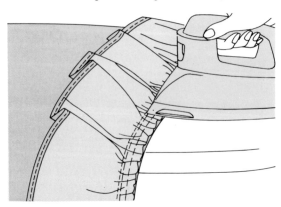

3. Press seam before joining to second garment section to prevent lumps or uneven stitching. Using just the point of the iron, press ruffle edge flat within the *seam allowance only*—do not let the iron go beyond the stitch line.

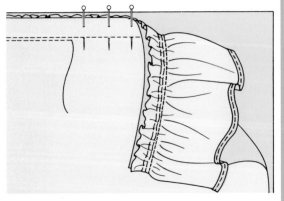

4. Pin edge with ruffle attached to second seam edge, right sides together, so ruffle is between the two garment sections. Stitch a thread width from first seam so no stitching will show on right side of garment or ruffle.

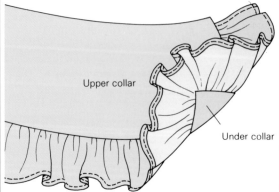

As the under and upper collar are being joined, the ruffle will be between the two garment sections. The final stitching should be slightly outside any other stitching so that no previous thread lines will show on finished collar.

Stitching a plain ruffle to an edge

Attaching headed or double ruffles

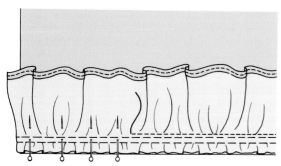

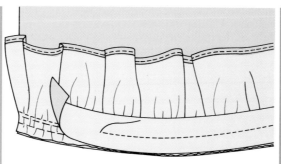

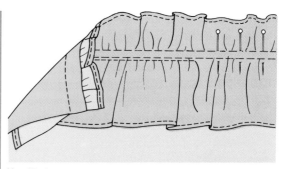

To attach a ruffle to a straight edge, pin the ungathered strip to the straight edge, gather it to fit, then permanently stitch in place. Trim the seam allowance *of the ruffle only* to 3 mm, leaving other seam allowances intact.

To stitch a ruffle to a curved edge, proceed as for gathering ruffle to edge; tack in place. Place right side of a 3 cm wide bias strip to wrong side of ruffle, raw edges even. Stitch through all thicknesses on seamline.

If ruffle is at an edge, place wrong side of ungathered ruffle against wrong side of garment, matching bottom row of gathering stitches to seamline on garment. Gather ruffle to fit; stitch, with the ruffle up, along the seamline.

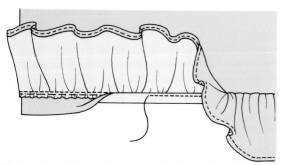

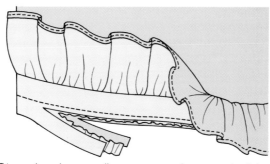

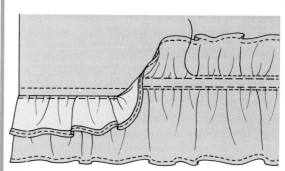

Fold untrimmed seam allowance under 3 mm, then fold again so that cut edge of ruffle is enclosed and inside fold of seam allowance is on seamline. Pin in place and topstitch along edge at stitch line through seam allowances only.

Trim and grade seam allowances, removing as much of the bulk of the ruffle seam allowance as possible. Bias strips are recommended here because they shape around curves better than the straight seam allowance could.

Trim seam allowance of garment to 3 mm. Turn ruffle to outside of garment and topstitch in place along top row of gathering stitches. The seam allowance will be completely enclosed by the second line of stitching.

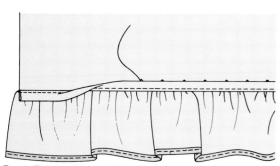

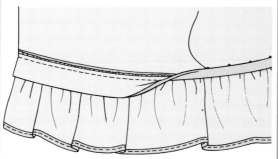

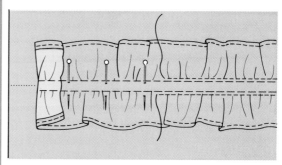

Turn ruffle away from straight edge and press the finished seam allowance toward garment so ruffle will hang properly. To be sure seam allowance will stay in that position, slipstitch the finished edge to the garment.

Turn ruffle away from edge and seam allowance toward garment so that ruffle is in proper position. Press seam allowance flat. Turn under remaining raw edge of bias strip 6 mm and slipstitch to garment.

If ruffle is not at an edge, first mark desired location for ruffle on right side of garment. Pin ungathered ruffle to garment, gather to fit, and topstitch to garment. Use gathering stitches as a guide, stitching just alongside them.

199

Ruffles

Circular ruffles

The deep fullness and the fluid look characteristic of circular ruffles are created by the way the fabric is cut rather than by means of gathering stitches. Circular ruffles can be used anywhere that gathered ruffles would be suitable; they are especially effective at necklines and when made of sheer, filmy fabrics. To make circular ruffles, a paper pattern is essential. Measure the length of the edge to which ruffle will be attached; this will be the circumference of the inner circle. Next, decide the width of the ruffle; this will be the distance between the inner and outer circles.

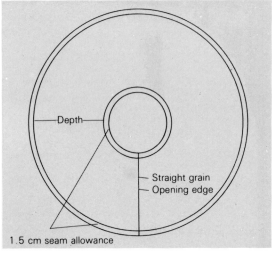

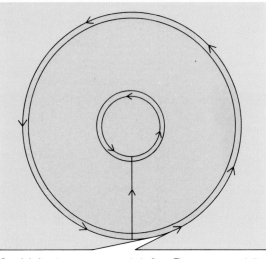

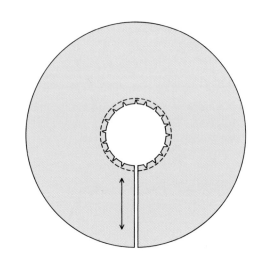

On paper, draw inner circle first. Draw outer circle at width of ruffle. Add 1.5 cm at edge of each circle.

Cut fabric along outermost circle first. Then cut on grainline to the innermost circle and cut it out.

Staystitch inner circle on seamline. Clip seam allowance repeatedly until inner edge can be pulled out straight.

Piecing to achieve length

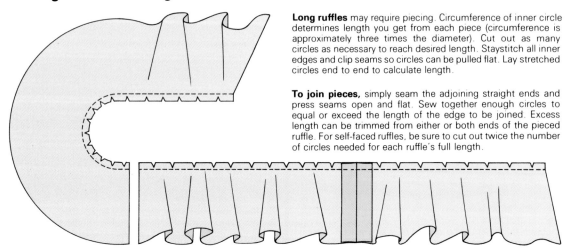

Long ruffles may require piecing. Circumference of inner circle determines length you get from each piece (circumference is approximately three times the diameter). Cut out as many circles as necessary to reach desired length. Staystitch all inner edges and clip seams so circles can be pulled flat. Lay stretched circles end to end to calculate length.

To join pieces, simply seam the adjoining straight ends and press seams open and flat. Sew together enough circles to equal or exceed the length of the edge to be joined. Excess length can be trimmed from either or both ends of the pieced ruffle. For self-faced ruffles, be sure to cut out twice the number of circles needed for each ruffle's full length.

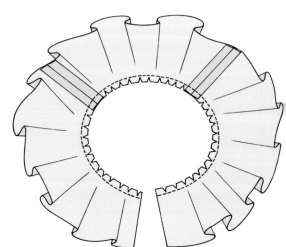

Finishing outer edge

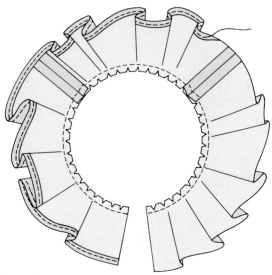

Single-layer circular ruffles are finished on outer edge, before attaching, with a narrow hem or decorative stitching. this creates a definite 'right' and 'wrong' side.

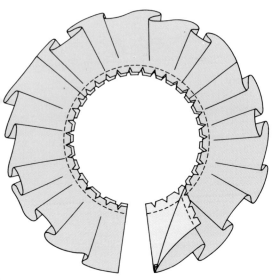

Self-faced circular ruffles require duplicate circles, or two identical pieced strips. With right sides together, stitch along outer edge. Trim seam and turn to right side.

Attaching to a garment

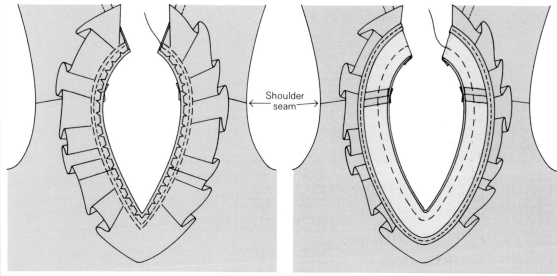

1. Place wrong side of ruffle against right side of garment with ruffle seam allowance flat and smooth (additional clips may be required). Tack layers together.

2. Join facing sections and seam-finish outer edge. Match facing to garment edge, seams and notches aligned. Tack, then stitch, reinforcing point with short stitches.

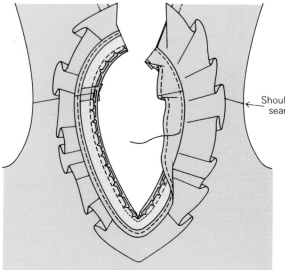

3. Trim and grade seam allowances, leaving garment seam allowance the widest. Clip seam allowances to stitching. Understitch to keep facing from rolling to right side.

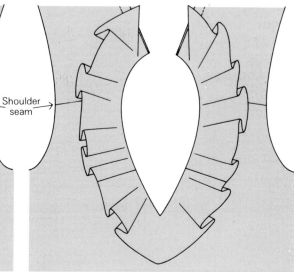

4. Turn facing to inside, finish ends and tack to zipper. Turn ruffle away from garment when pressing neckline seam; do not press ruffle flat onto garment.

Ruffles

Finishing ends

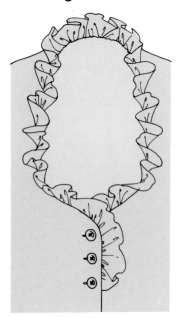

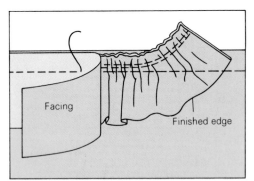

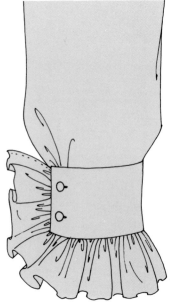

Tapering ends into the garment seamline is a common method for finishing off ruffles, especially when the ruffle does not continue the full length of the seam. Position the ruffle on the seam, drawing it beyond the seam allowance until the outer finished edge crosses the seamline where the ruffle will end. Only this outer edge will be visible on garment as ruffle ends slant inward.

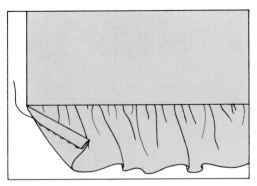

Tiny hems are used to finish a ruffle edge not caught into a seam, as might be the case at a cuff. In such instances, attach ruffle on its normal seamline; at end of ruffle turn fabric to wrong side and slipstitch in place with tiny hand stitches. In cases where the flat ends of two ruffles meet, fold ends under and seam together by hand.

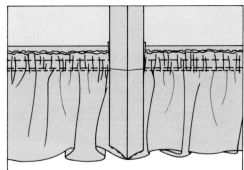

Sewing into cross seams automatically finishes off the ends of some ruffles. The ruffle is usually attached first, then handled as a continuation of the straight seam being joined. Fold seam allowances under at bottom edge and slipstitch them in place to finish off the hem edge.

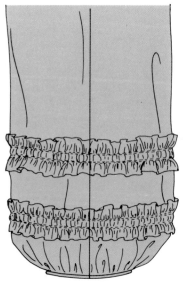

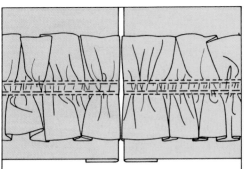

Ruffles not applied to an edge are almost always incorporated into a cross seam. Before stitching the cross seam, make sure the gathering or topstitching rows are aligned with one another so that the ruffles match perfectly when the seam is completed.

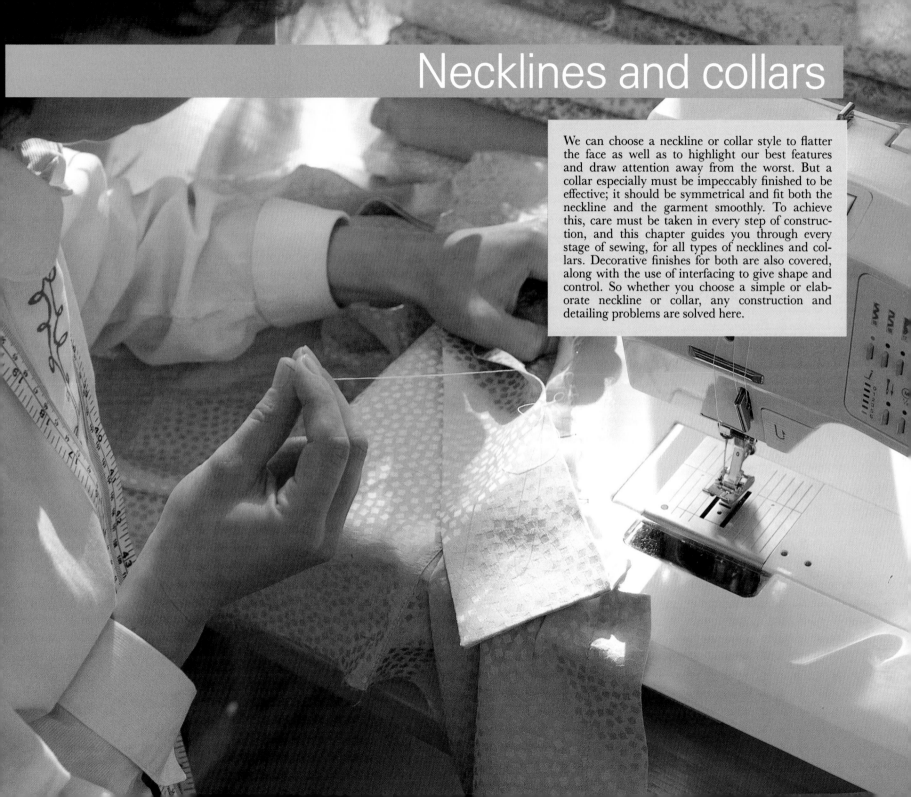

Necklines and collars

We can choose a neckline or collar style to flatter the face as well as to highlight our best features and draw attention away from the worst. But a collar especially must be impeccably finished to be effective; it should be symmetrical and fit both the neckline and the garment smoothly. To achieve this, care must be taken in every step of construction, and this chapter guides you through every stage of sewing, for all types of necklines and collars. Decorative finishes for both are also covered, along with the use of interfacing to give shape and control. So whether you choose a simple or elaborate neckline or collar, any construction and detailing problems are solved here.

Neckline finishes

Neckline facings

A facing is the fabric used to finish raw edges of a garment at such locations as neck, armhole, and front and back openings. There are three categories of facings: shaped facings, extended facings (essentially shaped facings), and bias facings.

A facing is shaped to fit the edge it will finish either during cutting or just before application. A **shaped facing** is cut out, using a pattern, to the same shape and on the same grain as the edge it will finish. A **bias facing** is a strip of fabric cut on the bias so that it can *be* shaped to match the curve of the edge it will be applied to.

After a facing is attached to the garment's edge, it is turned to the inside of the garment and should not show on the outside.

In order to reduce bulk, both shaped and bias facings can be cut from a fabric lighter in weight than the garment fabric. Because the extended facing is cut as one with the garment, garment and facing fabric are always the same.

The illustrations at the right show some examples of neckline-shaped facing pieces and a bias facing.

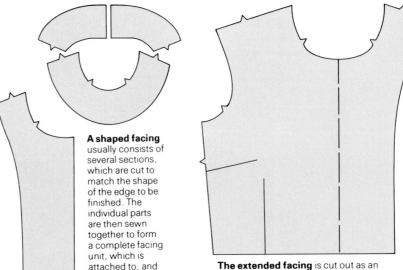

A shaped facing usually consists of several sections, which are cut to match the shape of the edge to be finished. The individual parts are then sewn together to form a complete facing unit, which is attached to, and serves as a finish for, the raw edge.

The extended facing is cut out as an extension of the garment; it is then folded back along the edge it finishes.

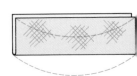

A bias facing is a narrow strip of lightweight fabric cut on the bias so it can be shaped to conform to the curve of the edge it will finish. Less bulky and conspicuous than a shaped facing.

Interfacing necklines

Depending on pattern and fabric, it may be necessary or desirable to interface a garment neckline before applying the facing. Interfacing will help to define, support, and reinforce the shape of the neck.

The type of interfacing is dictated by the garment fabric; the method of application will depend on both the pattern instructions and the type of interfacing selected. If the pattern does not include separate pattern pieces for cutting out the inter-facing, use the facing pattern pieces, but trim away 1 cm from the outer edges of the interfacing so that this edge will not extend beyond the completed facing (see below).

When it is an extended facing, the inner edge of the interfacing may either meet the garment foldline or extend 1 cm beyond it into the facing portion. If edge and foldline meet, herringbone-stitch the edge to the foldline; if the edge extends, match the garment and interfacing foldlines and stitch the two together along the fold, using very short stitches approximately 1 cm apart.

If a zipper will be inserted, reduce bulk of interfacing by trimming it away at the placket seamline. If the zipper has been applied, trim the interfacing as close to the placket seamline as possible (see below). Topstitching on zipper determines how far *in* the interfacing can extend.

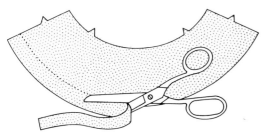

If the facing pattern was used to cut out interfacing pieces, trim 1 cm from the outer edge of each.

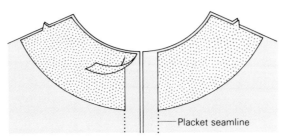

Placket seamline

If zipper has not been applied to the garment, trim away the unnecessary interfacing along the placket seamline.

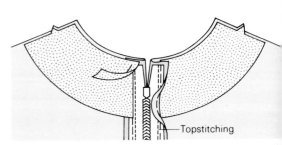

Topstitching

If zipper has been applied, trim interfacing along placket top stitching; position cut edges under seam allowances.

Construction of shaped neckline facings

Shown and explained below are the three most typical examples of shaped neckline facings. Although they look different, they are similarly constructed. If interfacing is being used at the neckline, apply it to the garment before attaching the facing. If any alterations have been made to the garment that affect the edges to be faced, be sure to alter facing and interfacing accordingly.

3. Keeping seam allowances open, apply a finish suitable to the fabric along the outer, unnotched edge of the facing unit. Some of the possible finishes are shown below. (Also see Seam finishes.)

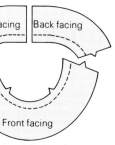

Round neck facing pieces

1. To help maintain the shape of the facing, staystitch 3 mm inside the neck seamline of each facing section. With an extended facing, staystitch inside the garment neck seamline as well. Lay the pattern pieces back onto the fabric sections to check whether the staystitched edges have retained their original measurements. If section is shorter, clip and release a few stitches; if longer, pull up on several of the stitches.

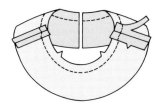

Round neck facing unit

2. With right sides together and the markings matched, seam the front facing sections to the back facing sections at shoulders. Press seams flat as stitched, then open. Trim the seam allowances to half-width; seam-finish if necessary, using a hand overcast stitch. A complete extended facing unit will consist of two garment fronts with each of their extended facings seamed, at the shoulders, to the back neck facing section.

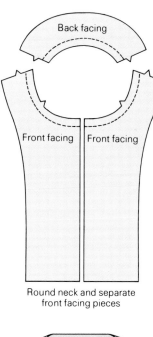

Round neck and separate front facing pieces

Round neck and separate front facing unit

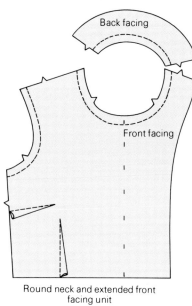

Round neck and extended front facing unit

Round neck and extended front facing unit

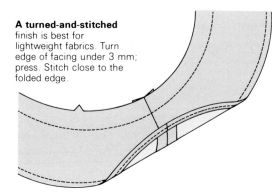

A turned-and-stitched finish is best for lightweight fabrics. Turn edge of facing under 3 mm; press. Stitch close to the folded edge.

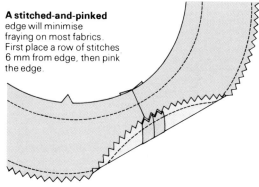

A stitched-and-pinked edge will minimise fraying on most fabrics. First place a row of stitches 6 mm from edge, then pink the edge.

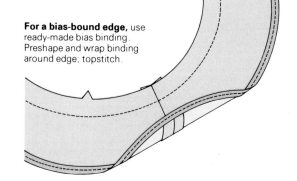

For a bias-bound edge, use ready-made bias binding. Preshape and wrap binding around edge; topstitch.

205

Neckline finishes

Applying shaped facing to neckline with zipper

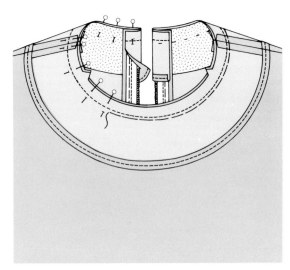

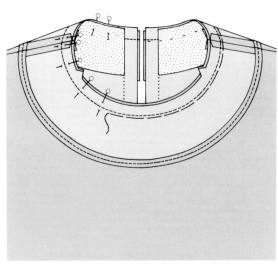

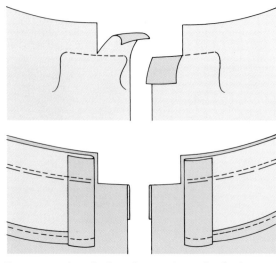

1. Right sides together, matching notches, markings, and seamlines, pin facing to neck. **If zipper has been inserted,** open zipper and wrap ends of facing to inside around each zipper half. Tack facing to garment along neck seamline.

If zipper has not been inserted, facing ends can be handled in two ways. To use the **first method,** shown above, keep centre back seam allowances of both facing and garment extended; then pin and tack them together in this position.

To use **second method,** reinforce neck seamline for 1 cm on each side of centre back seam. Clip seam allowance along centre seamline to reinforcement stitches; fold ends down to inside of garment. Fold facing seam allowances back; tack.

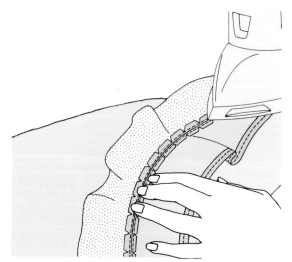

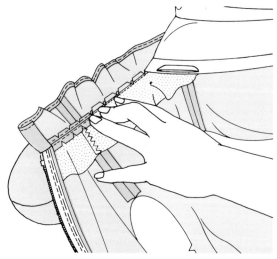

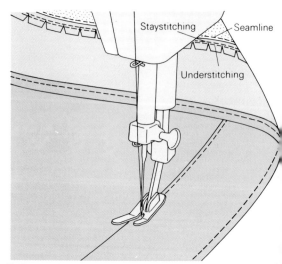

4. Place seam, wrong side up, over a tailor's ham or the curved edge of an ironing board. Using the tip of the iron, press seam open. Press carefully to prevent the seam edges from making an imprint on right side of garment.

From the wrong side, with the facing extended away from the garment, place seam over a seam roll. Press all seam allowances toward the facing. Press carefully to avoid creasing either the facing or the garment.

5. To keep facing from rolling to outside of garment, the seam should be understitched. With facing and seam allowances extended away from garment, stitch from right side close to neck seamline, through facing and seam allowances.

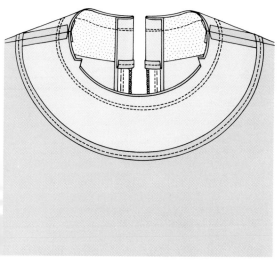

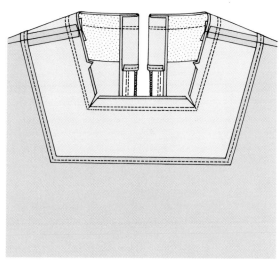

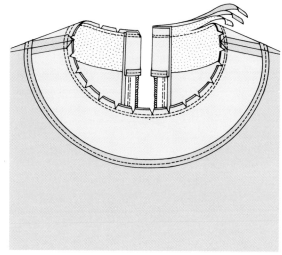

2. With facing side up, stitch facing to garment along the neck seamline; secure stitching at both ends. Check to be sure that the neck seamlines will align with each other when the zipper is closed. Remove tacking. Press seam flat.

If it is a **square neckline,** apply the facing in the same way but reinforce the corners by using short stitches for 2 cm on both sides of each corner. To relieve strain when facing is turned to inside of garment, clip into the corners.

3. Trim and grade seam allowances, making garment seam allowance the widest. Trim diagonally across centre back seam allowances and cross-seam allowances at shoulders. Clip curved seam allowances. If not already in, insert zipper.

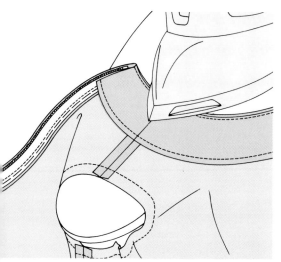

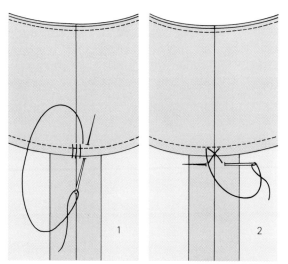

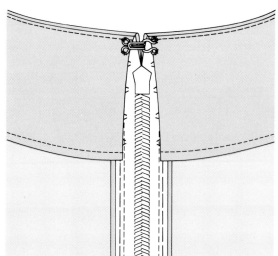

6. Turn facing to inside of garment, allowing seamline to roll inside slightly. Align facing and garment seamlines and centre markings, then press along neck edge. To hold edges in place, it may be helpful to diagonal-tack along neck edge.

7. With facing and garment seamlines aligned at shoulders, tack facing in place. Use either several closely spaced whip-stitches (1) or a cross-stitch tack (2), catching only facing edge and seam allowances of garment.

8. With ends folded under, pin facing to zipper tape. Make sure that the facing will not be caught in the zipper. Open zipper and slipstitch facing to zipper tape. Close zipper and attach fastener at top of placket.

Neckline finishes

Applying shaped facing to neckline and garment opening

Some designs require facing of both the neck *and* a front or back opening. The facing used for the opening may be a separate piece or an extended facing. Buttonholes are the usual closure. Bound buttonholes are constructed *before* facing is applied; machine buttonholes, *after* application.

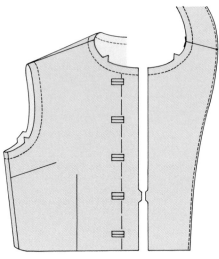

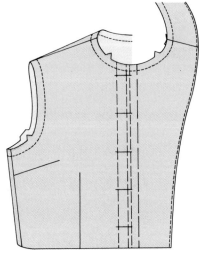

Neck and separate front facing

Neck and extended front facing

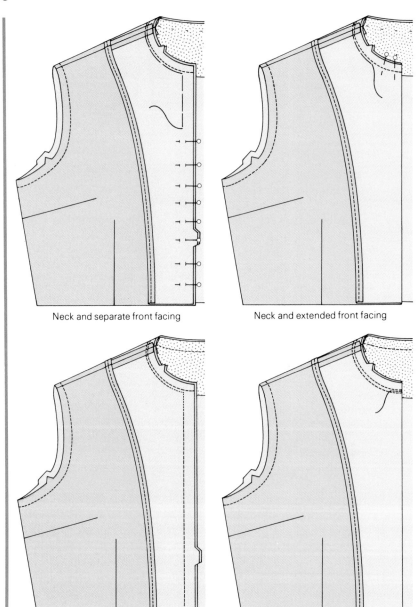

Neck and separate front facing

Neck and extended front facing

Neck and separate front facing

Neck and extended front facing

1. With right sides together, matching markings and notches, pin and tack the facing to the garment along the neck seamline. When it is a **separate front facing,** pin and tack down the opening edge. With an **extended facing,** the facing has been folded back onto the garment, producing a fold rather than a seam. In this situation, there is no need to match, pin, and tack.

2. Stitch facing to garment along the seamline. With the **separate front facing,** it may be advisable to stitch directionally, starting at centre back and stitching to lower edge of front facing on each side. Reinforce corners formed by the neckline and opening edge seamlines, by taking small stitches for 2 cm on both sides of each corner. With the **extended facing,** just the neck seamline is stitched; backstitch at both ends to secure stitching. After appropriate stitching, remove tacking and press the seam flat as stitched. Do not press the fold of an extended facing.

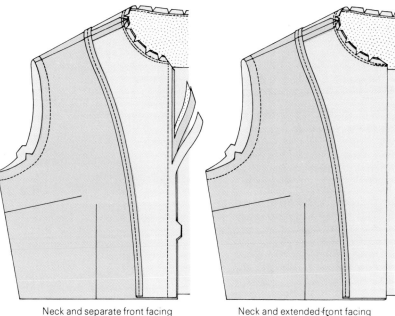

Neck and separate front facing

Neck and extended front facing

3. Trim, grade, and clip the seam allowances, making the garment seam allowance the widest. Trim diagonally across the seam allowances at the corners and cross seams.

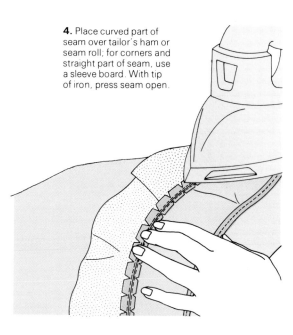

4. Place curved part of seam over tailor's ham or seam roll; for corners and straight part of seam, use a sleeve board. With tip of iron, press seam open.

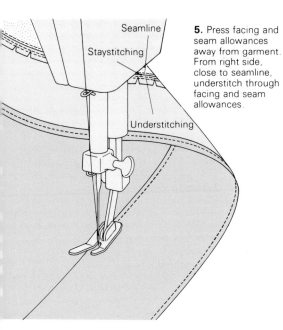

Seamline

Staystitching

Understitching

5. Press facing and seam allowances away from garment. From right side, close to seamline, understitch through facing and seam allowances.

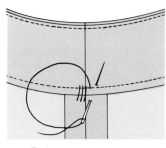

6. Turn facing to the inside; align centre markings and seamlines. Diagonal-tack along neck, if needed, to hold layers together; press.

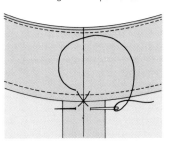

Tacking with whipstitches

Cross-stitch tack

7. With seamlines and centre markings aligned, tack facing to garment at shoulders, using either closely spaced whipstitches or a cross-stitch tack. Catch only the facing and the seam allowances of the garment. Finish the backs of bound buttonholes with the facing, or make machine buttonholes through garment and facing. (See Bound and machine-worked buttonholes.)

Pressing 15
Cross-stitch tack (single) 146
Whipstitch 14#
Reducing seam bulk 15#

Neckline finishes

Combination facings

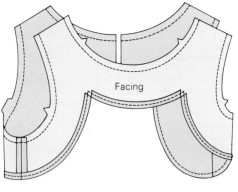

Facing

1. A combination facing is a shaped facing in which both the neck and armholes are finished by the same facing unit. Staystitch neck and armholes of both facing and garment. Construct facing unit and garment, leaving all the shoulder seams open. Zipper may be inserted before or after the facing is applied.

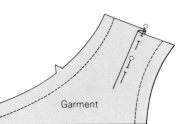

Garment

2. Pin a narrow tuck in fronts and backs of *garment* shoulders, as shown. This tuck, which is released later, ensures that the facing and seams will not show on the outside of the garment.

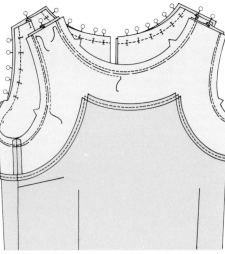

3. Right sides together, pin and tack facing to garment along the neck and armhole seamlines of the *facing*. (For facing treatment at zipper placket, see p. 206.) Facing side up, stitch facing to garment, starting at shoulder seamlines.

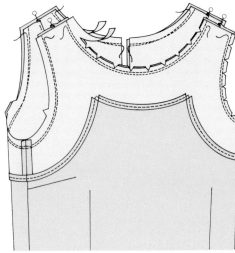

4. Remove the tacking; press seams flat. Trim grade, and clip seam allowances. Trim cross-sear allowances diagonally. Place seams over a seam ro and carefully press all seams open. Then press al seam allowances toward facing.

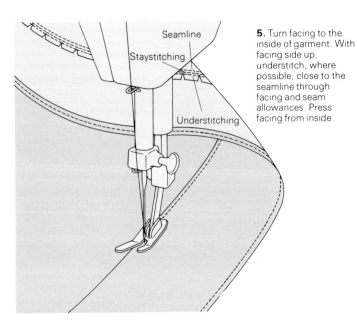

Seamline

Staystitching

Understitching

5. Turn facing to the inside of garment. With facing side up, understitch, where possible, close to the seamline through facing and seam allowances. Press facing from inside.

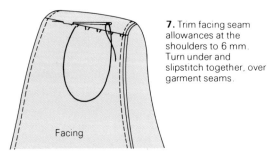

Garment

Facing

6. Release tucks at shoulders. With neck and armhole seam allowances folded back and the facing out of the way, tack then stitch the garment shoulder seams. Tie thread ends. Press seams flat, then open; push through opening.

Facing

7. Trim facing seam allowances at the shoulders to 6 mm. Turn under and slipstitch together, over garment seams.

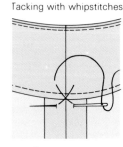

Tacking with whipstitches

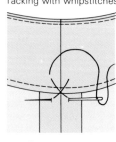

Cross-stitch tack

8. Press facing shoulder seams. Witl side seams aligned, tack the facing to garment seam allowances, using either a few closely spaced whipstitches or a cross-stitch tack At zipper placket slipstitch the turned-under facing ends to the zipper tapes. Attach fastener at top of placket.

Constructing and applying a bias facing

A bias facing is a narrow rectangular strip of lightweight fabric, cut on the bias so that it can be shaped to conform to the curve of the edge it will be sewn to and finish. This shaping is done with the aid of a steam iron. For details, see Step 1.

The bias facing is often used instead of a shaped facing on garments made of sheer or bulky fabrics. A conventional shaped facing, because of its width, might be too conspicuous on a garment made from sheer fabric; a shaped facing cut from garment fabric might be too bulky when the fabric is thick or heavy.

The finished width of a bias facing is generally from 1 to 2.5 cm. The *cut* width of the strip, however, must be twice the finished width plus two seam allowances. (The strip is folded in half lengthwise. The folding automatically gives the facing one finished edge.) The total length needed equals the length of the seamline of the edge being faced plus 5 cm for ease and finishing. It may be necessary to piece bias strips to obtain the required length; see pages 310–311 for the method.

The zipper should be inserted in the garment before applying a bias facing.

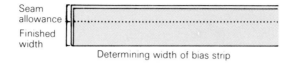

Determining width of bias strip

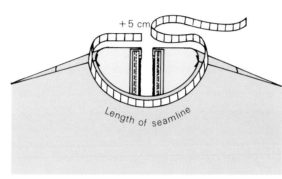

Determining length of bias strip

Length and width. Bias strip should be twice the desired finished width plus two seam allowances, each the same width as the garment seam allowance. Length equals length of edge being faced plus 5 cm for ease and finishing.

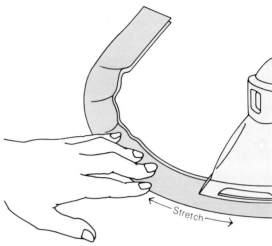

1. Cut out strip; fold it in half lengthwise. Using a steam iron, press strip flat. Shape by pressing again, stretching and curving folded edge to mould raw edges into curve that matches edge being faced. Keep raw edges even.

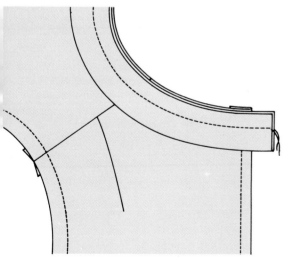

2. With all edges even, pin and tack facing to right side of garment. If edges of facing are slightly uneven from the shaping, trim and even them before pinning to garment. Stitch along seamline. Remove tacking and press.

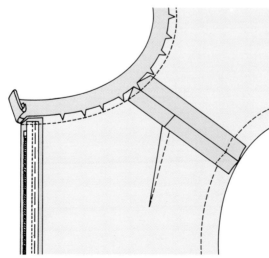

3. Trim and grade seam allowances, making sure that the garment seam allowance is the widest. Clip seam; trim ends of bias to 6 mm. Extend facing up and away from garment and press along seamline. Fold ends of facing to inside.

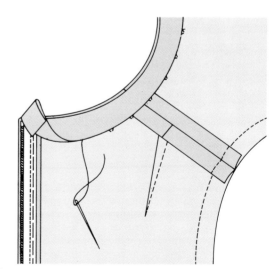

4. Turn facing to inside of garment, letting the seamline roll slightly beyond the edge. Pin in place along folded edge. Slipstitch edge and ends of facing to inside of garment. Remove pins. Press. Attach fastener at top of placket.

Neckline finishes

Corded necklines

The application of cording, made from self or contrasting fabric, gives a decorative finish to a neckline edge. Note that although cording is sometimes referred to as piping, the two are different. The difference is explained on page 312.

There are two application methods for cording. The more common method is to stitch the cording to the garment and then apply a separate facing. The second requires a specially constructed cording that is made with knit fabric and is a combination cording and facing. The way the ends are finished depends on whether or not the neckline has a placket opening. If cording is applied to a neckline that does not have a placket, the finished neckline must be large enough to slip easily over the head.

Narrow or wide cord may be used as a filler for the cording. If a woven fabric is used to cover the cord, cut it on the bias; knit fabric can be cut on

the cross or bias. If applying to a *neckline that will be faced,* cut fabric for cording wide enough to encase the cord plus two seam allowances.

When using the *special knit combination* cording and facing, cut the fabric wide enough to encase the cord plus 2.5 cm. The length of cording needed for any application, regardless of placket presence or absence, is the length of the neck seamline plus 3 cm. Before applying any cording, finish all garment details at the neck seamline.

Application of cording to faced neckline

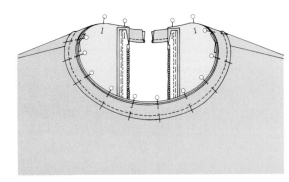

1. With zipper open, pin the cording to right side of garment, with cord just outside seamline and the cording stitch line just inside seamline. Leave excess cording at ends.

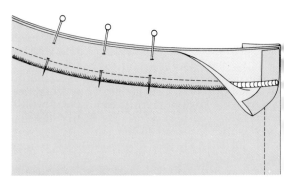

2. At ends, release enough of stitching holding cord to open fabric, then cut cord even with placket edges. Trim fabric ends to 6 mm; fold in, even with cord; re-wrap around cord.

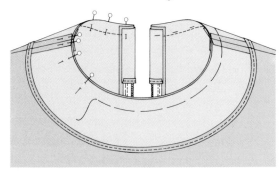

4. Remove tacking. Construct facing unit (p. 205). With right sides together, pin and tack facing to garment. Wrap ends of facing around zipper halves to inside of garment.

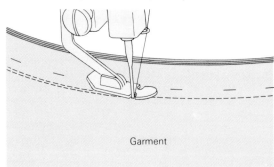

5. With wrong side of garment up, stitch facing to garment along seamline. Crowd stitching between cord and the row of stitching from Step 3. Secure thread ends. Remove tacking.

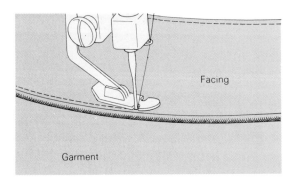

7. Extending facing and seam allowances away from garment, understitch along neck seamline. Use zipper foot; stitch from right side of facing, through all seam allowances.

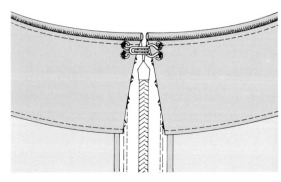

8. Turn facing to inside and press. Tack facing to garment at shoulders. Tack fabric at ends of cording closed. Slipstitch facing ends to zipper tapes. Attach fastener at top.

Application of knit combination cording and facing

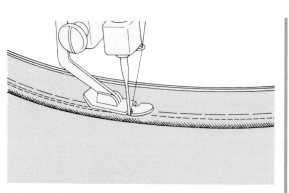

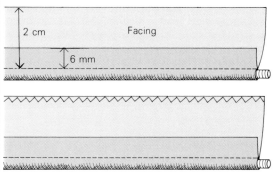

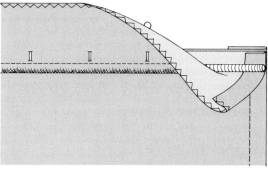

3. Tack cording to garment; remove pins. Using a zipper foot adjusted to right of needle, stitch cording to garment. Stitch between cord and the stitching encasing the cord.

1. Wrap strip around cord as shown (for size of strip, see p. 212). Using a zipper foot, stitch close to cord. Seam-finish 'facing' edge. Trim garment seam allowance to 6 mm.

2. Pin the 6 mm wide side of cording to right side of garment, aligning its edge with garment edge, its stitch line along garment seamline. Treat ends as in Step 2, opposite.

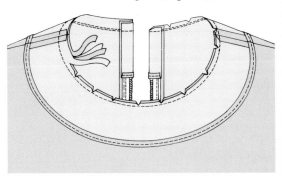

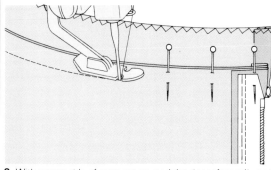

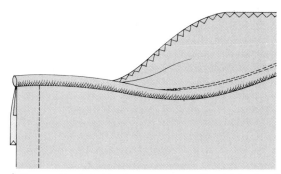

6. Press seam flat. Trim, grade, and clip the seam allowances. Trim diagonally at cross seams and corners. Press seam open, then press facing and seam allowances away from garment.

3. With wrong side of garment up, and the zipper foot adjusted to right of needle, stitch cording to garment on the 6 mm seamline. Remove pins as you stitch.

4. Turn cording to inside of garment; press. Sew fabric closed at ends of cording. Tack cording to garment at shoulders and zipper; attach fastener.

Cording necklines without plackets

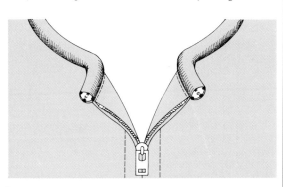

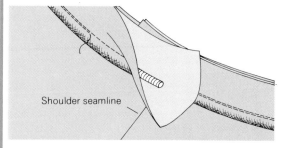

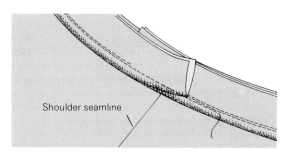

If heavy cord has been used, instead of tacking the fabric closed at ends, attach a large snap to ends of cording. This will serve as a finish and as a fastener for neckline as well.

To cord a neckline with no placket opening, apply cording as required by its type, but allow the ends to overlap at a shoulder seamline. Release stitching at each end and trim cord

to shoulder seamline. Overlap ends, easing empty part of casing away from seamline. Stitch across ends through all layers. Turn cording to inside and tack.

213

Neckline finishes

Bound and banded necklines

The illustrations below are designed to show how finished bound and banded necklines differ from each other and from a plain faced neckline. The essential difference lies in where the upper edge of the finish falls; this is dictated by where and in what manner the finish is stitched to the neckline.

Supposing all four necklines were based on the same simple jewel neckline, as these are, the *uppermost edge* of the **faced, bound** and **shaped-band** necklines would be at the same level; the *seamline* of the **strip band** would be at this level, but its uppermost edge would be above.

With a plain **faced** neckline, the facing is stitched to the neck seamline, which becomes the finished edge when the facing is turned to the inside. With a **bound** neckline, the original seam allowance is trimmed from the garment, and the upper edge of the binding ultimately falls where the original seamline was.

A shaped band is an additional, but integral, part of the garment; its upper edge forms the finished neckline edge without changing the location. **A knit band** is an extension above the original neckline, very much like most collars are.

Faced neckline

Bound neckline

Shaped-band neckline

Strip-band neckline

Bound necklines

A neck edge can be finished by binding it with a strip of self or contrasting fabric. The finished width of the binding, which should be no more than 2.5 cm, is the same as the width of the seam allowances used in application. If finished width is to be 2.5 cm, the seam allowances are also 2.5 cm, which places the seamline 2.5 cm below cut edge.

If pattern is not designed for binding, cut away the original seam allowance so that the top edge of the bound neckline finish will fall along the original seamline. The actual width of the strip will depend on whether it is to be a *single-layer binding* or a *double-layer binding*. The **length needed** is the length of the seamline plus 5 cm. Cut the strip on the grain with the most stretch—on the bias for woven fabrics, on the crosswise grain for knits.

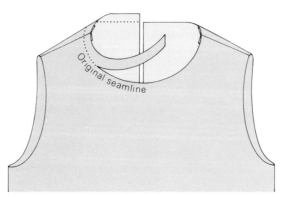
If your pattern is not designed for a bound neckline finish, trim away the seam allowance. This permits the top edge of the finished neckline to fall along the original *seamline*.

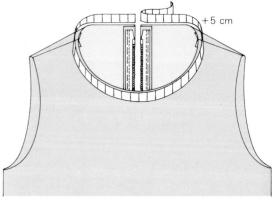
The length of the binding strip equals the length of the garment seamline plus 5 cm for ease and for finishing the ends. Take this measurement after the zipper has been inserted.

Applying a single-layer binding

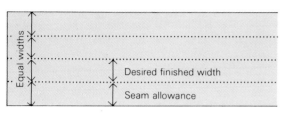

1. For a single-layer binding, cut strip four times the desired finished width and the length of the neck seamline plus 5 cm. Have seam allowance widths the same as finished width.

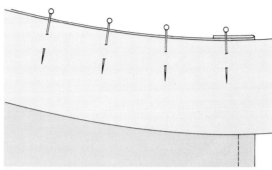

2. Open zipper. With right sides together and edges even, pin the binding to the garment along the seamline. Stretch binding if necessary to fit smoothly around curves.

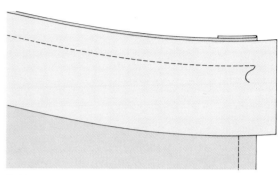

3. With binding up, stitch to garment along the seamline, removing pins as you stitch. Secure thread ends. Press flat. Trim excess binding at ends to 1 cm.

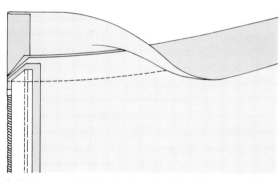

4. Fold ends of binding back, even with placket edges. Trim across corners and cross-seam allowances. Bring binding up over the seam allowances to inside of garment. Press.

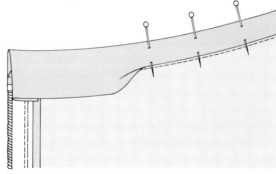

5. If binding strip is made of a **woven** fabric, turn under the raw edge along the seamline. Press with fingers to shape the binding to the curve; pin in place.

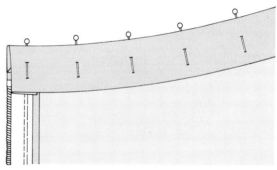

If it is a **knit** binding, let the raw edge lie flat, extending to the inside of the garment. Pin binding in place, but from the *right side*, through all thicknesses, along seamline.

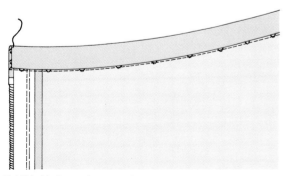

6. With bindings of **woven** fabric, slipstitch ends of binding closed. Slipstitch folded edge to garment along entire neck seamline. Stitches should not show on right side.

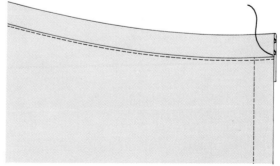

On **knit** bindings, slipstitch ends closed. Then, from right side of garment, stitch in seam groove through all thicknesses, remove pins as you stitch. Trim off excess binding.

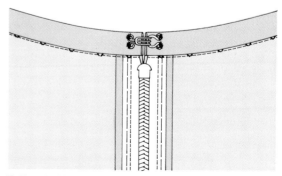

7. From inside, press the neck edge. Close zipper and attach a hook and round eye to binding ends. The ends of the binding should meet when hook and eye are fastened.

215

Neckline finishes

Applying a double-layer binding

Binding a neckline without placket

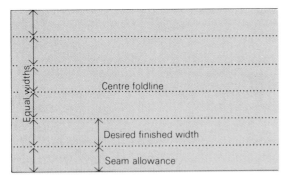

1. For a double-layer binding, cut the strip six times the desired finished width and the length of neck seamline plus 5 cm. Have seam allowance widths the same as finished width.

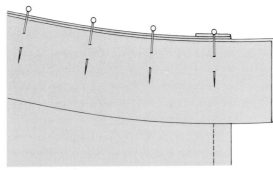

2. Open zipper. Wrong sides together, fold binding strip in half lengthwise. Keeping all edges even, pin to garment along seamline. Stretch binding to fit around curves.

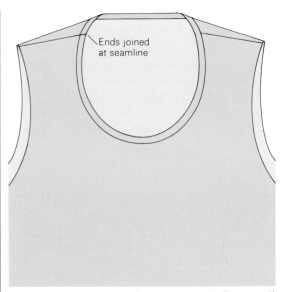

Ends joined at seamline

Single or double-layer binding may be used. The only difference from the basic applications is in the handling of the ends and that they should be joined at a garment seamline.

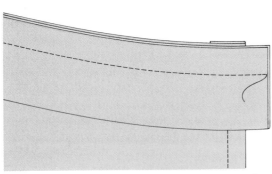

3. With binding up, stitch to garment along the seamline, removing pins as you stitch. Secure thread ends. Press flat. Trim excess binding at ends to 1 cm.

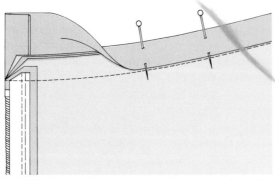

4. Fold ends of binding back, even with placket edges. Trim across corners and cross-seam allowances. Bring binding up over seam allowances to inside of garment. Pin in place.

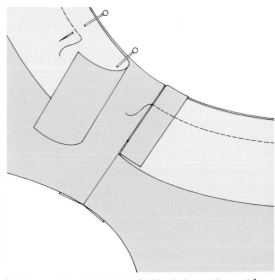

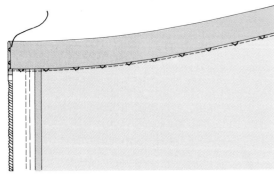

5. Slipstitch ends of binding closed. Then slipstitch the folded edge of binding to garment along the entire neck seamline. Stitches should not show on right side of garment.

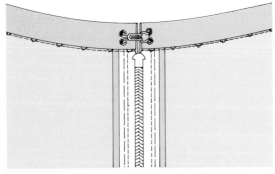

6. From the inside, press the neck edge. Close zipper and attach a hook and round eye to binding ends. The ends of the binding should meet when hook and eye are fastened.

1. When applying the binding, fold back the starting end 1 cm and align the fold with the garment seamline. Pin binding in place and stitch to within 8 cm of starting point.

Ready-made binding

Narrow hem facing and **fold-over braid** can both be used to bind necklines. Fold-over braid is already folded off-centre; if you are using narrow hem facing (2.5 cm width) you will have to press the off-centre fold first. The off-centre fold ensures that, when the tapes are positioned properly, both edges will be caught in the same stitching. These tapes can also be preshaped to match the curve they will be applied to. Other tapes can be used, provided they have finished edges and can be shaped.

When **shaping tape** to fit an inward curve, which necklines generally are, stretch the open edges while easing in the folded edge. To shape an outward curve, do the reverse: stretch the fold while easing in the open edges.

Narrow hem facing folded off-centre

Fold-over braid

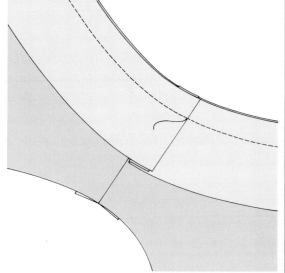

2. Trim away excess binding at this end to 1 cm beyond fold of starting end. Lap this end over the beginning fold and stitch the rest of the way across, through all thicknesses.

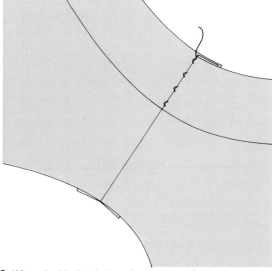

3. When the binding is turned up, the end folded first will be on top. Slipstitch ends together as they lie. Finish according to binding type (single-layer or double-layer).

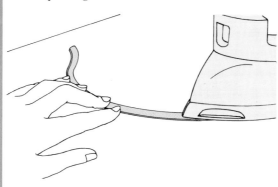

1. These bindings should be shaped to match the curve of the neck edge before application to garment. With your hand and a steam iron, mould the binding into the proper curve.

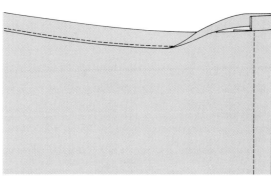

If neckline has a placket opening, fold ends back even with edges of placket. Then topstitch binding to neckline and attach fastener at ends (see Step 6, opposite page).

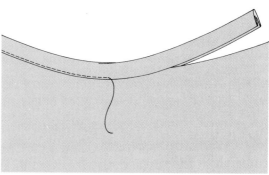

2. Wrap shaped binding around neck edge with wider half to inside of garment and the fold along the neck edge. Topstitch along outer edge of narrower half, handling ends as below.

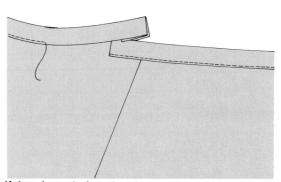

If there is no placket, place the starting end 1 cm ahead of a garment seamline. Stitch to within 8 cm of start. Fold second end under to align with seamline, and complete stitching.

Neckline finishes

Shaped bands and knit bands

Another way to finish a neckline is with a separate fabric band. The two basic types are the **shaped band** and the **knit band.** The shaped band, which is cut to a precise shape according to a pattern, has two main parts: the band and its facing (sometimes an extended facing).

The knit band is a strip of knitted fabric folded in half lengthwise; it is shaped to conform to the neckline curve before or during application. Used on both woven and knit fabrics, how a knit band is applied depends on the amount of stretch in the fabric and on size of neckline (see pp. 220–221).

Shaped-band neckline finish

Knit-band neckline finish

Shaped-band neckline finish

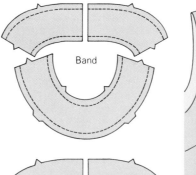

Band

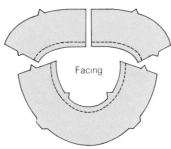

Facing

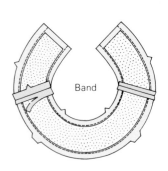

Band

1. To help maintain their shapes, apply staystitching along the neck and outer edges of the band, the neck edge of the facing, and the top edge of garment. If neckline is a V or square, reinforce the corners with short stitches for 2 cm on both sides of corners, then clip into the corners. Do not insert zipper.

2. Select an interfacing appropriate to the garment fabric and apply it to the band. Interfacing illustrated is iron-on type. With right sides together, match and then seam the band sections to form complete band. Press seams flat, then open. Trim seam allowances to half-width. Construct facing unit as described on page 205.

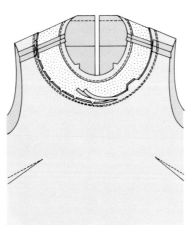

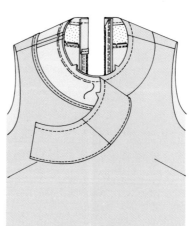

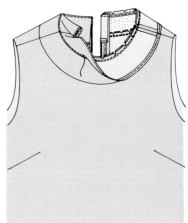

3. With right sides together, matching all markings, notches and cross seamlines, pin and tack the band to the garment. Stitch along seamline. Remove the tacking and press seam flat. Trim, grade, and notch the seam allowances. Press the seam open; then press the seam allowances and the band up, away from the rest of the garment.

4. Insert the zipper, positioning the top stop 1 cm below neck seamline, being sure to match the cross seams within the placket. Open zipper. With right sides together, and matching all markings, notches, and seamlines, pin and tack the facing to the band along neck edge. Stitch. Remove tacking and press the seam flat.

5. Trim, grade, and clip the seam allowances. Press seam open, then press seam allowances and facing away from garment. With facing right side up, understitch along seamline through all layers. Turn facing to inside; secure it to garment at shoulder seams and slipstitch the ends of the facing to the zipper tapes. Attach appropriate fastener at top.

Placket bands

The **placket band** is a variation of the shaped band, in that it is cut from a pattern and applied in a similar way. Both a type of garment opening and its finish as well, it is most often straight, which permits both the band and its facing to be cut out as one piece. Such a facing is an extended facing.

Sometimes the unit will be a **combination neck and placket band,** as in the second illustration below. When this is the case, it is applied by a combination of techniques from those used for the neckline shaped band, on the opposite page, and the placket band, shown and explained at the right.

Straight placket band

Combination neck and placket band

Straight placket band

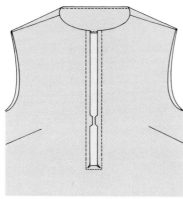

1. Staystitch the opening a thread width from the seamline, using shorter stitches for reinforcement at corners and across the bottom. Clip into corners.

4. Turn each band and facing to the right side; pull out the corners. Using a press cloth, press the entire band from the facing side.

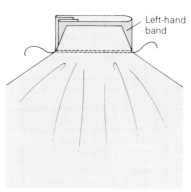

7. With right sides together, match, pin and stitch lower edge of left-hand band to garment at end of placket. Press seam flat, then downward.

Band / Facing

2. Apply interfacing to wrong side of each placket band. Placket band illustrated is interfaced with an iron-on interfacing; facing is an extended facing. If bound buttonholes are planned, construct them in the right-hand placket band at this point.

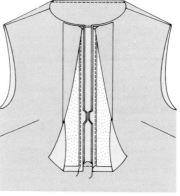

5. With right sides together, matching markings, notches, and seamlines, pin and tack each band to the garment. With band side up, stitch in place. Press.

Left-hand band
Right-hand band

8. At lower end of right-hand band, trim and turn in seam allowances; slipstitch them together. Press flat. Apply machine buttonholes now if they are being used.

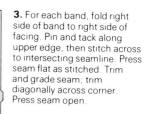

3. For each band, fold right side of band to right side of facing. Pin and tack along upper edge, then stitch across to intersecting seamline. Press seam flat as stitched. Trim and grade seam; trim diagonally across corner. Press seam open.

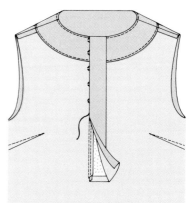

6. Trim and grade seam allowances. Press seams open, then toward bands. Finish backs of bound buttonholes. Turn under edge on each facing; slipstitch to band.

9. Match centre lines and lap right-hand band over left. Sew buttons to left band.

Neckline finishes

Knit bands

Knit bands are a suitable neckline finish for knit and woven fabrics. Two application techniques have been devised. The first is for knits with **limited stretch,** e.g., most double knits, and woven fabrics; the second is for **very stretchy** knits, such as sweater knits. Bands cut from slightly stretchy (limited stretch) knits are shaped to match the curve of the neck *before* being applied.

If the neckline is high, it may be necessary to insert a zipper (see pp. 222–223). If it is a wide or low neckline, like the one at right, a zipper is not needed. Stretchy knit bands, which are ideal for higher necklines, are shaped to the neck edge *during* application. In these cases, a zipper is optional. When a woven fabric that does not stretch has been used in a garment with a low neckline, a knit band may be used to finish the neckline.

Neckline finished with a slightly stretchy band

Neckline finished with a very stretchy band

Applying a limited-stretch knit band

Finished width

Seam allowance

1. Cut strip twice the desired finished width plus two seam allowances. Length is equal to the length of neckline seam plus two seam allowances. Cut on crosswise grain.

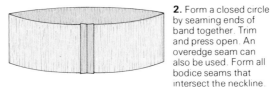

2. Form a closed circle by seaming ends of band together. Trim and press open. An overedge seam can also be used. Form all bodice seams that intersect the neckline.

3. Fold strip in half lengthwise, with its wrong sides together and edges even. Tack edges together. Pin-mark centre back (the seam) and centre front (at opposite halfway point in band).

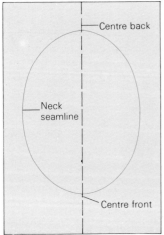

Centre back

Neck seamline

Centre front

4. On a piece of calico or heavy paper, draw exact shape of the entire neckline seam. Mark on it centre front and back. Pin this guide to ironing board.

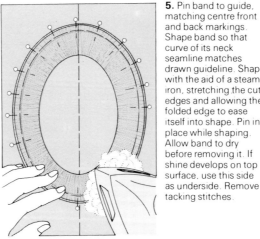

5. Pin band to guide, matching centre front and back markings. Shape band so that curve of its neck seamline matches drawn guideline. Shape with the aid of a steam iron, stretching the cut edges and allowing the folded edge to ease itself into shape. Pin in place while shaping. Allow band to dry before removing it. If shine develops on top surface, use this side as underside. Remove tacking stitches.

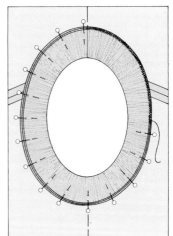

6. Turn the garment inside out. Pin band to right side of garment, matching seamlines and centre markings. With band side up, stitch to garment, using an overedge or double-stitched seam (see Seams). Remove pins as you stitch. Press seam allowances toward the garment; band extends away from the garment.

Stretchy knit bands

A stretchy knit band can be cut from the same fabric as the garment or cut from a purchased banding called ribbing. Ribbing is a stretchy knit fabric that is sold by the metre, cut and finished to a specific width. Many colours and designs are available. Whether you use the garment fabric or a bought ribbing, the knit should be stretchy but have the ability to recover (return to its original shape after being stretched).

Most typical of the necklines to which stretchy bands can be applied successfully are the **crew neck,** the **mock turtleneck** and the **turtleneck.** The width of the band will be determined by the neckline type. Examples of suitable finished widths are 2.5 cm for a crew neck, 5 cm for a mock turtleneck, and 10 cm for a turtleneck (5 cm when it is turned back on itself). All purchased ribbings are a precise width and can be used only at that

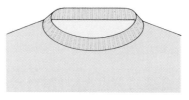
Crew neck

Mock turtleneck

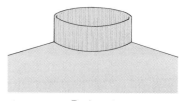
Turtleneck

width. If you are cutting the band yourself, cut it twice the finished width plus two seam allowances. Then fold it in half lengthwise, producing one finished edge.

The length of the band is determined by (1) the stretch and recovery capabilities of the knit; (2) measurements at the parts of the body it must first pass over and then fit snugly (that is, the head and neck); (3) tension required for close fit during wear.

To give an example, a turtleneck band applied to a neckline without a zipper must have the right combination of stretch and recovery, and be of sufficient length, to pass over the head, yet hug the neck when worn. Generally such a band is cut from 5 to 10 cm shorter than the neck seamline. If the neckline has a zipper opening, the band can be very nearly the same length as the neckline because it will only have to hug the neck.

Applying a stretchy knit band

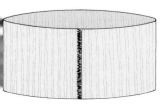

1. With right sides together, seam ends of band to form a closed circle. Use overedge or double-stitched seam (see Seams). Form bodice seams that intersect neck seamline.

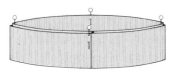

2. Fold band in half lengthwise, wrong sides together and edges even. Divide the band into four equal parts; mark with pins. One mark, the centre back, is at the seam formed in Step 1.

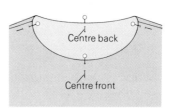

3. To ensure equal distribution of band over garment edge, divide the garment's neckline into four equal parts. Two marks are at centre front and back, others are halfway between.

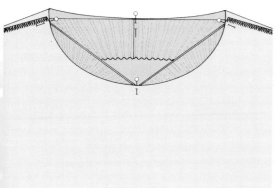

4. Turn the garment inside out. Place band to right side of garment, matching pin marks and neck seams. Stretch band to fit garment neckline; pin in place. Take care to keep raw edges of band and garment even.

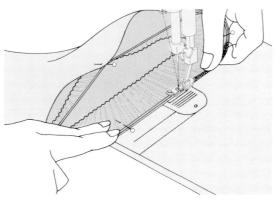

5. With band side up, stitch band to garment, using either an overedge or double-stitched seam (see Seams). Stretch the band so that it lies flat against the garment's edge; do not stretch the garment. Remove pins as you stitch.

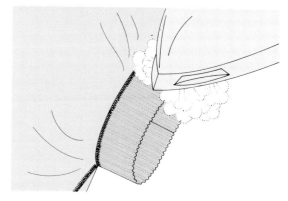

6. Holding the iron above the seam, allow the steam to return the seam and band to their unstretched state. Then press the seam allowances toward the garment. Let the band dry thoroughly before handling so that it will not stretch out of shape.

Neckline finishes

Zippers in knit band necklines

If necessary, a zipper can be added to a knit-band neckline. This is done by applying the band to the garment, according to the type of fabric it is cut from, while making allowances for the insertion of the zipper. Follow one of the band applications from pages 220–221, but allow for the exceptions explained in the zipper methods on these two pages. Techniques described here will place the zipper between the two layers of the band.

If you use a single-layer ready-made ribbing, the top of the zipper is finished differently. Use the exposed zipper method if garment has no placket seam; centred zipper method if there is a seam.

Exposed zipper application

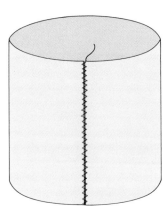

1. Cut band according to type of neckline and fabric (see pp. 220–221). Temporarily seam band into closed circle, using a butted seam, as follows: trim away seam allowances, then butt seamlines and join with a zigzag stitch, catching both of the edges in the stitching.

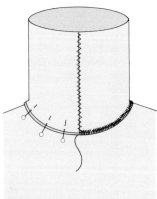

2. Apply band to garment, using appropriate method (see p. 220 or 221), except stitch only one band edge, the one facing the right side of garment. Press seam up toward band. If a slightly stretchy band is the type being applied this will require removal of the tacking stitches holding the edges together.

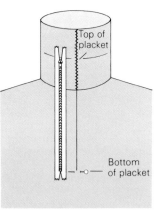

3. To locate centre of placket, lightly press a crease, from the right side, along the centre back of the garment. To determine how long placket opening should be, place zipper along crease, with top stop just below the foldline of band (the top of the placket), and insert a pin just below the bottom stop to mark bottom of placket.

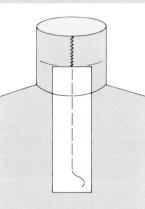

4. Cut a piece of stay fabric 8 cm wide and 5 cm longer than placket opening. Draw a line or press a crease in stay fabric the length of the placket opening. Centre this line over crease in garment; pin and tack in place along line.

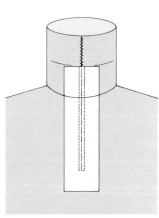

5. Sew stay fabric to garment by stitching 3 mm from both sides of centred lines and across the bottom of the placket.

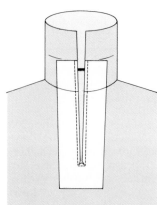

6. Slash through and remove stitching of the butted seam in the band and cut along the centred lines to within 1 cm from end of placket. Then cut to the stitching at each corner, forming a wedge at bottom.

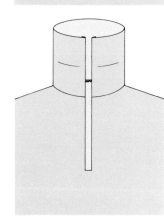

7. Turn all the stay fabric to inside of garment; press so that none of it shows on the right side of the garment.

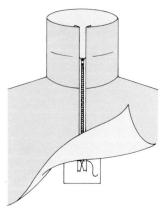

8. Position zipper under opening with top stop at fold of band and bottom stop at the end of placket opening; pin. Slip-tack zipper to edges of opening. Lift garment up to expose the wedge and bottom of zipper. Using a zipper foot, stitch across base of wedge, through the wedge, stay fabric and zipper tapes.

Centred zipper application

9. With zipper closed, fold back one side of garment to expose zipper and stitching from Step 5. Using a zipper foot, sew zipper to garment by stitching, from bottom to top, along the stitching line. Fold back other side of garment and stitch other zipper tape to garment in the same way. Trim away the excess stay fabric.

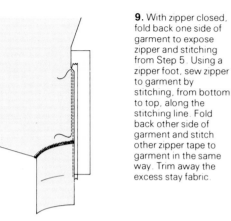

1. Cut band according to type of neckline and fabric (see pp. 220–221). Apply band to garment according to the appropriate method chosen (p. 220 or 221), except do not seam band into a circle, and sew only one of its edges—the one closest to the garment's right side—to the garment. Press seam up toward band.

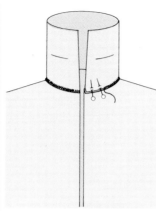

2. With band extended away from garment, machine-tack entire placket seam closed. Positioning the top stop just below fold of band, insert zipper, using the centred zipper application (see Zippers).

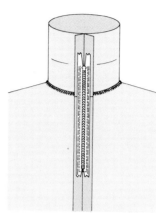

10. Trim excess zipper tape at top of placket. Open zipper and extend one tape, its seam allowance and stay fabric. Fold free half of band down to right side of band, matching ends. Pin in place and stitch along zipper stitching line. Repeat process for other half of zipper.

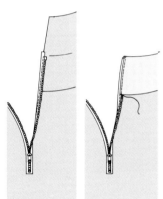

3. Open zipper and fold free half of band to inside of garment. Match the neck seamlines of band and garment; pin in place from right side. Fold under edges of band at each zipper tape and slipstitch them to the tapes.

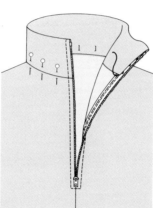

4. Stitch from the right side, in the seam groove, through all layers; remove pins as you stitch. Use a straight stitch for this, stretching the fabric, if necessary, as you stitch.

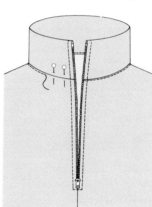

11. Turn band to inside of garment and match neck seamlines of band and garment; pin in place from right side. Stitch from the right side, in the seam groove, removing pins as you stitch. Use a straight stitch for this, stretching the fabric, if necessary, as you stitch.

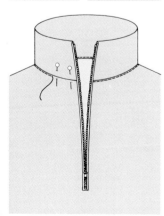

Ready-made ribbing

If you are using a length of ready-made ribbing, you will have only one layer to work with. Because of this, the part of the zipper that extends into the band cannot be stitched between layers, as was specified in the two preceding zipper applications.

When positioning a zipper for a neckline that has a single-layer band, place its top stop at the top edge of the band and turn under the upper ends of the tapes. Then apply the zipper, catching the turned-under tapes in the stitching (1). To finish the zipper within the band area, and ensure that it will lie flat against the band, sew the edges of the zipper tape to the band with herringbone stitches (2).

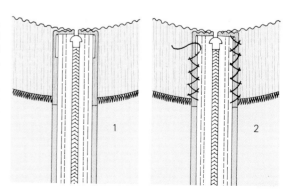

Collars

Types of collar

Though they come in many shapes and sizes, all collars are basically one of three types: **flat, standing** or **rolled**. And different as they may be in other respects, collars are alike in one way that is important to understand. Each has a top and bottom portion, usually called the *upper* and *under* collar, sometimes the *collar* and *collar facing*. It does not matter how the outer edge of a collar is shaped; this shape does not affect its basic construction. The curve of the inner edge, however, is important. It is the relation of the curve at this edge to the neckline curve that determines the collar's type.

The more alike the two curves are, the less the collar will stand up from the neck edge (flat collar). The more these curves differ, the more the collar will stand up (standing collar). If the curves differ slightly, the collar will stand up to some extent, then fall (rolled collar).

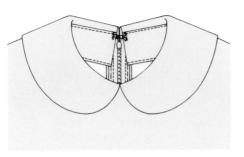

A flat collar emerges from the neck seamline to lie flat against the garment, rising only slightly above the garment's neck edge. Examples are Peter Pan and sailor collars. Flat collars occur most often in untailored garments, such as dresses, and in children's wear.

A complete flat collar may consist of two separate units or one continuous unit. When a collar has two units, one is intended for the right-hand portion of the neck, the other for the left-hand portion. The construction of a flat collar is explained on page 226; its application is described on page 227.

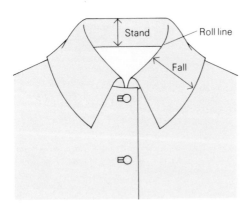

A rolled collar first stands up from the neck edge, then falls down to rest on the garment. The line at which the collar begins to fall is called the *roll line*. The positioning of this line determines the extent of the stand, and thus the fall, of the collar. Examples of the rolled collar, other than the one shown, are the notched and the shawl collars.

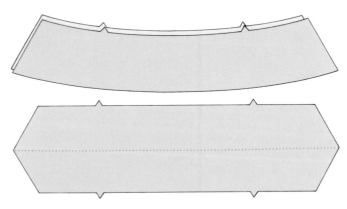

Rolled collars are usually constructed from separate upper and under collars. Some, however, are constructed from one piece, which, when folded back onto itself, forms the entire collar. Either type may or may not have a seam at the centre back. Construction and application methods for the rolled collar are on pages 228–236.

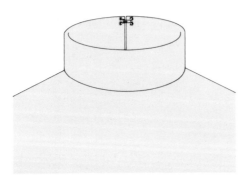

A standing collar extends above the neck seamline of the garment either as a narrow, single-width band or as a wider, double-width band that will fold back down onto itself. Most standing collars are straight, but they can be curved so that they stand up at a slight angle. A shirt collar with a stand is a variation of the standing collar.

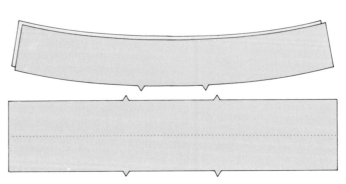

A standing collar may be either rectangular or slightly curved in shape. Some have a separate upper and under collar; others are formed from one piece that folds back on itself to form the entire collar. The methods for the construction and application of standing collars are detailed on pages 237–240.

Interfacings

Interfacing is an important part of any collar because it helps to define and support the collar's shape. If a collar is to be tailored, the best interfacing choice is the appropriate weight of an iron-on interfacing or a hair canvas. It adds firmness but relatively little shape to the collar. On collars that will not be tailored, any type of interfacing can be used, so long as its weight is compatible with that of the garment fabric. For adequate support, interfacing should be firm-grade woven or non-woven. It is applied before pattern markings are transferred. For general guidance in the selection of interfacing types, see pages 88–96.

This book deals only with those collars that will not be tailored. As a general rule, interfacing is applied to the wrong side of the under collar; there are exceptions to this, however, and these are clarified as they arise in the collar construction methods that follow. Basic methods of applying interfacing to an under collar are given below.

Where to apply the interfacing

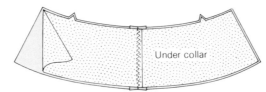

Interfacing is generally applied to the wrong side of the under collar. Some exceptions to this rule are discussed in connection with the adjoining three illustrations.

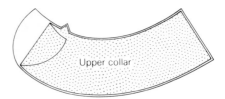

If constructing a flat collar from a very lightweight fabric, apply interfacing to wrong side of *upper* collar. This prevents seams from showing through to the finished side.

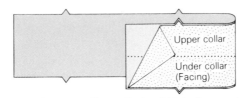

If constructing a standing collar in which both parts of the collar are one piece, interfacing can be applied to *wrong side of entire piece* if garment fabric is not too bulky.

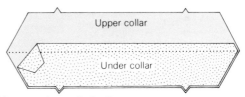

With a one-piece rolled collar, interfacing is applied to wrong side of the under collar area but, if you prefer, it can *extend 1 cm beyond foldline* into the upper collar.

Interfacing applications

The method chosen for the application of interfacing depends upon the type of interfacing being used. Shown at the right are the methods appropriate for lighter-weight and heavy conventional interfacings, and for iron-ons. Some general rules, however, apply to them all. (1) Transfer all pattern

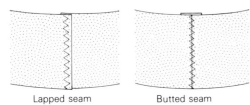

Lapped seam   Butted seam

markings to the interfacing. (2) If there is a centre back seam, and the interfacing is a sew-on, join the interfacing, before application, with either a lapped or butted seam (see Seams in interfacing on p. 88). (3) Reduce bulk at corners by trimming across them 2 mm inside the seamline.

On collars that are to be tailored, the interfaced under collar requires padstitching (see Padding stitches, hand or machine).

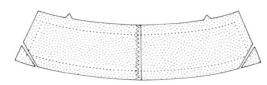

Lighter-weight interfacings: Transfer markings. Form seam if necessary. Trim across corners 2 mm inside seamline.

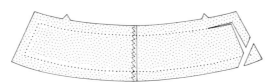

Heavy interfacings: Transfer markings. Form seam if necessary. Trim away all seam allowances and across corners.

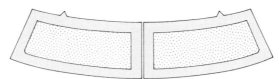

Iron-on interfacings: Transfer markings. Trim all seam allowances and corners. Iron onto wrong side of under collar.

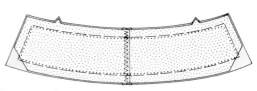

With the interfacing to the wrong side of the under collar, match, pin and tack inside the seamline.

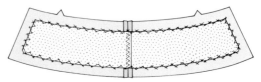

Match and tack the interfacing to wrong side of under collar. Herringbone stitch to under collar over all the seamlines.

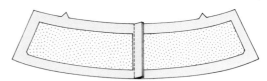

If necessary, form centre back seam in garment fabric (do not catch interfacing in seam). Press seam flat, then open.

225

Collars

Flat collars

Flat collars are the easiest type to construct and apply. One of the most familiar forms is the Peter Pan collar, being made and applied on these two pages. It is made up of two separate collar units, one applied to the left-hand portion of the neck and the other to the right-hand portion. The techniques used here can be followed for any kind of flat collar, including those that consist of only one unit that spans the entire neck edge, such as a sailor collar.

A zipper is the usual garment closure; insert it before applying the collar. If bound buttonholes will be used, construct them before applying the collar and finish their backs after application; make worked buttonholes after applying collar.

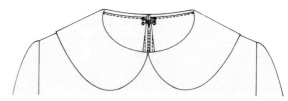

Construction of a flat collar

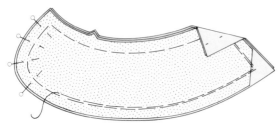

1. Apply interfacing to wrong side of each under collar. Right sides together, match, pin and tack each upper collar to each under collar, leaving neck edges open.

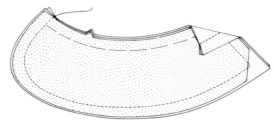

2. Stitch each unit along outer seamline, again leaving neck edges open. Use short reinforcement stitches at corners; stitch across corners to blunt them (see Seams). Press.

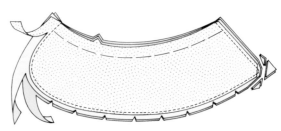

3. Trim and grade seam allowances; trim across corners and taper seam allowances on both sides of each; notch or clip the curved seam allowances (see Seams).

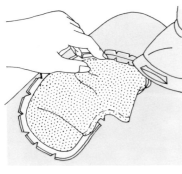

4. Press all seams open. Use a seam roll to press the curved areas of the seams and the corners; the ironing board for straight portions.

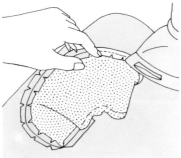

5. Using a seam roll and ironing board as explained in Step 4, press seam allowances toward the under collar.

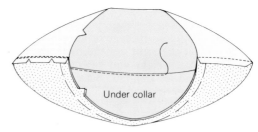

6. If desired, understitch the outer edge of each collar unit. With under collar right side up, understitch along the seamline, catching the seam allowances underneath.

7. Turn collar units right side out. To pull out corners, push a needle, threaded with a double, knotted length of thread, out through corner point. Pull on thread.

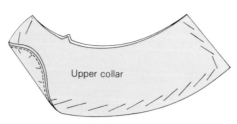

8. With the fingertips, work each outer seamline slightly toward the under collar side; hold edges in place with diagonal tacking. Using a press cloth, press collar.

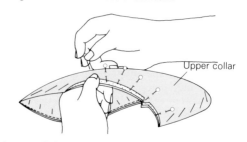

To form a slight roll, hold each collar unit, as shown, over hand, upper collar on top. Pin neck edges together as they fall; tack together along seamline of under collar.

Applying a flat collar

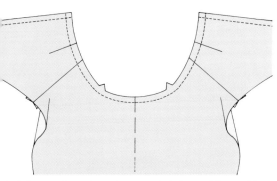

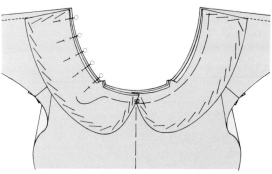

1. Before applying the collar, staystitch the neckline and form all seams and darts that intersect the neck seamline. Apply interfacing to the garment if necessary.

2. If collar consists of two units, as this Peter Pan flat collar does, align and join the two where their neck seamlines meet (seam allowances may overlap).

3. Match, pin and tack the collar to the garment along the neck seamline. Be sure that the point at which the two units are joined falls at the garment centre.

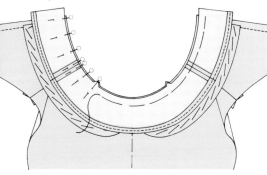

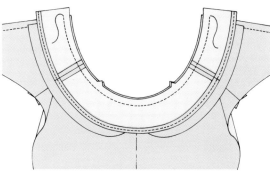

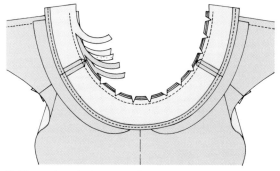

4. Form facing unit (see page 205). With the right side of facing toward upper collar, match, pin and tack unit to collar and garment at neck seamline (ends will extend at placket).

5. Facing side up, stitch facing and collar to garment at neck seamline; secure stitching. Be sure ends of seamline align when zipper is closed. Remove tacking; press.

6. Trim and grade the seam allowances, making the garment seam allowance the widest. Trim diagonally across the cross-seam allowances. Notch or clip the seam allowances.

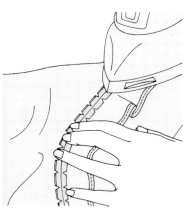

7. Place seam over a seam roll. Press the entire seam open, running tip of iron between facing and collar seam allowances

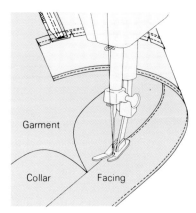

Garment

Collar   Facing

8. Press facing and all the seam allowances away from the garment. With facing side up, understitch close to the neck seamline.

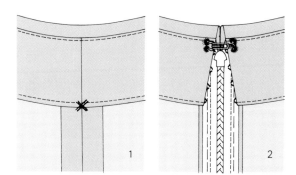

9. Press facing to inside of garment. Cross-stitch tack facing edge in place at shoulder seamlines (1). Turn facing ends under at zipper and slipstitch in place; attach fastener (2).

Interfacing 84–85, 88–91
Pad stitches 142, 152–153

Rolled collars

Rolled collars are differentiated from flat collars by a **roll line** that breaks the collar into **stand** and **fall** areas. The position of the roll line determines the location and size of both stand and fall. Typical examples of rolled collars are illustrated below, the second being the classic notched collar. Another is the shawl collar (pp. 238–240).

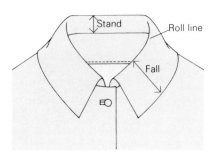

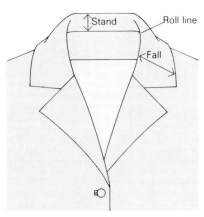

Methods are given on these two pages for the construction of both the two-piece form of the rolled collar (upper and under collars separate) and the one-piece (upper and under collars set apart by a fold). Methods of application appear on pages 230–233; the choice of method depends upon the weight of the garment fabric and whether or not there is a back neck facing.

On tailored garments, a collar may be interfaced with hair canvas or iron-on interfacing. Padstitching will give firmness and some shape.

Construction of a two-piece rolled collar

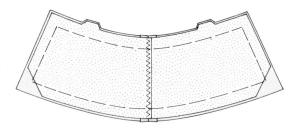

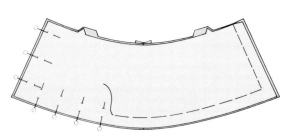

1. Apply interfacing to wrong side of under collar. If there is a centre back seam: for the garment fabric, use a plain seam trimmed to half-width and pressed open; for the interfacing, use a lapped or butted seam.

2. Right sides together, match, pin and tack the upper collar to the under collar along the outer seamline, leaving the neck edges open. If necessary, slightly stretch the under collar to fit the upper collar.

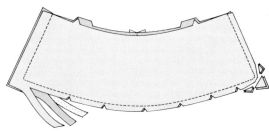

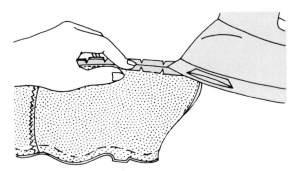

4. Trim and grade the seam allowances, making the seam allowance nearest the upper collar the widest. Trim across corners and taper seam allowances on both sides of corners. Notch or clip curved seam allowances (see Seams).

5. Carefully press the entire seam open. Use a seam roll for the curved areas of the seam and for the corners; use the ironing board for the straight portions of the seam. Try not to press a crease into the collar itself.

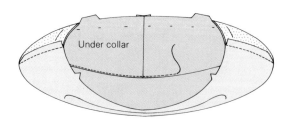

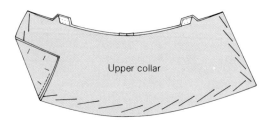

7. If necessary, understitch the outer seamline. With the under-collar-side up, understitch close to the seamline, catching all of the seam allowances underneath. Turn collar right side out; to pull out corners, see Step 7, page 226.

8. Work the outer seamline slightly toward the under collar side so that it will not show from the upper side. Hold outer edges in place with diagonal tacking; leave neck edges open. Using a press cloth, press the collar.

Construction of a one-piece rolled collar

Collars

In one-piece rolled collars, the upper and under collars are areas defined at their outer edges by a fold rather than separate pieces joined by a seam. One half of the collar piece is designated the upper collar, the other half the under collar. (There are some one-piece collars that begin, literally, as two pieces because of a centre back seam; when it is joined, the two form one piece.)

The fold between the upper collar and under collar areas makes the construction of a one-piece rolled collar different from that of the two-piece version, the one-piece collar being formed when the two halves are folded together and seamed at the sides. The application of both collars, however, is the same (see pp. 230–233).

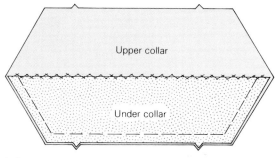

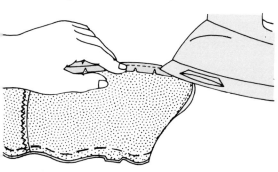

3. Stitch upper collar to under collar along outer seamline, leaving neck edges open. Use short reinforcement stitches at corners; stitch across corners to blunt them (see Seams). Remove tacking from outer seamline; press.

1. Apply interfacing to the under collar area. If edge of interfacing meets the foldline, herringbone stitch in place over the foldline; if edge extends beyond the foldline, hold in place along foldline with small stitches spaced 1 cm apart.

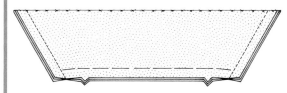

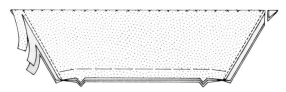

6. Press all of the seam allowances toward the under collar, again placing the curved, straight and cornered parts of the seam over a seam roll or the ironing board. Take care not to crease the rest of the collar.

2. Fold collar in half along the foldline so that the right sides of the upper and under collars are facing. Match, pin and tack along the side seams; stitch along the seamlines and secure stitching at ends. Remove tacking from side seams.

3. Press the seam flat as stitched. Trim and grade the seam allowances, making the one nearest the upper collar the widest. Taper the seam allowances at the corners, being careful not to cut into the stitching.

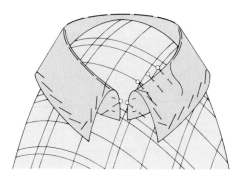

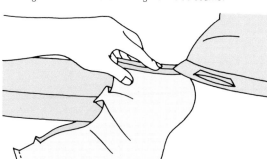

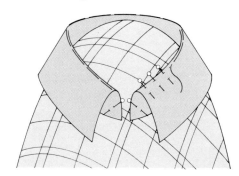

9. Mould collar, over a tailor's ham, into shape intended by pattern. Pin and tack through all layers along roll line. Steam collar; let dry. Remove from ham; pin and tack neck edges together as they fall. Remove diagonal tacking stitches.

4. Using a seam roll, press the seams open, then press all the seam allowances toward the under collar. Turn the collar right side out; to pull out the corners, see Step 7, page 226. Using a press cloth, press the collar.

5. Mould collar, over a tailor's ham, into the shape intended by the pattern. Pin and tack through all layers along the roll line. Steam collar; let it dry. Remove from ham; pin and tack neck edges together as they fall.

229

Collars

Applying a rolled collar (lightweight to mediumweight fabrics)

This method of collar application can be used if the garment fabric is light to medium in weight. With this method, both the upper and under collars are sewn to the garment at the same time that the facing is being attached to the garment. If the garment needs interfacing, apply it before attaching the collar. If bound buttonholes are being used, construct them before applying the collar; finish their backs (or construct worked buttonholes) after the collar and facing have been applied to the garment. Construct the collar according to one of the methods from pages 228–229.

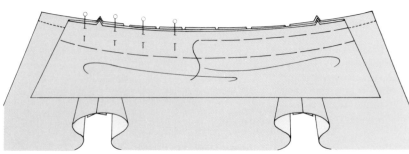

1. Staystitch garment neck edges and form all seams and darts that intersect neck seamline. With under collar toward right side of garment, match, pin and tack collar to garment, clipping garment seam allowance, if necessary, so collar will fit easily.

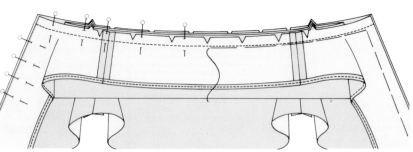

2. Construct facing unit (p. 205). With right side of facing toward right side of garment and upper collar, match, pin and tack facing through collar and garment at neck and garment opening. Clip facing seam allowance at neck, if necessary, so facing fits easily.

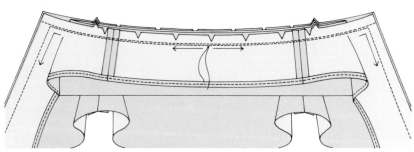

3. Facing side up, stitch facing and collar to garment. Stitch each side directionally, from centre back to the bottom of the garment opening. Use shorter reinforcement stitches for 2 cm on both sides of each corner. Remove tacking. Press seam flat as stitched.

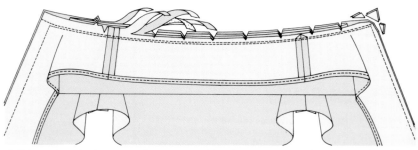

4. Trim and grade the seam allowances, making the one nearest the garment the widest. Trim diagonally across the cross-seam allowances and corners; taper the seam allowances on both sides of each corner (see Seams). Notch or clip the curved seam allowances.

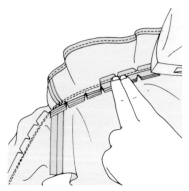

5. Press the entire seam open over a seam roll, running tip of iron between the facing seam allowance and collar or garment seam allowance, depending on area being pressed.

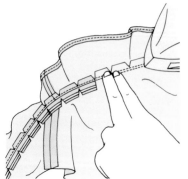

6. Still using the seam roll, press all the seam allowances toward the facing.

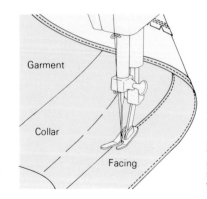

7. Understitch the neck and garment opening seamlines where necessary. Facing side up, stitch close to seamline, through all the seam allowances. Press facing to inside of garment; attach to shoulder seams with a single tack.

Garment

Collar

Facing

Applying a rolled collar (heavy or bulky fabrics)

This is the method to use if the garment fabric is bulky or heavy. In this technique the under collar is sewn to the garment and the upper collar to the facing. The resulting seams are then pressed open and allowed to fall onto each other as they will. Attaching the collar in this manner causes the bulk at the neckline to be divided between the two seams. If necessary, interface the garment before attaching collar. If bound buttonholes are being used, construct them before applying the collar; finish their backs (or construct worked buttonholes) after collar and facing have been applied.

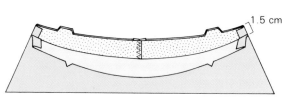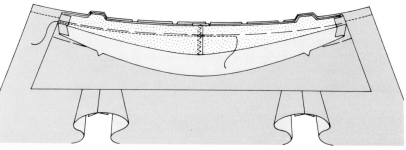

1.5 cm

1. Construct the collar, following the appropriate construction method from pages 228–229, but ending stitching at the sides 1.5 cm from the neck edge.

2. Mould the collar as in Step 9 or 5, page 229, but do not tack neck edges together.

3. Staystitch garment neck edge; form all seams and darts that intersect neck seamline. Right sides together, match, pin and tack under collar to garment; clip garment seam allowance if necessary for collar to fit. Stitch along seamline; secure stitching. Press.

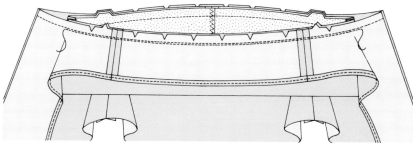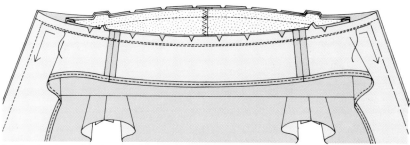

4. Construct facing unit (p. 205). With right sides together, match, pin and tack facing to upper collar only; clip facing seam allowance if necessary for facing to fit. Upper-collar-side up, stitch facing to upper collar; secure stitching. Remove tacking stitches.

5. Match, pin and tack remaining portions of facing to garment. Directionally stitch each side: starting at a collar end, stitch to bottom of garment opening; secure stitching. Use short reinforcement stitches at corners. Remove tacking stitches.

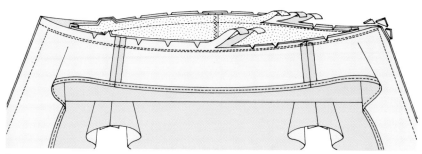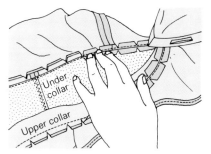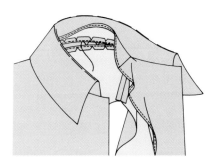

6. Press all seams flat; trim. Trim across corners and taper seam allowances on both sides of each corner. Grade seam allowances beyond the collar ends to the bottom of each opening side. Notch or clip all seam allowances.

7. Using a seam roll, press all seams open; then press the seams beyond collar and along garment opening toward facing.

8. Turn facing to inside. Allow neck seamlines of collar to fall as they may; pin, then tack in place with catchstitch.

231

Collars

Applying a rolled collar to garment without back neck facing

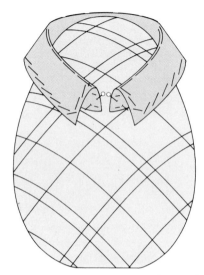

1. Construct the collar, following appropriate method from pages 228–229. Mould the collar over a tailor's ham as in either Step 9 or Step 5 on page 229. Remove collar from ham as directed but do not tack neck edges together.

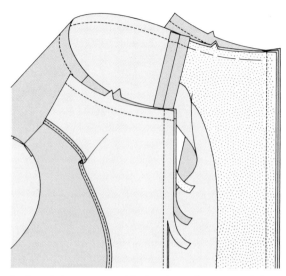

2. Staystitch garment and facing; form all seams and darts that intersect garment neck seam. Interface garment; construct round buttonholes. Sew facing to garment at opening edges. Press seams flat; trim and grade; press seams open.

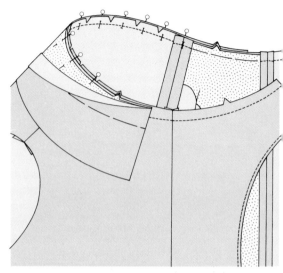

3. Right sides together, match and pin the under collar to the garment neck seamline from one shoulder to the other, clipping the seam allowance of the garment where necessary so that the collar will fit smoothly.

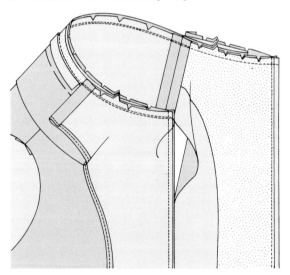

7. Keeping the upper collar seam allowance free across the back, stitch the facing and collar to the garment along the neck seamline. Secure stitching at both ends. Remove all of the tacking stitches; press the seam flat.

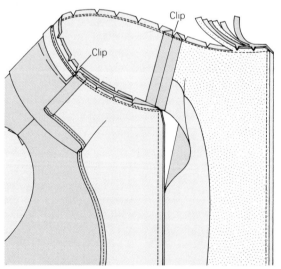

8. Trim and grade seam allowances, making seam allowance of garment the widest. Trim across corners and taper seam allowances on both sides of each corner; at both shoulders, clip into all seam allowances. Clip or notch curved areas.

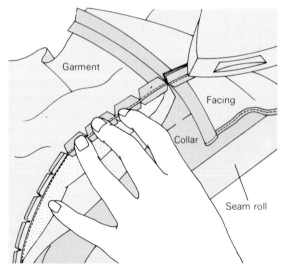

9. Using a seam roll, press the entire seam open, pressing between the facing and the collar or garment from each shoulder to front edge; between under collar and garment across the back neck from shoulder to shoulder.

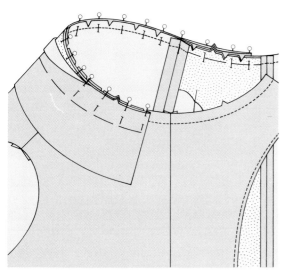

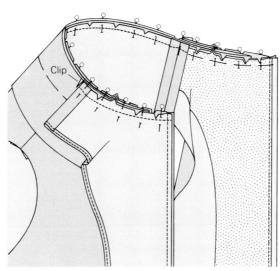

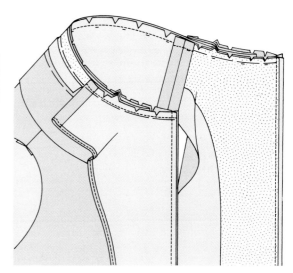

4. Match and pin both the under collar and the upper collar to the garment neck seamline from each shoulder to corresponding end of collar. Clip the garment seam allowance if this is necessary for the collar to fit.

5. At both shoulders, clip upper collar to seamline. Right sides together, match and pin facing to garment and collar along neck seamline, clipping facing seam allowance if necessary. Fold back facing ends at shoulder seamlines.

6. Fold back the free portion of the upper collar seam allowance. Tack through all layers along the neck seamline, taking care to keep the upper collar seam allowance free along the entire back neck edge. Remove all pins.

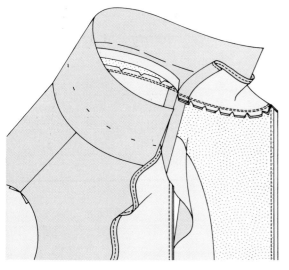

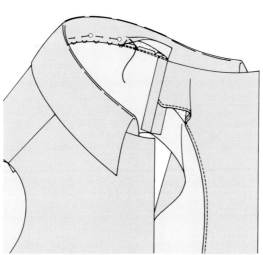

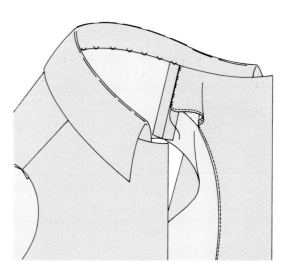

10. Place seam over a seam roll and press the front parts of the seam down, toward the garment; the back portion of the seam up, toward the collar. Press seams at opening edges toward facing; turn facing to inside of garment.

11. Let the collar fall into position along its roll line; smooth the upper collar over the under collar. Turn under the free upper collar seam allowance; pin, then slipstitch in place along the garment neck seamline. Press.

12. Slipstitch turned-under ends of facing in place along garment shoulder seamlines; press. If necessary, finish the backs of bound buttonholes (or construct worked buttonholes). Remove tacking stitches from collar at roll line.

Collars

Shawl collar

The shawl collar is like the standard notched collar in that the completion of both these collar styles involves the formation of lapels (see illustration below and on p. 228). The shawl is different from the notched collar in that its upper collar and lapels are cut from a single pattern piece; this eliminates the need for the seam between collar and lapels that is characteristic of a notched collar. The outer edge

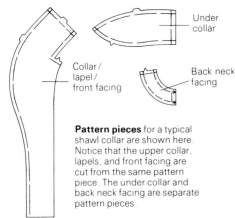

Under collar

Collar/lapel/front facing

Back neck facing

Pattern pieces for a typical shawl collar are shown here. Notice that the upper collar, lapels, and front facing are cut from the same pattern piece. The under collar and back neck facing are separate pattern pieces.

of a shawl collar is usually an unbroken line, but on some patterns this edge will be scalloped or notched to give the impression of a notched collar.

As a rule, the shawl collar is attached to a wrapped-front garment that is held together by a tie belt. In double-breasted garments, buttons or some other kind of fastener will be used.

Constructing and applying a shawl collar

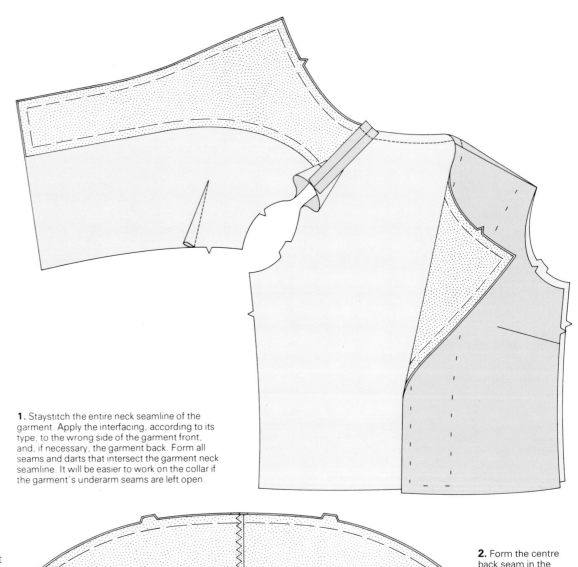

1. Staystitch the entire neck seamline of the garment. Apply the interfacing, according to its type, to the wrong side of the garment front, and, if necessary, the garment back. Form all seams and darts that intersect the garment neck seamline. It will be easier to work on the collar if the garment's underarm seams are left open.

2. Form the centre back seam in the under collar. Press seam flat, trim to half-width, then press open. Apply interfacing to wrong side of under collar (see p. 225).

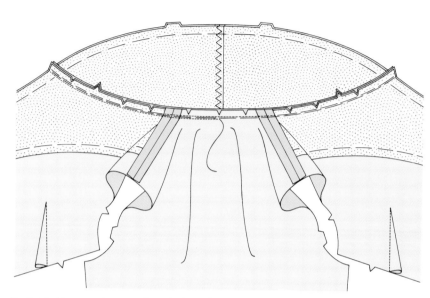

3. Right sides together, match and pin under collar to garment along neck seamline; clip garment seam allowance if necessary for collar to fit smoothly. Tack along neck seamline. Garment side up, stitch under collar to garment. Remove tacking; press seam flat.

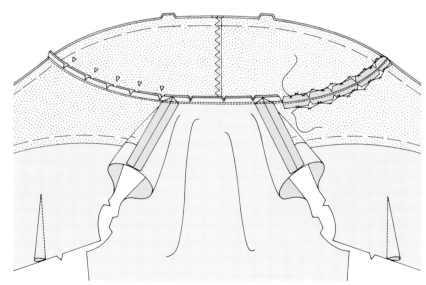

4. Trim seam allowances to 1 cm; diagonally trim the cross-seam allowances. Finger-press seam open; clip garment seam allowance and notch under collar seam allowance until they both lie flat. Press seam open; herringbone stitch over both edges to hold seam open.

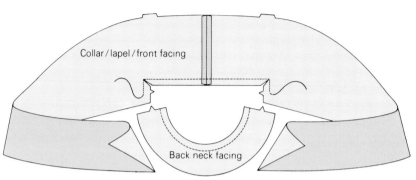

Collar / lapel / front facing

Back neck facing

5. Staystitch neck seamline of the collar/lapel/front facing pieces and reinforce corners with short stitches. Seam the two pieces together. Press seam open, then flat; trim to half-width. Clip into both corners. Staystitch neck seamline of back neck facing piece.

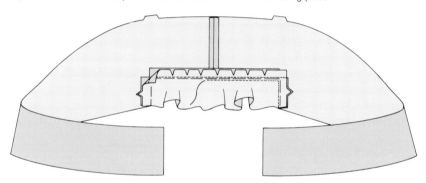

6. Match and tack the back neck facing to the collar/lapel/front facing; clip back neck facing seam allowance where necessary and spread collar/lapel/front facing at corners. Collar/lapel/front facing side up, stitch the seam, reinforcing and pivoting at corners.

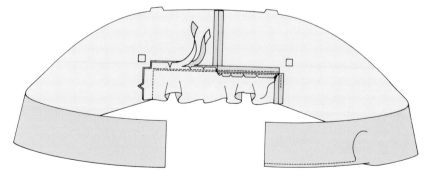

7. Press seam flat, trim to 6 mm, then press seam open. Notch out both corners of the back neck facing seam allowance; whipstitch these edges together. If necessary, apply a seam finish to the outer, unnotched edge of the entire unit. *(Continued next page)*

Collars

Constructing and applying a shawl collar (continued)

8. With right sides together, match and tack the collar/lapel/facing unit to the under collar. Stitch the seam directionally, from centre back down on each half. Press seam flat; trim. Clip into seam at both ends of lapel roll line. Grade seam *above* the clips, making seam allowance of collar/lapel/facing unit the widest; grade seam *below* clips so that the garment seam allowance is the widest. Clip and notch the seam; press open. Press seam above clips at roll line toward the under collar; press the seam below these clips toward the facing.

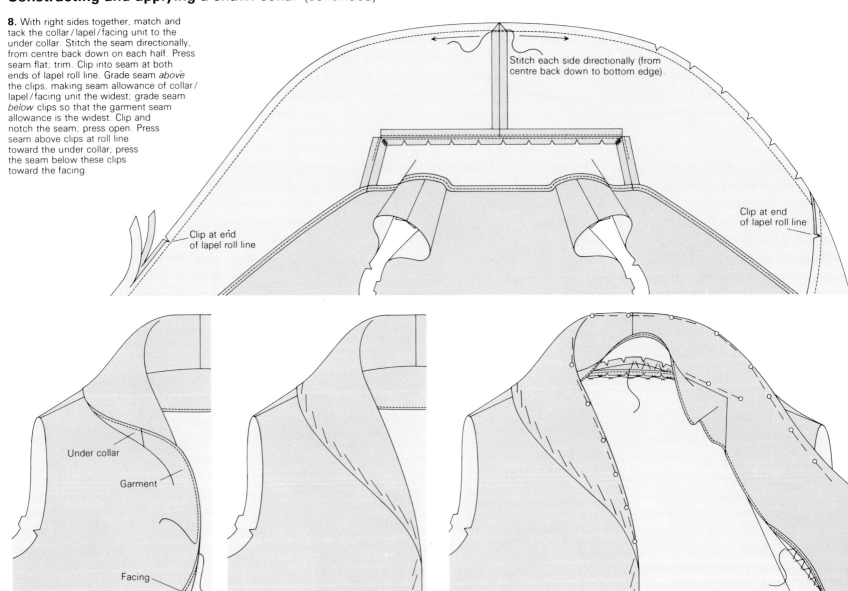

Stitch each side directionally (from centre back down to bottom edge).

Clip at end of lapel roll line

Clip at end of lapel roll line

Under collar

Garment

Facing

9. With under collar and garment side up, understitch outer edge of collar and lapels. With facing side up, understitch each edge of garment opening below the lapels.

10. Turn collar/lapel/facing unit to right side. Roll outer edge of collar and lapels toward under collar; roll edges of garment opening toward facing. Diagonal-tack along edges.

11. Allow collar, lapels and the facing unit to fall smoothly into place. Pin through all layers along the roll line and just above the back neck seamline. Lift up back neck facing and, using catchstitch, stitch facing and garment neck seamlines together as they fell. Remove pins. Attach lower edges of facing to garment with tacks.

Collars

Standing collars

Standing collars extend up from the neck seamline and are of two types: (1) the **plain standing collar,** also called the band or Mandarin collar; (2) the **turn-down standing collar,** sometimes known as the turtleneck or roll-over collar. The basic difference between the two is their initial width, the turn-down collar being twice as wide as the band style so that it can turn back down onto itself.

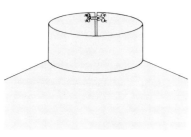

Plain standing collar

Turn-down standing collar

Standing collars are either rectangular or curved. Those that are rectangular, which either type can be, may be constructed from either one or two pieces. If a collar is curved, as only the plain collar can be, it will consist of two pieces.

Names given to the parts of a standing collar vary. The parts of the collars shown on the next few pages have been identified as either *collar* or *facing*. Sometimes only the collar is interfaced; if it is a one-piece unit, secure interfacing at foldline (see Interfacings). Both collar and facing can be interfaced if desired. Such interfacing decisions depend on the weight of the garment fabric.

For a variation of the standing collar, a shirt collar with a stand, see pages 239–240.

Constructing a one-piece standing collar

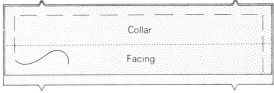

1. Interfacing for plain band collar is trimmed along neck seamline of facing, then applied to wrong side of collar and facing. (If garment fabric is bulky, interface collar only.)

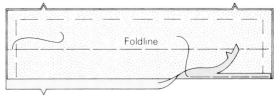

2. If necessary, tack interfacing in place along foldline. Fold up facing edge along its neck seamline; tack in place along seamline. Press; then trim to 6 mm.

3. Fold section along its foldline with right sides of collar and facing together. Match and stitch together along side seams. Press flat; trim and grade seam allowances.

4. Press the seams open, then toward the facing. Turn collar right side out. Using a press cloth, press the collar. Remove tacking stitches at foldline.

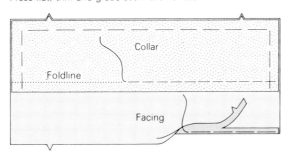

Turn-down collar is cut twice as wide as it would be if it were a plain band collar. So that the finished turn-down collar will not be too stiff or bulky, apply interfacing to the collar portion and 1 cm into the facing area. Hold in place at the foldline with short stitches, spaced 1 cm apart. Proceed with construction, following Steps 2, 3, and 4 above.

Constructing a two-piece standing collar

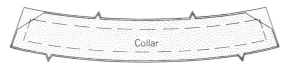

Whether the two-piece collar is curved, as shown, or rectangular in shape, the construction procedure is the same.
1. Apply interfacing to the wrong side of the collar section.

2. Fold up the facing's edge along its neck seamline and toward the wrong side of the facing. Tack in place near fold. Press; then trim to 6 mm.

3. With right sides together, match, tack and stitch collar to facing along the side and upper seamlines. Press seams flat. Trim, grade, and notch or clip seam allowances.

4. Press seams open, then toward the facing. Understitch the upper seamline if necessary. Turn collar right side out. Using a press cloth, press the collar.

Collars

Applying a standing collar to a garment

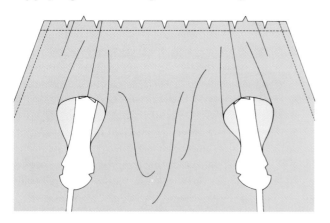

1. Staystitch the neck seamline of the garment. Form all seams and darts that intersect the neck seamline. Insert the zipper. Clip into the neck seam allowance at 2 cm intervals; this will permit the collar to fit smoothly onto the garment.

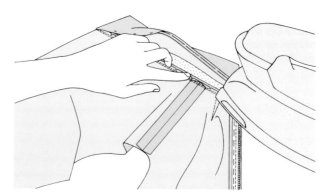

4. Using a seam roll, press the seam open, then press it up, toward the collar.

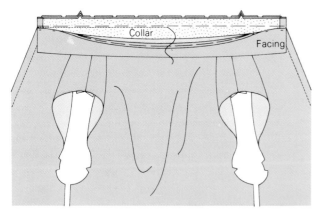

2. With right sides together, match, pin and tack the edge of the collar to the garment along the neck seamline. Stitch the seam and secure stitching at both ends.

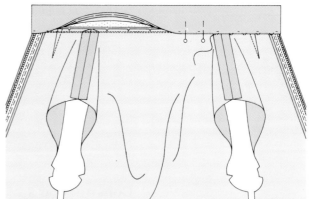

5. Bring the facing edge down to align with the neck seamline; pin in place. Slipstitch facing to garment along the neck seamline, removing pins as you stitch. Remove tacking stitches at facing edge and press neckline seam.

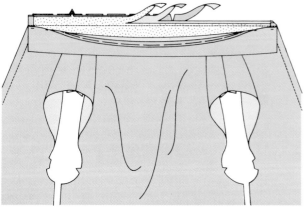

3. Press seam flat. Trim and grade seam allowances, making the collar seam allowance the widest. Trim diagonally across the corners and cross-seam allowances.

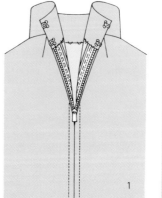 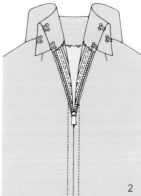

6. Attach fasteners so that the ends of collar meet when fastened. With a plain standing collar (1), sew two sets to the inside of collar, placing one set at neck, the other at the top of collar. For a turn-down collar (2), attach two sets as for the plain collar but sew another set to the centre of the turned-down portion.

Collars

Shirt collar with a stand

A shirt collar with a stand is commonly found on men's shirts but can also be used for jackets and for women's wear. This type of collar can be thought of as having two sections, *collar* area and *stand* area. The stand may be cut as a separate piece or it may be an extension of the collar. Whether the stand is cut as one with the collar or separately, the collar unit is applied to the garment the same way as any other standing collar.

As a rule, it is the under collar that is interfaced, but if the fabric is very lightweight or sheer, interfacing can be applied to the upper collar; this will prevent the seams from showing through to the finished side of the collar. It is always advisable to interface the stand. If the stand area is an extension of the collar, the interfacing is applied to *both* under collar and stand in a single piece.

The usual garment closure is buttonholes. Since a buttonhole is generally constructed in the collar stand after it has been applied to the garment, it may be more convenient to construct all of the buttonholes for both the garment and the stand after applying the collar.

Topstitching of the collar and stand is optional, but it is usally necessary if the placket of the garment has been topstitched.

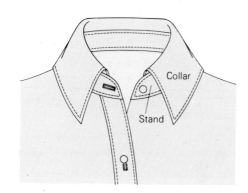

Collar

Stand

Constructing a shirt collar with a separate stand

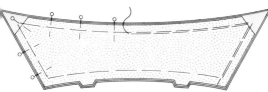

1. Interface the under collar (and stand, if it was cut out as part of under collar). Tack upper collar to under collar along side and upper seamlines. (If stand's facing was cut out as part of upper collar, handle neck edge as in Step 5.)

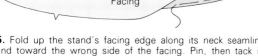

2. Stitch the seam. Use shorter stitches at the corners; stitch across corners to blunt them. Press seam flat. Trim, grade and clip the seam allowances. Trim across corners and taper seam allowances on both sides of the corners.

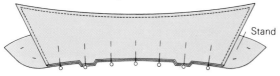

3. Press seam open, then toward the under collar. Turn the collar to the right side; pull out the corners (see Step 7, p. 226). Press collar from the under collar side. If desired, topstitch along the outer finished edges.

Stand

4. Apply the interfacing to the wrong side of the collar stand. (If the collar stand was cut out as a continuation of the collar, the stand was interfaced in Step 1 when the interfacing was applied to the under collar.)

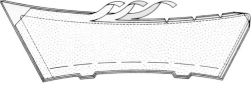

Facing

5. Fold up the stand's facing edge along its neck seamline and toward the wrong side of the facing. Pin, then tack in place close to the fold. Remove pins. Press; then trim the seam allowance to 6 mm.

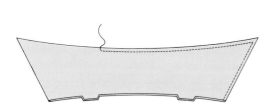

Stand

6. With the right side of the under collar toward the right side of the stand, match and pin the collar to the stand along the lower edge of the collar. The stand will extend beyond the ends of the collar.

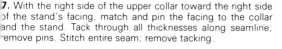

Facing

7. With the right side of the upper collar toward the right side of the stand's facing, match and pin the facing to the collar and the stand. Tack through all thicknesses along seamline; remove pins. Stitch entire seam; remove tacking.

8. Press seam flat. Trim and grade the seam, making the facing seam allowance the widest. Notch and clip the curved seam allowances. Press the seam open, guiding point of iron between the facing and upper collar seam allowances.

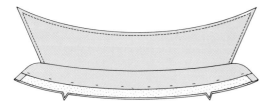

9. Turn stand and facing to the right side. Using a press cloth, press the seam, facing and stand down, away from the collar. If necessary, diagonal-tack through all thicknesses to hold them in place during pressing.

Collars

Applying a shirt collar with a stand to a garment

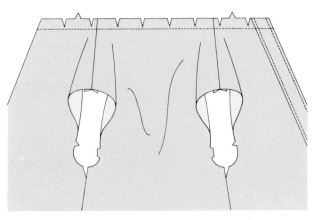

1. Staystitch garment neck seamline and form all seams and darts that intersect the neck seamline. Clip into the neck seam allowance at 2 cm intervals; this will permit collar to fit smoothly onto the garment.

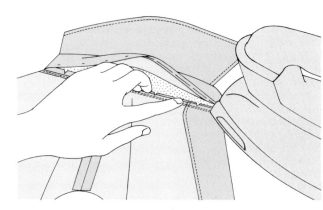

4. Using a seam roll, press the seam open, then up, toward the collar.

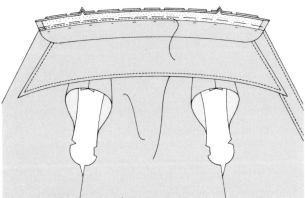

2. With right sides together, match and pin the stand to the garment along the neck seamline. Stitch the seam; secure the stitching at both ends.

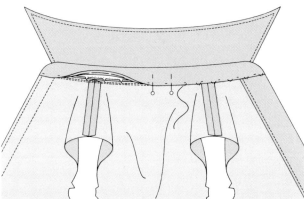

5. Bring the facing edge down to align with the neck seamline; pin in place. Slipstitch facing to garment along the neck seamline. Remove pins and all tacking stitches.

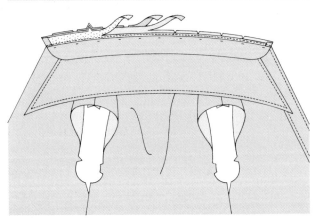

3. Press seam flat. Trim and grade the seam allowances, making the seam allowance of the stand the widest. Clip or notch seam if necessary.

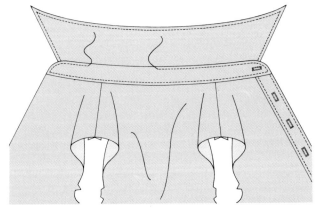

6. From the facing side, press the neckline seam. If desired, topstitch along all edges of the stand. Start and end topstitching on upper edge of stand at centre back. Bring threads to the inside and tie. Construct buttonhole in the stand (and buttonholes in garment if postponed until this stage).

Waistline seams may fall at the natural waistline, or almost anywhere between the bust and the hip. Wherever this essential design detail falls, and regardless of whether it is intended to be closely or loosely fitted, its treatment can range from the simple to the elaborate, from straightforward seams to casings, waistbands and all kinds of belts. All these are covered in this chapter, along with the use of knitted fabrics for insets and waistbands, for dresses, skirts, pants and tops. Here are tips for ensuring correct placement of the waistline and details of how to finish the seam itself and all its variants. The chapter closes with a helpful section on making belts and belt carriers.

Waistline joinings

Waistline seams

Waistline seams that join the top and the bottom of a garment may be located almost anywhere on the body between the hip and the bust. A garment waistline may fall, as many do, at the natural waistline, but it may also lie just underneath the bust, as it does in an Empire style, or be placed on the hips, as it is in a dropped-waist style. The waistline may be either closely or loosely fitted.

Some waistlines are formed not with an actual seam but by means of an attached casing or an insert of fabric or ribbing. The basic procedure for constructing a joining, an insert, or a casing remains the same regardless of location or fit.

Waistline seams are not always straight horizontal seams; they may be curved or angled sharply toward the bust or hips. It is generally best to fit the bodice and skirt individually to the body before joining them with the waist seam.

Preparation

Before the waistline seam is sewn, the following steps must be completed: (1) waistline edges on both bodice and skirt staystitched; (2) all darts, tucks, or pleats made; (3) all vertical seams stitched, seam-finished, and pressed open; (4) skirt waistline seam easestitched. Do the last step, easestitching, from the right side on the skirt waist seamline, breaking stitching at side seams and leaving 8 cm thread ends. If bodice ease is called for, follow pattern instructions.

If zipper placket intersects the waistline, zipper can be inserted only after forming waist seam.

Joining a bodice to a fitted skirt

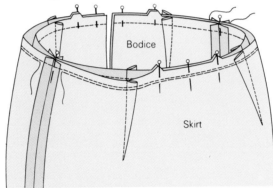

1. Turn the skirt to the wrong side and the bodice to the right side. Slip the bodice into the skirt (work is done with bodice inside skirt, their right sides together). Align and pin cut edges, carefully matching side seams, centre front and back, all notches. The skirt may be slightly larger than the bodice; easestitching will correct this.

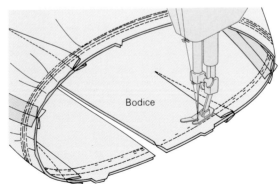

3. Stitch the waistline seam from placket edge to placket edge. Reinforce seam by beginning and ending it with backstitching. The garment is easiest to handle at this point if bodice is placed inside the skirt as it was for pinning and tacking, and the seam stitched from the inside, along the bodice seamline, as illustrated.

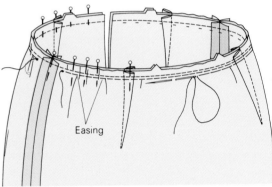

2. Pull on bobbin threads of easestitching until each skirt section exactly fits corresponding bodice section. Secure ease threads by knotting. Distribute fullness evenly, avoiding gathers, tucks, or any fullness within 5 cm of either side of centre front and back. Pin at frequent intervals; tack. Try on garment and make any necessary adjustments.

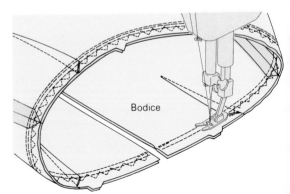

4. Trim ends of darts and cross-seam allowances. Remove tacking. Press seam as stitched. Finish seam in one of the two following ways: stitch seam allowances together with a zigzag or multistitch zigzag; or apply a waistline stay. Pull the bodice out of the skirt and press the seam again, with both seam allowances directed toward the bodice.

Applied casings

An applied casing may be sewn onto a one-piece garment that has no waistline seam; in effect, it substitutes for the seam by providing some fit at the waistline. The applied casing may also act as a facing for the top edge of pants and skirts and the lower edge of blouses and jackets.

It may be sewn to either the inside or the outside of a garment. If it is sewn outside, the casing may be made either of the garment fabric or of a contrasting trim. A casing sewn inside is usually made of a lightweight lining fabric or a ready-made bias binding to reduce unnecessary bulk. If an inside casing has a drawstring that is to be led to the outside, it is necessary to provide buttonhole or in-seam openings. An applied casing is most easily shaped to a garment if casing is cut on the bias.

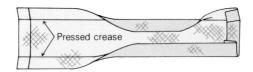

To prepare casing from fabric, first determine the width that the finished casing should be. It must be equal to the width of the elastic or drawstring plus 6 mm ease for freely threading the elastic or drawstring through the casing. In addition to these finished width requirements, 6 mm seam allowances are required on the edges; for this, allow an additional 12 mm in your width calculation. Length is determined by the circumference of the garment at the place where the casing will be applied plus 12 mm for finishing ends.

Determine true bias of the fabric, then pencil the dimensions of the casing onto the fabric to ensure accurate cutting. After cutting the casing, fold under and press 6 mm to the wrong side on all edges. Press ends under before pressing down sides.

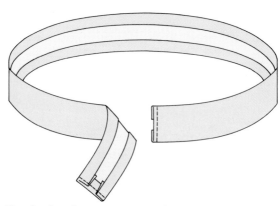

If casing is to be sewn to a one-piece garment, edgestitch both ends (turned under in preparation described above).

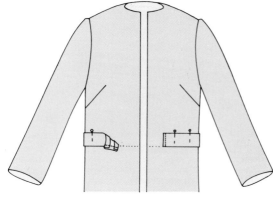

Pin casing to garment with lower edge on waistline marking on inside or outside of garment as pattern instructs

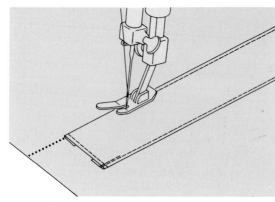

Edgestitch casing to garment on long sides. Backstitch at both ends of stitch lines to strengthen. Press casing flat.

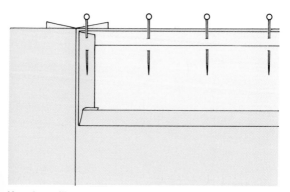

If casing will also serve as facing, first trim seam allowance at garment edge to 6 mm. With right sides together and starting at a vertical seam, pin casing to garment.

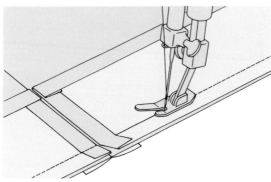

With ends of casing turned back as shown, machine-stitch along pressed crease of casing, which is 6 mm from cut edge. Overlap stitching at ends for reinforcement.

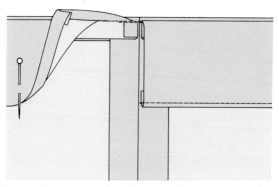

Turn casing to wrong side of garment, letting garment edge roll slightly inside. Pin casing in place. Edgestitch along lower edge, again overlapping stitching. Press flat.

247

Waistline casings

Threading elastic and drawstrings

Casings are threaded with elastic or drawstrings that, when drawn or tied, fit snugly around the body. Elastic for this purpose should be a firm, flat type or non-roll waistband elastic.

The exact length depends upon the elastic's stretchability, but it should be slightly less than the measurement of the body at the casing position plus 1 cm for lapping. Drawstrings may be cord, fabric tubing, braid, leather strips, ribbons, even scarves. Elastic can be combined with fabric or ribbon tie ends to give comfort and a pretty finish; the length of the ribbon ends depends upon the type of tie you have in mind.

If the area behind the drawstring opening needs reinforcement, iron a patch of interfacing, about 3 cm wide and slightly longer than the opening, to it.

Finishing a full casing

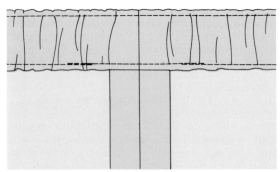

On a fold-down casing, close the opening by edgestitching. Keep area flat by stretching the elastic slightly as you sew. Take care not to catch the elastic in the stitching.

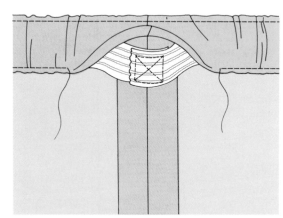

To insert elastic into a casing, attach a safety pin to one end of the elastic; secure other end to garment so it will not be pulled through the casing as the pin is worked around the waistline. Take care not to twist the elastic.

To join ends of elastic, first overlap them 1 cm and pin. Stitch a square on the overlapped area, crisscrossing it for strength. Or make several rows of zigzag stitching on all sides of this area. Pull joined ends inside casing.

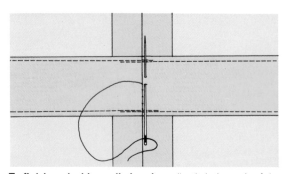

To finish an inside applied casing, slipstitch the ends of the casing together by hand. Make certain that the drawstring or elastic is not caught in the stitching.

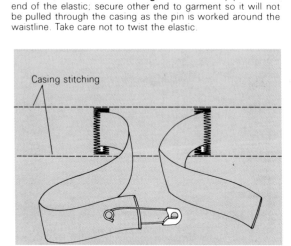

Casing stitching

A drawstring can be threaded through a casing with the help of a safety pin. If it is an inside casing, the drawstring can be led in and out through two vertical buttonholes, worked on the garment before the casing is applied.

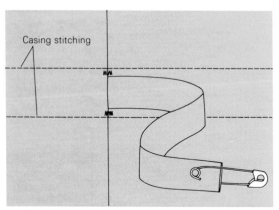

Casing stitching

A drawstring can also be led through an inside casing by way of in-seam openings. Simply leave openings in seams the width of the drawstring; reinforce with bar tacks at ends or small squares of seam binding stitched into seam.

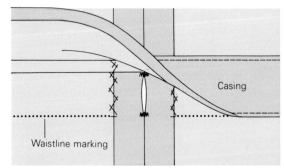

Casing

Waistline marking

To hold seam allowances flat in an in-seam opening, herringbone-stitch them to the garment. Be sure to do this before the casing is applied, taking care that the stitches do not show on outside of garment.

Finishing a partial casing

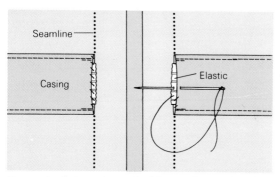

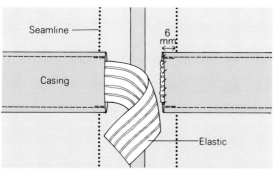

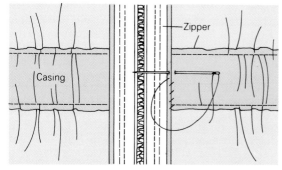

If a centred zipper is used with a casing, casing should stop at zipper seamlines. Apply casing; insert elastic or drawstring; whipstitch ends of elastic to ends of casing.

If an invisible zipper is used with a casing, extend the casing 6 mm beyond zipper seamlines as it is applied. Sew ends of elastic or drawstring to ends of casing.

Insertion of either zipper will secure ends of casing and elastic or drawstring. To finish, press zipper seam allowances flat over casing; whipstitch to casing as shown.

Mock casings

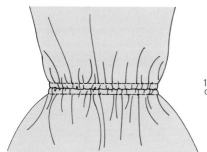

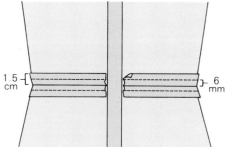

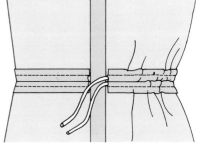

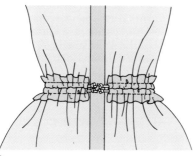

Plain seams, threaded with round elastic or fine strong cord, can substitute for conventional casing. Effect resembles shirring.

1. Stitch waistline seam; press open. Form casings' by stitching seam allowances to garment 6 mm on each side of seamline.

2. Using a tapestry needle or bodkin, thread cord or elastic through the casings. Adjust the shirring to the desired waist measurement.

3. Knot the ends of the cord or elastic, then stitch over them when inserting the zipper or closing the centre back seam.

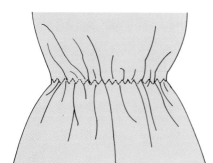

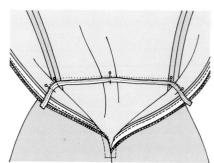

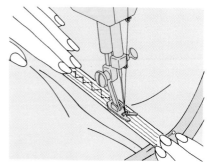

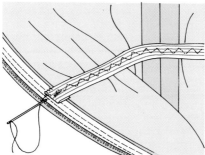

Narrow elastic can be stitched to the wrong side of a garment that has no waist seam. The result is very similar to that of a casing.

1. Cut elastic the desired length plus 2 cm; divide it and waistline into eighths. Pin elastic in place, with 1 cm ends at openings.

2. Stretch the elastic between pins as you stitch. Use either a narrow multistitch zigzag or two rows of straight stitching.

3. Turn the loose ends of the elastic under 1 cm and whipstitch them securely to the seam allowances or zipper tapes.

Waistline finishes

Waistbands and facings

There are several ways to finish the waistline edge of a garment. The straight waistband is the most familiar finish, but a contour waistband, stretch waistband or facing may be used. The pattern will specify a waistline treatment, but a different finish can often be substituted if desired.

Straight and contour waistbands are stable, inflexible finishes. They are made to fit the body's waist measurement plus some allowance for wearing ease. Straight waistbands are rectangular in shape and should be no wider than 5 cm. Contour waistbands are wider than 5 cm and are shaped to accommodate the difference in girth between the waist and rib cage or waist and hips.

Stretch waistbands are flexible and can be used on knit or woven fabrics. They can be made of a combination of fabric and elastic or of a decorative elastic. If a stretch waistband is to be used on a garment without a zipper, the hips should be no more than 25 cm larger than the waist; if the difference is greater, the garment will not pull over the hips and still fit the waist snugly.

A facing provides a clean, smooth finish that does not extend above the waistline edge. Made of a lightweight fabric, it can help reduce bulk.

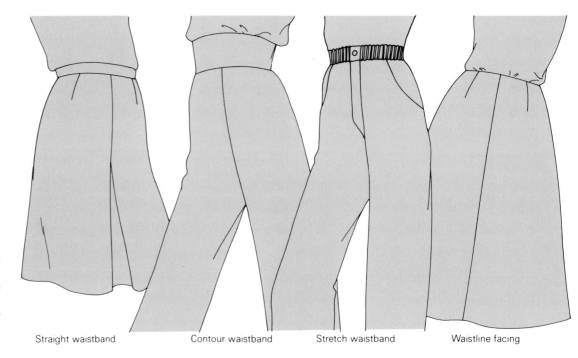

Straight waistband   Contour waistband   Stretch waistband   Waistline facing

Waistline placement

The waistline finish acts as an anchor for the garment, holding it in the proper position on the body. Exact placement of the waistline seam should be determined with the garment on the body. Try it on after all vertical seams and darts have been stitched and before the zipper is inserted; pin the zipper placket closed.

Tie a string snugly enough around the waistline to hold the garment up. Settle the garment around the body so that the seams and darts all lie in the proper positions. Pull the waist seamline above or below the string until the garment rides smoothly over the hips and the darts end at the correct position. When adjusting pants, pull them up until they fit well in the crotch and seat area.

After fitting, measure up 1.5 cm from the new seamline and trim away any excess to create a new seam allowance. Apply machine easestitching on the new seamline, then insert the zipper.

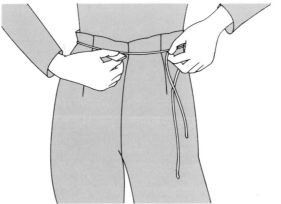

Mark waist seamline location directly beneath the string, with pins or chalk, after garment has been adjusted so that it fits properly. Seamline may not be level all around the body. Help may be needed for accurate marking.

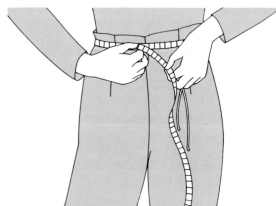

Measure the waistline circumference while the garment is still on the body and before removing string. Measure with lower edge of the tape measure along chalked mark. Use this waistline measurement to determine waistband length.

Interfacing 84–85, 88–91   Buttons 361–362
Worked buttonholes 355–358   Fasteners 364, 367

Cutting the waistband

Before cutting the waistband, decide where the waistband opening will fall and how much extension will be needed on each end of the waistband. The extensions at the ends of the waistband depend on the location of the placket opening on the garment. The ends of the waistband lap right over left when the opening is on the front or left side, and left over right on a centre back opening.

The overlap end is most often straight and finished flush with the edge of the garment opening. If a special decorative effect is desired, the end may be shaped into a point or a curve, in which case extra length must be allowed. Underlaps have straight ends, and must extend at least 3 cm beyond edge of opening to accommodate fasteners.

Patterns will include a piece for the waistband if called for by the design, but it may be easier to cut the waistband without a pattern, especially if the waistline has been altered. The length of the waistband should equal the waistline measurement as determined on the opposite page, plus 3 to 4 cm for ease, plus two 1.5 cm seam allowances, plus whatever is desired for overlap and underlap.

Waistband width is determined by the style of the waistband and how its back is to be finished. A straight waistband should be a maximum of 5 cm wide when finished; contour waistbands may be considerably wider.

A straight waistband can be finished with a separate or extended (self) facing; for a self facing, cut the waistband twice the finished width plus seam allowances. When waistband is folded in half, the facing forms the back.

Contour waistbands require a separate facing. A fabric facing is cut to the same dimensions as the waistband; petersham ribbon (for curved or straight waistbands) is purchased in the desired finished width.

If the waistband is cut without a pattern, locate and mark the foldline, seamlines, overlap and underlap, centre front, centre back and side. Waistbands should be cut on the lengthwise grain for greatest stability. If crosswise grain has to be used instead, the waistband must be interfaced.

Finishing. The waistband opening can be fastened with hooks and eyes, a button and buttonhole, or special waistband fasteners that either clamp or sew on. Multiple sets are used except when the fastener is a button; then a snap is added. The inner set of fasteners takes most of the strain; the outer set holds the top edge flat.

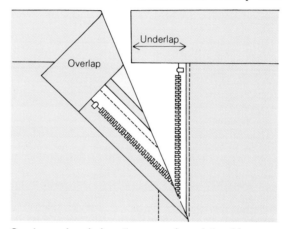

Overlap and underlap allow space for waistband fasteners.

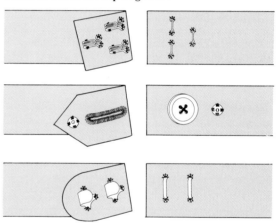

Fastener combinations most often used to close waistband.

Reinforcing the waistband

So that the waistband will hold its shape and strength throughout the life of the garment, it must be *reinforced with interfacing* or professional waistbanding. (Stretch waistbands, naturally, are exceptions to this.) In addition to reinforcement, an *underlining* may be needed to prevent seams from showing through and to add support to a delicate fabric. A waistband is not lined, but sometimes, to reduce bulk, a lining fabric will be used to make the waistband facing.

The type of interfacing used in a waistband is determined by the garment fabric. It should be sturdy but flexible, crease-resistant and durable, and it should have the same care properties as the garment fabric. The interfacing that is used in other areas of the garment may be adequate; if it is not, consider using two layers of that interfacing or one layer of a heavier interfacing.

If only one layer is needed, it should be attached to the waistband side of the unit (the one that will be outermost in the finished garment). If two layers are required, apply one layer to the waistband and one to the waistband facing. If the waistband has a self facing and the entire unit is interfaced, hold the interfacing to the waistband by machine-tacking through both layers slightly below the foldline, on the facing side.

Professional waistbanding can be used in place of regular interfacing. This is a flexible woven synthetic stiffener that has been heat-set in specific widths, ranging from 1 to 7 cm. It should be purchased in the exact width that the finished waistband is to be; it should not be cut down to size, as this will remove the finished edge and expose the sharp cross-yarns, which can scratch the skin. Professional waistbanding is applied differently from regular interfacing; exact instructions follow in this section (see p. 254).

251

Waistline finishes

Straight waistband formed as it is applied

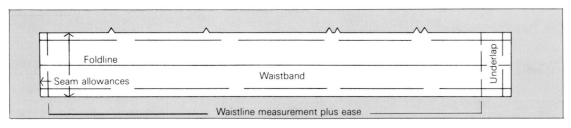

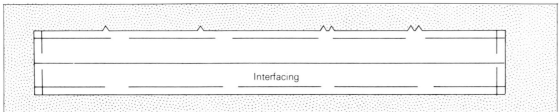

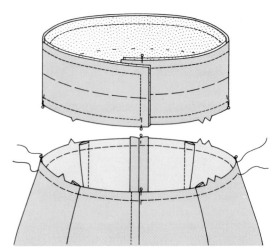

This is perhaps the most basic and traditional of all the waistband techniques. The waistband for this method is cut with an extended (self) facing and is then applied to the garment as a flat piece. The ends are formed and finished while it is being applied to the garment. If the waistband is to be cut without a pattern, determine the correct length and width as described on the preceding pages. The length of the waistband should be placed on the lengthwise grain of the fabric for greatest stability. Cut and apply the interfacing according to the type of interfacing that has been chosen and the number of layers being used. Mark the foldline of the waistband by tacking by hand through all thicknesses.

1. Pin-mark waistband and garment into sections (mark the edge of the waistband that will be sewn to the garment). Place a pin at beginning of overlap or seam allowance, another at beginning of underlap. Divide remainder of band into quarters. Pin-mark the garment waistline also into four equal parts, using the zipper opening as the starting point.

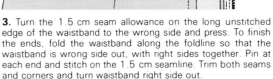

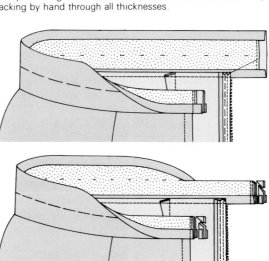

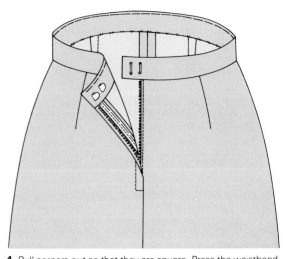

2. With right sides together, pin waistband to garment, matching pin marks and notches. Draw up the ease thread on garment between pins so that the fullness is evenly distributed and the garment lies flat against the waistband. Tack, then stitch, on the seamline. Press seam flat. Grade the seam allowances. Press the waistband and seam up.

3. Turn the 1.5 cm seam allowance on the long unstitched edge of the waistband to the wrong side and press. To finish the ends, fold the waistband along the foldline so that the waistband is wrong side out, with right sides together. Pin at each end and stitch on the 1.5 cm seamline. Trim both seams and corners and turn waistband right side out.

4. Pull corners out so that they are square. Press the waistband facing to the inside of the garment along the foldline, keeping the turned-under seam allowance intact. Pin turned-under seam allowance to garment. Slipstitch folded edge to the seamline, making certain that no stitches show through to the outside. Attach suitable fasteners to ends of waistband.

Straight waistband made before application

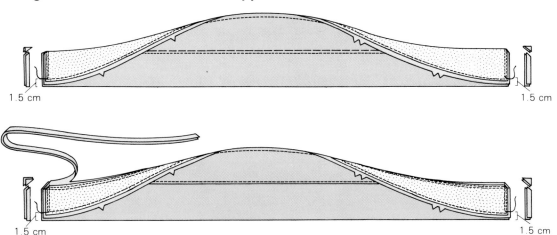

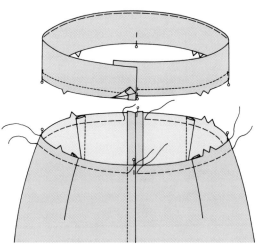

1. This waistband may be cut with an **extended facing,** as in the method opposite, or with a **separate facing.** Apply interfacing according to type and the number of layers being used, making sure it is attached to the side that will be outermost in the finished garment. To construct the waistband with an extended facing, fold the waistband in half lengthwise, right sides together, and stitch across each end from the fold to within 1.5 cm of the opposite edge. Secure the stitching. If the band has a separate facing, place right sides of facing and waistband together and stitch across ends and top. Stop and secure stitching 1.5 cm from lower edge on ends. Press seams flat, then grade seams and trim corners.

2. Turn the waistband to the right side and press. To simplify matching waistband to garment, pin-mark both into four equal sections. On the waistband, first place a pin at the beginning of the underlap, then divide remainder of band into quarters. Pin-mark the garment seamline evenly into quarters as well, starting at the actual opening of the zipper.

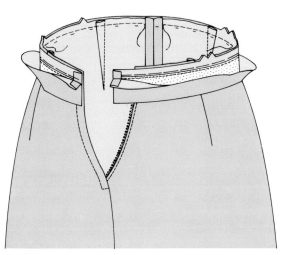

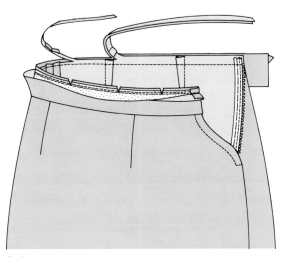

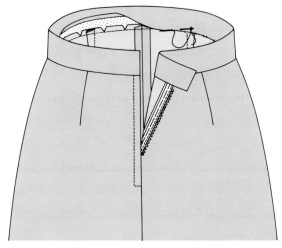

3. With right sides together, pin the waistband to the garment edge. Carefully match all notches and pin marks, making sure that the finished edge of the waistband overlap is flush with the edge of the zipper closing. Pull up the ease thread and adjust fullness evenly between pins so the skirt lies flat against the waistband. Tack along seamline.

4. Stitch the waistband seam from placket edge to placket edge. Be careful that no tucks are formed in the garment ease and caught in the stitching. Press the seam as stitched, then grade the seam allowances. Clip the seam allowances so they will lie flat when encased in the waistband. Remove any tacking that might show from the right side.

5. Turn the waistband right side out. Press along foldline and ends. Turn under 1.5 cm along the unstitched edge and pin to the garment. Slipstitch the fold of the seam allowance to the garment around the waist seamline and underlap. Sew carefully so that no stitches are visible on the right side of the garment. Attach suitable fasteners to ends of waistband.

Waistline finishes

Straight waistband with professional waistbanding

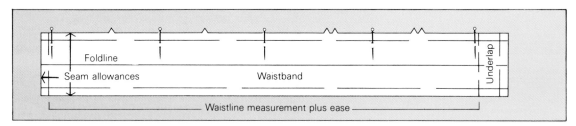

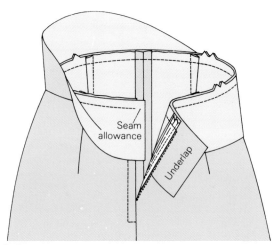

The waistband used for this technique is the straight waistband with self facing. Cut the waistband twice the width of the professional waistbanding plus two seam allowances. The length of the waistband equals the body waist measurement, plus ease allowance, plus two seam allowances, and at least 3 cm for underlap (allow extra length for an overlap).

1. Pin-mark the areas between underlap and overlap or seam allowance into quarters. Cut waistbanding (which has been purchased in the exact width the finished waistband is to be) the length of the waistband minus two seam allowances; extend waistbanding through underlap and overlap but not into seams at ends. (See Cutting the waistband, p. 251).

2. Pin-mark garment waistline into quarters. Pin waistband to garment, matching all marks. Place beginning of underlap to back edge of zipper opening, and overlap or seam allowance to front edge of zipper opening. Distribute garment ease evenly; tack and stitch seam. Press as stitched, then press seam and waistband up. **Do not grade seam.**

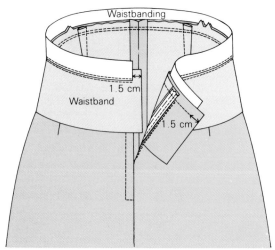

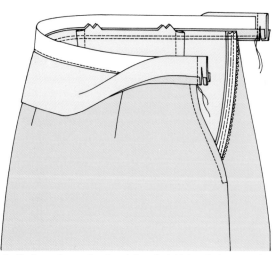

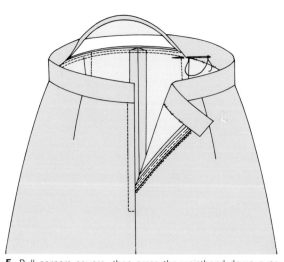

3. With waistband down over garment, lap the waistbanding over seam allowances. Place so that the width of the waistbanding is away from the garment, one edge is aligned exactly to the seamline, and the ends are 1.5 cm away from the ends of the waistband. Sew along edge of banding, through both seam allowances. Grade now if desired.

4. To form the ends of waistband, fold band along centre foldline so that right sides are together. Pin once at each end to hold the fold in place. Stitch along each end of waistband as close as possible to the waistbanding without actually stitching through it. Trim seams and corners. Turn waistband right side out, over banding.

5. Pull corners square, then press the waistband down over the banding. Turn under the 1.5 cm seam allowance along the unstitched edge and press in place. Pin the folded edge to the waistband; slipstitch this fold to the waistband seam or just above it. Stitching should not show on the right side. Finish the ends by attaching fasteners.

Constructing a straight ribbon-faced waistband

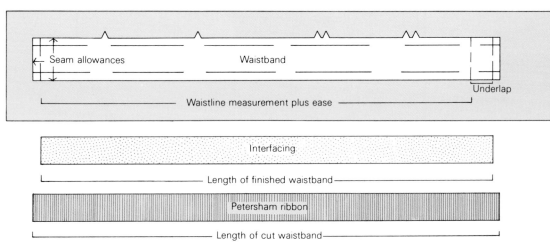

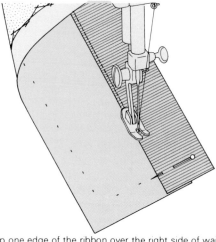

A ribbon facing on a waistband reduces bulk without sacrificing stability, making it a practical choice for nubby or heavy fabrics. Cut the waistband on the lengthwise grain of the fabric. The width should equal that of the finished waistband plus two seam allowances. The length should total the waist measurement, plus ease, two seam allowances, overlap if desired, and at least 3 cm for underlap (or to equal zipper underlay, if there is one—see illustration for Step 4). Purchase straight petersham ribbon for the facing the width of the *finished* waistband and the length of the *cut* waistband. Cut interfacing the width and length of the finished waistband. Herringbone-stitch (or iron) to wrong side of waistband (p. 251).

1. Lap one edge of the ribbon over the right side of waistband upper seam allowance. Align edge of ribbon with the seamline and match the cut ends of the ribbon with the ends of the waistband. For accuracy in stitching, it is best to pin or tack the ribbon in place. Stitch as close to the edge of the ribbon as possible, using a short stitch.

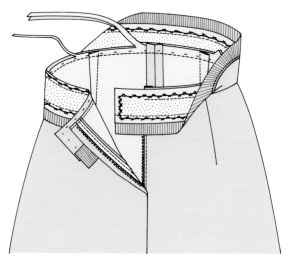

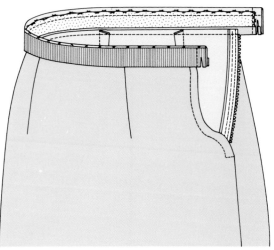

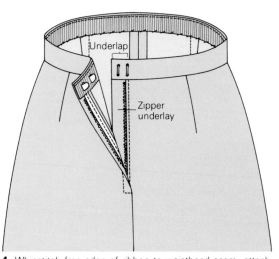

2. Pin-mark the waistband and garment into four equal sections, as described on page 252. Pin waistband to garment, right sides together, matching pin marks and notches. Draw up the ease thread so garment lies flat against waistband; keep ease evenly distributed. Tack and stitch the seam. Press seam as stitched; grade the seam allowances.

3. Press waistband and seam allowances up. To finish ends, fold right sides of the waistband together along the edge of the ribbon. Pin ends in place and stitch across them on the seamlines. Trim seams and corners; turn waistband to the right side. Press ribbon facing to wrong side along folded edge. Pin free edge of ribbon to waist seam.

4. Whipstitch free edge of ribbon to waistband seam; attach the fasteners. The zipper underlay illustrated here is used for fine tailored garments, often in conjunction with a ribbon-faced waistband. If this zipper application is used, allow for an underlap equal to the zipper underlay when cutting the waistband, ribbon and interfacing.

Waistline finishes

Topstitched straight waistband

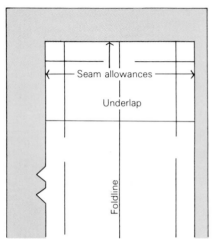

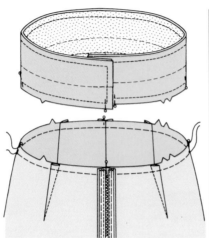

1. This quick and secure waistband is suitable for casual garments. Cut the waistband length to equal the waist measurement, plus ease, seam allowance, underlap, and overlap if desired. Width is twice the finished width plus seam allowances. Apply interfacing (p. 251).

2. Divide waistband and garment into sections. On the waistband, place a pin at beginning of underlap and another pin at overlap or seam allowance; pin-mark space between pins into quarters. Pin-mark the garment waistline into quarters, starting at zipper.

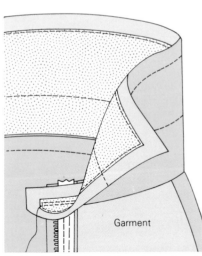

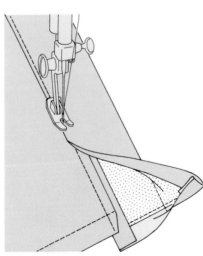

3. Pin the *right* side of the waistband to the *wrong* side of the garment, matching all pin marks and notches. Draw up ease thread and distribute any fullness evenly. Stitch the seam. Press as stitched, then press both seam and waistband up. Grade seam; trim corners.

4. Turn under seam allowance on free edge and ends of waistband; press. Turn waistband down to right side on foldline and pin turned-under edge over waistline seam, covering first stitching. Topstitch close to the edge through all thicknesses. Attach fasteners.

Straight waistband formed with selvage

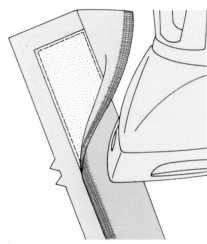

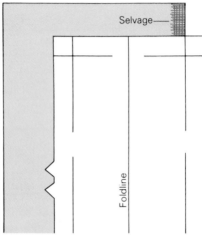

2. Not merely quick, this waistband technique helps to reduce bulk by eliminating a seam allowance. Determine size of waistband as directed on page 250, then cut the waistband so that the *seamline* of one long edge falls on the selvage. This provides one finished edge.

2. Fold the waistband lengthwise along foldline, wrong sides together (the long raw edge should extend 1.5 cm below the selvage); press. Interface the half of the waistband that has the raw edge. Interfacing should not extend into any seam allowances.

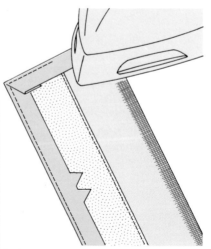

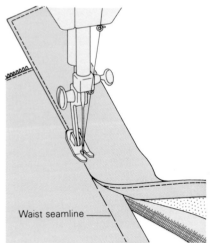

3. Turn the long raw edge and the ends to the wrong side on the seamlines and press. Make certain that pressed-under-edge does not extend below selvage edge when waistband is folded in half. Pin-mark waistband and garment into quarters as directed on page 253.

4. To enclose the garment edge within the waistband, place selvage to the inside and fold along waist seamline. Match all pin marks; pin if desired. Topstitch close to fold, from end to end, catching selvage in stitching. Press waistband flat. Attach fasteners.

Construction and application of a contour waistband

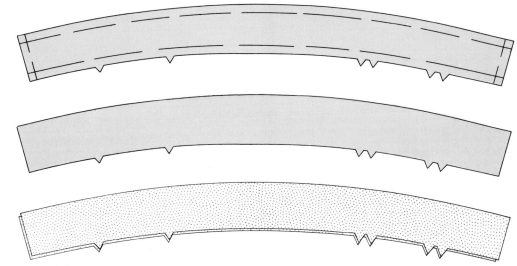

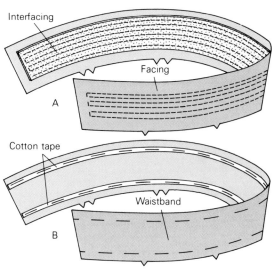

A contour waistband is at least 5 cm wide and is formed to fit the body's curves; it is often decoratively shaped along the top edge as well. The width and shape of this waistband requires a separate facing and a double layer of interfacing (hair

canvas if outer fabric permits). The interfacing is not applied to the waistband, as is usual, but to the waistband facing. This permits padstitching of the facing, which builds in and holds a permanent shape. (See Padstitching.)

1. Apply the two layers of interfacing to wrong side of waistband facing and padstitch through all layers by machine (A). To prevent stretching of the long edges, tack 6 mm cotton tape over seamlines on wrong side of waistband (B).

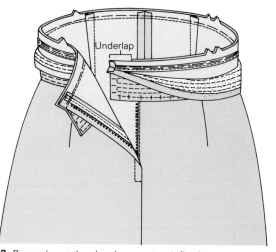

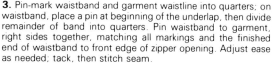

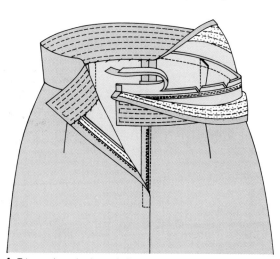

2. Right sides together, pin and tack waistband to facing along ends and upper edge. Starting and ending 1.5 cm from lower edge, stitch as tacked, pivoting at corners and stitching through centre of cotton tape. Press seam flat. Trim and grade seam allowances. Turn the waistband right side out; diagonal-tack around all three finished edges and press.

3. Pin-mark waistband and garment waistline into quarters; on waistband, place a pin at beginning of the underlap, then divide remainder of band into quarters. Pin waistband to garment, right sides together, matching all markings and the finished end of waistband to front edge of zipper opening. Adjust ease as needed; tack, then stitch seam.

4. Trim and grade the waistline seam; press it and waistband away from garment. Turn under seam allowance on lower edge of the facing and slipstitch the fold to the waistline seam and underlap. Remove all tacking. Press the finished waistband. Apply fasteners; the width of the waistband determines the number of sets and their placement.

Waistline finishes

Waistline finished with shaped facing

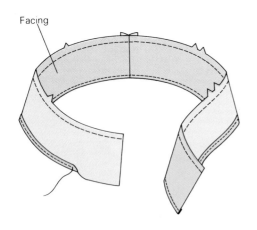

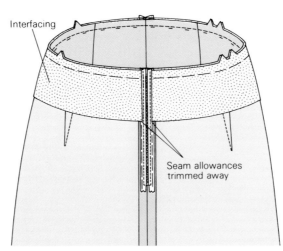

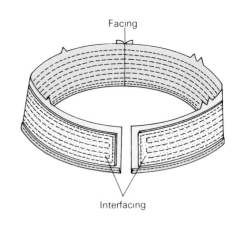

1. Cut facing from garment fabric; if this fabric is heavy, facing may be cut from a sturdy lighter-weight fabric to reduce bulk. Staystitch facing sections 3 mm inside waist seamline. Stitch sections together, leaving open the seam that corresponds to the placket opening. Apply appropriate seam finish to outer edge of facing. (See Seam finishes, pages 160–161).

2. Interfacing method depends on garment fabric. **For medium to lightweight fabrics,** apply one layer of interfacing to garment. Seam interfacing the same as facing; trim away 1 cm from outer edge and all of seam allowances at ends. Tack wrong side of interfacing to wrong side of garment, matching markings and positioning ends over zipper tapes.

If fabric is heavy, the combination of two layers of interfacing plus padstitching will support the waistline area and reduce wrinkling during wear. Cut the interfacing from facing pattern minus waistline seam allowance; trim lower edge of interfacing to same width as facing. Stitch interfacing seams and apply to wrong side of facing; padstitch. (See Padstitching.)

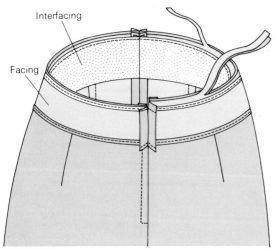

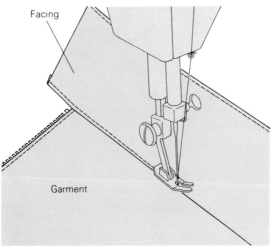

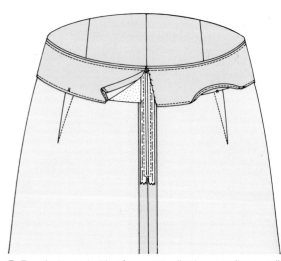

3. To apply facing of either type, first pin facing to garment, right sides together, matching all seams and notches. Match seam allowances at ends of facing to edges of placket opening. Pin 6 mm wide cotton tape over waist seamline; tack through all thicknesses. Stitch seam and press flat. Trim, grade and clip the seam allowances.

4. From the wrong side, with the facing extended away from the garment, press all seam allowances toward the facing. Understitch the seam to keep facing from rolling to the outside of the garment. With facing and seam allowance extended away from garment, stitch from right side close to waist seamline, through facing and seam allowances.

5. Turn facing to inside of garment, allowing seamline to roll inside slightly. Press along waist edge. Tack facing to garment at seams and darts. Turn seam allowances of facing ends to wrong side, making sure facing is turned in such a way that it will not catch in zipper; slipstitch to zipper tape. Attach a hook and eye or hanging snap fastener at top of placket.

Waistline finished with ribbon facing

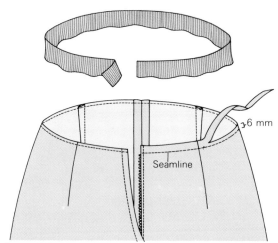

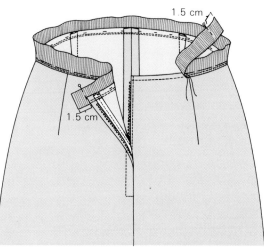

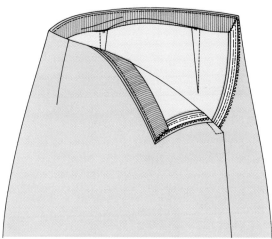

1. Use 2.5 cm wide curved skirt petersham, available by the metre or in prepackaged quantities. Cut it to a length equal to the garment waistline measurement plus 3 cm. Staystitch the garment waistline on the seamline and trim the seam allowance to 6 mm.

2. Place a pin 1.5 cm from each end of ribbon. Lap wrong side of ribbon over right side of garment waistline so that the edge of the *inside* curve of the ribbon is over the staystitched seamline. Match pins at ribbon ends to placket edges. Tack in place. Stitch close to edge of ribbon.

3. Turn the ribbon to inside of garment, allowing garment edge to roll in slightly. Fold under ribbon ends on 1.5 cm mark so that they clear zipper, and press entire edge of ribbon. Tack ribbon to garment at all seams and darts; whipstitch ends to zipper tape. Attach fasteners.

Waistline finished with extended facing

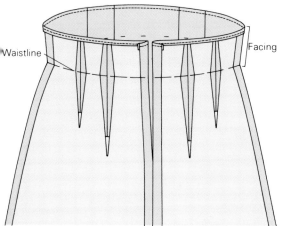

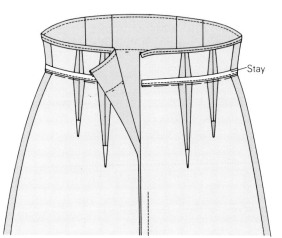

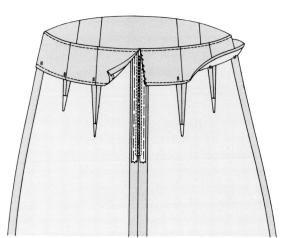

Some patterns are designed with an extended (self) waistline facing. Garment darts extend through the waistline into the facing; pattern foldline marks finished waistline edge.
1. Stitch darts and seams on both the garment and facing. Press the seams open; slash and press open the darts. Finish facing edge as required for fabric. (See Seam finishes.)

2. No interfacing is used; instead, a stay is applied to the waistline. Measure the garment along the foldline from edge to edge; cut a length of seam binding or cotton tape to that measurement. With width of tape on facing, pin the stay along the foldline; have ends of stay even with open edges. Stitch through stay and garment 3 mm from foldline.

3. Turn the facing to the inside of the garment along the foldline; press. Insert the zipper as recommended by the pattern. Turn in the ends of the facing, being sure to clear the zipper; slipstitch them to the zipper tape. Tack the facing to the garment at all seams and darts. Finish top of closure with hook and eye or hanging snap fastener.

259

Waistline finishes

Applied elastic waistband (self-band)

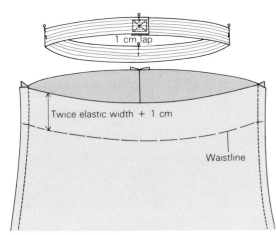

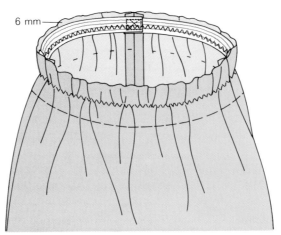

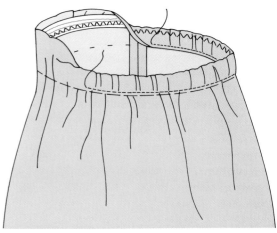

1. This technique can be used only when the garment has not been dart-fitted at waistline. Cut garment with an extension above waistline that is twice the width of the elastic plus 1 cm. Mark waistline with tacking stitches. Cut a length of elastic to fit snugly around waist plus 1 cm. Overlap ends and stitch securely; pin-mark elastic into quarters.

2. Pin elastic to the inside of extension, matching each pin mark to a side seam, centre back, or centre front. Place top edge of elastic 6 mm down from top edge of the extension. Stitch along the lower edge of the elastic, stretching it between pins as you stitch to fit the fabric. A wide zigzag stitch is best but a short straight stitch may be used.

3. Turn elastic and fabric to inside of garment along stitched edge of elastic. The elastic will be completely covered. If fabric does not fray, raw edge may be left as it is. If fabric frays, turn under 6 mm on raw edge. Stitch along the waistline marking through the waistband, elastic and garment, stretching elastic during stitching.

Applied elastic waistband (separate band)

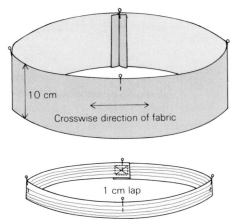

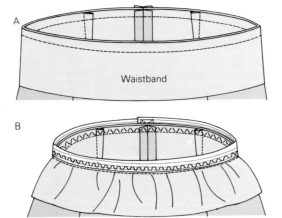

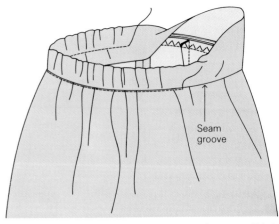

1. This method is suitable only for knits with stretch; waistline may be dart-fitted. Cut waistband on the crosswise grain of the fabric, 10 cm wide and the same length as *garment* waist measurement plus seam allowances. Join ends with a 1.5 cm seam. Cut 2.5 cm-wide elastic to fit *body* waist snugly plus 1 cm. Overlap 1 cm at ends; stitch securely. Pin-mark waistband, elastic and waistline into quarters.

2. Matching pin marks and seams, pin waistband to skirt with right sides together. Stitch a 1.5 cm seam, stretching both pieces of fabric as you sew (A). Press seam as stitched. Lap elastic over waistline seam allowance with the bottom edge of the elastic just above first row of stitching. Using a zigzag stitch, sew elastic to seam allowance, stretching it to fit between pins (B) as you stitch.

3. Fold waistband over elastic to the inside of garment. Working from the outside, pin the waistband in place, inserting pins just below the seamline so the excess length of the waistband, on the inside, is caught in the pinning. Stitch from right side in the seam groove, stretching elastic so waistband is flat. Trim away excess seam allowance from lower edge of waistband inside garment.

Decorative stretch waistbands

Decorative stretch waistbands are made with specially designed elastic products available in solid colours, plaids or stripes. Variously woven, braided, or shirred, they come in several different widths from 2.5 cm upwards. Choose a decorative elastic as close as possible to the fabric weight.

The **woven elastics** are called webbings, and their stretchability varies from limited to moderate.

Webbings are quite firm and will not roll over during wear. The limited-stretch webbing should be used only when the garment has a placket opening—the stretch is not sufficient to fit over the hips or bust and still fit snugly at the waist.

Braided elastics have a moderate amount of stretch and can often be used without a placket opening. The **shirred bandings** are any fabric (includ-

ing jute) stitched with elastic thread; their stretch is limited by the amount of shirring, but they are usually stretchy enough to be used without a placket opening.

Edge finishing. On some products, both edges are finished; on others, only one. This determines how the banding is applied. On an unfinished edge, a stitching line will be indicated.

Attaching decorative elastic

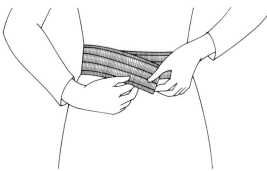

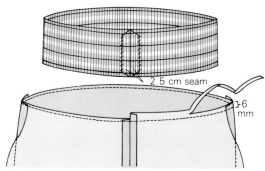

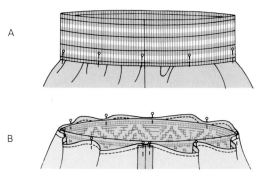

1. Purchase decorative elastic or shirred banding in a length to fit around the waistline snugly, allowing an additional 5 cm for finishing ends. Width choice depends on the effect desired. To avoid fraying during construction, always cut straight across elastic. As an extra precaution, stitch across cut ends with a straight or zigzag stitch.

2. Sew all garment seams that form the waistline. Staystitch on garment waistline seam and trim the seam allowance to 6 mm. If no closure is being used, seam the ends of the elastic or banding by placing right sides together and stitching a 2.5 cm seam. Press open. Turn top edges of seam allowance in diagonally and whipstitch seam allowances to waistband.

3. Divide garment waistline and elastic or banding into four or eight equal parts; pin-mark. If both edges of elastic are finished, lap wrong side of elastic over right side of garment. Place waistband seam at centre back and match pins (A). If one edge is unfinished, place elastic inside garment, right sides together, matching pins and stitch lines (B).

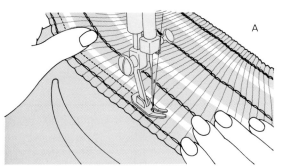

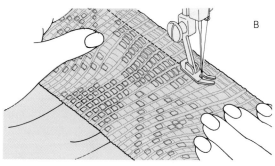

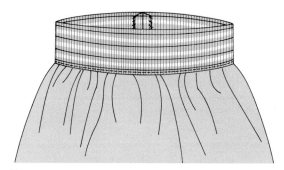

4. Stitch elastic with either a straight stitch set at 2 mm stitch length or a zigzag stitch of medium length and width. For a lapped waistline seam (A), stitch just inside the first elastic thread if sewing banding, close to the finished edge if elastic webbing is being used. If the elastic has one unfinished edge, sew along indicated stitch line (B). Sew between elastic threads if possible. With one hand behind presser foot and the other

in front, carefully stretch elastic between pins as you stitch, to fit the garment. Make certain that stitch line of elastic remains aligned with seamline of skirt. Remove pins as you reach them; do not stitch over them. Overlap stitching at ends. Press seam carefully as it was stitched; test iron temperature first on a scrap to make sure that the heat you use will not damage the elastic.

5. Press waistband up. The finished waistband pulls the garment into size by forming soft gathers; the number of gathers depends on size difference between waistline of garment and waistband. If a closure is included in the garment, finish the ends of the elastic by turning them under the desired amount and tacking down. Underlap should extend under overlap enough to allow for fasteners (p. 251).

261

Belts

Tie belts

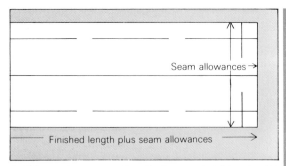

1. Belt may be cut on either the bias or straight grain. Cut it twice the desired finished *width* plus seam allowances, and the necessary *length* plus seam allowances. Length should equal waist circumference plus enough extra to tie ends.

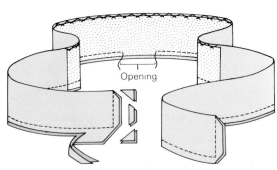

2. If belt is to be interfaced, apply interfacing only to portion that encircles waist. Fold belt in half lengthwise, right sides together. Stitch ends and long edge, leaving an opening for turning. Trim and grade seams and corners.

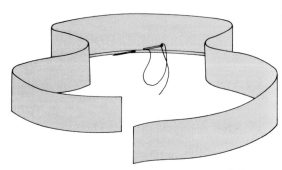

3. Turn belt to the right side through the opening. Pull corners out so that they are square, and press edges carefully. Press in the seam allowances at opening and slipstitch opening closed. Give finished belt a final pressing.

Reinforced belts

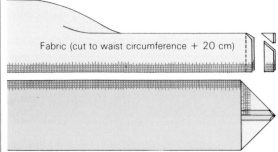

To hand-finish: 1. Cut fabric for belt twice the width of belting plus 1 cm, with one long edge on the selvage. To form a point at one end, fold fabric in half lengthwise and stitch end with 1 cm seam. Press seam open as illustrated.

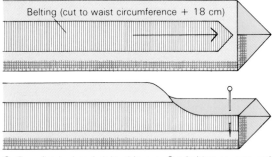

2. Turn finished end right side out. Cut belting so one end has the same point as the fabric. Insert pointed end of the belting into fabric point. Press flat. With belting centred on fabric, pin raw edge of fabric over belting.

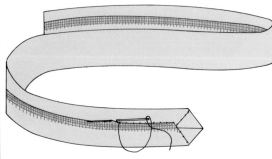

3. Pin selvage edge over raw edge, pulling fabric taut around belting. Slipstitch at point, then along selvage edge. Finish belt by attaching buckle to unfinished end. If a prong buckle will be used, work eyelets (p. 264).

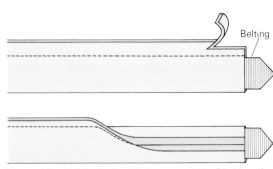

To machine-finish: 1. Cut fabric twice width of belting plus 3 cm. Shape one end of belting. Fold fabric over belting, wrong side out. Stitch close to belting, using a zipper foot. Trim seam allowances to 6 mm; move seam to centre of belting.

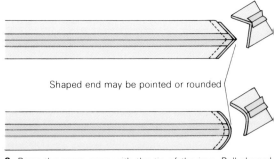

2. Press the seam open with the tip of the iron. Pull shaped end of belting into position inside stitched fabric tube. Carefully stitch close to, but not through, the belting. Trim seam. A closely fitted cover for the belting has now been made.

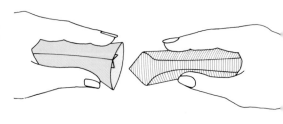

3. Remove the belting and turn the fabric tube right side out. Do not press. Cup belting and slip it into belt, shaped end first. Attach buckle to unfinished end. If a prong buckle will be used, work eyelets in shaped end of belt (p. 264).

Shirt sleeves

One form of the set-in sleeve is attached by the shirt-sleeve method, which permits the sleeve to be sewn into the armhole before the garment side and sleeve seams are stitched.

Sleeves eligible for this method are less rounded than usual along the shoulder line because the cap is not so steeply curved; there is less difference between the measurement of the armhole and the up-

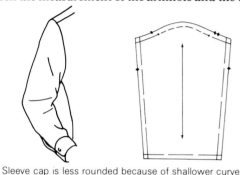

Sleeve cap is less rounded because of shallower curve.

per sleeve curve, which means easestitching along that curve is usually not necessary. Flat-felled seams are often used in this method; because of the armhole curve, they should be narrow and, contrary to most seam situations, made on the wrong rather than the right side. A popular method for men's shirts, where it originated, the shirt-sleeve technique is also an easy way to handle children's sleeves.

Shirt-sleeve method

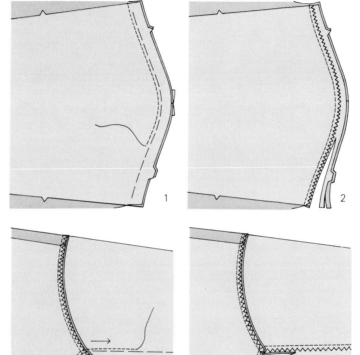

1. With right sides together, match and pin sleeve to armhole; ease in sleeve's slight fullness as it is being pinned (easestitching is not necessary). Tack as pinned, and stitch with sleeve side up.

2. Diagonally trim cross-seam allowances at shoulder. If a flat-felled seam is desired, construct at this time (see Seams). For regular seam finish, place another row of stitches (straight or zigzag) within seam allowance 6 mm from the first row. Trim the seam allowance close to the second row of stitching. Overlock stitch may also be used to neaten the seam edge.

3. With right sides facing, match, pin and tack underarm seams (turn armhole seam allowances toward sleeve). Stitch in one continuous seam from bottom of garment to bottom of sleeve.

4. Diagonally trim cross-seam allowances. If a flat-felled seam is desired, construct at this time (see Seams). For regular seam finish, place another row of stitches (straight or zigzag) within seam allowance close to second row of stitching 6 mm from first row. Trim seam allowance.

Elbow shaping

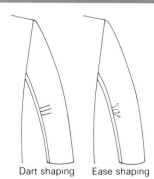

Dart shaping   Ease shaping

A close-fitting sleeve that extends beyond the elbow usually requires darts or easestitching along the sleeve seam to give the shaping and ease necessary for the elbow to bend comfortably.

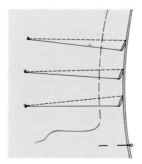

Sleeves with elbow darts: With right sides together, form each elbow dart, stitching from wide end to point; leave 10 cm thread ends and tie knot at each point (see Darts). Extend each dart and press flat as stitched. With wrong side up, place darts over tailor's ham and press them toward sleeve bottom. With right sides together, match, pin and tack sleeve seam.

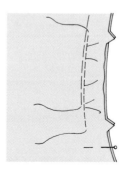

Sleeves with easestitching: Between designated markings on back seamline of sleeve, place a row of easestitching within seam allowance, a thread's width from seamline. Pin sleeve seams together, right sides facing, at all matched markings. Pull bobbin thread ends of easestitching line to draw up fullness along back seam; distribute fullness evenly. Pin in place and tack.

Sleeves

Raglan sleeves

A raglan sleeve is attached to the garment by a seam that runs diagonally down from the front neckline to the underarm, and up to the back neckline. This sleeve covers the entire shoulder and needs some shaping device to make it conform to the shoulder's shape. One device is a dart that extends from

neckline to shoulder edge; here the sleeve pattern is one piece. Another is a shaped seam that runs from the neckline over the shoulder to the sleeve bottom; this sleeve is made from two pieces. Whichever method is used, the deepest part of the curve should fall over the edge of the shoulder without protruding.

1. With right sides facing, match, pin and stitch shoulder darts from wide end to point; leave 10 cm thread ends. Knot thread ends. Press dart flat. Slash darts if necessary and press open over a tailor's ham. Match, pin and stitch underarm seams, right sides together. Press flat, then press open.

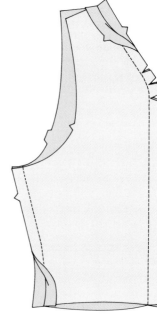

For a two-piece sleeve, place front and back together, right sides facing. Match, pin and stitch the shoulder seam. Press the seam flat to embed stitches, then finger-press open. Notch out fullness from seam allowance along shoulder curve. Press seam open over a tailor's ham. With right sides together, match, pin and stitch the underarm seams. Press flat, then open.

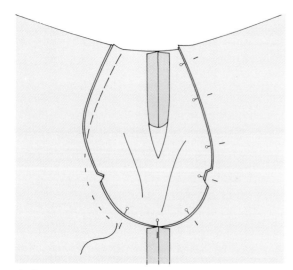

2. Garment side seams should be permanently stitched and pressed open. With right sides together, pin sleeve to armhole, aligning underarm seams, and matching all markings; work with wrong side of sleeve toward you. Tack as pinned.

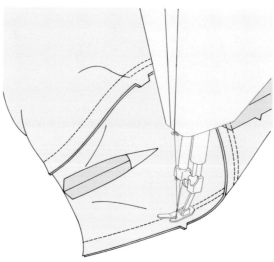

3. With sleeve side up, stitch as tacked. Diagonally trim cross-seam allowances at underarm seams. Between front and back notches of underarm curve, place another row of stitching (either straight or zigzag) 6 mm from first row.

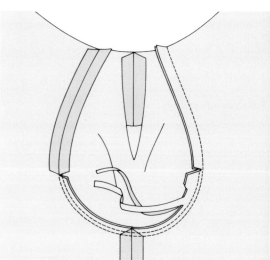

4. Press the seam flat as stitched to embed the stitches. Clip into the seam allowances at the point of each notch. Trim underarm seam allowances close to the second row of stitching. Press seams open above the clips.

Kimono sleeves

Method 1

A kimono sleeve, which is cut as an extension of the main bodice piece, can be either loose or close-fitting, depending on the degree of the sleeve's shoulder slope and underarm curve. If the sleeve fit is very close, a gusset is probably needed for comfort

(see pp. 272–273). To construct a kimono sleeve without a gusset, follow one of the methods here, using regular seam binding or 12 mm cotton tape for reinforcement under the arm. The first method is easier, but the second is less bulky.

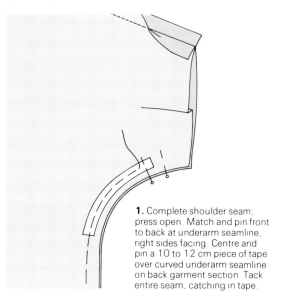

1. Complete shoulder seam; press open. Match and pin front to back at underarm seamline, right sides facing. Centre and pin a 10 to 12 cm piece of tape over curved underarm seamline on back garment section. Tack entire seam, catching in tape.

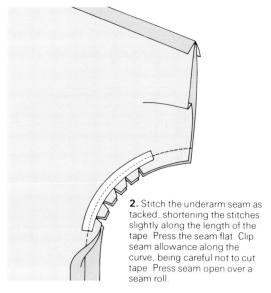

2. Stitch the underarm seam as tacked, shortening the stitches slightly along the length of the tape. Press the seam flat. Clip seam allowance along the curve, being careful not to cut tape. Press seam open over a seam roll.

Method 2

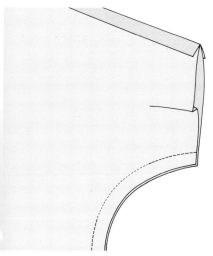

1. Complete shoulder seam and press open. With right sides facing, match, pin and tack front to back at underarm seamline. Stitch, shortening stitches along curve. Press flat.

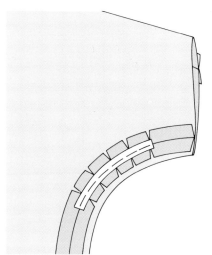

2. Clip seam allowances along curve. Press seam open. Centre, pin and tack a 10 to 12 cm piece of reinforcing tape along curved seamline. Make sure stitches go to right side.

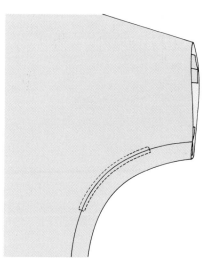

3. From the right side, stitch through all the thicknesses, approximately 3 mm on each side of tacked line. Secure thread ends on wrong side. Remove tacking, and press.

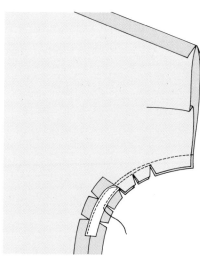

If exposed stitching is not wanted, stitch the tape from wrong side, catching the *tape and seam allowance only* on each side of tacked line. Remove tacking, and press.

271

Sleeves

Gussets

A gusset is a small fabric piece inserted into a slashed opening, usually under the arm of a close-fitting kimono sleeve, to provide ease for a comfortable fit. Although gusset shapes vary, there are two

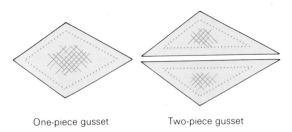

One-piece gusset   Two-piece gusset

basic gusset types, **one-piece** (usually diamond-shaped) and **two-piece** (usually triangular).

The one-piece type is the more difficult to insert because the entire gusset must be sewn into an enclosed slashed opening after underarm and side

seams have been stitched. In the two-piece gusset, each piece is separately inserted into a slashed opening on each bodice piece; underarm, both gusset sections, and side seams are then stitched in one seam. Because a two-piece gusset is easier to insert, you may want to convert a one-piece to that type (see next page). Occasionally a gusset will extend into a main garment section; when it does, this is more of a design than a functional feature.

For maximum ease of movement, cut the gusset so that its length is on the bias. Transfer all pattern markings accurately, especially at gusset corners and garment slash points.

Reinforce point at marked gusset opening before slashing. For lightweight fabrics or those that fray, use a bias square or seam binding as described below. A lightweight iron-on interfacing can also be used; iron it over slash point on garment's wrong side. If the fabric is firm, staystitching is usually sufficient reinforcement.

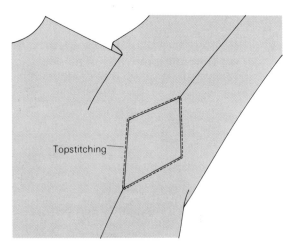

Topstitching

In a well-constructed gusset, all points are precisely related to shape of slashed opening; joining is accurate and smooth. For greater strength, topstitching may be added.

Reinforcing point of slash opening

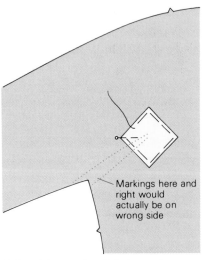

Markings here and right would actually be on wrong side

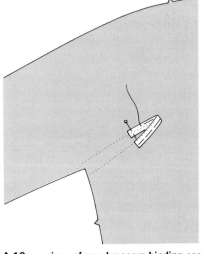

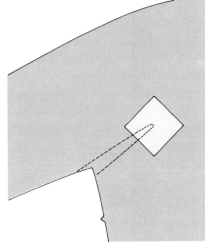

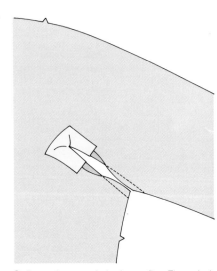

1. To reinforce point of slash opening, cut a 5 cm square of bias (garment or underlining fabric). On right side of garment, position the centre of the fabric square over the slash point; pin and tack patch in place.

A 10 cm piece of regular seam binding can be used in place of bias square; fold tape into a V. Position and pin tape to right side of garment so the V of the tape coincides with the V of the slash point. Tack.

2. Staystitch a thread's width from marked stitching line (shorten stitches around the point). Start at wide end, stitch up one side to point, pivot, take one stitch across point, pivot again, stitch down other side.

3. Press the staystitched area flat. Then slash through centre of opening (between stitching lines) up to reinforced point; cut through fabric square as well. Turn square to wrong side; press lightly so it lies flat.

Inserting a one-piece gusset

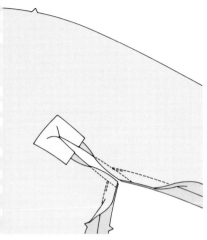

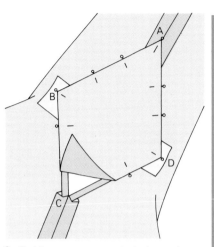

1. With right sides together, match, pin and tack garment front to back at underarm seams and side seams. Stitch from sleeve bottom to intersecting lines of gusset opening; secure stitches. Stitch from lower edge of bodice to intersecting lines of gusset opening; secure stitches. Press seams flat, then open.

2. Position gusset over slashed opening so marked points of gusset (designated here as A, B, C, D) match corresponding markings of opening. With right sides together, pin the gusset into the slashed opening; match all points accurately and align stitching line of opening to gusset seamline.

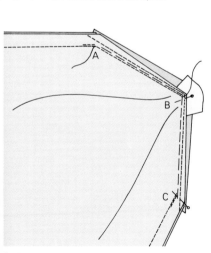

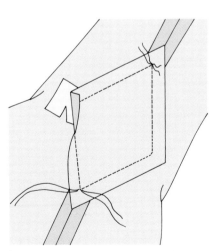

3. Tack, but do not remove pins from corners. Garment side up, stitch from point A to B (shorten stitches going around point B); pivot, take one stitch across point, pivot again, and stitch to point C. Leave 10 cm thread ends at beginning and end. Stitch other side of gusset (C to D to A) the same way.

4. Pull all thread ends to wrong side of gusset and knot. Press seams toward garment. Trim extending edges of fabric squares to 1 cm, re-press seams toward garment. If desired, top-stitch close to seamline on right side of garment (see preceding page); pull threads to wrong side and knot.

Inserting a two-piece gusset

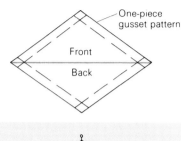

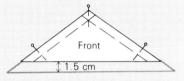

One-piece gusset pattern

Front
Back

Front
1.5 cm

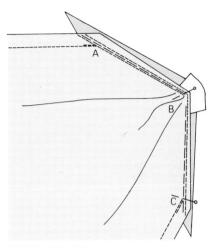

1. To convert a one-piece into a two-piece gusset, determine which halves of gusset pattern correspond to front and back bodice pieces; divide with a line; cut in half. Pin triangular pattern pieces to fabric; add 1.5 cm to cut edge (for underarm seam allowance). Cut out pieces and transfer markings.

2. With right sides together, match and pin gusset to slashed opening of front bodice; align seamlines of opening and gusset. Tack, but do not remove pins from corners. Garment side up, stitch from edge A to B (shorten stitches around B); pivot, take one stitch across point, pivot, stitch to edge C.

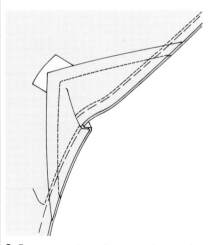

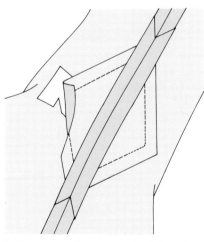

3. Press seams toward garment. Insert other triangular gusset piece into slashed opening of back bodice in same way as for front bodice. With right sides together, pin garment back to front at underarm seam; match intersecting lines of gusset edge and other markings as well. Tack and stitch.

4. Press seam flat to embed stitches, then press seam open. Trim extending edges of fabric squares at gusset points to 1 cm; re-press seams toward garment. If desired, top-stitch close to seamline on right side of garment (see illustration on preceding page); pull threads to wrong side and knot.

273

Sleeve finishes

Types of sleeve finish

The finishing of a sleeve edge usually depends on pattern design. It may be a simple **self-hem** or **faced finish** (shaped or bias), or decorative **double binding** of self or contrasting fabric, or a **knit band** (pp. 276–277). The finish is sometimes a design feature, as a **casing** (pp. 276–277) or **cuff** (pp. 278–284) would be.

For successful completion of any sleeve, follow these guidelines. (1) Mark the hemline to length to suit wearer; sleeve length helps determine total garment silhouette and can add to or detract from it. (2) Use proper pressing techniques throughout. (3) Reduce bulk wherever possible.

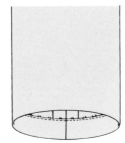

A self-hemmed edge is a simple sleeve finish. A facing can also be used.

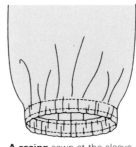

A casing sewn at the sleeve edge can be self-faced or it can be separately applied.

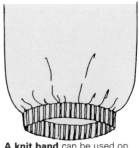

A knit band can be used on knit or woven fabrics to give a firm yet comfortable fit.

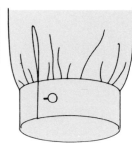

A cuff can have a placket opening or be loose-fitting with no opening.

Self-hem

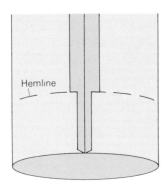

1. Mark sleeve hemline. To reduce bulk at seamline within hem width, trim seam allowance below marked hemline to half width.

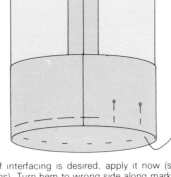

2. If interfacing is desired, apply it now (see Hems). Turn hem to wrong side along marked hemline; pin and tack near fold.

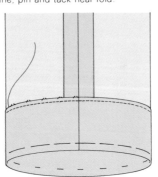

3. To even hem allowance, measure from fold to desired width, and mark that distance around entire hem. Trim along marked line.

4. Finish raw edges of hem (see Hems). Pin edge to sleeve and secure, using appropriate hand stitch. Remove tacking. Press.

Shaped facing

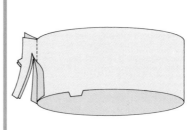

1. With right sides together, match, pin and stitch facing ends. Press flat, then open. Trim seam allowances to half width.

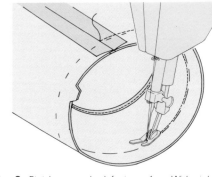

2. Finish unnotched facing edge. With right sides together, match, pin and tack facing to sleeve edge. Stitch with facing side up.

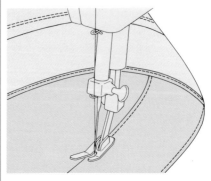

3. Press seam flat. Trim and grade seam allowances; clip if needed. Extend facing and seam allowances; understitch along facing.

4. Turn the facing to wrong side; roll edges in slightly. Press. Diagonal-tack in place if necessary. Pin edge to sleeve and secure.

Bias facing

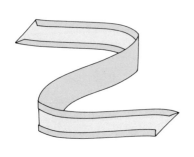

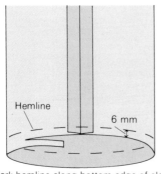

1. Cut a strip of 4 cm bias to sleeve circumference plus 5 cm. Press under long edges 6 mm. If desired, use narrow hem facing.

2. Mark hemline along bottom edge of sleeve. To facilitate application of bias facing, trim hem allowance to 6 mm width.

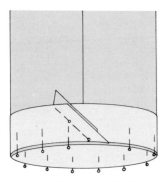

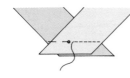

3. Open folded edges and pin facing to sleeve edge, right sides together; pin ends together in diagonal seam (straight grain).

4. Remove facing from sleeve, keeping ends pinned. Stitch ends along straight grain. Trim seam allowances to 6 mm and press open.

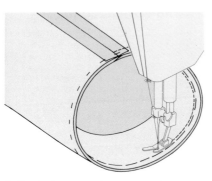

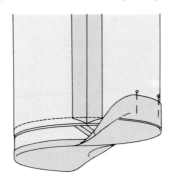

5. Re-pin facing to sleeve, raw edges even. Tack in place; stitch 6 mm from raw edge, using foldline as guide. Press flat.

6. Turn facing to wrong side; roll edges in slightly and press. Pin folded edge of facing to sleeve and slipstitch in place.

Double-fold bias binding

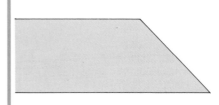

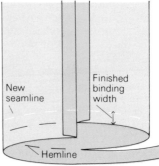

1. Cut a strip of self-fabric bias equal in *length* to the sleeve edge circumference plus 5 cm, in *width* to 6 times the finished width.

2. Mark sleeve hemline, trim away hem allowance. Mark new seamline a distance from cut edge equal to the finished binding width.

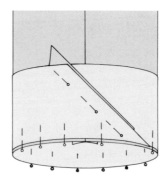

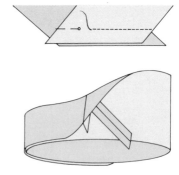

3. With right sides together, pin binding to sleeve, raw edges even. Pin binding ends together in diagonal seam (straight grain).

4. Remove binding; keep ends pinned. Stitch. Trim seam allowances to 6 mm; press open. Fold binding in half, wrong sides together.

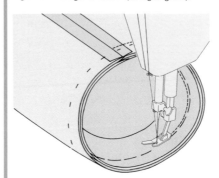

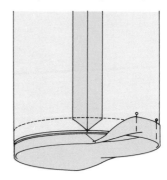

5. Pin binding to right side of sleeve, raw edges even; tack in place along new sleeve seamline. Stitch with binding side up.

6. Press seam flat. Extend binding up and press; turn to wrong side so fold meets the stitching line. Pin and slipstitch in place.

Sleeve finishes

Casings

A casing is a fabric tunnel through which elastic or drawstring can be passed; either will draw up sleeve fullness, creating a puffed effect. Casings are a popular sleeve finish for children's wear, blouses and sportswear.

There are basically two casing types. The first is a **self-faced casing;** in this type the tunnel is created by turning the sleeve edge to the inside. Some self-faced casings are positioned above the sleeve edge so that a gathered flounce, known as a *heading*, will hang below. To construct a self-faced casing (with or without heading), an adequate fabric allowance must be provided below the hemline. The second type of casing is an **applied casing,** actually a separate bias strip that is sewn to the sleeve edge to form the tunnel. The applied type is generally used when there is not enough hem allowance for a self-faced casing or when fabric bulk makes a casing of thinner fabric desirable. Ready-made bias binding can be used for this purpose; select the width closest to but slightly wider than the elastic.

For both types of casing, it is wise to select a narrow elastic (3 mm to 12 mm) that is appropriate for tunnelling (see Elastics).

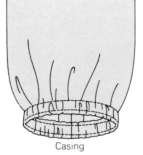
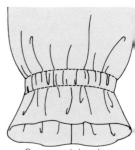

Casing.   Casing with heading.

Self-faced casing

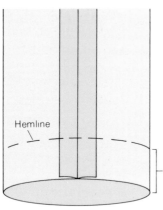

1. Mark hemline on sleeve. Allow enough casing width below hemline to equal width of elastic plus 1 cm. Along the raw edges of the sleeve, turn a scant 3 mm to the wrong side and press.

Hemline

Elastic width plus 1 cm

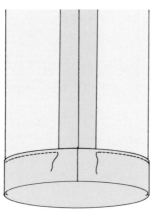

2. Turn casing width to wrong side along marked hemline; pin and tack close to free edge. Stitch along tacked line, leaving a small opening at the sleeve hemline.

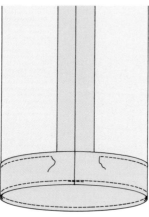

3. Stitch close to fold on lower edge of sleeve, overlapping for a few stitches. Fit the elastic around arm where the casing will be worn; add 1 cm and cut.

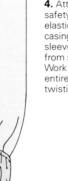

4. Attach a bodkin or safety pin to one end of elastic and insert into casing. Pin other end to sleeve to keep that end from slipping through. Work safety pin around entire casing; avoid twisting the elastic.

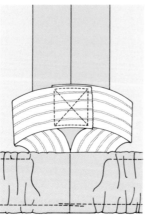

5. Unpin both elastic ends; overlap them 1 cm and pin together. Stitch a square on overlapped area, crisscrossing it for strength. Pull joined ends inside the casing. Edgestitch opening to close it, stretching elastic slightly as you sew.

Self-faced casing with heading

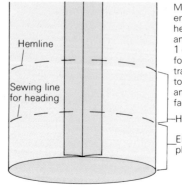

Hemline

Sewing line for heading

Mark hemline. Allow enough width below hemline for both heading and elastic widths plus 1 cm. Mark sewing line for heading. Thread-mark traced lines. Turn 6 mm to wrong side and press, and proceed as for self-faced casing.

Heading width

Elastic width plus 1 cm

Sleeve finishes

Applied casing

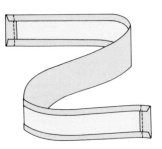

1. To make casing, cut a strip of bias equal in length to circumference of sleeve edge plus 2 cm and equal to the elastic width plus 2 cm. (If using ready-made bias, select one slightly wider than the elastic.) Turn under 1 cm on both ends of the bias strip and stitch across. Press under 6 mm on both long edges.

Knit bands

Knit bands are suitable sleeve finish for knit fabrics that stretch. In the case of woven fabrics, the band may be applied to a loose-fitting sleeve to reduce width at the cuff. Knit bands are a popular choice to finish sleeves on sweatshirts, tracksuits, T-shirts, pyjamas and children's wear.

The type of sleeve will determine the method of application. A sleeve may be fitted with a limited-stretch band, for example, a T-shirt cuff, or with a stretchy band, for example, a tracksuit cuff.

A stretchy band may be cut from the same fabric as the garment or cut from a purchased band called ribbing (see Neckline finishes, knit bands).

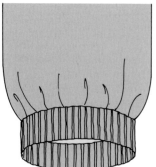

A knit band is a convenient finish for sleeves of knit or woven fabric on sportswear and children's wear. The band stretches and recovers to allow comfortable control of the sleeve width.

Applying a stretchy knit band

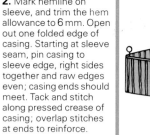

2. Mark hemline on sleeve, and trim the hem allowance to 6 mm. Open out one folded edge of casing. Starting at sleeve seam, pin casing to sleeve edge, right sides together and raw edges even; casing ends should meet. Tack and stitch along pressed crease of casing; overlap stitches at ends to reinforce.

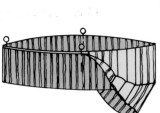

1. With right sides together, seam ends of band to form a closed circle. Use overedge or overlock stitch seam (see Seams). Fold band in half lengthwise, wrong sides together, and edges even.

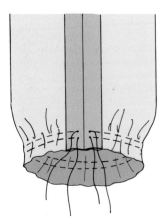

2. Form sleeve seam. To gather lower edge of sleeve, machine-baste 1.5 cm and 12 mm from raw edge. Pull up threads and adjust gathers evenly to measure 2.5 cm less than sleeve pattern. Fasten thread ends.

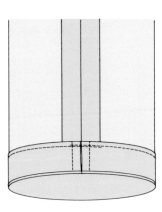

3. Turn casing to wrong side; roll sleeve edge slightly inside. Press. Pin folded inner edge of casing in place and tack; edgestitch along fold, overlapping stitches at end. Fit elastic around arm where casing will be worn; add 1 cm and cut. Complete as for self-faced casing (p. 276).

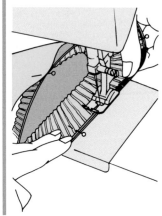

3. Pin cuff to sleeve right sides together, matching seams. Baste, stretching cuff to fit. With band side up, stitch band to sleeve. Stretch the band so that it lies flat against the garment's edge; do not stretch garment. Remove the pins as you stitch.

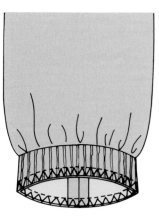

4. Finish the seam allowance with a zigzag-stitched seam or two rows of stitching. Cut the seam allowance close to the second row of stitching or use an overlocker machine (serger) to neaten edge. Press seam allowances toward the garment.

277

Cuffs

Cuffs with plackets

Cuffs are fabric bands at the bottoms of straight, gathered, or pleated sleeve edges. Although cuff styles vary according to the garment design, any cuff will basically be one of two general types.

The first type can be used on both long and short sleeves, and is made large enough around for the hand or arm to slip in and out easily without a cuff-and-placket opening. (For more information about cuffs without plackets, see pp. 282–284).

The second type of cuff is generally attached to a full-length sleeve and, unlike the first type, it requires a cuff-and-placket opening fastened snugly around the wrist. Of this cuff type, the three most popular styles are the **lapped cuff, shirt cuff** and **French cuff.** Each is constructed and applied to the sleeve (see pp. 280–281) after the placket opening is made at the sleeve edge.

The three most commonly used plackets are the **faced placket, continuous bound placket** and **shirt placket.** Note that edges of the faced placket meet at the opening, while edges of the other two plackets lap. The continuous bound placket is finished with a single fabric strip to create a narrow lap; the shirt placket is finished with two separate pieces to create a wider lap.

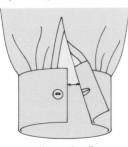

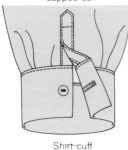

Lapped cuff

The **lapped cuff,** here with a continuous bound placket, has one end projecting from placket edge. The **shirt cuff** is sewn with its ends aligned to the underlap and overlap edges of the shirt placket. The **French cuff,** here with a faced placket, is sewn to the placket edges so cuff ends meet rather than lap; the cuff is cut wide to double back onto itself.

Shirt cuff   French cuff

Faced cuff plackets

1. Cut a rectangular facing that is 6.5 cm wide and as long as the length of the slash plus 2.5 cm. If garment fabric is heavy, use underlining for facing. Apply a seam finish to the raw edges of the facing except on the bottom edge.

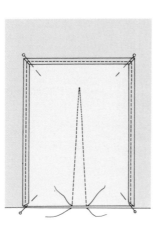

2. Centre facing over marked opening, right sides together and raw edges even. Pin at each corner. From wrong side of sleeve, stitch along marked lines; start from one edge, stitch to point (shorten stitches for 2 cm on either side of point), pivot, and stitch down to other edge. Press flat.

3. Slash to point; be sure not to clip threads. Press seam open, then toward facing. Turn facing to wrong side of sleeve; roll edges slightly inside. Press. Slipstitch top edge of facing to sleeve.

Continuous bound cuff plackets

1. Cut binding from self-fabric to measure 3 cm wide and twice the length of the marked slash. Along one long edge of cut binding, press under 6 mm to wrong side. Mark 6 mm seam allowance along the other long binding edge.

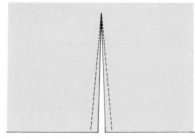

2. Reinforce stitching line of placket opening. Within a thread width of seamline, stitch to point (shorten stitches for 2 cm on either side of point), pivot, and stitch down. Press flat. Slash to point; take care not to clip threads.

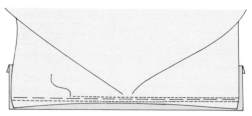

3. Spread slash and pin to unfolded edge of binding, right sides together; align reinforced stitching line to marked 6 mm seamline on binding. Tack, then stitch with sleeve side up. Press seam flat to embed stitches.

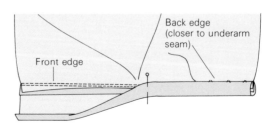

Front edge

Back edge (closer to underarm seam)

4. Extend binding and fold it to the wrong side, encasing raw edges; folded edge of binding should meet stitching line. Pin in place and secure with slipstitching. Turn front edge of binding to wrong side of sleeve and press.

Shirt cuff plackets

    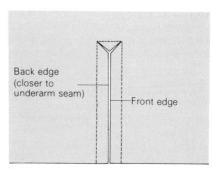

1. To construct overlap, fold in half, right sides together; pin and stitch around top edge to matching point at side. Press seam flat. Clip seam allowance at matching point; trim and grade; taper corners and point (A). Turn right side out; pull out corners and points. Press flat (B). Press under seam allowance along unnotched edge (C).

2. To prepare underlap piece, simply press seam allowance to the wrong side along unnotched edge. Trim this pressed-under seam allowance to about half-width.

3. Place reinforcing stitches within placket seamline; shorten them at corners. Slash to within 1 cm of placket top, then to corners. Determine front and back edges of opening.

In the third image: "Back edge (closer to underarm seam)" and "Front edge"

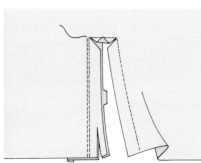 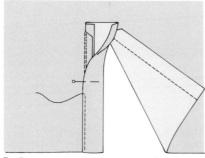 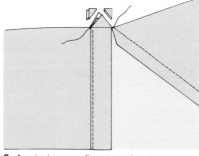 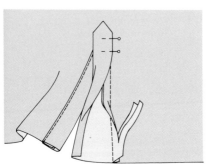

4. With seamlines aligned, pin and stitch right side of underlap raw edge to wrong side of the back placket edge; secure stitches at top corner of placket. Press flat; trim.

5. Press seam allowance toward underlap. Fold underlap to right side; pin its folded edge over stitch line. Edgestitch through all thicknesses; stop at corner; secure stitches.

6. At placket top, flip triangular piece up and pin to underlap. Stitch across base of triangle, securing stitches at beginning and end. Taper square corners of underlap.

7. Pin right side of overlap's extended edge to wrong side of remaining (front) placket edge, align seamlines, and keep raw edges at bottom even. Stitch; secure stitches at top.

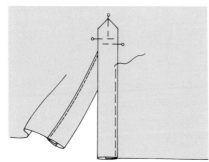 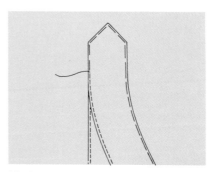 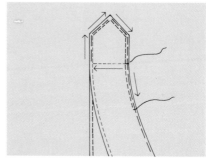

8. Press seam flat. Trim seam allowance to about half-width and press toward overlap. Bring folded edge of overlap to stitching line and pin it in place.

9. Pin the top portion of overlap to sleeve, completely covering the top portion of underlap; pin down as far as placket corner. Tack along all pinned edges.

10. Topstitch along untacked fold of overlap (make sure not to catch any part of underlap in stitching); pull threads to wrong side at stopping point and knot.

11. Topstitch (through all the thicknesses) across overlap and around tacked edges; follow direction of arrows. Secure stitches at beginning. Remove tacking; press.

Cuffs

Construction of cuffs with plackets

Cuffs actually consist of a cuff and a facing section, which may be cut all-in-one or as two pieces (see below). Bound buttonholes, if any, should be made before cuff is constructed; worked buttonholes, after cuff is applied to sleeve. Before starting cuff application, complete underarm sleeve seams and prepare pleats or gathers at sleeve edge if called for. Note the placement of cuff end to placket edge. A lapped cuff will have one end flush with and one end projecting from the placket edges; both ends of the **shirt cuff** and the **French cuff** will be flush with the placket edges.

One-piece and two-piece cuff construction

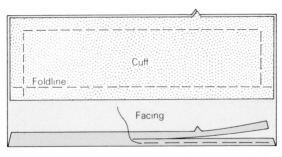

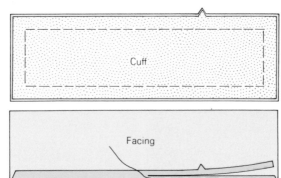

For one-piece cuff, apply interfacing to cuff section. Interfacing can come to foldline or, for a softer fold, extend 1 cm beyond it into facing section (see Interfacing). Turn and press seam allowance to wrong side along facing edge and trim to 1 cm; uneven-tack along folded edge.

For two-piece cuff, apply interfacing to wrong side of cuff section. Turn, trim, tack notched edge of facing section.

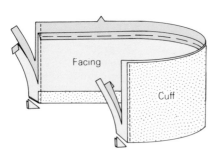

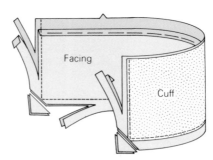

For one-piece cuff, left, fold in half along marked foldline, right sides together, and pin the two ends. **For two-piece cuff,** right, pin cuff to facing, right sides together, leaving notched edge open. Tack either one as pinned, and stitch. Press seam flat. Trim and grade seam allowances; taper corners.

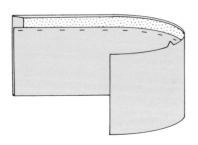

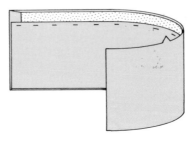

For both one-piece and two-piece cuffs, press seam allowances open, then toward facing. Turn cuffs right side out; pull out the corners. Roll facing edges slightly under, and press. If necessary, diagonal-tack around edges of two-piece cuff.

Shirt and French cuff construction

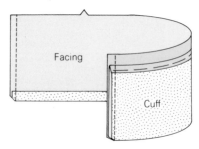

A shirt cuff differs slightly from the cuff constructed at left. Because of the shirt cuff application method (see opposite page), the edge of the *cuff* section rather than the facing section is turned under and tacked. Before turning the interfaced cuff edge under, trim away the interfacing seam allowance along that edge. Complete cuff construction as directed at left.

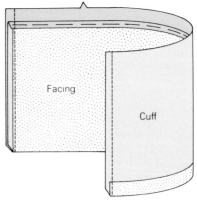

A French cuff is cut double the width of a standard cuff so that it can fold back onto itself. This turnback action exposes the facing, and so the *facing* section, rather than the cuff section (as described at left), is interfaced. Before turning the facing edge under, trim away the interfacing seam allowance along that edge. Complete cuff construction as directed at left.

Lapped cuff application

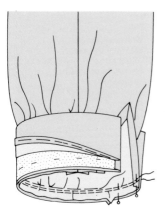

1. Pin cuff to sleeve at all matched markings, right sides together. Cuff end at back placket edge (edge closer to underarm seam) should project out to create underlap; other end should be flush with remaining placket edge. Pull gathering threads (if any) to ease in fullness of sleeve; distribute gathers evenly while pinning. Tack in place.

2. Stitch as tacked; secure thread ends at beginning and end. Press seam flat. Trim cross-seam allowances diagonally. Trim and grade seam allowances so widest is next to cuff.

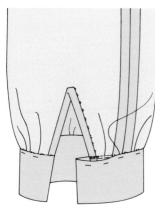

3. Pull cuff down; press seam allowances toward cuff. Bring folded edge of facing to stitching line on wrong side of sleeve; pin and slipstitch entire folded edge to sleeve. Remove tacking and press. Complete underside of bound buttonholes or make worked buttonholes. Topstitch if desired.

Shirt cuff application

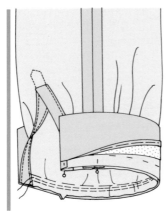

1. Pin right side of cuff facing to wrong side of sleeve at all matched markings. Cuff ends should be flush with the underlap and overlap edges of the shirt placket. Pull gathering threads (if any) to ease in fullness of sleeve; distribute gathers evenly while pinning. Tack in place.

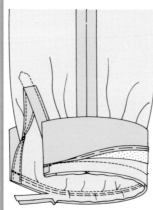

2. Stitch as tacked; secure thread ends at beginning and end. Press seam flat. Trim cross-seam allowances diagonally. Trim and grade seam allowances so widest is next to cuff.

3. Pull cuff down; press seam allowances toward cuff. Bring folded edge of cuff just over stitching line on right side of sleeve; pin and tack in place. Edgestitch along tacked edge; continue stitching around entire cuff if desired; secure thread ends. Remove tacking and press. Make worked buttonholes. Topstitch if desired.

French cuff application

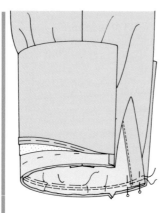

1. Pin cuff to sleeve at all matched markings, right sides together; cuff ends should be flush with both edges of the placket. Pull gathering threads (if any) to ease in fullness of sleeve; distribute gathers evenly while pinning. Tack in place.

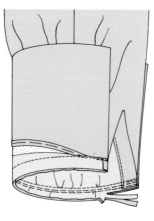

2. Stitch as tacked; secure thread ends at beginning and end. Press seam flat. Trim cross-seam allowances diagonally. Trim and grade seam allowances so widest is next to cuff.

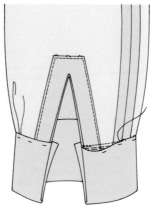

3. Pull cuff down; press seam toward cuff. Bring folded edge of cuff facing to stitching line on wrong side of sleeve; pin and slipstitch folded edge to sleeve. Remove tacking and press. Complete underside of bound buttonholes or make worked buttonholes. Fold cuff in half and press lightly.

Cuffs

Cuffs without plackets

Because cuffs without plackets have no openings, they are cut large so the hand or arm can slip easily in and out. There are three basic styles of this cuff type: the **straight band cuff, straight turnback cuff,** and **shaped turnback cuff.**

The straight band cuff is made with a separate cuff attached to the sleeve bottom; the straight turnback cuff is made by turning up the deep finished hem of a sleeve. Sometimes, instead of the deep self-hem, a **separate extension piece** is added to the sleeve bottom to form the turnback cuff. The shaped turnback cuff is a separately constructed cuff that is attached to the sleeve with a facing.

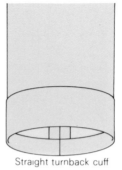
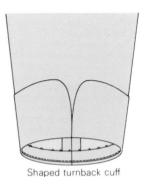

Band cuff   Straight turnback cuff   Shaped turnback cuff

Illustrated at left are the three basic styles of cuffs without plackets: the **straight band cuff,** here attached to a full gathered sleeve; the **straight turnback cuff;** and the **shaped turnback cuff** applied with a facing.

Straight band cuff construction and application

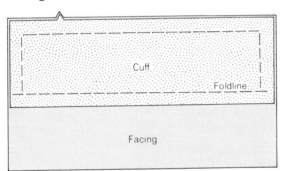

Cuff

Foldline

Facing

1. To construct cuff, apply interfacing to the wrong side of cuff section. Interfacing can come right to foldline or extend about 1 cm into facing section for a softer crease (see Interfacing).

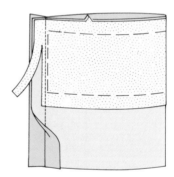

2. With right sides together, match and pin cuff ends together. Stitch and press flat. Trim interfacing seam allowances close to stitching line. Press seam open.

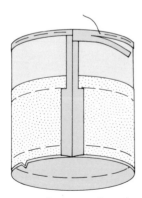

3. Trim seam allowances along the stitched facing section to half-width. Turn and press seam allowance along facing edge to wrong side; trim seam allowance to 1 cm; tack.

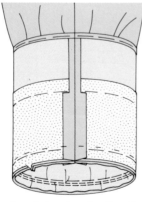

4. Match and pin edge of cuff section to the sleeve edge, right sides together. If sleeve is full, pull gathering threads to ease in fullness. Tack cuff in place.

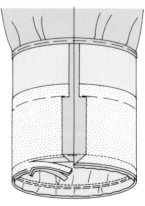

5. Stitch cuff as tacked, overlapping a few stitches at the end. Press to embed stitches. Diagonally trim cross seams. Trim and grade so cuff seam allowance is widest.

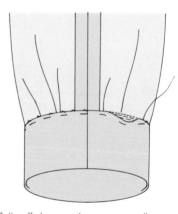

6. Pull cuff down and press seam allowances toward cuff. Fold facing section up to wrong side of sleeve, folded edge meeting stitch line; pin and slipstitch to sleeve. Press.

Straight turnback cuff (self-hem)

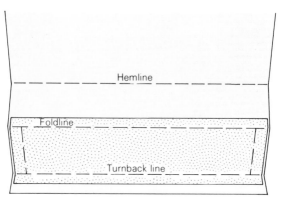

1. Note foldlines for cuff on sleeve bottom. If sleeve needs adjusting, do so above these lines. Trace and thread-mark each line. Apply interfacing between 'foldline' and 'turnback line' extend interfacing 1 cm beyond lines for softer crease (see Interfacing).

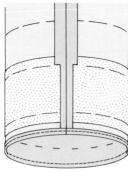

2. With right sides together, match, pin and tack underarm sleeve seam. Stitch. Press seam flat, then open. Trim seam allowance below 'foldline' to half-width. Finish edge.

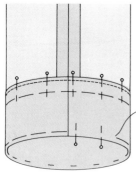

3. Fold sleeve hem to wrong side along 'foldline' markings; hold hem in line (do not let it pull) by pinning free edge to sleeve. Pin, then tack close to fold.

4. Remove pins at free edge. Form the cuff by folding sleeve to right side along 'turnback line.' Pin, then tack through all thicknesses along fold to hold in place.

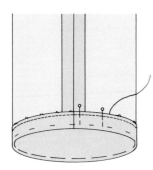

5. Pin hem edge in place on wrong side of sleeve. Secure with an appropriate hemming stitch (see Hemming stitches). Remove all tacking stitches, and press cuff lightly.

Straight turnback cuff (separate extension)

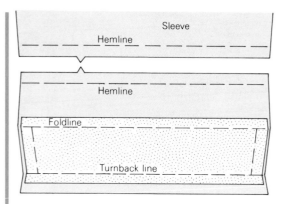

1. Note foldlines for cuff on sleeve extension; trace each line, thread-marking the 'foldline' and 'turnback line'. If sleeve needs adjusting, do so above the hemline marking on sleeve. Apply interfacing between 'foldline' and turnback line on extension piece; extend interfacing 1 cm beyond these lines for a softer crease (see Interfacing).

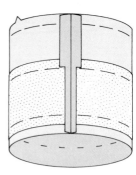

2. Complete sleeve seam. Press open. Right sides together, match, pin and stitch extension ends. Press flat, then open. Trim seam allowances below 'foldline' to half-width.

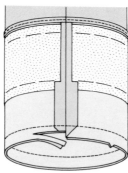

3. Finish unnotched edge of extension. With right sides together, match, pin and tack extension to sleeve along 'hemline'; stitch. Press flat. Trim and grade seam allowances.

4. Pull extension down; press seam open. Fold extension to wrong side along 'foldline'. Pin free edge of extension to sleeve to hold in place. Pin, then tack close to fold.

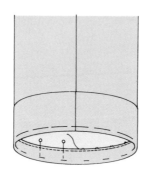

5. Remove pins. To form cuff, fold sleeve to the right side along 'turnback line'. Pin, then tack through all thicknesses. Pin and secure free edge to sleeve. Remove tacking; press.

Cuffs

Constructing shaped turnback cuff

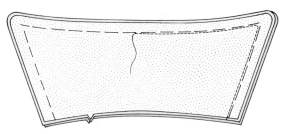

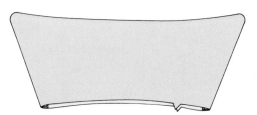

1. Cut and mark cuff and facing sections from pattern. Apply interfacing to wrong side of cuff section. With right sides together, match, pin and tack cuff to facing; leave the sleeve edge open. Stitch as tacked.

2. Press cuff flat. Trim, then grade seam allowances so widest is next to the cuff section. Clip into or notch out excess fabric from curved seam allowances, as necessary, so seam will lie smooth when cuff is turned.

3. Press seams open over a seam roll, then press seam allowances toward facing section. Turn cuff right side out; roll seams toward facing side. Press, and diagonal-tack if necessary to hold stitched edges in place.

Applying cuff with facing

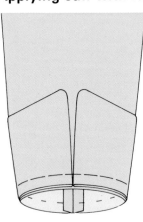

1. Complete underarm sleeve seam; press open. Match and pin the facing side of cuff to the right side of sleeve. Tack in place along seamline.

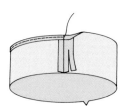

2. With right sides together, pin and stitch ends of sleeve facing. Press seam flat, then open. Trim seam allowances to half-width. Apply seam finish to unnotched edge of facing.

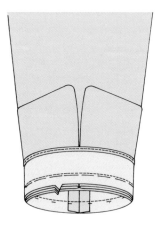

3. Match, pin and tack sleeve facing to cuff and sleeve. Stitch along seamline. Press to embed stitches.

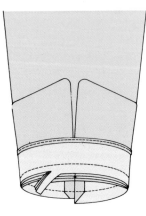

4. Diagonally trim the cross-seam allowances. Trim and grade seam allowances so widest is next to the sleeve.

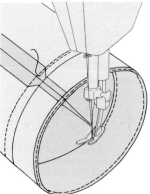

5. Extend the facing and seam allowances and, with right side up, understitch on facing side of seamline. Press seam flat.

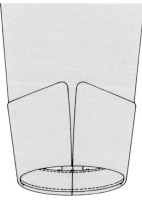

6. Turn facing to the inside, rolling edges slightly inward. Press seamline. Pin free edge of facing to sleeve. Secure in place.

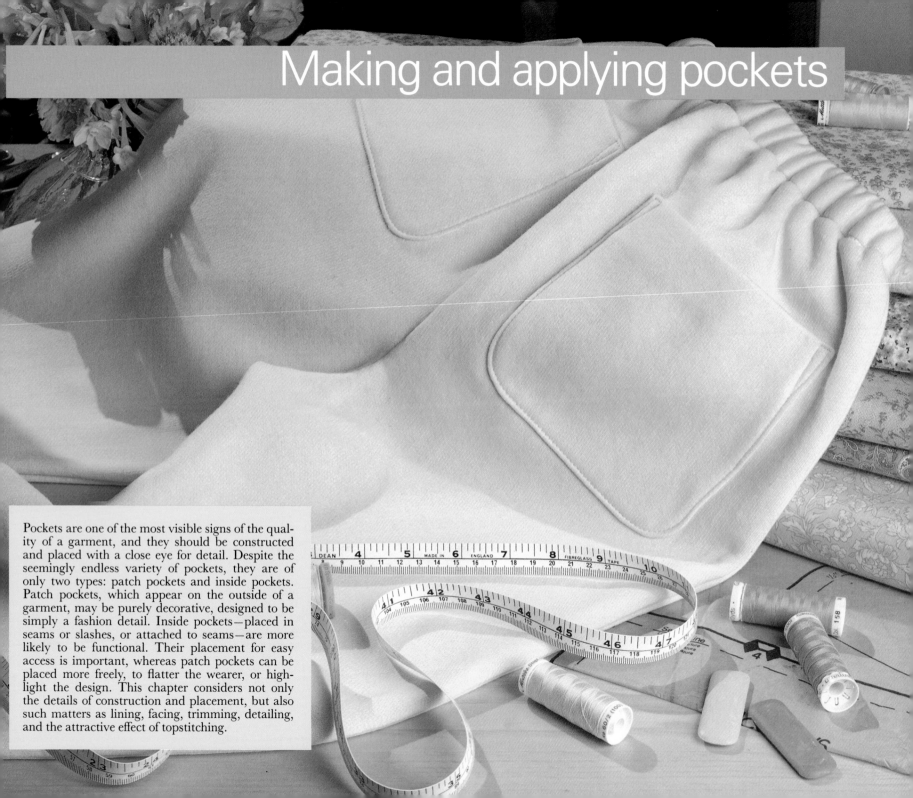

Making and applying pockets

Pockets are one of the most visible signs of the quality of a garment, and they should be constructed and placed with a close eye for detail. Despite the seemingly endless variety of pockets, they are of only two types: patch pockets and inside pockets. Patch pockets, which appear on the outside of a garment, may be purely decorative, designed to be simply a fashion detail. Inside pockets—placed in seams or slashes, or attached to seams—are more likely to be functional. Their placement for easy access is important, whereas patch pockets can be placed more freely, to flatter the wearer, or highlight the design. This chapter considers not only the details of construction and placement, but also such matters as lining, facing, trimming, detailing, and the attractive effect of topstitching.

Patch pockets

Comparison of types

There are two general pocket classifications for women's wear, patch pockets and inside pockets.

Patch pockets appear on the outside of the garment. They are made from the fashion fabric, can be lined or unlined, and may be attached either by machine or by hand. They can be square, rectangular, pointed or curved and may be decorated with topstitching, lace or braid trims, or construction details such as tucks.

Inside pockets are usually made from a lining fabric; they are kept on the inside of the garment, and the opening to the pocket can be either invisible or decorative. There are three types of inside pockets: the **in-seam** pocket, which is sewn to an opening in a seam; the **front-hip** or **front curved** pocket, which is attached to the garment at the waist and side seams; and the **slashed pocket,** which is identified by a slit in the garment, variously finished with the pocket itself, or with a welt, a flap, or a combination of both the welt and the flap. **Placement of the pocket** on the garment depends on whether the pocket is functional or strictly decorative. A pocket to be used should be located at a level that is comfortable for the hand to reach. If a pocket is only decorative, as pockets above the waist usually are, it should be placed where it will be most flattering.

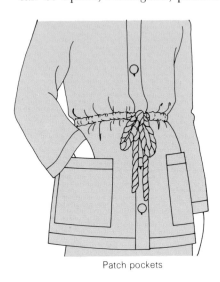

Patch pockets

In-seam pockets

Front-hip or front curved pockets

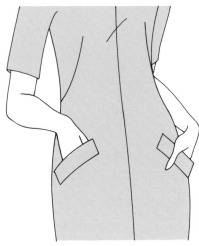

Slashed pockets with welts

Important preliminaries

Pockets are one of the most visible signs of a garment's overall quality and, as such, should be constructed with a close eye to detail.

Begin by double-checking the pocket location, particularly if you have made pattern alterations. Transfer pocket location and stitch lines to fabric with careful marking techniques; follow with precise stitching, taking care to neither stop short of nor run beyond the indicated stitch lines.

Trim and grade wherever it is possible, and press well at each step.

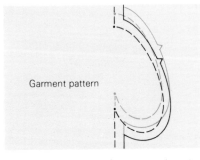

If a pocket is re-located to be more flattering or more accessible, be sure to transfer all pocket markings to the new position.

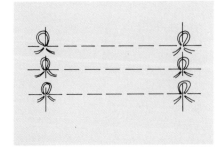

Mark the pocket first with tailor's tacks for positioning, then with thread-marking for all stitching lines.

Add interfacing if pocket fabric is lightweight or loosely woven. This adds strength and helps preserve the pocket's shape.

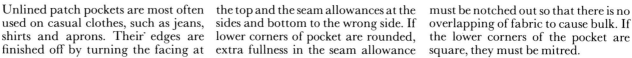
Patch pockets explained

Patch pockets are essentially shaped pieces of fabric that are finished on all sides, then attached to the garment by hand or machine. They may be lined or unlined, and may also be decorated in any of several ways before being attached to the garment.

If pockets are to be used in pairs, take care that the finished pockets are the same size and shape; a cardboard template cut to that size is helpful for guiding stitching and pressing.

If a plaid, a stripe or a print is to be matched, the pocket must be cut so that this is possible; a striped or plaid pocket may be cut on the opposite grain from the garment or on the bias for added contrast.

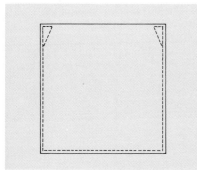

Plain patch pocket, attached with topstitching

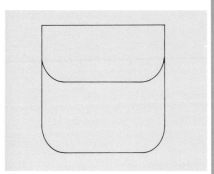

Patch pocket with flap, attached by hand

Unlined patch pockets

Unlined patch pockets are most often used on casual clothes, such as jeans, shirts and aprons. Their edges are finished off by turning the facing at the top and the seam allowances at the sides and bottom to the wrong side. If lower corners of pocket are rounded, extra fullness in the seam allowance must be notched out so that there is no overlapping of fabric to cause bulk. If the lower corners of the pocket are square, they must be mitred.

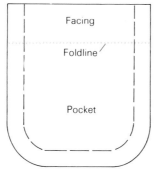

Unlined patch pockets usually have a self-facing at the opening edge, which is turned to the inside during construction.

1. Turn under raw edge of pocket facing and edgestitch. Fold facing to the right side along foldline and stitch each side on seamline.

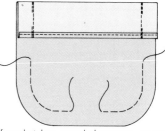

2. If pocket has rounded corners, easestitch at each corner a thread width into the seam allowance from the seamline.

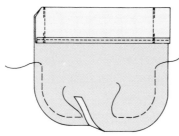

3. Trim entire pocket seam allowance to 1 cm and cut diagonally across each corner at top. Turn facing to wrong side; pull corners out.

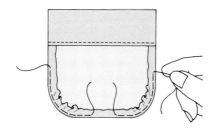

4. Press top edge. Pull easestitching at corners to draw in seam allowance and shape pocket curve. Notch out excess fabric.

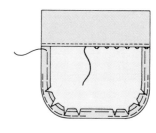

5. Press pocket seam allowances and facing flat. Hand-tack around entire pocket edge and slipstitch facing to pocket.

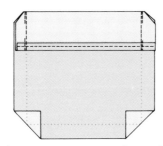

To mitre a square corner, first make a diagonal fold to the right side across the junction of the seamlines. Press to crease.

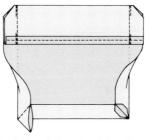

Open the fold and place the *right* sides of the seam allowances together. Stitch on the crease from raw edge to corner. Trim.

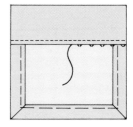

Turn corners and facing to wrong side and press entire pocket flat. Hand-tack around all edges and slipstitch facing to pocket.

287

Patch pockets

Lined patch pockets

Lining gives patch pockets a neat custom finish. Also, it adds opaqueness to loosely woven or sheer fabrics, which is a great benefit for working pockets that are made of such fabrics. Lining should not be expected to take the place of interfacing, however; it does not support the outer fabric well enough. Often you will need to interface *and* line a patch pocket.

The lining should always be colour-matched to the outer fabric, and can be of either the garment fabric itself (if it is not too heavy) or a traditional lining fabric. The lining may extend to all edges or, if the pocket has a facing, it may go only to the facing.

If a pocket is lined to all edges, use this trick to ensure that no lining shows at the edges. First, cut the lining slightly smaller than the pocket by trimming 3 mm from all its cut edges. Centre the lining on the pocket so edges correspond, and stitch on the seamline. When the pocket is turned, the lining will pull the finished edge slightly to the wrong side. Press, remembering that the objective is crisp, sharp edges with no lining visible on the right side.

Patch pocket lined entirely to edge

Patch pocket lined to edge of facing

Lining entire pocket

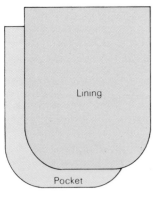
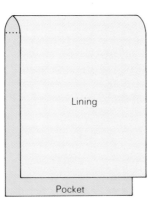

1. Cut pocket pieces out. For a **separately lined pocket,** cut lining exactly like pocket piece. For a **self-lined pocket,** cut pocket double size, with a fold at the top edge.

2. For a **separately lined pocket,** place right sides of pocket and lining together and pin along all edges. For a **self-lined pocket,** fold pocket in half, with right sides together, and pin the edges together. Stitch on seamline around raw edges, leaving small portion of bottom edge open. Press flat.

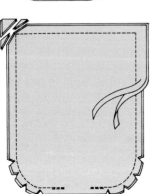

3. Trim and grade seam; taper corners. If pocket is rounded, notch out excess fabric so that when pocket is turned, there is no excess fabric in seam allowances.

4. Turn pocket to right side, gently pushing it through the open portion in the seam at the bottom edge. Pull out all corners; roll seam to the edge so that it is not visible from the right side. Press. Slipstitch opening at bottom closed.

Patch pockets

Separate lining applied to facing

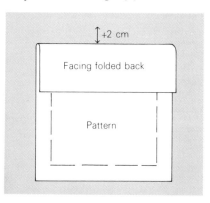

1. Cut lining from the pocket pattern, first folding the facing down out of the way along the foldline. Add 2 cm to lining piece at folded edge of pattern.

2. Pin top of lining to pocket facing, right sides together. Stitch a 1 cm seam, leaving a small opening in the centre of the seam for turning. Press seam toward lining.

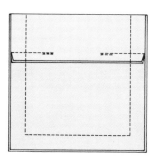

3. With right sides still together, match the bottom and side edges of lining and pocket. Pin, then stitch around the marked seamline. Press flat to embed the stitches.

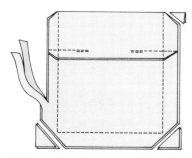

4. Trim and grade seam; trim diagonally across corners at top of pocket and at lower edges so that seam allowances in corners will not be folded back on themselves.

5. If pocket has rounded corners, first trim and grade the seam. Then trim diagonally across corners at top and notch out excess fabric in lower rounded corners.

6. Gently turn pocket to right side through opening in facing/lining seam. Press, rolling seam to underside so it will not show on right side. Slipstitch opening closed.

Adding details

Trimming details, such as topstitching, rick-rack, lace or Russia braid may be added to pockets during their construction. Topstitching is the most frequent decorative addition.

Topstitching will be most successful when it is done to the pocket before the pocket is applied to the garment (as compared with using the topstitching step as both a decorative measure and a means of attaching the pocket). For a better look, use a longer stitch

Patch pocket decorated with topstitching

Make tucks before pocket is constructed.

length (about 3 mm) when topstitching.

A patch pocket can also be trimmed with buttons and buttonholes, or with appliqués. Studs on jeans and denim skirts contribute decoration along with reinforcement.

Apply any kind of decoration to the pocket before applying it to the garment. Construction details, such as tucks and pleats, should be formed before the pocket is constructed.

Applying patch pockets

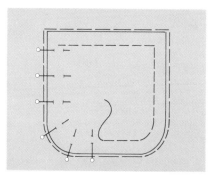

1. Pin and hand-tack finished patch pocket to the right side of the garment, carefully matching it to traced markings.

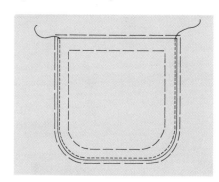

2. To sew pocket on **by machine,** set machine for a regular stitch length; stitch as close as possible to edge of pocket.

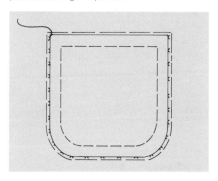

To sew pocket on **by hand,** use an uneven slipstitch. Take care not to pull the stitches too tight, or pocket will pucker.

Patch pockets

Zigzag stitching 30–33   Hand bar tack 147; whipstitch 148
Interfacing 84–85, 88–91   Tying thread ends 149

Corner reinforcement

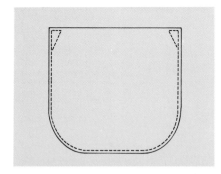

Small, identical triangles stitched at each top corner. This is the pocket reinforcement seen most frequently on shirts.

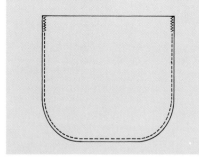

A zigzag stitch about 3 mm wide and closely spaced, run down 1 cm from the top of each side. Good for children's clothes.

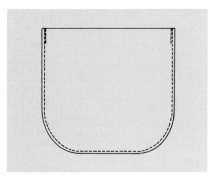

A backstitch for 1 cm on each side of the pocket's opening edge, with thread ends tied. This method is often used on blouses.

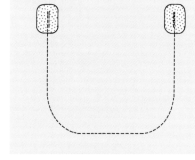

A patch of fabric or iron-on interfacing, placed on the wrong side of garment under reinforcement stitching, adds strength.

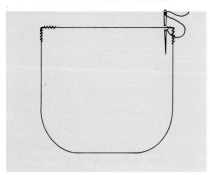

Hand reinforcement may be preferable. One method is to **whipstitch** invisibly for 6 mm on each side of top corners.

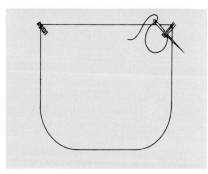

Another hand method is a **bar tack**—6 mm long straight stitches diagonally across corner with blanket stitches worked over them.

Patch pockets with flaps

In addition to such decorative devices as topstitching, patch pockets can be varied by means of flaps. These are finished, and sometimes intricately shaped, additions that are free-hanging and located at the top of the pocket. There are two methods for constructing a flap. One is to cut an extra-deep pocket facing, which is turned back over itself to the right side to create a self-flap; the opening of the pocket is above the flap.

In the second method, a separate flap is attached to the garment above the opening for the pocket, then pressed down over the opening.

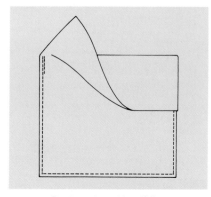

Patch pocket with self-flap

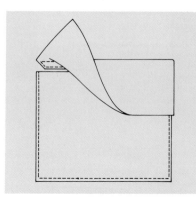

Patch pocket with separate flap

Patch pocket with self-flap

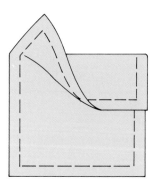

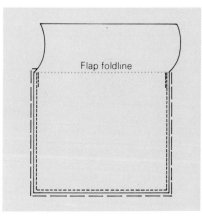

Flap foldline

1. Using pattern, cut out the pocket and construct as for any lined or unlined patch pocket with facing. Hand-tack around entire pocket. Fold pocket top down to the right side along line marking depth of flap; press.

2. Attach pocket to the garment and reinforce corners as for a regular patch pocket, keeping flap up out of the way. Start and end stitching at the flap foldline. Remove all tacking; give pocket a final pressing.

Patch pocket with separate flap

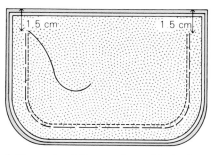

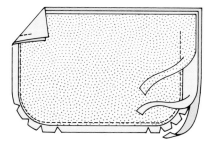

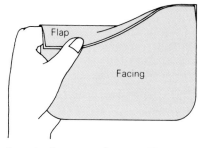

1. To construct flap, cut flap and facing from same pattern; interface flap. Pin flap to facing, right sides together, and stitch on seamline, starting and ending 1.5 cm from base of flap. Press to embed stitching.

2. Trim and grade the seams; clip or notch curves if the flap has shaped or rounded corners. Interfacing should be trimmed away completely to seamline; the seam allowance of the flap should be left widest.

3. Turn flap right side out, easing seamed edge slightly to facing side so that seam will not show on finished flap. **If fabric is bulky,** roll seam allowances at top edge over your finger, with the flap side up, to get additional width

from the flap seam allowance. This will help the flap to lie flat and prevent curling on lower edge. Pin, then hand-tack, across the opening a scant 1.5 cm away from the raw edges. Carefully press the flap flat.

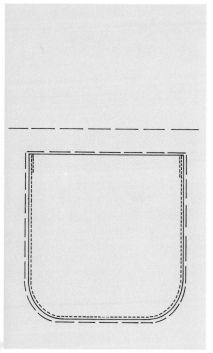

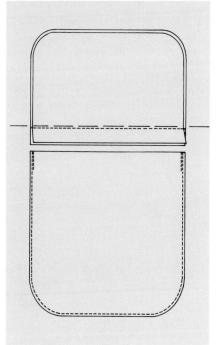

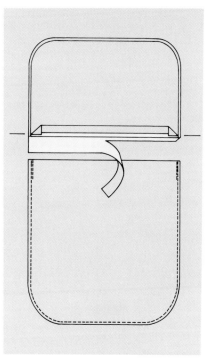

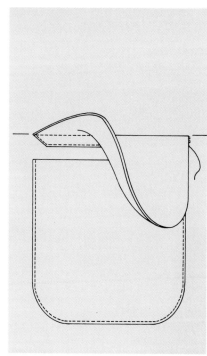

4. To attach pocket and flap to garment, pin finished pocket onto garment within tacked markings and sew in place, using any of the methods on page 289. Reinforce top edges of pocket. Press pocket. Mark flap seamline with tacking 1.5 cm above top of pocket.

5. Pin flap to garment, right sides together, with flap extended away from pocket. Edge of seam allowances should be aligned with top of pocket; seamline of flap should be on marking. Stitch on flap seamline. Pull thread ends to wrong side of garment and tie.

6. With the uppermost seam allowance of the flap held out of the way, carefully trim the lower seam allowance close to stitching. Fold under 6 mm on long edge of upper seam allowance and fold in the ends diagonally to eliminate all raw edges in finished flap.

7. Pin upper seam allowance over the trimmed seam allowance and edgestitch around the ends and along the long side. Tie thread ends. Fold flap down over pocket and press. If necessary to hold flap flat, slipstitch the upper corners of the flap to the garment.

291

Inside pockets

In-seam pockets

Although all finished in-seam pockets look the same from the right side of the garment, they may be constructed in three different ways, depending on how the pattern is designed. In the **all-in-one** in-seam pocket, the pocket is part of the garment, so the two are cut as one and there is no seam at the opening of the pocket. The **separate**

in-seam pocket is made up of separate pocket and garment pieces that are joined in the seamline to create the pocket. The **extension** in-seam pocket is made up of a separate pocket piece and a garment piece that has a small projection designed to extend into the pocket opening.

Because inside pockets generally receive a great deal of wear, the seam into which they are set must be re-inforced with a stay to prevent stretch-ing. Use a sturdy lining fabric for the pocket to reduce bulk.

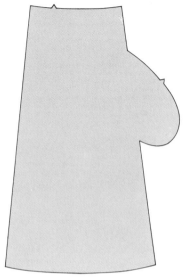

All-in-one in-seam pocket

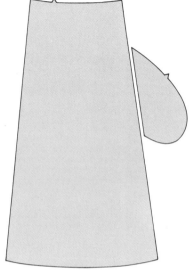

Separate in-seam pocket

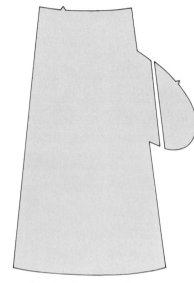

Extension in-seam pocket

Reinforcing in-seam pockets

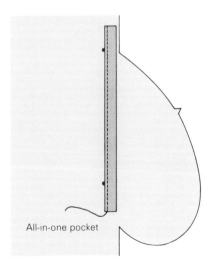

All-in-one pocket

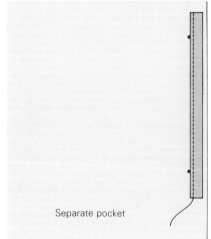

Separate pocket

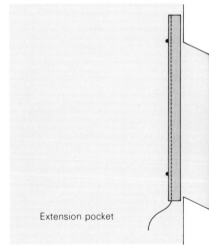

Extension pocket

Seamline of front garment section must be reinforced before any in-seam pocket is sewn in, regardless of type. Cut a length of seam bind-ing equal to the pocket opening plus 5 cm.

Position tape on the *wrong* side of the pocket seamline, centring it next to the marks for the pocket opening. (Drawings show position for each pocket type.) One edge should be aligned

with seamline; the width of the tape should be on the seam allowance or extension of gar-ment. Tack, then stitch tape in place 3 mm from edge nearest seamline.

All-in-one in-seam pocket

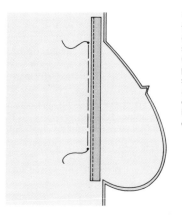

1. Reinforce garment front along pocket opening. With right sides together and markings matched, pin the front and back sections together along pocket opening. Tack by hand along pocket opening.

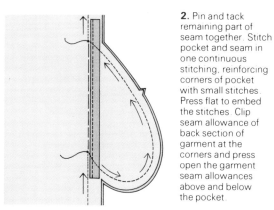

2. Pin and tack remaining part of seam together. Stitch pocket and seam in one continuous stitching, reinforcing corners of pocket with small stitches. Press flat to embed the stitches. Clip seam allowance of back section of garment at the corners and press open the garment seam allowances above and below the pocket.

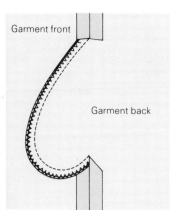

Garment front

Garment back

3. Finish and reinforce raw edges of pocket with an overedge stitch, catching in garment front seam allowance at the top and bottom. Press pocket toward garment front and remove tacking at opening.

Separate in-seam pocket

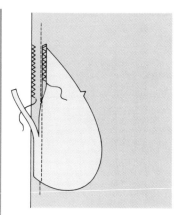

1. Reinforce garment front. Pin one pocket section to front garment piece, right sides together, matching markings. Stitch a scant 1.5 cm seam. Grade the *front* pocket seam allowance only and finish each seam edge separately. Pin, stitch and seam-finish other pocket section and back garment piece in same way, but do not trim seam allowance.

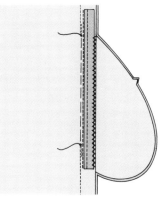

2. With right sides together and pockets extended, match markings and pin front and back sections together along pocket opening; hand-tack across opening. Pin and stitch side seams above and below pocket opening; reinforce with backstitches at pocket markings. Press flat.

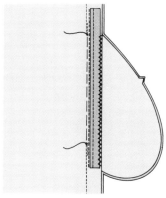

3. Press back pocket seams open and front pocket seams toward pocket. Pin pocket sections together, matching raw edges, and stitch around pocket, backstitching at pocket markings and catching front seam in stitching. Press flat.

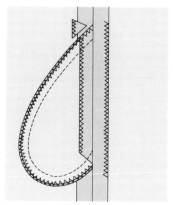

4. Seam-finish edges of pocket together, using the same stitch as on seam allowances. Catch front seam allowance into the seam-finishing at top and bottom of pocket. Press pocket toward garment front and remove tacking from opening. Trim off point of pocket at the top.

Adding a facing to the opening edge of the pocket will keep any of the pocket fabric from showing if pocket gapes open.
1. Cut two strips of garment fabric on the straight grain, each measuring 5 cm wide by the length of the pocket opening plus 8 cm. Turn under and press 6 mm to the wrong side on one long edge of each facing strip.

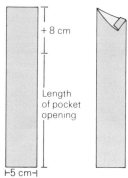

+ 8 cm

Length of pocket opening

⊢5 cm⊣

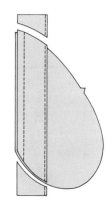

2. Apply facing to pocket before sewing pocket into garment. Place wrong side of each facing on the right side of each pocket piece, with the raw edges even at opening. Edgestitch along pressed-under edge, then stitch other long edge of pocket facing to pocket 1 cm from raw edge. Trim away excess facing fabric at top and bottom of pocket.

Inside pockets

Extension in-seam pocket

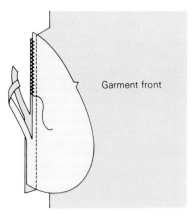

1. Reinforce garment front along pocket opening. Pin and stitch one pocket section to front garment piece, right sides together, matching markings and having raw edges even. Press flat. Trim seam to 6 mm and overcast edges together.

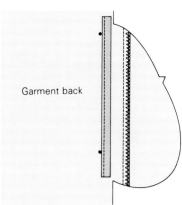

2. With pocket extended away from garment, press seam toward the pocket. Pin and stitch other pocket section to back garment piece as for front.

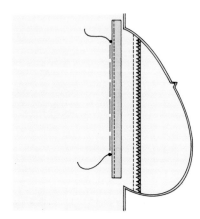

3. With right sides together and all markings matched, pin the front and back sections together along pocket opening; hand-tack across opening.

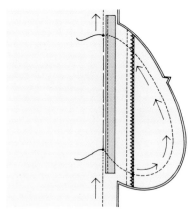

4. Pin and tack remainder of side and pocket seam together and stitch in one continuous seam, reinforcing the corners with small stitches.

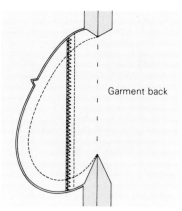

5. Press flat to embed stitches. Clip seam allowance of back garment section to corner and press seam open above and below the pocket.

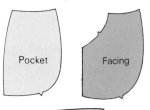

6. Seam-finish edges of pocket together, using the same stitch as on the pocket seam allowance edges. Catch in the garment front seam allowance at the top and bottom. Press pocket toward garment front and remove tacking at opening.

Front-hip pockets

Front-hip pockets are attached to the garment at the waist and side seams and must be included in any waist or hip alterations made in the garment.

Although these hip pockets can vary greatly in shape and detailing along the opening edge, they are all made up of two pattern pieces, a pocket piece and a facing piece. The shapes of the two are never the same because the facing piece finishes off the pocket opening, while the pocket piece becomes part of the main garment at the waistline.

The pocket piece must be cut of garment fabric, but lining fabric may be used for the facing.

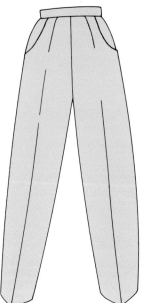

Construction of front-hip pocket

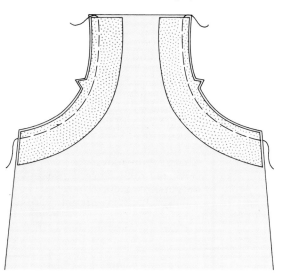

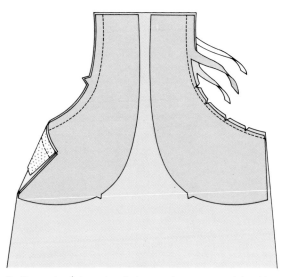

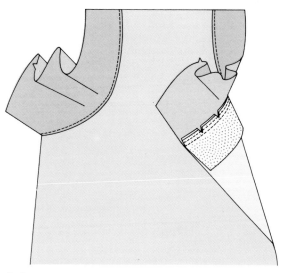

1. Cut a strip of interfacing 5 cm wide and shaped to follow the opening edge of pattern piece for pocket facing. Tack to wrong side of garment at opening edge of pocket—the 'wearing' edge, where reinforcement is most needed.

2. Pin and stitch pocket facing to the garment, right sides together, along opening edge of pocket. Press flat to embed stitches. Trim and grade the seam, leaving garment seam allowance the widest. Clip or notch curves.

3. Press seam open, then press both seam allowances toward facing. Understitch the facing to keep it from rolling to the right side: with garment right side up, stitch close to seamline through facing and seam allowances.

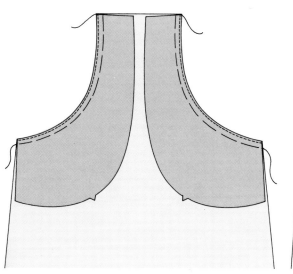

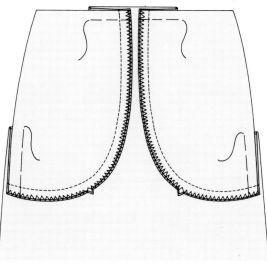

4. Turn facings to inside along seamline and press. Tack around curved edge. If topstitching is desired for a decorative effect, apply it now. (Flaps, if being used, should be made and tacked in place before facing is applied.)

5. Pin pocket to facing, right sides together, and stitch as pinned around seamline to the side of the garment. Press. Seam-finish raw edges. Tack side edges of pocket to side seam of garment and top edge of pocket to waistline.

6. Pin together and stitch side seams of garment, catching in pocket and facing seams. Press seams flat, then open. Treat the upper part of the pocket as part of the waistline seam when applying bodice or waistband.

Inside pockets

Slashed pockets

There are three types of slashed pocket, which differ only in the way the pocket opening is finished. When the pocket acts as a finish, the result is a **bound** pocket, which looks like a large bound buttonhole. A second method is with a **flap,** which covers the pocket after insertion into the upper edge of the slash. Flaps are usually, but not necessarily, rectangular. The third finish, a **welt,** is a rectangular piece, cut separately or as a part of the pocket, that fits over the pocket opening and is sewn into the lower edge of the slash. (A variation is a double welt—one at each edge of the slash.) The three finishes may be used together in almost any combination.

Bound pockets

Bound pockets are those in which the pocket itself is used to finish off, or bind, the edges of the slash in the garment. From the right side of the garment, the pocket looks like a large bound buttonhole. Although lining fabric is generally recommended for inside pockets, in this pocket type the pocket fabric will show on the outside, so the garment fabric is preferable for the purpose.

When the pocket is completed, arrowhead tacks may be worked at each end for a tailored look (see Hand stitches). Check any pattern you plan to use to be sure that the pocket pieces meet the specifications below. If they do not, alter them to conform.

Bound pocket

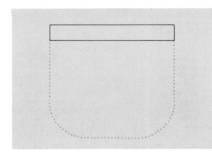

Pocket with flap on top edge

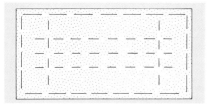

Single welt pocket

Marking and cutting slashed pockets

Slashed pockets are thought to be the most difficult of the inside pockets to construct. Actually, they are only a matter of precise marking and exact stitching, combined with very careful cutting. Construction is very much like that of a bound buttonhole, although the finished result is much larger. The pocket back and front are not joined until they have been attached to the opening edge, which is the slash in the garment. The seams of the pocket itself are then formed.

Carefully thread-mark the opening for the pocket on the right side of the garment, using a very small hand stitch. Be sure markings are exactly on grain (unless the pockets are diagonally placed) and that centre and stitching lines are exactly parallel. All permanent machine stitching should be done with a very short stitch. Press carefully at each step of construction; a final pressing by itself is not sufficient to set sharp edges.

Tack across ends to mark *width* of opening, then through centre line and on parallel stitching lines to mark *depth* of opening; extend marks about 2 cm beyond the actual limits. Be sure lines are on-grain and parallel.

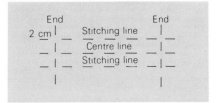

Stitch rectangle precisely for any type of slashed pocket. Begin stitching at centre of one side and pivot at corners. Take same number of stitches across each end; overlap stitches at starting point to secure.

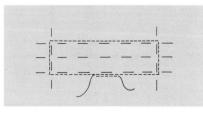

If garment fabric is lightweight or loosely woven, add a stay of lightweight interfacing for stability and crispness. Cut it about 10 cm long and 5 cm wider than opening; centre it behind pocket opening and tack in place.

Curve pocket corners if they are square on the pattern, to prevent any lint buildup in the pocket from repeated wearings and washings. Instead of pivoting when stitching the pocket, simply round the corners off.

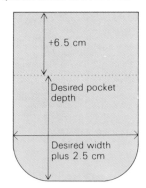

Pieces for bound pocket: Two pocket pieces are needed. The first should measure desired pocket depth plus 6.5 cm; the second, pocket depth plus 1 cm. Cutting width of both: desired width plus 2.5 cm for side seams.

Constructing bound pockets

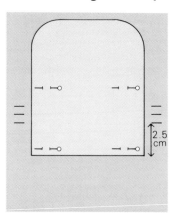

1. With right sides together, pin the long pocket section over pocket markings on garment, with straight (top) edge of pocket 2.5 cm below the lower marked stitching line.

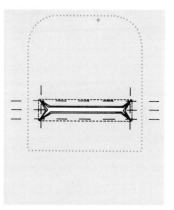

2. Turn garment side up for stitching. Following tacked markings, stitch a rectangle as shown on preceding page. Slash through all thicknesses between stitching lines; stop 1 cm before ends and slash diagonally into the four corners.

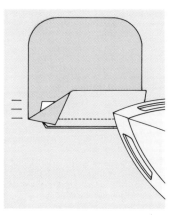

3. Gently push pocket section through slash to the wrong side of the garment. Pull on the small triangles at each end to square the corners of the rectangular opening. Press triangular ends and seam allowances away from the opening. Press straight end of pocket up over the opening.

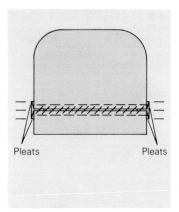

4. Fold pocket to form even pleats that meet in the centre of the opening. Check from the right side to make sure that the pleats (or 'lips') are equal in depth to one another across the entire width of the pocket. Tack through folded edges and whipstitch lips together. Remove the tacked markings from garment.

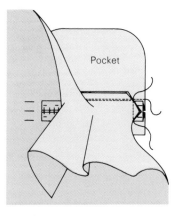

5. Turn garment right side up and flip back garment so that the side edge of the pocket is exposed. Stitch over the triangle and the ends of the lips at each side of pocket. Fold garment down so that top seam allowance of opening shows and stitch through the seam allowances and the pocket, as close as possible to first stitching.

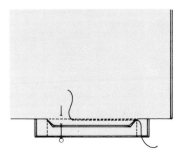

6. Slip remaining pocket section under one sewn to garment and pin along outer edges. Flip garment up so that bottom seam allowance of opening is exposed and stitch through seam allowance and both pocket sections.

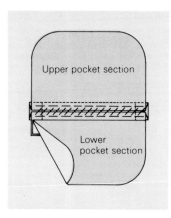

7. Turn garment to wrong side. Unpin pocket edges and turn lower pocket section down. Press in place.

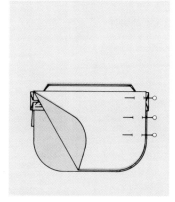

8. Turn upper pocket section down; bottom raw edges of both sections should be even. If they are not, trim them to the same length. Pin sections together.

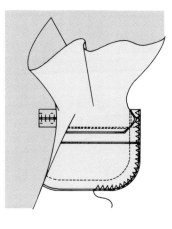

9. Turn garment to right side again and fold garment in such a way that side of pocket is exposed. Stitch around pinned pocket on the seamline, starting at the top and stitching across triangular ends as close as possible to original stitching. Backstitch at beginning and ends. Press flat. Seam-finish outer raw edges. Remove all tacking.

Inside pockets

Flap and separate welt pockets

In these two pockets, either a flap or a welt is completely constructed, then attached to one of the seam allowances of the pocket opening. The **flap** is attached to the top seam allowance, the **welt** to the bottom one. This is the only difference in the construction of the two pockets.

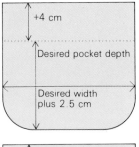

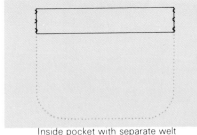

Inside pocket with flap

Inside pocket with separate welt

Making the pocket

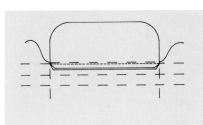

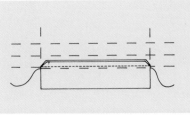

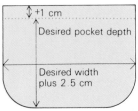

1. Cut two pocket sections, one to desired depth of pocket plus 4 cm, the other to desired depth of pocket plus 1 cm. Both pocket sections should be the desired pocket width plus 2.5 cm for side seam allowances.

2. Tack right side of welt or flap to right side of garment over pocket markings. If a flap is being used, the seamline of flap should align with **upper** stitch line; if a welt is used, match its seamline to **lower** stitch line.

Making the flap or welt

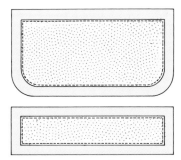

1. Cut welt or flap and its facing from pattern and interface wrong side of welt or flap. Trim interfacing seam allowance.

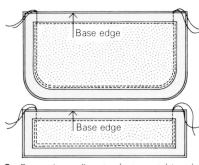

2. Pin welt or flap to facing, right sides together, and stitch around marked seamline, leaving base edge open. Press flat.

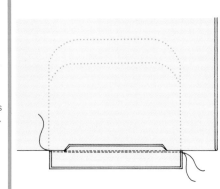

7. With garment right side up, flip up garment to expose pocket edge. Slip remaining pocket section under opening, right side up, matching raw edges of pocket sections; pin. Stitch, as shown, on first stitch line.

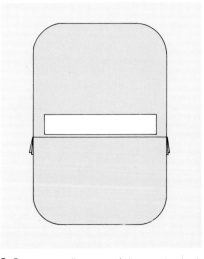

8. Press seam allowance of the opening back away from opening, then turn garment to the wrong side and bring down lower pocket section. Press flat. One edge of pocket is now completely finished.

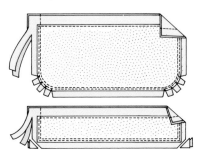

3. Trim and grade seam, clip or notch curves if corners are rounded. Turn and press, easing the facing under slightly.

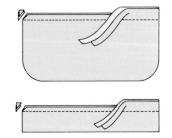

4. Trim base edge to 6 mm. Machine-stitch 6 mm from raw edge to hold layers together. Trim across corners diagonally.

Slipstitch 143; hand bar tack 147   **Reducing seam bulk 159**
Securing thread ends 149   **Slashing buttonholes 344**

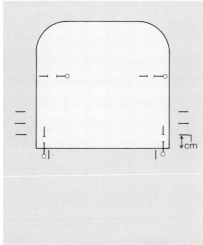

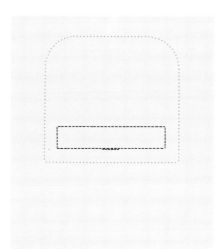

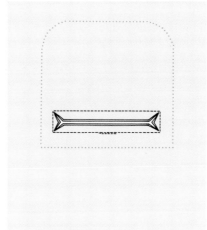

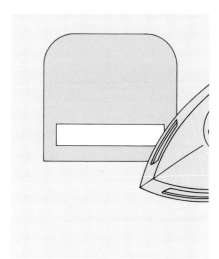

3. With right sides together, pin long pocket section over pocket markings, extending edge 1 cm below lower marked stitching line. (Note: the flap or welt will be between the pocket and the garment at this step.)

4. Turn garment section to the wrong side. Following tacked marking precisely, stitch a perfect rectangle, pivoting at corners and overlapping stitching on one long side. Remove all tacking stitches.

5. Very carefully slash through all the thicknesses at centre of rectangle; stop 1 cm before ends and cut diagonally into the four corners, forming small triangles at each end. Do not cut into stitching.

6. Gently push pocket through slash to wrong side. Turn a flap *down* over opening; turn a welt *up*. Pull on small triangles to square corners of opening. Press triangles and seam allowances away from opening.

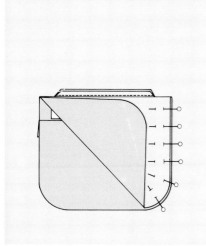

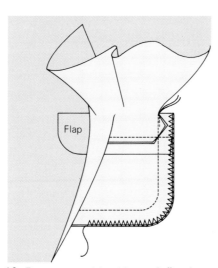

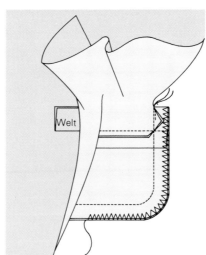

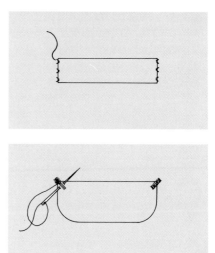

9. Turn the upper pocket section down over the opening. Bottom raw edge of both pocket sections should be even. If they are not, trim them to the same length. Pin sections together, taking care not to catch garment.

10. Turn garment right side up. A **flap** (see above) should be in a downward position, pocket opening completely covered. A **welt** (above right) will point upward and also cover pocket opening. Flip garment back so pocket is exposed. Stitch around pinned pocket, starting at top. Stitch across triangle ends as close as possible to original stitching; back-stitch at beginning and end. Press flat. Seam-finish outer edge of pocket.

11. To finish off the **welt** pocket (top), slipstitch ends of the welt invisibly to garment. This will hold the welt in an upright position. To finish the **flap**, make a tiny bar tack by hand to hold the flap down.

Inside pockets

Self-welt or stand pocket

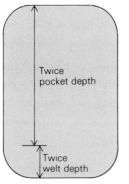

Twice
pocket depth

Twice
welt depth

Width of pocket opening plus 2.5 cm

In this method, a welt
is formed of pocket
fabric during pocket
construction.
1. Cut pocket from
garment fabric on the
lengthwise grain.
Pocket length should
be twice the desired
depth of the finished
pocket plus twice the
desired depth of the
welt; pocket width
should equal that of
the pocket opening
plus 2.5 cm for side
seam allowances.

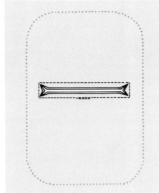

4. Carefully cut
through garment and
pocket at centre of
rectangle; stop 1 cm
before ends and cut
diagonally into the
four corners, forming
a small triangle at
each end of opening.

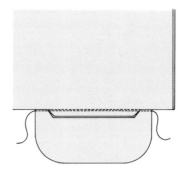

7. Turn garment right
side up. Flip up
bottom portion of
garment to expose
lower seam
allowances of
opening. Stitch
through seam
allowances and
pocket.

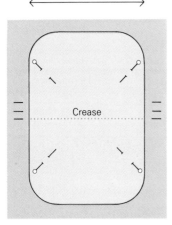

Crease

2. Fold pocket in half
horizontally and press
in a crease at the
fold. With right sides
together, pin pocket
section to the
garment, aligning
crease with marked
lower stitching line.

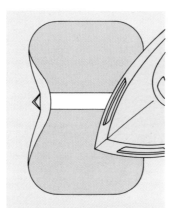

5. Gently push
pocket through slash
to wrong side. Pull on
small triangular ends
to square the corners
of the opening. Press
triangular ends and
pocket opening seam
allowances away
from the opening.

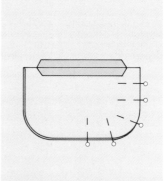

8. Turn garment back
to wrong side and
fold upper portion of
pocket down over
bottom section.
Right sides of pocket
should be together
and the edges should
be even. Pin around
pocket. Press open
the seam allowance
at the top.

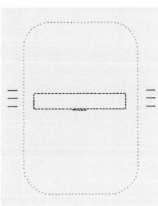

3. Turn garment to
the wrong side.
Following tacked
guidelines, stitch
around pocket,
forming a perfect
rectangle (see
p. 296). Remove
tacking stitches.

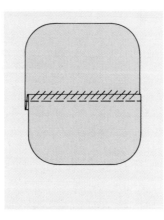

6. Form a pleat to
cover the pocket
opening by folding
lower pocket section
up. Check from the
right side to see that
pleat depth is even
and covers the entire
opening. To hold
pleat in place, tack
through the fold,
then whipstitch
folded edge to top of
opening. (Pleat
becomes the welt.)

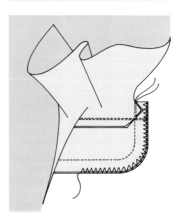

9. Turn garment right
side up again and flip
it out of the way to
expose the pocket.
Stitch around the
pinned pocket,
starting at the top
and stitching across
triangular ends as
close as possible to
original stitching;
backstitch at
beginning and end.
Press flat.
Seam-finish outer
raw edges of pocket.
Remove all tacking.

Hems and other edge finishes

Hemlines have always been a focus of fashion, but today, when a multiplicity of dress lengths are worn, you can choose a length to suit you and your clothing. The hemline has a vital effect on the appearance of an outfit, and it can be chosen to flatter the wearer. The hem is a sewing basic that not only provides a neat finish, but also helps a garment hang well when worn. This chapter takes you step-by-step through all the kinds of hems and the different finishes that you will need, from the first step of marking the hem to the finishing touches. Both hand and machine techniques are covered, along with the newer fusible products. Also included are decorative touches and special techniques for special fabrics, including knits, lace, leather, fake furs, velvet and sheers.

Hems

Types of hem

A hem is a finish for any bottom edge of a garment. There are three basic forms—a **turned-up edge** (the most common), a **faced edge** and an **enclosed edge.** Although all are dealt with here as hem treatments,

any of them might be used for other edges as well.

Selection of a hemming method depends largely on garment style and fabric. Whatever the choice, certain criteria should always be met: (1) The gar-

ment should hang evenly and gracefully; (2) there should be no lumpiness in the hem allowance; (3) unless meant to be decorative, finished hems should be totally inconspicuous.

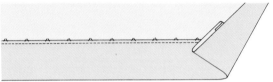
Turned-up hem

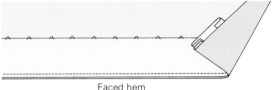
Faced hem

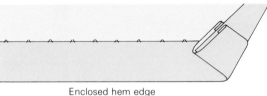
Enclosed hem edge

Marking the hemline

The first step, common to all hem finishes, is marking the hemline. Except for certain pleated styles, marking is done after garment construction has been completed. Though a garment's finished length is largely determined by the pattern style and current fashion, it should be modified if a dif-

ferent length will be more flattering to the wearer. It is wise to check the hemline location before cutting the pattern, in case a change is required.

Basically, there are two ways to mark a hem—on a flat surface or on the wearer. The first is suitable for a hem on the hipline or above, the second for

any length below the hip. If someone is marking a garment for you, it is best to wear the undergarments and shoes you will wear with it, and to stand in one place while your helper moves around you to mark. Before marking a bias or circular garment, allow it to hang for 24 hours.

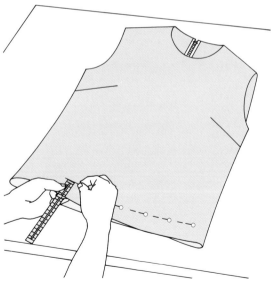

Before marking a hemline at the hip or above (also pants legs), check the pattern to see how much hem allowance has been provided. Measure and turn up this amount, pinning fabric from right side. Try on garment; adjust length if necessary. Remove garment; measure and mark the hemline.

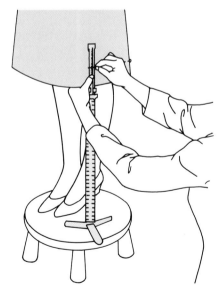

To mark a hemline below the hips, put garment on over appropriate undergarments; wear shoes and belt that go with it. Stand on a low stool, while a helper moves around you with a marker (pin marker as shown, metre rule, or suitable substitute), placing pins or marks every few centimetres.

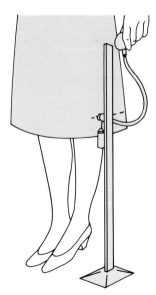

To mark a hemline without help, use a marker of the chalk type shown here. Test it on a scrap beforehand; the chalk cannot be removed from some fabrics. Standing straight, with feet together, move the marker around you, marking every few centimetres. Try to avoid changing posture as you work.

Turning up the hem edge

In a turned-up hem, a certain width of fabric, the *hem allowance,* is folded inside the garment, then secured by hand, machine, or fusing. This is the hem type usually provided for in pattern designs, with the amount of turn-up indicated on the pattern by a line or written instructions. It is wise to check this allowance before cutting out the garment, should a change be desirable.

The hem's shape, straight or curved, generally determines how much should be turned up. As a rule, the straighter the edge, the deeper the hem allowance; the more it curves, the shallower the allowance. Exceptions are sheer fabrics, in which a very deep or a narrow rolled hem (p. 326) may be preferable, and soft knits, where a narrow turn-up will minimise sagging (p. 306 and p. 326).

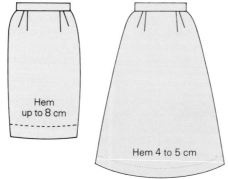

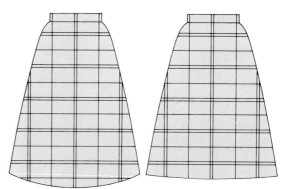

Hem allowance varies according to garment shape. Up to 8 cm is usually allowed for a straight garment, 4 to 5 cm for a flared one. Fabric weight should also be considered.

A hemline may look distorted if the hem curve is too extreme for, or does not align with, the fabric design. A slight adjustment may be necessary, for a better effect.

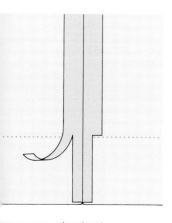

1. Before turning up the hem, reduce bulk within the hem allowance by trimming seam allowances to half their original widths. This will make the hem smoother at the seamlines.

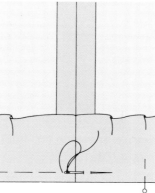

2. With wrong side facing you, fold hem on the marked line, placing pins at right-angles to the fold about every 5 cm. (If a mark should be greatly out of line with the others, ignore it, and align the fold with the marks on either side.) Try on garment; make adjustments if necessary. After removing the garment, tack close to the folded edge.

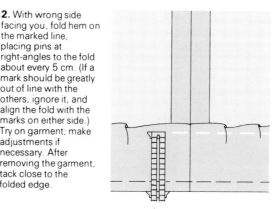

3. Make the hem allowance an even width all around by measuring the desired distance from the fold then marking with chalk. The ironing board is an ideal place to work, as it lets you deal with a small part of the hem at a time. A sewing gauge is the easiest measuring device to use.

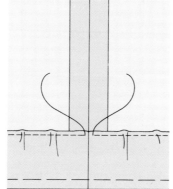

4. Trim excess hem allowance along the marks. At this stage, you can see whether or not the hem edge lies smoothly against the garment. If there are ripples, the fullness should be controlled by easing, a step that is usually necessary with gored skirts and other flared styles.

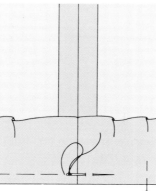

5. Ease the hem by machine-tacking 6 mm from the edge, beginning and ending stitches at each seam. Draw up fabric on easestitching until each section of the hem edge corresponds with that part of garment. Take care not to draw the edge in too much, or it will pull against the garment when finished.

6. Press the hem lightly to shrink out excess fullness, keeping the hem allowance grainlines aligned with those of the garment. Heavy paper inserted between hem and garment will prevent the hem edge from leaving a ridge.

Hems

Sewing hems by hand

Before a hem is secured by hand, the raw edge should be neatly finished. The finish chosen depends first on fabric characteristics and garment style, second on personal preference.

The edge can be left uncovered on fabric that does not fray, also where a lining will cover the hem; use a covered edge for fabric that frays a great deal, and in those situations where a more finished look is wanted.

There are two basic hand-hemming methods—*flat*, where stitches pass over the hem edge to the garment, and *blind*, where stitches are taken inside, between hem and garment. Blind hems are best for heavier fabrics and knits because the hem edge is not pressed into the garment. (See Hand stitches for techniques.)

Uncovered hem edges

A turned-and-stitched edge is suitable for all lightweight fabrics, especially crisp sheers; an excellent, durable finish for washable garments.

A stitched-and-pinked edge is a quick hem finish for fabrics that fray little or not at all; it is a particularly good choice for knits.

A zigzagged edge is a fast and relatively neat finish usable for any fabric that frays; also for knits, taking care not to stretch the edge.

An overlocked (serger) edge gives a professional look as it cuts, sews and neatens in one operation; it is suitable for all knits and woven fabrics.

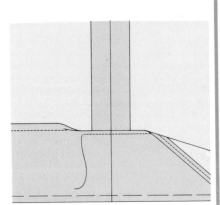

Turn the hem edge under 6 mm and press. (If using an easestitch, turn the edge along the stitching line.) Topstitch 3 mm from fold.

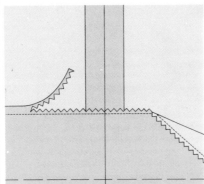

Stitch 6 mm from the hem edge, using regular stitching or easestitching (see p. 303) as required. Trim edge with pinking shears.

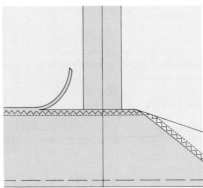

Stitch close to hem edge with a zigzag of medium width and length. If necessary, easestitch just below zigzag. Trim excess fabric.

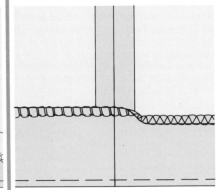

Stitch 6 mm from the hem edge, using an overlock stitch to suit the type of fabric (see p. 39) as required.

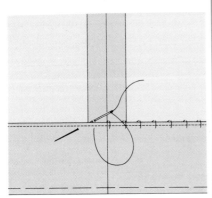

Secure hem with vertical hemming stitches (shown) or use slip hemming, spacing the stitches 1 cm apart. Do not pull thread taut.

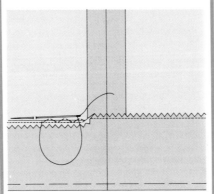

Turn hem edge back 6 mm; secure with a blind-hemming stitch, as shown, or with the blind herringbone stitch (for a heavy fabric).

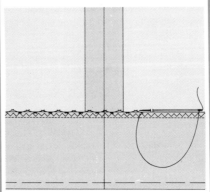

Secure hem with herringbone stitch if material is lightweight or tends to curl. For heavier fabric, use a blind-hemming stitch.

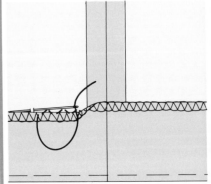

Turn hem edge back 6 mm; secure with a blind-hemming stitch, as shown, or with the blind herringbone stitch (for a heavy fabric).

Hems

Covered hem edges

Double-stitched hem

Seam binding provides a clean finish for fabric that frays. Use the woven-edge type for a straight-edge hem, a stretchy lace for a curved shape and for knit or other stretch fabric.

Bias binding is a neat hem finish for garments with a flared shape—the bias adjusts to curves. Use the 12 mm width, in matching colour if available, otherwise a neutral shade.

Hong Kong finish is suitable for any garment style or fabric, but especially good for heavy or bulky fabrics; recommended also for velvet or satin, using net in place of a bias strip.

This technique is recommended for very wide hems, also for heavy fabrics, as it gives better support. The edge is left uncovered as a rule, but a Hong Kong finish is also appropriate.

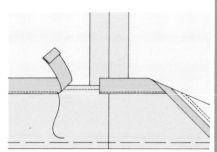

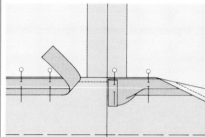

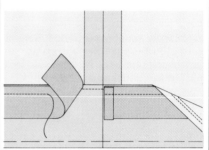

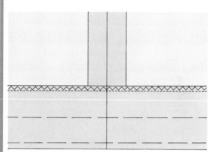

Lay seam binding on right side of hem, lapping it 6 mm over the edge. Edgestitch, overlapping ends at a seam, as shown.

Open one fold of binding; place crease just below easestitching on right side of hem. Fold end back 6 mm; align with a seam; pin.

Cut 2.5 cm bias of underlining fabric, or use packaged 12 mm width. Stitch to the hem, 6 mm from edge, lapping ends.

After finishing the hem edge, place a row of tacking stitches halfway between the edge and the fold at the hemline.

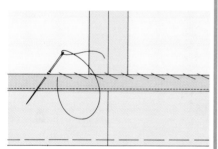

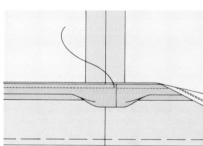

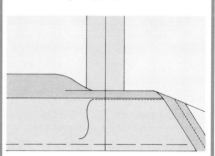

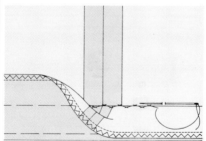

For **light to mediumweight fabric,** secure hem with one of the flat hemming stitches—slant (shown), vertical, or herringbone stitch.

Stitch to within 8 cm of starting point. Trim tape to lap 6 mm beyond fold of starting end; stitch the rest of the way across.

Wrap bias over the raw edge and press. From the right side, stitch in the groove formed by the first row of stitching.

Fold the hem back along this tacking and secure the fold with the blind herringbone stitch, spacing the stitches 1 cm apart.

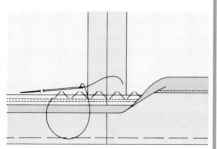

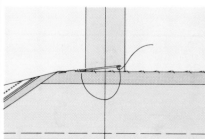

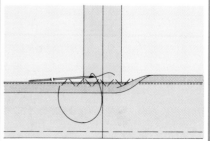

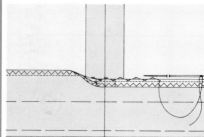

For **bulky fabric,** fold back tape and hem edge; blindstitch, as shown, catching the stitches through the hem edge only.

Secure hem edge with slip hemming stitches, as shown, or use either vertical or slant hemming stitches to secure it.

Secure the hem with the blind-hemming stitch, or use blind herringbone stitch. Be careful not to pull thread too tight.

Turn the upper half of the hem up again, and secure the edge with a blind herringbone stitch. Do not pull the thread too tight.

Hems

Sewing a hem by machine

The major assets of machine hems are speed and extra sturdiness. They can also provide a decorative touch, and are especially appropriate if topstitching is part of the design. Machine stitches are more apparent on a hem than hand stitches. Of the several methods, the blindstitched hem is the least conspicuous because only about every sixth stitch catches the right side of the fabric. For blindstitching a hem on a knit or on fabric that does not fray, see page 149. For fabric that frays, see the method below.

Use machine hems only on garments where easily seen stitches do not detract from the overall appearance. Take special care with all types of machine-stitched hems to keep stitching an even distance from the hemline.

Types of machine-stitched hem

Blind hemming by machine is a sturdy yet fairly inconspicuous finish; used mainly for children's clothing, very full skirts and household items.

A narrow machine-stitched hem is suitable where neither a deep nor an inconspicuous hem is required; best for blouses, shirts and dress linings.

A topstitched hem is essentially a decorative finish, particularly appropriate where topstitching is used elsewhere in garment construction.

A narrow topstitched hem is fine for knits, especially soft ones, which may sag with a hand finish; suitable for any fabric that does not fray.

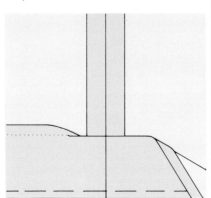

Mark, fold and tack hemline. Make the hem allowance even; turn edge under 1 cm; press. Adjust machine for blind-hemming stitch.

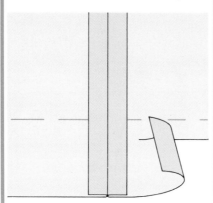

Mark the hemline. Trim hem allowance to 12 mm. Turn edge under 6 mm and press. Turn edge again and press along hemline.

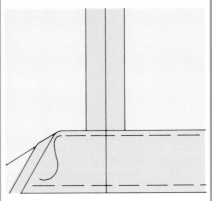

Mark, fold and tack hemline. Adjust hem allowance to desired width. Fold hem edge under 1 cm. Tack to garment along fold.

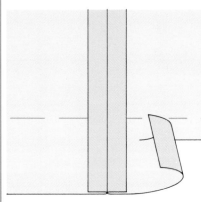

Mark the hemline. Trim the hem allowance to 1.5 cm. Turn the hem up on the hemline and press. Tack 1 cm from the edge.

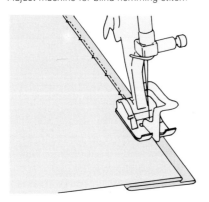

Lay hem allowance face down; fold garment back to reveal the hem edge. Stitch, catching only the garment in the zigzag stitch.

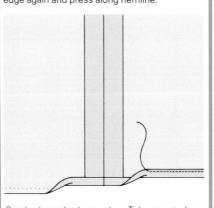

Stitch along the hem edge. Take care to keep the hem and garment grainlines aligned; if edge is allowed to slant, hem will ripple.

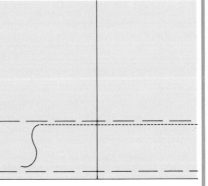

Topstitch from the right side, using a straight stitch or, if desired, a zigzag or another of the decorative stitch patterns.

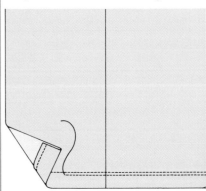

Topstitch, 1 cm from fold. Stitch a second row 3 mm below the first one (or use a twin needle to stitch both rows at once).

Fusing a hem

A fast and inconspicuous way to secure a hem is to bond it with fusible web (a sheer nonwoven material that melts with application of heat and moisture). This web is available in packaged pre-cut strips, suitable for most hem jobs, and also in larger sheets, from which you can cut strips.

A hem can be fused on any fabric that can be steam-pressed, but pressing time varies with different fabrics, so a test is essential. Check on a scrap to see if the bond is secure and the appearance satisfactory.

If properly done, the fusing lasts through normal washing and dry-cleaning procedures. Removal is possible, but messy, so adjust your hem carefully before application. The following additional precautions are necessary: (1) avoid stretching a fusible web during application; (2) do not let it touch the iron; (3) do not glide the iron over the fabric.

Using iron-on hemming tape

Iron-on hemming tape is a bias-cut strip of lawn which can be ironed directly over the raw edge of a hem to hold it to a garment. There is no need to stitch or overcast the edge of the fabric, as the raw edge is enclosed within the hemming tape and the fabric cannot fray.

If you are hemming a flared garment, run a gathering thread along the edge of the hem. After turning up the hem edge, pull in the gathering thread to fit before ironing the hemming tape over the top.

Use a *dry* iron, set to the temperature suitable for the fabric you are using, and iron the tape on *slowly*. Make sure that the bonding side of the tape is facing downwards.

Iron-on hemming tape is useful when you have a very shallow hem allowance, and produces a much less bulky hemline on garments made with heavy fabrics.

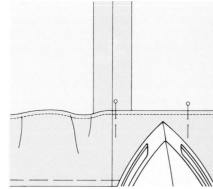

1. Slip a 2 cm strip of fusible web between hem allowance and garment, placing top edge of strip just below hem edge; pin.

2. With iron at steam setting, fuse the hem lightly in place by pressing between pins with the tip of the iron. Remove pins.

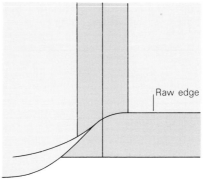

1. Make sure that the hemline is even and the exact length you require. Fold up the hem allowance and press carefully.

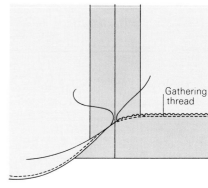

For flared hemlines, run a row of gathering stitches along the raw edge. Pull gathering thread up to fit when hem is folded.

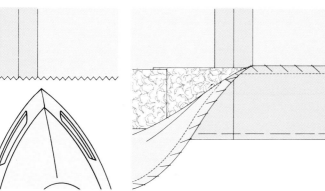

3. Cover hem with damp press cloth. Press a section at a time, holding iron on cloth until dry. Let fabric cool before handling.

To fuse heavy fabric, use 5 cm strip of fusible web to support extra weight. This may take extra pressing time, especially at seams.

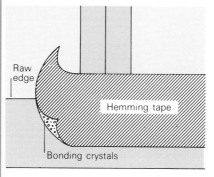

2. Centre the hemming tape, bonding side down, over the raw edge of the hem and the wrong side of the garment fabric.

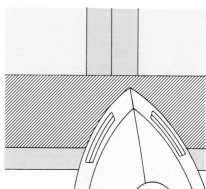

3. Press slowly with a dry iron set to the temperature suitable for the fabric you are using. Hem is bonded when tape crystals melt.

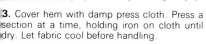

Hems

Hemming a faced opening

There are two ways to finish the hem edge of a faced opening. One is to hem the facing itself, then fold and secure it inside the garment. This is appropriate for all light to medium-weight fabrics, and permits later lengthening of the hem.

In the second method, the hem allowance is trimmed at the facing and the part of the garment that is covered by it. The bottom of the facing is then sewn to the garment by hand or machine. This technique is

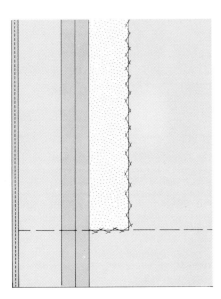

suitable for any fabric, but is especially good for a heavy one because it eliminates so much bulk. It does not, however, permit the hem to be lengthened.

Whichever method is used, the lower edge of the completed facing should be smooth and flat. The easiest way to achieve this is to trim the interfacing at the hemline and sew it in place with a flat herringbone stitch, as shown in the diagram above.

Method 1

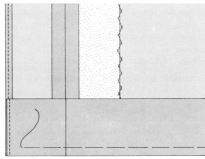

After marking the garment hemline, make sure faced edges are the same length. Press facing seam open; fold and tack hemline.

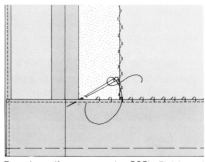

Ease hem if necessary (p. 303). Finish and secure hem edge in appropriate way (see pp. 304–305), hemming to the edge of the facing.

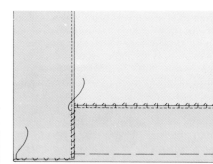

Fold facing inside the garment and press. Slipstitch bottom edge of facing to hemline. Whipstitch free edge of facing to hem.

Method 2

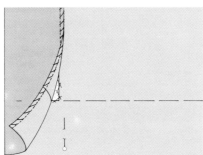

1. Mark hemline with thread; make sure the faced edges are the same length. On the hem allowance, pin-mark where facing ends.

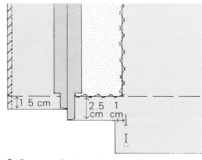

2. Open out facing; trim hem allowance of facing to 1.5 cm, of garment to 2.5 cm; end 1 cm from pin. Trim seam allowances as shown.

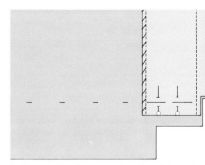

3. Turn facing back so that the right side is toward the garment. Pin and tack the bottom edge, aligning traced hemlines.

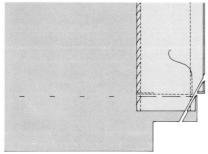

4. Stitch from inner edge of facing to seam at garment edge; pivot, and stitch up seam for 2 cm. Trim corners diagonally.

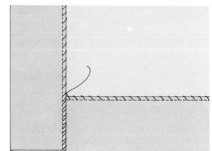

5. Turn facing inside garment; whipstitch inner facing edge to hem allowance. Secure hem with appropriate stitch (pp. 304–305).

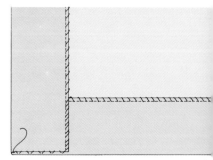

If preferred, omit the stitching in Step 4, and slipstitch the lower edge. On a very heavy fabric, this edge can be left open.

Mitring topstitched binding (outward corner)

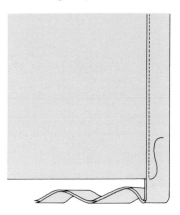

1. Prepare binding for topstitching application (see p. 315). Insert one garment edge into the fold of the binding; pin and stitch along inner edge of binding; stop at the bottom of the garment.

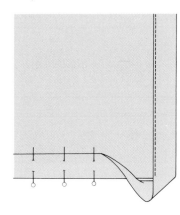

2. Bring binding around the corner, encasing bottom raw edge of garment; pin in place, forming mitre around corner.

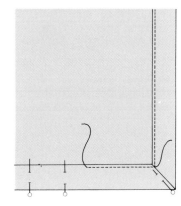

3. Pin mitred fold in place. Resume stitching at last stitch in inner corner. Pull threads through at starting point and knot. Slipstitch mitred fold if necessary.

Mitring topstitched binding (inward corner)

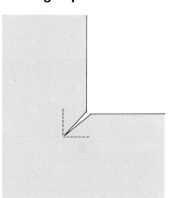

1. Reinforce the inner garment corner with small stitches: stitch within a thread's width of the seamline for 2 cm on either side of the corner. Clip into the corner, being careful not to cut threads.

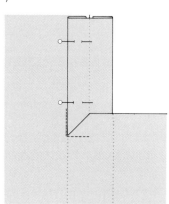

2. Prepare binding for topstitching application (see p. 315). Open out centre fold and pin binding to one side of corner, smooth side out, aligning centre fold with raw edge.

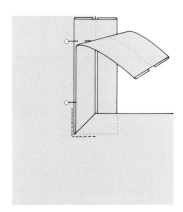

3. Fold the binding straight back on itself so that the fold is aligned with the garment's stitching line.

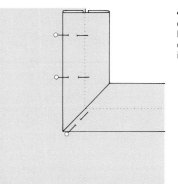

4. Then fold binding diagonally; press lightly. Pin the diagonal fold to hold it in place.

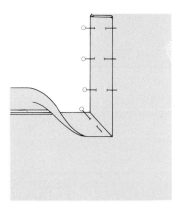

5. Fold binding over raw edge, mitring corner on the wrong side of the garment; pin in place.

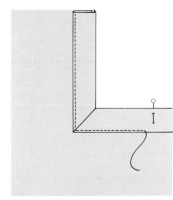

6. From the right side, stitch along binding edge through all thicknesses. Slipstitch mitred fold in place if necessary.

Special hemming techniques

Problem hems

Special techniques are required on some garments to achieve a satisfactory hem finish. Sometimes the garment itself creates the need. An even, smooth hem on pants cuffs, for example (see right), demands careful handling of the lines that form the cuff and hem. A long evening gown may need help to hold its hemline flare; a good quality interfacing added to the hem fortifies it (see opposite page).

Hems in standard garments may need special handling because of unusual fabric characteristics, mainly texture or structure. Pages 324–326 suggest techniques for such problem fabrics: lace, fake fur, leather, velvet, stretchy knits and sheers.

Another category of fabrics can be treated normally except for small special considerations at the hemline. For example, permanent press and tightly woven fabrics are both difficult to ease. When a garment made of such hard-to-ease fabrics has a shaped hem, the hem allowance should be kept narrow; it will be far easier to control the excess fullness.

Brocade and fabrics like it can quickly become worn-looking; as a preventive measure, use a light touch when pressing the hem fold. Some such fabrics may even waterspot; this can be avoided by pressing with a dry iron set low. To retain the reversibility in garments of double-faced fabrics, hems can be either banded or bound (see pp. 313–315).

Adding cuffs to an uncuffed pants pattern

To make cuffed pants using a favourite pants pattern not designed for cuffs, alter the pattern as follows:
1. Make all pattern alterations that occur in the waist-to-hip area (the waist, crotch, etc.) and width of leg.
2. Determine finished pants length from the waistline; have a friend measure you along the side, or take the side seam measurement from another pair of pants that fits well.
3. Measure this same distance down from the waistline marking on pattern pieces and mark them.
4. Decide on the cuff depth; double this measurement and add it to the pattern (if necessary, tape tissue paper to bottom for added length).
5. To this amount, add another 3 cm for a hem allowance.
6. Mark and identify each line.
7. Cut out pants; thread-mark hem, foldlines and turn-up lines.
8. Construct and hem the cuff as directed above right.

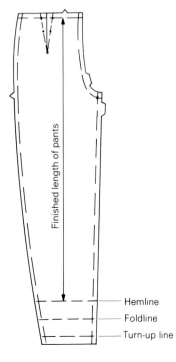

Finished length of pants

— Hemline
— Foldline
— Turn-up line

Hemming pants cuffs

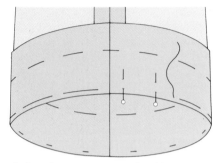

1. Complete pants construction. Press seams open. Turn hem allowance to wrong side along foldline; pin, then tack close to fold.

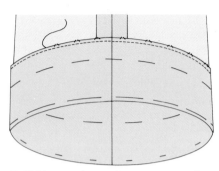

2. Finish raw edge, and secure to pants leg; if desired, machine-stitch in place (stitching will not show when cuff is turned).

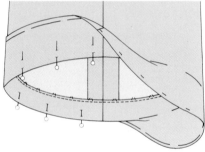

3. Turn cuff up to the right side along turn-up line; pin in place. Tack close to fold, through all thicknesses. Press gently.

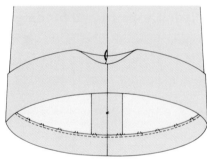

4. To keep the cuff from falling, sew a short French tack at seams, 1 cm below top edge of cuff. Remove all tacking; press.

Adding cuffs to shaped pants

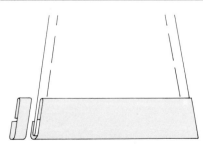

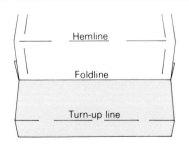

Hemline

Foldline

Turn-up line

To add cuffs to a shaped pants pattern, add length to pattern as explained at left; fold pattern according to the line indications; make cutting edges at bottom continuous with those above. Open out pattern piece; use to cut and mark pants.

Stiffened hemlines

Interfacing adds body and support to a hem, and can also serve as a cushion to keep the edge from being pressed sharply against the garment.

Hem interfacing is cut on the bias (see pp. 310–311 for the method) from underlining fabric or from a fairly heavy grade of good quality cotton interfacing, whichever best suits the garment fabric. Make sure that the interfacing material you use does not lose its resilience after washing.

You can interface the hem of a lined or an unlined garment. In a lined, tailored garment, the interfacing can be cut very wide even if the hem allowance is narrow, as the lining will cover the part of the interfacing above the hem edge. The interfacing extends below the hemline before it is folded. This method is also suitable for velvet or satin garments as the hemline has a softly rolled or padded look.

In an unlined garment, the hem allowance must be deep enough to enclose the interfacing. Cut the interfacing the depth of the hem allowance minus 1 centimetre.

Stiffening the hem of a lined garment

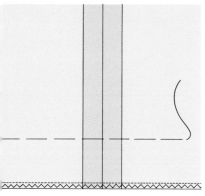 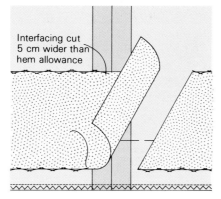 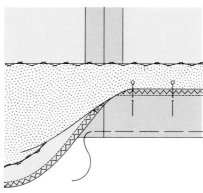 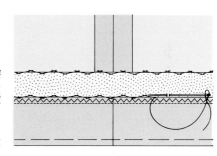

Interfacing cut 5 cm wider than hem allowance

1. Tack hemline with contrasting thread. Make the hem allowance even; finish the edge. Lay garment with wrong side toward you.

2. Pin interfacing in place with lower edge extending 2 cm below hemline. Herringbone-stitch both edges. Overlap ends where they meet.

3. Turn hem up along tacked line and pin, then tack close to the fold. (Interfacing will extend above the hem edge about 2 cm.)

4. Secure hem edge with herringbone stitches, as shown, taking the stitch that is above the hem edge through interfacing only.

Stiffening the hem of an unlined garment

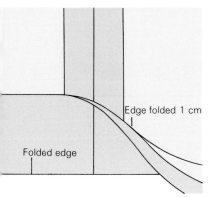 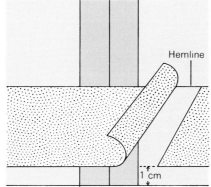 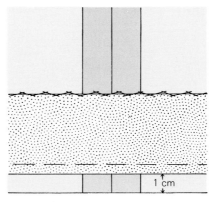 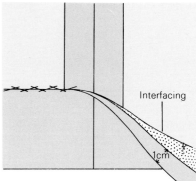

Edge folded 1 cm

Folded edge

Hemline

1 cm

1 cm

Interfacing

1cm

1. Fold up hem allowance to desired hemline, making sure that it is even. Fold under the top edge 1 cm; press carefully.

2. Lay garment out flat. Place interfacing, cut to depth of hem allowance less 1 cm, between folded edges. Overlap edges where they meet.

3. Tack the interfacing in place, then catch the interfacing to the garment with herringbone stitches along the hemline fold only.

4. Turn up hem allowance and interfacing; fold the top edge over the interfacing and herringbone-stitch in place. Remove tacking stitches.

323

Special hemming techniques

Hemming laces

Lace fabrics range from lightweight to heavy, and are made in a variety of patterns with either straight or scalloped edges. The hemming method depends upon the lace. Laces that are backed can be finished by one of the turned-up hem methods described on pages 304–305, hems for heavy laces can be faced (see pages 310–311). For lightweight laces, a rolled hem (see page 326) is recommended; an alternative is a lace trim appliquéd to the hemline (see below). If the lace is already scalloped, the finished edge can be used as the hemline (see below).

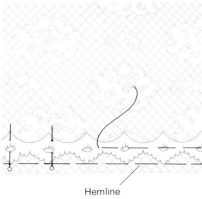

To appliqué a lace trim to the edge, mark hemline. Place trim on right side of garment, aligning lower edge with garment hemline. Pin, then tack through centre of trim.

Stitch trim to garment by the appliqué method (whipstitch along inner edge of trim's motif, or use a narrow machine zigzag). Cut away hem allowance underneath the lace trim.

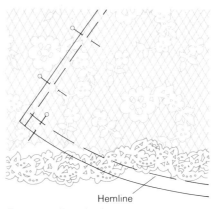

To use scalloped edge as hem, pin pattern to fabric; align hemline with bottom edge of scallop motif. Cut above scallop to separate part of motif that falls below hemline curve.

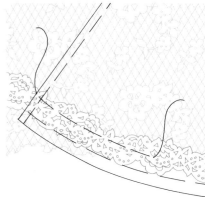

Reposition separated portion of scallop to follow hemline curve; pin and tack. Cut out garment. Secure repositioned part of scallop with whipstitching or machine zigzag.

Hemming fake furs

The problem associated with hems in fake fur is usually caused by the bulk and weight of the fur's long hairs. When a fake fur has short hairs, as many do, it can be handled like a mediumweight fabric. A turned-up hem is the finish to use; the raw edge is covered with seam binding and the hem secured with double stitching (p. 305). Garments of exceptionally heavy or dense fake fur require a bias hem facing, either the packaged type or one made from lining fabric (p. 311). The facing method for such fake furs (see below) is similar to the standard facing technique.

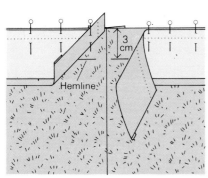

Mark hemline. Trim hem allowance to 3 cm. Open one folded edge of facing; fold end back 6 mm. Starting at garment seam, pin facing to hem, right sides together.

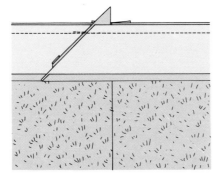

Stitch on crease of fold to within 8 cm of the starting point, removing pins as you go. Cut excess facing to overlap the first end, and continue stitching across. Press flat.

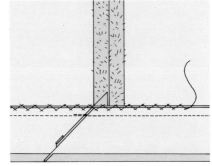

Turn hem up to wrong side along marked hemline on garment; pin and tack through hem fold to hold in place. Herringbone-stitch raw edges of fabric and facing to the garment.

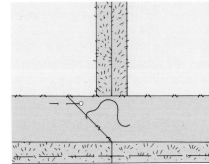

Press facing up, and pin to back of fur fabric; secure. Slipstitch lapped ends in place. Remove all tacking stitches. If necessary, steam-press gently, using a press cloth.

Types of application

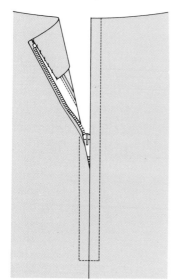

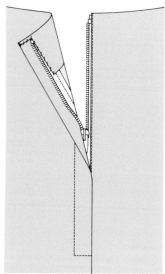

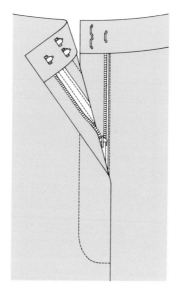

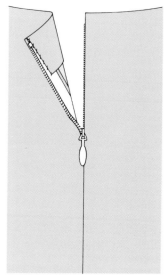

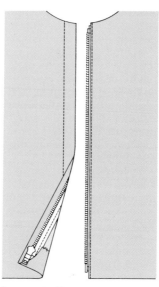

Centred: Application involving a conventional zipper. Used at centre front or back of garment, at edges of sleeves and in home decorating.

Lapped: This application, too, takes a conventional zipper. Most often used at the left side seam of pants, skirts and dresses.

Fly-front: This traditional trouser application is used on men's pants and on women's pants and skirts. Requires a conventional zipper.

Invisible: Possible only with the special invisible zipper, this application can substitute for either a lapped or centred application.

Open-end: The open-end zipper may be sewn in with either a centred or lapped application. For jackets, tracksuit tops, waistcoats or skirts.

Installation tips

Before any zipper is sewn into a garment, the placket seam should be **seam-finished** and then, in most cases, tacked open. **Staystitch** any curved or bias placket seamlines about 6 mm from the cut edge to prevent possible stretching.

It is not generally necessary to preshrink zippers as the garment fabric and the zipper tape will shrink in unison when laundered. But if you are using a **stretch fabric** which is washed before stitching, preshrink the zipper by immersing it in hot tap water for a few minutes; roll it in a towel to absorb excess moisture, then allow it to air-dry.

To **shorten a zipper,** use the method described here or use a wide machine zigzag stitch with care.

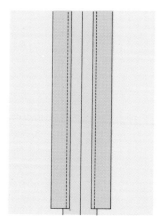

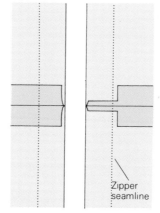

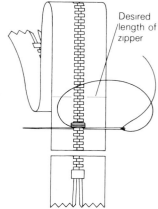

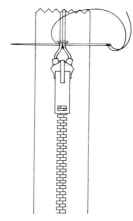

Enlarging seam allowances: This is necessary if they are less than 1.5 cm wide. Edgestitch woven seam binding to edge of seam allowances only.

Reduce bulk in cross-seam allowances at, for example, yokes and waistlines. Trim seam allowances slightly past zipper seamline as shown, and press open.

To shorten a zipper, whipstitch several times over ladder or chain as shown, 2 cm below desired new length, then cut off the excess zipper and tapes.

For some dress plackets, a zipper must be closed above the top stop. Whipstitch edges of tapes together 6 mm above top stop, or attach a straight-eye fastener.

329

Zippers/centred

Centred application

The method for applying a centred zipper is the same regardless of the garment type; the only variable is in the placement of the zipper below the top edge of the garment. Where it is placed depends on how this edge will be finished. If a facing is to be used, you should place the top stop of the zipper *1 cm below* the seamline of the garment. This allows extra space for turning down the facing and for attaching a hook and eye.

If the finish does not require seam allowances to be turned down, for instance at a waistband or on a standing collar, place the top stop *just below* the seamline (a scant 6 mm).

All work is done on the *inside* of the garment except for topstitching. **Work from bottom to top** of placket, in both preliminary tacking and topstitching. Keep the zipper closed, except in Step 3, and slider tab up.

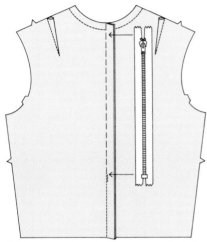

1. Measure and mark the exact length of the placket opening, using the zipper as a guide. Close the seam with machine stitching: stitch up to the mark for bottom of zipper with a regular stitch length, backstitch, then change to machine tacking for placket seam.

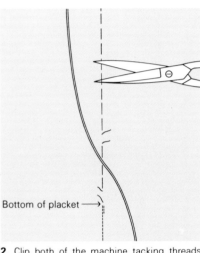

Bottom of placket →

2. Clip both of the machine tacking threads at the bottom of the placket; then clip only the bobbin thread at 1 cm intervals—this will make removal of tacking easier. Press the seam open and, if necessary, seam-finish the edges with a finish suitable for the fabric.

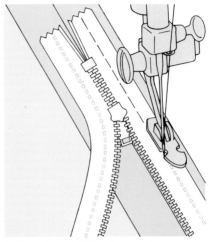

3. Extend the right-hand seam allowance and place zipper face down, with the top stop at mark and the edge of the opened ladder or chain along the seamline; pin in place. Using a zipper foot, machine-tack along stitching guideline on zipper tape.

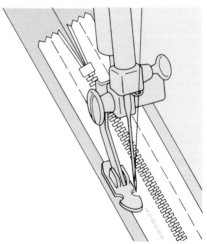

4. Close the zipper and keep the pull tab up. Extend the remaining seam allowance. Position the zipper foot to the left of the needle and machine-tack the unstitched zipper tape, from bottom to top, to the seam allowance, following the guideline on the tape.

5. Turn garment right side up and spread it as flat as possible. Starting at the centre seam, hand-tack across bottom and up one side, 6 mm from the seamline, catching garment, seam allowance and zipper tape in tacking. Repeat for the other side.

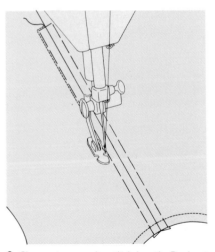

6. Change to a regular stitch length. Begin at the bottom of the placket, just outside the tacking, and topstitch through all three layers—garment, seam allowance and tape. Take two or three stitches across bottom of placket, pivot, and stitch to top.

7. Position the zipper foot to the right side of the needle and topstitch the remaining side in the same way, taking the same number of stitches across bottom of placket. Pull thread ends to wrong side and tie. Remove hand tacking stitches and open the placket.

Prickstitch 136; slipstitch 143   Neckline finishes 204–223
Blind hemming (machine blindstitch) 145   Waistline finishes 246–261

Zippers/centred

Finishing centred application

Centred application of open-end zipper

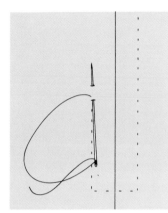

Hand-finishing gives a custom look to a garment. Follow basic procedure through to Step 5. Then remove machine tacking to open placket seam. See Prickstitch for formation of stitch. Work from centre seam across bottom of zipper, then up one side; repeat for other side. If fabric is heavy, work second set of stitches, placing them between first stitches for strength.

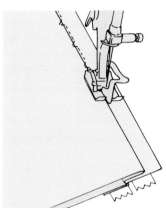

Machine blindstitching is a quick, durable way to simulate hand stitching. Follow basic procedure through to Step 5. See Machine blindstitching for detailed instructions on formation of stitch. In this method, the action of the zigzag stitch requires that you stitch from bottom to top on one side of the zipper and from top to bottom on the other.

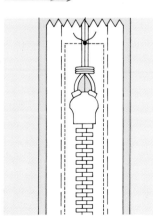

In some dresses, both ends of the zipper placket are closed. The zipper must therefore be closed at the top by whipstitching tapes together before insertion of zipper. Follow the basic procedure with one exception: when doing final stitching, continue across top of zipper placket to vertical seam. Pull thread ends to wrong side and tie.

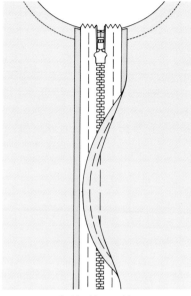

1. Machine tacking

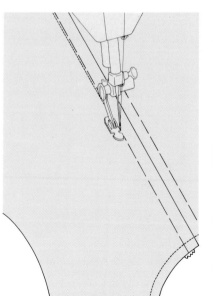

3. Topstitching

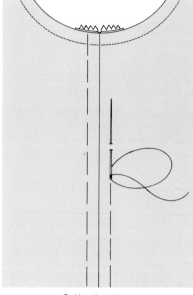

2. Hand tacking

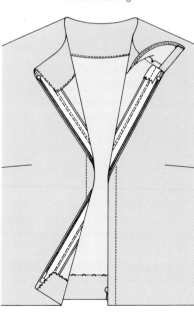

4. Finishing

An open-end zipper is best sewn in before any facings or hems are in place.
1. First **machine-tack** opening closed. Press seam open; finish if necessary. Position closed zipper face down on seam allowances, centring zipper teeth over seam. Extend seam allowance and tape; machine-tack down centre of tape. Keeping pull tab turned up, machine-tack free side of tape in the same way.
2. Next, **hand-tack** seam allowances and zipper to garment from right side, 6 mm on either side of seamline (1 cm from seamline for the heavy, large-toothed jacket zippers). Do not stitch across the bottom.

3. Then **topstitch** each side of the zipper, stitching slightly outside the hand tacking. Keep stitching straight and same distance from centre seam the entire length of the seam. Pull thread ends to wrong side of garment; tie. Remove hand tacking, then open the centre seam.
4. If facing and hem are in place, as they would be in a replacement application, release the hem, but not the facing. Push facing out of the way during zipper application. Turn top tape ends under at a slight slant so that they will not be caught in the teeth. After application, turn under and slipstitch the facing or hem edges to the zipper tapes.

Zippers/exposed

Exposed application

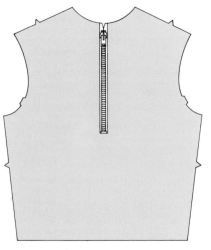

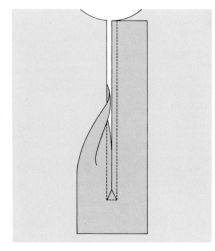

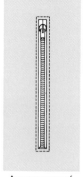
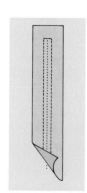

The exposed zipper can only be applied where there is no seam. Although it can be used on woven fabrics, it is most often seen on sweater knits. Before installation of the zipper, a stay is sewn to the placket area, which prevents sagging and stretching.

1. Cut a stay 8 cm wide and 5 cm longer than the zipper from lightweight, firmly woven lining fabric. Mark opening down centre of garment and stay to equal the length of zipper ladder or chain plus 1.5 cm. Right sides together, match markings and tack stay to garment.

2. The opening for the zipper should be wide enough to expose only the zipper ladder or chain. Stitch 3 mm on each side of the centre line and across bottom at end of centre marking. Remove tacking. Slash down centre line to within 1 cm of bottom; cut into corners.

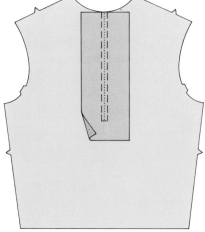

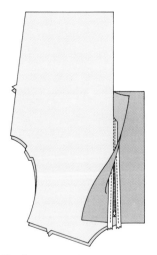

3. Turn stay to inside and press, making sure that none of the stay shows on right side of garment. Centre zipper under opening with bottom stop of zipper at bottom end of opening. Slip-tack zipper to garment along the folds on each side and at bottom of zipper.

4. Lift the bottom part of the garment to expose the ends of the zipper tape and the triangle of garment and stay fabric at the bottom of the opening. Using a zipper foot, stitch across the base of the triangle to secure it to zipper tapes and stay.

5. Fold back one side of the garment until the original stitching line is visible. Working from bottom to top, stitch the garment to the zipper tape along this stitching line. Repeat for the other side of the zipper. Remove the slip tacking that held zipper in position.

Enclosed exposed zipper

Appearance of   Stay-tacked on
finished zipper   all sides

If both ends of the zipper opening are closed, as in a pocket or a cushion cover, follow the basic procedure opposite, with these exceptions:
Cut the stay 8 cm wide and 10 cm longer than opening. Centre stay over mark for opening. Stitch across both ends when stitching stay onto fabric.

Corners slashed   How triangular
after stitching   ends are secured

Slash after stitching as in Step 2, but cut into corners at both ends.
Close the zipper tapes above top stop with a bar tack. Tack the zipper into finished opening as in Step 3, tacking top as well as bottom.
Stitch triangles at both top and bottom (see Step 4) to zipper tape.

Zippers/exposed

Decorative exposed zipper

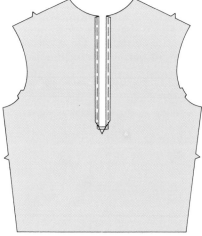

1. Length of opening equals length of zipper ladder or chain (plus 1.5 cm if facing has not been applied). Mark opening down centre of garment. Stitch around opening 3 mm from centre mark on both sides and at bottom.

2. Cut carefully along centre line to within 1 cm of bottom, then cut diagonally into each corner. This will form a 3 mm seam allowance on each of the long sides of the opening and a small triangle at the bottom.

3. Turn the 3 mm seam allowance on the long sides to right side of garment. Tack seam allowances in place and press opening flat. When application is completed, seam allowances will be covered by the decorative trim.

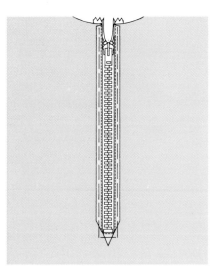

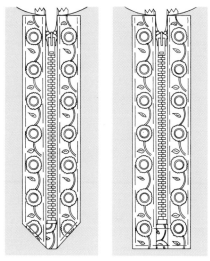

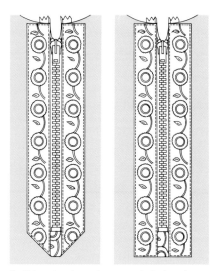

4. Centre the zipper under the opening with the bottom stop at bottom end of opening and top stop at finished edge (1.5 cm from upper edge if facing has not been applied). Using a zipper foot, edgestitch zipper from garment side through all thicknesses.

5. Trim should be at least 6 mm wide to cover seam allowances. Position the trim around the zipper; mitre trim to make a square or pointed end, as you prefer. Try, if possible, to match the design horizontally across zipper. Tack trim in place by hand.

6. Using the zipper foot, topstitch the trim to the zipper, first next to ladder or chain, then on outer edge. (If the trim contrasts in colour with the garment, choose thread and zipper colours to match the trim.) If facing is not already in place, apply it now.

Mitring the trim

For mitring purposes, trim should be twice the length of the zipper tape plus whatever extra is required to match a design. Some additional length is also needed for finishing the ends: **twice** the width of the trim for a pointed end; **four times** the width of the trim for a square end.

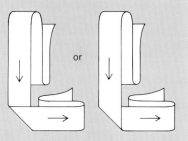

For a point, first fold the trim straight across itself, making a 45° angle.

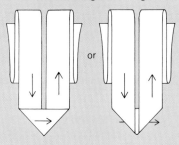

Then fold again, forming an opposite 45° angle, to complete the mitre.

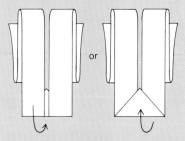

For a square end, complete steps for triangular mitre; then fold point either under or back onto trim.

Zippers/lapped

Lapped application

A lapped zipper is applied the same way regardless of garment type; the only variable is in the placement of the zipper in relation to the garment edge. If there will be a facing finish, place the top stop *1 cm below* the seamline. If the garment will have a waistband or standing collar, place the top stop *just below* the seamline. Do all work on inside of garment, except topstitch-ing; keep zipper closed throughout application. **Work from the bottom to the top** on all steps; this will ensure that the lap goes in the proper direction on the garment.

Enclosed lapped application

Before beginning the basic application, whipstitch zipper tapes together above top stop. The length of the placket should be the distance from bottom stop to whipstitches.

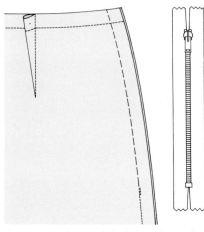
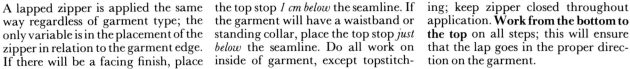
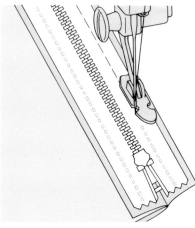
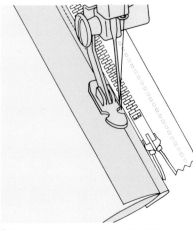
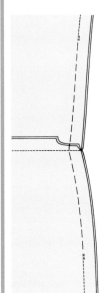
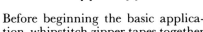

1. Mark exact length of placket opening, using the zipper as a guide. Stitch seam up to bottom of zipper placket with a regular stitch length, backstitch, then change to machine tacking for placket. Clip tacking thread at intervals. Press seam open; seam-finish.

2. To position the zipper, extend the right-hand seam allowance and place zipper on it face down, with top stop at mark and edge of ladder or chain along the seamline; pin in place. Using a zipper foot, positioned to right of needle, machine-tack on stitching guideline.

3. Position zipper foot to the left of the needle. Turn the zipper face up, forming a fold in the seam allowance. Bring the fold close to, but not over, the zipper ladder or chain; pin if necessary. Stitch along edge of fold through all thicknesses.

If placket intersects a cross seam, such as a waistline, make sure the seam is matched perfectly before tacking the placket opening. Trim cross-seam allowances as shown to reduce unnecessary bulk. Stitch from bottom of seam to bottom of placket using a regular stitch length, backstitch, then change to machine tacking and stitch to top of placket. At top of placket, return the stitch length to normal, backstitch two stitches, and complete the seam. Press the seam open.

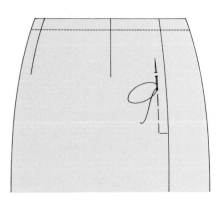
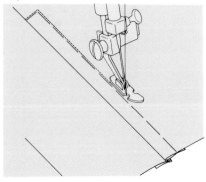
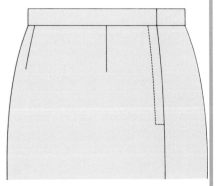
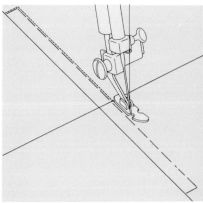

4. Turn garment to right side; spread fabric as flat as possible over unstitched zipper tape. Hand-tack across bottom of zipper, then up along the side, about 1 cm from seamline. This should place tacking close to stitching guide-line on zipper tape.

5. Position zipper foot to the right of the needle. Topstitch close to the tacking across the bottom of the zipper and up along the side, pivoting at the corner. Take care not to stitch over the tacking. Bring thread ends to under-side and tie. Remove tacking stitches.

6. Open the zipper placket by removing the machine tacking in the placket seam. Tweezers are helpful for getting out any stubborn thread ends. Finish top edge of garment with appro-priate finish—facing, collar, or waistband—as pattern directs.

Start and stop topstitching at the vertical seam. Stitch from seam across bottom of zip-per, up along the side, then back across top. Pull thread ends to wrong side and tie.

Finishing lapped application

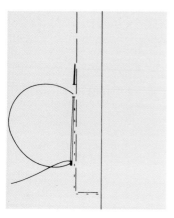

Hand-finishing is a sign of careful work. Follow basic instructions to Step 5. See Prickstitch for formation of the hand stitch. Work from bottom to top of zipper. For extra strength, turn garment to inside and machine-stitch edge of front *seam allowance* to zipper tape.

Machine blind-stitching gives the appearance of hand finishing, but is more durable.
1. Allow 2.2 cm seam allowances when cutting out garment. Follow instructions for basic application up to Step 3. Tack free zipper tape to remaining seam allowance through centre of tape.

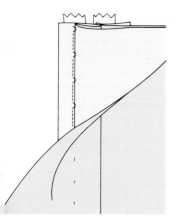

2. Set the sewing machine for a short narrow blindstitch. Keep foot to right of needle. Fold back garment on tacking line and, with bottom of placket away from you, position zipper tape over machine feed. With zipper foot on seam allowance, blindstitch full length of placket, closely following fold. Prickstitch by hand across bottom. Remove tacking.

Lapped application of open-end zipper

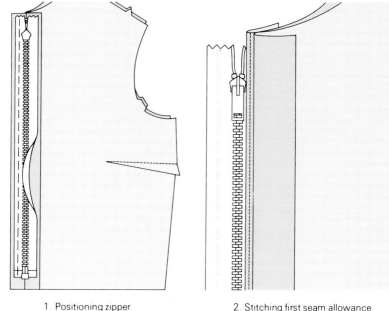

1. Positioning zipper

2. Stitching first seam allowance

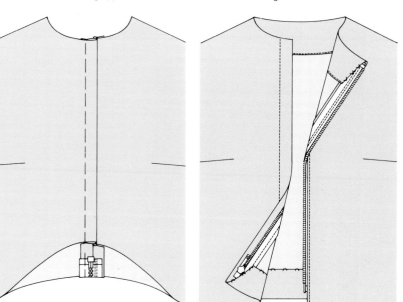

3. Hand tacking before topstitching

4. Finishing

An open-end zipper should be sewn in before facings or hems are in place.
1. Machine-tack placket seam closed. Press open and seam-finish if necessary.
Position closed zipper face down on seam allowances, with zipper teeth centred over the seam and bottom stop at bottom of opening. Keeping tab turned up, machine-tack right-hand tape to seam allowance from bottom to top.
2. Turn the zipper face up, forming a fold in the seam allowance. Bring the fold close to, but not over the zipper teeth; pin if necessary. Change to a zipper foot, positioned to the left of the needle.
Stitch along edge of fold through all thicknesses.

3. Turn garment right side up and spread as flat as possible. Starting at the bottom of the placket, **hand-tack** up the length of the zipper, through garment, seam allowance and zipper tape, about 1 cm from seamline. This should place tacking close to stitching guideline on tape. Position zipper foot to right of needle; topstitch close to tacking. Remove hand tacking.
4. Open zipper placket by removing tacking from seam. Apply any facings, hems or linings to garment, and slipstitch any edges near the zipper so that they will not be caught in zipper teeth during wear.

335

Fly-front zipper application

The fly-front zipper is the traditional zipper application for men's trousers. It is often used on women's clothes as well, however, because it provides such a neat and durable closing. Traditionally, the placket has a definite lap direction: in women's clothes it laps right over left as shown here; in men's garments it laps left over right (see Sewing for men/trousers).

A special trouser zipper is often recommended for use with this application. If a trouser zipper is not suitable because of its weight, or the limited colour range, a skirt zipper can be used. No matter what type of zipper is used, it will probably require shortening; fly-front plackets are not as long as most other zipper plackets. See instructions at right.

It is best to buy a pattern designed with a fly-front closing—it will supply all the necessary pattern pieces.

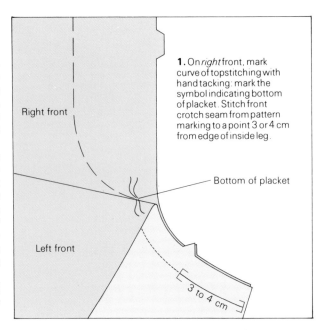

1. On *right* front, mark curve of topstitching with hand tacking: mark the symbol indicating bottom of placket. Stitch front crotch seam from pattern marking to a point 3 or 4 cm from edge of inside leg.

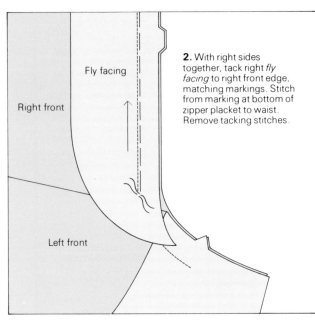

2. With right sides together, tack right *fly facing* to right front edge, matching markings. Stitch from marking at bottom of zipper placket to waist. Remove tacking stitches.

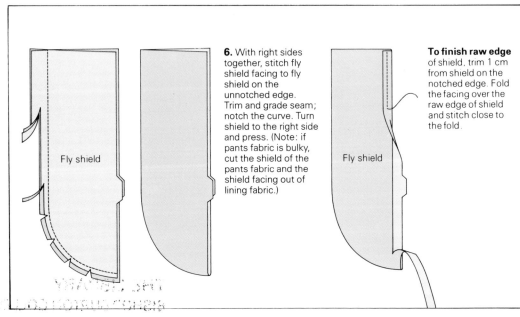

6. With right sides together, stitch fly shield facing to fly shield on the unnotched edge. Trim and grade seam; notch the curve. Turn shield to the right side and press. (Note: if pants fabric is bulky, cut the shield of the pants fabric and the shield facing out of lining fabric.)

To finish raw edge of shield, trim 1 cm from shield on the notched edge. Fold the facing over the raw edge of shield and stitch close to the fold.

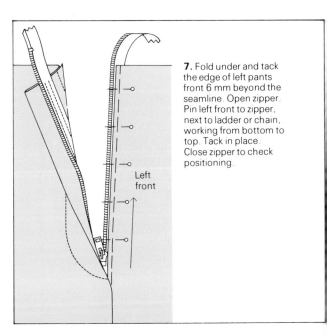

7. Fold under and tack the edge of left pants front 6 mm beyond the seamline. Open zipper. Pin left front to zipper, next to ladder or chain, working from bottom to top. Tack in place. Close zipper to check positioning.

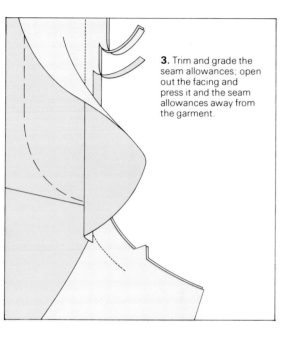

3. Trim and grade the seam allowances; open out the facing and press it and the seam allowances away from the garment.

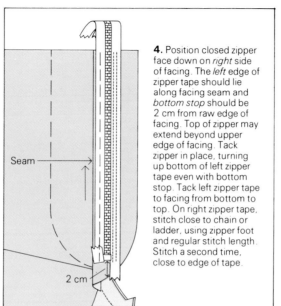

Seam

2 cm

4. Position closed zipper face down on *right* side of facing. The *left* edge of zipper tape should lie along facing seam and *bottom stop* should be 2 cm from raw edge of facing. Top of zipper may extend beyond upper edge of facing. Tack zipper in place, turning up bottom of left zipper tape even with bottom stop. Tack left zipper tape to facing from bottom to top. On right zipper tape, stitch close to chain or ladder, using zipper foot and regular stitch length. Stitch a second time, close to edge of tape.

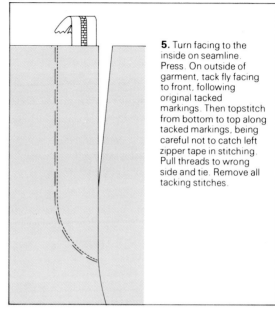

5. Turn facing to the inside on seamline. Press. On outside of garment, tack fly facing to front, following original tacked markings. Then topstitch from bottom to top along tacked markings, being careful not to catch left zipper tape in stitching. Pull threads to wrong side and tie. Remove all tacking stitches.

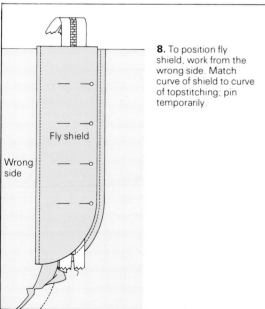

Fly shield

Wrong side

8. To position fly shield, work from the wrong side. Match curve of shield to curve of topstitching; pin temporarily.

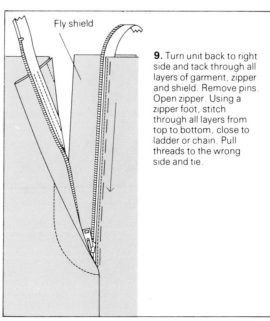

Fly shield

9. Turn unit back to right side and tack through all layers of garment, zipper and shield. Remove pins. Open zipper. Using a zipper foot, stitch through all layers from top to bottom, close to ladder or chain. Pull threads to the wrong side and tie.

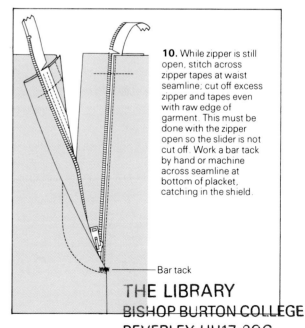

Bar tack

10. While zipper is still open, stitch across zipper tapes at waist seamline; cut off excess zipper and tapes even with raw edge of garment. This must be done with the zipper open so the slider is not cut off. Work a bar tack by hand or machine across seamline at bottom of placket, catching in the shield.

Zippers/invisible

Invisible zippers

The invisible zipper is different from a conventional zipper in both appearance and installation. When this zipper is closed, all that shows on the garment is a plain seam and tiny pull tab. Invisible zippers are applied to an open seam, to seam allowances only—there is no stitching on the outside of the garment. They can be used wherever conventional zippers are.

Manufacturers supply a special zipper foot, designed to fit all makes of sewing machine, for installing this zipper. A conventional zipper foot may also be used to apply a synthetic coil invisible zipper.

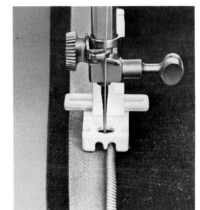

Press synthetic coil invisible zippers from wrong side with the zipper open so that the tapes are smooth and the coils stand away from tapes. Zipper will then feed smoothly through grooves in the foot. Do not close the zipper until both sides have been stitched in place.

A special foot for invisible zippers is designed with grooves that hold the coil or chain upright and out of the way so needle can stitch right alongside chain or coil. This foot will fit any make of sewing machine. A conventional zipper foot may also be used.

Application of invisible zipper

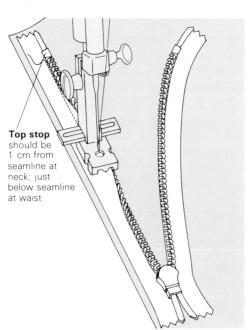

Top stop should be 1 cm from seamline at neck; just below seamline at waist.

1. Seam-finish garment edges, if needed. Place open zipper, face down, on the right side of garment—coil along seamline, top stop at appropriate mark. Pin if necessary. Fit right-hand groove of the foot over coil. Stitch to slider; backstitch; tie thread ends at top.

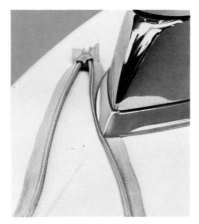
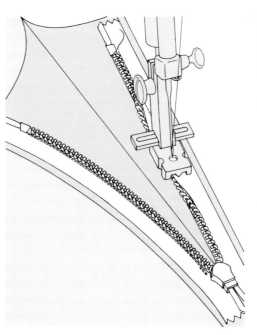

2. Pin the unstitched tape, face down, to right side of other garment piece. Width of zipper tape should be on garment seam allowance. Position top stop at appropriate mark and coil along seamline. Fit left-hand groove of foot over coil. Stitch as in Step 1.

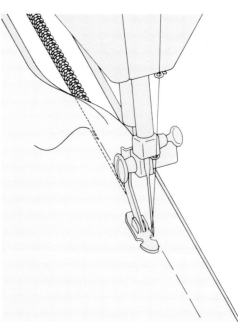

3. Close zipper. Attach conventional zipper foot and position to left of needle. Pin and tack seam below zipper. Lower needle into fabric at end of stitching, slightly above and to the left of the last stitch. Stitch seam to lower edge. Tie thread ends.

4. To hold zipper ends down, stitch each tape end to a seam allowance only, not garment.

Keep coil in rolled-back position for easy sliding.

5. Open up zipper; stitch across tops of tapes with the coil held upright as shown.

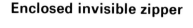
Zippers/invisible

Application of invisible zipper: optional steps

Enclosed invisible zipper

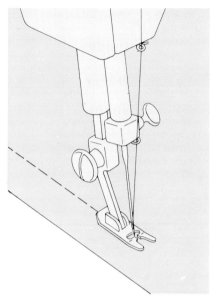

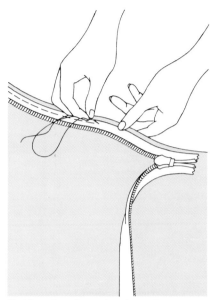

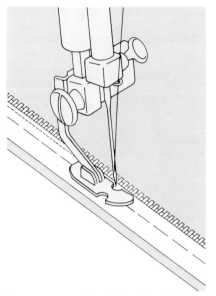

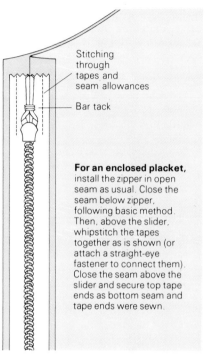

Stitching through tapes and seam allowances

Bar tack

Tacked guideline: To help in positioning the zipper, hand-tack or machine-tack a seam guideline on both garment pieces. Place coil exactly on this line, and use it for matching the seamlines below zipper.

Tacking the zipper in place: Done before machine stitching, tacking is especially helpful when applying an invisible zipper with a conventional zipper foot. Tack, then stitch, one tape at a time from top to bottom.

To use a conventional zipper foot: Tack first tape in place; with foot to left of needle, stitch close to teeth. Move foot to right of needle and repeat the process for other side. Finish as in Steps 3, 4, 5, left.

For an enclosed placket, install the zipper in open seam as usual. Close the seam below zipper, following basic method. Then, above the slider, whipstitch the tapes together as is shown (or attach a straight-eye fastener to connect them). Close the seam above the slider and secure top tape ends as bottom seam and tape ends were sewn.

Special tips for applying invisible zippers

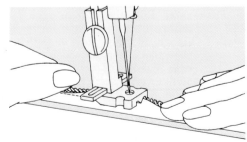

New length

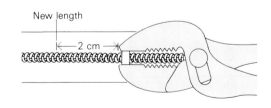

2 cm

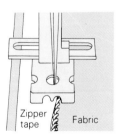

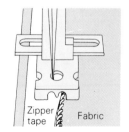

Zipper tape   Fabric   Zipper tape   Fabric

To reduce puckering: Puckering may occur when sewing fabrics with a permanent press finish and some sheers. To avoid this, hold fabric and zipper firmly behind and in front of zipper foot and keep them taut as they pass under the needle. Let the feed dog move the fabric; do not pull it.

To shorten zipper, measure and mark new length on tape. Make new bottom stop by whipstitching several times over chain about 2 cm below mark. (Zipper shown above has an adjustable bottom stop, which can be clamped in place with pliers.) Cut off zipper 1 cm below new bottom stop.

Adjusting for different fabrics: For average-weight fabrics, the needle should stay in centre of needle hole on the invisible zipper foot. It may be advisable, however, to move the foot so needle is off-centre—*closer* to coil for lightweight fabrics (left, above), *farther away* for heavy fabrics (right, above).

Zippers/special applications

Seam and pattern matching (invisible zipper)

The situations below may occur in the installation of an invisible zipper. The extra matching steps are necessary because this zipper is applied to an *open* seam. When zippers are applied to a closed seam, as is usually the case, matching is easily taken care of when the seam is tacked before zipper installation. The method for matching diagonals can also be used to match garment seams, or to match a large print motif, such as a floral. The fabric must, of course, be cut so that it is possible to match the stripe, plaid or design.

Knits, leather, fake fur

Knits: Stabilise a zipper opening in a moderately stretchy knit by staystitching 1 cm from cut edges (see Staystitching for knits). If fabric is very stretchy, stabilise zipper area on both seams with woven seam binding. Stitch it to the wrong side, over the seam allowance, with the stitching 1 cm from cut edge.

Leather, suede and vinyl: A centred application is recommended. The zipper placket seam cannot be tacked closed because punctures from the needle would remain. To close the placket temporarily for installation of zipper, turn back the seam allowances on the seamline and glue them down to wrong side of garment. On outside of garment, hold the placket edges together with a length of masking tape. Use crosswise strips of masking tape to position zipper face down on seam allowances. Stitch on *inside* of garment from bottom to top, taking the same number of stitches across bottom of zipper on each side of seam. Pull thread ends to wrong side; tie. Remove masking tape.

High-pile fake fur: Use petersham ribbon to form a smooth, flat facing between zipper and fur fabric. First, clip pile from the placket seam allowances. Edgestitch 2.5 cm wide petersham ribbon, cut 2 cm longer than zipper, to right side of both seam allowances, aligning edge of ribbon with seamline. Trim the fabric seam allowances underneath the ribbon to 6 mm. Place opened zipper face down on ribbon with bottom stop at end of opening and zipper teeth even with seamline; tack and stitch. Repeat for other side. Turn ribbon and zipper inside garment along the seamline. Hand-backstitch the zipper tape and ribbon on the fur fabric *backing* only. Herringbone-stitch the ribbon edge to the backing.

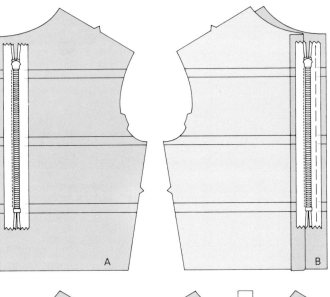

Plaids or stripes: Sew the first side of the zipper in place, then close the zipper. Let unstitched side of zipper lie face down on outside of fabric (drawing A). With a pencil, mark the zipper tape at each predominant cross bar or stripe. Open the zipper and tack the second zipper tape in position, matching the marks on the tape to the plaid or stripe on the second side of the garment (B). Close the zipper and check on right side of garment for a precise match. If correct, open zipper and stitch second side; complete the installation.

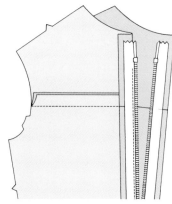

Yoke or waistline seam: Follow procedure at left for matching plaids or stripes, first trimming the cross-seam allowances to eliminate bulk.

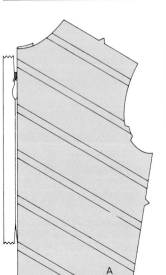

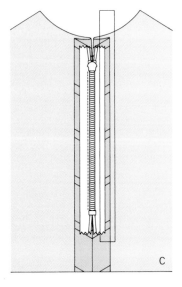

To match diagonals or large designs, stitch the first side of the zipper in place, then fold back fabric so that right side of zipper and fabric are both visible (A). Fold back seam allowance of unstitched side. Match second side to first side, taping in place temporarily (B). Turn fabric to wrong side and tape unstitched side of zipper tape to fabric seam allowance (drawing C). Remove tape from face side of fabric. Open zipper; stitch the taped side of zipper; finish application.

Running stitch 142; whipstitch 148 **Pleat terms 178**
Seam finishes 160–161 **Staying a waistline joining 244**

Zippers/special applications

Zippers in pleated skirts

When sewing a zipper into a pleated skirt, the main objectives are to make sure that the zipper is as inconspicuous as possible and that it does not interfere with the fold or hang of the pleats. Therefore, the positioning of the zipper seam must be considered when the pattern is laid out on the fabric.

If the pleats are box or inverted, try to position the zipper seam down the centre of the pleat *underfold*; then install the zipper with either the centred or invisible method.

If the garment is knife pleated, try to position the seam where the pleat *backfold* will fall; then insert the zipper by means of the special lapped application that is shown and described at right. (See the section on pleats for definition of terms.)

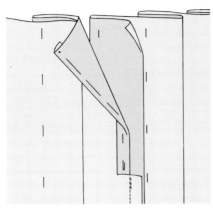

For knife pleats: 1. Stitch the zipper seam at the pleat backfold after the pleats have been formed. Leave the top part open for the zipper. Clip into the left seam allowance; turn it to the wrong side of the garment and tack in place, as shown above.

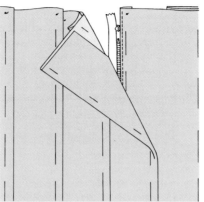

2. Turn garment to right side. Working with the open part of the seam, position closed zipper under tacked seam allowance with the folded edge close to the teeth and top stop just below top seamline. Tack. Then, using a zipper foot, stitch close to fold.

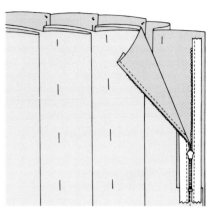

3. Turn garment to wrong side; extend the unclipped (right-hand) seam allowance. Place unstitched half of zipper face down on seam allowance with teeth 6 mm beyond seamline. Pin and tack. Open zipper and stitch to seam allowance only, not to top fold of pleat.

Zipper underlays and stays

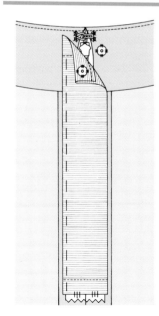

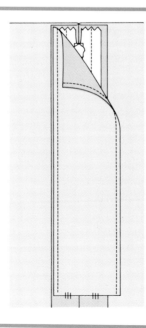

A ribbon underlay can be added to any zipper application after garment is completed. To make it, cut 2.5 cm wide petersham ribbon 2 cm longer than zipper chain or ladder. Fold under and finish top and bottom edges. Centre over back of zipper, with top just above slider, and stitch to left seam allowance only. If attaching at a neck edge, hand-stitch, using a running stitch, to facing and then to seam allowance. Whipstitch across bottom to both seam allowances. Attach snap fastener at top of ribbon as shown.

A fabric underlay is added to a skirt or pants before waistband is applied. (Waistband must be cut long enough to extend across entire width of underlay at top.) For underlay, cut a strip from garment fabric the length of the zipper tape and 6 cm wide. (For a self-facing, cut fabric 12 cm wide and fold in half lengthwise.) Seam-finish raw edges. From wrong side, place underlay over zipper with top edge meeting waistline edge and lengthwise edge even with the left seam edge. Pin, then stitch underlay to seam allowance only. Whipstitch across bottom to both seam allowances.

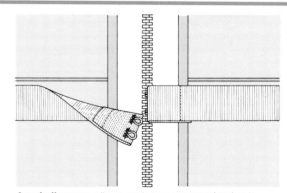

A waistline stay relieves strain on a zipper and makes it easier to close. To make the stay, cut a length of petersham ribbon equal to the measurement of the garment at waistline plus 5 cm. Finish the ends by folding them back 2 cm, then turning raw edges under 6 mm and machine-stitching in place. Sew hooks and round eyes to ends. Position ribbon at waistline with ends at either side of zipper. Leaving 5 cm free at each end for easy fastening, tack stay to waistline seam allowance if there is one; to seams and darts if there is not.

Buttonholes

Types of buttonhole

All of the many buttonhole methods are variations of two basic types, worked and bound. The method you choose for a garment will depend on the design of that garment, the fabric, and your particular level of sewing ability.

Bound buttonholes are made by stitching strips or patches of fabric to the buttonhole location in any of several ways. The garment fabric is then cut as specified, and the strips or patches are turned to the wrong side, thus 'binding' the edges of the opening. Bound buttonholes are particularly suited to tailored garments, but are not recommended for sheer or delicate fabrics where the patch might show through or add bulk.

Machine-worked buttonholes consist of two parallel rows of zigzag stitches, and two ends finished with a bar tack. They can be made by using a special buttonhole attachment (see p. 355) or the built-in buttonhole capabilities (see p. 356). A machine-worked buttonhole is opened only after stitching is completed. These buttonholes are used on sportswear, washable garments, children's clothes and men's jackets.

Hand-worked buttonholes are made by edging a cut in the fabric with hand buttonhole stitches. The two ends can be finished with a bar tack or a fan-shaped arrangement of stitches. Hand-worked buttonholes are used on men's jackets and women's tailored garments, and are a good choice for fabrics too sheer for bound buttonholes.

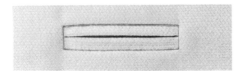

Bound buttonhole

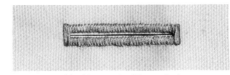

Machine-worked buttonhole

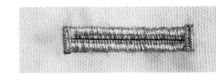

Hand-worked buttonhole

Determining and testing buttonhole length

It is important to make your buttonholes exactly the right length, so that they allow the button to pass through easily, yet hold the garment securely closed. The **length of the buttonhole opening** should equal the diameter of the button plus its height. On a bound buttonhole, this measurement will be the total length of the buttonhole from end to end; on a worked buttonhole, however, because of the finishing that is involved at each end, the space allowed for must be 3 mm greater than the actual opening.

To check buttonhole length, make a slash in a scrap of the garment fabric equal to the length desired for the buttonhole opening. If the button slips through easily, buttonhole length is correct.

Test the buttonhole method on a scrap of fabric before working on the actual garment; be certain to include all the layers of fabric, such as interfacing and underlining, that will be present in the finished garment. Also, go through all construction steps when testing the technique.

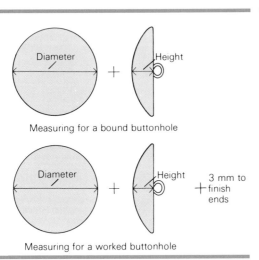

Measuring for a bound buttonhole

Measuring for a worked buttonhole

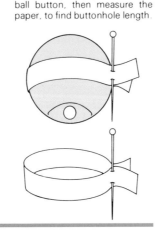

Pin a strip of paper around a ball button, then measure the paper, to find buttonhole length.

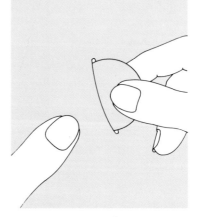

Test the proposed buttonhole length by slipping the button through a slash cut in a scrap of the garment fabric.

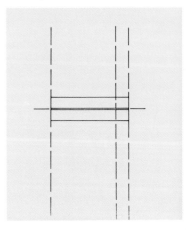

Make a practice buttonhole to test the technique, using all layers of fabric that will be in the final garment.

Positioning buttonholes

Buttonholes in women's garments are placed on the right-hand side of a garment that closes at the front; if a garment closes at the back, the buttonholes go on the left-hand side.

Buttonholes must be positioned on the garment in relation to the button placement line, which, in turn, is located according to the centre line of the garment. The button placement line must be marked on each half of the garment so that the centre lines of the garment will match when the garment is closed.

The three key placement points for buttonholes are at the neck, the fullest part of the bust, and the waist. Additional buttonholes are evenly spaced between these points. The lowest buttonhole must always be above the bulk of the hem.

Altering buttonhole positions

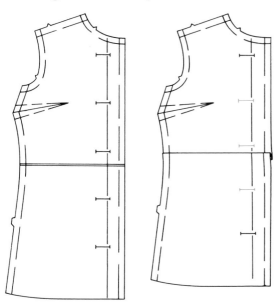

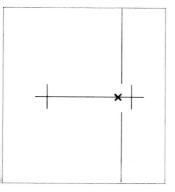

Horizontal buttonholes are the most secure, therefore used on most garments. When buttoned, the pull of the closure is absorbed by the end of the buttonhole, with very little distortion. These buttonholes are placed to extend 3 mm beyond the button placement line.

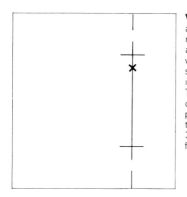

Vertical buttonholes are often used with a narrow placket, such as a shirt band, or when there are many small buttons involved in closing the garment. They are placed directly on the button placement line, and the top of the buttonhole is 3 mm above the mark for centre of button.

If a pattern with a button closing is altered lengthwise, the buttonholes must be re-spaced on the pattern itself after the alteration is complete. Shown above is the procedure for a shortened pattern; when one is lengthened, the procedure is reversed. In either case, a buttonhole may have to be added or subtracted for the sake of design. Remember the three key positioning points when re-spacing.

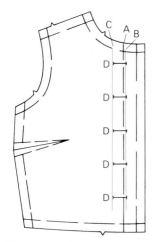

Markings for horizontal buttonholes: Marking A is the button placement line of the garment; B and C mark the ends of the buttonhole (B is 3 mm from button placement line); D marks the centre of the buttonhole. These markings should all be transferred to the garment before the construction begins.

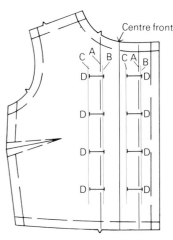

On **double-breasted** garments, the two rows of buttons must be equidistant from the centre line of the garment. If buttons are to be 8 cm from the centre line, locate the B line of the left-hand row of buttonholes 7.7 cm from centre and the B line of the right-hand row 8.3 cm from centre line. Mark remaining lines.

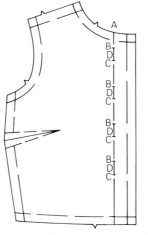

The markings for vertical buttonholes are placed directly on the button position line A. The D lines should be marked first, on top of the A line to prevent confusion between buttonholes and spaces. The B and C lines mark the ends of the buttonhole, with the B line placed 3 mm above the mark for the button centre.

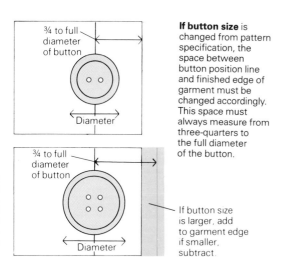

If button size is changed from pattern specification, the space between button position line and finished edge of garment must be changed accordingly. This space must always measure from three-quarters to the full diameter of the button.

If button size is larger, add to garment edge if smaller, subtract.

Bound buttonholes

Construction principles

A well-made bound buttonhole is flat, and the inner fabric edges, or 'lips', are set into a rectangle that has perfectly square corners and is no wider than 6 mm. (The exception to the 6 mm width is made when a fabric is very bulky. A slightly wider rectangle may look better.)

Each of the buttonhole lips should be no wider than 3 mm, and they must meet exactly in the centre of the buttonhole. In most cases, the lips will be cut on the straight grain of the fabric, but the bias grain can be an attractive contrast if a plaid or stripe is being used. Cut one continuous strip of fabric for all the buttonhole lips, and make all of them at one time.

When constructing the buttonholes, **complete the same step on all buttonholes** before proceeding to the next step. This is much more likely to produce

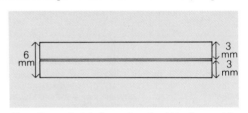

If total buttonhole is 6 mm, lips should be 3 mm wide.

a look of uniformity than if the buttonholes are finished one at a time.

Use spun polyester thread for all tacking in the bound buttonholes; it is least likely to mar the fabric. Machine-tack all markings unless the fabric shows stitch marks. When doing the permanent stitching, use a short stitch (1 to 1.5mm) to add strength and to help achieve sharper corners. Do not backstitch; backstitching can inadvertently get off the stitching line. Instead, pull all thread ends

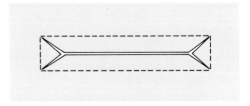

Opening cut first in centre, then into corners.

through to the wrong side and tie them securely.

At some point in the construction of the buttonhole, a rectangular-shaped opening must be cut through the garment. Before cutting, make sure

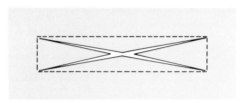

Opening cut straight into corners from centre.

that all stitching for the buttonhole is in precisely the right place and that all rows are straight and parallel to one another. It is extremely difficult to correct stitching once the slash has been made.

There are two different ways of cutting a buttonhole. One is to cut in the centre to within 6 mm of each end, then diagonally into each of the four corners. This produces the small triangles at each end that are eventually stitched to the buttonhole patch or lips.

The other way of cutting, suggested for fabrics that fray easily, is to cut directly into the corners from the centre of the buttonhole area. The tri-

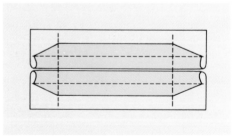

Reduce bulk by grading edges of lips.

angular ends produced by this method are much larger and easier to work with. Whichever method you use, take care to cut exactly to, but not through, the stitching lines.

The edges of the patches or strips must be graded to reduce bulk when the buttonhole is finished. The layer of fabric nearest the outside (or next to the gar-

ment) is left widest. Successive layers should be trimmed 3 mm narrower.

Support fabrics in the buttonhole area must be treated very carefully. If the garment is underlined, work the buttonholes through the underlining. If the garment is not underlined, a strip of support fabric may be added underneath the buttonhole area only. Cut a strip of lightweight underlining or interfacing fabric (an iron-on fabric may be used) 3 cm wider and 3 cm longer than the buttonhole area. Centre it over the area and tack in place before beginning any construction, including marking, on the buttonholes.

Bound buttonholes should never be worked

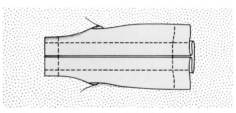

Cut hair canvas to fit under back of buttonhole.

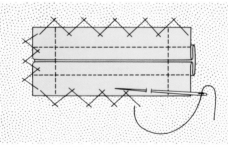

Herringbone-stitch buttonhole lips to hair canvas.

through hair canvas interfacing because of the difficulty in pressing and because of the excess bulk. Instead, work the buttonholes in the garment, then cut openings in the hair canvas the same size as the buttonhole rectangles and in exactly the same position as the buttonholes. The interfacing should fit up close to the buttonhole stitching. Pull the back of the buttonhole through the opening, then herringbone-stitch the outer edges of the buttonhole patch or strip to the interfacing.

Corded method

In this method, corded bias strips are used for the buttonhole lips. The cord produces soft, rounded edges instead of crisp ones, making this method particularly suitable for spongy fabrics that do not hold a sharp crease well, such as textured knits.

The bias strip for each lip should be 4 cm wide by the length of the buttonhole plus 3 cm. Save time by cutting and sewing the lips for both sides of all buttonholes at the same time. Use a cable cord not over 3 mm in diameter; consider the thickness of the fabric and make sure that the finished lips have body but not too much bulk.

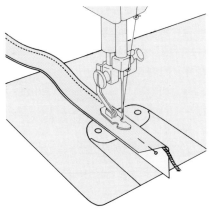

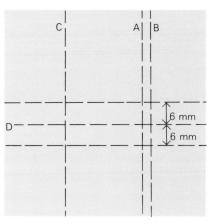

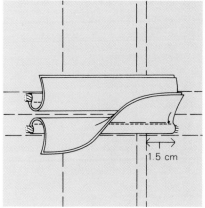

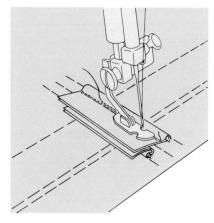

1. Fold bias piece, right side out, around the cable cord and pin the edges together to hold the cord in place. Stitch close to the cord, using a zipper foot. Cut into individual strips for buttonholes, each strip 3 cm longer than width of buttonholes.

2. Thread-mark the four positioning lines on garment as described on page 343. Tack additional marking lines 6 mm above and below the buttonhole position line. If the fabric is very heavy, tack these lines 8 mm from the buttonhole positioning line.

3. Centre strips over markings on right side of garment so ends extend 1.5 cm beyond lines for ends of buttonhole. Corded edges should lie along the outer 6 mm markings, with excess fabric of strips toward centre of buttonhole. Tack each strip in place by hand.

4. Attach zipper foot to machine. Lower needle through strip and garment precisely on the mark for end of buttonhole and just to the inside of the existing stitching. Stitch with a 1 mm stitch length, stopping at mark for other end. Repeat for remaining side.

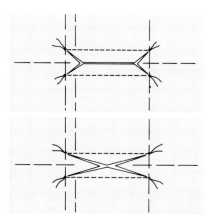

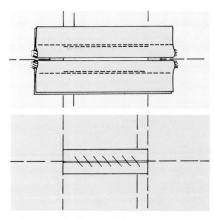

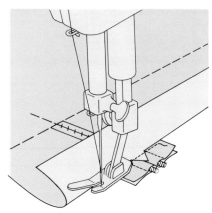

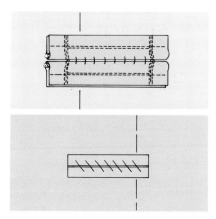

5. Bring thread ends to the wrong side of the garment and tie. Cut along the centre line of the buttonhole to within 6 mm of each end, then cut diagonally into each corner. Or, cut directly from centre into each corner. Take care not to cut through stitching.

6. Remove the hand tacking that was used to hold the strip to the garment. Turn the strips through to the wrong side and pull the triangular ends into place. Press as directed on page 351. From the right side of the garment, diagonal-tack lip edges together.

7. Attach the straight stitch presser foot. With the garment right side up, fold back enough of the garment to expose one triangular end. Stitch back and forth across triangle several times to secure it to ends of strips. Repeat for other end of buttonhole.

8. Remove all the tacked markings except centre front markings. Trim the strips to within 6 mm of the buttonhole stitching lines. Press the entire area. The diagonal tacking stitches holding the lips together should stay in until the garment is completed.

Bound buttonholes

Patch method

The patch method involves making a rectangular opening the size of the buttonhole, with a patch of garment fabric as the facing. The patch facing is then folded so as to create the buttonhole lips.

This method is a good choice for buttonholes in fabrics that are light to medium in weight, do not fray, but do retain a crease readily. For each buttonhole, cut a patch of fabric 5 cm wide and 3 cm

longer than the buttonhole. To mark the centre of the patch, fold it in half lengthwise and finger-press the fold. Straight grain is preferred for the patch, although bias may be used.

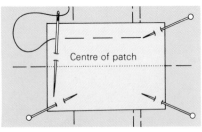

1. With right sides together, centre patch over buttonhole markings, placing the crease of the patch along the buttonhole position line. Tack in place over markings.

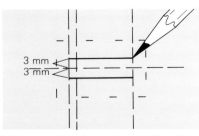

2. On wrong side of garment, mark lines 3 mm above and below the buttonhole positioning lines. On heavy fabric, mark these lines 5 mm to 1 cm away from the positioning lines.

3. Using a 1 mm stitch length, stitch around the 'box' made by the pencil markings and the buttonhole length markings. Begin on one of the long sides and pivot at the corners.

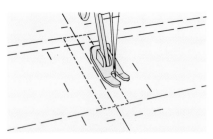

4. For an exact rectangle, take the same number of stitches (5 or 6) across each of the short sides. Overlap several stitches at the end. Remove hand tacking and press.

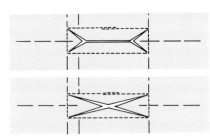

5. Cut through patch and garment along centre to within 6 mm of the ends, then diagonally to corners. Or cut directly into the corners from the centre. Do not cut stitching.

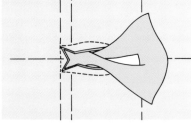

6. Gently turn patch through opening to wrong side of garment. A properly stitched opening will be a perfect rectangle. Pull on the ends to square the corners.

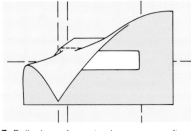

7. Roll edges of opening between your fingers until the seam is precisely on the edge of the opening. Press carefully so that none of the patch shows on the right side.

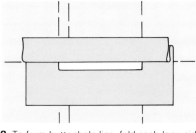

8. To form buttonhole lips, fold each long side of the patch over the opening so that the folds meet exactly in the centre. For accuracy, fold along a true grain line.

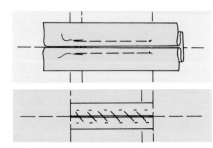

9. From right side, check accuracy of lips and manipulate them until exactly right. Tack along the centre of each lip to hold the fold in place. Then diagonal-tack the lips together at their fold lines and press.

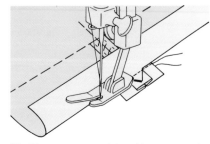

10 Place garment right side up on the machine. Flip back enough of the garment to expose one of the triangular ends, then stitch back and forth across both it and the patch. Repeat at the other end.

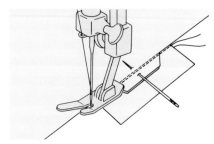

11. With the garment still right side up, turn it back to expose one of the horizontal seam allowances. Stitch through the seam allowance and the patch, just slightly inside the original stitching line. Repeat on other seam.

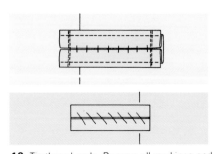

12. Tie thread ends. Remove all markings and tacking except centre front line. The diagonal tacking holding the lips together should remain in place until the buttons are added. Trim patch to within 6 mm of machine stitching.

Simplified patch method

This buttonhole method is an ideal choice for a beginner because both the positioning and the formation of the lips are done in one easy step. Also, there is an easy way to check that the lips and stitching lines are properly located before the buttonhole is cut, which virtually ensures success. Because this method relies on machine-tacked markings, it cannot be used on fabrics that are easily marred by a machine needle. Cut a patch of fabric for each buttonhole that is 5 cm wide and 3 cm longer than the buttonhole, on either the bias or the straight grain.

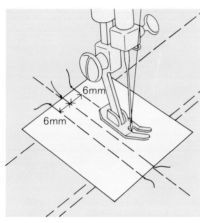

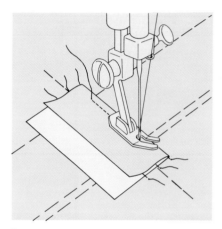

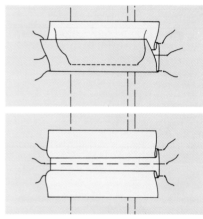

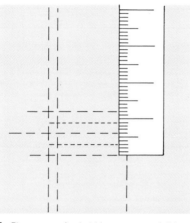

1. Placing right sides together, centre the patch over the buttonhole markings on the garment. Machine-tack through centre of patch along the buttonhole position line, then exactly 6 mm above and below this line.

2. Fold one long edge of patch toward centre on the 6 mm tacked line and finger-press it in place. Using a 1 mm stitch length, sew precisely 3 mm from fold; begin and end exactly on buttonhole length markings.

3. Fold other edge of patch toward centre on 6 mm tacked line. Finger-press it in place and stitch as above. The lips have now been formed and stitched in place. Press edges of lips away from centre line of buttonhole.

4. Five rows of stitching are now visible on wrong side of garment. Use a ruler to check that all five are precisely 3 mm apart along their entire length. Re-stitch if necessary; tie thread ends. Remove machine tacking.

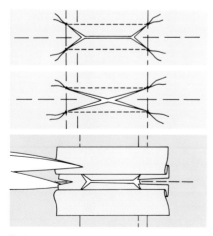

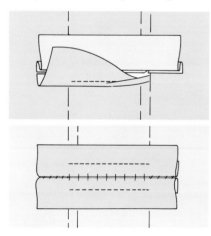

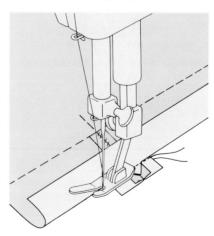

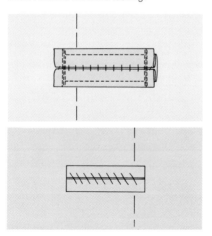

5. From wrong side, cut along centre line to within 6 mm of ends. Then cut diagonally into corners. Or cut directly into corners from centre. From the right side, cut through ends of patch so there are two strips.

6. Carefully push the lips through the opening to the wrong side and press. Diagonal-tack them together. From wrong side, slipstitch the ends of the lip strips together on the fold lines, beyond buttonhole area.

7. Place garment on the machine, right side up. Fold back just enough of the fabric to expose one tiny triangular end of buttonhole. Stitch back and forth across this end, attaching it to strips. Repeat at other end.

8. Remove all markings except centre front line and press. Trim ends and sides of strips to within 6 mm of stitching lines. The diagonal tacking holding lips together should stay in until garment is finished.

Bound buttonholes

One-piece folded method

This buttonhole method is recommended for light to mediumweight fabrics that crease easily and do not fray. Like regular patch buttonholes, it involves a patch of fabric, but it differs from them in that the lips are formed before the patch is attached to the garment. In addition to ensuring uniform lip widths, this method eliminates almost all bulk from the buttonhole area.

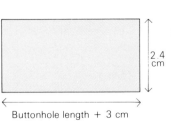

1. For each buttonhole, cut a patch of garment fabric 2.4 cm wide and 3 cm longer than the buttonhole. For best results, cut the patch on the straight grain.

2. With wrong side inward, fold along edges so they touch. Tack through centre of each fold; press. Patch is now 12 mm wide; open side has two 6 mm sections.

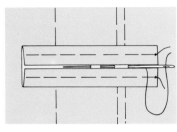

3. Centre the patch, open side up, on the right side of the garment directly over the buttonhole markings. Tack the patch in place through the centre.

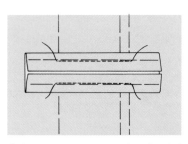

4. Selecting a 1 mm stitch length, stitch through exact centre of each half of the patch, starting and stopping exactly on markings for end of buttonhole.

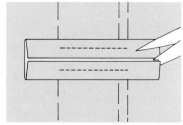

5. Pull thread ends to the wrong side of the garment and tie. Remove tacking threads; press. Cut through the centre of the patch to form two strips.

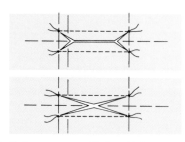

6. Turn to wrong side to cut into corners. Cut along centre line and then into corners. Or cut directly into corners from centre. Stop short of stitching.

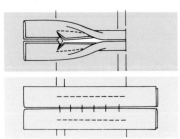

7. Carefully push the buttonhole strips through the opening to the wrong side. Pull on the ends of the strips to square off the corners of the rectangle. Tack the lips together diagonally from the right side of the garment. Press.

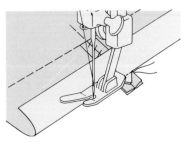

8. Place the garment right side up on the machine. Fold back enough fabric to expose one of the triangular buttonhole ends. Stitch back and forth across this triangle to secure it to the strips. Repeat at the other end.

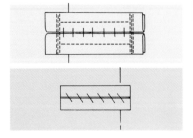

9. Remove all markings except centre front line. Trim the edges of the buttonhole strips to within 6 mm of the ends of the buttonhole. Press. The diagonal tacking should remain in place until the garment is completed.

One-piece tucked method

This method is the same as the one at the left, except that the lips are stitched before the patch is sewn to the garment. For each buttonhole, cut a patch (bias or straight) 3.6 cm wide and 3 cm longer than

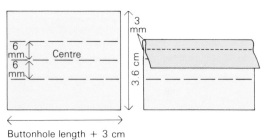

the buttonhole. Mark the lengthwise centre of the patch, then mark lines 6 mm above and below the centre. Fold the patch, wrong sides together, on the 6 mm lines. Press, then stitch 3 mm from the folds. Proceed with Step 3, left.

Cording bound buttonholes

If the lips of a buttonhole seem limp and somewhat thin in relation to the rest of the garment, both problems can be remedied by drawing wool or soft cord into the lips. This extra step is taken after the lips have been formed, but **before** the triangular

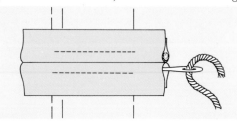

ends of the buttonholes are stitched. Also, note that the only buttonhole methods adaptable to this are the simplified patch and the one-piece folded and tucked methods.

Choose a wool or soft cord in a diameter that will just nicely plump the lips. If the garment fabric is washable, choose an acrylic wool. Use a loop turner or a blunt-pointed (tapestry) needle to pull the wool through the lips. Cut the wool even with ends of the patch strips, then stitch across the ends.

Bound buttonholes

Two-piece piped method

In this procedure, a completely faced 'window' is made in the garment, then the buttonhole lips are constructed and sewn in behind the 'window'. An advantage of the method is that the corners of the buttonhole, sometimes a troublesome area, can be made perfectly square before the lips are sewn in. It is an excellent choice for fabrics that tend to fray, because the raw edges of the garment are finished off early in construction. The lips in the finished buttonhole are slightly wider than in other buttonhole techniques, which makes it an excellent choice for heavy, bulky fabrics.

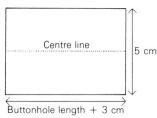

1. Cut a facing for the 'window', 5 cm wide and 3 cm longer than buttonhole, from a sheer, lightweight fabric, colour-matched to garment fabric. Finger-press centre crease.

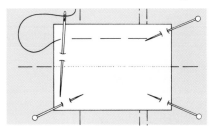

2. Centre the sheer patch over the buttonhole markings on the right side of the garment. Carefully pin at each of the corners, then hand-tack in place.

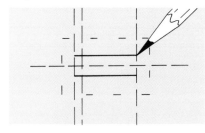

3. On the wrong side of the garment, pencil-mark lines 4 to 6 mm above and below buttonhole positioning line. These lines and buttonhole end lines together form a rectangle.

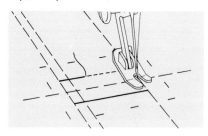

4. Using a 1 mm stitch length, stitch around the rectangle. For best results, start at the centre of one long side, pivot at the corner, then stitch across the end.

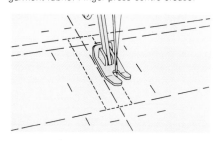

5. Continue stitching, pivoting at corners and making sure that the same number of stitches are taken across each end. Overlap about four stitches at the starting point.

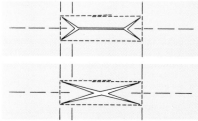

6. Next cut into corners. Cut through centre of rectangle to within 6 mm of each end, then into corners. Or cut directly into corners from centre. Do not cut through stitching.

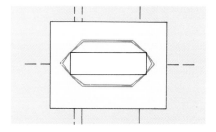

7. Push the patch through the opening to the wrong side of the garment. Square off the corners and press, making certain that none of the patch shows on the right side.

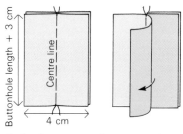

8. For lips, cut two fabric strips 4 cm wide and 3 cm longer than buttonhole. Right sides together, machine-tack strips through centre. Open out on tacking; press flat.

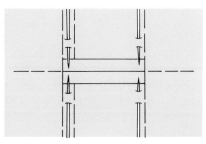

9. With the garment right side up, position the lips underneath the 'window' so that the joining of the lips is aligned with the centre of the buttonhole opening. Use fine needles instead of pins to hold lips in place so that presser foot can get next to the ends.

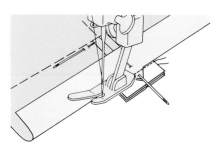

10. With garment right side up, fold back fabric on buttonhole end marking. The triangular end, and the ends of the sheer patch and the lips, will be exposed. Use a needle to pin triangle to other layers. Stitch triangle back and forth exactly on end of buttonhole.

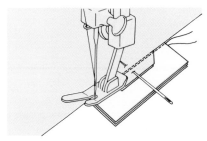

11. After both buttonhole ends are stitched, sew top and bottom to buttonhole lips. Use a needle to hold seam allowances of opening to the lips, and stitch through all layers as close as possible to the first stitching; take care to keep stitching straight.

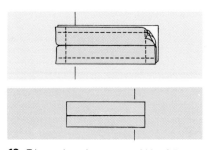

12. Trim and grade excess width of lips and patch so the layer nearest the garment is 1 cm and the top layer 6 mm from the stitching. Remove all markings except centre front line and press. Leave machine tacking in centre of lips until garment is complete.

Bound buttonholes

In-seam method

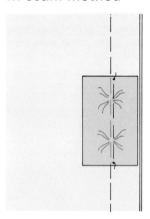

In-seam buttonholes are actually nothing but finished openings in a seam. Mark each end of the buttonhole opening, then tack the seam, going across the buttonhole opening. For each buttonhole, cut two stays from lightweight fabric 3 cm wide and 3 cm longer than the opening, and on the same grain. Centre and tack a stay on each side of the seam, over buttonhole markings.

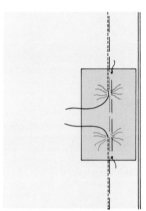

Stitch the garment seam, interrupting the stitching at the buttonhole markings. Leave long thread ends at each end of the buttonhole. Pull thread ends to one side of the garment and tie them together.

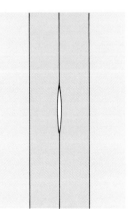

Press seam open and trim stay so that it is slightly narrower than the seam allowances. If the buttonhole is in a horizontal seam that also runs through the facing, remember to leave a similar space in the facing. Make the opening in the facing the same way as the buttonhole, eliminating the stays. Then slipstitch facing and garment together.

Facing finishes

After bound buttonholes have been constructed the interfacing is attached (see p. 344) and the garment facing is ultimately sewn into the garment. The areas in the facing that lie behind the buttonholes must then be opened, finished off, and finally attached so that the buttonhole is ready to be used.

There are three principal methods for finishing a facing. Which you choose depends mainly on the type of garment fabric, but also on the amount of time you want to spend. The **oval method** is a quick

Oval method

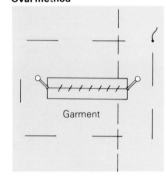

Position facing in garment exactly as it will be worn. Tack around each buttonhole through all the garment layers to hold the facing in place. Insert a straight pin from the right side through the facing at each end of the buttonhole.

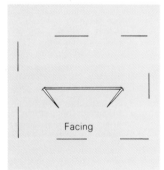

Working from the facing side, cut the facing between the two pins. This slash must not be longer than the buttonhole, and it should be on the straight grain if possible. Remove pins.

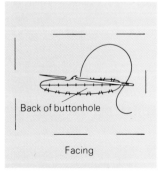

Carefully turn under the raw edges of the slash enough to clear the opening of the buttonhole; the slash will take an oval shape. Slip-hem the facing in place around the buttonhole, making sure that no stitches show on the right side of the garment. Remove tacking.

Rectangle method

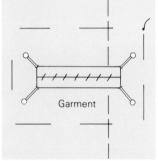

Position facing in garment exactly as it will be worn. From the right side, tack around each buttonhole through all garment layers. Insert a straight pin from the right side through the facing at each of the four corners of the buttonhole.

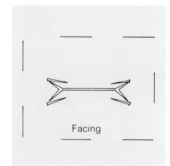

Working from the facing side, cut along the centre of this pin-outlined area to within 6 mm of each end. Then cut diagonally to each of the four pins. Remove pins.

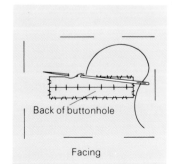

Turn under the raw edges so that the fold is even with the stitching on all four sides of the buttonhole. The slash will take a rectangular shape. Slip-hem the facing to the back of the buttonhole.

Bound buttonholes

and easy finish, good for fabrics that fray easily because little handlng is involved. The **rectangle method** is similar to the oval method, except that the shape is more exacting, and requires more manipulation. For this reason, it is recommended

only for tightly woven fabrics that will not fray easily. The **windowpane method** can be used for all types of fabric. It is the neatest of all the facing finishes, but requires more time in the execution than either of the other methods.

Pressing during construction

Pressing during construction is essential for a well-made bound buttonhole. To avoid imprints or shine on the right side, place strips of brown paper between the patch or strips and the garment, and use a soft press cloth between the garment and the ironing board. Choose the proper temperature setting and amount of moisture for the particular fabric you are using.

Press carefully at each of the following stages: (1) after initial stitching of patch or strips to garment; (2) when the patch or strips have been pulled to the wrong side (press triangular ends with the tip of the iron and top and bottom seams with the side); (3) after tacking lips together; (4) when edges of patch or strip have been trimmed and/or graded; (5) after facing has been completely attached.

Windowpane method

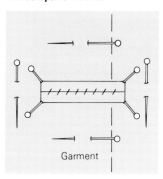

Garment

1. Position facing in garment exactly as it will be worn. From the right side, pin the garment to the facing around the buttonhole. Insert a straight pin from the right side through the facing at each of the four corners of the buttonhole.

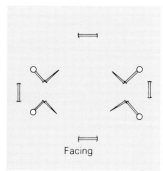

Facing

2. Turn the garment to the facing side and insert four more pins at the corners. Then remove the pins originally inserted from the right side. Facing and garment can then be opened out and the facing will still be pin-marked.

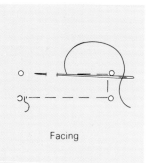

Facing

3. Remove the pins that hold the garment and facing together and carefully lift the facing away from the garment. Thread-mark the rectangular outline of the buttonhole on the facing, using the pin markings as a guide. Remove pins when outline is completed.

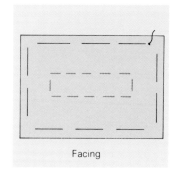

Facing

4. Using a lightweight fabric colour-matched to the garment, cut a patch 5 cm wide and 3 cm longer than the buttonhole. Centre the patch over the tacked outline of the button-hole and tack in place.

Facing

5. From the wrong side of the facing, stitch the patch in place along the tacked outline of the buttonhole. Cut, turn, and press the patch to the wrong side as described for the two-piece piped method. Steps 4, 5, 6, 7, page 349.

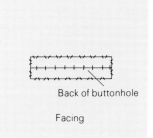

Back of buttonhole

Facing

6. When all windowpane openings have been made, replace the facing in its permanent position on the garment. Pin the openings in place at the buttonholes and slip-hem the edges of the opening to the buttonhole.

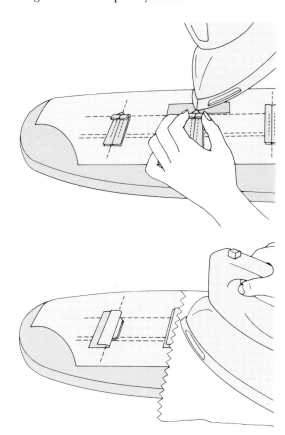

351

Bound buttonholes

Buttonholes for fur, leather and similar materials

Real and fake fur, leathers and vinyls cannot accept regular bound buttonhole techniques, for several reasons. One is that usually they cannot be marked on the right side, either because marking would damage the face of the material, as in leathers, or that the markings would not show, as in deep pile furs. Other considerations are the bulk inherent in some of these materials, and the fact that self-material often cannot be used for the lips. The result of these special limitations is that bound buttonholes in these fabrics quite often do not look like regular bound buttonholes, and are not made in the same way.

To mark for buttonholes in leather, fur and similar materials, use chalk, pencil, or a felt tip pen on the back side of the material. Some leathers and vinyls can be marked with a tracing wheel. If a deep pile fur must be marked on the right side, use T-pins or extra-long coloured-head pins. Cut these materials with a sharp razor blade or craft knife, using a metal ruler as a guide if needed.

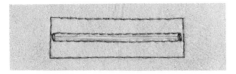

A false buttonhole, for real or fake leathers

A buttonhole for fur made with petersham lips

This fur buttonhole is merely a finished slit

False buttonholes for real and fake leathers

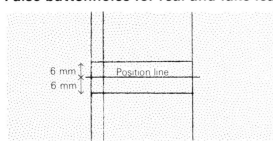

6 mm
Position line
6 mm

This is not a bound buttonhole in the true sense; it is actually two rectangles stitched to look like a buttonhole, with a slit in the centre. **1.** Apply a suitable interfacing and pencil-mark buttonhole (see p. 343). Draw additional lines 6 mm or 1 cm above and below buttonhole position line.

2. Transferring of markings to right side of fabric must be done carefully to avoid puncture marks from needles and pins that would show in the finished garment. Tacked markings must be placed so needle punctures will be hidden in final stitching. This is done with three hand stitches, in this way: using the

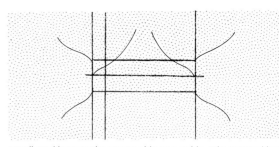

pencil markings on the wrong side as a guide, take one tacking stitch across each end and a third, longer stitch along the centre of the buttonhole. Leave long thread ends on all stitches. This makes only six puncture marks, which will be covered by machine stitches.

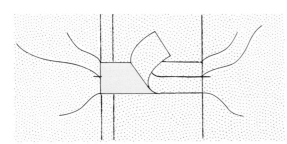

3. Remove the interfacing from within the rectangular buttonhole area carefully so as not to disturb the three long tacking threads. To do this, trim out interfacing along the pencil marks for buttonhole sides and ends. To remove an iron-on interfacing, slit with a razor blade on markings, then apply a warm iron to the area to soften the adhesive.

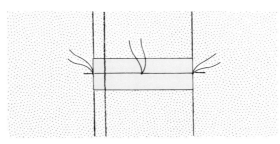

4. Now tie the thread ends together so that the thread markings on the right side of the garment are straight, taut, and secure. Before continuing with the buttonholes, apply the garment facing. Turn the facing to its permanent position, and anchor it securely in place, with either leather glue or topstitching, before stitching the buttonholes.

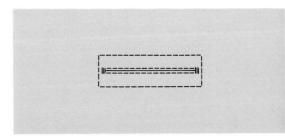

5. Stitch buttonhole from right side of garment as shown above. Stitch outer rectangle first, then one side of centre to within one stitch of end. Pivot on the needle and take one stitch forward, then one back; repeat for a total of five stitches. Stitch other side and end. Tie all thread ends. Cut buttonhole between centre stitches. Remove tacking stitches.

Strip method for real and fake leathers

This is a true bound buttonhole, made in a way much like the strip method for fabric, except that several stitching steps are eliminated to avoid weakening the leather with excess needle punctures. Vinyls and leathers vary greatly in thickness and suppleness, which affects the width of the lips in the finished buttonhole. The thicker the material, the wider the lips. Use the guide, right, to select the correct width, then make a test buttonhole. The length of each strip should be 3 cm greater than the length of the buttonhole to provide a 1.5 cm extension on each end.

Buttonhole width	Lip width	Strip width
6 mm	3 mm	12 mm
1 cm	5 mm	2 cm
12 mm	6 mm	2.4 cm

If garment facing is leather, use Step 6 to finish back of buttonhole; for fabric see pages 350–351.

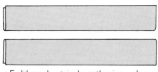

Fold each strip lengthwise; glue.

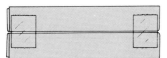

Tape strips together at ends.

1. Cut two strips for each buttonhole in the recommended width for the size of buttonhole you are making. Fold strips in half lengthwise, apply leather glue or rubber cement to wrong side and allow to dry, weighted if necessary. Butt the folded edges and tape together 1 cm from ends.

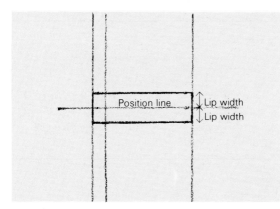

2. Mark the ends and the buttonhole position (centre) line on the back of the fabric with chalk or a felt tip pen (see p. 343). Mark additional lines above and below the centre line, making them the same distance from the centre line as the recommended lip width.

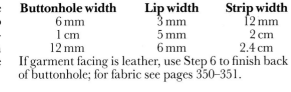

3. Draw additional lines into the corners from a point on the centre line 1 cm from each end. Cut along the centre of the buttonhole to within 1 cm of the ends, then cut diagonally into each of the four corners, following the marked lines. Use a razor blade or craft knife and metal ruler for a clean cut.

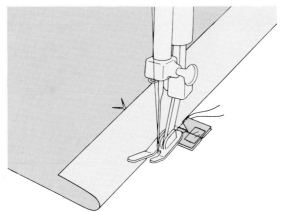

4. Centre the buttonhole strips behind the cut, with the butted edges of the lips exactly in the centre of the buttonhole. With right side up, fold garment back to expose the end of the buttonhole. Turn out the little triangle so that it is on top of the strips and stitch exactly on the drawn line at the base of the triangle. Repeat at the other end.

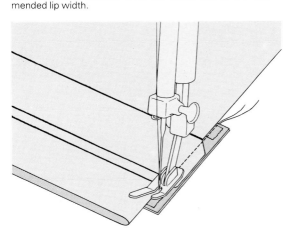

5. Fold the garment down to expose one side of the buttonhole. Match the edge of the seam allowance of the slash to the edge of the buttonhole strips and stitch exactly on the marked line of the base of the seam allowance. Repeat on the other side of the buttonhole. Tie all thread ends; do not backstitch. Remove tape from strips.

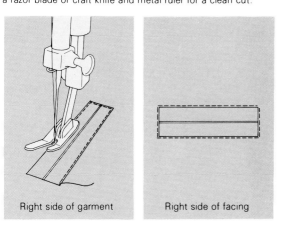

Right side of garment   Right side of facing

6. Apply interfacing, trimming it out of buttonhole area (see p. 344). Sew facing to garment. To finish the facing, stitch the lips to facing from the right side of the garment by sewing in the seam crevices that form the buttonhole rectangle. Tie all thread ends. Trim away the facing inside the stitching lines to open the buttonhole.

Bound buttonholes

Taped method for real and fake furs

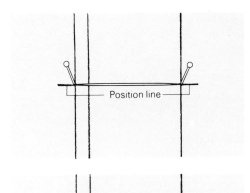

This easy buttonhole method for fur can also be used as a facing finish for the strip method described at right.

1. Using a pen or pencil, mark the buttonhole length and position lines on the wrong side of the material. Place a pin at mark for each end and cut between pins on buttonhole position line. Use a razor blade so that only the leather back, not the fur, is cut.

2. Cut four strips of 12 mm cotton tape for each buttonhole, each piece 3 cm longer than the buttonhole. On the wrong side, centre a strip of tape along one edge of slash, aligning edge of tape exactly to edge of slash. Herringbone-stitch tape to skin. If a regular needle will not penetrate the skin, use a special wedge-shaped leather needle. Repeat on other edge.

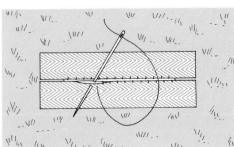

3. The remaining two pieces of cotton tape are stitched on from the right side. Centre them at slit in the same way as explained above. Sew edges of tape to buttonhole edges with a small overhand stitch. Push fur away from slit to ensure that it is not caught in stitching.

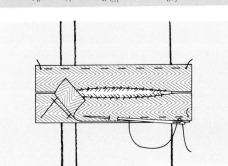

4. Turn both pieces of tape to the inside. Using a running stitch, secure these pieces to the corresponding herringbone-stitched tapes. This method may also be used for a facing finish. (An alternative facing finish involves simply slashing a marked opening in the facing and whipstitching edges of slash to the back of the buttonhole.)

Strip method for real and fake furs

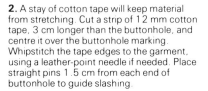

1. Mark buttonholes (see p. 343), drawing additional lines 3 mm above and below the centre line to extend beyond length lines. Cut two strips of petersham ribbon, of light or dark shade to match the fur, 3 cm longer than the buttonhole. To form lips, fold pieces of ribbon in half and press. Whipstitch strips together for 1.5 cm at ends.

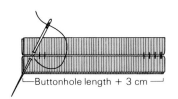

2. A stay of cotton tape will keep material from stretching. Cut a strip of 12 mm cotton tape, 3 cm longer than the buttonhole, and centre it over the buttonhole marking. Whipstitch the tape edges to the garment, using a leather-point needle if needed. Place straight pins 1.5 cm from each end of buttonhole to guide slashing.

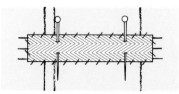

3. Slash through tape and fur between the pins, using a single-edge razor blade. Place a pin in each of the four corners of the buttonhole—exactly where the 3 mm lines above and below centre cross the buttonhole length lines. Slash diagonally into each corner.

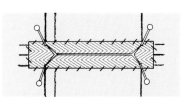

4. Carefully cut hair away from the buttonhole seam allowances formed by the slashing. Centre the ribbon lips at the slash so that the opening in lips exactly matches the slit in the fur. Whipstitch edges of the little triangle at each end to the ribbon lips. Hand-backstitch across base of triangle.

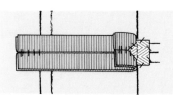

5. Match the edge of one seam allowance of slash to outside edge of the ribbon lip so that the sheared area lies against the ribbon. Whipstitch these edges together for the entire length of the buttonhole. Repeat on other seam allowances.

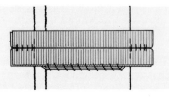

6. Stitch along each side of the opening, 3 mm from the edge. Use a short machine stitch or a hand backstitch. To finish garment facing behind buttonhole, use the taped method at the left and slipstitch facing opening to back of buttonhole.

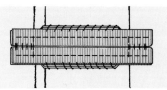

Worked buttonholes

The two types

A worked buttonhole is a slit in the fabric finished with either hand or machine stitches. It has two sides equal in length to the buttonhole opening, and two ends finished with bar tacks (as illustrated at right) or with a fan-shaped arrangement of stitches (see page 357).

A worked buttonhole is stitched through all fabric layers, after interfacing and facing are in place; the colours of all the fabrics should match or blend to avoid a colour clash at the cut edge. A hand-worked buttonhole is slit first, then stitched;

a machine-worked buttonhole is stitched then slit.

Mark the fabric for worked buttonholes as described on page 343. The measurements for the actual buttonhole opening and for the stitched but-

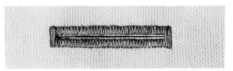

Machine-worked buttonhole with bar-tacked ends

tonhole are, however, different. The finished length of a worked buttonhole will equal the opening plus an extra 3 mm for the stitches used to finish each end (see p. 342).

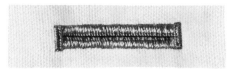

Hand-worked buttonhole with bar-tacked ends

Machine-worked buttonholes

There are various ways in which a machine-worked buttonhole may be made.

One way is with **built-in buttonhole stitches** that come with the machine (see p. 356); by means of a few movements of a lever or turn of a dial, a buttonhole with finished ends is stitched. There is no need to turn the fabric by hand. This method is used when the machine has a built-in zigzag stitch capability.

A second method makes use of a **special attachment** that clamps onto the needle bar and presser foot of the machine. This attachment moves the fabric in the buttonhole shape, while the machine does the zigzag stitching. Attachments will vary

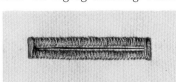

Rectangular buttonhole made with two widths of zigzag stitches, with fabric turned by hand.

Elastic buttonhole made with overedge stitch; suitable for stretch fabrics.

Reinforced buttonhole made with two rows of stitching for extra durability.

Buttonhole attachment for machine

from machine to machine, but in most cases the size and shape of the buttonhole is determined by a button placed in the attachment. Buttonhole size is limited by the capability of the attachment.

Most sewing machines offer a range of buttonholes to suit many different garments and fabric types. Consult your machine booklet for the buttonholes available to you.

A useful buttonhole offered by some machines is the elastic buttonhole, made with overedge stitch or with triple stretch stitch set to zigzag. This buttonhole is stretchable and is suitable for knits and stretchy fabrics.

When you are working buttonholes on very stretchy fabric, a piece of interfacing placed between the fabric and the facing is essential, whether or not your machine offers the elastic buttonhole. The interfacing acts as a stay and prevents the but-

tonhole from stretching out of shape during use.

Reinforcing a machine-worked buttonhole is advisable when you are using a tough or a loosely woven fabric, and is also suitable for children's clothes. Simply stitch the buttonhole twice with the same stitch; for a decorative effect, use the blind hemming stitch at satin stitch length for the second stitching (see illustration at left).

Always practise machine-worked buttonholes, through all fabric layers involved, before beginning buttonhole work on the garment. This is particularly advisable if you are not an experienced user of sewing machines.

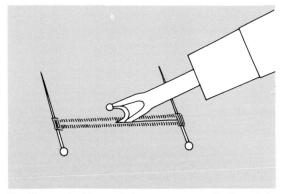

Machine-worked buttonholes are opened only after stitching is completed. Place pins at each end of the buttonhole opening to prevent cutting through the bar tacks. Slit the fabric down the centre on the buttonhole position line to the pins. Use a seam ripper, as shown; *never* use scissors to cut open a worked buttonhole.

Worked buttonholes

Buttonholes from built-in capabilities

Most sewing machines have built-in mechanisms that stitch buttonholes automatically. There is no need to pivot, change needle position or turn the fabric when a machine has these built-in capabilities. By the manipulation of a single control, each step of the buttonhole is automatically positioned and stitched. Half of the buttonhole is stitched forward, the other half is stitched backward.

Before stitching is begun, all buttonhole position and length marks must be made (see p. 343). The markings are then located under the presser foot as directed by the machine booklet.

Depending upon the machine, the buttonhole is stitched in two, four or five steps as described at the right. The instructions will vary according to the number of steps; directions in the machine booklet must be followed carefully. Also check the booklet to see whether there is a presser foot designed expressly for stitching buttonholes.

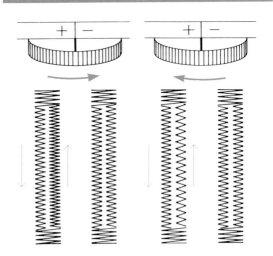

An unevenness in the spacing between stitches can occur when a machine sews in reverse, causing sides of buttonhole to look mismatched. The satin stitch probably needs adjusting; consult your machine booklet for instructions. As a rule, if reverse stitches are too close together, the satin stitch is adjusted to a minus setting; if they are too far apart, toward a plus setting. *Do not confuse this adjustment with the tension adjustment;* check your machine manual carefully.

The four-step buttonhole
With a four-step built-in buttonholer, the two ends and the two sides are each stitched separately. The dial is turned or the lever pushed for each of the four steps. There can be a difference in the starting points according to the type of machine being used—check the instruction book carefully before beginning.

The five-step buttonhole
Each side and end is stitched separately. In some machines, straight stitches (in reverse) return the stitching to the beginning of the buttonhole after one side and end are stitched. This allows both sides to be stitched forward. Other machines have a final securing step, which is merely straight stitches in the same place.

The six-step buttonhole This is positioned and stitched in the same way as the five-step buttonhole.

Cording machine-worked buttonholes

Cording a buttonhole reinforces its edges, making it more likely to withstand the strains of constant use. It also provides an attractive finish. Corded machine buttonholes are made by stitching over a filler cord, which may be embroidery or crochet thread, or a double strand of ordinary sewing thread.

Different types of cording feet are illustrated below. The cord may be looped around a 'toe' at the front or back of the cording foot, or threaded through an eyelet. Consult your machine booklet.

When stitching is completed, the looped end of the cord is pulled under one end of the buttonhole. At the other end, loose ends are tied, trimmed, then hidden under the bar tack.

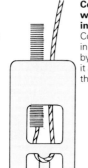

Cording foot with toe in the front. Cord is held in place by looping it around this toe.

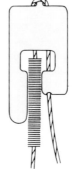

Cording foot with toe at the back. The cord is looped over the toe before stitching.

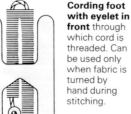

Cording foot with eyelet in front through which cord is threaded. Can be used only when fabric is turned by hand during stitching.

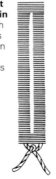

When the buttonhole is completely stitched, tie ends of cord, cut off extra length, and hide the knot under bar tack.

Hand-worked buttonholes

Hand-worked buttonholes are made by cutting a slit in the fabric equal in length to the buttonhole opening, then stitching over the edges with a combination of buttonhole and blanket stitches.

Horizontal buttonholes usually have a fan arrangement of stitches at the end where the button will rest and a straight bar tack at the other; a fan accommodates a button shank better. The tailored form of a horizontal buttonhole, the keyhole buttonhole, has an eyelet at the fanned end.

Vertical buttonholes are made like horizontals, except that both ends are finished in the same shape, either fanned or bar-tacked.

Test the buttonhole through all layers of fabric that will be in the finished garment. Stitch with a single strand of buttonhole twist or regular sewing thread. (If you prefer a double strand of the regular thread, take great care to pull up both strands uniformly with each stitch.) Stitch depth can be from 2 to 3 mm, depending on the fabric type and

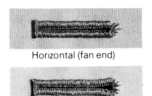

Horizontal (fan end)

Horizontal (keyhole)   Vertical (fan and bar tack)

the size of the buttonhole. A deeper stitch is used on loosely woven fabrics and large buttonholes. The stitch depth must be taken into consideration when determining the buttonhole length, because it affects the ends as well as the edges. Note that the markings for the ends of the buttonholes should be a stitch depth away at each end from the actual end of the cut opening.

Keep the stitches closely spaced and uniform when working buttonholes; do not pull them too tight. Fasten the stitching on the wrong side by running the thread under a few completed stitches. Remove markings only after all buttonholes are completed. To start a new thread, come up through the last purl, and continue stitching.

Fan-end buttonholes worked by hand

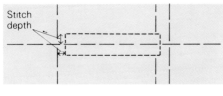

Stitch depth

Horizontal (shown) and vertical buttonholes are alike, except ends of verticals are finished the same way.
1. Decide stitch depth (2 to 3 mm). Mark necessary position lines. Stitch (1 mm stitch length) a rectangle that is the stitch depth away from centre line and end markings.

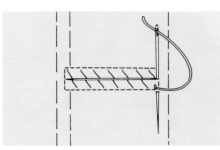

2. Cut along the buttonhole position line from one end of the rectangle to the other. Overcast the raw edges of the slit by hand, using a thread colour that matches the fabric. Turn the buttonhole in such a way that the end to be fanned is to the left. Take a short backstitch at opposite end between slit and machine stitching to fasten thread for hand stitching.

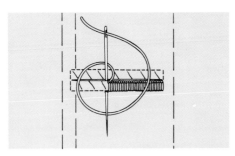

3. Working from right to left with the needle pointing toward you, insert the needle from underneath, with point coming out at the machine stitching. For first and each succeeding stitch, loop thread from previous stitch around to left and down to right, under the point of the needle. Pull needle through fabric, then away from you, to place the purl on the cut edge.

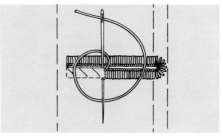

4. Take successive stitches very close together, continuing until that entire side is covered. Then fan the stitches around the end, turning the buttonhole as you work. Take 5 to 8 stitches around the fan, keeping them an even depth. When fan end is completely stitched, continue along the second side.

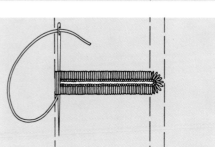

5. Stitch along second side until other end of the opening is reached. Then insert the needle down into the purl of the first stitch to wrong side of buttonhole; bring needle out just below the last stitch, at outer edge of buttonhole. Take several long stitches close together across the width of the two rows of buttonhole stitches to form the base for the bar tack.

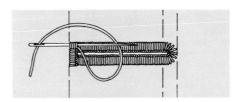

6. Working with point of needle toward buttonhole and beginning at one end of the bar tack, insert needle into fabric under long stitches. Keep thread from previous stitch under needle point; draw up stitch. Continue, completely covering long stitches. Secure on wrong side.

Worked buttonholes

Keyhole buttonholes worked by hand

The tailored worked buttonhole, or keyhole buttonhole, is similar to the horizontal hand-worked buttonhole on the preceding page. The difference is an eyelet, or enlarged resting place for the button shank, at one end instead of the usual fan arrangement of stitches. By providing more room for the shank, the eyelet ensures that the buttonhole will not be distorted when the garment is buttoned. This makes the tailored buttonhole the best choice for men's jackets and other finely tailored garments.

Remember, when working on a man's coat or jacket, that the buttonholes are placed on the opposite side from the side used for women's garments.

Use a single strand of buttonhole twist or heavy-duty thread for buttonhole stitches. For a professional touch, it is suggested that a tailored worked buttonhole be corded. The filler can be heavy-duty thread, buttonhole twist or fine string.

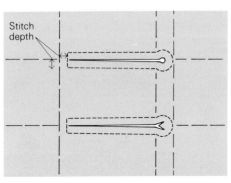

Stitch depth

1. Machine-stitch at 1 mm stitch length around the buttonhole the stitch depth away from the buttonhole position line and ends. There are two ways to open the buttonhole and eyelet: Use an awl to punch the eyelet hole, then cut along the position line to within 3 mm of the other end; or cut along position line to within 3 mm of keyhole end of opening, then cut two tiny diagonal slashes to stitches.

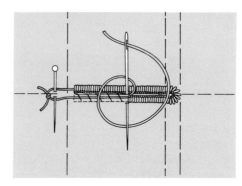

4. Continue the buttonhole stitches around the keyhole, keeping the purls close together along the edge. To form a smooth line, the stitches may have to be fanned slightly apart around the curve. Turn the buttonhole as work progresses and cover cut edge completely with buttonhole stitches.

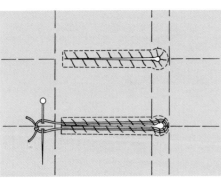

2. Overcast the edges of the slash by hand. If the buttonhole is to be corded, cut a length of cord and knot it to fit loosely around the buttonhole. Place the cord around the buttonhole so that the knot is at the end that will be bar-tacked; secure with pins. Overcast as above, enclosing the cord in the stitching.

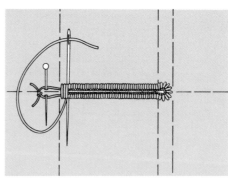

5. To make a bar tack at the unfinished end, take several long stitches across the end to equal the combined width of the rows of buttonhole stitches. Work blanket stitches across these long stitches, catching in fabric underneath, and keeping thread from previous stitch under the point of the needle with each new stitch.

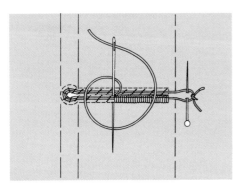

3. Work the buttonhole stitches with the keyhole opening at the left when work begins. Use the machine stitching as a guide for stitch depth. For each stitch, make sure thread from the needle eye goes around and under needle point. To form a purl on the edge, draw the needle straight up. Place stitches close together so that the edge is covered with purls.

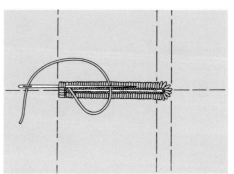

6. Cover long stitches completely with blanket stitches. When finished, fasten the thread on the underside. Pull slightly on the tied ends of the cording so that the buttonhole looks smooth and taut. Tie a new knot if necessary. Cut off excess cord; tuck knot into bar tack.

Button loops

Button loops can often be substitued for buttonholes, provided loops are compatible with the overall styling of the garment. They are particularly useful for fabrics such as lace, where handling should be kept to a minimum. Although any type of button can be used, ball buttons fit best.

Button loops may be set into the seam at the opening edge of the garment, or they may be part of an intricate, decorative shape called a frog, which is sewn in place on the outside of the finished garment. Frogs are most frequently used in pairs, with one frog containing the button loop and the frog opposite sewn under the button, which is usually the Chinese ball type (see p. 363).

Because loops go at the edge of the garment, the pattern may need some slight adjustment before the fabric is cut. First, cut the side of the garment to which the buttons will be sewn according to the pattern. Then mark the centre line of the side to which the loops will be sewn, add 1.5 cm for a seam allowance, and draw a new cutting line at this spot. Adjust the facing in the same way. (This adjustment eliminates any overlap.)

Always make a test loop to see how the fabric works into tubing and to determine the proper size for the loop. Sew a button onto a scrap of fabric to make sure that the loop will slip easily but also fit snugly over the button, which it must if it is to hold the garment edges securely closed. Also check the diameter of the tubing to see whether it is suitable for the button size.

Frog closure

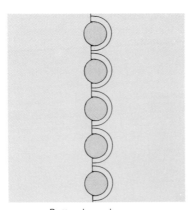

Button loop closure

How to make tubing

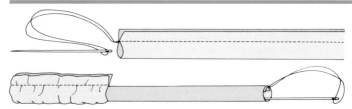

Self-filled tubing: Cut true bias strips 2.8 cm wide; fold in half lengthwise, right sides together. Stitch 6 mm from fold, stretching bias slightly; do not trim seam allowances. Thread a bodkin or large needle with a length of heavy-duty thread. Fasten thread at seam at one end of tubing, then insert needle, eye first, into tube and work it through to other end. Gradually turn all the tubing to the right side. This can be accomplished by pulling on thread and feeding seam allowances into tube.

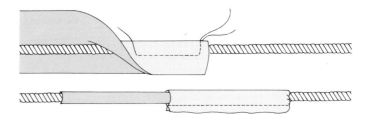

Corded tubing: Cut a length of bias equal in width to the diameter of cord being used plus 2.5 cm. Cut cord twice as long as bias. Fold the fabric around one half of the length of the cord, right sides together. Using a zipper foot, stitch across end of bias that is at centre of cording, then stitch down long edge close to cord, stretching bias slightly. Trim seam allowances. To turn right side out, simply draw enclosed cord out of tube; free end will go into tube automatically. Trim off excess cord, including stitched end.

How to make frogs

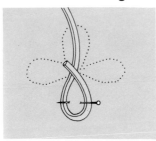

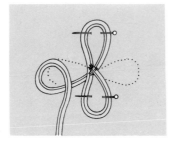

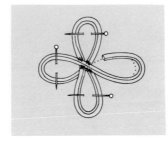

Draw the design for frog on paper. Place end of tubing at centre of the design, leaving a 6 mm end.

Pin the tubing to paper, following design and keeping seam up. Conceal first end on wrong side of frog.

Whipstitch the crossing securely, making sure that stitches and ends do not show on right side.

Remove frog from paper and place it face up on garment with button loop extending over the edge. Then

slipstitch to garment from underside. Make another frog for button and attach at button position.

Fabric closures

How to make button loops

Button loops are used on cuffs of sleeves, as well as at the front or back of blouses and dresses as the main garment closing. Button loops with pearl buttons are the traditional closure for brides' dresses. Though loops are most often made of self-fabric tubing, Russia braid can be used instead.

If you are substituting button loops for some other type of closure, be certain to adjust your pattern as instructed on the preceding page. In addition to adjusting the pattern, you will need to make a diagram to establish the spacing and size of the button loops. This is explained in detail in the step-by-step instructions.

When making your paper diagram, you must decide whether the button loops will be applied individually or in a continuous row. The choice depends on fabric weight and desired spacing. Use single loops when the buttons are large, or if the loops are to be spaced some distance apart. Continuous loops are advisable when buttons are small. The smaller the buttons, the closer together they should be to close the garment effectively.

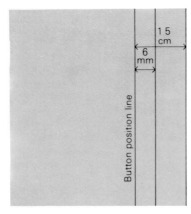

Making the paper diagram: On a strip of paper, draw a line 1.5 cm from the edge to represent the button position line (the line on which the buttons will be sewn). Draw a second line 6 mm from the first, into the seam allowance. This is where the ends of each loop should be placed for either application.

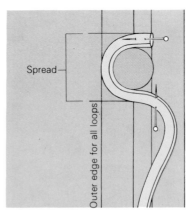

Place exact centre of button on position line and lay the tubing around it, with seam side up. Pin the end of the tubing at the 6 mm line, then pin again below the button where tubing meets the 6 mm line. Mark at edge of tubing above and below button; this is the *spread* (top-to-bottom spacing). Mark outer edge.

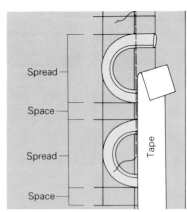

To make individual loops, mark entire length of placket, indicating spread of each loop and space between loops. Place tubing on guide and mark it at both places where it crosses 6 mm line to determine tubing length needed for each loop. Position loops on guide, tape in place. Machine-tack.

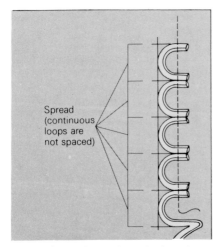

For continuous loops, determine loop size as with individual loops; prepare a paper guide marked with seamline and lines for loop formation. (Omit the spaces between the loops.) Place tubing on paper guide, turning it at 6 mm marks in seam allowance. Trim or clip at turns so the loops lie flat and close together. Tape loops in place, then machine-tack.

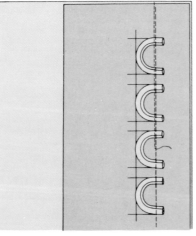

To attach loops of either type to garment, pin paper guide to appropriate side of garment on right side of fabric, matching 1.5 cm line to seamline of garment. Remove tape and machine-tack next to first machine-tacked line. Stitch carefully, making certain that the machine goes over the tubing without skipping. Then carefully tear the paper away.

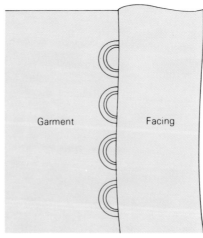

Pin and tack facing to garment, right sides together. Loops will be between facing and garment. Then, from garment side (so you can use the previous stitching as a guide), stitch on the seamline. This will conceal previous rows of tacking. If your sewing machine has a 'top feed' assist, it is helpful to use it. Grade seam allowances; turn facing to inside.

Trim and grade seam allowances. Fold the facing to the inside along seamline. Understitch, then press. Loops will extend beyond the garment edge. Lap this side of garment over opposite side, carefully matching *finished* edge to the button position line on the button side. Mark button locations, then sew buttons to garment at correct positions.

Button placement

Button positions should be marked when the garment is nearly completed and after the buttonholes or button loops are made. Although button position line should be marked at the beginning of construction and button location can be tentatively marked, the location should be finally determined when buttonholes are finished. Lap buttonhole side of garment over button side as garment will be worn, matching centre front or centre back lines; pin securely between buttonholes.

For *horizontal* buttonholes, place a pin through buttonhole opening, 3 mm from the end that is nearest the finished garment edge, into fabric beneath. For *vertical* buttonholes, button should be positioned 3 mm below the top of the buttonhole opening. Carefully lift buttonhole over pin and refasten the pin securely at the proper location. Centre button at pin mark, directly on centre line, and sew in place according to the type of button you are using. Be especially careful in double-breasted garments that layers are completely smooth and flat before positioning pins.

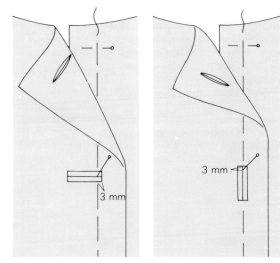

To establish button position, first lap garment sections with buttonholes on top and match up centre lines. Push a pin through buttonhole 3 mm from end to locate place for button.

Thread / needle choices

Buttons can be attached with any of several thread types, depending on the weight of the fabric. With **fine fabrics,** use spun polyester thread or a general-purpose sewing thread compatible with the fibre content of the fabric. For **light to mediumweight fabrics,** use silk buttonhole twist or a general-purpose thread compatible with the fibre content of the fabric. For all **heavy fabrics,** use silk buttonhole twist, or heavy-duty thread, or button and carpet thread. Thread should match the button in colour unless a contrast is wanted for its effect with sew-through buttons.

A single strand of thread is generally the best; double thread has a greater tendency to knot. Waxing with beeswax will strengthen thread and smooth its 'glide' through the fabric (especially recommended for silk twist). To wax thread, pass it across beeswax through slots in the container.

Your needle should be long enough to reach easily through the several thicknesses of button and fabric, but the diameter should not be greater than the holes in the button.

Shank buttons

There are two basic types of buttons, shank buttons and sew-through buttons. Shank buttons are those that have a little 'neck', or shank, with a hole in it, on the lower side. The shank allows the button to rest on top of the buttonhole instead of crowding to the inside and distorting the buttonhole. The shank button is especially recommended for closures in heavy and bulky fabrics. If the garment fabric is very bulky, as in a coat, it may be necessary to make an additional shank of thread below the regular shank to allow enough space for the buttonhole to fit under the button.

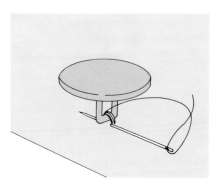

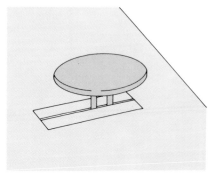

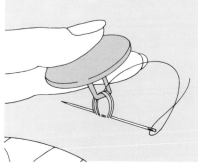

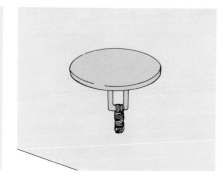

To sew a shank button onto fabric that is not very thick, take enough small stitches through fabric and shank to make the button secure. Position the button so that threads are parallel to the opening edge and the shank aligns with the buttonhole. This will keep the shank from spreading the buttonhole open. Fasten the thread between garment and facing with several stitches. Buttons used only as decoration are also sewn this way.

To make an additional thread shank, first take a few stitches where button is to be placed on the garment's right side. Holding forefinger between button and garment (this keeps the two apart until the button is secure), bring thread several times through shank and back into fabric. On last stitch, bring thread through button only, then wind thread tightly around stitches to form thread shank. Fasten securely on underside.

Attaching buttons

Sew-through buttons

A sew-through button has either two or four holes through which the button is sewn to the garment. When sewn flat, this button can be used as a closure only for very thin, lightweight fabrics, or as a decorative button. If a thread shank is added, the button can be used to close heavy or bulky fabrics as well. The shank permits the closure to fasten smoothly and will keep the fabric from pulling unevenly around the buttons. The shank length should equal the garment thickness at the buttonhole plus 3 mm for movement.

Buttons with four holes can be sewn on in a number of interesting ways. Use thread in a colour that contrasts with the button and treat the four holes as a grid for different arrangements of stitches. The thread can be worked through the holes to form a cross, a square, a feather or leaf shape, or two parallel lines.

If the holes are large enough, a button can be attached with narrow ribbon, braid or cord. (This may require an eyelet to be worked in the garment.) Run the ribbon or braid through the holes in the button and tie it in a secure knot on the wrong side of the garment or on top of the button.

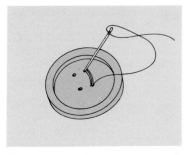

To sew button flat to a garment, take several small stitches at mark for the button location, then centre button over marking and sew in place through holes in button. Fasten stitches on wrong side or between garment and facing.

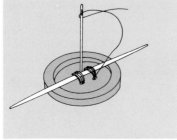
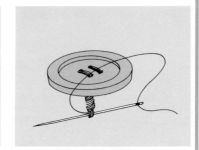

To make a thread shank, secure thread at button mark, then bring needle up through one hole in button. Lay a pin, toothpick or matchstick across top of button. Take needle down through second hole (and up through third then down through fourth, if a 4-hole button); make about six stitches. Remove pin or stick, lift button away from fabric so stitches are taut, and wind thread firmly around stitches to make shank. Backstitch into shank to secure.

Alternative thread shank method

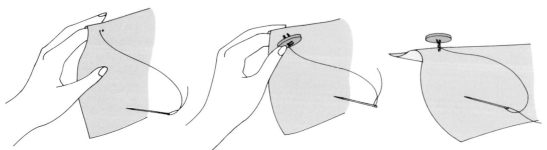

1. Take a stitch where the button is to be sewn, then place fabric over index finger of left hand.

2. With thumb, hold button against fabric, but well away from the button mark, and sew on button.

3. When enough stitches are made, lift button and wind thread around them. Secure with backstitches.

Sewing on buttons by machine

A zigzag sewing machine can be used to sew on sew-through buttons. Check machine booklet for exact instructions. A four-hole button may have to be sewn with two separate stitchings.

A button foot is included in some machine accessory boxes (some machines do not need special feet for sewing on buttons). The button foot holds the button in place while the needle stitches from side to side. Stitch width must equal the space between the holes in the button.

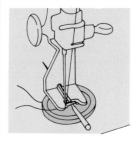

Some machines have button feet with adjustable shank guides. If your machine does not have such an attachment, push a machine needle into the groove on the ordinary button foot. The stitches pass over the shaft of this needle and form a shank. The thicker the needle shaft, the longer the shank.

Reinforcing buttons

Reinforcing buttons are useful at points of great strain and on garments of heavy materials. By taking the stress that would otherwise be on the fabric, they keep top buttons from tearing it.

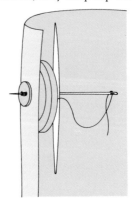

To add a reinforcing button, follow steps for attaching a sew-through button with a shank, additionally placing a small flat button on inside of garment directly under outer button. Sew as usual through all sets of holes (buttons should have same number of holes). On last stitch, bring needle through hole of top button only and complete shank. (If fabric is delicate, substitute a doubled square of fabric or seam binding for the small button.)

Making buttons

Fabric buttons

Fabric buttons made to match the garment are the answer when suitable ready-made buttons cannot be found. Full instructions come with each of the many kits available for making fabric-covered buttons. Covered buttons can also be made using plastic or bone rings, sold at haberdashery counters.

1. Select a ring of the diameter required for the finished button. Cut a circle of fabric slightly less than twice the diameter of the ring.

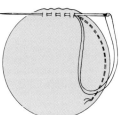

2. Using a double thread, sew around fabric circle with a small running stitch, placing stitches close to the edge. Leave thread and needle attached to fabric at the end of stitching.

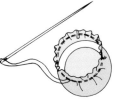

3. Place the ring in the centre of fabric circle. Gather fabric around the ring by pulling on the needle and thread until the hand stitches bring the cut edges of fabric together.

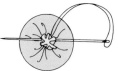

4. Secure gathered-up fabric around ring by pulling up hand stitches tightly. Fasten with several short backstitches.

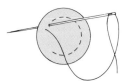

5. Decorate button by taking small backstitches around and close to ring, through both fabric layers. Use buttonhole twist. Attach button to garment with a thread shank.

Leather buttons

Leather buttons can be made at home using commercial cover-your-own kits. The easiest forms to cover are those with prongs all around the inside of the rim. Almost any type of leather, even fairly thick ones, can be used. This is a practical way to use small scraps and remnants.

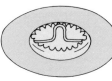

1. Use pattern in kit to cut a circle of leather for each button.

2. Centre button front on wrong side of leather; shape leather over button, hooking it underneath small prongs on inside of rim. Work across the diameter of the button, securing edges that are opposite one another.

3. When all excess leather is turned to the inside of the button, place button back over button front. Make sure that all cut edges are between button front and back, and that leather is stretched smoothly over the front.

4. Position a cotton reel over the button back, with shank of button in hollow centre of reel. Rap the reel sharply with a hammer to force button back into place. This will flatten the button, and should lock the back permanently in place. If back is not secure, rap it again, using reel and hammer as before.

Chinese ball buttons

Chinese ball buttons can be made with ready-made cord or braid, or your own tubing (p. 359). Always make a test button, keeping size of tubing proportionate to the button size you want. For example, use 5 mm tubing for a 12 mm button, 1 cm tubing for a 2.5 cm button.

1. Pin one end of tubing securely to a piece of paper. Loop the cord once as shown.

2. Loop a second time over first loop, then go under end. Keep seam of tubing down at all times as you work.

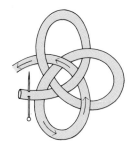

3. Loop a third time, weaving through previous two loops. Take care tubing does not become twisted at any point in either looping or weaving.

4. Gradually tighten up on loops, easing them into a ball shape. Trim the ends of the tubing and sew them flat to the underside of the button.

Hooks and eyes

Types and uses

Hooks and eyes are small but comparatively strong fasteners. Though they are most often applied at single points of a garment opening, such as a waistband or neckline, they can also be used to fasten an entire opening.

There are several types of hooks and eyes, each designed to serve a particular purpose. General-purpose hooks and eyes are the smallest of all the types and are used primarily as supplementary fasteners; a familiar example is the hook and eye at the top of a zipper placket. This type ranges in size from fine (0) to heavy (3); finishes are either black or nickel. Special-purpose hooks and eyes are larger

and heavier, and so can withstand more strain than those of the general-purpose type. Included in this group are plain and covered hooks and eyes for use on coats and jackets. The covered ones are advisable where a less conspicuous application is desired. Covered fasteners can be bought ready-made, or standard hooks and eyes can be covered with blanket stitches as explained below, right.

Another special-purpose type is the waistband hook and eye, different in form from all the other types, but also made with either a black or nickel finish. This can be used on a skirt or pants.

Two eye shapes are made for most hook types, the

purpose being to accommodate both lapped and butted garment openings. The *straight eye* is intended for use on lapped edges; the *round eye* for those that are butted. An exception is the special-purpose hook and eye designed for waistband use. The eye in this case is always straight, because the fastener will be used only on a lapped edge.

Standard hook   Straight eye   round eye

Attaching hooks and eyes

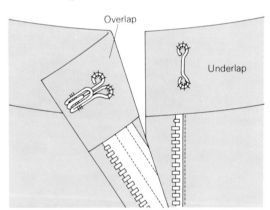

With lapped edges, the hook is sewn on the inside of the garment, the eye on the outside. Place *hook* on the underside of overlap, about 3 mm from the edge. Whipstitch over each hole. Pass needle and thread through fabric to end of hook; whipstitch around end to hold it flat against garment. Mark on the outside of underlap where the end of the hook falls—this is the position for the eye. Hold *straight eye* in place and whipstitch over one hole. Pass needle and thread through fabric and whipstitch other hole.

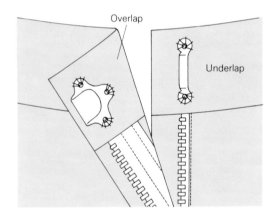

For use on waistbands of skirts or pants, special hook and eye sets are available. They are strong and flat, and designed so that the hook cannot easily slide off the eye. They can be used only for lapped edges. Position and sew on the hook and eye as for a lapped application of a standard hook and eye (end of hook need not be secured).

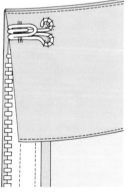 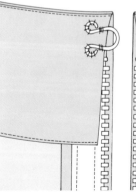

With butted edges, both the hook and the eye are sewn to the inside of the garment. Position *hook* 2 mm from one of the edges. Whipstitch over both holes. Pass needle and thread through fabric to end of hook; whipstitch over end to hold it flat against garment. Position *round eye* on other edge so that loop extends slightly beyond edge. Whipstitch over both holes. Then pass needle and thread through fabric toward edge and whipstitch both sides of loop to garment.

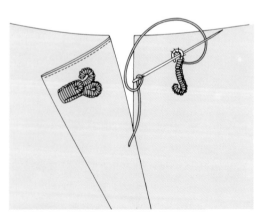

Covered hooks and eyes are used as a fine finishing touch. They can be purchased ready-made but you can cover your own as follows:
Sew a large hook and eye to the garment, by the lapped or the butted method, whichever is appropriate. Then, using a single strand of silk buttonhole twist that matches the fabric, cover both hook and eye with closely spaced blanket stitches. Do not catch fabric between the holes of the eye. Secure stitches.

Thread eyes

Essentially, a thread eye is a substitute for the metal eye. A thread eye is not as strong, however, as a metal eye and so should not be used at places where there is much strain.

There are two ways to form a thread eye: (1) the **blanket stitch method** (the stronger of the two) and (2) the **thread chain method.** For both, use a single

Straight eye   Round eye or loop

strand of heavy-duty thread or buttonhole twist in a colour that matches the fabric. A *straight eye* should be as long as the space between its two placement marks; a *round eye* should be longer than the space between placement marks, actual length depending on the fit of the garment.

These two methods can also be used for forming button loops and belt carriers. For a button loop, the length should be equal to the combined total of button diameter and thickness. A straight belt carrier should be as long as the belt is wide, plus 6 mm to 1 cm for ease.

Blanket stitch method

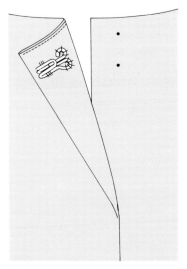

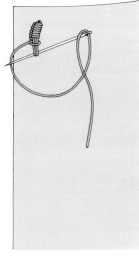

Sew hook to one edge of the garment by either the lapped or butted method (see opposite page) as required. Close the placket and mark beginning and end positions for eye on other edge.

Insert needle into fabric at one mark and bring it up at other mark. Take 2 or 3 more stitches in the same way; secure. (If the eye is round, let the thread curve into the intended size.)

Being careful not to catch the fabric, cover all of the strands of thread with closely spaced blanket stitches. When finished, bring needle and thread to the underside and secure stitching.

Thread chain method

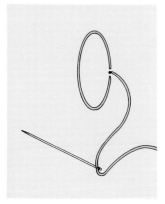

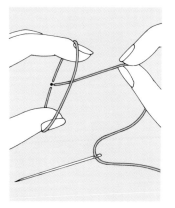

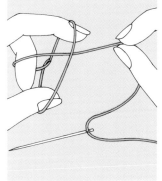

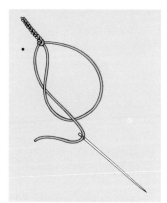

Mark on garment where thread chain will begin and end. Bring needle and thread up through one mark; take a small stitch over this mark, leaving a 10 to 15 cm loop.

As shown above, hold the loop open with the thumb and index finger of left hand; hold supply thread taut with the thumb and index finger of the right hand.

Bring second finger of left hand through loop to grasp the supply thread. Pull supply thread through loop; let loop slide off finger and be drawn down to fabric.

Repeat Steps 2 and 3 until chain is desired length. For straight eye, marked space and chain length are equal; for a loop, chain is longer than space between marks.

To secure the last loop of chain, pass needle and thread through final loop and pull taut. Fasten the free end of the chain to the garment at the second (end) mark.

Hooks and eyes

Hooks and eyes on fur garments

Large, covered hooks and eyes are sometimes used as fasteners for fur garments. Because of the difficulty of hand-sewing through furs, a special lapped method has been developed for attaching hooks and eyes (see below). The hooks are inserted into the seamline of the overlapping edge, and the ends of the eyes passed through punctures to the underside of the opposite edge. (If the garment edges are butted, both hooks and eyes can be inserted into the seamlines.) To facilitate the sewing of hooks and eyes, it is recommended that the garment opening be underlined or interfaced. The seamlines should not be machine-understitched; they can be hand-understitched after the hooks and eyes have been attached.

Attaching the hooks

Hooks in fur garments extend out from the seamline of the overlapping garment edge. Before stitching this seam, mark on the seamline the position of each hook. When stitching this seam, leave a 6 mm opening at each mark. Then proceed as follows.

1. Working from the wrong side of the garment, open out the facing. With curve of hook toward the facing, insert hook through a 6 mm opening and allow curve of hook to wrap around to right side of facing.

2. Pass an 8 cm length of 6 mm cotton tape under the stem of the hook. Cross the tape ends, then pull on them to bring the stem of the hook to the garment. Pin tape ends to garment and whipstitch in place. Make sure that the hand stitches do not show on the finished side of the garment.

3. Repeat Steps 1 and 2 for each hook. Then secure the facing to the cotton tape, using small, close whipstitches.

Attaching the eyes

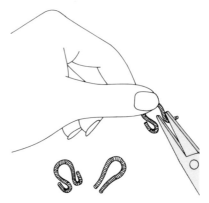

1. Using long-nose pliers, straighten the ends of each eye. This prepares the ends so that they can be passed through to the inside of the garment and then sewn in place.

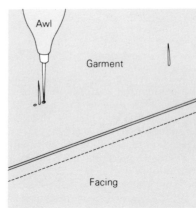

2. Pin-mark position for each eye on the underlap. From garment inside, pierce garment 6 mm to each side of each pin. If necessary, hand-finish holes (make eyelets).

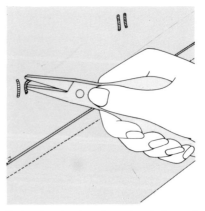

3. Insert ends of each eye into holes until just enough of the eye remains on garment right side for the hook to catch. Using the long-nose pliers, re-shape ends of each eye to form open loops.

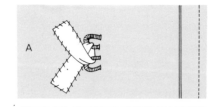

4. Pass an 8 cm length of 6 mm cotton tape under the stem of the eye and cross the ends. Pin the tape to the garment and whipstitch in place (A), making sure the stitches do not show on the finished side (B).

Types of snap fastener

Snap fasteners, another kind of small fastener, have less holding power than hooks and eyes. Each snap has two parts—a *ball* half and a *socket* half. General purpose metal snaps range in size from fine to heavy; finishes are either nickel or black. Clear nylon snap fasteners are also available.

Another type is the no-sew snap, a strong fastener which is not sewn to the garment but cleated into the fabric. No-sew snap fasteners also come in heavy-duty forms for use on overalls and canvas or leather garments, and with decorative tops for jeans and shirts. See packages for instructions. Covered snap fasteners are a good idea for jackets; instructions for making them are given at far right.

Basic application

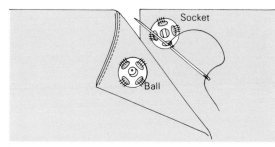

To attach a snap, position ball half on underside of overlap far enough in from edge so it will not show; whipstitch over each hole. Position socket half on right side of underlap to align with ball; whipstitch over each hole.

Covering snap fasteners

Fabric-covered snap fasteners are useful on jackets as they are not apparent when the garment is worn open. Cover large snaps with a lightweight fabric that is colour-matched to the garment. Follow the instructions below, then attach the fastener to the garment. To keep the fabric covering from fraying, lightly coat the edges with clear nail polish or a commercial anti-fray solution before sewing to garment.

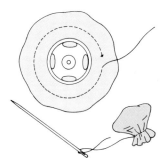

1. For each snap half, cut out a circle of fabric twice the diameter of the snap. Place small running stitches around and close to edge of fabric. Place snap half face down on fabric and draw up on stitches.

Special applications

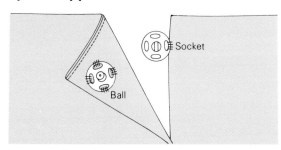

An extended snap fastener is used on butted garment edges. Attach ball half of snap to underside of one garment edge. Position socket half at the other garment edge; whipstitch over only one of the holes to secure socket to edge.

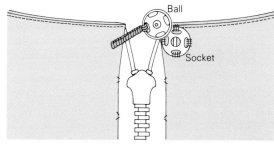

A hanging snap fastener can also be used for butted garment edges. Attach socket half to underside of one garment edge. To attach the ball half to the other edge, use the blanket stitch method for forming a thread eye (p. 365).

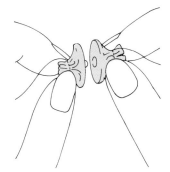

2. Push covered ball half into covered socket half—this will cut the fabric and expose the ball.

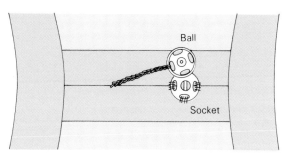

Lingerie strap guards are attached to the underside of a shoulder seam. Sew socket half of snap fastener to seam, 2 cm from centre of shoulder, toward neck edge. For a *thread chain guard* (above), start chain in garment about 4 cm from snap socket. Form a 4 cm chain (p. 365). Take a few whipstitches over

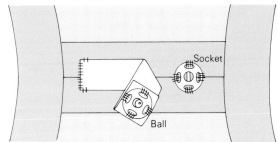

one hole of a ball half of snap; pass needle and thread through chain and fasten in garment. For a *tape guard* (above), use a 6 cm length of tape. Turn under one end 5 mm; whipstitch to garment 4 cm from snap socket. Turn under free end of tape 1.5 cm and sew ball half to underside.

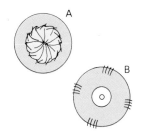

3. Pull snap apart. Draw stitches up tightly and secure. Trim excess fabric on the underside; whipstitch over edges if necessary (A). Attach snap to garment (B).

Tape fasteners

Types and uses

Tape fasteners are made in three types, **snap, hook and eye** and **hook and loop.** Tapes are practical fasteners for cushion covers and loose-covers, for children's clothing, and for such items as quilt covers, because they permit easy removal for laundering.

Since uses and applications differ, it is difficult to specify rules about extra fabric allowances for finishing edges. If a pattern calls for a tape fastener, as those for infants' clothes sometimes do, these allowances will be given. When you must determine for yourself how to cut fabric pieces, as with loose-covers, the fabric allowances become your decision. Allow, for example, a double seam allowance for the underlap in a lapped application.

The top and bottom edges of tape fasteners are usually caught into cross seams and need no further finishing. Never let the metal parts of any fastener extend into such seams.

Snap fastener tape has the ball halves of snaps on one tape, the socket halves on the other. Halves snap together and pull apart just like regular snap fasteners.

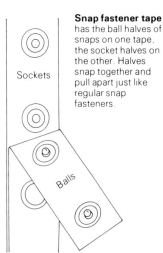

Hook and eye tape comes with the hooks on one tape, the eyes (usually round) on the other. Fastens like ordinary hooks and eyes.

Hook and loop tape fasteners consist of one tape with looped nap, a second with hooked nap. Hooks lock onto loops when the two are pressed together; unlock when pulled apart.

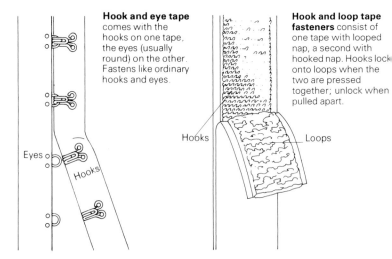

Applying tape fasteners

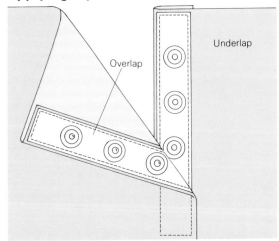

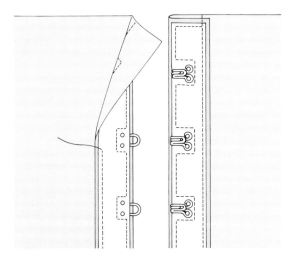

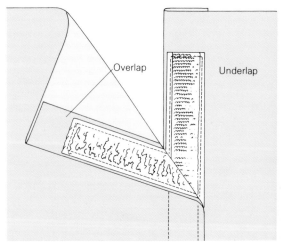

Snap fastener tape requires a lapped application because of the way the ball half must enter the socket half. Both garment edges should be wider than the tapes; for greater strength, cut a double-width seam allowance for the underlap. Position socket tape on underlap and stitch around all edges through all layers. Place ball tape on underside of overlap, align ball halves with sockets, and stitch around all edges through all layers. For a less obvious application, stitch ball tape to underlayer of overlap, fold edge under, and stitch along free edge through all layers.

Hook and eye tape calls for a centred application because hooks and eyes must butt to be fastened. As with snap fastener tape, both garment edges should be wider than the tapes. To apply, position hook tape on the underlayer of one edge, with hooks along fold. Stitch through both layers around each hook. Fold edge and stitch through all layers along the free edge (make sure needle does not hit hooks). Stitch eye half to the opposite edge in the same way, aligning eyes with hooks and positioning eyes just beyond fold. Again, make sure that the needle does not hit the metal parts of the fastener.

Hook and loop tapes must be lapped for the two halves to fasten. Because the hooks and loops lock on contact, application to an open seam is best; this lets them stay separate during application. Garment edges should be wider than tapes; for extra strength, cut a double-width seam allowance for the underlap. Position hook tape on underlap; stitch around all edges through all layers. Align and position loop tape on overlap; stitch around all edges through all layers. For a less obvious application, stitch the loop tape to underlayer of overlap, fold the edge under, and stitch along the free edge.

A good fit and wearing comfort are essentials in making clothes for men and children, as they are goals of sewing for women. For children's wear, the special requirements are speed of construction, durability, ease of wear and an allowance for growth. The special techniques for sewing for men and children are detailed here, starting in each case with the all-important matters of taking measurements and choosing patterns. For men's clothing, there are clear, step-by-step instructions for making casual wear, trousers, shirts and even ties, designed to complement the information from your commercial pattern. For children's clothing, the special techniques needed to achieve your sewing goals are covered, and there is a special section on making a child's coat. The chapter concludes with a section on encouraging children to sew, and includes suggestions for simple projects to arouse their interest.

Sewing for men and boys

What to aim for

When sewing clothes for men and children, some of the goals and certain techniques differ from those for women's garments. It is the intent of this chapter to deal with those aspects that vary from the usual. To make clear how these variations fit into the customary procedure, a step-by-step checklist has been provided for each of several garment types. These lists are not intended to take the place of your pattern direction sheet, but to supplement it, and to guide you in locating techniques that are to be found elsewhere in the book. Page numbers are listed alongside each step.

In sewing casual clothes, the aim is to make comfortable garments for informal wear. Simple methods are preferred for ease of sewing and quick results.

In the construction of men's more formal garments, where the goal is individual styling with good fit, the procedures are adapted from manufacturers' and tailors' methods. The results are intended to resemble ready-to-wear or custom tailoring. It is advisable to have some sewing experience before undertaking these more complex projects.

In sewing for children, two primary aims are durability and allowance for growth. Speedy completion of the garment is also important. Hints and techniques in the children's section, which begins on page 386, are based on these criteria.

Selecting pattern size

Pattern sizes for men and boys are grouped in three categories, each of them related to body build. A comparison of body types is shown at the right. (For Toddlers' and Little boys' sizes, see p. 386.)

To determine the correct size, first take and record measurements on a chart like one on the opposite page. Compare the starred measurements with those in the size charts below.

Select a **jacket or coat** size according to chest measurement, a **shirt** by the neckband size or ready-made size, **trousers** according to waist measurement. If measurements fall between two sizes, buy the larger size for a husky build, the smaller size for one that is slender. When pattern types are grouped (a jacket or a shirt plus trousers, for instance), choose the pattern size by the chest measurement and adjust the trousers to fit, if necessary.

Size range charts (in centimetres)

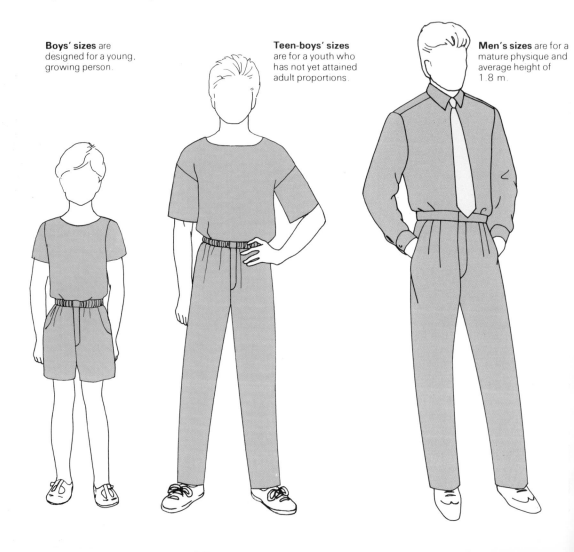

Boys' sizes are designed for a young, growing person.

Teen-boys' sizes are for a youth who has not yet attained adult proportions.

Men's sizes are for a mature physique and average height of 1.8 m.

BOYS'				TEEN-BOYS'			
Size	7	8	10	12	14	16	18	20
Chest	66	69	71	76	81	85	89	93
Waist	58	61	64	66	69	71	74	76
Hip (Seat)	69	71	75	79	83	87	90	94
Neckband	30	31	32	33	34.5	35.5	37	38
Height	122	127	137	147	155	163	168	173

MEN'S							
Size	34	36	38	40	42	44	46	48
Chest	87	92	97	102	107	112	117	122
Waist	71	76	81	87	92	97	107	112
Hip (Seat)	89	94	99	104	109	114	119	124
Neckband	35.5	37	38	39.5	40.5	42	43	44.5
Sleeve	81	81	84	84	87	87	89	89

How to take measurements

Directions for taking two sets of measurements are given below; for convenience, all can be taken at one time. Those in the **first group** (marked with asterisks) are used primarily for choosing a pattern size (see opposite page). They might also indicate the need for pattern adjustments. If the 'difference' column shows an amount of 1 cm or more, the pattern needs to be adjusted by that difference (see Pattern alterations section for methods).

Measurements in the **second group** (no asterisks) are useful for achieving good fit. These can be compared with actual pattern dimensions to see if the pattern needs adjusting in these areas.

The best way to take measurements is over an undershirt and lightweight trousers—no belt. Use a flexible tape measure, and pull it snug, but not too tight. When measuring *waist*, *outseam* and *inseam*, trousers should be adjusted to the preferred wearing position. The *crotch depth* can be measured by the method that is given on page 387, or it can be calculated instead by subtracting the inseam from the outseam measurement.

Measurements for growing boys should be checked often to keep pace with growth spurts. Arms and legs can grow longer without an accompanying change in girth. If this happens, a lengthening of the present size may be all that is needed.

Measurement chart

MEASUREMENT	YOURS	PATTERN	DIFFERENCE
Height*			
Chest*			
Waist*			
Hip (seat)*			
Neckband*			
Shirt sleeve*			
Shoulder			
Arm length			
Trouser outseam			
Trouser inseam			
Crotch depth			

FOR PATTERN SIZE:

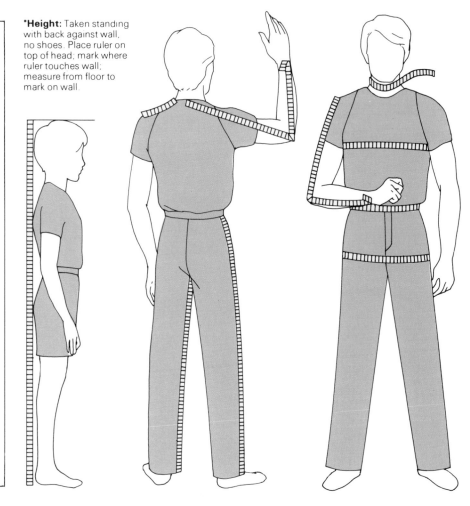

*Height: Taken standing with back against wall, no shoes. Place ruler on top of head; mark where ruler touches wall; measure from floor to mark on wall.

Shoulder length: From base of neck (shrug shoulders to locate it) to top of arm (raise arm shoulder high to locate the joint).

*Shirt sleeve length: From neck base at centre back, along shoulder, over bent arm to the wrist.

*Neckband: Around neck at Adam's apple plus additional 1 cm.

Arm length: From top of arm, over bent elbow, to wristbone.

*Chest: Around the fullest part.

*Waist: With pants adjusted to wearing position, measure around area where waist seam rests.

*Hips (seat): Around the fullest part.

Trouser inseam: Along seam on inside of leg to the hem (or desired length).

Trouser outseam: With trousers adjusted to comfortable height, measure along the side seam from waistline to hem (or desired length).

Sewing for men and boys/casual wear

Making pull-on shorts or pants

The sewing techniques required for casual wear are less complex than tailoring methods. Only a basic knowledge of sewing is required to make these garments, although some special techniques are listed here. For other methods that apply to construction of pull-on shorts and pants, follow up the references given in the procedure checklist on the right.

The most suitable fabrics for pull-on shorts or pants are lightweight weaves, or stretch knits such as jerseys or napped knits. These fabrics make a light or flexible garment for comfort and convenience. Leisurewear is loose-fitting, so that, although a good fit is recommended, measurements need not be as exact as with more formal wear.

Tracksuit pants are a very popular pull-on style, featuring a casing with elastic and drawstring at the waist, patch or inside pockets, and stretchy knit bands at the ankle.

Checklist / Pull-on pants procedure

Check pattern measurements 371

Adjust pattern fit: increase waist 118; decrease waist 119; finished length 115–116

Cut out and mark 96–106

Stitch and finish seams: knit seams 168; zigzagged, overlocked, overedged 160–161, 163

Construct pockets: patch 87–91; inside 292–294

Apply zipper: in ready-made knit cuffs 223; centred in leg seam 330; invisible zipper in leg seam 338–339

Finish waistline: drawstring in casing 248; threading elastic in casing 248; stretch waistband 250; applied elastic waistband 260; decorative stretch waistband 261

Finish cuffs: overlocked edges 304; turned and stitched 304; machine stitched 306; casings 276; stretchy knit bands 276–277

Pull-on shorts, in knit or woven fabrics, make comfortable and convenient leisurewear.

Pull-on pants, with inside or patch pockets, are easy to make and wear.

Elastic and drawstring casing

1. Stitch centre seam, leaving 2 cm gap, 5 cm from top on front to allow opening for elastic and drawstring insertion. Hand-baste seam allowance to garment in casing area for 7.5 cm for easier insertion of elastic. To make casing, turn upper edge down 4.5 cm to wrong side of garment. Hand-baste close to fold; press. Stitch 3.8 cm from fold. Make two more rows of stitching above the first, at 1.3 cm intervals, to make three casings.

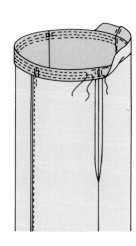

2. Cut two lengths of 1 cm elastic, each a comfortable waist measurement, plus 1.3 cm. Fasten a safety pin to one end of a length of elastic; insert through the opening in the upper casing and pull the elastic through; lap ends 1.3 cm and stitch. Repeat process for second elastic, threading it through the lower casing. Slipstitch openings in upper and lower casings.

3. Cut a length of 3 mm wide cord, a comfortable waist measurement, plus 40 cm. Fasten a safety pin to one end of the cord, insert through drawstring opening and thread through the middle casing. Knot both ends of cord. The waistband or casing is made the same way for pull-on shorts or pants. When the garment is worn, drawstring is adjusted and tied to allow a comfortable fit at the waist.

Making trousers

The construction of men's trousers involves a few techniques and some terminology (see Glossary of terms below) that are not encountered elsewhere. Directions for special techniques begin here and continue to page 383. For other methods that apply to trouser construction, see pages listed in the Checklist for procedure, below right.

A good fit is essential to well-made trousers. The best and easiest way to achieve it is by adjusting the pattern dimensions to those of a pair that fits well. (The chart, right, indicates which measurements should be compared.) If you do not have such a well-fitting pair, take the appropriate body measurements, as directed on page 371, and compare these with the pattern's. If lengthwise adjustments are needed, consult the Fitting chapter. Adjustments of up to 5 cm in waist or hip circumference can usually be made at the centre back seam. If you re-style the leg, be careful to make equal adjustments on both inseam and outseam so that the crease-line position will not be changed.

Glossary of terms

Bar tack: A reinforcement tack used at points of strain. Bar tacks can be made by hand (refer to Hand stitches for method) or by machine (see Machine facsimiles of hand stitches).
Inseam: The seam on the inside of the leg.
Outlet: Extra fabric allowance in trousers, which is usually added to the centre back seam and the top of the front inseam.
Outseam: The seam that falls along the outside of the leg (the side seam).
Overtacking: Three or four hand stitches in the same spot; used to hold two areas together.
Pin-tack: Several machine stitches in the same stitch, made by lifting the presser foot slightly so the fabric does not feed; used to reinforce machine stitching where the usual backstitching would be unsightly.
Pocketing: A tightly woven, lightweight fabric of cotton or cotton-synthetic blend; used for inside pockets, the zipper fly stay and shield lining, also waistband facing in men's trousers.
Stay: A piece of fabric (usually pocketing) used to reinforce an area and prevent stretching.

Trouser measurement chart

PLACE TO MEASURE	TROUSERS	PATTERN	DIFFERENCE
Waist (at the seamline)			
Crotch front (from waist to inseam)			
Crotch back (from waist to inseam)			
Hips (18 cm below waist)			
Thighs (7.5 cm below crotch seam)			
Outseam (waist to hemline)			
Inseam (crotch to hemline)			
Circumference of leg at knee*			
Circumference of leg at hem*			

*These measurements are needed only where an exact duplication of the trouser style is desired.

Checklist / trouser procedure

Check pattern measurements 371

Adjust pattern: crotch seam 122; crotch allowance 374; centre back seam allowance 374

Cut out and mark: trousers 96–106; crotch stays 374

Establish crease lines 374

Stitch back darts 171

Construct back pockets; patch 287–291; inside 375

Construct front pockets: patch 287–291; front-hip 304–305; in-seam 376

Stitch outseams: plain 157; with in-seam pocket 376

Apply zipper: boys' fly 336; men's fly 378–379

Stitch inseams 157

Attach waistbands 380–383

Construct change pocket 377

Anchor pocket tops 381

Stitch crotch seam 381

Finish waistband facings 380–383

Construct belt carriers 383

Attach trouser hooks 364

Hem trousers: turned-up hem 302–307; cuffed 322

Cutting additions for trousers

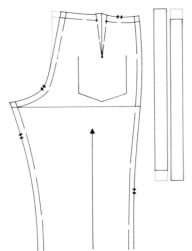

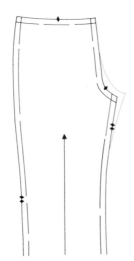

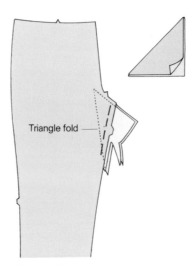

Triangle fold

Establishing the crease line

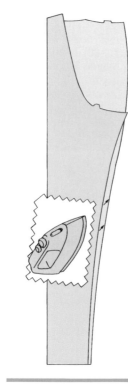

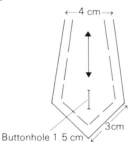

Trouser crease lines should be established before proceeding with the construction. Begin with back sections, folding each in half and aligning the inseam with the outseam. (To bring seam edges together at the top, it may be necessary to stretch the crotch area slightly upward. This can be done gently, and will give the crotch a slightly better curve.) Using a dampened press cloth, press the crease from the leg edge to 8 cm above crotch level. Repeat the procedure for trouser fronts, pressing the creases from the leg edge to the waistline.

Extra back waist allowance is usually provided at the centre back seam of men's trousers. This makes adjustments possible in the waist and upper hip areas where they are most often needed in case of a weight gain. If your pattern does not have this provision, add it yourself before cutting out the trousers: Draw a line, starting 2.5 cm from the cutting line at the waist and tapering to the existing cutting line at the seat. Add the same amount (2.5 cm) to the waistband pieces.

Extra crotch allowance should be added to the trouser left front (or the right, if a man prefers) so they will fit comfortably. Do this by drawing an addition on the pattern piece at the centre front seam and the inseam, as is shown. The addition is 2 cm at the crotch, and tapers to existing cutting lines at the waist, and at a point 12 cm below crotch on the inseam. Cut both trouser sections from the altered pattern piece, then trim the opposite side back to the original cutting line.

The addition of crotch stays gives extra life and durability to trousers by limiting the possibility of stretching or ripping in this area. To add stays, cut two 15 cm squares of pocketing; fold each square diagonally to form a triangle. Position one triangle on the wrong side of each trouser front, with the fold extending 6 cm from the inseam edge at the crotch, and tapering to meet the inseam edge about 15 cm below the crotch. Tack. Trim raw edges of the stay to match the seam edges.

Trouser pockets

Several different pocket styles are used for men's trousers. Three types of inside pockets—a *back-hip* pocket, a *front in-seam* style, and a *change* pocket—are dealt with in this section. Directions for other types, such as front-hip and patch pockets, are described in the chapter on Pockets.

Men's trouser pockets are rarely just decorative. To satisfactorily serve their many purposes, they should be smooth and sturdy, with opening edges neatly finished and reinforced. For smoothness, an inside pocket is usually made of pocketing (see Glossary, p. 373), cut so that it extends to, and is later attached to, the waistline; the pocket sections are joined with a French seam. Constructed in this way, the pocket is strong and well supported to better

withstand the downward thrust frequently exerted on it. For good appearance, opening edges are faced with trouser fabric; the opening ends are bartacked for reinforcement.

For ease in handling, most trouser pockets are attached before the trouser sections are joined—back pockets first, then the front ones. One exception is the change pocket, which is added after the waistband is attached, but before the waistband facing is anchored inside.

Instructions for the back-hip pocket (opposite page) and the change pocket (p. 377) include explanations of how to cut the needed pieces and mark the placement. If you wish, you can add these pockets to trousers not designed to include them.

The pocket tab

The back left pocket often has a tab closure to protect the man's wallet. The way to construct it is explained below. Its insertion in a double-welt pocket is illustrated on the opposite page.

←—4 cm—→

Buttonhole 1.5 cm

3cm

From trouser fabric, cut two pieces shaped as illustrated. Dimensions are 8 cm long; 4 cm across top; 5 cm across widest part; 3 cm each side of 'V'. Right sides together, stitch all but the top with a 6 mm seam. Trim corners diagonally; turn unit right side out; press. Make 1.5 cm long buttonhole by hand or machine.

Sewing for men and boys/trousers

Back-hip pocket

A typical back-hip pocket has edges finished with trouser fabric; the inside is cut from pocketing and extends to the waistline. Instructions are given here for a double-welt style. If you prefer a single-welt or a flap style, cut the pocket sections as specified below, then follow directions in the chapter on Pockets for finishing the edges.

Instructions below include a tab for securing the opening. An alternative is a hand-worked buttonhole, centred vertically 1 cm below pocket opening.

Preparation: (1) Stitch the back trouser darts, if any; slash them to within 1 cm of the points; press the darts open. **(2)** Thread-mark the pocket placement. (If your pattern gives no placement indication, place the pocket 9 cm below waist, or at the bottom of the dart. Opening begins 4 cm from the outseam, is 14 cm long, and aligns with the cross grain.) **(3)** From pocketing, cut two rectangles, each 28 cm by 18 cm (cut twice as many if you are constructing two pockets). **(4)** From trouser fabric, cut three rectangles (six for two pockets), each 16 cm by 4 cm. Two of these will be used for facings (welts) to bind the pocket edges; the third, for an underlay that fits behind the pocket opening.

1. On wrong side of the left trouser back, position one pocket section so that the top edge extends 2.5 cm above the placement mark, the sides 2 cm beyond each end. Tack it to the trousers just above the mark. (This is called the inside pocket; the other section, added later, is called the outside pocket.) If you are making two pockets, repeat for right trouser back.

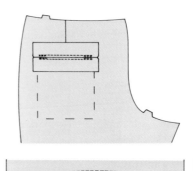

2. Tack facings to right side of trousers, having lengthwise edges meet at the placement mark, and ends extending 1 cm beyond the mark at each end. Stitch facings 3 mm from the mark, beginning and ending stitches 1 cm from each end. Starting at centre of the mark, cut to each end, slashing through the trousers and inside pocket. Take care not to cut beyond stitches.

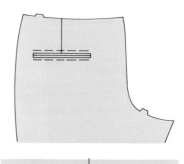

3. Gently push the facings through the slash to the wrong side. Working from the right side, fold and press facings to form 3 mm welts, with their folds meeting at the centre of the opening. Tack facings to hold them securely in place. Stitch each welt in the seam groove, pin-tacking at both ends (see Glossary, p. 373, for method). Bar-tack both ends of the opening.

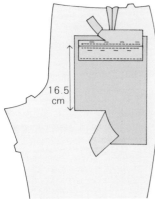

4. Inside trousers, trim upper facing to 1 cm above pocket opening. On lower part of pocket, measure 16.5 cm down from opening and trim excess fabric at bottom. Pin lower facing to pocketing. Pull pocket away from trousers; stitch along bottom edge of facing. Keep facing flat as you stitch; do not let it slide toward pocket opening.

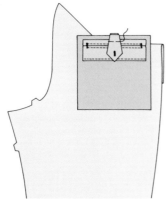

If attaching a pocket tab, centre it on upper facing, inside trousers, buttonhole at bottom. Tack or pin in place, then push tab through pocket opening; see if buttonhole is far enough below lower welt to be easily buttoned. (If upper end of buttonhole aligns with bottom of lower welt, this is adequate.) Reposition pocket tab if necessary.

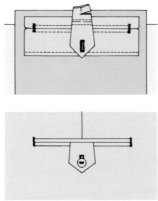

In order to stitch the tab, pull upper facing and pocket away from trousers; stitch through all layers (tab, facing and pocket), close to the previous stitching. Stitch again, 6 mm above the first stitching. Trim excess fabric from top of tab. Push tab through the opening; mark the button position; sew the button securely in place.

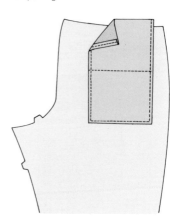

5. Position underlay on outside pocket section so that one lengthwise edge (will be bottom) is 14 cm from one end of pocket. Pin, then stitch bottom edge of underlay. Flip inside pocket toward top of trousers; lay outside pocket over it, with underlay face up, its lower edge at top. Stitch sides and lower edges with 6 mm seam.

6. Trim corners diagonally; turn pocket wrong side out (underlay is now inside); work seams out to edge. Press seam edges, then press under the top side edges of the outside pocket 6 mm. Stitch sides and bottom of pocket again, 3 mm from edge. Upper edge will later be trimmed to align with the waist seam allowances (see p. 381).

Sewing for men and boys/trousers

Trouser in-seam pocket

A front in-seam pocket is found most often in trousers of a traditional or tailored style. The inside sections are cut from pocketing, and the pocket opening (which is sewn to the outseam) is faced with the trouser fabric.

Construction of this pocket is begun after the back-hip pockets are completed and before the trouser outseam is stitched. Instructions include the addition of a back stay, which serves to both reinforce and finish the back inside edge of the pocket. Ends of the opening are reinforced with bar tacks.

This particular pocket fits well only in trousers with a certain cut. It should not be attempted unless the pattern style is designed to incorporate it. If your pattern has front-hip or patch pockets, see the chapter on Pockets for directions.

Preparation: (1) From pocketing fabric, cut four pocket sections, carefully indicating the opening edge with notches. **(2)** From the cross grain of pocketing, cut two pocket stays, each 4 cm wide and the length of the pocket opening plus 3 cm. **(3)** From the lengthwise grain of the trouser fabric, cut four pocket facings, each 6 cm wide and the length of the pocket opening plus 3 cm. Cut notches on all of the facings to indicate pocket openings. (If your trouser pattern provides separate pieces for the cutting of pocket facings, use the pattern pieces instead.)

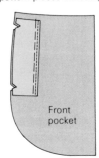

Front pocket

Back pocket

Lay front and back pocket sections, right side up, as shown. Tack a facing to each section, positioning the front pocket facing along the edge and the back pocket facing 1 cm from the edge, matching notches carefully. Stitch along each inside facing edge. Repeat the procedure for the second pocket, reversing the pocket positions so that the back pocket is on the left, the front pocket on the right.

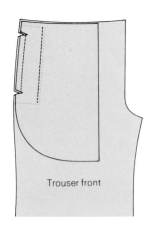

Trouser front

1. With right sides together, stitch the front pocket to the trouser front, between notches, *1.2 cm from the edge.* At each end of the stitch line, clip to the stitches and 3 mm beyond (the clip should be 1.5 cm deep).

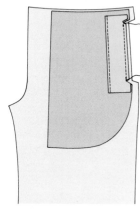

2. Press the seam open, then fold the pocket to the wrong side and press again, placing the seam 3 mm from the fold. Stitch in groove formed by first seam, pin-tacking at beginning and end of stitching. (See Glossary, p. 373, for pin-tack method.)

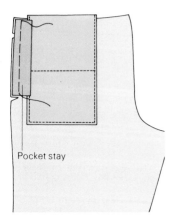

Pocket stay

3. Tack the pocket stay to the wrong side of the trouser back, aligning the bottom of the stay with the lower end of the pocket opening.

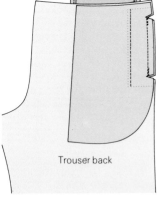

Trouser back

4. With right sides together, stitch the back pocket to the trouser back, between notches, 1.5 cm from the edge. Clip to the stitches at each end.

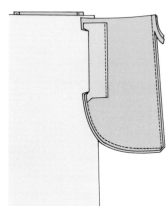

5. Pull the two sides of the pocket away from the trousers. Wrong sides together, stitch pockets with 6 mm seam, from the top edge to the lower notch for the pocket opening. Trim seam allowances to 3 mm. Trim the corners diagonally.

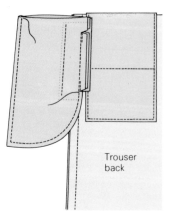

Trouser back

6. Press the pocket seam open. Turn the pocket wrong side out, work the seam out to the edge, then press again. Stitch the pocket a second time, 6 mm from the edge. Next, stitch front and back of trousers together along the outseam, above and below the pocket opening; reinforce with backstitches at each notch.

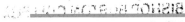

Change pocket

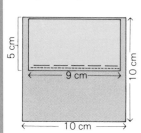

The change pocket, sometimes called a watch or a ticket pocket, is an in-seam type, inserted just under the waistband on the right trouser front; its opening is in the waist seam. An optional addition to any trouser style, the change pocket is constructed after the waistband is attached, but before the waistband facing is completed.

Preparation: (1) Trim seam allowances to 1 cm on trouser waist and waistband. **(2)** On the right front waist seam, mark pocket position with first edge 2 cm from outseam. (Opposite end of pocket will be 12 cm from outseam.) **(3)** From pocketing, cut two 10 cm squares. **(4)** From trouser fabric, cut a facing 5 cm by 9 cm.

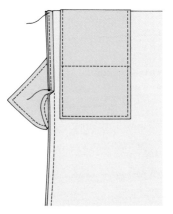

7. Between the bottom of the pocket opening and the top of the trousers, trim the back seam allowance to 3 mm. Press the outseam open. Fold the pocket stay over the back seam allowance and press. Also fold and press the edge of the back pocket over the back pocket facing.

Edge of back pocket / **Pocket stay**

8. Bring together the two folded edges of the stay and back pocket; tack. Stitch along the edge of the fold. This makes a neat finish for the pocket and, at the same time, reinforces it.

9. On the right side of the trousers, pull the front edge of the pocket toward the outseam. Bar-tack the ends of the pocket opening, either by hand or machine, taking one stitch beyond the outseam.

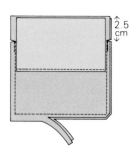

1. With right sides up, tack the facing to one pocket section with the top edges aligned, as shown. Stitch the lower edge of the facing.

5 cm / 9 cm / 10 cm / 10 cm

2. Wrong sides together, stitch the two pocket sections with a 6 mm seam, beginning and ending the stitching 2.5 cm from the top on each side; clip to the stitching. Trim corners diagonally; trim sides to 3 mm. Press seams open.

2.5 cm

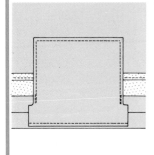

3. Turn pocket wrong side out; work seams out to edge; press. Stitch again, 3 mm from the edge. Fold back and pin the faced side out of the way. Place the unfaced side against the trouser waist (faced side underneath), aligning sides with pocket placement marks, top edge with edge of trouser waist seam. Stitch, 6 mm from the edge, through pocket and waist seam allowance.

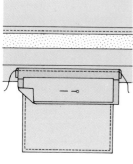

4. Fold the pocket down toward the trousers; press; stitch along the edge of the fold, through both the pocket and the waist seam allowance.

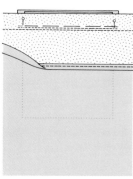

5. Unpin the facing side of the pocket; tack it to the waistband seam allowance. With the wrong side of the waistband face up, stitch across top of the pocket, as close as possible to the waistband seam. Insert two pins through the waistband seam, in line with the outside edges of the pocket.

6. From the trouser right side, make a bar tack at each pin mark, extending the tack 3 mm above and below the waist seam. To open the pocket, carefully remove the stitches from the waist seam, between the tacks.

Sewing for men and boys/trousers

Trouser zipper

A man's trouser zipper is applied in a fly closing that laps from left to right, the fly completed before the crotch seam is stitched. The method shown here is adapted from one used by many tailors and trouser manufacturers. To follow these directions, you will need to cut a fly facing, shield and shield lining, using your trouser pattern for a guide, and substitute these pieces for the ones included in the typical pattern. The dimensions are suitable for all men's sizes up to 112 (metric size).

A trouser zipper is recommended for use with this application. If this type is not available, or not suitable for your fabric, a 28 cm skirt zipper can be substituted. The zipper will be cut to the length of the fly opening when the application is complete. Besides a zipper, you will need half a metre of pocketing for fly stay and shield lining (see cutting instructions, right).

For the fly front in boys' trousers, the method in the Zipper section is more suitable than the one here. Be sure, however, when using that technique, to reverse the opening from right to left.

Cutting fly facing and shield

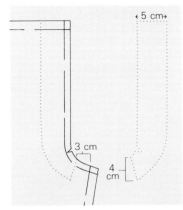
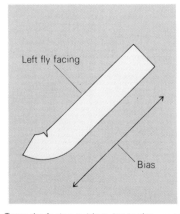
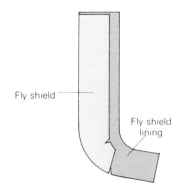

Before cutting fly facing and shield, trim the centre front seam to 1 cm on both trousers and trouser pattern; cut a notch on the front seam allowance, 4.5 cm from the inseam. On the trouser pattern, draw a guide for the facings—5 cm wide at the top and 4 cm wide at the bottom, ending 3 cm from the inseam.

Trace the facing guide twice to the wrong side of trouser fabric (see first drawing). Mark one tracing left (L), the other right (R); cut them out. The left facing is usually interfaced with pocketing, cut on the bias, using facing as pattern (above). This is called the *fly stay* because it reinforces and also supports the fly.

The right facing becomes an extension of the trousers called a *fly shield*. From the cross grain of pocketing fabric, using the facing as a guide, cut a fly shield lining, making it 8 cm longer at the bottom and 2 cm wider along the inside (notched) edge. Clip into the lining 3 mm at the bottom end of the shield.

Stitching the left fly front

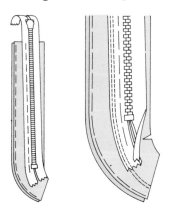
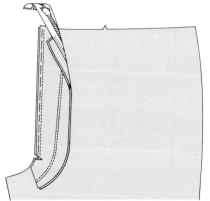
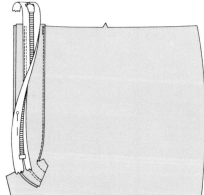
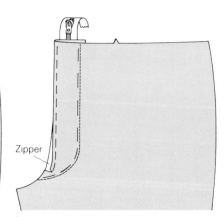

Tack the stay to the wrong side of the left facing. Place closed zipper on the facing, face down, with bottom stop 1 cm above the notch. Tack the zipper so that right edge of tape aligns with the facing edge at the bottom and is 6 mm away at the top. Stitch zipper tape along left edge, then again 3 mm from edge.

With right sides together, tack facing to left trouser front, taking care not to catch zipper. (Fold zipper back and, if necessary, pin to hold it out of the way.) Stitch facing from notch to waist edge, taking 6 mm seam. Carefully cut the notch to 9 mm, so that it extends 3 mm beyond the stitch line.

Pull the facing out and away from trousers, and press seam allowances toward it. If necessary, notch seam allowances on the curve so that the facing lies flat. From right side, stitch through the facing and all seam allowances, close to the seam. End the stitching and reinforce with a pin-tack at the notch.

Fold the facing inside the trousers, placing the seam 3 mm from the fold. Tack close to the seam to hold facing in position. From the right side, tack a guideline 4 cm from the fold, tapering the line to 1 cm opposite notch and extending it to trouser edge 2 cm below the notch. Topstitch close to tacking.

Sewing for men and boys/trousers

Stitching the right fly (shield)

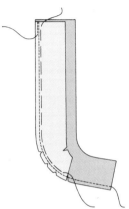

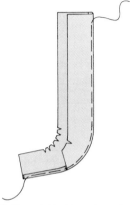

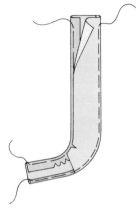

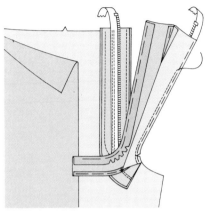

1. With right sides together, tack right fly facing and lining along the outside edge. Stitch with 6 mm seam, beginning at the top of the facing and ending at bottom edge of lining. Notch curve. Press seam open.

2. Turn right side out, work seam out to the edge and press, at the same time folding the lining edge under 6 mm. Tack. Clip inside edge of lining along the curve as shown, making the clips 1 cm deep and 6 mm apart.

3. Fold under the front edge of the lining 2 cm, aligning the fold with the edge of the facing. (The seam allowance should lie between the facing and the lining.) Press the fold, then tack it close to the edge.

4. With the zipper open, tack the right side of the fly shield to the back of the unattached half of the zipper. The zipper should be positioned so that the tape aligns with the facing edge, and the bottom stop is 1 cm above the notch. Stitch through zipper and shield, 6 mm from the edge. Do not catch the shield lining in the stitching.

Final zipper steps

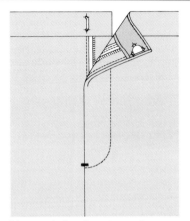

After waistband and crotch seam have been stitched, pull the bottom of the left fly slightly to the right so fly shield seam is covered. Bar-tack by hand or machine, extending the tack one or two stitches into the right front.

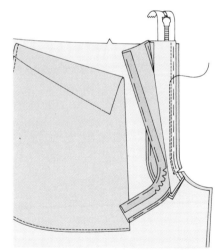

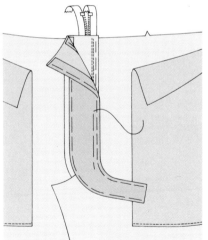

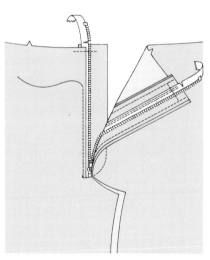

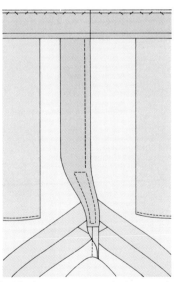

5. Close the zipper. With right sides together, tack shield and zipper to the right trouser front from notch to waist edge. (Do not catch the shield lining in the tacking.) Stitch through all layers, from notch to waist, placing stitches just to the left of the previous stitch line. Clip the notch to the stitching.

6. Open the zipper. Inside the trousers, press shield lining flat. Tack close to the fold, through all layers—shield, trousers and zipper. The upper lining should completely cover the back of the shield. The lower lining is left free and will be finished when trousers are completed (see Final steps, right).

7. From right side of trousers, stitch close to the left fly seam, pin-tacking at the notch, keeping the zipper tape and fly shield flat as you stitch. On each side of the zipper, stitch across the top of the tape, 1 cm from the edge of the trousers. Trim the tops of the zipper even with the trouser edge.

Inside the trousers, sew the lower end of the fly lining to crotch seam allowances with tiny backstitches.

Sewing for men and boys/trousers

Trouser waistbands

The methods for constructing a waistband for men's trousers vary according to the pattern, the fabric and the waistband material. The following directions, however, are common to all methods.

The waistband is cut of garment fabric in two sections, one for the right side of the body and one for the left. Each section is sewn to the corresponding trousers half, then the back seam of garment and waistband are sewn in one step. This makes any future waist alterations easier. (The top 2 to 3 cm of the back waistband seam may be left open in a 'V' for greater comfort.)

The left waistband must be cut longer than the right so that it equals fly facing and whatever extension is allowed for waistband fasteners.

The facing for the waistband is rarely of the garment fabric; instead, a firmly woven, lightweight fabric, such as pocketing, is used. The reinforcement is often a special stiffener, similar to buckram, instead of regular interfacing.

The waistband seam holds the front and back pocket tops securely in place.

Follow our instructions carefully; the cutting of the pieces and the point at which the waistband is applied may differ from the pattern's specifications. Leave crotch seam unstitched until directed to join waistband sections at centre back.

Using professional waistbanding

There are several products available for supporting a trouser waistband. Professional waistbanding is a flexible woven synthetic product that has been heat-set to precise widths from 1 to 7 cm. Purchase it in the exact width desired for the finished waistband. Do not cut it to make it narrower; this will remove the folded edge and expose sharp cross-yarns that could penetrate fabric and scratch skin. (Note: technique using this product is shown with a left front extension.)

Cutting: Cut the *left waistband* in a length to fit from the raw edge of the back seam to the finished edge at the front plus 8 cm. Cut the *right waistband* to fit from the edge of the back seam to the finished edge of the fly shield plus 1.5 cm. The width should equal the width of the professional waistbanding plus 4 cm. Cut *facing sections* the same length but 5 cm wider than the waistbanding, placing them on the true bias of the pocketing. Cut *waistbanding* to equal the length of the waistband sections minus 1.5 cm.

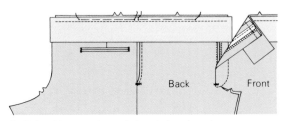

1. Right sides together, stitch waistband sections to garment sections. Tack pockets to waist seam.

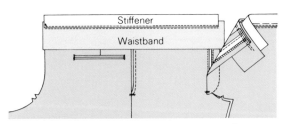

2. Lap the waistbanding over waistband seam allowances, aligning long edge with the stitching-on seamline. End of waistbanding should be 1.5 cm from front edge of each section. Stitch close to edge through all layers.

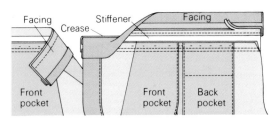

3. Stitch facings to waistbands with a 1.5 cm seam, right sides together. Grade seam allowances; press toward facing. Turn free edge of facing under 2.5 cm; press. Fold facing down; press a crease where waistband touches stiffener.

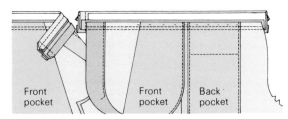

4. Turn facing back to the right side. Match inside of pressed crease to the top edge of the stiffener. Stitch across the front ends on each section. Trim seam and clip across corners diagonally, as shown.

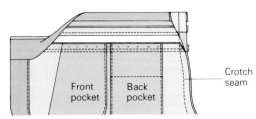

5. To sew centre back seam and waistband, lift facing up; pin seam, matching cross seams. Stitch; press open; fold facing to inside of waistband. (For a V-shaped opening at top of waistband, see Step 6, opposite page.)

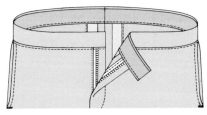

6. Press facing into position on inside of garment, keeping seam allowances of waistline seam toward top of waistband. Tack facing to trousers along waistline seam. From right side, stitch in seam groove, through the facing.

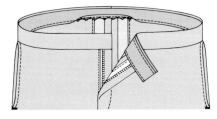

An alternative method: Machine-stitch 1 cm from lower edge of facing to hold fold in place. Secure facing to waist seam with a blind herringbone stitch, using machine stitches as a guide for placement of stitches on facing.

Sewing for men and boys/trousers

Tailored waistband

This smooth, flat, flexible waistband, made with hand-finishing, is the one used by professional tailors in the trousers of fine suits.

The stiffener should be more flexible than for other methods. Professional tailors use buckram, sold by the metre in haberdashery shops and departments. If buckram is not available, you can substitute a very heavy grade of hair canvas.

Instructions are given here for a finished waistband width of 4.5 cm; this method works best when the finished waistband width is kept under 5 cm.

The zipper should be in the trousers, but the crotch seam should still be open, when construction is begun. Cut the buckram strips on the bias. Cut the waistband sections from the garment fabric on the lengthwise grain (see Grain in fabrics, pp. 96–97).

Cutting: *Waistband sections* should be cut to length equal to waist seamline from edge to edge of each half plus 1.5 cm. Width is 7 cm. *Facings and finishing strips* are cut the same length as waistband sections, from cross grain of pocketing. Facings are 6.5 cm wide, finishing strips 4 cm wide. *Buckram:* same size as waistband; cut on the bias grain.

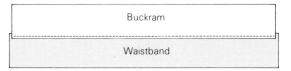

1. Lap one long edge of the buckram or hair canvas 6 mm over the **wrong** side of the waistband section. Stitch through centre of lapped edges. When folded, this is the top edge.

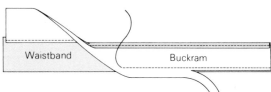

2. Turn buckram to wrong side of waistband; 6 mm of waistband fabric is now at top edge of buckram. At lower edge, trim buckram even with fabric; stitch the two together.

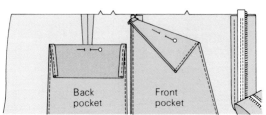

3. So that pockets will not be caught into the waistline seam when the waistbands are stitched on, pin the top edges of the pockets down out of the way.

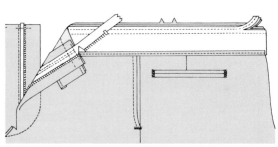

4. Working with the waistband side up, pin left waistband to left trouser half. Front edge of waistband should extend 1.5 cm beyond finished edge of trousers. Stitch, then trim seam allowances to 1 cm. Repeat for right side.

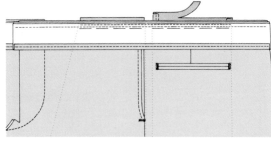

5. To secure pockets to waistline seam, first adjust them so they lie flat. Tack top edges to waist seamline. Waistband up, stitch through centre of waistband seam allowance, catching pockets. Trim pockets to 6 mm above seam allowance.

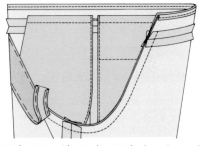

6. Sew crotch seam with one leg inside the other, right sides of fabric together. Stitch, beginning at bottom of zipper and ending 3 cm from top edge of waistband (for the comfort 'V'), stretching seat area slightly as you stitch.

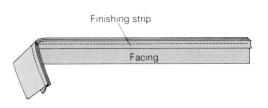

7. Fold facing finishing strips in half lengthwise. With right sides together, stitch them to one long edge of each of the facings, taking a 6 mm seam. Press seam flat to embed the stitches, but do not press strips away from facing.

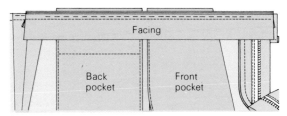

8. With finishing strip between wrong side of pants and facing, hand-sew facing seam allowance to seam allowance of waistband, using a running stitch. Facing will cover centre back seam. Leave facing loose at back seam and zipper.

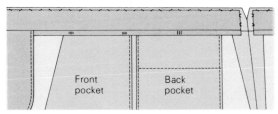

9. Press under remaining edges of facing 1 cm all around, and slipstitch to waistband edges at tops and ends. Overtack facing finishing strips to pockets at each side on front pockets, at centre on back pockets (see p. 373).

Sewing for men and boys/trousers

Using trouser waistbanding

This technique employs a specially designed product called men's trouser waistbanding with extremely durable results. It is a combination of waistband stiffener and facing; the stiffener is a sturdy interfacing and a woven insert edged with rubber, the facing is nylon. Facing and stiffener are joined at the lower edge; the top is left open for sewing to the waistband.

In this method, the ends of the waistbanding are machine-stitched to waistband seam allowances at centre back and front for maximum durability. Waistbanding is secured all around the waist seam.

Cutting: *Waistband sections* should be cut to length equal to the waist seamline of each half from edge to edge plus 1.5 cm; to a width 3 cm wider than the facing part of the waistbanding. *Waistbanding:* Same length as waistband sections.

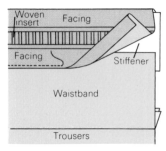
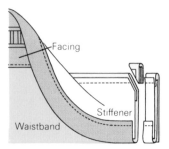
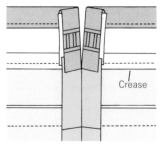
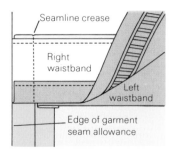
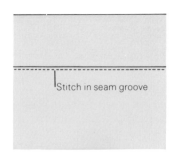

1. Right sides together, stitch waistband section to trouser section with a 1.5 cm seam. Press under free edge of facing part of waistbanding 1 cm. Place waistband top between facing and stiffener so it overlaps stiffener 1.5 cm. Stitch close to facing fold through all thicknesses.

2. Repeat for other half of waistband. Finish front edge of each section by turning waistband so right sides are together, and stitching across ends with a 1.5 cm seam. Trim and grade seam; clip corner diagonally. Turn band right side out, press; press a crease at top edge.

3. To form centre back seam, first open out waistbanding so it will not be caught in seam. Stitch entire seam from crease at top of waistband (or from 3 cm below for a comfort 'V') to zipper in the front. Press *seam* open, seam *allowances* back on unstitched waistbanding.

4. To finish back edges, fold the waistband so right sides are together. Work on half of garment at a time. Open out centre back seam allowance; match its edge to edge of waistbanding. Stitch in pressed seam allowance crease of waistbanding the width of waistband.

5. Turn the waistband right side out. To finish the waistband, stitch in the groove of the seam from the right side of the garment. Stitch through all thicknesses. The rubber edging on the woven insert of this trouser waistbanding will grip a shirt and keep it from riding up.

Using elastic waistbanding

This waistband method can be used with knit fabrics. It is ideal for them because it takes advantage of the fabric's stretchability, and at the same time gives the waistband a sturdy support that will not roll over. The elastic used, a strong waistband elastic, serves as both facing and interfacing. It is sold by the metre, in various colours, and is 3 cm wide; even when stretched a great deal, this elastic will not decrease in width.

You should purchase enough elastic to fit both waistband sections. Usually, the waist measurement plus 20 centimetres is sufficient. The left waistband is cut with an extension to allow for finishing the front edge with garment fabric.

Cutting: *Waistband sections* should be cut to length equal to the waist seamline of each half, plus an extra amount equal to the zipper fly facing on the left half and an additional 1.5 cm on the right. Width is that of the elastic plus 3 cm. *Elastic:* Length equal to waistbands minus zipper facing on left.

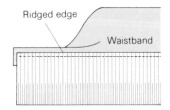
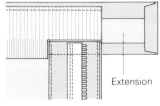
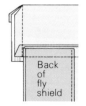
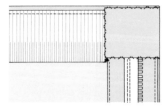
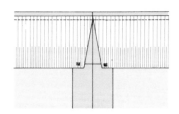

1. Lap wrong side of ridged edge of elastic 6 mm over right side of one long edge of waistband. On left half, match end of elastic to beginning of extension. Stitch.

2. Right sides together, sew waistband to trousers; trim seam allowances to 1 cm. Fold elastic and 6 mm of waistband to wrong side. On left side, trim elastic over zipper.

3. Fold the extension to inside of waistband; turn under seam allowances all around and slipstitch in place. Whipstitch cut end of elastic to zipper facing.

4. To finish right-hand side, fold waistband, right sides together. Stitch across end, aligning stitching with edge of trouser front. Trim seam and turn waistband right side out.

5. Stitch centre back seam, leaving elastic open. Turn waistband to inside; turn ends of elastic in on a diagonal, and tack each securely to centre back seam allowances.

Sewing for men and boys/trousers

Waistband with iron-on interfacing

In this method, the width of the waistband is not limited by the width of the stiffener; the interfacing may be cut to any desired width. Select a sturdy grade of iron-on interfacing. The construction method is the same as for the tailored waistband, page 381, beginning with Step 3.

Cutting: Waistband sections, facings and finishing strips: Cut these the same as for a tailored waistband, page 381, in the chosen width. *Interfacing* should be cut to the *finished* size of the waistband; trim away all seam allowances.

Match edges of interfacing to seamlines of wrong side of waistband. Iron in place; proceed with technique.

Belt carriers

Belt carriers appear on most men's trousers, the exception being those made with an elastic waistband. There are usually seven such carriers, evenly spaced around the waistline seam, with one carrier located at centre back. If the waist is very large more carriers should be added.

Carriers vary in width and length to suit trouser style and belt width. In general, the wider or heavier the belt, the wider the loops should be to support the weight. The total length of a carrier should equal the belt width plus 3 centimetres to allow the belt to slip through easily.

There are three ways to make belt carriers. The first method is quick and easy, and the selvage need not be used if the fabric is a firmly constructed knit. The second method is preferred for fine, tailored trousers in any fabric. The third method is an alternative suitable for very crisp, firmly woven, lightweight fabrics only.

Preparation of belt carriers

Method 1. Cut a strip of garment fabric along the selvage, three times the desired finished width, and the total length needed for all carriers. Fold strip into thirds, with raw edge of fabric on the inside and the selvage on the outside. Stitch close to edge on both long sides, through all thicknesses. Cut into lengths for individual carriers.

Method 2. Cut a strip of garment fabric along the selvage, twice the desired finished width of the carriers plus 6 mm, and the total length needed for all carriers. Press under 6 mm on raw edge. Lap selvage over turned edge and stitch in place with an uneven slipstitch, being careful not to stitch through to right side. Take a few securing stitches at beginning and end of each carrier length. Cut strip into carriers.

Method 3. If strips cannot be placed on the selvage, cut a strip of fabric twice the desired width of the finished carrier plus 12 mm, in a length sufficient for all carriers. Press under 6 mm on both long edges. Fold strip in half lengthwise, carefully matching the folded edges. Press. Topstitch close to both edges. Cut strip into the individual lengths needed for each carrier.

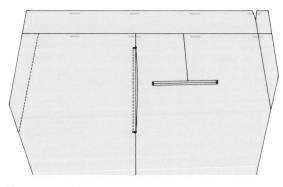

Marking location of carriers: Locate a carrier at centre back, one at each side seam, and halfway between each side seam and centres front and back. Tack a mark 6 mm below top edge of waistband and 6 mm below waistline seam (or lower, if the belt is wider than the waistband).

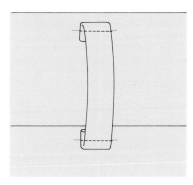

To attach carriers (except at centre back), fold each end under 6 mm; press. Place one fold 3 mm above top waistband mark, the other fold 3 mm below lower mark. Machine-stitch in place.

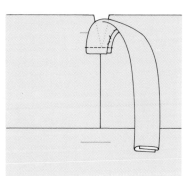

To attach centre back carrier where there is a V-shaped opening at the top of waistband, place one end of the carrier wrong side up just below the end of the V. Stitch across the width of the carrier

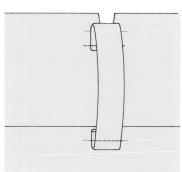

at the bottom of the V-shaped opening, as shown. Bring the carrier down over the waistband, fold the other end under 6 mm, and sew in place below the waistline seam. Press.

Sewing for men and boys/shirts

Making a shirt

Although a man's shirt may seem a masterpiece of precision, it requires little more than regular sewing techniques, very carefully executed.

Listed at the far right are the steps, in order, for constructing a shirt. The numbers after each step are the pages on which an explanation of that technique can be found. Because styles vary, not all steps will apply to every shirt.

The traditional seam choice for men's shirts is the flat-felled seam, preferred because it gives a uniformly clean finish. The fell, or overlap, is usually on the inside of the shirt, the exact opposite of most other applications, in which the flat-felled seam is formed on the right side. The result is one visible row of stitching (rather than two) on the right side of the garment. This and the other recommended techniques ensure that there are no exposed raw edges anywhere in the shirt.

The direction of the fell, or overlap, is very important. On the sleeve seam and the side seam, the overlap goes toward the back; on the shoulder seam, the overlap goes toward the front; on the armhole seam, away from the sleeve.

Checklist/shirt procedure

Adjust pattern fit 113–116, 118–121
Lay out pattern, cut out shirt 96–105
Transfer pattern markings 106
Attach pockets and shirt tabs 287, 289
Attach yoke 384–385
Construct collar: insert collar stays 385; attach interfacing 385; join collar sections 239; attach to band 239; attach band to neckline 240
Construct sleeve plackets 279
Set in the sleeves 269
Stitch underarm seams of sleeves and shirt 269
Construct and attach cuffs 280–281
Hem shirt 306
Make buttonholes 355–357
Attach buttons 361–362

Classic shirt yoke

The classic shirt yoke is fully lined so that all seams are enclosed. In the first of these two techniques, the yoke is topstitched in place along the front seam; it may also be topstitched at the back seam, if you like. The second method uses machine sewing throughout, but no topstitching. It is not difficult, but demands care in positioning for the stitching of front shoulder seams. Make fitting pleat at centre back before starting either yoke.

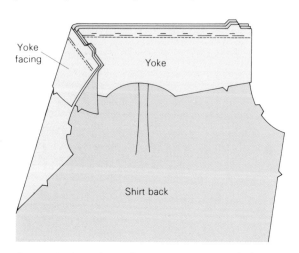

Step 1, both methods: Right sides together, tack the yoke to the shirt back. Tack the right side of the yoke facing to the wrong side of the shirt back. Stitch a 1.5 cm seam, sewing through all three layers. Grade seam allowances, leaving yoke seam allowance the widest. Press yoke and facing up, away from shirt, into yoke's permanent position.

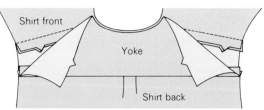

Topstitched method: Topstitch yoke seam if desired (not shown). Tack right side of yoke facing to wrong side of front shoulder seams. Stitch; press seam toward facing. Trim 5 mm

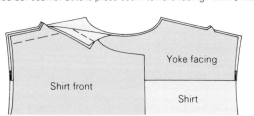

Couture method: Do not topstitch yoke seamline. Tack right side of yoke facing to wrong side of shirt fronts at shoulder seam. Right sides together, match shoulder seams of yoke and

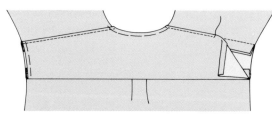

from the yoke shoulder seam; turn under and press the remaining 1 cm. Match folded edge to yoke facing seamline; topstitch. Tack neck and shoulder edges together.

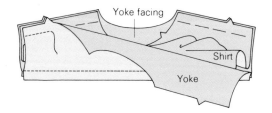

shirt front. (Shirt will be between yoke and yoke facing.) Stitch through yoke, shirt front and yoke facing. Turn shirt to right side and press.

Sewing for men and boys/shirts

Western shirt yoke

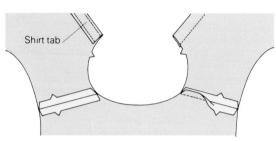

Shirt tab

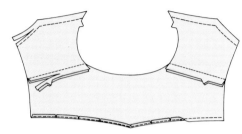

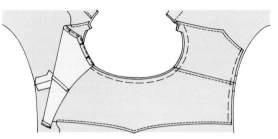

The western-style shirt yoke is basically a big appliqué sewn on over the shoulder area of the shirt. Unlike the traditional yoke, it is not an integral part of the shirt.
1. With wrong sides together, stitch the shoulder seams of the shirt and press them open.

2. Right sides together, stitch yoke sections together at shoulder. Trim and grade, making front seam allowance the widest; press toward back. Stitch on seamline of pointed edges; trim seam allowances to 6 mm. Press under, rolling stitching slightly to underside; clip as needed.

3. Pin yoke to right side of shirt as shown, matching markings and shoulder seams and carefully aligning edges of neck and armholes; tack yoke in place. Topstitch yoke along shoulder seams, then along folded seam allowances on front and back. Tack neck and armhole edges together.

Shirt collar stay

Collar stays are plastic strips with one pointed end that are used to support the front of a collar and prevent the collar point from curling upward.

Stays are an optional detail, but you must decide before beginning collar construction if you will use them. Collar stays are not readily available in shops, but you can make your own quite easily using a sheet of fairly rigid plastic. Cut the stay in the shape illustrated at right, long enough to reach diagonally from the collar roll to the finished collar point (the topstitching, on most collars). Round off the cut edges with an emery board.

Note: Iron-on interfacing cannot be used in a stayed collar, because the pocket for the stay is formed between interfacing and under collar.

1. On the right side of the under collar, centre a stay diagonally between the collar edges at each corner, with the point 1.5 cm from the corner. (Place it 1 cm from the corner if there is to be no topstitching.) Lightly, with a lead pencil, mark each side of the stay. Then mark straight across the end, making mark slightly longer than the width of the stay. Using a ruler, draw parallel lines from the end mark to the collar point.

Tips on making men's ties

1. A tie is cut on the bias, so any fabric choice should be viewed from this angle before purchase. A stripe, for example, will become a diagonal.
2. Because a tie is cut from the bias grain, it is more economical (because it avoids wasted fabric) to purchase an extra 10 centimetres and make two ties from the same piece of fabric.
3. There are two types of interfacing especially for ties; one is made of wool (or a wool and rayon blend) and can be dry-cleaned only; the other is made of synthetic fibres and is washable. If you have to use another type of interfacing, choose one that has a fair amount of body without being too stiff, or use two layers of a type that is of medium weight and softness.
4. When any tie is being worn, the bottom tip should reach to the top of the belt. After determining the proper length for the tie, compare it with that of the pattern adding or subtracting length as needed at the centre seam. Remember to alter the interfacings by the same amount.
5. For easier control in hand-stitching and pressing, cut cardboard pieces to the finished shape of each end of the tie, and place them inside the tie until stitching and pressing are completed.
6. The finished edges of the tie should be rolled, not flattened; do not put the full weight of the iron on the tie while pressing. Use a lightweight press cloth and, holding the iron just above it, allow steam to penetrate for a few seconds.
7. To keep the narrow end in place when the tie is worn, sew a loop of ribbon or fabric to the underside of the wide end about 15 cm from the point. Make the loop equal to the width of the narrow end plus 1 cm. Turn the ends of the loop under 6 mm and slipstitch each in place.

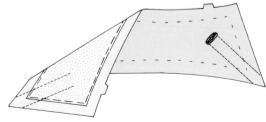

2. The mark at the end of the stay is for a buttonhole. Tack or iron a small square of interfacing onto wrong side of under collar under the buttonhole mark. Make machine or hand-worked buttonholes on right side exactly at mark on under collar. Carefully open buttonholes.

3. Tack interfacing to the wrong side of the under collar. Stitch along the parallel lines so that a pocket is formed for the stay. Complete collar construction. Slip stay into pocket. The end should protrude about 6 mm from the button-hole to permit easy removal for laundering.

385

Sewing for children

Special considerations

There is probably no sewing activity as immediately satisfying as sewing for children. You get quick results, for one thing, because the garments have smaller dimensions. Also, more shortcuts can be taken in techniques. Children's garments should be constructed to survive vigorous activity and endless washings. Other special considerations include providing room for sudden growth spurts, and planning garments that are easy to put on.

Size range charts (in centimetres)

BABIES

Age	Newborn (1–3 months)	6 months
Weight	3–6 kg	6–8 kg
Height	43–61	61–67

TODDLERS'

Size	½	1	2	3	4
Breast or Chest	48	51	53	56	58
Waist	48	50	51	52	53
Approx. height	71	79	87	94	102
Finished dress length	35.5	38	40.5	43	46

CHILDREN'S

Size	1	2	3	4	5	6
Breast or Chest	51	53	56	58	61	64
Waist	50	51	52	53	55	56
Hip	—	—	—	61	64	66
Back waist length	21	22	23	24	25.5	27
Approx. height	79	87	94	102	109	117
Finished length	43	46	48	51	56	61

GIRLS'

Size	7	8	10	12	14
Breast	66	69	73	76	81
Waist	58	60	62	65	67
Hip	69	71	76	81	87
Back waist length	29.5	31	32.5	34.5	36
Approx. height	127	132	142	149	155

CHUBBY

Size	8½c	10½c	12½c	14½c
Breast	76	80	84	88
Waist	71	74	76	79
Hip	84	88	92	96
Back waist length	32	34	35.5	37.5
Approx. height	132	142	149	155

Selecting pattern type and size

Patterns for children's clothes are grouped into several types, intended to reflect in their styling the size and physical development of the average child at certain ages. For purposes of identification, the pattern groupings are named to correspond with the different stages in a child's growth.

You should not assume, however, that just because your child is a toddler, he or she will automatically fit into the toddler size range. A child who is not yet walking may be larger than the largest set of measurements in the toddler range. To make an accurate size selection, you must measure your child and compare his or her individual measurements with those listed for each pattern type to see which type and what size most closely approximates the child's own measurements. The object is to choose a pattern type and size that fits with as few alterations as possible.

The captioned figures below represent the groupings of pattern types for children's wear. (For boys, see p. 370.) To make an accurate choice, measure your child and compare body measurements with those listed in the chart at left to determine which pattern type and size is suitable.

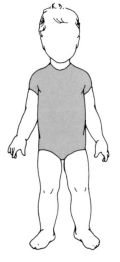

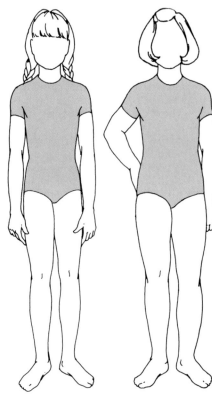

Babies' patterns are for infants who do not yet walk. There is a nappy allowance, and styles are usually suitable for both boys and girls.

Toddlers' sizes are for the stage of development between a baby and a child. A nappy allowance is included, and styles often suit both boys and girls.

Children's sizes have the same breast and waist measurements as Toddlers' but are meant for a taller child, so shoulder, arm and dress lengths are longer.

Girls' sizes are for the figure that has not yet begun to mature. Sizes are comparable to those for boys (see p. 370) but the height is greater for girls.

Chubby sizes are for the growing girl whose weight is above average for her age and height. The height range is approximately the same as for Girls'.

Taking measurements

Two sets of measurements must be taken for children's clothes. One set is used to select the correct pattern size (and to help with alterations); the other is used only for the alterations that may be needed to make the pattern fit better.

When using the two sets of measurements, it is important to remember that the first set is compared with the measurements on the *back of the pattern envelope*, the second set with measurements of the *actual pattern pieces*. When comparing the second set, you will need to know how much you should add for ease; on the first set, ease will be taken care of when differences, if any, between the body and the measurement on the pattern envelope are reconciled. This reconciliation is accomplished through basic pattern alterations.

Another way to check measurements is to compare the pattern's with those of a garment that fits the child well. Otherwise, measure the child over undergarments only. Use a tape measure that will not stretch. Check a child's measurements often; they can change rapidly. Also, height can sometimes increase with no change in circumference.

If a child's measurements fall between sizes, it is generally wiser to choose the larger size. Record measurements on your chart in pencil, to allow for frequent re-recordings as changes occur.

Measurement chart

Measurements for pattern selection

MEASUREMENT	CHILD	PATTERN ENVELOPE	DIFFERENCE
Weight (for babies)			
Height			
Breast			
Waist			
Hips			
Back waist length			
Finished dress length			

Measurements for pattern alterations only

MEASUREMENT	CHILD	PATTERN PIECE	EASE	DIFFERENCE
Arm length			None*	
Shoulder length			None	
Crotch depth			Up to 1 cm	
Pants inseam			Up to 1 cm	
Pants outseam			None	

*For fitted sleeve; add extra length for full sleeve.

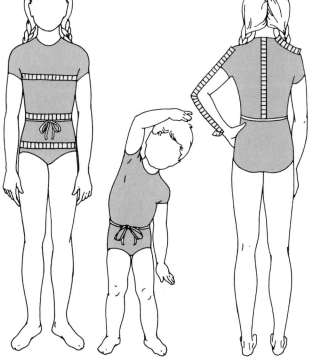

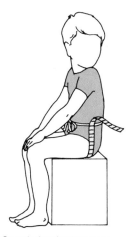

Breast: Under arms over fullest part of chest at front, just under the shoulder blades at back.
Waist: Around natural indentation (tie string around middle and have child bend sideways; the string will settle at the waistline).
Hips: Around fullest part of buttocks.

Back waist length: Prominent bone at base of neck to waist.
Shoulder length: Base of neck (have child shrug shoulders to locate it) to prominent bone at outer shoulder.
Arm length: From top of arm, over bent elbow, to wrist.

Height: Have child stand with back against wall, no shoes. Place ruler on top of head; mark where ruler touches; measure from floor to mark.

Crotch depth: With child seated on a firm chair, feet flat on floor, measure from waist to chair seat. Or measure a pair of pants that fits the child well and subtract the inseam from the outseam.

Sewing for children

Special sewing hints

1. For speed, modifications of mass production techniques can be applied. The basic idea is to group similar tasks, doing as much of one as is practical before changing to another. For example, you might cut out several garments at once; complete as much stitching as possible (even on unrelated units) before pressing; press a number of areas before returning to the machine; set hand work aside for a time when you will be sitting still anyway—when you are watching television, for instance.

2. For durability, substitute machine for hand stitches wherever it is practical and not unsightly to do so. (To tack down facings, for example.)

3. For extra strength, stitch areas of strain, such as armholes, twice.

4. For ease in handling really small garments, attach the sleeves before closing the underarm seam.

5. For ease of care, choose fabrics that are washable; also check the care requirements of white or pastel colours. Although cottons and synthetic blends are usually the first choices for children's garments, washable wools are also suitable.

6. To please the child, pick bright colours and lively prints. Be careful, though, to keep patterns in scale with the child's size. Too large a design can be overwhelming.

7. For convenience, always provide a pocket or two, even if the pattern does not include them. Children like places to keep small possessions.

8. A good safety precaution is to sew reflective tape strips to all outer garments, especially if they are dark in colour. As this tape is available only in large quantities from specialist safety device firms, purchasing a roll might be a worthwhile project for parents' or mothers' groups. The tape can be seen by motorists when children are outdoors during twilight and after dark.

9. To make a handed-down garment different for the younger brother or sister, add a special appliqué, pocket or monogram. Also, consider changing the garment's style: could a dress with sleeves be made into a pinafore dress for the new owner?

Providing room to grow

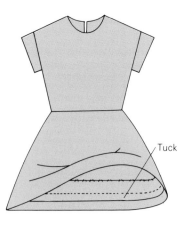

Three ways are described on this page to build some provision for sudden growth spurts into children's garments. The adjoining page tells how to add life to outgrown or worn garments.

A hem tuck introduces extra fabric into a skirt or dress hem without adding too much extra bulk. Illustration at the left shows how the finished garment looks from the right side.

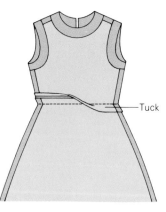

A bodice tuck is a way of providing extra length in the waist-to-shoulder area. This tuck is made before the zipper is inserted; to release the tuck, zipper stitching must be taken out to the bottom of the placket. The extra length that the released tuck adds to the centre back seam will make the zipper space too long. To remedy this, sew up a part of the seam at placket bottom equal to tuck depth. Re-stitch zipper.

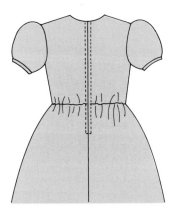

An expandable waistline can be made for any garment by adding extra fabric to the waistline, then controlling the fit with elastic. This is particularly suited to children's wear because it makes movement less constricted as well as allowing for growth. The elastic is generally put only in the back waist seam. Omit any darts in the back bodice or skirt.

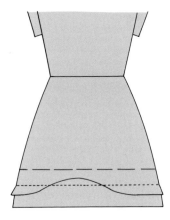

To make a hem tuck, add 2 to 10 cm of extra hem allowance when cutting garment. Mark hemline, then make the tuck within hem allowance, far enough above the hem edge so that it will not show. Sew tuck with the most easily removed stitch on your machine. Complete the hem; press tuck toward hemline. To lengthen garment, release the tuck stitching and either re-stitch a narrower tuck or use all of the tuck allowance.

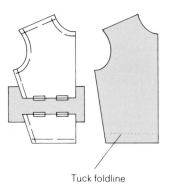

Tuck foldline

To make a bodice tuck, add 4 cm to bodice length; cut out garment. On the wrong side of each bodice section, mark a tuck foldline 2 cm above waist seam. Stitch bodice to skirt, then fold along tuck foldline and press. With skirt up, tack through waist seam and folded bodice. Machine-stitch just below waist seamline, using most easily removed stitch. Press tuck and seam allowances toward bodice.

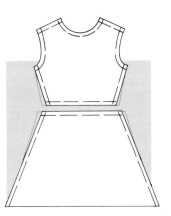

To make such a waistline, first add 1 cm to the side seams at waist, front and back, on bodice and skirt. Taper to original cutting line at hip and chest. Construct garment as usual; it will be about 4 cm too big in the waist. Sew a casing of bias binding to the back waist seam allowances; insert a length of narrow elastic (this will pull in the waistline); secure elastic ends at centre back and side seams.

Snap fasteners and snap fastener tape 17   **Slip hemming 139**
Hemming with banding 313

Extending garment life

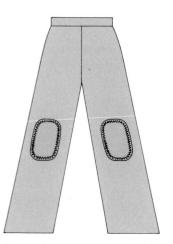
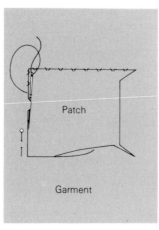

To lengthen a garment with little or no extra hem allowance, you can add a band of fabric. It could be a matching or contrasting plain fabric, or a harmonising print. (See Hem finishes for methods of adding bands.) This same technique will work equally well for lengthening sleeves at the lower edges.

To repair worn pants or make pants knees last longer, fuse a patch to the outside of the pants over the knee area. Use iron-on patches or scraps of fabric bonded to the garment with fusible web. After fusing, stitch around the outside edges of the patch with a decorative machine or hand stitch.

Insert a patch into a worn or torn area by first cutting away the damaged areas, then sewing new fabric in its place. Cut the worn spot into a square; clip 6 mm into each corner; press edges under 6 mm all around. Place patch under hole, matching grain or design; slip-hem folded edges to patch.

Active wear

Tracksuits – sweatshirts or T-shirts worn with trackpants – make comfortable and attractive wear for boys and girls of all ages. With no buttons or zippers, they are easy for even small children to put on and take off. They are quick to sew and their loose, simple shapes mean no fitting is needed. Several garments can

also be made at one time, using mass production methods. The range of fabric weights and colours now available means they can mix and match to create a variety of outfits, and single items can be easily replaced as they wear out. Easy laundering and no ironing make tracksuits easy to care for as well.

Making garments easy to put on and take off

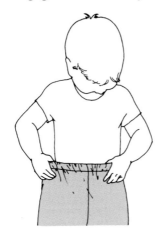

Elasticised pull-on pants and skirts can be managed by even young toddlers (sewing is easy, too). If garment front and back are different, mark back with ribbon or tape.

Hook and loop tape makes dressing easy for little ones, as fastening needs little dexterity. The tape can be sewn on in a long strip or in smaller pieces at button spacing.

A pinafore with a low neck and deep armholes is simple to pull on and off. Its easy fit makes it comfortable on hot days, and on cooler days, a T-shirt can be worn underneath.

No-sew snaps are the easiest type for small fingers to cope with, and they have good holding power. Use single snap fasteners for spot closings and snap fastener tape for plackets.

Sewing for children

Necklines

For necklines on children's garments, special finishes are recommended. Some are advised because they are easier to handle with the tiny neck seams and neck openings. A **bias finish** is simpler to work with than a tiny facing. A **combination facing** incorporates what would be three small neck and armhole facings into one facing of manageable size. It must be applied while the centre back seam is still open or the garment cannot be turned right side out. Some finishes are preferred just for their charm and appropriateness—**scallops,** for example, at the necklines of little girls' clothes.

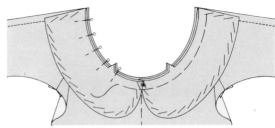

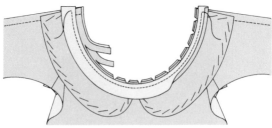

A bias finish for a neckline with collar is much easier to work with than a shaped facing on very small sizes. Construct collar and tack it to garment neckline. Cut a strip of 12 mm bias binding to fit neckline seam (or a true bias strip, 2.5 cm wide, from collar fabric). Tack to the neck seam, using 6 mm seam allowance. Stitch neckline; trim, grade and clip seam allowances. Turn under remaining edge of bias 6 mm and press. (This edge in purchased tape is already pressed.) Slipstitch the bias to the inside of the garment at neckline seam.

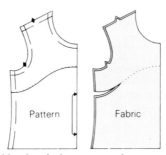

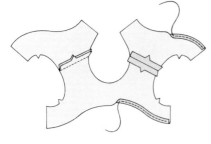

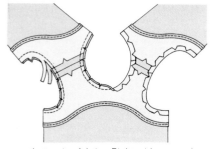

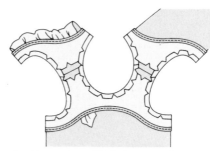

Combination facings are cut from patterns for garment front and back. Measure and mark several points 8 cm below neck edge and armhole; connect marks with curved lines. Lay pattern on fabric and transfer the curved lines with dressmaker's carbon paper. Cut out neck, shoulder and armhole edges; remove pattern and cut curved lines. Stitch and press garment darts and shoulder seams. Stitch and press facing shoulder seams. Seam-finish lower edges in a way that suits fabric. Right sides together, stitch facing to garment at neckline and armholes. Trim, grade and clip seam allowances. Press seams toward facing. Turn garment right side out by pulling backs of garment through shoulders to front. Lift facings away from garment and stitch side seams of garment and facings in one continuous seam; press open. Tack facings to seam allowances at underarm and to zipper at centre back.

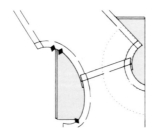

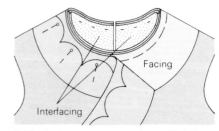

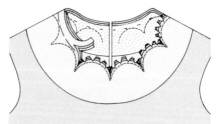

Scalloped edges begin with a paper pattern. Pin front and back pattern pieces together, overlapping and aligning the shoulder seams. Trace the neck seamline onto tissue paper. Calculate the size and number of scallops that will fit along the seamline, keeping scallop size proportionate to the garment. Height of scallop should be about one-third its width at base. Draw scallops with curves at seamline, using a sewing gauge. Centre pattern at front so that finished edges are at centre back. Tack interfacing to wrong side of garment at neck edge. Right sides together, tack neck facing to garment; pin tissue pattern on right side of garment over facing with scallop edges at seamline. Stitch through tissue and all fabric layers, using small (2 mm) stitches. Remove tissue. Trim, grade and notch curves; clip to stitch line at points. Turn all scallops right side out and press carefully.

Making a child's coat

Making a child's coat can be a real money-saver. It is worth investing in a durable fabric so that the coat can be handed on to another child. To make the coat adaptable for both boys and girls, work buttonholes on both sides (see below, right).

Because there is relatively little shaping in a child's coat, there is no need for the time-consuming traditional methods of shaping a tailored garment. A machine method for attaching the lining is not only quicker, it is more secure; it actually stands up better to active wear.

Interfacing can be done with iron-on fabrics, which should be chosen according to the coat fabric weight and the function the interfacing is to perform. For light to mediumweight coat fabric, use soft to medium grade iron-on interfacing; for a heavy coat fabric, use firm grade. With firm grade, it may be advisable to trim away all seam allowances and across corners of interfacing before use.

A quick hemming method for sleeves is to use fusible web. Before using this method, however, consider whether you might later wish to alter the sleeve length; it is best to fuse hems only when you do not expect to change them. Fusing directions here are general; for specific directions, see information accompanying the product.

Special techniques for making a child's coat are discussed on this page; refer to the checklist at the right for techniques covered elsewhere.

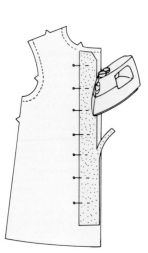

Gently anchor interfacing in place with the tip of the iron. Take care not to press over pins. Remove all pins, then lay a dampened press cloth over the whole interfacing section and press with an iron set for wool. The iron should be held in place for at least ten seconds. It is important to allow each piece to dry thoroughly before handling it—the garment piece will retain the shape in which it dries.

Checklist / child's coat procedure

Adjust pattern fit 113–121	
Lay out pattern, cut out coat 96–105	
Cut out lining 92, 100–101	
Transfer pattern markings 106	
Attach interfacing 391	
Stitch side, shoulder and under collar seams 156–158	
Attach under collar, upper collar and facings 224–227	
Set in sleeves 268	
Fuse sleeve hems 391; sew hem 302–309	
Make lining 391; attach lining 391	
Make buttonholes 355–358; attach buttons 361–362	

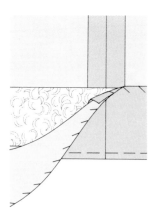

To fuse a sleeve hem, first decide the sleeve length and hem depth; seam-finish the fabric edge using an appropriate method. Cut fusible web to a width 1 cm less than the hem depth and long enough to go around the hem. Following the manufacturer's instructions, fuse hem in place. Press sleeves over narrow end of sleeve board or a sturdy cardboard tube.

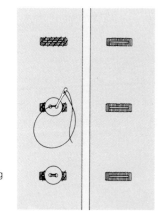

Dual buttonholes–that is, separate sets worked on both the left and right sides of the garment–can greatly lengthen the garment's life. Open buttonholes only on the side where they are needed, and sew buttons right over the unopened ones. If the coat is handed on to a child of the opposite sex, the closed set can be opened and the other set closed with tiny whipstitches. Buttons can then be re-attached over the newly closed set.

Lining the coat

It is advisable to choose a pattern for a coat with a lining, as this will help keep the garment's shape and provide extra warmth. The lining should fit smoothly within the garment, providing a neat, clean inside finish. At the lining stage, all construction on the coat should be complete, including hems and tacking in place of front facings.

Do all lining construction by machine, including setting in of sleeves and formation of centre back pleat, if pattern calls for one. Press all seams open. Fuse the lining hem into place, after measuring and adjusting it to hang 3 cm above the coat hemline.

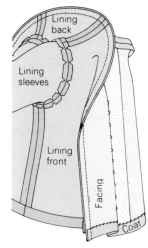

Pin lining to coat facings with right sides together, beginning at the hem on one front and ending at the opposite front hemline. Match shoulder seams and centre back. Stitch with a 1.5 cm seam. Clip all curves. Press seam allowances toward the lining.

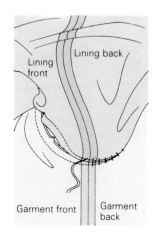

The lining is tacked to the coat at the underarm armhole seams to keep the lining in place. Lift the lining up at side seams so that underarm area of armhole seams is exposed. Match the seamlines of lining and coat at underarm; make sure seam allowances are all going toward sleeve. With a double thread, whipstitch lining seamline to coat seamline. Use French tacks between lining and coat hems at side seams. Whipstitch front facings to coat hem.

Sewing for children

Encouraging children to sew

It is likely that when a child sees you working at your sewing machine, especially if you are making something for him or her, the youngster will show an interest in learning to sew. The way you treat the first spark of interest can make all the difference to the child's future attitude toward sewing. Nurture this curiosity by answering questions as patiently as possible and by initiating simple sewing projects that the child can complete with a sense of achievement.

What projects a child can do will depend on the diligence and physical abilities he or she brings to them. Some children will spend more time with their sewing, and do more of it, so their capabilities will develop faster than those of children whose attention tends to wander. Also, some youngsters will be able to cut out intricate shapes, while others of the same age will be doing well to manage simple hand stitches.

Just when to start a young person using the sewing machine depends on the individual child's coordination and desire, but around nine years old is usually a good time. It is a good idea to approach the machine as part of a whole project, where the preparation has been done by the child, and there is a specific goal in view. At first, children need constant and patient adult supervision at the machine to make sure their fingers are not caught under the needle, and to ensure encouraging results.

Stitches and projects for different age groups

AGE	STITCHES TO LEARN	SUITABLE MATERIALS	SUGGESTED PROJECTS
2–3	None	Spools, trim and fabric scraps, zippers, fabric glue	Free play Make a collage
4–5	Simple embroidery, such as cross stitch, outline	Sewing cards: large needlepoint canvas, tapestry needle, wool	Embroidered pictures
	Sewing buttons	Medium to large buttons Large needle Wool	Sew buttons on a toy or favourite garment
6–7	Basic hand stitches, such as whipstitch, running stitch, backstitch	Felt Cotton fabrics that are not too tightly woven	Pocket animals Spectacle case Dolls' clothes Bib Patchwork Longstitch sampler
8–9	Advanced embroidery stitches, such as chainstitch, blanket stitch, buttonhole stitch Begin use of standard sewing machine, plain straight seams	Linen Cotton Terry cloth (woven) Needlepoint canvas Washable soft toy filling	Cushion cover Potholder Tote bag Tapestry Stuffed toys
10–12	Progress with sewing machine techniques —curved seams, gathers, casings or hems	Cottons and cotton blends	Simple-to-sew pattern, such as skirt, pull-on pants, shorts

Sample projects

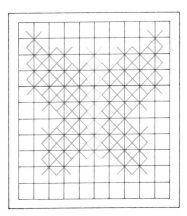

Sewing cards are made with the needlepoint canvas that has the fewest holes per centimetre (often called quickpoint canvas). Bind raw edges with masking tape. Using coloured marking pens, draw a simple stitch pattern on the canvas. The child stitches over markings with blunt needle and wool.

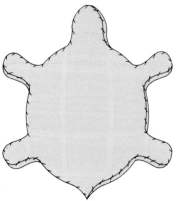

Pocket animals are made by cutting a bottom and top of a simple, familiar animal shape. The child sews the top and bottom pieces together (wrong sides of fabric together), leaving a small opening for stuffing. Good stitches for young hands: whipstitch and blanket stitch. After stuffing, sew up the opening.

A simple garment is a good first project at the sewing machine. It should have few pattern pieces, no set-in sleeves, and casings instead of shaped facings or waistbands. Teach the child to use fusible web for hems, or machine stitch; hand-stitch control is not likely to be good enough for a really invisible hem.

Sewing for the home is both enjoyable and economical, and it requires just the same basic skills as sewing for yourself and your family. This chapter gives you tips on dealing with the large fabric quantities required, as well as guidance on the choice of fabric, how to take measurements, estimate fabric quantities and make patterns, as well as how to choose what will best suit your home. The home decorating projects included here begin with loose-covers for chairs, followed by cushion covers and pillow cases. For the bedroom, there are bedspreads, bedcovers, and quilt covers. For beautiful windows throughout the house, you will find detailed instructions on how to make all kinds of curtains, draperies and blinds. Whether you are revitalising an existing decorating scheme, or starting from scratch in your new home, you will find here the style to suit your taste as well as all the techniques for achieving a professional look.

Advance considerations

In this chapter, you will find various methods for making major home decorating items—loose-covers, cushion covers, bedspreads, curtains and draperies. Sewing for the home calls for the same basic skills as dressmaking does, but they are often applied differently. For example, the 'pattern' for cutting out loose-cover fabric may be the uphol-stered chair or sofa being covered. With curtains and draperies, it will be a set of key measurements.

In most home decorating projects, you must re-member to add your own seam and hem allow-ances. Some techniques normally done by hand are here better done by machine, for example, hems in loose-covers, curtains and draperies. The machine not only does such jobs faster, but the results are more durable.

Often large quantities of fabric must be handled, and the working area should be modified or enlarg-ed to accommodate the extra bulk. It is also helpful to arrange things so that the sewing machine, the work area and the project being worked on are close to each other.

CHOOSING FABRICS

Certain fabrics are made specially for sewing for the home. Generally classified as 'decorator fabrics', they are usually at least 120 cm wide and often are treated to resist creases, stains or fading. Fabrics meant for use in clothing, if they share these same qualities, are just as appropriate.

Choosing the correct fabric for any project means relating the fabric's weight and weave to the day-to-day wear the fabric will get, the construction methods that will be used, and the final appearance you want from it.

Fabric for a loose-cover, for instance, should be closely woven and heavy enough to hold its shape. If the fabric is also treated to resist creases and stains, it will be practical as well as durable. The fabric's design is also a factor. Loose-cover fabric might well be cut into pieces of many sizes, causing the design to look very different from the way it did as uncut fabric. The best way to picture the effect is to test-drape a large swatch of fabric over the areas to be covered.

Test curtain or drapery fabric by holding it up to the window to see how its design and texture look when they are backlit. Sheers, semisheers and open weaves will filter the light gently. If you want to block the light, choose an opaque fabric or consider adding a lining to make the fabric more opaque at the window. Drape the fabric in folds as you test to check its appearance as a window covering. Fabrics for curtains and draperies should also be resistant to sun fading.

Bedspreads, curtains and draperies are most effective when constructed with a minimum of seams. The best choice, to provide a large, unbroken expanse of fabric, is a fabric with a generous width. Wide fabrics are the most economical, as a rule, for any major home sewing project.

Consider also how the colour, design and texture of the fabric will blend with the rest of the room. This becomes very important when the item being made is massive or will span a large area. Be sure, too, that the fabric suits the mood of the room. It will help, when shopping for new fabric, to carry samples of fabrics already in the room. You can often get a sample by carefully trimming a scrap from a seam allowance or hem. If this cannot be managed, buy a small swatch of the fabric you are considering and test it at home before making a final purchase. Such testing is a good precaution in any case because the light in the store may well be different from that in your room.

Finally, is the fabric's cost in proportion to the value you put on the project? A fabric must be right for its purpose, and durable enough to justify the time you spend sewing. But you may want more from bedroom than from kitchen curtains, for example, and be willing to invest more in them.

EQUIPMENT AND SUPPLIES

In addition to your basic equipment, you should consider other tools that might come in handy when sewing for the home. For example, you can cut upholstery fabrics better and more comfortably with heavy-duty shears. When fitting a loose-cover to a chair, use long (3 cm) coloured-head pins or T-pins—their length and large heads make it easier to pin heavy fabrics together and to pin fabric to upholstery.

A carpenter's folding rule is ideal for long, straight, above-the-floor measurements for cur-tains and draperies. For curves, use a flexible rule or tape measure.

There are also supplies designed specially for home decorating—some to be stronger, others to stream-line construction or to give a quality finish to your project. Examples of such special items are cushion forms for making covered cushions; metal weights that, when sewn to the bottom of curtains, will make them hang properly; pleater tapes and hooks for easy construction and automatic pleating of both curtains and draperies; co-ordinated trims to give a professional look to your room.

SEWING

You will undoubtedly use your sewing machine more often than usual when sewing for your home, because so much traditional hand work can be done by machine—hemming, for example. To use your machine to its fullest, investigate feet and attach-ments available for it that can save you time.

These are just a few useful examples. A zipper foot is indispensable for inserting a zipper or form-ing corded seams. The narrow hemmer foot enables you to stitch a narrow rolled hem fast and effici-ently, with neat results. An adjustable seam gauge or a quilter guide-bar is helpful if you are stitching a wider-than-normal seam allowance.

The gathering foot makes quick work of gather-ing long lengths of fabric. The binder attachment lets you stitch a binding to a raw edge in one opera-tion, without pinning. A roller foot or other 'top feed' assist attachment can help to make difficult fabrics feed evenly; a 'no snag' foot is good for open weave fabrics.

The appropriate seaming method can vary, de-pending on your fabric and the project you are engaged in. For most situations, a plain seam is all that is required; it can be seam-finished if necessary. If the fabric is a sheer, say a voile for kitchen cur-tains, a French seam is recommended. A flat-felled seam is valuable mainly as a sturdy seam for heavy fabrics, but it also gives an attractive informal look to fabrics of other weights. It is best confined to straight seams.

For any sewing, choose the proper needle, thread and stitch length for the fabric. Test and adjust ten-sion before starting, and whenever the items being sewn are changed. Be sure to use the proper foot pressure, especially when matching motifs at seams or stitching extra-long fabric lengths.

What you will need

A loose-cover is a practical and economical way to restore a worn piece of furniture or to give it a new look. If the loose-cover is to be a replacement for an old cover, an easy way to cut the new one is to take the original apart and use the resulting pieces, first for a trial layout to determine the amount of fabric needed, and then as patterns for cutting the new loose-cover.

If you are starting afresh, fabric requirements are ascertained by measuring the piece of furniture (see below), then adding various amounts for any specific requirements of the fabric, for the loose-cover's skirt, and for making cording for the seams if necessary (see next page). The fabric is pinned directly to the furniture to develop the sections that make up the loose-cover. An advantage of this method is that it allows for the fitting of any irregularities in the furniture's shape.

In a third cutting method for a loose-cover, you first make a trial loose-cover in calico, then use the calico pieces as a pattern.

In choosing a fabric, the basic requirements are that it be sturdy, resistant to dirt and easily cleaned. Generally, a mediumweight fabric is better than a heavy one because it is easier to handle where several layers must be joined, and adds less bulk when layered over upholstery. To check your fabric choice for colour and design, take home a small swatch (about 0.2 of a metre or one design motif) and drape it over the furniture. Some stores will lend you a sample; if your store will not, a swatch could prove a good investment by preventing a costly mistake.

In addition to the fabric, you will need thread and machine needles suitable for it, and heavy-duty loose-cover zippers for both the loose-cover and cushions (see p. 399 for length requirements). If the loose-cover will not have a skirt, get either snap fastener tape or hook and loop tape, or tacks, to secure the loose-cover to the frame. Other items that you might need are cable cord for the cording, seam or cotton tape to reinforce occasional seams, and T-pins. T-pins are better than regular straight pins because they are heavier and longer, and their tops are easier to hold for this kind of pinning.

Taking measurements

An estimate of the fabric needed for a loose-cover can be arrived at by measuring the piece of furniture to be covered. The three key measurements to take are shown and explained at the right; the tape direction corresponds to the lengthwise grain of the fabric. Extra fabric will be needed for matching or special placement, for making cording and for a gathered or pleated skirt (p. 396). Add these extra amounts to the basic measurement to get the total amount required.

Record all measurements on a chart similar to the one below. If you need to convert the centimetre measurements to metres, move the decimal point back two places.

Measurements for total quantity	cm	m
Measurement A_____ x_____ sections		
Measurement B_____ x __2__ (both arms)		
Measurement C_____ x_____ cushions		
Allowance for special fabric needs		
Allowance for covering cord		
Allowance for skirt		
Total		

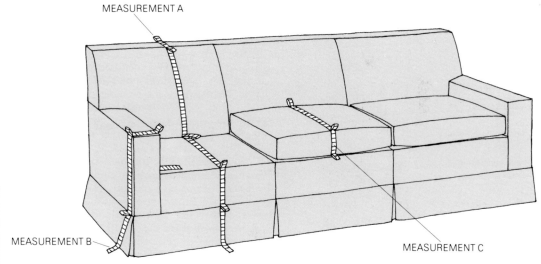

MEASUREMENT A

MEASUREMENT B

MEASUREMENT C

Measurement A (back and front): Remove cushion. *For cover with skirt,* measure from floor at back, over furniture top, then down to floor at front; add 30 cm for tuck-in, 5 cm for each seam crossed, and an allowance for skirt finish. *For cover without skirt,* measure just to bottom edges of furniture; add 28 cm for facings. For a wide piece (sofa), multiply length by number of fabric widths needed.

Measurement B (sides and arms): *For cover with skirt,* measure from inside arm at seat, over the arm, then to floor at side; add 15 cm for tuck-in, 5 cm for each seam crossed, and an allowance for skirt finish. *For cover without skirt,* measure just to the bottom edge of furniture and add 14 cm for facing. Double either of these measurements to arrive at total length needed for both arms.

Measurement C (cushions): Measure around the entire cushion from the back to the front; add 5 cm for each seam crossed by the tape measure. For two or more cushions the same size and shape, multiply this total by the number of cushions that need to be covered. For cushions of varying sizes, measure each cushion separately, then add all of these measurements together.

Loose-covers

Special fabric considerations

Basic fabric needs are estimated by measuring the furniture to be covered (see the preceding page). Some adjustments may be needed in this basic estimate because of the construction, design or width of the fabric, as well as for variations in loose-cover style. The following should be considered before any fabric is actually purchased.

The width of many upholstery and loose-covering fabrics is 120 cm, which is usually sufficient for each lengthwise section of a chair or sofa. If the fabric is narrower, more than one fabric length might be needed for each section; if the fabric is very wide, less than the full width of a fabric length might suffice. If a section should take less

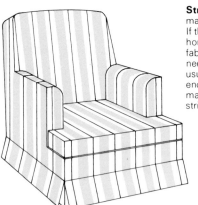

Stripes need to be matched at seams. If the stripe is horizontal, extra fabric length is needed; fabric is usually wide enough to permit matching of vertical stripes.

Motifs on fabrics should be placed at strategic points on the various sections of the loose-cover. Such positioning will requre extra fabric.

than a full fabric width, the excess may be usable on the front of an arm, as a boxing strip, and so on. Before buying your fabric and while measuring your furniture, carefully appraise both fabric and furniture to see if a smaller amount will do. Be careful, though, not to skimp.

An extra amount will be needed when the fabric has a large motif that must be centred strategically on the loose-cover, or a horizontally striped design that must be matched at the seamlines. The supplementary amount is usually the length of one extra motif for each section of the loose-cover.

If the seams of the loose-cover are to be corded, extra fabric is required to cover the cord. For an average-sized chair, allow 1 metre; for a large chair, 1.4 m; for a sofa, 1.8 m. The cord requirement can be calculated by measuring the seams of the upholstery. If you want to cover the cording in a fabric other than the loose-cover fabric, this amount is of course a separate quantity.

The amount needed for a skirt depends on the style of the skirt and the method chosen for finishing its lower edge (see pp. 400–401). Skirts can be plain, pleated or gathered. Two measurements are necessary, total skirt length and total skirt width.

Total skirt length is the finished skirt length (the distance from the floor to the seamline where the skirt is joined to the loose-cover), plus a 2.5 cm top seam allowance, plus an allowance for finishing the lower edge.

Total skirt width is the finished skirt width (equal to the measurement of the skirt's top seamline) plus allowances for pleats or gathers, plus 2.5 cm seam allowances for finishing ends and joining fabric lengths. To arrive at the approximate number of fabric lengths that are needed to produce the total skirt width, divide the width of the fabric that is being used into the total skirt width.·

The illustrations at the right show a range of typical furniture types that lend themselves to loose-covering; the adjoining captions give the approximate amounts of fabric that would be needed to cover each one.

These measurements are intended to give you an idea of the different amounts needed for different types of furniture. They are not intended to replace actual measurement of the piece of furniture you are going to cover.

Approximate quantities

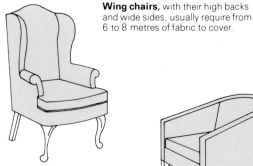

Wing chairs, with their high backs and wide sides, usually require from 6 to 8 metres of fabric to cover.

Occasional chairs are small chairs which usually need 4 to 5.5 metres of fabric.

Club chairs can take from about 5.5 to 7 metres of fabric.
Ottoman like the one shown requires about 1.8 metres.

Small sofas can require multiple lengths of fabric. Amounts average 7 to 9 metres.

Sofas call for multiple fabric lengths. Requirement is usually about 10 to 13 metres.

Fitting and cutting loose-covers / the unit method

An accurate way to make a loose-cover is to use the piece of furniture being covered as a guide, fitting and cutting each section to correspond to the seams of the furniture's upholstery. With this method, the fabric is pinned to the furniture with its right side out. This permits precise placement of the fabric's motifs, matching of fabric at seamlines and accurate fitting of any of the furniture's irregularities.

Although some loose-covers will have more seams and sections than others, most can be divided into units, and the units cut, fitted and sewn in the following order: (1) **top and inside back,** (2) **seat platform and apron,** (3) **arms,** (4) **outside back,** (5) **cushion** and (6) **skirt.**

The general procedure is to pin the fabric to the centre of a section, then smooth it toward each side, then upward and downward, keeping the grain-lines straight and pinning to the furniture as you progress. Lengthwise grain should run from top to bottom of each vertical section, from back to front of horizontal sections (cushions).

Cut out the section, allowing 2.5 cm seam allowances on all edges, and tuck-ins (extra fabric) where necessary. Tuck-ins are needed at points where movement occurs when furniture is sat upon—where back and arms meet at the seat plat-form, for example, or where wing and back meet in a wing chair.

If fabric is plain and of a solid colour, you can mark and remove each section after its fitting. It is better, however, to pin the entire loose-cover before removing any part of it, especially when the fabric requires careful placement of a motif or matching at the seamlines.

Where two or more sections must be cut identically, such as the top and bottom of a cushion, you can cut one and then unpin it to use as a pattern for cutting the other. When the other piece is cut, pin-fit all of the sections to check their fit.

When the fabric has a motif, centre it on the front and the back and on each side of the arms, a little bit more than halfway up from the centre point. Centre a motif on each side of a cushion so that it becomes reversible.

With directional fabrics (naps, one-way prints), be sure to place fabric consistently on all sections—from top to floor on vertical sections, from back to front on horizontal sections.

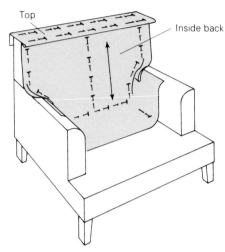

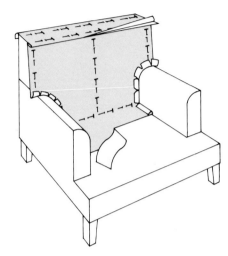

Top and inside back: With right side out and lengthwise grain running vertically, drape fabric over top and back. (Centre design if necessary.) Pin in place down centre. Then working from the centre out, smooth fabric until it is taut and pin at sides. Leaving a 5 cm fold between back and top, pin fabric across top; pin along seamline.

Leaving 2.5 cm seam allowances, trim the back of the top, the sides and the arms (if tuck-ins are necessary between back and arms, allow an extra 8 cm of fabric). Clip and notch seam allowances where this is necessary for fabric to fit. Trim at seat, allowing 15 cm for tuck-in. Cut fabric along fold between top and inside back.

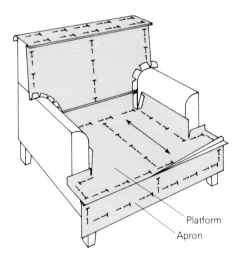

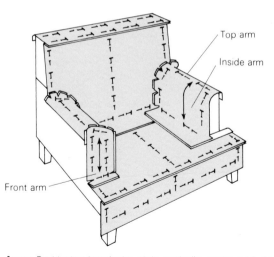

Seat platform and apron: Allowing 15 cm to extend up the back, position fabric on seat as was done for inside back. Leaving a 5 cm fold between seat and apron, pin fabric to apron. At back and arms, trim fabric, allowing 15 cm for tuck-ins. Trim other edges, except bottom, to 2.5 cm seam allowances (5 cm at bottom). Cut along fold at seat and apron.

Arms: Positioning lengthwise grain vertically, centre and pin fabric to top of arm, then down inside of arm. Trim all edges that do not need tuck-ins to 2.5 cm seam allowances (at seat, allow 15 cm for tuck-in; if tuck-in is needed at back of arm, allow 8 cm). Position and pin fabric to front of arm; trim to 2.5 cm seam allowances. *(Continued next page)*

Loose-covers

Fitting and cutting loose-covers/the unit method (continued)

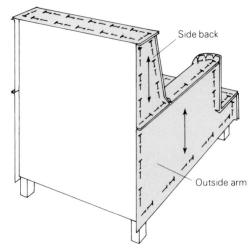

Side back

Outside arm

Outside arm and side back: Depending on upholstery seams, these may be cut as one piece, or as two (shown). With the lengthwise grain vertical, drape fabric down arm, then up side back (if two pieces, allow an extra 5 cm between). Centre as needed; pin. Trim edges, allowing 2.5 cm for seams (5 cm at bottom). If necessary, cut along fold between sections.

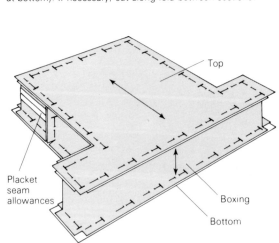

Top

Placket seam allowances

Boxing

Bottom

Cushion: Placing lengthwise grain as shown, centre and pin fabric on cushion top (match motif with rest of loose-cover). Cut, leaving 2.5 cm seam allowances. Cut an identical piece for cushion bottom; pin in place. Cut and fit boxing pieces; allow for two placket seam allowances at centre of piece to contain zipper. Trim edges to 2.5 cm seam allowances.

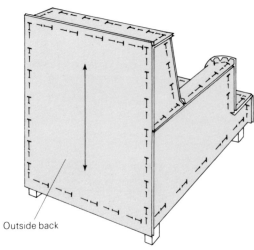

Outside back

Outside back: With the lengthwise grain vertical, drape the fabric down the back. Centre the fabric and pin it down the centre. Working from the centre, smooth the fabric toward the sides and top and bottom edges, pinning as you progress. Trim the top and side edges, providing for 2.5 cm seam allowances; trim bottom edge, leaving a 5 cm seam allowance.

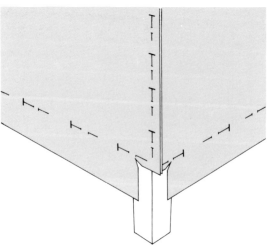

At each leg: After checking to see that all sides of the loose-cover fit and are pulled taut, re-pin the entire bottom edge of the loose-cover. At each leg, trim away fabric, leaving 1 cm seam allowances and forming a three-sided edge as shown. Clip diagonally into corners of top seam allowance, being careful not to clip beyond seamline.

Special shaping techniques

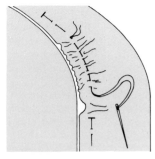

Gathering is one way to control fullness at a curve. Pin both layers of fabric along seamline up to curved area. Then, using a double thread, place hand-gathering stitches along seamline of edge to be gathered. Draw up on fabric to fit other fabric edge; secure gathers.

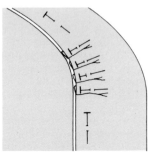

Folds can also be used to control fullness around a curve. Pin both fabric layers up to the curved area. Then, working from the centre out, form narrow, equal folds along the longer fabric edge until it fits the shorter edge. Pin folds in place.

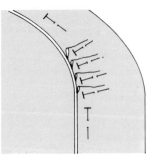

Darts are another method of controlling fullness at curved edges. Pin fabric layers together up to the curved area. Then, working from the centre out, form narrow, equal darts in the longer fabric edge to fit it to the shorter edge. Pin darts in place.

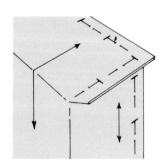

A mitre can be formed to shape a continuous piece of fabric around a corner. With lengthwise grain placed as shown, pin fabric to sections on both sides of corner. Then pin the fabric along the corner. Trim excess fabric to the 2.5 cm seam allowances.

Needle / thread / stitch length selection 27
Seams 156–161, 165, 167
Making cording 310–312
Centred zipper application 330

Preparing to sew

After the loose-cover has been satisfactorily fitted and pinned, mark the seamlines (see the adjoining drawing and explanation). It may also be useful to label each section by writing its name and location on a piece of paper or tape and placing the label on the top seam allowance.

Arrange the work area so that the furniture being worked on is reasonably near the sewing machine. To support the quantity of fabric you will be handling, it is helpful to have a large table at the machine. If your machine is a portable, set it on the table; if the machine is in a cabinet, move the table to the side or back of the machine as necessary.

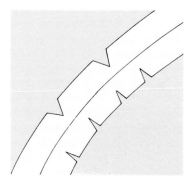

Mark seamlines by spreading seam allowances open and running chalk down seamlines. Every 8 to 10 cm make a mark perpendicular to the seamline; these serve as matching points, much like the notches in ready-made patterns.

Sewing the loose-cover

The most accurate way to sew loose-covers is to handle one unit at a time. Remove a unit from the furniture and unpin the pieces. Lay them out flat and trim the seam allowances even. Stitch the unit together and put it back in place to make sure that it fits the furniture and the adjoining units. Then remove, stitch and check the next unit.

Where possible, it is best to use corded seams. They are stronger than plain seams and better define a loose-cover's edges. To construct the required quantity of cording (welting), cut continuous bias strips, then cover the cord. For all stitching, use a needle, thread and stitch length suitable for the fabric. Shorten the stitch length around curves and corners.

It is best to apply the cording to the half of the seam that needs control and staystitch the other seamline. For instance, apply the cording to larger rather than smaller sections; cord the gathered seamline rather than the ungathered one. As the cording is being applied, clip and notch its seam allowances so that it will fit around curves and corners. Where ends of cording meet, treat them as explained below. When constructing a corded seam, use a zipper foot and place successive rows of stitching between the preceding row and the seamline bringing each row closer to the seamline.

Form plain seams where seams will not be corded—joining boxing pieces, for example. Trim, grade, clip or notch seam allowances where necessary; press all seams open; seam-finish as needed. Leave placket seam of loose-cover open for zipper.

The zipper of a cushion cover should be inserted in a part of the boxing before the boxing unit is formed. For reinforcement, tape the seams at the ends of any zipper placket.

Applying zippers

On a chair cover, the zipper is usually applied to a side back seam; on a sofa cover, to one or both side back seams. If the sofa will stand against a wall the zipper can be installed in one or two of the lengthwise seams between loose-cover sections.

A zipper should span at least three-quarters of the seam and should not extend into the skirt. The zipper for a cushion cover should be at the back of the boxing unit, and should be long enough to go across the back and around at least one corner.

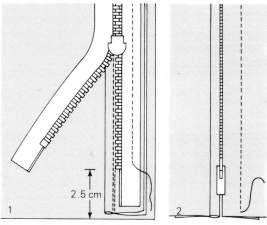

Zipper at loose-cover back: (1) Open zipper. With face down and top stop 2.5 cm above bottom seamline, place teeth along stitching that holds cording. Stitch. (2) Turn back corded edge; close zipper. Turn under and butt other placket edge to cording; stitch other zipper half to this edge.

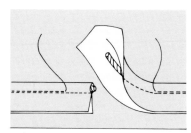

When cording ends meet, start stitching 1 cm from end. At the other end, trim *cord* to meet first cord, *fabric* to 1 cm

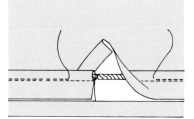

Fold the trimmed fabric edge under 5 mm. Wrap the fold around the starting end of cording, letting cord ends meet

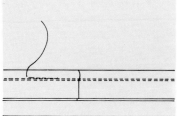

Stitch across both ends to 1 cm beyond the point where stitching was started. If necessary, backstitch to reinforce

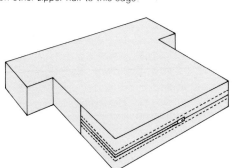

Zipper in cushion cover is usually applied by the centred method to a part of the boxing. Entire boxing unit is then formed and attached to cover pieces (see p. 430)

Loose-covers

Finishing bottom loose-cover edge

When the loose-cover is completely sewn, try it on the furniture to check the fit and to mark the bottom seamline. For a facing, mark the seamline along the bottom edge of the furniture; for a skirt, an equal distance from the floor on all sides.

To construct and apply a **facing,** see the opposite page. If the finish is a **skirt,** first cut enough fabric lengths to produce the finished width (see below and p. 396). Whether these are joined immediately or later depends on the skirt style.

For a *gathered skirt,* join the lengths first, finish the skirt's lower edge, then apply gathering stitches to the top seamline. Pin and gather the skirt to fit the loose-cover; pin the cording to the skirt. Remove the skirt and stitch the cording; remove the loose-cover and attach its skirt.

For a *pleated skirt,* work first with unjoined strips so that you can place the joining seams at the backs of pleats. Pin the strips to the loose-cover, forming and marking the pleats and the joining seams as you go. Remove the marked strips and open them out flat. Join the lengths and finish lower edge of skirt. Re-pin skirt to loose-cover, re-pleat, and pin cording to skirt. Remove skirt to stitch cording; remove loose-cover to attach skirt.

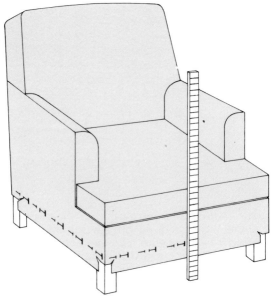

Before facing or skirt is constructed and applied, mark seamline at lower edge of loose-cover: for facing, at bottom of furniture; for skirt, an even distance from floor.

Calculating total skirt widths

Single pleats: Allow for finished skirt width, plus joining seams and twice the depth of each pleat. Position pleats at the corners and at lengthwise seams of loose-cover.

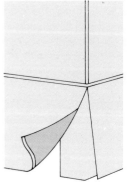

Separate underlay pleats: Finished skirt width, plus joining-seam allowances, the depth of each pleat, seam allowances at all pleat ends for a lined finish.

Continuous pleats: Three times the finished skirt width, plus joining-seam allowances. Place a pleat at each corner and at centre front and back, then form pleats in between.

Gathers: This type of skirt calls for twice the finished skirt width, plus joining-seam allowances. Fullness should be evenly distributed around the entire skirt.

Finishing lower edge of skirt

A machine-stitched hem can be the finish for skirt's lower edge. Start with 4 cm hem; for methods, see Hemming.

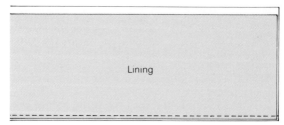

For self-lined skirt, cut skirt twice the finished length, plus two seam allowances. Fold at hemline; tack at top.

Skirt to be separately lined has 6 mm hem allowance; cut lining 6 mm shorter than skirt. Right sides together, sew lining to skirt at lower edge. Trim seam; press toward lining.

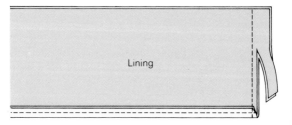

To seam the free ends, fold in half, right sides together, and align top edges; stitch, trim and press seams. Turn skirt right side out; align and tack top edges.

Skirt closures

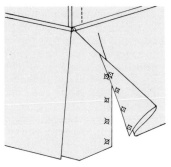

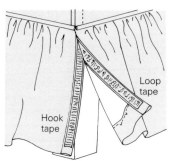

Hook tape

Loop tape

The lapped edges of pleated skirts can be held closed with hook and loop tape or snap fasteners. When applying the skirt, leave underlap of pleat free beyond the placket and finish its top edge. The overlap can be sewn to the loose-cover. Sew tape or snap fasteners to back of pleat.

The butted edges of gathered skirts can be fastened with hooks and round eyes, or hook and loop tape. When applying skirt, turn back placket seam allowances so the placket edges will meet; if necessary, turn under or seam-finish placket seam allowances.

Skirtless (faced) finish

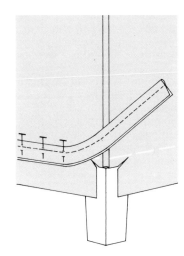

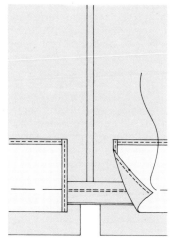

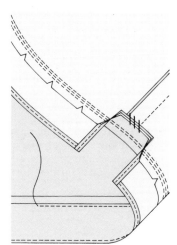

When seamline has been marked at bottom of furniture, pin the cording in place along markings. (See p. 398 for an explanation of cutting around the legs.) Sew cording to loose-cover.

For each side of loose-cover, cut a facing that will be, with outer edges finished, the length of the side from leg to leg, and 8 cm wide. Finish edges; apply facing to loose-cover.

Clip into seam allowances at each end of facings. Trim, grade and notch seam allowances; understitch the seamlines. Turn unfaced parts of seams to inside; whipstitch in place.

Securing bottom edge of loose-cover

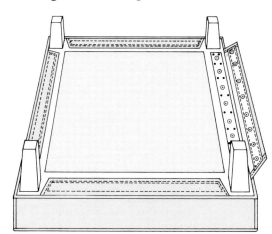

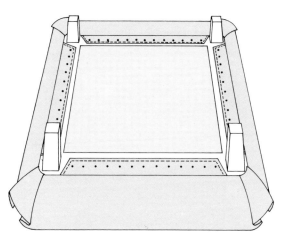

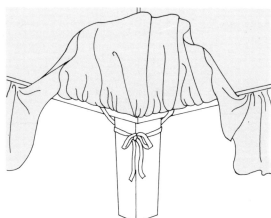

A skirtless finish can be held in place with snap fastener tape or nylon tape. Sew one half of fastener to wrong side of facings; align and nail the other half to the frame.

Skirt can be secured to the frame by nailing loose-cover and skirt seam allowances to it. Another way is to add a facing to seam of loose-cover and skirt, then nail facing to frame.

Tapes tied at each leg are another way of holding a skirted loose-cover in place. Simply insert 30 cm lengths of cotton tape at sides of legs as skirt is being stitched to cover.

401

Cushions

Types of cushion

Though cushions vary greatly in size and shape, there are basically only two types, knife-edge and box-edge.

A **knife-edge cushion** is one that is thickest at the centre and tapers off to the edges, so that there is very little side depth.

A **box-edge cushion** is uniform in thickness from centre to edges, and so has a side depth that must be covered with a boxing strip. The bolster, to the surprise of many, is actually a type of box-edge pillow. Typical shapes for any of these cushions are rectangular and circular; one bolster form is wedge-shaped. The forms for cushions can be preshaped (cut foam shapes and polyester-filled covers are examples), or you can buy or make a fabric cover and fill it with kapok or foam.

To arrive at the basic measurements of the fabric pieces for the cushion cover, measure the cushion form (see below); allow for a seam at each edge. If a placket will fall at one of the seams already allowed for in the basic measurements, no additional allowances are necessary. If a placket opening will be within a section, for example in a part of the boxing strip, extra allowances are needed; these are explained as they occur on the next few pages.

When a cushion shape is intricate, it is best to make a pattern for cutting the fabric sections. When fabric is expensive or fragile, a calico test cover is advisable; it can serve later as an inner cover for the cushion. If the cushion is to be trimmed, apply the trimmings before constructing the cover. Some trims, such as ruffles, can be added to the outside seams so that they extend out from the edges and increase the cover's size.

Knife-edge cushion covers

The cover for a basic knife-edge cushion consists of a top and a bottom section. To allow for insertion of the form, an opening must be provided in one of the cover's seams. The opening can be closed with hand slipstitches but a zipper inserted in the seam makes it easier to remove the cover and put it back on.

The instructions at the right are for inserting a zipper into a seam of a rectangular cover. It is easier, in a circular cover, to insert the zipper across the centre of the bottom. This requires creating a placket seam. Allow for it by cutting two semicircles with an extra seam allowance along their straight edges. Insert the zipper, then sew the bottom to the top.

If cording will be used in the seams, prepare a suitable quantity of covered cord. Use a zipper foot to apply cording and to stitch the seams.

Tufting a knife-edge cushion, besides adding a decorative touch, keeps the cover and form from shifting. It is done after the form is inserted into the cover.

Once a cushion is tufted, the cover is rarely, if ever, removed, and so a zippered opening is not needed. Tufting can be done with thread only, or with thread and buttons.

Pillow cases are relatively loose-fitting knife-edge decorative covers for bed pillows. To be most attractive, a pillow case should cover the full width of a single bed or half the width of a double bed. Extra size is added to the body of the pillow case by means of trims or borders that extend out from the cover portion.

The placket for a pillow case is placed along the centre of the bottom; it should be finished before the top and bottom sections are joined. Remember to allow for the placket when cutting out the bottom section.

Taking measurements

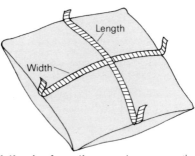

Knife-edge form: If *rectangular*, measure the length and width; if *circular*, measure diameter. Add seam allowances to all edges.

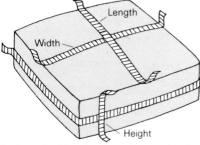

Rectangular box-edge form: Measure length, width, height, then around form for length of boxing. Add seam allowances to edges.

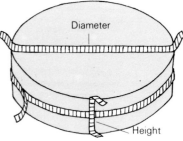

Circular box-edge form: Measure diameter and height, then around form for length of boxing. Add seam allowances to all edges.

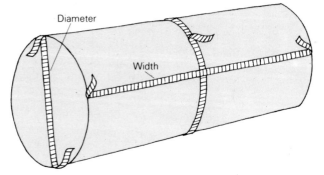

Circular bolster form: Measure diameter of ends, width of bolster, then around bolster. Add seam allowances to all edges.

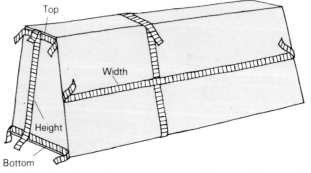

Wedge bolster form: Measure height, top and bottom widths of ends, width of bolster, around bolster. Add seam allowances to edges.

Constructing a knife-edge cushion cover

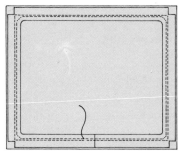

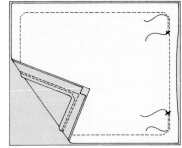

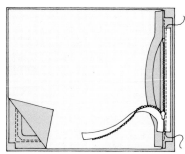

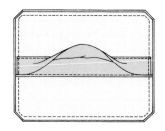

Pillow cases

1. Tack cording to right side of cover top, along the seamline (to join cording ends, see p. 399). Clip into cording seam allowances at corners. Stitch the cording in place, stitching across corners to blunt them.

2. On wrong side of cover top, mark top and bottom of placket opening. With right sides together, stitch cover top to cover bottom above and below placket. Start at each marking and stitch to each corner's seamline.

3. Extend placket seam allowance of top section. Open zipper and place half of it face down on seam allowance, with teeth along cording and top and bottom stops at top and bottom of opening. Stitch in place.

Pillow case is a loose-fitting knife-edge cover unique for its placket opening, which is placed along centre of case bottom. Placket is finished before top and bottom are joined; usually takes the form shown—4 cm wide overlapping hemmed edges. See other forms below.

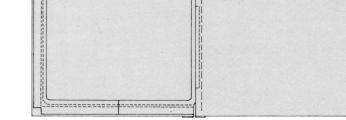

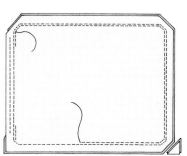

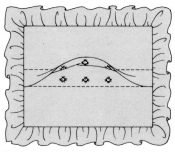

4. Close zipper; form bar tack across tapes at top. Spread open the cover sections and placket seam. From right side, tack, then stitch the free zipper tape to bottom of cover; stitch across ends and along the side of the zipper. Remove tacking stitches; open zipper.

5. Right sides together, stitch cover top to the bottom (begin and end at placket seam). Sew across corners to blunt them; trim seams.

Ruffle, attached to case top before top is sewn to bottom, increases case size. Here snap fasteners secure placket's overlapping edges.

Tufting cushions

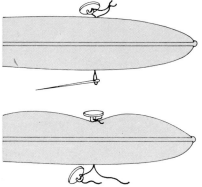

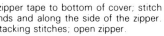

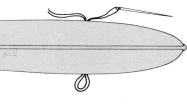

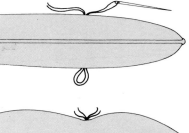

To tuft with buttons, thread a long needle with a double strand of strong thread. Tie thread ends to button shank. Push needle down through cushion.

Clip the thread to remove needle. Tie a second button opposite the first; draw up knot and button tightly to dimple the cushion. Clip thread ends.

To tuft with thread only, push a long needle, threaded with a double strand of strong thread, down through cushion, then up, coming out next to starting point.

Clip thread to remove needle. Tie the thread ends, forcing knot down so it presses into and dimples the cushion. Clip, leaving some thread ends.

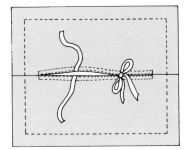

For case with flat self-border, cut sections to allow for both pillow and border width. Do not extend placket into border. With placket open, sew top to bottom; turn right side out; topstitch on line between pillow and border. Placket may have lapped zipper or fabric ties.

Cushions

Box-edge cushion covers

A box-edge cushion cover consists of top and bottom sections, plus a boxing strip to cover the sides. A zipper is usually inserted into a part of the boxing strip and applied before the strip is sewn to the cushion top and bottom. If cording will be used in the seams, prepare the necessary quantity of covered cord before constructing the cushion. A boxed effect can be achieved on a rectangular cover without a separate boxing strip. For this method, both top and bottom sections must be cut to include half the cushion depth along each edge.

Rectangular box-edge cover

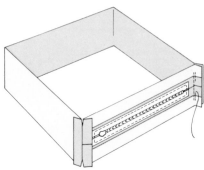

1. To provide for a placket, cut one part of boxing the length of the cushion side plus two seam allowances, by the height of the cushion plus four seam allowances. Insert zipper along the lengthwise centre. Then seam the boxing strip unit as shown at left.

2. If cording the cushion, sew cording to top and bottom seamlines of boxing. Position cording to right side of boxing with raw edges of cording toward raw edges of boxing. Join cording ends as on page 399; clip into seam allowances at the corners.

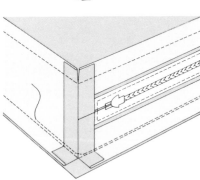

3. With right sides together and the boxing side up, stitch bottom section to the bottom seamline of the boxing. Stitch just inside stitching that holds cording to boxing. Spread the boxing seam allowances open at the corners; stitch across the corners to blunt them.

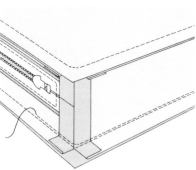

4. Open zipper. With right sides together and the boxing side up, sew top section to the top seamline of boxing, using techniques in Step 3. Trim seams if necessary. Turn cover to right side through zipper opening; push out on fabric at corners.

Boxed effect without boxing strip

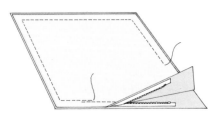

Cut top and bottom to include side depth. Apply invisible zipper to one seam; open. Sew top to bottom from one placket end to other.

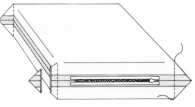

Fold cover at corners to align cross seams; stitch across as shown, and trim. Length of stitch line should be equal to height of cushion.

Turn the cover to the right side through the zipper opening. Push out on the seamlines to shape the corners and their edges.

Circular box-edge cover

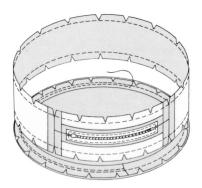

1. Allow for and insert the zipper into about a quarter of the boxing (Step 1, left). Staystitch and clip both edges of boxing. Stitch cording as shown to top and bottom pieces.

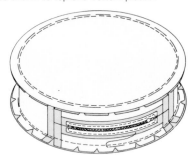

2. Open zipper. With right sides together, tack top section to the top seamline of the boxing; tack bottom section to the bottom seamline of the boxing.

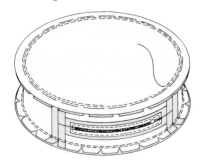

3. With boxing side up, stitch top and bottom to the boxing. Trim seams if necessary. Turn cover to right side through zipper opening. Push out on seamlines to shape edges.

Cushions

Bolster covers

A bolster is a type of box-edge cushion in which the boxing strip area has become the largest part, actually the body of the cushion, and the top and bottom merely the cushion ends. The two most typical bolster shapes are round and wedge. Since both are relatively complicated to cover, it is best to make a pattern for cutting the fabric pieces. As shown below, the closures occur in joining seams and thus need no special provision. In a **round-bolster** cover, the zipper is inserted into the seam that joins the ends of the body piece. In a **wedge-bolster** cover, the placket opening spans that joining seam and the bottom seam of both end pieces. Snap fastener tape is the easiest closure to apply; see example below.

Cover for round bolster

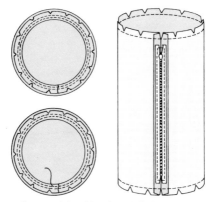

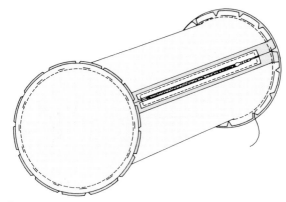

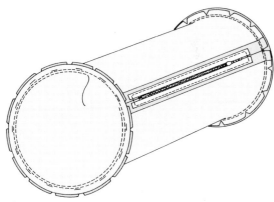

Stitch cording to right side of each bolster end piece; clip into seam allowances of cording so it will curve. Insert zipper in seam that will join ends of body piece; staystitch and clip into seam allowances of both edges of body.

Open the zipper. With right sides together, tack an end piece to one edge of the body; spread the clipped seam allowances of the body so that seamlines can be matched. Tack the other end piece to the other edge in the same way.

With body part of cover nearest the needle, stitch both of the end pieces to the body. Remove tacking; trim seams if necessary. Turn cover to the right side through the zipper opening. Push out on seamlines to curve the edges.

Cover for wedge bolster

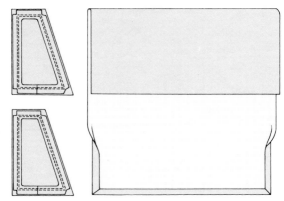

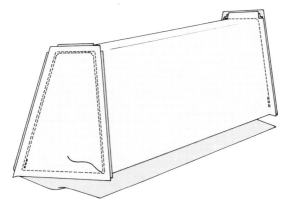

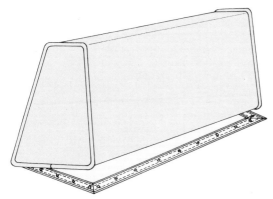

Stitch cording to right side of both ends; clip seam allowances of cording so that it will go around corners. At one end of the body piece, fold in and mitre the corner seam allowances (this prepares edge for snap fastener tape).

Right sides together, stitch both end pieces to body piece, starting and ending stitching at bottom seamlines. Clip into seam allowances of body pieces at top corners; stitch across corners to blunt them. Turn cover right side out.

Sew ball half of snap fastener tape to upper seam allowance of open seam; mitre tape at corners (keep snaps free of mitres). Position socket half on lower seam, aligning sockets and balls; mitre at corners; topstitch through all layers.

Types of spreads and covers

Basically, there are three bedspread styles—*throw*, *flounced* and *tailored*. The first is simply a flat piece that drapes over the bed. The second two have fitted drops (sides) that may be gathered, pleated or straight.

Whatever the style, a spread is made with a full fabric width in the centre and seams an equal distance from the centre. Unless covered by lining, seam allowances should be neatly finished, preferably self-enclosed or bound, but they can be zigzag-stitched or overlocked. Because of the many metres involved, machine-finished hems are the most practical.

Any fabric will do for a spread, but generally, the more body it has the better. If the bed is to be used for lounging during the day, the spread fabric should be sturdy and easy to clean. Lining is optional, but a soft or sheer fabric will probably need one. Any nap (or one-way design) should run the same way on all throw sections.

Any of the basic styles can be adapted for a *coverlet*—a short spread that ends 8 cm below the mattress. A coverlet edge is more visible than one that hangs to the floor, so lining and/or cording would be appropriate.

A quilt- or duvet-cover is a large knife-edge cover into which a quilt or duvet is slipped. The opening at the base of the cover may be fastened with buttons, snap fasteners, self ties, hook and loop tape or a zipper.

Coverlets and quilt- or duvet-covers are usually combined with a *dust cover* or *valance*—a fitted top piece with a straight, pleated or gathered skirt—that conceals the box springs and legs. For economy, the top can be calico or some other inexpensive fabric.

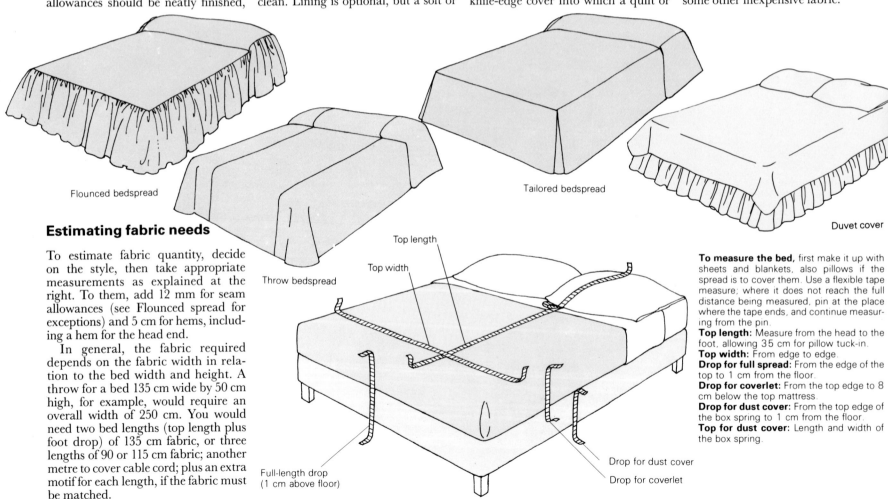

Flounced bedspread

Throw bedspread

Tailored bedspread

Duvet cover

Top length

Top width

Full-length drop
(1 cm above floor)

Drop for dust cover

Drop for coverlet

Estimating fabric needs

To estimate fabric quantity, decide on the style, then take appropriate measurements as explained at the right. To them, add 12 mm for seam allowances (see Flounced spread for exceptions) and 5 cm for hems, including a hem for the head end.

In general, the fabric required depends on the fabric width in relation to the bed width and height. A throw for a bed 135 cm wide by 50 cm high, for example, would require an overall width of 250 cm. You would need two bed lengths (top length plus foot drop) of 135 cm fabric, or three lengths of 90 or 115 cm fabric; another metre to cover cable cord; plus an extra motif for each length, if the fabric must be matched.

To measure the bed, first make it up with sheets and blankets, also pillows if the spread is to cover them. Use a flexible tape measure; where it does not reach the full distance being measured, pin at the place where the tape ends, and continue measuring from the pin.

Top length: Measure from the head to the foot, allowing 35 cm for pillow tuck-in.

Top width: From edge to edge.

Drop for full spread: From the edge of the top to 1 cm from the floor.

Drop for coverlet: From the top edge to 8 cm below the top mattress.

Drop for dust cover: From the top edge of the box spring to 1 cm from the floor.

Top for dust cover: Length and width of the box spring.

Throw style

A **throw bedspread** is made of three panels that form a flat rectangle, long and wide enough to cover the entire bed. The centre panel is the width of the top or less, and long enough to include foot drop and pillow tuck-in. Side sections extend from centre panel to floor on each side; corners at the foot end are often rounded so that they do not touch the floor.

Any bulky or heavy fabric, especially a quilted one, is a good choice for a throw. Heavy fabrics are less inclined to wrinkle or to become rumpled.

Basic procedure is to join the sections, then hem all around. Unless a throw is lined, self-enclosed seams are most suitable. Two types, *flat-felled* and *French*, are shown below. For two others, *mock French* and *self-bound*, consult the Seams chapter.

For more emphasis on seams, cording or a flat trim can be added. If cording is used, finish seams with a zigzag stitch or bias binding. If a flat trim is added, it is simplest to topstitch the trim over the seam allowances on the right side (see below).

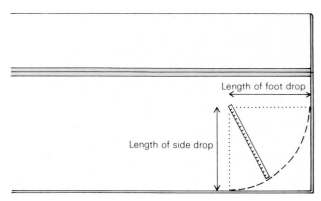

To round off corners, fold spread in half lengthwise; mark a square on the outer corner at the foot end. Sides of square should equal the drop depth plus hem allowance. Using a tape measure or metre rule, measure from the inner corner out, marking a cutting line in an arc. Cut one corner, then mark and cut the second one.

Length of foot drop

Length of side drop

Recommended seams

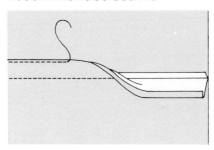

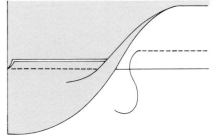

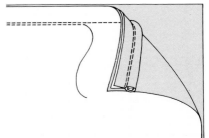

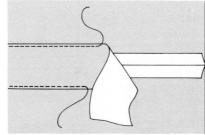

For a flat-felled seam, stitch on seamline, wrong sides together. Trim one seam allowance to 3 mm. Fold under 3 mm of second allowance; fold second over first; topstitch.

For a French seam, stitch 6 mm from seamline, wrong sides together. Trim seam allowances. Fold fabric right sides together, stitched line on fold; stitch 6 mm from fold.

For a corded seam, stitch cording to right side of one seam allowance, crowding stitches between cording and stitches that hold it. Stitch seam, placing this row closer to cording.

For a seam with trim, stitch on the seamline, wrong sides together. Press seams open; trim seam allowances, if necessary. Topstitch the trim over the seam.

Suggested edge finishes

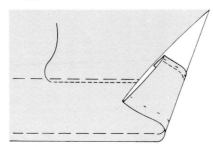

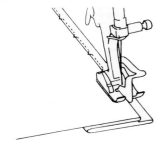

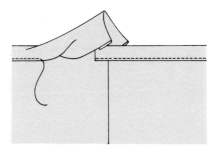

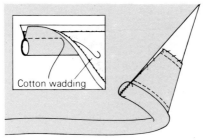

For topstitched hem, turn up hem allowance; fold hem edge under 1 cm; tack hem. Topstitch from right side, close to tacking.

For blindstitched hem, turn up hem allowance; fold edge under 1 cm. Blindstitch as shown, catching only the spread with zigzags.

For topstitched binding, wrap binding over hem edge, wider side underneath. Edgestitch as shown, catching both sides of binding.

For a padded edging, cover a strip of cotton wadding with bias (see inset); attach filled bias in the same way as cording (see Hems).

Cotton wadding

Bedspreads and bedcovers

Fitted spread with flounce

A **flounced bedspread** has a fitted top and drops that are gathered or pleated all around. Mediumweight or lightweight fabric is best for this style.

The top is cut the length and width of the bed, plus seam allowances and a hem allowance for the head end. If fabric must be pieced, use a full width for the centre panel and a split width (or portion) for each side. The top will fit better if you blunt the corners at the foot end by taking a few stitches diagonally when joining top to drops. Corners can also be rounded, using the mattress for a pattern.

The drop is cut in several sections, joined with French seams (see p. 407) or interlocking fell seams (p. 415). Allow twice the length to be covered for a gathered drop, three times this length for pleats. Sections are usually cut from fabric width so that lengthwise grain goes from top to floor. For a fuller look, or special effect (stripes running horizontally, for example), cut sections lengthwise.

A ruffled flounce can be made with or without a heading. For a style with no heading, cut the top with 2.5 cm seam allowances; cut the flounce with 2 cm allowances at top edge, 5 cm for bottom hem. For a headed ruffle, allow 5 cm seams at the top, 2 cm for top of ruffle and 5 cm for a hem.

The usual procedure is to join the flounce sections, hem the bottom and the free edges, then gather and join the flounce to the top. Before gathering, divide the drop into 10 or 12 equal parts and mark the divisions with notches. Do the same with the top. Align the notches when joining.

Cording, if desired, can be added to a style with no heading; attach it to the flounce before stitching flounce to top. Instead of self-binding (near right), zigzag seam edges or line the top (opposite page).

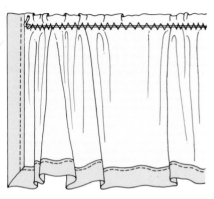

For a plain flounce, place a thin cord 1 cm from top edge on the wrong side; stitch over it with widest zigzag. Pull the cord to form gathers, adjusting flounce to fit top section. (If your machine does not have a zigzag, make two rows of straight-stitch gathering, or use a gathering foot.)

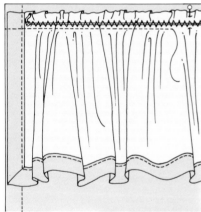

Right sides together, pin flounce to the top section, with edge of flounce 6 mm below edge of top. Stitch just below the cord, or 2.5 cm from the top edge.

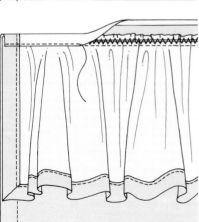

Trim flounce seam allowance to 6 mm. Fold under the edge of untrimmed seam allowance 3 mm, then fold again, aligning fold with seamline and enclosing the edge of the flounce; press. Stitch folded edge through seam allowances only.

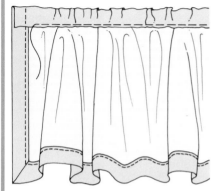

For headed flounce, fold and press the top edge 3 cm to the wrong side. Place one row of straight-stitch gathering 3 mm from the raw edge (or use a gathering foot). Do not gather over the hem at the end. Draw up gathers to fit the top of the spread.

Wrong sides together, pin flounce to the top section, extending flounce 1.5 cm beyond the edge of the top. Stitch 3 mm below the gathering line. (This distance might be a little more than 3 mm, but should not be less, or the raw edge of the flounce will not be covered.)

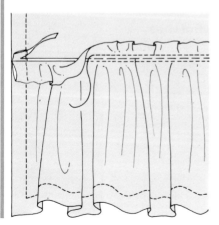

Trim seam allowance on the top section to 3 mm. Fold flounce to right side of the top, and stitch in place 3 mm above gathering stitches. All seam allowances are now enclosed.

Fitted spread with tailored drops

A **tailored bedspread** has a fitted top and straight drops. The top is the same as for a flounced spread (see opposite page). The drops, where they meet at corners, can be (1) stitched together; (2) pleated; (3) hemmed, with an underlay backing; or (4) hemmed, with no underlay.

Stitched corners produce a snug fit, and a trim look if the fabric is heavy or the spread is lined.

Inverted pleats permit a more flexible fit; work best with light or medium-weight fabric. Sections should be cut so that seams will be at the edge of a backfold, allowing 24 cm for each side of pleat (12 cm folded).

Hemmed edges with an underlay resemble pleats, but are better to use with bulky fabric. Cut each drop section to fit the top, plus 5 cm for hems. Cut underlays 30 cm wide (omit them if the bed has corner posts).

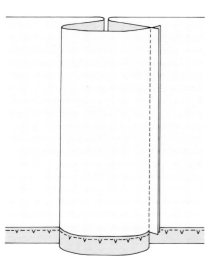

For drop with corner pleats, join sections with 1 cm seams, having each seam fall at the backfold of a pleat. Finish hem at the bottom, clipping seams above the hem edge.

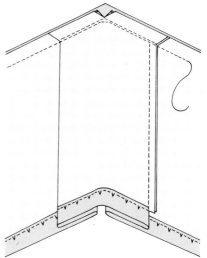

Stitch top of pleat close to seamline; clip centre back to stitching. Right sides together, pin sides to top, aligning pleat folds with corners and spreading back of pleat; stitch.

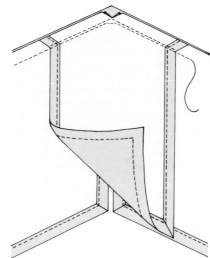

For corner with underlay, hem side and bottom edges of drop sections and underlays. Stitch top of underlay behind opening; clip to stitching at centre. Join sides to top.

Lining a bedspread

A bedspread lining can serve several purposes at once. It can add body, enclose seam allowances, take the place of a hem, even, if desired, make the spread reversible. A lining also adds durability when fabric is loosely woven, or has loose floats on the back (as brocade would have, for example).

Lining fabric should be compatible with the spread in care requirements, and at least as wide, so that seams will correspond. A bed sheet might be used, eliminating lining seams.

A throw style is lined from edge to edge. In tailored styles there are three choices: the top only can be lined; the drops only can be lined; or both top and drops can be lined. Directions for lining a fitted top are given at far right. See following two pages for ways to line side sections.

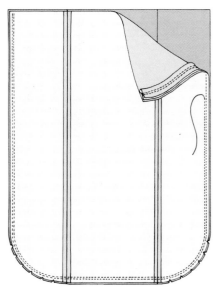

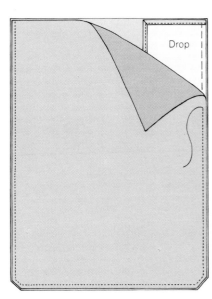

To line a throw, substitute seam allowances for hems on all edges. Cut lining sections to match. Join throw and lining sections separately; press all seams open. If throw is being corded, stitch cording around the edge on the right side of the throw. With right sides together, seams aligned, and throw on top, stitch sides and foot end, placing stitches to left of first stitch line. Notch curves. Turn right side out; fold in edges of open (head) end; stitch folds together.

To line fitted top only, cut lining to fit the top. With right sides together, tack side and foot sections to the top. Place lining over the top with right sides together, with the drop in between. Stitch side and foot edges, taking three stitches diagonally at each corner. Trim corners diagonally. Turn spread right side out. Fold in edges along the open (head) end and stitch folds together.

Lining fitted drops and attaching to an unlined top

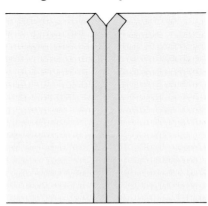

1. Pin, tack and stitch drops of spread together; stop stitching and secure each seam 1 cm from raw edge at top. Remove tacking and press seams open.

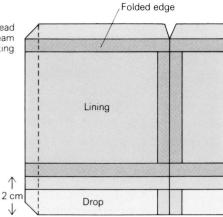

4. Fold lining and drop so that right sides are facing again and bring folded edge of lining to meet seamline of drop. Stitch the ends together at each side; trim corners diagonally. Turn right side out; press. The lining should be about 2 cm shorter than the drop along the bottom edge.

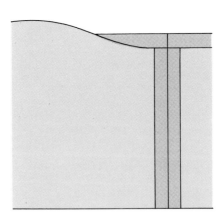

2. Cut lining for drops 4 cm shorter in height than spread drops. Join lining sections together; press the seams open. Along one long edge, press a 1 cm seam allowance to the wrong side.

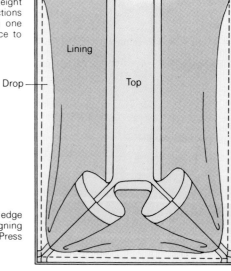

5. Stitch seam allowance of drop to top of spread, right sides together. Keep lining out of the way. Pivot at each corner as shown (or blunt if corners are to be rounded).

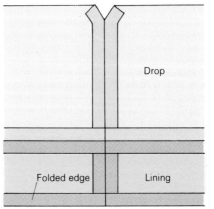

3. With right sides together, pin bottom edge of drop to unfolded edge of lining, aligning seams. Tack and sew a 1 cm seam. Press seam open as shown.

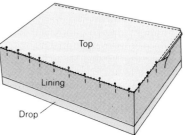

6. Pull drop down and press seam allowance down; trim away excess fabric at corners. Bring folded edge of lining to seamline and slipstitch in place. Turn under a narrow double hem at head of bed and slipstitch in place. Turn bedspread right side out.

Lining fitted drops and attaching to a lined top

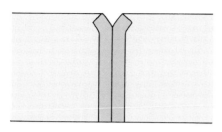

1. Line drops completely before starting to line top. Pin, tack and sew drops of spread together; stop stitching and secure each seam 1 cm from raw edge at top. Press.

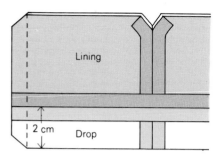

4. Fold lining and drop so that their right sides are facing again and bring top edge of lining to meet top edge of drop. Stitch the ends together at each side; trim corners diagonally. Turn right side out; press. The lining should be about 2 cm shorter than the drop along the bottom edge.

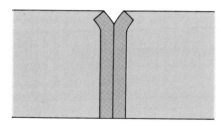

2. Cut lining for drops 4 cm shorter in height than spread drops. Join lining sections together, stopping and securing each seam 1 cm from raw edge at top. Press.

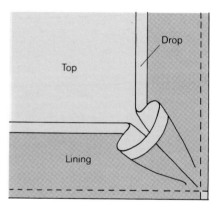

5. With right sides of top and drops facing, tack drops and their lining to spread top, pivoting at each corner (or blunting if they are to be rounded).

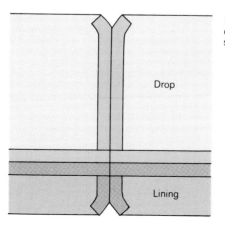

3. With right sides together, stitch lining to drop along bottom edge, aligning seams. Press seam open as shown.

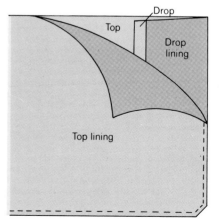

6. Place lining over the top with right sides together and the lined drops in between. Stitch side and foot edges, taking 3 stitches diagonally at each corner, or stitch in curve if they are to be rounded. Trim corners. Turn spread right side out. Fold in edges along the open (head) end and stitch folds together.

Curtains, draperies and blinds

What you will need

Curtains, draperies and blinds are sewing projects even a novice can undertake. Success depends less on sewing skill than it does on careful measuring and thoughtful relating of style and fabric.

The procedure is basically the same for all window treatments in this section. When you have decided on a style, install the hardware and measure this and the window area to determine fabric needs (p. 414). Before buying a particular fabric, appraise its impact on the room. Borrow a sample from the store, if possible, or buy half a metre. See how it looks at the window; light behind a fabric can change its look considerably. Check whether the fabric is resistant to sun fading and deterioration and to wrinkles, and make sure you know exactly what sort of cleaning it will require.

If you choose to make blinds, you will only need to purchase the fabric and a kit containing all the fittings and accessories required as well as detailed instructions for making and installing.

When you shop for rods, tracks, tapes, mounting fixtures and accessories for curtains and draperies, look for the kind that will support the fabric as well as create the effect you want. The illustrations opposite show the basic range but a much larger range is available and constantly changing; those below show some typical uses. It is well worth consulting the many free brochures and booklets provided by manufacturers before deciding on a style.

Before you start cutting or sewing, make sure that your work area is adequate for the large amount of fabric you will be handling. A table next to the machine to support fabric weight will help. Prepare fabric by straightening ends, re-aligning grain if necessary, and pressing. See page 415 for special considerations when cutting fabric to be matched.

Choosing the style

To decide on a window treatment, you must consider far more than mere looks. First, there is the view. Do you want to conceal it or frame it? Will an uncovered window create a privacy problem? Should sunlight be controlled? Does the window type limit your choice (a French window, for example, that opens in)? Might the look be improved by tracks set above or to the sides of the frame? Finally, will the style harmonise with the room itself?

Window coverings classify into these basic types:

Sheer curtains. Sheer or semi-sheer fabric; not lined; top casing (or channel heading) slips directly over rod. Styles: *panel* curtain has top casing, bottom hem; *casement* has hems top and bottom; *ruffled* has ruffles at sides and bottom, and is often tied back to window frame.

Café curtains. Any fabric type and heading style; may be lined. Cover only part of window lengthwise, providing privacy at one level, light at another; best in informal settings. Upper tier can overlap heading of lower tier, or form a short valance above uncovered space.

Draperies/heavyweight curtains. Usually made with heavier fabrics; may be lined; heading pleated, gathered or looped. May be teamed with sheers to provide light during the day, insulation against cold at night, and privacy at all times. *Panel* draperies cover only the sides of the window; *draw* draperies span entire width.

Blinds. Any fabric may be used; lining adds support. Offer full light when open, complete privacy when closed. Types include *roller* and *Roman* blinds, and *balloon* or *Austrian* drapes.

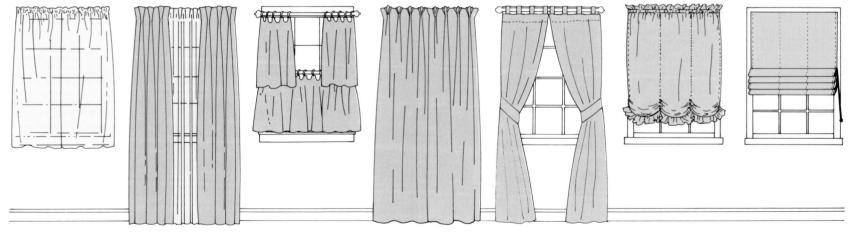

Sheer panel curtains with a casing at the top, slipped over a flat curtain rod.

Sheer panel on extensible track, plus pleated draw draperies on traverse track.

Double café curtains are hung with brass rings on the traditional café rod.

Full length draw draperies with triple pinch pleats on a two-way traverse track.

Draw draperies with looped heading on decorative rod are tied back to window frame.

Balloon drape with ruffled hem is hung from a café rod mounted on a board.

Roman blind is drawn up by a cord through rows of rings on the back.

Rods, tracks and fixtures

Flat curtain rod, used mainly for stationary curtains; comes in standard and heavy-duty weights, adjustable length.

Nylon ring tape, used in the construction of Roman blinds and balloon drapes.

Flexible track made of strong PVC is suitable for bay windows.

Café rod, suitable for straight or pleated curtains; comes in a variety of thicknesses.

Decorative rod supports plain or pleated draperies; wood or metal with elaborate finials.

Sash rod for lightweight curtains. Holders fix rod between two walls or window frame without screws or glue.

Extensible track adjusts to fit window without need of trimming.

Traverse track holds draperies to be opened and closed; available in one-way or two-way draw.

Accessories

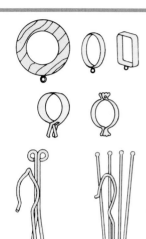

Rings with eyes must be sewn to curtain or drapery; come in a variety of shapes and sizes to suit different rod styles.

Café clips are quickly attached and easily removed for laundering; used mainly for café curtains.

A ring-and-hook combination is used with a pleater tape heading.

Metal, nylon and plastic hooks for use with corded ruffle or pleater tape.

Pleater tape hooks slip into pleater pockets; types for regular or ceiling traverse, to hold pleats or ends.

Weights improve hang of draperies or curtains; individual weights are tacked to corners; lead weight tape is inserted in the hem fold.

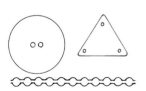

Anchors (toggle, screw, molly) hold bolts or screws securely to support drapery weight.

Curtains, draperies and blinds

Estimating fabric needs

Two measurements are basic for estimating fabric needs for window coverings: finished length and finished width. Install all hardware before measuring; fabric is sewn to fit the supporting device rather than the window. For most accurate results, use a steel tape or folding ruler. If more than one window is being covered, measure each one, even if they all appear to be the same. General measuring procedure is given here. See illustration below for the specifics of measuring for various styles.

Finished length: Measure from the top of the rod or track to the place where the hem will fall; standard choices are *sash*, *sill* bottom of *apron*, or *floor* (see right). For a floor-length style, subtract 1 centimetre to clear the floor.

Finished width: Measure the entire span of the rod or track. If it projects from the wall or frame, include the *return* (distance from fixture to bend in rod). On a traverse track measure each half separately from end of *slide* (overlap) to the fixture.

To ensure adequate fullness, double the finished width figure; triple if for sheers or other lightweight fabrics. (To achieve the necessary fullness, you may have to join one or more fabric widths—see opposite page.) From this calculate the *number of panels* you will require.

To determine the *length* that each panel should be cut, add hem and heading allowances to the finished length measurement. These will vary with the window treatment. An overall allowance of 30 cm would certainly be adequate. In general, it is better to be generous than too exact; some length is always taken up by the fullness of the fabric. Allow extra fabric if you plan to include a shrinkage tuck at the hem. If the heading will extend above or fall below the top of the rod or track (see below), further adjustments in length must be made. When fabric must be matched to allow for uninterrupted flow of design, add one extra motif for each length required.

To estimate fabric needs, multiply the *total length* for each panel times the *number of panels* needed for each window. (If your measurements are in centimetres, it will be necessary to divide by 100 to convert to metres.) For blinds, follow the directions supplied with the construction kit.

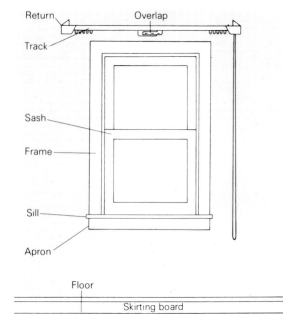

Measuring

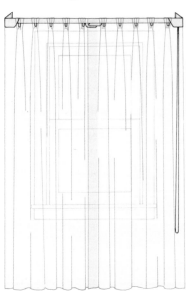

Floor-length draperies on a traverse track: Measure finished length from top of track to 1 cm above the floor; add 30 cm for hem and heading extension above the track. For width, measure each half of track separately, from end of slide to the mounting fixture, including the return.

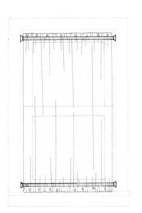

Casement curtains on sash rods: Measure length from top of upper rod to bottom of lower one; add 1 cm for heading extension at each end. Measure width across inside of frame.

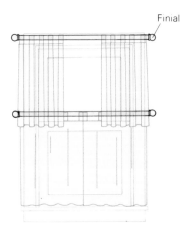

Double café curtains on café rods: Measure upper tier from top of rod to bottom of lower rod; measure lower tier from top of rod to sill. Measure width between finials.

Roller blind sitting on window frame: Measure finished length and width to fit window frame. Extra fabric is required for the roll; refer to blind kit instructions for the exact amount.

Curtains, draperies and blinds

Matching techniques

When a fabric requires matching, the design should flow without interruption from heading to hem and from side to side. Treatment of the design must be duplicated exactly for each window in the room. Always relate motif placement to finished edges. If the fabric has a vertical repeat, make sure that you allow for the overlap, if any. See below for matching and placement of horizontal motifs.

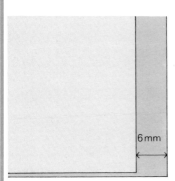

To match panels horizontally, first decide on the best placement for motifs. The ideal is a complete motif at both heading and hem. Cut one panel; align remaining fabric with this first one to cut each subsequent piece.

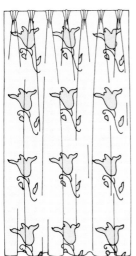

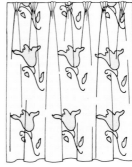

If a partial repeat must be used at one edge, place it at the hem for a floor-length treatment, at the heading for a shorter length. Use a full motif at the opposite end. Such placement makes the cut-off less noticeable.

Joining panels

A simple and neat way to join curtain sections is with the interlocking fell seam, illustrated below. In this technique, one edge is pressed and then machine-hemmed over another. An interlocking seam can also be made using a hemmer foot, which will fold the extending edge while you stitch. For better control of fabric that must be matched, use a French or mock French seam.

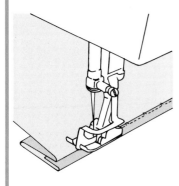

For interlocking fell seam, lay sections with right sides together, and top piece 6 mm from edge of piece beneath (a bit more for heavy fabric).

6 mm

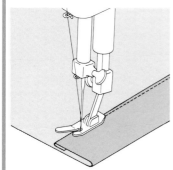

Fold extended edge of under layer over the top one, and press. This job is easier if you set a table next to the ironing board to support bulk of fabric. Or work directly on a large table, carefully protecting its surface.

Fold both layers a second time and press again. Pin every 10 or 12 cm to hold layers in place. If fabric is very slippery, tack instead. Stitch edge of inside fold, as shown. This one line of stitching holds all edges enclosed.

Side hems

Side hems for unlined panels are generally made before the heading or the bottom hem are undertaken. Machine techniques and fusing are both suitable. Side hems can be single, as below, or double (p. 419). Standard finished width is 2.5 cm. Clip selvage at 5 cm to 8 cm intervals to prevent sagging. Sheers can be left with selvage unhemmed, provided it does not pull. If desired a ruffle can be added.

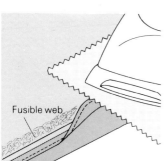

For blindstitched hem, turn and press hem allowance; press the hem edge under at least 1 cm. Adjust your machine for blind-hemming stitch. Fold back curtain or drapery portion to reveal hem edge. Stitch, catching curtain only in the zigzag stitch.

For straight-stitched hem, turn and press the hem allowance; press the hem edge under at least 6 mm. Adjust machine for 2.5 to 3 mm stitch length. Stitch along the hem edge, taking care to keep grainlines of hem and curtain aligned.

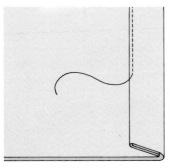

For a fused hem, turn and press the hem allowance; press the hem edge under at least 6 mm; stitch close to fold. Slip fusible web between hem and curtain. Set iron for steam; fuse, covering hem with damp press cloth (see Hems for more details).

Fusible web

415

Curtains, draperies and blinds

Casings

The fullness of a sheer curtain is generally controlled with a casing. This is a hem that slips over the curtain rod, forcing the fabric to gather in soft folds. The casing can be plain or have a heading that extends above the rod (see below).

Fabric allowance for a plain casing should equal diameter of rod, plus 1 cm for turning under the edge, plus an ease allowance so that fabric will slip easily over rod. Ease should be 6 mm to 1 cm, depending on fabric thickness; pin fabric over rod to determine right amount. If you want a heading, add twice desired depth to above measurements. To provide a shrinkage tuck (if you want to avoid pre-shrinking washable fabric) add another 5 cm.

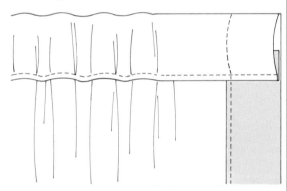

Plain casing: Press raw edge under 1 cm; turn down a casing equal in depth to half rod diameter, plus half the suitable ease allowance. Stitch in place on pressed edge.

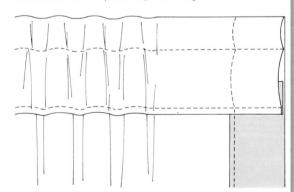

Casing with heading: Decide casing width, adding half total heading allowance. Turn raw edge under 1 cm, press and stitch. Stitch again at heading depth.

Heading tapes

Formerly, decorative headings of curtains had to be made by hand—a laborious and time-consuming task. Now, however, the easiest method of making pleated and gathered headings for most drapery styles is to use pleater tapes. These can be corded or cordless. Although corded tapes are easier to use, cordless hook tapes can also produce a number of interesting pleats. Instruction booklets printed by manufacturers will greatly assist you to select a style of pleated or gathered heading to suit the curtains you have chosen.

There are styles of tape designed for draperies that are to conceal the tracks, and others for curtains that are to be suspended below the tracks or decorative poles. The latter can also be used for curtains where the track is fixed to the ceiling. Lightweight pencil pleating tape is available for sheers and semi-sheers.

The pockets on heading tapes are on one side only, so it is important to check that they will be facing you once the tape is sewn on. Stiffening the top of the curtain is not necessary as these tapes have built-in stiffening.

Plastic and nylon hooks are available for corded tapes and are easier to remove than those made of metal. Pleater hooks are made only in metal.

Illustrated below are various styles of heading that can be made with pleater tapes.

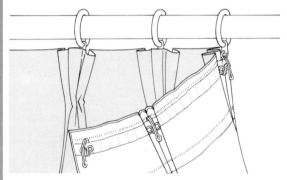

Deep fanned pinch pleating made with cord tape. This style of tape can be used for curtains that conceal the track or for those that are suspended below.

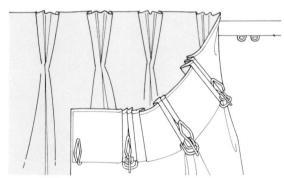

Triple pleats made with pleater hooks. By inserting the four prongs of the hook into different pockets, single and double pleats can also be made.

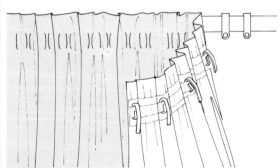

Gathered heading made with standard cord tape. This tape is made in a wide range of colours and is also available in nylon for sheers.

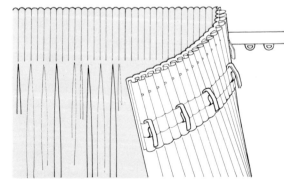

Deep heading pencil pleating on sheers. This style of corded tape is specially made for sheers, and is suitable for tracks mounted close to ceiling or with space above.

Corded tapes

The directions given here are for pencil pleating. Before sewing on tape, pull out 4 cm of each cord at one end, knot ends together and trim off surplus tape. Turn this end under, enclosing knotted cords under tape. At other end of tape free 5 cm of the cords and leave for pleating up. Tack a 1.5 cm hem at top of curtain. Making sure that hook pockets are facing you, tack the whole outer edge of the tape to the curtain, then stitch, leaving 5 cm between top of tape and curtain. Pleat up but do not cut off surplus cord; this allows curtain to be pulled flat for easy cleaning. (Cord tidies are available for hanging surplus cords neatly out of sight.) Insert hooks each end and at 8 cm intervals.

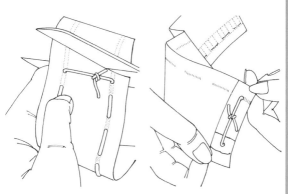

Before sewing on tape pull out 4 cm of each cord at one end, knot the ends together and trim off surplus tape. Turn end under, enclosing knot.

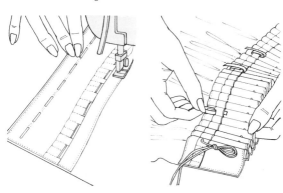

Making sure that hook pockets are facing you, tack tape to curtains. Stitch around the outer edge of the tape and pleat up, but do not cut off the surplus cord.

Hook pleater tape

With cordless tape the pleats are formed by inserting four-prong pleater hooks. Multi-pocket tapes are used to make single, double or triple pleats. (Refer to manufacturers' booklets for instructions.) There are tapes for making pinch pleats on double-fullness curtains; other tapes have double the number of pockets for fuller pleats and greater flexibility of spacing.

Hooks are made in two stem heights; the longer are used for tracks with space above or decorative rods and tracks, the shorter are used for tracks fixed to the ceiling. Buy tape to match the length of the unpleated curtain, plus an extra 40 cm to allow for exact placement of the pockets.

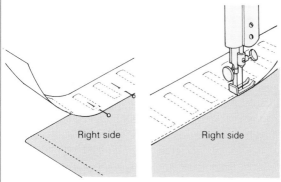

Lay tape wrong side down to right side of curtain, overlapping the edges by 1 cm, with open pocket edge pointing away from curtain. Pin, tack and stitch.

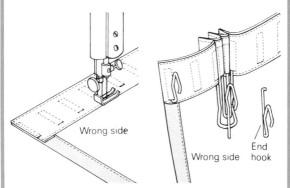

Turn tape over to wrong side of curtain. Turn under both ends of tape and stitch in place, then stitch along bottom of tape below the pockets. Pleat up.

Other pleating methods

If you wish to pleat the heading of a curtain by hand it is necessary to use a stiffener (either nonwoven interfacing or buckram). Attach to the curtain in the same way as shown for hook pleater tape.

Cartridge pleats can most easily be made using pleater tape and pleater hooks. Insert the two inner prongs of the hook into tape, leaving one pocket between them. Into this large pleat insert cylinders of stiff paper or buckram.

Clip-on rings, usually used for café curtains, hold a simple pleat that is not stitched. These rings can be easily removed, enabling the curtain to be flattened for cleaning and ironing. Allow 5 cm for each pleat, 8 cm in between.

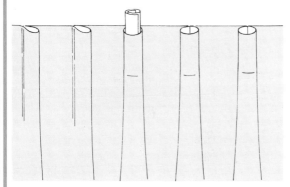

Cartridge pleats: Cut 10 cm wide strips of buckram or stiff paper then cut into 8 cm lengths. Form rolls and insert into pleats. Rolls will expand to fill pleats.

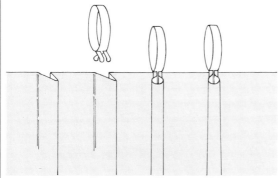

Clip-on rings: The pleat is simply held in place by the ring which is attached as shown; no stitching is required. Press crease at centre of each pleat.

Curtains, draperies and blinds

Scalloped heading

A graceful finish for the top of café curtains, scallops can be used on a plain or a pleated heading. There should be an *uneven* number on each panel, with at least 1.5 cm or a pleat width between them. To make your own pattern, cut a strip of paper the width of the hemmed curtain. Across the top mark scallop widths and spaces between them, centring the first scallop. Make the scallops half as deep as they are wide, using a compass or a sewing gauge to draw them. When cutting the curtains, allow for a self-facing at the top equal to the scallop depth plus 6 cm. Cut the stiffening (from nonwoven interfacing) the length and depth of the facing less 1 cm. The rod will be visible, so it is important to choose one that complements your fabric.

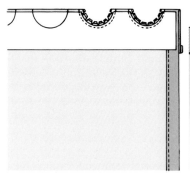
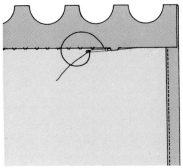
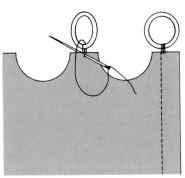

1. Turn facing edge under 1 cm; press. Fold facing allowance to right side. Tack stiffener to wrong side. Trace scallops over stiffener; stitch. Trim stiffener; clip curves.

2. Turn the facing to the wrong side, over the stiffener. Slip-hem the facing to the curtain along the folded edge and at the side hems. Machine-stitch, if preferred.

3. Press the heading carefully, using a pin, if necessary, to pull out corners at the top of each scallop. Attach rings (clip-on or sew-on) between the scallops.

Looped heading

Loops add interest to plain window treatments. Plan enough loops to support the curtain adequately, and make them long enough to slip easily over the rod. When planning panel length, include finished loop length in the total and allow 1 centimetre for a top seam. Fabric loops may be made the same way as belt carriers, or you could use braid loops, which require less preparation.

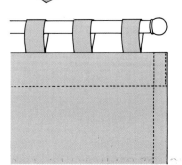

Fabric loops. Prepare loops. Fold and tack to right side of curtain, raw edges aligned. Stitch 6 mm from the edge. Apply a facing over the loops, stitching 1 cm from edge.

Press the facing to the wrong side. Machine-stitch side and lower edges of facing to the curtain or, if preferred, slip-hem them. Slip the curtain over a café or decorative rod.

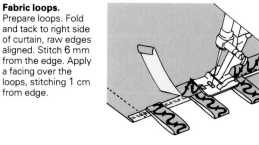

Braid or ribbon loops. Cut the loops. Press top of curtain 1 cm to right side. Tack loops over folded edge, as shown. Stitch them 6 mm from fold. Cut a length of braid equal to the width of the curtain plus 2 cm, fold the ends under 1 cm. Position top edge close to fabric fold and stitch, then stitch ends and lower edge. All loop ends will be neatly enclosed.

Roman blind and balloon drape

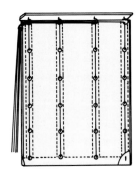

Roman blind: Stitch vertical rows of rings or ring tape to the back of the firm fabric blind. The space between the rows depends on the size of the window and the depth of the fold required. Attach threaded cord to headboard with screw eyes.

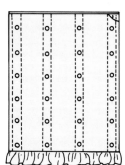

Balloon drape: Stitch rings or ring tape along the side edges and along the horizontal lines. Tie cords to the bottom rings and thread through to screw eyes. Draw drape up to create billowing effect.

Curtains, draperies and blinds

Hem allowances and methods

To ensure accuracy in the finished length of curtains or draperies, fold and tack hem allowances, hang panels a few days, then adjust if necessary. A hem at the sill should just clear; one at the floor should clear by 1 cm; combined curtains and draperies should be the same length. If using weights, pin or tack them in place to test the effect.

Average hem allowances are 5 cm for curtains, 8 to 15 cm for draperies, depending on length. While a single hem is adequate for mediumweight or heavy fabric, a double hem is recommended for sheers, and will improve the hang of any fabric. Of the various ways to finish hems, machine methods and fusing are the most practical, but many people prefer hand-finished draperies.

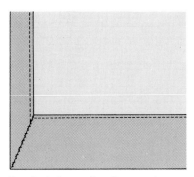

For single hem, allow 6 mm to 1 cm to turn under at edge. At each corner, turn edge in diagonally to form a mitre.

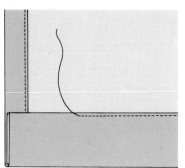

For double hem, allow turn-under equal to hem depth. Keeps edge from showing through sheers, and adds weight.

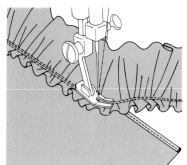

For ruffled hem, allow 1 cm to make a narrow machine-stitched hem, folded to right side. Topstitch ruffle over hem.

Weighting and anchoring hems

Curtains and draperies hang better when hems are weighted or anchored. Individual weights are used for heavier fabrics. They are attached at the corners and at the bottom of seams to prevent drawing.

Lead weight tape is run through the hems of sheer and lightweight panels to encourage even hanging and minimise billowing. Cup hooks can also be used to hold side hems straight and stationary.

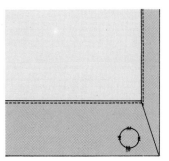

For unlined curtains, weights should be covered before being sewn to hem. Trace shape of weight onto a double thickness of curtain fabric; add 6 mm for seaming. Stitch, leaving an opening for turning. Turn right side out, slip weight in and close opening. Sew to hem at corners and seams.

For sheer curtains, the best choice is lead weight tape. It should be purchased in a length to equal the width of the curtain. Slip tape through the hem, then tack it in place with a few stitches at the side hems and at any seams.

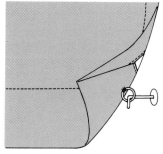

For lined draperies, cover the weight with lining fabric as described above for unlined panels. Sew the weight to the drapery hem, high enough so that lining hangs over it. If preferred, the weight can be sewn on with no covering, as you would a button.

To anchor curtains so that outside edges will remain straight and taut, use small plastic rings and cup hooks. Sew rings to bottom hem of curtains at outer edge then screw cup hooks into the wall behind the rings. Hooks should point down to hold the rings most securely.

Setting pleats

To hang gracefully, pleat folds may need setting: When draperies are hung, arrange the folds carefully. Pin them in position at the bottom, or tie them loosely with soft cord or tape, using T-pins to support tape if necessary. Leave them in place for a few days.

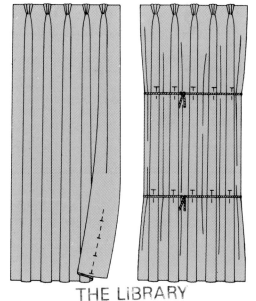

419

Curtains, draperies and blinds

Making a lining

Lining gives a more finished look to draperies or café curtains and, at the same time, adds opaqueness, protects fabric from fading and helps to insulate a room against cold or heat.

Lining fabric is usually an opaque cotton, such as sateen or calico, in white or off-white. Specially treated fabrics are also available for extra insulation. When cutting panels to be lined, allow 10 cm for self-facings at sides, 8 cm for a bottom hem, and 1 cm for the top seam. Cut the lining 10 cm narrower than the full curtain width, and 8 cm shorter so that it hangs above the curtain.

The hem allowances given above are for short curtains. For floor-length panels, allow more depth—at least 12 to 15 cm for the drapery panels, and about 8 cm for the lining.

Hem the lining first, then stitch it to each side of the drapery panel (when drapery is turned right side out, it will have a 4 cm self-facing on each side). Next, form the pleats as directed on pp. 416–417. Finish the lower edges as shown below.

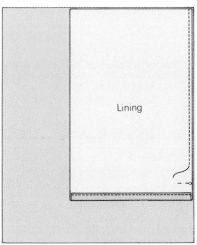

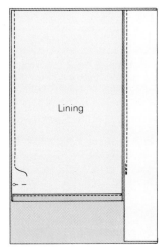

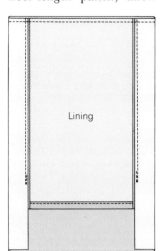

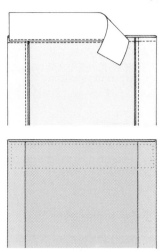

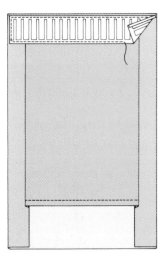

1. Make a 2 cm hem at lining bottom. Place lining on drapery, right sides together, top and right edges aligned. Stitch 1 cm seam from top to 5 cm above lining hem.

2. Pull lining over to left side, aligning edge with that of drapery. Stitch 1 cm seam, starting at top, ending 5 cm above lining hem.

3. Centre lining on the drapery; press seams toward the lining. Stitch across top of lining and drapery, 1 cm from the edge.

For covered heading, align edge of stiffener with top seam, as shown; stitch the edge. Turn panel right side out. Press sides.

For pleater tape heading, do not stitch top as in Step 3. Turn drapery right side out; tack top edges. Sew tape round outer edge.

Finishing lower edges of lined draperies

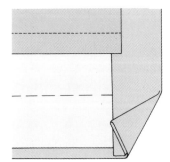

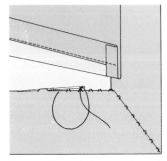

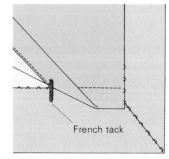

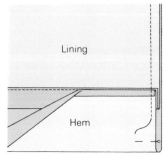

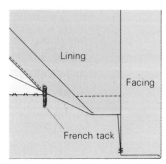

To hand-finish lower edges, fold and press hem edge under 1 cm; turn corner in diagonally. (For bulky fabric, trim excess from corner.)

Turn up hem; slip-hem in place. If a different hand or machine finish is preferred, consult the Hems chapter for suitable method.

Slip-hem remainder of lining to the facing and hem. Anchor lining to drapery hem every 25 cm to keep the layers aligned.

To machine-finish lower side edges, have panel wrong side out, as in Step 3, above. Fold right side of hem over drapery and lining; pin.

Stitch side seam down to hem fold. Turn drapery right side out. Slip-hem the hem. Tack bottom end of facing to hem. French-tack the lining.

Curtains, draperies and blinds

Making a detachable lining with tape

Detachable linings can be easily and quickly made by using lining tape. This method is particularly useful as it allows the lining to be hooked on and off for separate washing. This style of tape can be used with almost all types of commercial pleater tape. The hooks which suspend the curtain from the track also attach lining to curtain. Plastic or nylon hooks are easier to remove than metal hooks.

Allow one and a half to double the width of the track when calculating fabric and tape needs. (You can reduce this to one and a quarter if you are using a heavy lining such as a metallic reflective fabric for insulation.) Allow approximately 10 cm for the hem. Make the lining hang slightly inside the curtain at the sides and have the hem 2 to 3 cm shorter than that of the curtain so that the lining will not show from the right side.

After stitching the side and bottom hems of the lining, sew the top edge between the two sides of the split skirt on the lining tape, as shown below.

Remember not to cut off the surplus cords once the lining is pleated up so that it can be flattened for easy cleaning. Surplus cords can be hung neatly out of sight using a specially designed cord tidy.

If desired, the lining can be anchored to the curtain at side hems and at the hem with tacks or French tacks. These stitches would have to be removed when detaching the lining for washing.

Pelmets and valances

A pelmet or valance will add that finishing touch and is useful if you wish to disguise an awkward feature of a window or curtain heading.

Any heavy fabric stiffened with buckram or similar material tacked to a headboard can form a pelmet. Use a paper pattern of the required depth cut to fit the front of the headboard and both returns. If a join is needed a better appearance will be achieved by having two side pieces of equal length, centring the main piece.

A valance is like a very short curtain and is usually hung on a valance rail or rod which must not interfere with the working of the curtain track behind it. Lining is advisable for pelmets and valances.

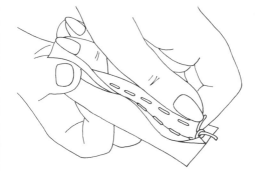

1. Taking the edge of the tape which will come to the centre of the track, knot freed cord ends together and trim off the surplus tape.

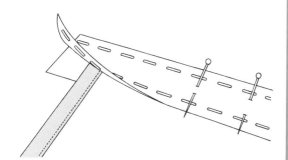

2. Slip top edge of lining between two sides of tape's split skirt. Turn under edge of tape to enclose knotted ends and stitch in place.

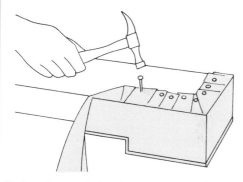

Fit the pelmet to the headboard with plated staples or small flat-headed brass nails. It can also be attached to a rod or rail with curtain hooks.

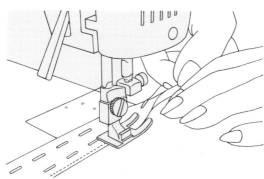

3. Machine a line of stitching to trap lining between the two tape skirts. Finish end of tape by turning under but leave cords free for pleating up.

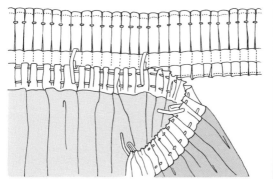

4. Attach lining to curtain by inserting stem of each hook through hole in top edge of lining tape, then through pocket on curtain, before turning over to final position.

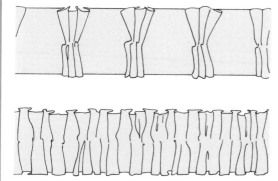

A valance heading is most easily made with pleater tape, but can also be pleated or gathered by hand. Lining will give a valance a more finished appearance.

Knitting for yourself and your family can be a most enjoyable pastime—and a productive one. This chapter will start you with the basics of choosing yarn and essential equipment. Six different ways of starting, or casting on, are described, so you can choose the best method for you and your project. Detailed instructions and step-by-step diagrams follow for working knit and purl stitches which form the basis of every knitted article, then for basic stitch patterns, selvage and finishing, or casting off. The mysteries of knitting terminology and the abbreviations used in patterns are all explained before the chapter moves on to increasing and decreasing, essential for shaping garments, and then to crossing stitches, which will open the decorative world of cables. Circular knitting (done with double-point needles), picking up stitches and correcting errors complete the chapter.

Knitting supplies

Yarns

Many yarns are suitable for use in knitting. Choices differ in fibre content, texture, weight and ply. The chart below gives the characteristics and uses of natural and artificial yarns that are widely available and frequently chosen for knitting. In addition to the basic types included in the chart, most yarn manufacturers produce artificial and blended yarns of their own design, which they sell under their own trade names. These names will become familiar to you after a few visits to well-stocked specialist yarn stores. To broaden your yarn choices beyond the recommendations in commercial pattern books, consult this chart and the sections on Selecting yarn (p. 427) and Checking the tension (p. 443).

NAME	WEIGHT	DESCRIPTION	USES
Babywool	Light 2–4 ply	Pure wool or synthetic; soft, light and hardwearing	Baby garments
Crêpe	Medium to heavy 4–12 ply	A cabled yarn, usually pure wool or a mixture; hardwearing and practical	General purpose; sportswear, schoolwear; everyday garments
Woollen	Wide range	A soft yarn, not cabled; may be pure wool or synthetic	General purpose and fashion garments
Mohair	Light	Pure mohair is soft and fluffy; when blended with wool may be smooth and firm	Fashion garments when a fluffy texture is desired
Bouclé	Medium	Natural and/or synthetic yarns plied with a textured effect	Fashion garments where extra texture is desired
Synthetic	Wide range	Chemically produced fibres; machine washable and economical	Fashion garments, children's wear
Ribbon	Various	Rayon or cotton; knitted or woven	Fashion garments
Metallic	Light	Shiny, smooth or textured	Fashion garments
Rovings	Medium to heavy	Pure wool single yarn, lightly spun; soft and bulky	Outdoor and hardwearing garments
Fashion yarns	Wide range	Natural or synthetic fibres blended and/or plied with other fibres or yarns	A wide range of yarns is available for all styles of fashion garments
Natural and handspun	Wide range	Natural undyed fibres including wool, angora, silk, alpaca	Many and various
Cotton	Medium to light 4–12 ply	Natural fibre; soft and smooth	Summer and between seasons garments

Selecting yarn

A knitting yarn should be appropriate for both style and intended purpose. Consider the differences in yarn characteristics and weigh the advantages and disadvantages for each project.

The most significant factor in yarn performance is fibre content. *Wool* and *acrylic* are warm yarns, the most versatile because they can be spun in many weights and types. Their resilience makes them especially desirable for garments. Of the two, wool gives the better results. *Linen* and *cotton* are cool yarns, used mostly for summer garments and household items. *Rayon* and *nylon* are incorporated into some blends for textural interest.

A yarn's construction is crucial to its suitability for a purpose. Highly twisted yarns are smooth, easy to work with, generally durable and suitable for any stitch pattern. Loosely twisted or handspun yarns are less durable, but have an appealing texture and give great warmth

due to their high loft (fluffiness). Fancy yarns, in which strands of different thicknesses or fibres are twisted together, are exciting in texture but less durable and suited only to simple stitch patterns.

Yarn ply is not related to the number of strands of yarn twisted together. Ply is, in general, an indication of the thickness of the yarn (4 ply being thicker than 2 ply), but it is not an indication of its strength. Neither is ply an indication of a yarn's weight—light, medium or heavy. Suggestions for suitable articles in each weight are in the chart opposite.

Good elasticity (stretch capacity) and recovery (return to original size) are desirable qualities in a yarn to be used for making a garment. Both comfort and fit retention depend on these qualities. In a yarn used for making a household item, ability to withstand many washings may be more important. Check yarn labels for the care requirements.

Tips for buying yarn

Most knitting projects represent a substantial investment in time and money. It pays to be an informed consumer when purchasing yarns.

1. Check yarn labels for dye lot number and purchase all yarn of one colour from the same dye lot. Each number represents a different dye bath and may differ slightly from another.

2. Buy enough yarn of the same dye lot to complete the article. This is an instance where too much is better than not enough. Some stores will accept the return of unused skeins within a reasonable time. Check this possibility at the time of purchase.

3. Check the yarn label for washability and other care information. If none is given, you should wash and block your tension swatch to see how the yarn responds to these procedures.

4. If a yarn label gives tension information, the needle size mentioned is the one recommended for that particular yarn. It is wise to stay within one size of the recommendation.

5. To duplicate the appearance and fit of your chosen pattern, it is simplest to buy the yarn recommended for it, though you can of course choose a colour other than the one shown.

6. If you choose to substitute another yarn for the one recommended, select yarn as close as possible to the original in weight and type. It is a good idea to buy a single skein first and knit a swatch to see how the tension and appearance compare with those of the pattern.

7. To calculate yarn needs for a substitution or your own design, see Designing a garment, p. 451.

8. Should you need to convert ounces to grams or vice versa, use this formula: 100 grams = 3.52 ounces. For example, if 16 ounces of yarn are called for, and you are substituting a yarn weighed in grams, divide 16 by 3.52 and multiply by 100. The quantity is 454 grams.

9. Before each purchase, check a yarn's recovery. Stretch and release a 15 cm length. If it does not return to its original size, you cannot expect the knitted article to hold its shape.

Winding yarn

The most convenient way to use yarn is from a ball or skein that can be pulled out from the centre. In this form it is less likely to tangle or to unwind too quickly. Yarn is often sold this way; if it is not, rewind the yarn before you use it. Before you begin rewinding a skein, slip it over the back of a chair and cut the anchoring string. Take care to wind the ball loosely. If yarn is pulled too tight, it will stretch and may lose some elasticity.

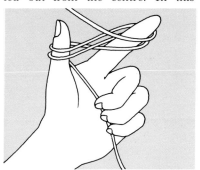

Grasp a loose end of yarn firmly between back fingers and palm of left hand, about 30 cm from the end. Wind yarn six or eight times around thumb and index finger in figure-of-eight fashion.

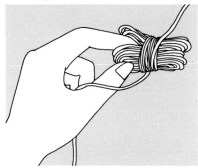

Slip yarn off fingers and fold it in half, end to end. Holding the folded bunch between thumb and index finger, wind the yarn loosely around both yarn and fingers about a dozen times.

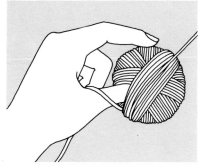

Keeping thumb in centre, continue to wind yarn, turning the ball constantly so it will be round. When it is 8 cm across, remove your thumb, but be careful not to wind over the centre yarn.

Continue winding loosely until all the yarn is taken up, then tuck the final end into the ball. Use the ball by drawing yarn out from the centre, as shown in the illustration.

Knitting supplies

Needles

There are three basic types of knitting needle—*single-point, double-point,* and *circular.* Examples of each needle type are illustrated below.

Needle thickness is expressed in millimetres (mm). The thicker the needle, the larger the stitch. While there are no precise rules for needle and yarn relationship, in general, thicker yarns should be worked with large needles, thinner yarns with small ones. If the needles are too large for the yarn, the structure of the knitted fabric will be flimsy; if they are too small, the structure will be too compact and inelastic. Some yarn labels include a recommended needle size; a safe approach is to stay within one size of this.

Needle length should be chosen according to a project's dimensions. In general, shorter ones are easier to use but they should hold all stitches comfortably. A circular needle should be at least 5 cm less than the circumference of the knitting.

Choice of needle material—plastic, metal or wood—is largely a matter of personal preference and availability. Plastic is quieter and somewhat easier for a beginner to manage. Metal is noisier, but stitches slide more readily; their rigidity may, however, cause problems for arthritic knitters. Bamboo or wood are more expensive, but this disadvantage is far outweighed by their superior feel and performance. In caring for needles, it is best to store them flat or in a tube with their points protected.

Needle size comparisons

Knitting needles (also called knitting pins) sold in the United Kingdom, Australia and New Zealand are sized in millimetres (mm). The number on the needle indicates the diameter of the needle in millimetres. Many people, however, still have in their possession needles marked in old English sizes; some may also have needles manufactured in the United States, where yet a third standard of sizing is used. Many patterns, too, are imported from other countries and may specify a needle size that is not metric. And many people keep and use knitting patterns published before the introduction of metric needle sizes.

The chart below gives the equivalent sizes for needles marked in metric, old English and American sizes. Note: Because knitting needles are produced by several manufacturers, there are very slight variations in sizes between different makes. The chart gives approximate comparisons. If you are in any doubt, try to contact the manufacturer of the needles you are using. If you are following a metric pattern and want to use non-metric needles, an alternative is to use a knitting needle gauge, shown on the opposite page.

Before starting any knitting project, however, make a test swatch to determine the size of the needles you should use to ensure that your tension matches the one specified in the instructions. See pages 437 and 443 for more information about tension.

METRIC	OLD ENGLISH	AMERICAN	METRIC	OLD ENGLISH	AMERICAN
2.00	14	0	5.00	6	8
2.25	13	1	5.50	5	9
2.50	–	–	6.00	4	10
2.75	12	2	6.50	3	10½
3.00	11	–	7.00	2	–
3.25	10	3	7.50	1	11
3.50	–	4	8.00	0	12
3.75	9	5	9.00	00	13
4.00	8	6	10.00	000	15
4.50	7	7			

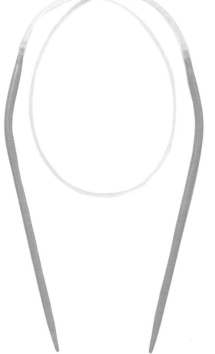

A circular needle is used to knit round, seamless garments, or in preference to straight needles for flat pieces. It consists of two nylon, aluminium or bamboo tips connected by a flexible nylon cord.

Single-point needles are used in pairs to knit flat pieces. Straight and rigid, they are used more frequently than other types, and are considered the standard needles. In fact, knitting instructions usually do not specify them by type, simply indicating what size to use.

Jiffy or **rocket needles** are large-sized (12–25 mm in diameter) single-point needles. Work proceeds rapidly and the fabric produced is quite thick and loosely structured.

Double-point needles are used in sets of four or more to knit seamless, circular items, such as socks or mittens. In some instructions, they are abbreviated as dp needles.

Knitting aids

There are many knitting aids available, each one designed to make a certain task easier. A selection of such aids is shown below. Besides those items specifically meant for knitting, a few other craft supplies are indispensable. Examples are the crochet hook and knitter's needles shown below, also scissors for cutting yarn. A knitting, or tension square gauge is useful for checking tension. Use coloured-head pins when assembling a knitted garment; they do not disappear into the pile. Graph paper and a notebook are useful for charting and keeping track of patterns.

A crochet hook is the best tool for recovering a dropped stitch that has run several rows down. It can also be used for casting off, or joining knitted sections with a slipstitch. A 3 or 4 mm hook is easiest to handle.

A cable needle holds a group of stitches waiting for a cable stitch pattern. Cable needles are essentially shorter versions of double-point needles (see opposite page). The size chosen (2 to 7.5 mm) should correspond as closely as possible to that of the working needle.

Knitter's needles have large eyes and blunt ends, which makes them ideal for sewing knitted sections together. They are also used for concealing yarn ends on a finished article. Sold in pairs, they are available in medium and large sizes.

A knitting gauge, or tension square gauge, is used to check tension—the number of stitches and/or rows per 10 cm as specified in the pattern.

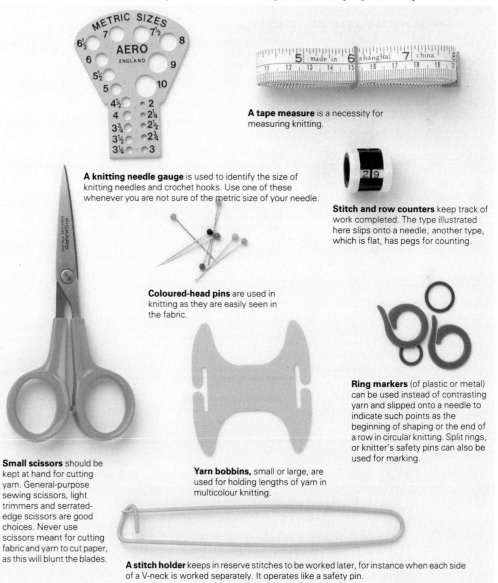

A knitting needle gauge is used to identify the size of knitting needles and crochet hooks. Use one of these whenever you are not sure of the metric size of your needle.

A tape measure is a necessity for measuring knitting.

Stitch and row counters keep track of work completed. The type illustrated here slips onto a needle; another type, which is flat, has pegs for counting.

Coloured-head pins are used in knitting as they are easily seen in the fabric.

Small scissors should be kept at hand for cutting yarn. General-purpose sewing scissors, light trimmers and serrated-edge scissors are good choices. Never use scissors meant for cutting fabric and yarn to cut paper, as this will blunt the blades.

Yarn bobbins, small or large, are used for holding lengths of yarn in multicolour knitting.

Ring markers (of plastic or metal) can be used instead of contrasting yarn and slipped onto a needle to indicate such points as the beginning of shaping or the end of a row in circular knitting. Split rings, or knitter's safety pins can also be used for marking.

A stitch holder keeps in reserve stitches to be worked later, for instance when each side of a V-neck is worked separately. It operates like a safety pin.

429

General knitting techniques

Casting on

Casting on is the first step in knitting. It forms the first row of stitches and one selvage of the finished article, usually the bottom, or hem, edge.

There are many methods for casting on; six of the most representative are shown here. Each method is best suited to a particular type of stitch or project, depending on the elasticity or firmness required in the finished article.

The character of a cast-on edge is determined not only by the way in which stitches are put on the needle, but also by the way they are to be worked. Knitting into the front of the stitch produces a looser edge than working into the back or between the stitches as in cable cast-on.

Stitches of the cast-on row should be uniform in size or the edge will be untidy. It is worth the time to re-do them if the first attempt is unsatisfactory. The cast-on stitches should also be moderately loose so they will be easy to work.

When casting on a large number of stitches, keeping count is easier if you slip a loop of contrasting yarn or a ring marker on the needle every 10 or 20 stitches.

To form slip knot for first stitch, make a loop 15 cm from yarn end; insert needle, draw through a loop from the ball end and tighten the knot.

Two-needle methods of casting on

KNITTING ON

Knitting on employs two needles and one yarn length. Each new stitch is formed as in knitting, then transferred to the left needle. A versatile selvage, it is soft when worked through loop fronts, firm if worked through loop backs. Suitable also for increasing stitches at one side or completing a buttonhole.

CABLE CAST-ON

Cable cast-on is produced the same way as knitting on, but for each new stitch, the needle is inserted between the two previous stitches. The resulting edge is decorative and elastic, nicely suited to ribbing and attractive for the edges of socks or hats. Stitches should be knitted off through the loop fronts only.

RIB CABLE CAST-ON

Rib cable cast-on produces a firm edge that also has good elasticity for single rib. The appearance closely resembles a machine cast-on as this method does not create the ridge effect typical of hand casting on. On the first row, work the knit stitches through the back loops. Begin and finish first row with knit 2.

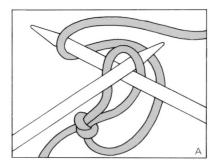

Hold needle with slip knot in left hand. Insert right needle and take yarn around it as for knitting (A); draw yarn through to form a new stitch, but do not

drop first loop from left needle (B). Instead, transfer new stitch to left needle and knit into it to form the next new stitch.

Make slip knot and first stitch as in knitting on (above). For each new stitch after that, insert the right needle between two stitches; take yarn

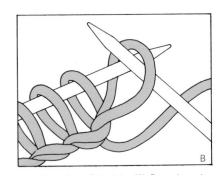

around needle as for knitting (A). Draw through a new stitch, then transfer it to left needle (B). Continue forming new stitches between two loops.

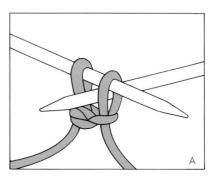

Cast on two stitches using knitting on. Insert right hand needle between two stitches purlwise. Wrap yarn around needle and draw new stitch

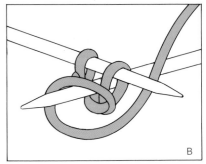

through (A). Transfer it to left hand needle (B). Continue forming new stitches alternately knit and purl, finishing with an odd number.

One-needle methods of casting on

SINGLE CAST-ON

Single cast-on is done with one needle and one length of yarn. It forms a loose selvage that is used for a hem edge or a buttonhole or for lace. This is a very easy cast-on method, but somewhat difficult to work off the needle evenly in the first row. For a beginner, the double cast-on is easier to control.

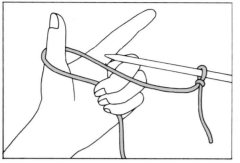

1. Make slip knot on needle held in the right hand. Wrap yarn from the ball around left thumb, as shown, then grasp yarn firmly between the palm and back fingers.

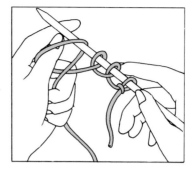

2. Turn thumb so the back of it is facing you; insert needle front to back through the loop that is formed by twisting the thumb.

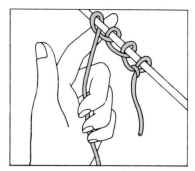

3. Slip thumb out of loop, at same time pulling yarn downward to close the loop around the needle. Repeat Steps 2 and 3.

DOUBLE CAST-ON

Double cast-on employs one needle and a double length of yarn; it is started a measured distance from the yarn end, allowing 2.5 cm per stitch. Firm, yet elastic, this method is suitable for any pattern that does not require a delicate edge. It is recommended for beginners, since no experience is needed.

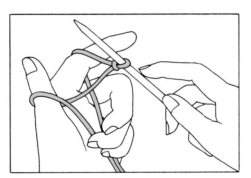

1. Make slip knot a measured distance from yarn end. Wrap short end over left thumb, yarn from ball over left index finger; hold both ends between palm and back fingers.

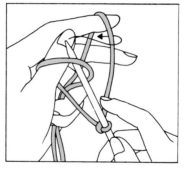

2. Slip needle up through the thumb loop, then scoop yarn from the index finger (see arrow) and draw a loop onto the needle.

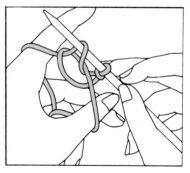

3. Release thumb loop; tighten loop on the needle by drawing the short yarn forward with the thumb. Repeat Steps 2 and 3.

PROVISIONAL CAST-ON

Provisional cast-on employs two needles held together and two yarns; the working yarn is wrapped around a foundation yarn, which is removed later when stitches are picked up for knitting or grafting. To begin, cut a length of yarn in a contrasting colour four times as long as the final width of work.

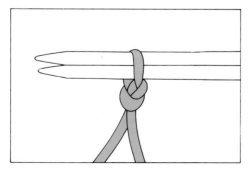

1. Make a slip knot in the working yarn (dark) and place it on two needles. Hold the contrasting yarn (the foundation yarn) beside the slip knot.

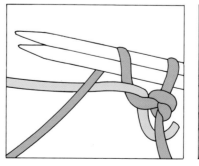

2. Take the working yarn under it and over the needles from front to back. Bring foundation yarn in front of working yarn.

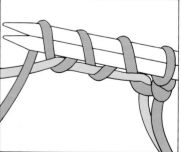

3. Repeat Step 2 until you have cast on the required number of stitches. Remove one needle and knit the first row.

Forming the knit stitch: English (right-handed) method

The **knit stitch** is one of two fundamental movements in knitting; it forms a flat vertical loop on the fabric face.

Knitting methods vary from one place to another; two widely used ones are shown below and opposite.

In both, the stitches are worked off the left needle onto the right, but in one, yarn is controlled with the right hand, in the other, with the left. Whatever your natural hand preference, you should be able to master either method, because the nature of knitting is basically ambidextrous.

In the right-handed technique, yarn is drawn around the right needle with the right index finger. Tension (control of yarn released with each stitch) is maintained between the two end fingers by wrapping yarn around the last. There are other correct ways to wrap yarn. The main thing is to feel comfortable with the method and to achieve even tension and speed.

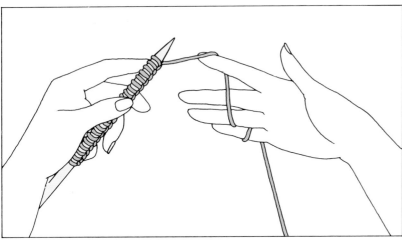

1. Grasp the needle with cast-on stitches in the left hand. The first stitch should be about 2 cm from the tip. Take yarn around little finger of right hand, under the next two fingers, and over the top of the index finger, extending it about 5 cm from the first stitch on the needle.

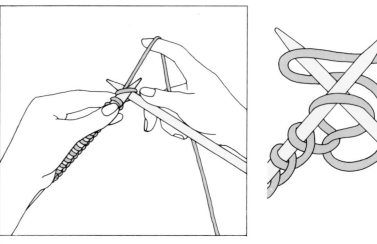

2. Holding yarn behind the work, °insert right needle into front of first stitch from left to right (needle tip points toward the back). With the right index finger, take yarn forward *under* the right needle, then backward *over* the top (see detail above right).

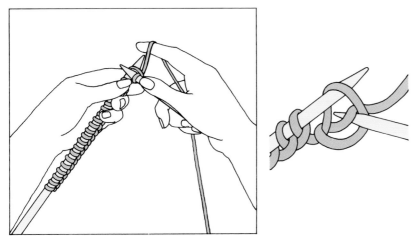

3. Draw the loop on the right needle forward through the stitch, at the same time pushing the stitch on the left needle toward the tip. (With the deftness that comes with practice, these two movements will become smoothly coordinated. When they do, your speed will increase.)

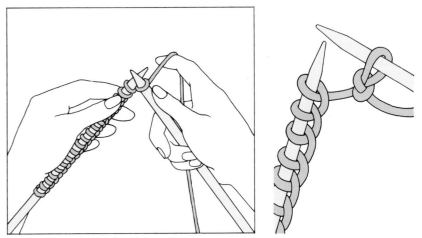

4. Allow first stitch to slide off left needle. New stitch (the loop just made) remains on right needle.° Repeat steps between asterisks, pushing stitches forward on left needle with thumb, index and middle fingers, moving stitches back on right needle with the thumb.

Forming the knit stitch: Continental (left-handed) method

Controlling yarn with the left hand is the customary knitting practice in many European and Eastern countries. In this method, the Continental, the fundamental action is to scoop yarn from the left index finger onto the right needle. There are several ways to position yarn. Here, tension is controlled partly with the last two fingers, and partly with the index finger, extending it to tighten yarn after the needle passes underneath.

Many experts believe that greater speed can be attained with the Continental than with the English method. Whatever your choice, you will find that speed is developed by holding the needles lightly and minimising all movements. For the right-handed method, nimble finger action is required; for the left-handed, the key is flexible wrist movement. If you learn both methods, you can knit some two-colour patterns more quickly.

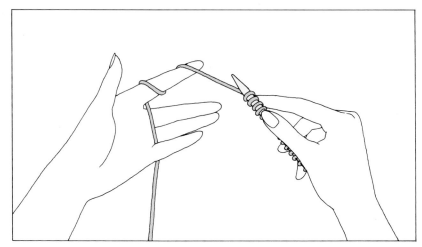

1. Hold the needle with cast-on stitches in the right hand and wrap yarn over the left, taking it between the fourth and fifth fingers, under the next two fingers, over the top of the index finger, then around it once more. The yarn should extend about 5 cm from the first stitch.

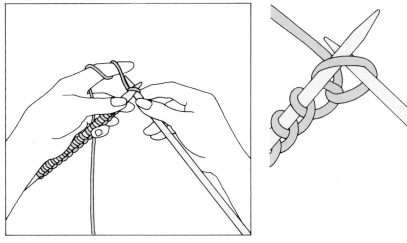

2. Transfer needle with stitches to the left hand and extend index finger slightly, pulling the yarn behind the needle. Push the first stitch up near the tip. °Insert right needle into front of first stitch from left to right (needle tip points toward the back).

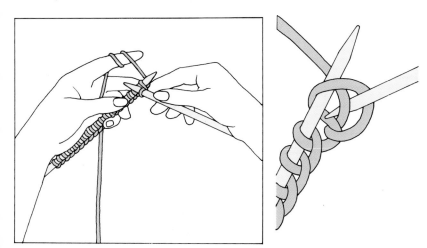

3. Twist the right needle and pull the tip *under* the yarn to draw a loop through the stitch. At the same time, push the stitch on the left needle toward the tip. (With the deftness that comes with practice, these two movements will become smoothly coordinated.)

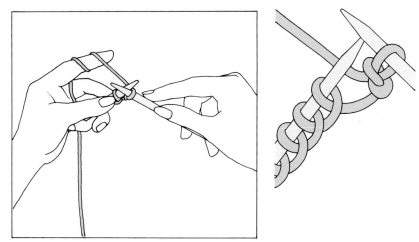

4. Allow first stitch to slide off left needle. New stitch (the loop just made) remains on the right needle.° Repeat steps between asterisks, pushing stitches forward on the left needle with thumb and middle finger, moving stitches back on right needle with the thumb.

Forming the purl stitch: English (right-handed) method

A **purl stitch** is the reverse side of a knit stitch. Its loop structure is a horizontal semicircle, whereas the knit loop is vertical and flat (see p. 434).

In forming a purl stitch, the movements are the reverse of those used for knitting. The needle enters the front of the stitch from right to left, and the yarn, held in front of the work, is cast over the needle back to front.

When yarn is controlled with the right hand (as shown below), purl stitches tend to be looser than the knit ones. This is because the yarn must be cast farther to form a purl stitch than is required for the knit movements. With experience, a natural compensation is usually developed, especially if the index finger is kept close to the work. Should the difficulty persist, a good exercise is to keep working a 1 × 1 rib (see p. 436 for directions) until an even tension has been established.

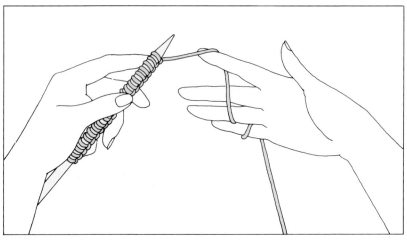

1. Grasp the needle with cast-on stitches in the left hand. First stitch should be about 2 cm from tip. Take yarn around little finger of the right hand, under the next two fingers, and over the top of the index finger, extending it about 5 cm from first stitch on needle.

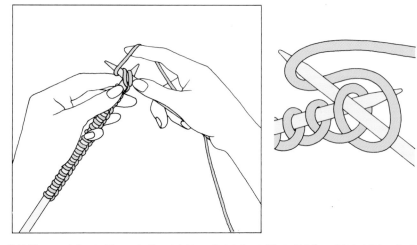

2. Holding yarn in front of the work, °insert right needle into front of first stitch from right to left (needle tip points upward slightly). With the right index finger, take yarn backward *over* the right needle, then forward and *under* it (see detail above right).

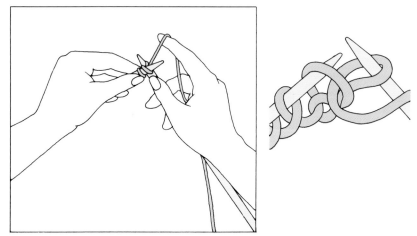

3. Draw the loop on the right needle backward through the stitch, at the same time pushing the stitch on the left needle toward the tip. (With the deftness that comes with practice, these two movements will become smoothly coordinated.)

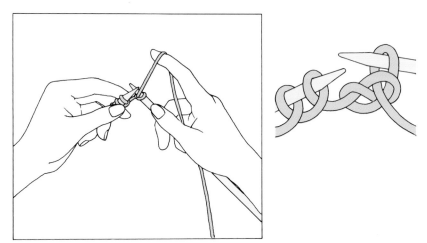

4. Allow first stitch to slide off left needle. New stitch (the loop just made) remains on the right needle.° Repeat steps between asterisks, pushing stitches forward on left needle with thumb, index, and middle fingers, moving stitches back on right needle with thumb.

Forming the purl stitch: Continental (left-handed) method

To form a purl stitch, yarn is held taut with the left index finger while a new loop is scooped up with the right needle. This action is facilitated by a forward twist of the wrist to release yarn, and by anchoring the working stitch with the thumb as the new stitch is drawn through it.

Shifting yarn from knit to purl position, and vice versa, can slow your working speed unless the manoeuvre is part of the working rhythm. With yarn held in the left hand, a shift is made by swinging yarn forward between needle tips to the purl position, and back again, the same way, to resume the knit position. Yarn in the right hand must be wrapped around the right needle, back to front, to work a purl stitch, then front to back again for the knit stitch. Less speed will be lost if you keep the index finger close to the work and the working stitches close to the needle tips.

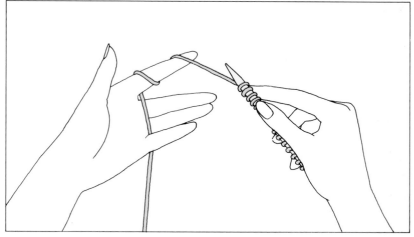

1. Hold the needle with cast-on stitches in the right hand and wrap yarn over the left, taking it between the fourth and fifth fingers, under the next two fingers, over the top of the index finger, then around it once more. Yarn should extend about 5 cm from the first stitch.

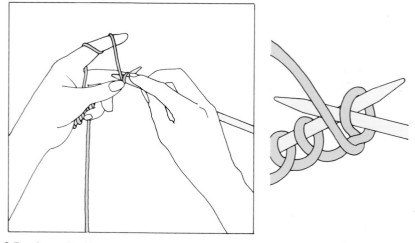

2. Transfer needle with stitches to left hand and extend index finger, pulling yarn in front of needle. Using thumb and middle finger, push first stitch up near tip. ° Insert right needle into front of first stitch, right to left (tip points upward slightly).

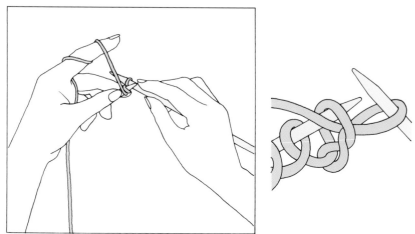

3. Turn left wrist so that yarn on index finger comes toward you, then push back and down with the right needle to draw a loop back through the stitch. At the same time, push stitch on left needle toward tip. (With practice, these movements become smoothly coordinated.)

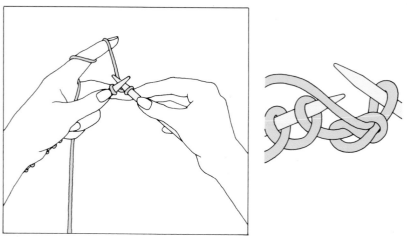

4. Allow first stitch to slide off left needle and straighten left index finger to tighten new stitch on right needle.° Repeat steps between asterisks, pushing stitches forward on left needle with thumb and middle finger, moving stitches back on right needle with the thumb.

General knitting techniques

Basic stitch patterns

The basic stitch patterns, shown below, are the most versatile and the easiest patterns to produce, ideal for a beginner. To practise these patterns, use mediumweight, general purpose knitting yarn with size 4 mm needles, and cast on 20 to 24 stitches. (**Note:** Each pattern has a *multiple*, which is the smallest number of stitches needed to complete one pattern unit. Work the first pattern row, then turn the needle and work the next row. As you knit, pay special attention to developing moderate and even tension (see opposite page), and always complete a row before setting the work down. Each time you try a new pattern or check tension, you can proceed this way. Eventually, if you like, squares can be joined to make something useful such as a cushion top or soft tote bag.

Each basic pattern is produced with plain knit and/or purl stitches (see Techniques, pp. 432–435) in which the stitch loop is positioned with the left side (thread) to the back of the needle, and the right side to the front. Plain stitch methods can be modified for the twisted variations illustrated opposite. These distinctions help you avoid twisting stitches accidentally, a not unusual occurrence when a dropped stitch has been retrieved or work put down with a row in progress.

Stocking stitch

Reverse stocking stitch

The garter stitch is normally produced by knitting every stitch of every row, though purling every stitch will give the same results. The simplest of all stitch patterns, it has a pebbly surface that is identical on both sides, and a somewhat loose structure that stretches equally in both directions. Use for jumpers, blankets, and accessories.
Multiple is any number of stitches
Every row: K

The stocking stitch is produced by knitting one row and purling the next. The most versatile of the basic stitch patterns, it is smooth on one (the knitted) side and pebbly on the other (the purled) side. The knit side is usually considered to be the right side, but the purled side can be used for this purpose if desired; it is then referred to as **reverse stocking stitch** (below left). The fabric stretches more in the crosswise than the lengthwise direction. Use it for jumpers and dresses, also for knitted accessories such as hats, gloves, and socks. See pp. 475–476 for the way stocking stitch is employed in jacquard patterns.
Multiple is any number of stitches
Row 1: K
Row 2: P

1 × 1 rib

2 × 2 rib

The moss or seed stitch is produced by alternating one knit and one purl stitch within a row, then knitting the knit stitches and purling the purl stitches on the return row. The texture of this pattern is similar to that of the garter stitch, but the fabric is firmer. Use it for blankets and garments, also as a contrasting texture for another pattern stitch.
Multiple of 2 sts plus 1
Every row: °K 1, P 1°, K 1

The rib stitch is produced by alternating knit and purl stitches on one row, then purling the knit stitches and knitting the purl stitches on the return row. The result is a pattern of vertical ridges that is identical on both sides when knit and purl stitches are interchanged in equal numbers, with no variations in technique. The ratio of knit to purl stitches may be even or uneven. It is frequently indicated by numbers. Examples are 1 × 1 and 2 × 2, shown left. These are the classic rib patterns often referred to as ribbing. They have considerable elasticity in the crosswise direction and are especially suitable for garment edges, where they provide a snug fit. For this purpose, ribbing is usually worked with needles a size or two smaller than those that are used for the garment.
For 1 × 1 rib, multiple of 2 sts
Every row: °K 1, P 1°
For 2 × 2 rib, multiple of 4 sts
Every row: °K 2, P 2°

Variations on basic stitch patterns

The performance and appearance of basic stitch patterns can be altered by entering the stitch or wrapping yarn contrary to the usual way. The resulting fabrics (examples shown below) are somewhat firmer and more elastic than those shown on the opposite page. You can knit swatches and compare them.

One variation is the **twisted stitch,** formed by entering the back instead of the front of a loop. This action twists the loop a half turn at the base so that it does not lie as flat as the regular stitch. Either knit or purl stitches can be twisted in a given pattern, but rarely both. For *twisted stocking stitch*, work into the back loop of all stitches on the knit row and work all purl stitches normally. For a *1 × 1 twisted rib*, work into the back loop of all the knit stitches and work all the

purl stitches in the normal way.

Another variation is the **plaited stitch,** produced by wrapping yarn *over* the needle for a knit stitch, *under* the needle for a purl stitch. Stitches formed this way are continually twisted and the resulting fabric is exceptionally firm. In the *plaited stocking stitch*, both knit and purl stitches are worked with the techniques shown below right. On the right side, vertical rows resemble 3 ply braid. For *1 × 1 plaited rib*, plaited knit stitch is alternated with plaited purl.

The plaited methods are convenient for working with beads or sequins. They are also practical for knitting with large needles and heavy yarns because the fabric is firmer. Tension for these stitches must be kept looser than normal because of the twist in the stitch.

Twisted stocking stitch

1 × 1 twisted rib

Plaited stocking stitch

Plaited rib

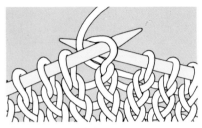

To form a twisted knit stitch, enter *back* of loop, take yarn under needle as for regular knit stitch. On the return row, purl normally.

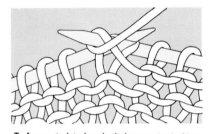

To form a twisted purl stitch, enter *back* of loop, take yarn over needle as for regular purl stitch. On the return row, knit normally.

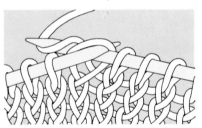

To form a plaited knit stitch, enter front of loop as for regular knit stitch, then take yarn *over* the needle to produce the new stitch.

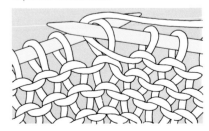

To form a plaited purl stitch, enter front of loop as for regular purl stitch, then take yarn *under* the needle to produce the new stitch.

YARN TENSION

Tension is resistance on the yarn as it passes through the fingers controlling it; it should be moderate, consistent, correct and exact. Moderate tension means that stitches can be worked easily, yet no space is visible between loops and needle. If stitches are too tight, inserting the right-hand needle is difficult. If loops are too loose, they tend to slip off the left-hand needle too soon.

Consistent tension results in an even fabric in which stitches are the same size throughout. Achieving this is a matter of practice. Correct tension is one that suits the yarn and the stitch. Loosely spun or thick yarns need an easy tension; tightly spun and inelastic yarns require a firm tension. Twisted, crossed and cable stitches need a loose tension; lace patterns should be tensioned more firmly.

Exact tension is the duplication of that specified in a knitting pattern. For more about this, see page 443.

ATTACHING NEW YARN

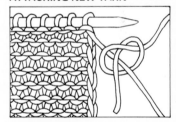

At beginning of row, tie yarn on as shown, then slide it close to the needle. Weave the end into the edge later.

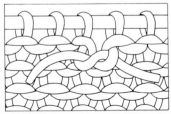

In circular knitting, introduce new yarn where side seam would be. Knit with new yarn for a few stitches, then loosely tie end to old yarn. Weave ends into reverse of work when completed.

437

General knitting techniques

Casting off

Casting off (also called **binding off**) is the removal of stitches from a needle in such a way that they will not unravel. It forms the last row of finished work and sometimes is used to begin the shaping of an armhole, or to produce one side of a horizontal buttonhole. A cast-off edge should be suitable for the type of knit and the purpose it will serve.

Of several casting-off methods, the most versatile are plain and suspended, shown below. Stitches are cast off in the same sequence in which

they were formed (that is, knitting the knit and purling the purl stitch). On the cast-off row, stitches should be moderately loose and uniform, or the edge may draw in or look distorted. If your stitches tend to be tight, you can avoid problems by casting off on a needle one size larger than the size that was used for the knitting.

The three techniques illustrated on the opposite page have limited uses. One should know them, however, to obtain the best results in those situations for which they are suitable.

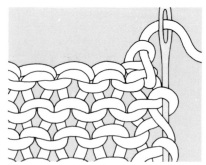

To secure yarn end after casting off, slip it through last stitch, pull to tighten loop.

Thread yarn end in a knitter's needle and weave it into a seam edge for 5–8 cm. Cut remainder.

Casting-off techniques

PLAIN CAST-OFF

Plain cast-off is the simplest, most frequently used method. It is suitable for any situation where an unadorned, firm selvage is required, for example a shoulder seam or buttonhole.

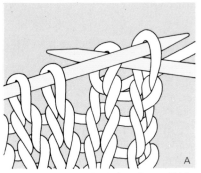

Work two stitches at beginning of row. °Holding yarn behind work, insert left needle in first stitch (A).

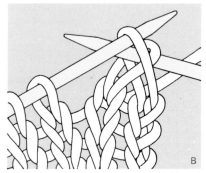

Pull the first stitch over the second stitch (B), and off the needle (C). Work the next stitch.° Repeat

instructions between the asterisks until desired number of stitches are cast off.

SUSPENDED CAST-OFF

Suspended cast-off is similar to plain cast-off, but more flexible. Use this method to finish ribbing, or as a substitute for the plain technique if your selvages tend to be tight.

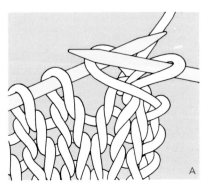

Work two stitches. °Pull first stitch over second as for plain cast-off, but keep pulled stitch on left

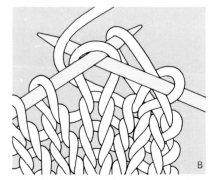

needle (A). Work the next stitch (B); drop both stitches off the left needle at the same time (C).°

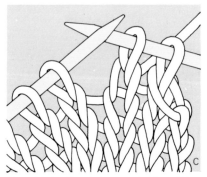

Repeat instructions between asterisks until two stitches remain; knit these together.

438

INVISIBLE CAST-OFF

Invisible cast-off makes an inconspicuous finish for 1 × 1 ribbing. To begin, cut yarn, leaving an end four times the knitting width; thread yarn in a knitter's needle.

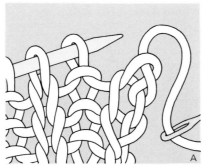

°Insert knitter's needle knitwise in knit stitch at end of needle; drop stitch off (A). Skip next purl stitch; insert needle purlwise in the next stitch;

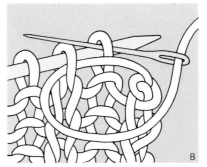

draw yarn through. Insert needle purlwise in purl stitch at end of needle (B), draw yarn through; drop stitch off. Take needle behind the knit stitch

and insert it knitwise in next purl stitch (bring yarn forward between stitches first) (C), draw yarn through.° Repeat from first asterisk.

CROCHETED CAST-OFF

In **crocheted cast-off,** the stitches are worked off in a chain stitch. The result is a firm and decorative edging suitable for a blanket or afghan, also a pretty finish for a hat or bootees.

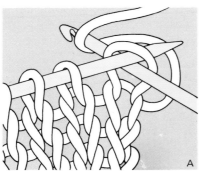

°Holding crochet hook as if it were a needle, insert it knitwise in first stitch; take yarn around

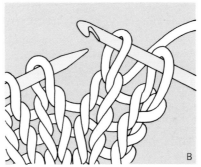

hook (A). Draw through a loop and let first stitch drop off needle. Draw a loop through next stitch

in same way (B). Draw a loop through two loops on hook (C).° Repeat from first asterisk.

THREE-NEEDLE CAST-OFF

Three-needle cast-off of two pieces forms a neat, seamless joining. It can be used for two straight edges having an equal number of stitches, or for shoulder edges shaped by turning.

°With right sides together and both pieces held in the left hand, work the first stitch on each needle

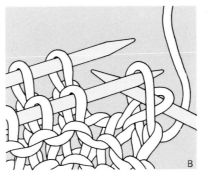

simultaneously (A).° Work the next two stitches together in the same way. Slip first stitch on right

needle over second (B).° Repeat from first asterisk. Ridge produced will be wrong side of seam (C).

General knitting techniques

Side selvages

A side edge, whether it is exposed or enclosed in a seam, should be neat and suited to its purpose. Usually, greater precision is attained by working a narrow border, known as a selvage, in addition to the pattern stitches.

Six ways to form selvages are shown below. For each method, you must add two or four stitches to the total when casting on; the instructions in a pattern do not normally make provision for selvage stitches.

One-stitch methods are used for edges to be seamed, or along which stitches will be picked up, for example, neck or arm bands. Two-stitch methods are more decorative, and also prevent the edges from curling.

They are especially suitable where no finish will be applied, for example, at the edge of a facing. If appropriate, different selvages might be used on the same piece—one type for the left side, another for the right.

Single chain edge 1: Use for stocking stitch and pattern stitches when seams are to be joined edge to edge or stitches are to be picked up later.

On *right* side, slip first stitch knitwise; knit the last stitch. On *wrong* side, slip first stitch purlwise; purl the last stitch.

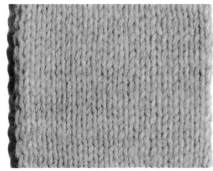

Double picot edge: A decorative and delicate edging; very pretty for baby things. See p. 445 for the way to take yarn forward at the beginning of a row.

On the *right* side, bring yarn in front of right needle (yarn forward), insert needle knitwise in first stitch and slip it, knit the next stitch, pass the slipped stitch over the knitted one. On the *wrong* side, take yarn behind right needle (yarn back), purl first two stitches together.

Single chain edge 2: Forms a neat and flat edge for garter stitch.

Holding yarn at the front of the work, slip the first stitch of each row purlwise, then take yarn behind the work for knitting.

Double chain edge: Use when a decorative as well as firm edging is required.

On the *right* side, slip first stitch knitwise, purl the second stitch. At the end of the row, purl 1, slip the last stitch knitwise. On the *wrong* side, purl the first two and the last two stitches.

Single garter edge: A firm border, especially good for a stocking stitch or a pattern stitch where edges tend to be loose. Use also as an alternative to a single chain edge.

Knit the first and last stitches of every row.

Double garter edge: A firm and even edge; will not curl.

On every row, slip the first stitch knitwise and knit the second stitch; knit the last two stitches.

Note: Double edges should not be used when seams are to be joined together.

Machine knitting

BUYING A KNITTING MACHINE

The major advantage machine knitting has over hand knitting is that tension is automatically controlled, giving the garment the appearance of having been manufactured professionally. Machines also allow you to knit garments much more quickly than by hand.

Buying a knitting machine can involve a considerable outlay, so it is wise to examine the various machines on the market before choosing. Machines offer different features; choose the one best suited to the type of garment you intend to make.

Knitting machines for home use are made by Jones-Brother, Singer, Toyota, Passap, Pfaff, Knitmaster and Silver Reed. The first three are single-bed machines, which means that a ribber attachment is needed for making tubular, ribbed and double-knit fabric. The other four are double-bed machines, so no attachment is needed to make these fabrics. All brands have various machines for fine gauge, standard, bulky or chunky knitting, ranging from 1 ply to 20 ply yarns.

A basic set of punch cards comes with all machines. The cards are fitted into a slot on the back of the machine and produce patterns. Electronic machines can produce hundreds to thousands of patterns at the touch of a button.

Accessories are available for all models for lace making and multi-colour knitting, and to simplify and speed up both designing and making your own garments.

A knit tray or tracer is built into some models but is an extra on the others. This allows you to see the design you are working to. The design is drawn on a Mylar graph sheet and placed in a holder on the back of the machine. It is moved as the work progresses and indicates where to increase or decrease.

Wool winders come with most machines. They wind the yarn on the cone with the correct tension.

USING A KNITTING MACHINE

Take advantage of the free lessons provided by the distributor or retailer to learn how to use your machine properly. Courses in machine knitting are also an invaluable means of making the most of the capabilities of your machine.

The manufacturers all produce pattern books for their machines. The styles are mostly everyday clothes for men, women and children, but there is sufficient variety to make a knitting machine a valid investment if you intend to make all the clothes for your family or take up a profitable hobby.

Once you become proficient on the machine, you can design your own garments. Use the body measurements of the person for whom the garment is intended to calculate the number of stitches and rows required. It is important to make a test swatch for the correct tension; see pages 437 and 443 for information on tension. The number of rows and stitches can be calculated from this tension swatch (see page 481). Then draw up a chart for your design as shown on pages 482–483.

If you use hand-knitting wool it is advisable to pre-wax it by holding a piece of paraffin wax against it as it unwinds. The wax will come off as the garment is made, but any remnants will easily come out with washing. Waxing the wool smoothes the fibres and binds them together. It also makes it easier for the wool to move through the needles, so helping to prevent needle breakage.

GUARANTEES

Most knitting machines carry a five year guarantee against faulty manufacture. All guarantees include a period of free service, usually twelve months. Make sure you keep a record of the serial number and model of your machine.

AFTER-SALES SERVICE

Availability of replacement parts should be considered when you choose a machine. Most distributors have agents in large towns and in the metropolitan areas who can provide spare parts and servicing.

LOOKING AFTER YOUR MACHINE

Always choose the appropriate ply and the correct quality yarn for the garment being made. A finer yarn is used in machine knitting than in hand knitting. For machine knitting, buy cone yarns or wind hand-knitting yarns onto a cone. Cone yarns are widely available.

Dusting and oiling are important for the smooth operation of your machine. Refer to your instruction booklet for the location of oiling points, but be careful not to over-oil.

When the machine is not in use, cover it with a dust cloth.

PARTS OF A TYPICAL KNITTING MACHINE

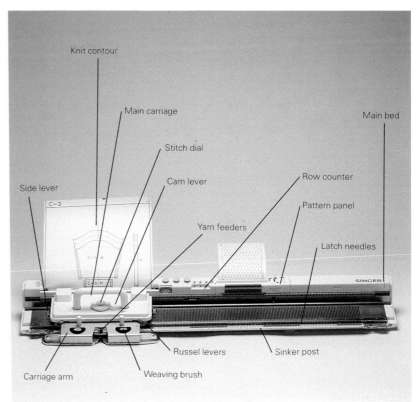

Knit contour
Main carriage
Stitch dial
Cam lever
Side lever
Yarn feeders
Row counter
Main bed
Pattern panel
Latch needles
Russel levers
Sinker post
Carriage arm
Weaving brush

Knitting terminology

For written knitting instructions there is a special vocabulary, much of it expressed in abbreviated or symbolic form. Listed below are abbreviations, symbols, and terms used in this book, in addition to some other commonly used abbreviations, with their definitions alongside. Also included are page references for illustrations of techniques.

These or similar abbreviations are in common use elsewhere. You may encounter terms that are expressed differently, or which are not included here, but an explanatory key for them will usually be provided with the relevant pattern.

An alternative to written instructions is a chart, which uses different symbols. Examples of chart symbols can be found on pages 477–478.

Some of the terminology used in knitting cannot be abbreviated, but may need some explanation. When a pattern instructs you to measure the knitting *above rib,* it means the length of work after the ribbed band, as opposed to *from the beginning,* when work is measured from the cast-on edge.

When the pattern says *cast off stitches at each side* (for example, at the start of sleeve shaping), always cast off at the beginning of two successive rows, never at the end of the row.

End with RS row means that the last row should be worked with the right side facing the knitter (a knit row if you are working stocking stitch). *End with a WS row* means work the last row with the wrong side facing (a purl row in stocking stitch).

Work the stitches as presented or *as they appear* means that you should knit the knit stitches and purl the purl stitches as they face you on the row being worked. This instruction is usually given for rows on the wrong side of textured knits.

K	knit pp. 432–433
P	purl pp. 434–435
K-wise	knitwise (insert needle as though to knit)
P-wise	purlwise (insert needle as though to purl)
KP, KPK, etc.	knit and purl, or knit, purl, knit into same stitch as many times as there are letters
K 2 (3) tog	knit 2 (or 3) stitches together p. 449
P 2 (3) tog	purl 2 (or 3) stitches together p. 449
tbl	through back of loop (enter stitch from the back instead of the front) p. 437
blw	below (work into the loop below the next stitch) p. 444
alt	alternate
beg	beginning
dec	decrease pp. 448–449
inc	increase pp. 445–447
patt	pattern
rep	repeat
rnd	round
foll	following
rem	remaining
cont	continue
sl	slip a stitch, without working it, from the left needle to the right one p. 444
st	stitch
psso	pass the slipped stitch over p. 448
sl 1, K 1, psso	slip 1 stitch, knit 1 stitch, pass the slipped stitch over the knitted one p. 448
SSK	Slip next stitch knitwise twice. Place the left hand needle into these two stitches and knit them together p. 448
dp	double-point (needles) p. 428
ybk	yarn back (take yarn to back of work) p. 445
yfwd	yarn forward (bring yarn to front of work) p. 445
yon	yarn over needle p. 445
yrn	yarn around needle pp. 444–445

wyab	with yarn at back
wyaf	with yarn at front
R	right
L	left
WSF	wrong side facing
RSF	right side facing
cross 2 RK	cross 2 stitches to the right, knitting p. 450
cross 2 LK	cross 2 stitches to the left, knitting p. 450
cross 2 RP	cross 2 stitches to the right, purling p. 450
cross 2 LP	cross 2 stitches to the left, purling p. 450
C4F	cable 4 front pp. 450, 468–469
C4B	cable 4 back pp. 450, 469
CC	contrasting colour
MC	main colour
DK	double knitting yarn (8 ply)
st st	stocking stitch p. 436
rev st st	reverse stocking stitch p. 436
g st	garter stitch
° °	instructions between asterisks should be repeated as many times as there are stitches to accommodate them
( )	instructions enclosed by parentheses should be repeated by the number of times indicated after the parentheses
[ ]	*for stitch patterns,* instructions within brackets explain the method of working a particular stitch or technique *in garment directions,* numbers between brackets are for additional sizes
yrn twice, etc.	wind yarn around the needle as many times as specified p. 444
tension	number of stitches and rows per 10 cm that should be obtained using designated yarn and needles
multiple	the number of stitches required to work one motif horizontally in a pattern stitch
selvage	a finished edge pp. 430–431, 438–440
work even	continue work without increasing or decreasing
M	make a stitch

Multiples and repeats

In knitting terminology, a **multiple** is the number of stitches needed to complete one segment of a pattern stitch horizontally; it appears as a sequence of stitches between two asterisks. Here is a typical example of how it works:

Multiple of 6 sts plus 3
Row 1: * K 3, P 3*, K 3
Row 2: P 3,* K 3, P 3*

The six stitches between asterisks comprise the multiple. The three stitches following or preceding an asterisk are added to balance the pattern, or permit moving it left or right for a diagonal.

The total number of stitches on the needle should be divisible by the multiple. For instance, if a multiple is 8 sts plus 3, the number to be cast on would be 16 plus 3, or 64 plus 3 and so forth. When following a pattern, the multiple is then repeated as many times as there are stitches to be worked.

As a rule, a multiple remains constant throughout a pattern. If a change does occur, as happens in some lace patterns, it is always temporary, and the count is restored eventually to the original.

If you want to substitute one pattern for another, the relation of the multiple to the cast-on stitches must be considered. If instructions are to cast on 126 stitches and the pattern multiple is 6, you could substitute a stitch with a multiple of 7, because it divides evenly into 126. If you choose one with a multiple of 8, which does not divide evenly into 126, you will have to adjust the stitch total.

The term **repeat** is sometimes used as a synonym for multiple. It can also denote the number of rows needed to complete one pattern motif vertically.

Checking the tension

Knitting instructions always specify **tension**—the exact number of stitches, and sometimes rows, per 10 centimetres, using the specified yarn, needles, and stitch pattern. *The size of a finished article is based on this tension, so to achieve the correct size it is essential to duplicate the tension exactly.*

Before beginning any new project, make a test swatch at least 15 centimetres square, using the recommended yarn and needles, and working in the specified stitch. Place the completed swatch right side up on a flat surface (the ironing board is a good place to work) and pin the edges, taking care not to stretch the sample out of shape. Using a ruler, tension square gauge or tape measure, count the number of stitches and rows that fall within a 10 centimetre span.

If there are too many stitches in your tension square, knit another sample using needles one size larger; if there are too few stitches, use needles one size smaller. The time will be well spent, because even one stitch per 10 centimetres multiplies to a substantial size difference over a wide area. But do not attempt to use needles more than one size away from that specified; if you cannot match the tension, choose another pattern. For more information about tension, see page 437.

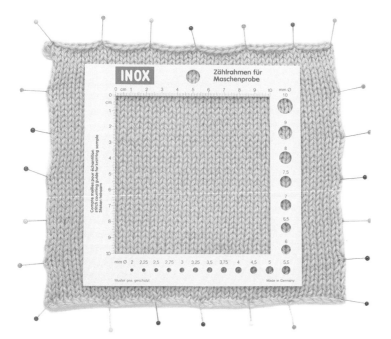

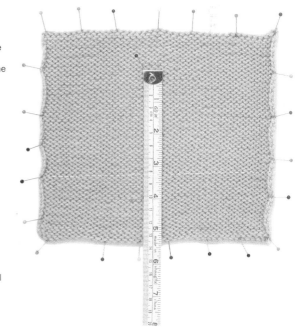

To check the tension horizontally, left, pin swatch to a flat surface, taking care not to stretch it. Using a tension square gauge or tape measure, place two pins 10 cm apart and count the stitches between them. It is easier to count stitches on the knit side of stocking stitch, where each loop represents one stitch. When counting stitches for garter stitch, count the loops in one row only.

To check the tension vertically, right, place two pins 10 cm apart and count the rows between them. It is easier to count rows on the purl side of stocking stitch, where every two ridges equal one row. In counting rows for garter stitch, every ridge equals one row and every furrow equals another.

Following knitting instructions

Elongating stitches

Unusual textures can be produced by making some stitches longer than others in a given knitting sequence. Three elongating methods are shown in the drawings below.

A **slipped stitch** is a lengthened loop made by moving a stitch from the left needle to the right one without working it. Slipping forms a long vertical loop on one side of the work, a loose horizontal ridge on the reverse side. Unless the instructions say otherwise, stitches are slipped *purlwise* when working a pattern stitch, and the yarn is held in the working position of the preceding stitch.

A **double stitch** is a knit stitch that is twice as long as a regular one. It is produced by knitting into the loop below the stitch on the needle. A double stitch is knitted just once, the upper and lower loops dropped off simultaneously. This method is limited to every other stitch in a row.

A **simple elongated stitch** is made by wrapping yarn more than once around the needle, then dropping the extra loop(s) on the next row. This technique may be used for an entire row and will result in a band of openwork, or it can be used singly, as in lace patterns.

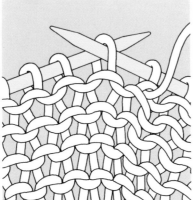

To slip one purlwise (sl 1 P-wise) in a knit row, hold yarn behind the work; insert needle into front of next stitch from right to left and slide the stitch onto the right needle.

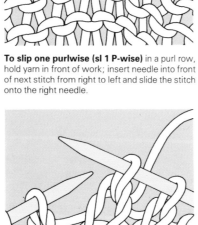

To knit one below (K 1 blw), also called double stitch, insert right needle front to back in centre of the loop just below next stitch. Take yarn around needle to make a knit stitch.

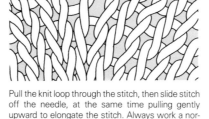

Pull the knit loop through the stitch, then slide stitch off the needle, at the same time pulling gently upward to elongate the stitch. Always work a normal stitch between two double stitches.

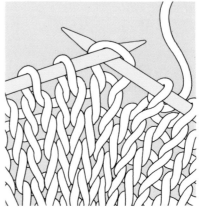

To slip one knitwise (sl 1 K-wise) in a knit row, hold yarn behind the work; insert needle into front of next stitch from left to right and slide the stitch onto the right needle.

To slip one purlwise (sl 1 P-wise) in a purl row, hold yarn in front of work; insert needle into front of next stitch from right to left and slide the stitch onto the right needle.

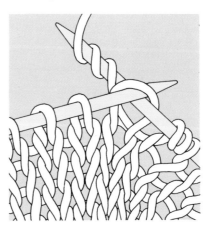

For a simple elongated stitch (yrn twice or **yrn 3 times)** wind the yarn two or three times around the needle as you work the stitch. The number of wraps is always specified in the pattern.

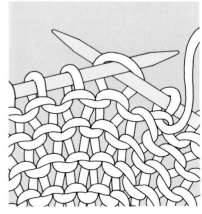

To slip one knitwise (sl 1 K-wise) in a purl row, hold yarn in front of work; insert needle into front of next stitch from left to right and slide the stitch onto the right needle.

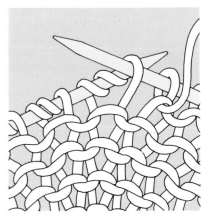

On the next row, let the extra loop(s) drop off the needle as you work each elongated stitch. Long stitches formed in this way are generally used as lacy bands between solid areas (see p. 463).

Increasing

An **increase (inc)** in knitting is the addition of a stitch. Its main function is to shape work by enlarging certain areas, but it is also used to produce fancy stitch patterns such as laces and bobbles. For pattern purposes it is combined with a decrease, in the same or a subsequent row, so the stitch total is constant.

There are four basic methods of increasing: **changing yarn position** (right), **raised** (page 446), **lifted** (page 446), and **bar** (page 447). **Casting on** (pages 430 to 431) is also used for increasing, principally to add three or more stitches at either side of the work. If you familiarise yourself with all methods, you can choose the one most appropriate.

Choice of an increase method is based largely on the appearance desired. Increasing by changing yarn position, which forms a hole in the fabric, is used only for a decorative effect. A bar increase is also decorative. It is a desirable choice when increases must be made in steps, because it is readily seen and easily counted. A lifted increase is nearly invisible. It is especially suitable for shaping a dart or any area where a subtle enlargement is called for. A raised increase can be decorative or inconspicuous, depending on how it is made.

When increasing gradually, to shape a sleeve, for example, the seam edge will be smoother if you place the additions two or three stitches in from the edge. With a complicated stitch, however, it is better to increase only one stitch from the edge to avoid disrupting the pattern.

When increasing rapidly, or shaping a chevron, **double increases** (page 447) are used. These are paired additions made on either side of a centre stitch.

INCREASING BY CHANGING YARN POSITION

Increasing by changing the position of the yarn between two stitches produces a hole, so this method is used for knitting or shaping when a lacy effect is desired. Abbreviations for the various types of this increasing method are **yfwd, ybk, yrn** and **yon.** The loops produced by these changes in yarn position must be knitted or purled on the next row.

Occasionally, directions specify a multiple **yrn** increase. All loops are worked on the return row, but must be worked alternately knit and purl.

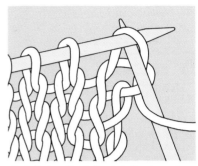

yfwd—before first knit stitch (for picot selvage, some laces): holding yarn *in front of* right needle, insert needle knitwise in first stitch and knit it. The made stitch can then be seen.

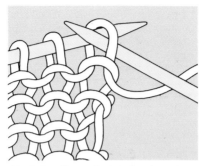

ybk—before first purl stitch (for picot selvage, some laces): holding yarn *behind* right needle, insert needle purlwise in first stitch and purl it. The made stitch can then be seen.

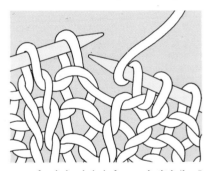

yrn—after knit stitch, before purl stitch (for rib patterns): bring yarn forward between needles, then back over right needle and forward under it into position for next purl stitch.

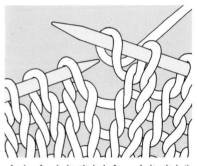

yfwd—after knit stitch, before a knit stitch (for stocking stitch and lace stitches): bring yarn forward *under* the right needle, then back *over* it into position for the next knit stitch.

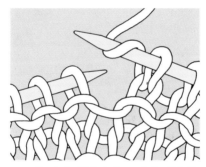

yrn—after knit stitch, before a knit stitch (for garter stitch): bring yarn forward *over* the right needle, then back *under* it again, into position for the next knit stitch.

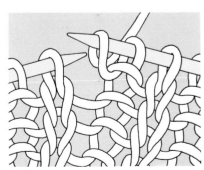

yon—after purl stitch, before a knit stitch (for rib patterns): take yarn over right needle from front to back. The made stitch can be seen after the next knit stitch is completed.

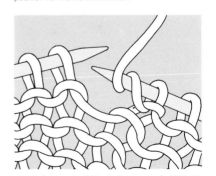

yrn—after purl stitch, before a purl stitch (for reverse stocking stitch and lace stitches): take yarn back *over* right needle, then forward *under* it into position for the next purl stitch.

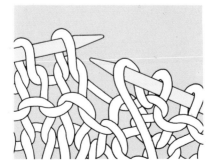

yon—after purl stitch, before a purl stitch (for garter stitch): take yarn back *under* right needle, then forward *over* it. The made stitch can be seen after purl stitch is completed.

Following knitting instructions

Increasing

RAISED INCREASE

A raised increase is made by picking up a horizontal strand between two stitches and working it as if it were a stitch. There are two ways to work the strand; each gives a very different result. If you knit or purl into the front of it, a hole is left beneath, a suitable approach for a lace stitch or wherever a decorative effect is desired. If you work into the back of the strand, the stitch thus made is twisted. This increase method can be used effectively where you want the shaping to be inconspicuous, for instance, after ribbed band.

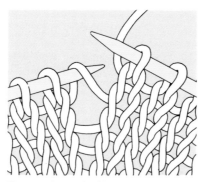

First step for a raised increase is to insert left needle front to back under the horizontal strand that lies between two stitches.

LIFTED INCREASE

A lifted increase is made by working into the loop below a stitch as well as into the stitch itself. The result is basically inconspicuous, but there is a definite slant to the new stitches formed, which makes them particularly suitable for paired increases to each side of a centre area, in sleeves, for example, (see illustration immediately on the right).

A lifted increase may be made on the right side of the work, two or three stitches from the selvage. It should be worked with a loose tension for best results.

To pair lifted increases on either side of a centre area, work a *left* increase as you approach the centre; work a *right* increase after it.

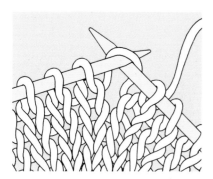

For a decorative raised increase on a knit row, knit into the front of the strand (a hole is formed under the stitch).

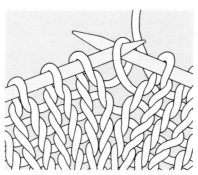

For an invisible raised increase on a knit row, knit into the back of the strand (the stitch is thus twisted; the result is inconspicuous).

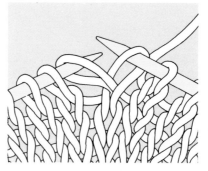

For lifted knit increase, right, insert *right* needle in top of loop just below next stitch, knit the loop, then knit stitch on needle.

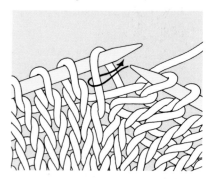

For lifted knit increase, left, insert *left* needle in top of loop below last completed stitch; pull back gently; knit into front of the loop.

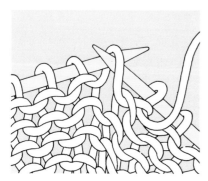

For a decorative raised increase on a purl row, purl into the front of the strand (a hole is formed under the stitch).

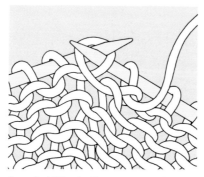

For an invisible raised increase on a purl row, purl into the back of the strand (the stitch is thus twisted; the result is inconspicuous).

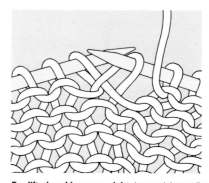

For lifted purl increase, right, insert *right* needle under loop just below next stitch; purl the loop, then purl the stitch on the needle.

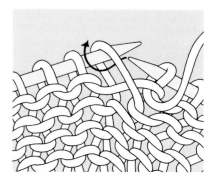

For lifted purl increase, left, insert *left* needle under loop below last completed stitch; pull back gently; purl into front of the loop.

BAR AND MOSS INCREASES

Bar and moss increases are produced by working into the same stitch twice. For a bar increase, knit into the front and back of a stitch; for a moss increase, knit and purl into the front. The decorative result, either a bar or a nub, makes it easy to keep track of the increases of several rows.

The bar follows the stitch on which an increase is made, a fact that must be allowed for in paired increases. For example, when an increase is worked three stitches from the end on the right edge, it must be made four stitches from the end on the left edge.

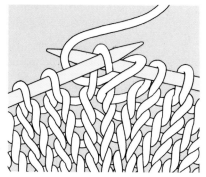

For a bar increase on a knit row, knit a stitch, but do not drop it off the needle; instead, knit again into the back of the same stitch.

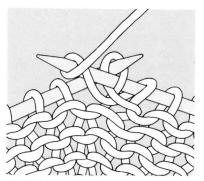

For a bar increase on a purl row, purl a stitch, but do not drop it off the needle; instead, purl again into the back of the same stitch.

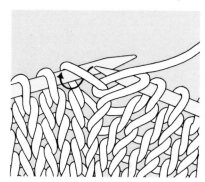

For a moss increase on a knit row, knit a stitch but do not drop it off the needle; instead, purl into the front of the same stitch.

Double Increasing

Double raised increase: Knit into back of horizontal strand before centre; knit centre stitch; knit into back of next strand.

Double lifted increase: In stitch before centre, make a lifted increase left; knit centre stitch; make a lifted increase right.

Double lifted increase into 1 stitch: Knit loop below centre stitch; knit into back of centre stitch; knit again into loop below centre.

Double bar increase: Knit into front and back of stitch before centre stitch; knit into front and back of centre stitch.

Double moss increase: Knit and purl the stitch before centre stitch; knit centre stitch; knit and purl the next stitch.

Double lace increase: Take yarn forward just before the centre stitch; knit centre stitch; yarn forward, knit next stitch.

447

Following knitting instructions

Decreasing

A **decrease (dec)** in knitting is the reduction of one or more in the number of stitches. Its purpose, generally, is to shape work by making it narrower, but it is used also, combined with increasing, to form stitch patterns such as lace and bobbles.

Two basic methods are shown below and at the top of the opposite page. There is little difference in the way they look, but the slip stitch method (below) draws in less snugly

than two stitches worked together (above opposite), and is easier to work when tension is snug.

Each decrease method pulls stitches on a diagonal to the right or the left. If decreases are worked randomly, or at the edge of a garment, the direction of this slant is not significant. It *is* important for symmetrical shaping, however, such as a raglan armhole or a V-neck where a line will be seen. The options are to slant

decreases to the right at the left side of the centre, slant them to the left at the right of it, or vice versa.

To use decreases for gradual shaping, stitches are reduced one at a time on the right side, which means that you work them every other row. If stitches must be reduced every row, then decreases can be worked on the wrong side, but care must be taken to keep direction of the slant (as viewed from the right side) consistent.

To shape a chevron or mitred corner, **double decreases** are used. These are paired decreases, worked on each side of a centre or axial stitch. They form a rather thick nub or ridge on the face of the fabric.

To decrease three or more stitches in succession, a plain cast-off is preferable (see page 438). This method may be used, for example, at the beginning of an armhole, or at the centre of a neckline.

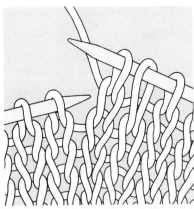

Knit decrease, left (sl 1, K 1, psso): Slip a stitch knitwise; knit the next stitch.

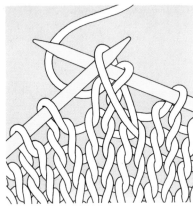

Insert left needle into the front of the slipped stitch and pull it over the knitted one.

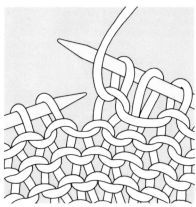

Purl decrease, right (sl 1, P 1, psso): Slip a stitch knitwise; purl the next stitch.

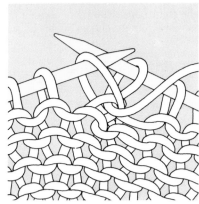

Insert left needle into the front of the slipped stitch and pass it over the purled one.

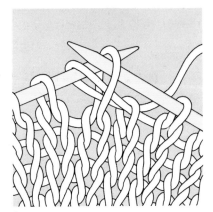

Knit decrease, right: Knit a stitch and return it to the left needle. Pass the next stitch over it.

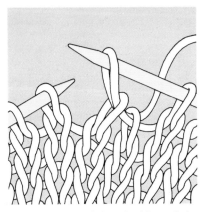

Replace the knitted stitch on the right needle by slipping it purlwise.

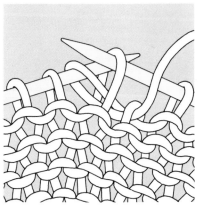

Purl decrease, left: Purl a stitch and return it to the left needle. Pass the next stitch over it.

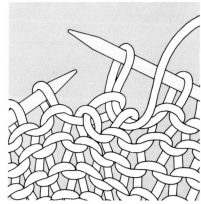

Return the worked purl stitch to the right needle by slipping it purlwise.

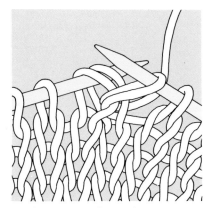

Knit decrease, right (K 2 tog): Knit 2 stitches together through the front of both loops.

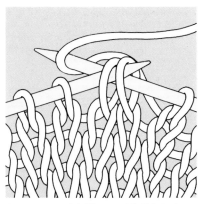

Knit decrease, left (K 2 tog tbl): Knit 2 stitches together through the back of both loops.

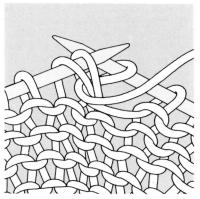

Purl decrease, right (P 2 tog): Purl 2 stitches together through the front of both loops.

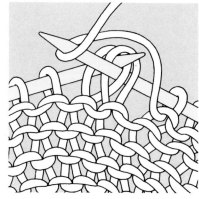

Purl decrease, left (P 2 tog tbl): Purl 2 stitches together through the back of both loops.

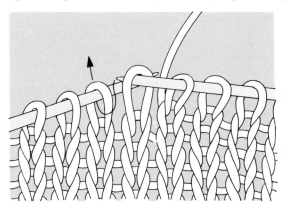

Knit decrease, left (SSK): (Slip the next stitch knitwise) twice.

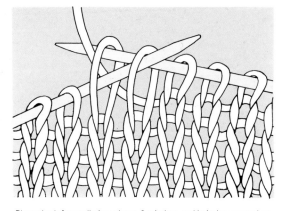

Place the left needle into these 2 stitches and knit them together.

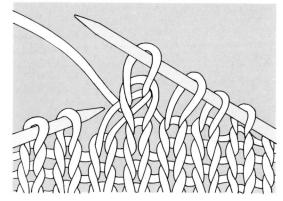

Slip both stitches off the needle together.

Double decreasing

Double decrease, left (sl 1, K 2 tog, psso): Slip a stitch knitwise, knit the next 2 stitches together, pass the slipped stitch over the knitted ones. This decrease is similar in appearance to the one above, but draws in a little less snugly. It is also a bit easier to work.

Double decrease, right (K 3 tog): Knit 3 stitches together through the front of all 3 loops. The result is a rather thick ridge with sharply slanted stitches on either side.

Crossing stitches

Crossing stitches is a way to produce certain decorative effects, such as a braid, basket weave, or honeycomb pattern. The crossed stitches appear to be twisted because they are pulled diagonally right or left. The twist direction is determined by the way stitches are worked—to the front or the back.

To cross two stitches, work the second stitch on the left needle, then the first. Three stitches can also be exchanged this way, working the third stitch, then the first stitch, and finally the second one. The crossovers are easier to manipulate and yarn is less strained if the tension is somewhat loose.

A variation of the above method is crossing through two stitches, as illustrated at the top of the opposite page. The results are subtly different from crossing two stitches, but close enough in appearance that you could substitute the variation for the regular crossing technique.

Crossing more than three stitches is called **cabling.** This is a technique that requires a double-point or cable needle to hold the first stitches out of the way until needed. The holding needle should be the same size or smaller than the working needle; a larger one might stretch the stitches. Most people work cable stitches from the holding needle, as illustrated opposite, but some find it easier to slip them back onto the left needle and work them from that position.

The look of a cable is varied by the number of stitches exchanged (this number can be even or uneven), the number of rows worked between twists, and the direction of the twist itself. If stitches are held to the front, a cable twists to the left; if stitches are held to the back, the twist will be to the right. Most cable patterns are complex, and so they are usually written out in full in the list of abbreviations and then abbreviated in the pattern itself.

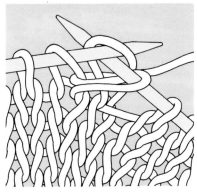

Cross 2 stitches right, knitting (cross 2 RK): Knit into the front of second stitch on the left needle, but do not drop the stitch off.

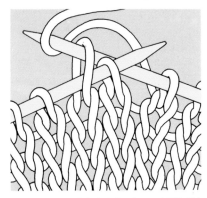

Knit into the front of the first stitch (the one that was skipped); allow both first and second stitches to drop off the needle together.

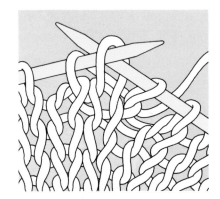

Cross 2 stitches left, knitting (cross 2 LK): Knit into the back of second stitch on the left needle, but do not drop the stitch off.

Knit into the back of the first stitch (the one that was skipped); allow both first and second stitches to drop off the needle together.

Cross 2 stitches right, purling (cross 2 RP): Purl into the front of second stitch on the left needle, but do not drop the stitch off.

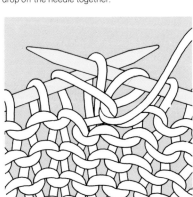

Purl into the front of the first stitch (the one that was skipped); allow both first and second stitches to drop off the needle together.

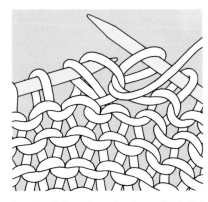

Cross 2 stitches left, purling (cross 2 LP): Purl into the front of second stitch on the left needle; pass it over the first stitch and off the needle.

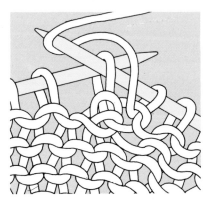

Purl into the front of the first stitch (the one that was skipped), then allow this first stitch to drop off the left needle.

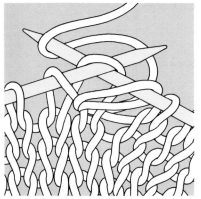

Cross through 2 stitches right, knitting (cross through 2 RK): Knit 2 stitches together through the *front;* knit the first stitch again, then drop both stitches off the left needle together.

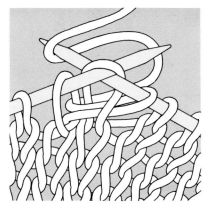

Cross through 2 stitches left, knitting (cross through 2 LK): Knit 2 stitches together through the *back;* knit the first stitch again, but through the *front;* drop both stitches off together.

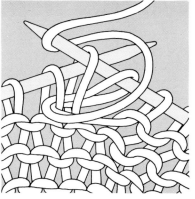

Cross through 2 stitches right, purling (cross through 2 RP): Purl 2 stitches together through the *front;* purl the first stitch again, then drop both stitches off the left needle together.

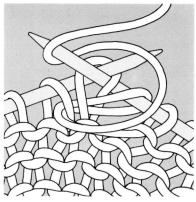

Cross through 2 stitches left, purling (cross through 2LP): Purl 2 stitches together through the *front;* purl the first stitch again, but through the *back;* drop both stitches off together.

Crossing stitches with a cable needle

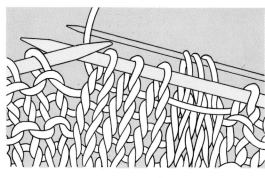

For a cable twisted right, slip the cable stitches onto a cable needle, or any double-point needle, and hold these at the back of the work while you knit the remaining stitches of the cable section.

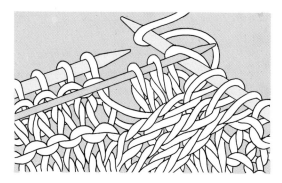

Knit the stitches from the cable needle, as shown, or if you prefer, slip them back onto the left needle and knit them from there. Continue with the rest of the pattern according to instructions.

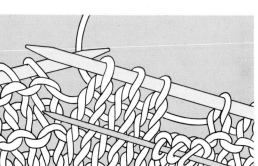

For a cable twisted left, slip the cable stitches onto a cable needle, or any double-point needle, and hold these at the front of the work while you knit the remaining stitches of the cable section.

Knit the stitches from the cable needle, as shown, or if you prefer, slip them back onto the left needle and knit them from there. Continue with the rest of the pattern according to instructions.

Following knitting instructions

Correcting errors

It may be necessary to correct a mistake in your knitting. The methods given here will help you to correct in the easiest and most suitable way. If an error is one row down, drop the stitch off the needle directly above it, then retrieve it using the knitting needles or a crochet hook. When it is a few rows down, let that stitch run, and pick it up with a crochet hook, as shown. Use the same methods to pick up a stitch that has dropped or run accidentally. To pick up a dropped stitch in a purl row of stocking stitch, turn the work around and retrieve the stitch from the right side.

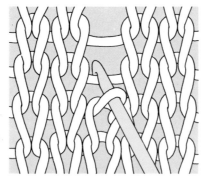

To retrieve a run in stocking stitch, insert a crochet hook front to back, hook it *over* the horizontal thread and draw through a loop.

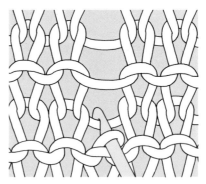

To retrieve a run in garter stitch, insert crochet hook front to back in each knit loop; pull through a loop as for stocking stitch.

For a purl loop in garter stitch, insert the crochet hook back to front, hooking it *under* the horizontal thread; draw through a loop.

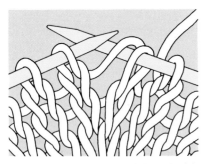

To retrieve a dropped knit stitch, insert the right needle through the loop and under the strand, as shown in the illustration.

Insert the left needle from back to front through the top of the loop only, then pull gently upward and forward on it.

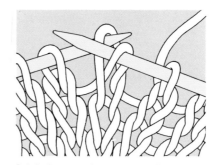

Pull the loop over the strand and off the needle. The stitch (which was the strand) remains on the right needle and is facing the wrong way.

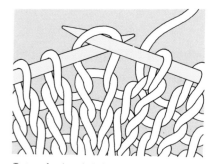

To transfer the stitch, insert the left needle from front to back and slip the stitch onto it. It will be in the correct position to knit.

Picking up new stitches

By picking up stitches along a finished edge (usually written pick up and K in instructions), you can add a collar, cuff, trim, even sleeves, without sewing sections together. There is more than one way to pick up stitches. All are equally good, but the one shown here is the simplest and the most widely used. Ideally, stitches that will be picked up should not have been cast off: they should be left on a piece of contrasting yarn. For instructions on picking up stitches on a selvage, see pp. 486–491.

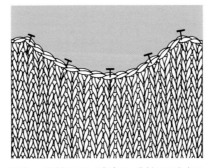

Before picking up stitches, divide work into equal sections, using pins or scraps of yarn. Tie on working yarn where stitches will begin.

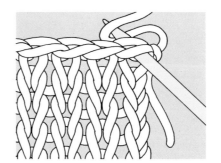

Hold work in left hand, right side facing you. °Insert right needle under the edge stitch; take yarn around needle as for knitting.

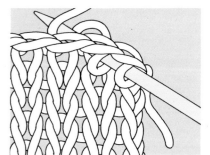

Bring stitch through to the right side. *Repeat from asterisk. Work proceeds from right to left; first row worked on the wrong side.

Circular knitting

Circular knitting is the way of making a seamless tube or a flat piece worked from the centre out. There are two methods, with a circular needle or with a set of double-point needles.

The **circular needle** is practical for any large item, tubular or flat. It holds a great many stitches and permits most of the weight to be supported in the lap, thus lessening strain on the arms. To knit a tube or flat circle, the circumference of the knit piece must be at least 5 cm larger than that of the needle for stitches to fit comfortably and without stretching. Available needle lengths range from 40 to 105 cm, so the smallest tube possible would be 45 cm. Anything smaller must be knitted on double-point needles.

A circular needle can also be used to knit any flat item that would normally be worked on straight needles, including garments. For this purpose, the stitches are worked back and forth as in regular knitting (see below right).

Double-point needles are used most often for small items, such as mittens, socks or a neck. A large piece of work is possible, however, if the needles are long enough, and there are enough of them, to ensure that stitches will not slide off. As a rule, double-point needles are sold in sets of four. You will need an extra set when five or more needles are required (the knitted square, next page, is an example).

When casting on for double-point needles, the stitches are divided evenly among the number of needles in use, leaving one needle for working. Some adjustment may be necessary to allow for the pattern multiple. For example, to knit a 2 × 2 rib, each needle would have to carry a multiple of 4 stitches. The cast-on method on the top of the next page is best for most purposes. The cast-on method below it is more convenient to use when the centre area is very small.

Almost any stitch can be knitted in the round, but an adjustment must be made in the row sequence as the right side always faces you. Knitting every row, for example, produces a stocking stitch; alternating knit and purl rows produces a garter stitch. Certain lace patterns and jacquards are easier to knit in the round because the pattern sequence becomes simpler.

While there are some differences in the handling of double-point and circular needles, the basic approach for knitting is the same with both.

Important points to remember

1. Before joining into a round, work the first row in the usual way. This helps prevent twisting and will bring the right side of the cast-on to the right side of the work.

2. A marker should be placed between the last and first stitches of each round. Pattern changes, for example a switch from knit to purl stitches, will occur at this point, and progression will be uneven if rounds are not clearly marked. (To mark other key points, such as locations of increases, without confusion, use markers of a different colour.)

3. Every joining stitch (the first one on a needle or round) must be pulled extra firmly to avoid a ladder effect.

4. The right side of a tube or flat motif always faces you, and the stitch pattern must be adjusted accordingly.

Knitting with a circular needle

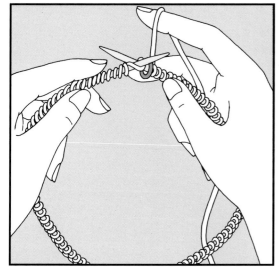

To knit a tubular fabric, hold needle tip with the *last* cast-on stitch (the one attached to ball of yarn) in your *right* hand, the tip with *first* cast-on stitch in your *left*. Knit the first stitch, pulling yarn firmly to avoid a gap where the tube is joined.

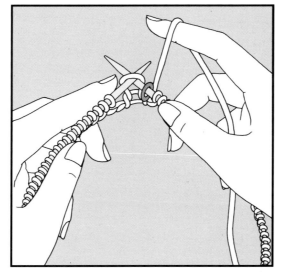

Knit around the circle until you reach the marker, then slip the marker and start the next round. At this point check for twisted stitches; if you find any, unravel the work and start again. A twisted edge cannot be corrected in any other way.

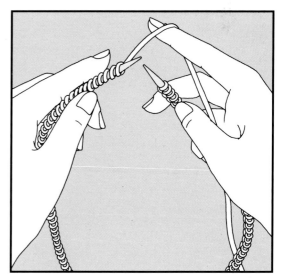

To knit a flat fabric, hold needle tip with the *last* cast-on stitch in your *left* hand, the tip with *first* cast-on stitch in your *right*. Knit to the last stitch then flip needle around so that wrong side faces you. Continue to turn work with each round.

453

Knitting with double-point needles

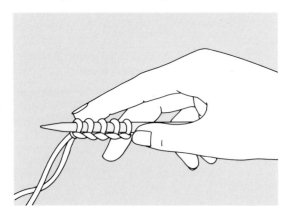

1. To knit a tube with four dp (double-point) needles, cast on all stitches on one needle. Knit off a third of the stitches onto each needle before joining into a ring. (To knit with five or more needles, use the same approach, dividing stitches evenly among the total, minus one needle for working.)

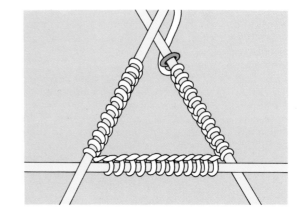

2. Lay the three needles in a triangle, with the bottom edges of all stitches facing the centre. Place a ring marker, or a loop of contrasting yarn, after the last stitch (where the ball end of the yarn is).

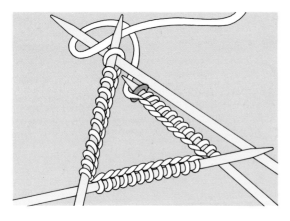

3. Using the fourth needle, knit into the first cast-on stitch, thus closing the triangle. Pull extra firmly on the yarn for this stitch, so there will not be a gap. When you have knitted all stitches off the first needle, use that one for the working needle, placing it behind the others as you knit the first stitch in the next group.

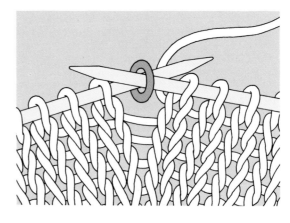

4. Knit each section of the circle until you reach the marker, then slip it and start the next round. Continue to slip the marker with each round; it marks regular progression of rows. This diagram shows meeting the marker on circular needles.

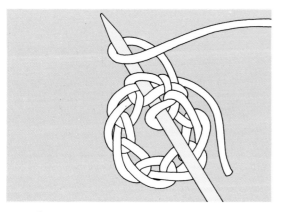

To knit a flat item, started at the centre (a tablecloth, for example, or a lace motif), cast on the stitches by this method: crochet a chain, having one loop for each stitch that is needed; join it in a ring. Transfer the loop that remains on the hook to one dp needle, then pick up stitches around the ring, setting the correct number on each needle. For a small centre area, this method is easier to manage than the one shown above.

To knit a square from the centre out, crochet 8 chains, join in a ring, and pick up 2 stitches on each of four needles. On first round, increase 1 stitch between each 2-stitch group. On the next and subsequent rounds, increase 2 stitches at the centre of each section. A triangle is worked in the same way, but with 6 stitches in three sections. A circle is made similarly, but started with 10 stitches on five needles; one increase is made in each section every round, moving its location 1 stitch forward each round.

The inventiveness of knitters throughout the world has produced an enormous variety of knitted patterns, all of which can be made using the two basic stitches of knit and purl. Once the simple techniques of knitting have been mastered, you will be able to knit almost anything, from the textures and cables of Aran styles, through delicate lacy patterns, to the multicoloured patterns of Fair Isle and picture knitting. All these are featured in this section, with full instructions for working and detailed photographs of the patterns produced. Combining these patterns will enable you to create original designs in knitted garments or the instructions may simply help you to interpret commercial patterns. But you might soon find yourself joining knitters from this craft's long history in inventing patterns of your own.

Knitting stitches

Using a pattern stitch

A pattern stitch (often called pattern for short) is the sequence of knitting techniques, repeated continuously, that forms knitted fabric. It consists of a *multiple,* stitches needed for one horizontal motif, and a *repeat,* rows required to form one vertical unit.

Most pattern stitches can be classified according to structure. Familiarity with basic structures will permit you to knit almost anything as your skill increases, even to invent your own stitch if you do not find one to suit your needs.

Patterns in this section are grouped according to type, though in a few cases a stitch may fit more than one category. The first group, *textures,* comprises those compact knits that are sometimes called fabric stitches. The first ten stitches in this group are ideal for beginners, since they require limited skill for success.

When choosing a pattern stitch, you will be influenced by its appearance, but other things should be considered, too. Is it suitable for the yarn? A highly textured yarn and a busy pattern, for instance, do not mix. Is it appropriate for the intended use? Few lace stitches would make a warm winter garment.

To knit a pattern, cast on a number of stitches that can be divided by the multiple; add any additional stitches indicated, plus selvage stitches. Follow instructions to the last row, then begin again at Row 1. Unless stated otherwise, the first row is the right side. The word *reversible* appears wherever a pattern is identical on both sides. For a reminder of what abbreviations mean, see page 442.

Textures

Simple seed: A stocking stitch interspersed with purl stitches; suitable for baby garments.
Multiple of 4 sts
Row 1: *K 3, P 1*
Row 2 and alt rows: purl
Rows 3 and 7: knit
Row 5: K 1, *P 1, K 3*, P 1, K 2

Chevron seed: Zigzags of purl stitches on stocking stitch background.
Multiple of 8 sts
Row 1: *P 1, K 3*
Row 2: *K 1, P 5, K 1, P 1*
Row 3: *K 2, P 1, K 3, P 1, K 1*
Row 4: *P 2, K 1, P 1, K 1, P 3*

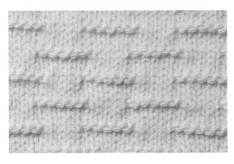

Tracks: Streaks of purl stitches on a face of stocking stitch.
Multiple of 10 sts
Row 1: *K 4, P 6*
Row 2 and alt rows: purl
Rows 3 and 7: knit
Row 5: *P 5, K 4, P 1*

Reverse triangles: Stocking stitch and reverse stocking stitch in triangles.
Multiple of 5 sts
Row 1 (right side): knit
Row 2: *K 1, P 4; rep from * to end
Row 3: *K 3, P 2; rep from * to end
Row 4: As 3rd row
Row 5: As 2nd row
Row 6: knit
Rep these 6 rows

Diamond seed: Purl stitches tracing diamonds on a stocking stitch face.
Multiple of 8 sts
Row 1: *P 1, K 7*
Rows 2 and 8: *K 1, P 5, K 1, P 1*
Rows 3 and 7: *K 2, P 1, K 3, P 1, K 1*
Rows 4 and 6: *P 2, K 1, P 1, K 1, P 3*
Row 5: *K 4, P 1, K 3*

Moss stitch squares: Blocks of stocking stitch, framed by moss stitch.
Multiple of 10 sts plus 3
Row 1 (right side): P 1, *K 1, P 1*
Row 2: P 1, *K 1, P 1*
Row 3: P 1, K 1, P 1, *K 7, P 1, K 1, P 1*
Row 4: P 1, K 1, P 9, *K 1, P 9*, K 1, P 1
Rep Rows 3 and 4 three times
Rep these 10 rows

Basket stitch (reversible): Chequer-board squares of stocking stitches and reverse stocking stitches.
Multiple of 10 sts
Rows 1 to 6: °K 5, P 5°
Rows 7 to 12: °P 5, K 5°

Gathered stitch: Shirred sections are created by doubling stitches, working even, then decreasing stitches to the original number. The section depths can be varied, also stocking stitch substituted for garter stitch if desired.
Multiple is any number of sts
Rows 1 to 6: knit
Row 7: K into front and back of each st
Rows 8, 10, 12: purl
Rows 9 and 11: knit
Row 13: K 2 tog all along the row
Rep from Row 2

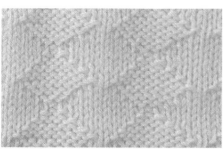

Quilted diamonds (reversible): The diamonds of reverse stocking stitch appear to be embossed on a background of stocking stitch. This pattern pulls inward slightly in much the same manner as a rib (see p. 458 for rib characteristics).
Multiple of 10 sts
Row 1: °K 9, P 1°
Rows 2 and 8: K 2, °P 7, K 3°, P 7, K 1
Rows 3 and 7: P 2, °K 5, P 5°, K 5, P 3
Rows 4 and 6: K 4, °P 3, K 7°, P 3, K 3
Row 5: P 4, °K 1, P 9°, K 1, P 5

Linen stitch: This has the appearance and firmness of a woven fabric; it is well suited to tailored garments.
Multiple of 2 sts
Row 1: °K 1, yfwd, sl 1, ybk°
Row 2: °P 1, ybk, sl 1, yfwd°

Ridge stitch: Horizontal ridges stand out in relief against stocking stitch.
Multiple of 2 sts
Row 1: knit
Row 2: °K 2 tog all across the row°
Row 3: K into front and back of each st
Row 4: purl

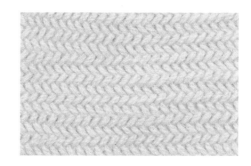

Herringbone: Very firm stitch, similar to a woven in appearance and elasticity. Tension must be kept fairly loose.
Multiple of 2 sts
Row 1: K 2 tog tbl dropping only first loop off left needle, °K 2 tog tbl (the remaining stitch and next stitch), again dropping only the first loop off the needle°, K 1 tbl
Row 2: P 2 tog dropping only the first loop off left needle, °P 2 tog (the remaining stitch and next stitch), again dropping only first loop off needle°, P 1

Waved welt (reversible): Undulating rows of stocking stitch and reverse stocking stitch. The emphatic horizontals give a feeling of width to the fabric.
Multiple of 8 sts plus 1
Row 1: °P 1, K 7°, P 1
Row 2: K 2, °P 5, K 3°, P 5, K 2
Row 3: P 3, °K 3, P 5°, K 3, P 3
Row 4: K 4, °P 1, K 7°, P 1, K 4
Row 5: °K 1, P 7°, K 1
Row 6: P 2, °K 5, P 3°, K 5, P 2
Row 7: K 3, °P 3, K 5°, P 3, K 3
Row 8: P 4, °K 1, P 7°, K 1, P 4

Waffle: A heavy, 3-dimensional stitch; worked in medium to heavyweight yarn, suitable for a jacket, coat, or afghan.
Multiple of 2 sts
Rows 1 and 2: knit
Row 3: °K 1, K 1 blw° (see p.278)
Row 4: °pick up the long (top) yarn produced by the K 1 blw and K it tog with the st on the needle, K 1°
Row 5: °K 1 blw, K 1°
Row 6: °K 1, K the next st tog with the long yarn as for Row 4°
Rep Rows 3 to 6 for the pattern

Knitting stitches

Introduction to rib stitches

Rib stitches are characterised by vertical ridges and great crosswise elasticity. The classic rib patterns are shown on page 436; the examples here give an idea of the many interesting variations.

A typical rib is formed by alternating knit and purl stitches in the same row. The ratio of knit to purl stitches may be even or uneven. The larger the numbers, the less elastic the fabric.

Because of its exceptional elasticity, a rib stitch is often used at garment edges. In this use, it is called *ribbing*. To ensure a snug fit, ribbing is usually worked with needles a size or two smaller than those used for the garment body. When you select a ribbing, make sure that it complements the fabric stitch.

Ribs

Tweed stitch rib: A nubby texture produced by slipping stitches on the knit portions; best suited to plain yarns.
Multiple of 6 sts
Row 1: *P 3, yfwd, sl 1 P-wise, ybk, K 1, yfwd, sl 1 P-wise*
Rows 2 and 4: *P 3, K 3*
Row 3: *P 3, K 1, yfwd, sl 1 P-wise, ybk, K 1*

7 × 3 flat rib: Less elastic than narrower rib patterns; can be used successfully for a garment fabric.
Multiple of 10 sts
Row 1: *K 7, P 3*
Row 2: *K 3, P 7*

Stocking heel stitch: Not a true rib structure, but has appearance and nearly the elasticity of one; often used for sock heels, as it withstands heavy wear.
Multiple of 2 sts plus 1
Row 1: *K 1, sl 1 *, K 1
Row 2: purl

Moss stitch rib: An attractive variation on a 5 × 6 rib pattern.
Multiple of 11 sts plus 5
Row 1: K 5, *(K 1, P 1) 3 times, K 5*
Row 2: *P 5, (P 1, K 1) 3 times*, P 5

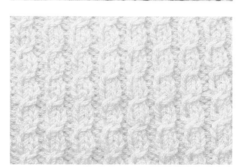

Changing rib: A pretty variation on a 1 × 3 rib; suitable for an all-over pattern as well as a rib trim.
Multiple of 8 sts
Rows 1 and 3 (wrong side): *K 3, yfwd, sl 1 P-wise, K 3, P 1*
Row 2: *K 1, P 3, ybk, sl 1 P-wise tbl, P 3*
Row 4: *K 1, P 3, K 1, P 3*

Broken ribbing: An interesting texture produced by fragmenting the rib stitches; suitable as a fabric stitch for jumpers.
Multiple of 4 sts plus 3
Row 1: °K 2, P 2, °K2, P1
Row 2 and subsequent rows: As Row 1

Cable rib: Worked as a 2 x 2 rib but stitches are twisted on every 4th row.
Multiple of 4 sts plus 2
Row 1: P 2 ° K 2, P 2°
Row 2: K 2 ° P 2, K 2°
Row 3: P 2 ° cross 2 RK, P 2°
Row 4: K 2 ° P 2, K 2°

Precautions in the use of diagonal stitches

Diagonals are patterns in which the stitch progression slants to the right, the left, or alternately right and left, produced by moving the repeat one stitch left or right on successive rows.

One-way diagonals have limited uses because they tend to stretch on the bias. This can be overcome to some degree by taking these precautions. (1) Choose firmly twisted yarns; avoid soft ones. (2) Use needles one size smaller than is normally recommended for the yarn choice. (3) Take special care in blocking and washing; do not wring, twist or tug.

Two-way diagonals resemble their woven counterparts in both looks and performance. They have limited stretchability and are suitable for tailored garments.

Diagonals

Oblique moss stitch: A simple technique produces an interesting texture.
Multiple of 5 sts
Row 1: *K 4, P 1*
Row 2: *P 1, K 1, P 3*
Row 3: *K 2, P 1, K 2*
Row 4: *P 3, K 1, P 1*
Row 5: *P 1, K 4*
Row 6: *K 1, P 4*
Row 7: *K 3, P 1, K 1*
Row 8: *P 2, K 1, P 2*
Row 9: *K 1, P 1, K 3*
Row 10: *P 4, K 1*

Ripple: A very subtle diagonal with the knit stitches twisted to the right on a stocking stitch face.
Multiple of 3 sts
Row 1: *K 2 tog, then K the first st again before slipping both sts off left needle, K 1*
Rows 2 and 4: purl
Row 3: *K 1, K 2 tog, K the first st again*

Diagonal rib: Typical of diagonals produced by moving the pattern one stitch to the right on alternate rows.
Multiple of 4 sts
Row 1: °K 2, P 2°
Row 2 and alt rows: knit the knit sts and purl the purl sts as they appear
Row 3: °K 1, P 2, K 1°
Row 5: °P 2, K 2°
Row 7: °P 1, K 2, P 1°

Steps: Small knots on stocking stitch face.
Multiple of 5 sts
Row 1 (wrong side): *P 2, (K front and back) 3 times*
Row 2: *(K 2 tog tbl) 3 times, K 2*
Row 3: *P 1, (K front and back) 3 times, P 1*
Row 4: *K 1, (K 2 tog tbl) 3 times, K 1*
Row 5: *(K front and back) 3 times, P 2*
Row 6: *K 2, (K 2 tog tbl) 3 times*
Continue moving pattern 1 stitch to the right every odd-numbered row. After 10 rows, pattern repeats from Row 1

Herringbone twill: Side-to-side zigzag.
Multiple of 4 sts
Rows 1 and 5: *K 2, yfwd, sl 2, ybk*
Rows 2 and 6: sl 1, *yfwd, P 2, ybk, sl 2*, P 3
Rows 3 and 7: *yfwd, sl 2, ybk, K 2*
Rows 4 and 8: P 1, *ybk, sl 2, yfwd, P 2*, ybk, sl 2, yfwd, P 1
Rows 9 and 13: *yfwd, sl 2, ybk, K 2*
Rows 10 and 14: sl 1, *yfwd, P 2, ybk, sl 2*, yfwd, P 2, sl 1
Rows 11 and 15: *ybk, K 2, yfwd, sl 2*
Rows 12 and 16: P 1, *ybk, sl 2, yfwd, P 2*, ybk, sl 2, yfwd, P 1

Chevron rib: An up-and-down pattern to the zigzag, rather than side-to-side as in the herringbone twill above.
Multiple of 12 sts
Row 1: °P 2, K 2, P 2, K 1, P 2, K 2, P 1°
Row 2, 4, 6, 8: knit the knit sts and purl the purl sts as they appear
Row 3: °P 1, K 2, P 2, K 3, P 2, K 2°
Row 5: °K 2, P 2, K 2, P 1, K 2, P 2, K 1°
Row 7: °K 1, P 2, K 2, P 3, K 2, P 2°

Diagonal couching stitch: The slant is produced by pulling an extra knit loop across two stitches on the knit row. Each increase is compensated for by a decrease in the purl row.
Multiple of 2 sts plus 1
Row 1: K 1, *insert right needle between next 2 sts, draw through a loop; keeping this loop on right needle, sl the first st K-wise, K the second st*
Row 2: P 1, *P 1, P 2 tog*
Row 3: K 2, *proceed as for Row 1*, K 1
Row 4: P 2, *P 1, P 2 tog*, P 1

Knitting stitches

Introduction to lace stitches

A **lace stitch** is basically any pattern with openwork. Its forms are numerous, ranging from eyelet bands in stocking stitch background to delicate lace networks. The structuring also varies, and includes some of the simplest and some of the most complex patterns. Those shown here are just a sampling of possibilities.

You can usually recognise a lace pattern by the frequent appearance of a yarn forward increase. This technique creates a hole. Elsewhere in the sequence, each increase is offset by a decrease to keep the stitch total constant. Another lace technique is the elongated stitch (see drop stitch lace, page 463), which forms more of a slit than a hole.

The casting on is important in lace knitting; it should be flexible and inconspicuous. The provisional method is recommended (page 431).

Lace stitches, especially the airy ones, look best knitted with fine yarns and the recommended needles. Medium-weight yarns can be used if a more tailored product is desired.

Lace stitches

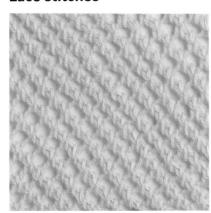

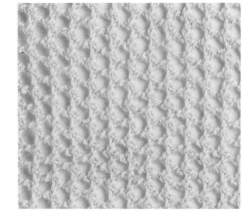

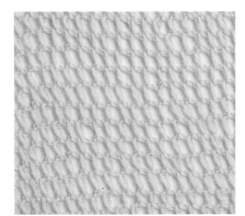

Oblique openwork: A stitch formation typical of many lace stitches, it is a combination of yfwd increase (which forms a hole) and K 2 tog decrease (which keeps the number of stitches constant). Has a tendency to slant on the bias.
Multiple of 2 sts
Row 1: K 1, *yfwd, K 2 tog*, K 1
Rows 2 and 4: purl
Row 3: K 2, *yfwd, K 2 tog*

Turkish stitch: Openwork similar to that in stitch above, but more delicate. Here the yfwd increase is combined with a decrease of sl 1, K 1, psso. (See p. 448 to review this last method.)
Multiple of 2 sts
All rows: *yfwd, sl 1, K 1, psso*

Eyelet stitch: Large holes formed by taking yarn twice around the needle for the increases. Taking the yarn around the needle at the beginning and end of Row 3 produces a delicate selvage. For a firmer edge, add one selvage stitch at each end.
Multiple of 4 sts
Row 1: *K 2, yrn twice, K 2*
Row 2: *P 2 tog, K 1, P 1, P 2 tog*
Row 3: *yrn, K 4, yrn*
Row 4: *P 1, (P 2 tog) twice, K 1*

Network (reversible): Chunky texture interspersed with large holes. Worked with fine yarn and medium needles, this is a very good stitch for a shawl. Tension should be kept fairly loose, in order to work the P 4 together.
Multiple of 4 sts
Row 1: P 2, *yrn, P 4 tog*, P 2
Row 2: K 2, *K 1, KPK into the yrn of the previous row*, K 2
Row 3: knit

Cellular stitch: An airy pattern resembling a type of crochet; very light and easy to execute; suitable for a baby blanket or shawl. For best results, work this stitch with medium or large needles and block carefully, as it has a tendency to stretch on the bias.
Multiple is any number of sts
Row 1 (wrong side): purl
Row 2: K 1, *K under the horizontal strand before the next st, K 1, pass the made st over the K 1*

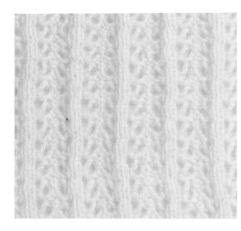

Lace rib: A combination of openwork and stocking stitch. The right side is shown, but the reverse side is just as pretty.
Multiple of 7 sts plus 2
Row 1 (wrong side): P 2, *yon, sl 1, K 1, psso, K 1, K 2 tog, yrn, P 2*
Rows 2 and 4: *K 2, P 5*, K 2
Row 3: P 2, *K 1, yfwd, sl 1, K 2 tog, psso, yfwd, K 1, P 2*

Travelling vine: Left edge is scalloped.
Multiple of 8 sts
Row 1: *yfwd, K 1 tbl, yfwd, sl 1, K 1, psso, K 5*
Row 2: *P 4, P 2 tog tbl, P 3*
Row 3: *yfwd, K 1 tbl, yfwd, K 2, sl 1, K 1, psso, K 3*
Row 4: *P 2, P 2 tog tbl, P 5*
Row 5: *K 1 tbl, yfwd, K 4, sl 1, K 1, psso, K 1, yrn*
Row 6: *P 1, P 2 tog tbl, P 6*
Row 7: *K 5, K 2 tog, yfwd, K 1 tbl, yrn*
Row 8: *P 3, P 2 tog, P 4*
Row 9: *K 3, K 2 tog, K 2, yfwd, K 1 tbl, yrn*
Row 10: *P 5, P 2 tog, P 2*
Row 11: *yfwd, K 1, K 2 tog, K 4, yfwd, K 1 tbl*
Row 12: *P 6, P 2 tog, P 1*

Lace zigzag: Both side edges are scalloped. Suitable for a shawl or afghan.
Multiple of 2 sts
Row 1: K 1, P 1, *yon, K 1, P 1*
Rows 2, 4, 6, 8, 10: *K 1, P 2 tog, yon*, K 1, P 1
Rows 3, 5, 7, 9: K 1, P 1, *yon, K 2 tog, P 1*
Rows 11, 13, 15, 17, 19: K 1, P 1, *sl 1, K 1, psso, yrn, P 1*
Rows 12, 14, 16, 18, 20: *K 1, yrn, P 2 tog tbl*, K 1, P 1
Row 21: K 1, P 1, *yon, sl 1, K 1, psso, P 1*
Rep pattern from Row 2

Bluebells: A delicate pattern suitable for a shawl or baby garments.
Multiple of 8 sts plus 5
Rows 1 and 3: K 1, *yfwd, 1 double dec [K 2 tog tbl, return st obtained to left needle, pass the next st over it, then put st back on right needle], yfwd, K 5*, yfwd, 1 double dec, yfwd, K 1
Row 2 and alt rows: purl
Row 5: K 1, *K 3, yfwd, sl 1, K 1, psso, K 1, K 2 tog, yfwd*, K 4
Row 7: K 1, *yfwd, 1 double dec, yfwd, K 1*, yfwd, 1 double dec, yfwd, K 1

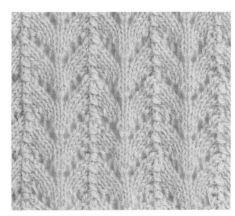

Horseshoes: One of many beautiful stitches that originated in the Shetland Islands in the nineteenth century, when gossamer laces were a favourite form of knitting.
Multiple of 10 sts plus 1
Row 1: K 1, *yfwd, K 3, sl 1, K 2 tog, psso, K 3, yfwd, K 1*
Row 2 and alt rows: purl
Row 3: K 1, *K 1, yfwd, K 2, sl 1, K 2 tog, psso, K 2, yfwd, K 2*
Row 5: K 1, *K 2, yfwd, K 1, sl 1, K 2 tog, psso, K 1, yfwd, K 3*
Row 7: K 1, *K 3, yfwd, sl 1, K 2 tog, psso, yfwd, K 4*

Hyacinths: Soft, bell-like clusters in an openwork background. This is a delicate stitch, suitable for a shawl. For best results, keep the tension fairly loose when working.
Multiple of 6 sts plus 2
Row 1 (wrong side): K 1, *P 5 tog, KPKPK into next st*, K 1
Rows 2 and 4: purl
Row 3: K 1, *KPKPK into next st, P 5 tog*, K 1
Row 5: knit, winding thread 3 times around the needle for each st
Row 6: purl, letting extra loops drop off the needle

461

Knitting stitches

Lace stitches (continued)

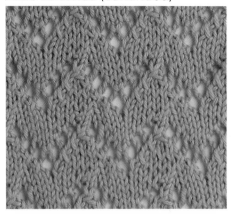

Chevron lace: Horizontal zigzags. Multiple is increased one stitch in Row 9, reduced one stitch in Row 11.
Multiple of 8 sts plus 1
Row 1: *K 5, yfwd, K 2 tog, K 1*, K 1
Row 2 and alt rows: purl
Row 3: *K 3, K 2 tog tbl, yfwd, K 1, yfwd, K 2 tog*, K 1
Row 5: K 1, *K 1, K 2 tog tbl, yfwd, K 3, yfwd, K 2 tog*
Row 7: *yfwd, K 2 tog tbl, return st to left needle, pass next st over it and put st back on right needle, yfwd, K 5*, K 1
Row 9: *K 1, K into front and back of next st, K 6*, K 1
Row 11: *K 2 tog, K 4, yfwd, K 2 tog, K 1*, K 1
Rep from Row 3

Diagonal lace stripe: A rib stitch pattern with diagonal bands of openwork.
Multiple of 10 sts plus 3
Row 1: *P 3, yon, sl 1, K 1, psso, K 5*, P 3
Row 2: *K 3, P 4, P 2 tog tbl, yrn, P 1*, K 3
Row 3: *P 3, K 2, yfwd, sl 1, K 1, psso, K 3*, P 3
Row 4: *K 3, P 2, P 2 tog tbl, yrn, P 3*, K 3
Row 5: *P 3, K 4, yfwd, sl 1, K 1, psso, K 1*, P 3
Row 6: *K 3, P 2 tog tbl, yrn, P 5*, K 3
Row 7: *P 3, K 7*, P 3
Row 8: *K 3, P 7*, K 3

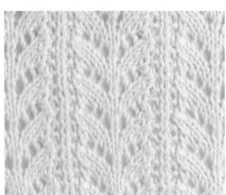

Baby fern: A very elegant lace pattern with the cast-on edge slightly scalloped. Suitable for baby clothing, a dress, or an afghan; use medium-weight yarn.
Multiple of 12 sts
Row 1 and alt rows (wrong side): purl
Row 2: *K 2 tog, K 2, yfwd, K 1, yfwd, K 2 sl 1, K 1, psso, P 1, K 1, P 1*
Row 4: *K 2 tog, K 1, yfwd, K 3, yfwd, K 1 sl 1, K 1, psso, P 1, K 1, P 1*
Row 6: *K 2 tog, yfwd, K 5, yfwd, sl 1, K 1, psso, P 1, K 1, P 1*

Fancy trellis: Crossbars in relief; suitable for a pullover or cardigan.
Multiple of 7 sts
Row 1: *K 2, K 2 tog, yfwd, K 3*
Row 2: *P 1, P 2 tog tbl, yrn, P 1, yrn, P 2, tog, P 1*
Row 3: *K 2 tog, yfwd, K 3, yfwd, sl 1, K 1, psso*
Rows 4 and 8: purl
Row 5: *yfwd, sl 1, K 1, psso, K 5*
Row 6: *ybk, P 2 tog, P 2, P 2 tog tbl, yrn, P 1*
Row 7: *K 2, yfwd, sl 1, K 1, psso, K 2 tog, yfwd, K 1*

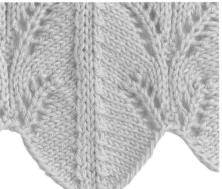

Fern stitch: Like baby fern but larger.
Multiple of 29 sts
Row 1: *K 1, sl 1, K 2 tog, psso, K 9, yfwd, K 1, yrn, P 2, yon, K 1, yfwd, K 9, sl 1, K 2 tog, psso*
Row 2 and alt rows: *P 13, K 2, P 14*
Row 3: *K 1, sl 1, K 2 tog, psso, K 8, (yfwd, K 1) twice, P 2, (K 1, yfwd) twice, K 8, sl 1, K 2 tog, psso*
Row 5: *K 1, sl 1, K 2 tog, psso, K 7, yfwd, K 1, yfwd, K 2, P 2, K 2, yfwd, K 1, yfwd, K 7, sl 1, K 2 tog, psso*
Row 7: *K 1, sl 1, K 2 tog, psso, K 6, yfwd, K 1, yfwd, K 3, P 2, K 3, yfwd, K 1, yfwd, K 6, sl 1, K 2 tog, psso*
Row 9: *K 1, sl 1, K 2 tog, psso, K 5, yfwd, K 1, yfwd, K 4, P 2, K 4, yfwd, K 1, yfwd, K 5, sl 1, K 2 tog, psso*

Vandyke stitch: V-shaped openwork in a stocking stitch background. An attractive stitch for a jumper.
Multiple of 10 sts
Row 1: *yfwd, sl 1, K 1, psso, K 8*
Row 2 and alt rows: purl
Row 3: *K 1, yfwd, sl 1, K 1, psso, K 5, K 2 tog, yrn*
Row 5: *K 2, yfwd, sl 1, K 1, psso, K 3, K 2 tog, yfwd, K 1*
Row 7: *K 5, yfwd, sl 1, K 1, psso, K 3*
Row 9: *K 3, K 2 tog, yfwd, K 1, yfwd, sl 1, K 1, psso, K 2*
Row 11: *K 2, K 2 tog, yfwd, K 3, yfwd, sl 1, K 1, psso, K 1*

Horizontal openwork: Lacy bands set at intervals in a stocking stitch.
In the example, lace stitches occur every ten rows; they could be set closer together or farther apart, or just one band used for a decorative touch.
Multiple of 2 sts
Rows 1, 3, 5, 7, 9, 10: knit
Rows 2, 4, 6, 8: purl
Row 11: ybk, P 2 tog, *yrn, P 2 tog*
Row 12: knit

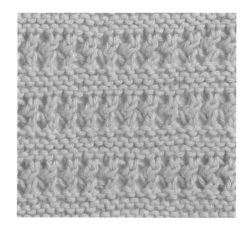

Lace insert: A double band of openwork alternating with strips of garter stitch (or moss stitch or stocking stitch). Can be used for trim or an entire fabric.
Multiple of 2 sts
Rows 1 to 6: knit
Rows 7 and 9: *yfwd, K 2 tog*
Rows 8 and 10: ybk, P 2 tog, *yrn, P 2 tog*

Striped faggoting: Openwork ribs combined with reverse stocking stitch. This stitch can be worked as shown, or one multiple of the lace could be used for a lacy insertion.
Multiple of 8 sts plus 4
Row 1: *P 4, K 2 tog, yfwd, K 2*, P 4
Row 2: *K 4, P 2 tog, yrn, P 2*, K 4

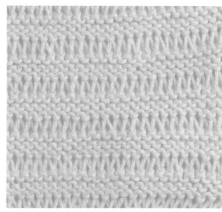

Drop stitch lace: Bands of elongated stitches alternating with bands of garter stitch (or moss stitch or stocking stitch). The open bands can be set close together or far apart, depending on the effect desired.
Multiple is any number of sts
Rows 1 to 4: knit
Row 5: knit, winding thread twice around the needle
Row 6: knit, letting extra loop drop

Butterfly: A very pretty stitch for a child's jumper.
Multiple of 10 sts plus 5
Rows 1 and 3: K 5, *K 2 tog, yfwd, K 1, yfwd, sl 1, K 1, psso, K 5*
Rows 2 and 4: *P 7, sl 1 P-wise, P 2*, P 5
Rows 5 and 11: knit
Rows 6 and 12: purl
Rows 7 and 9: *K 2 tog, yfwd, K 1, yfwd, sl 1, K 1, psso, K 5*, K 2 tog, yfwd, K 1, yfwd, sl 1, K 1, psso
Rows 8 and 10: *P 2, sl 1 P-wise, P 7*, P 2, sl 1 P-wise, P 2

Double drop stitch: Two rows of elongated stitches, back to back, make an attractive lacy insert. Use one row as a trim, or several for an airy fabric, as shown here.
Multiple is any number of sts
Rows 1, 3, 5, 7: knit
Rows 2, 4, 6: purl
Row 8 (wrong side): knit, winding thread twice around the needle
Row 9: rep Row 8, letting the extra loop drop
Row 10: knit, letting extra loop drop

Knitting stitches

Lace stitches (continued)

Feather stitch: Cast-on edge is scalloped.
Multiple of 10 sts plus 2
Rows 1 to 4: knit
Rows 5, 7, 9, 11: K 2, * yfwd, K 2, K 2 tog, K 2 tog tbl, K 2, yfwd, K 2 *
Rows 6, 8, 10, 12: K 1, purl to last st, K 1

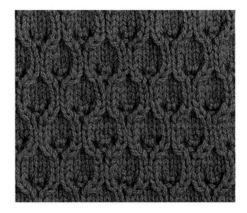

Snowball stitch: A neat stitch suitable for jumpers and children's wear.
Multiple of 6 sts plus 1
Rows 1 and 3: K 3, * P 1, K 5 *, P 1, K 3
Rows 2 and 4: P 3, * K 1, P 5 *, K 1, P 3
Row 5: * K 1, K 2 tog, yfwd, K 1, yfwd, sl 1, K 1, psso *, K 1
Rows 6, 8, 10: P 6, * K 1, P 5 *, P 1
Rows 7 and 9: K 6, * P 1, K 5 *, K 1
Row 11: * K 1, yfwd, sl 1, K 1, psso, K 1, K 2 tog, yfwd *, K 1
Row 12: P 3, * K 1, P 5 *, K 1, P 3

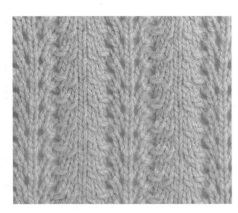

Wave stitch: A delicate stitch suitable for baby wear.
Multiple of 12 sts plus 1
Row 1: * K 1, (K 2 tog) twice, (yfwd, K 1) 3 times, yfwd, (sl 1, K 1, psso) twice *, K 1
Rows 2 and 4: purl
Row 3: knit

Fan stitch: An airy, undulating pattern. Cast-on edge is scalloped.
Multiple of 18 sts
Row 1: * (K 2 tog) 3 times, (yfwd, K 1) 6 times, (K 2 tog) 3 times *
Rows 2 and 4: purl
Rows 3, 5 and 6: knit

Diamond fern stitch: A variation of fern stitch (see p. 462) with distinctive diamond pattern. Cast-on edge is very slightly scalloped.
Multiple of 12 sts plus 9
Row 1: K 5, ° K 2 tog, yfwd, K 1, yfwd, sl 1, K 1, psso, K 7 °, K 2 tog, yfwd, K 2
Row 2 and alt rows: K 1, purl to last st, K 1
Row 3: K 4, * K 2 tog, (K 1, yfwd) twice, K 1, sl 1, K 1, psso, K 5 *, K 2 tog, K 1, yfwd, K 2
Row 5: K 3, * K 2 tog, K 2, yfwd, K 1, yfwd, K 2, sl 1, K 1, psso, K 3 *, K 2 tog, K 2, yfwd, K 2
Row 7: K 2, * K 2 tog, K 3, yfwd, K 1, yfwd, K 3, sl 1, K 1, psso, K 1 *, K 2 tog, K 3, yfwd, K 2
Row 9: K 1, K 2 tog, * K 4, yfwd, K 1, yfwd, K 4, sl 1, K 2 tog, psso *, K 4, yfwd, K 2
Row 11: K 2, * yfwd, sl 1, K 1, psso, K 7, K 2 tog, yfwd, K 1 *, yfwd, sl 1, K 1, psso, K 5
Row 13: K 2, * yfwd, K 1, sl 1, K 1, psso, K 5, K 2 tog, K 1, yfwd, K 1 *, yfwd, K 1, sl 1, K 1, psso, K 4
Row 15: K 2, * yfwd, K 2, sl 1, K 1, psso, K 3, K 2 tog, K 2, yfwd, K 1 *, yfwd, K 2, sl 1, K 1, psso, K 3
Row 17: K 2, * yfwd, K 3, sl 1, K 1, psso, K 1, K 2 tog, K 3, yfwd, K 1 *, yfwd, K 3, sl 1, K 1, psso, K 2
Row 19: K 2, * yfwd, K 4, sl 1, K 2 tog, psso, K 4, yfwd, K 1 *, yfwd, K 4, sl 1, K 1, psso, K 1
Row 20: K 1, purl to last st, K 1

Knotted stitches

Popcorn: A medium-sized knot made by knitting several times into the same stitch, then slipping all extra loops over the first one. Knot size can be varied by working fewer or more times into a stitch. The number and spacing of popcorns in a pattern can also be varied according to the effect desired.
Multiple of 6 sts plus 3
Rows 1 and 5: knit
Row 2 and alt rows: purl
Row 3: K 1, *make popcorn in next st [(K front and back of loop) twice, then slip the 2nd, 3rd, and 4th sts over the 1st], K 5*, make popcorn, K 1
Row 7: K 4, *make popcorn, K 5*, make popcorn, K 4

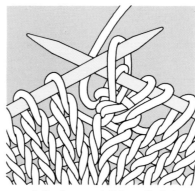

Pulling the second stitch over the first

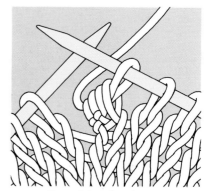

Three stitches slipped over one

Bobble: A dramatic-looking knot made by working several times into the same stitch, knitting back and forth on the increases, and finally slipping the extra stitches off the needle in the same way as for a popcorn (above). The bobble size can be varied, but it is essentially a large knot, suitable for a trim or accent, or to be used sparingly in an all-over pattern.
Multiple is any number of stitches
On stocking stitch or other background, work bobble as follows: (K front and back of same st) twice, (turn work and P these 4 sts, turn work and K them) twice, slip the 2nd, 3rd and 4th sts over the 1st. Space bobbles as shown or as desired.

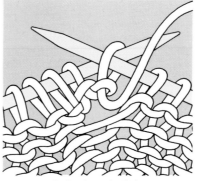

Purling the made stitches

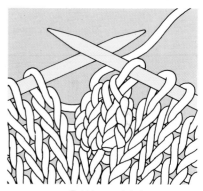

Bobble completed

Trinity stitch: A smaller, less complicated knot than either a popcorn or bobble. It is formed by making a double increase in one stitch followed by a double decrease in the next. Trinity (also called blackberry) is a popular choice for one panel in an Aran motif. Note that at the end of Row 2 there are 2 stitches fewer than you started with. At the end of Row 4, the pattern returns to the starting number.
Multiple of 4 sts plus 3
Rows 1 and 3: purl
Row 2: *P 3 tog, KPK into next st*, P 3 tog
Row 4: *KPK into first st, P 3 tog*, KPK into last st

Hazelnut stitch: A flatter and broader knot than either a popcorn or a bobble; it looks embossed. The knot is produced by making a double increase and working it over all stitches for 2 more rows.
Multiple of 4 sts
Row 1: °P 3, (K 1, yfwd, K 1) in next st°
Rows 2 and 3: °P 3, K 3°
Row 4: °P 3 tog, K 3°
Rows 5 and 11: purl
Rows 6 and 12: knit
Row 7: °P 1, (K 1, yfwd, K 1) in next st, P 2°
Row 8: K 2, °P 3, K 3°, P 3, K 1
Row 9: P 1, °K 3, P 3°, K 3, P 2
Row 10: K 2, °P 3 tog, K 3°, P 3 tog, K 1

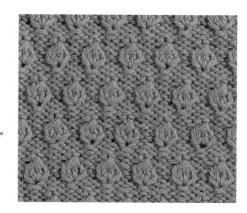

465

Knitting stitches

Introduction to crossed stitches

Richly embossed **cross-stitch patterns** are produced by switching the working order of two or three stitches, which pulls knitted loops on a diagonal. Some of these patterns are actually cables in miniature (see pages 468–469 for cable stitches), but are easier and faster to work because there are fewer steps. Other crossed-stitch patterns resemble woven fabrics, in both appearance and performance. In basket weave, right, crossing locks the stitches, limiting stretch.

To cross two stitches, work the second stitch on the left needle, then the first one, slipping both stitches off the needle together. To do this comfortably and without stretching the yarn, tension should be kept fairly loose.

After stitches are crossed, they slant either to the left or right. The direction depends on the way the loops are worked—to the front or back. Review crossed-stitch methods before starting (pages 450–451).

Because the technique provides so much textural interest, these patterns are best worked with smooth yarns.

Basket weave: Stitches crossed left and right to form a sturdy fabric that is similar to a woven structure.
Multiple of 2 sts
Row 1: *cross 2 LK*
Row 2: P 1, *cross 2 RP*, P 1

Crossed stitches

Wasps nest: A 3-dimensional texture produced by crossing knit stitches alternately to the right and the left. It looks very much like smocking.
Multiple of 4 sts
Row 1: *cross 2 RK, cross 2 LK*
Row 2 and alt rows: purl
Row 3: *cross 2 LK, cross 2 RK*

Basket weave rib: A very wide decorative pattern, more suitable for a fabric than for ribbing, or one panel of the rib could be used as a decorative insert on a garment worked in stocking stitch or reverse stocking stitch.
Multiple of 12 sts plus 5
Row 1: *P 5, K 1, (cross 2 LK) 3 times*, P 5
Row 2: K 5, *P 1, (cross 2 RP) 3 times, K 5*

Knotted cross stitch: The crossed stitches slipped over two increases form a moderate-sized nub on a stocking stitch background.
Multiple of 4 sts plus 2
Rows 1 and 3: knit
Row 2 and alt rows: purl
Row 5: *K 2, cross 2 LK, (yrn, pass the second st on right needle over the first st and the yrn) twice*, K 2

Crossed-stitch ribbing: Forms a very elastic fabric that retains its springiness through many washings.
Multiple of 3 sts plus 1
Row 1: P 1, *cross 2 RK, P 1*
Row 2: K 1, *P 2, K 1*

Chain stitch: Resembles a cable rib but is much easier to execute.
Multiple of 8 sts plus 4
Row 1: *P 4, cross 2 LK, cross 2 RK*, P 4
Row 2: *K 4, P 4*, K 4
Rows 3 and 5: *P 4, K 1, P 2, K 1*, P 4
Rows 4 and 6: *K 4, P 1, K 2, P 1*, K 4

Small diamonds: A lattice pattern in a scale small enough for a child's jumper.
Multiple of 6 sts plus 2
Row 1: K 3, *cross 2 RK, K 4* cross 2 RK, K 3
Row 2 and alt rows: purl
Row 3: *K 2, cross 2 RK, cross 2 LK*, K 2
Row 5: K 1, *cross 2 RK, K 2, cross 2 LK*, K 1
Row 7: *cross 2 RK, K 4*, cross 2 RK
Row 9: K 1, *cross 2 LK, K 2, cross 2 RK*, K 1
Row 11: *K 2, cross 2 LK, cross 2 RK*, K 2

Double rick-rack: Can be used effectively as an all-over pattern (shown), or one rick-rack panel would make an interesting accent or trim.
Multiple of 9 sts plus 5
Row 1: °P 5, cross 2 RK, cross 2 LK°, P 5
Rows 2 and 4: K the P sts and P the K sts of the previous row
Row 3: °P 5, cross 2 LK, cross 2 RK°, P 5

Twigs: Delicate branches traced on a stocking stitch background.
Multiple of 13 sts plus 2
Row 1: *K 1, cross 2 RK, K 2, cross 2 RK, K 1, cross 2 LK, K 3*, K 2
Row 2 and alt rows: purl
Row 3: *K 4, cross 2 RK, K 3, cross 2 LK, K 2*, K 2
Row 5: *K 3, cross 2 RK, K 1, cross 2 LK, K 2, cross 2 LK, K 1*, K 2
Row 7: *K 2, cross 2 RK, K 3, cross 2 LK, K 4*, K 2

Twill rib: A very elastic as well as an attractive stitch, produced by crossing through two stitches (p. 451).
Multiple of 9 sts plus 3
Row 1: °P 3, (cross through 2 RK) 3 times°, P 3
Row 2 and alt rows: °K 3, P 6°, K 3
Row 3: °P 3, K 1, (cross through 2 RK) twice, K 1°, P 3

Palm fronds: Leaves appear to be embossed on the stocking stitch background.
Multiple of 14 sts plus 6
Rows 1 and 5: K 6, *K 2, cross 2 RK, cross 2 LK, K 8*
Row 2 and alt rows: purl
Row 3: K 6, *K 1, cross 2 RK, K 2, cross 2 LK, K 7*
Row 7: K 6, *K 3, sl 1, K 1, psso and K it before dropping off the needle, K 9*
Row 9: knit
Rows 11 and 15: *K 1, cross 2 RK, cross 2 LK, K 9*, cross 2 RK, cross LK, K 1
Row 13: *cross 2 RK, K 2, cross 2 LK, K 8*, cross 2 RK, K 2, cross 2 LK
Row 17: K 2, *sl 1, K 1, psso and K, K 12*, sl 1, K 1, psso and K, K 2
Row 19: knit

Knitting stitches

Introduction to cable stitches

A **cable** is one of the most handsome of the pattern stitches. Coordinating its technique requires practice, but once that is mastered, the applications are numerous and fascinating. Although versatile, cables are mainly used for sportswear in heavier yarns.

Like a crossed stitch, a cable results from an exchange of stitch positions, usually four or more. A double-point or cable needle is used to hold the first stitches while the next group is worked. Holding stitches to the front produces a cable twist left; to the back, a cable twist right. To make it sharper, the raised portion of a cable is usually knitted, the stitches on each side of it purled. Exceptions are the pattern types below, in which cables are continuous.

Cables

Lattice stitch: Embossed crisscrosses, produced by cabling right and left on alternate rows.
Multiple of 4 sts
Row 1: knit
Row 2 and alt rows: purl
Row 3: K 2, *sl 2 sts on cable needle and leave at back of work, K 2, K 2 sts from cable needle*, K 2
Row 5: *sl 2 sts on cable needle and leave at front of work, K 2, K 2 sts from cable needle*
Rep from Row 2

Sand tracks: Continuous cables form a deeply waved all-over pattern.
Multiple of 12 sts
Rows 1, 5, 9: knit
Row 2 and alt rows: purl
Row 3: *sl next 3 sts on cable needle and leave at front of work, K 3, K 3 sts from cable needle, K 6*
Row 7: *K 6, sl next 3 sts on cable needle and leave at back of work, K 3, K 3 sts from cable needle*
Rep from Row 3

Wild oats: A softly contoured pattern in low relief.
Multiple of 4 sts plus 1
Rows 1 and 5: *K 2, sl 1 P-wise, K 1*, K 1
Rows 2 and 6: P 1, *P 1, sl 1 P-wise, P 2*
Row 3: *sl 2 sts on cable needle and leave at back of work, K the sl st of 2 rows previous, K 2 sts from cable needle, K 1*, K 1
Rows 4 and 8: purl
Row 7: K 1, *K 1, put the sl st on cable needle and leave at front of work, K 2, K st from cable needle*

Simple cable rib: The classic cable on a background of reverse stocking stitch.
Multiple of 7 sts plus 3
Rows 1 and 3: *P 3, K 4*, P 3
Rows 2, 4, 6: *K 3, P 4*, K 3
Row 5: *P 3, C 4F (sl 2 sts on cable needle and leave at front of work, K 2 sts, K 2 sts from cable needle)*, P 3

Coiled rope: A spiral, the result of twisting the cable continuously to the right.
Multiple of 9 sts plus 3
Rows 1 and 3: *P 3, K 6*, P 3
Rows 2, 4, 6: *K 3, P 6*, K 3
Row 5: *P 3, sl 3 sts on cable needle and leave at back of work, K 3, K 3 sts from cable needle*, P 3

Minaret stitch: Slender cabled towers.
Multiple of 12 sts plus 4
Rows 1, 3, 5: P 4, *K 2, P 4*
Rows 2 and 4: K 4, *P 2, K 4*
Row 6: K 4, *yfwd, sl 2 P-wise, ybk, K 4*
Row 7: P 4, *sl 2 sts on cable needle and leave at front of work, P 2, yon, K 2 tog tbl from cable needle, put next 2 sts on cable needle and leave at back of work, K 2 tog, yrn, P 2 from cable needle, P 4*
Row 8: K 4, *P 2, K 1 tbl, P 2, K 1 tbl, P 2, K 4*

Braided cable: A very wide pattern, suitable where a bold accent is desired.
Multiple of 23 sts plus 5
Rows 1 and 5: *P 5, K 18*, P 5
Row 2 and alt rows: *K 5, P 18*, K 5
Row 3: *P 5, (sl 3 sts on cable needle and leave at back of work, K 3, K 3 sts from cable needle) 3 times*, P 5
Row 7: *P 5, K 3, (sl 3 sts on cable needle and leave at front of work, K 3, K 3 sts from cable needle) twice, K 3*, P 5

Crossed ribs: A bold, rather large pattern.
Multiple of 16 sts plus 2
Row 1 and alt rows (wrong side):
K 2, P 2, K 2
Rows 2, 4, 6, 8: *P 2, K 2*, P 2
Row 10: P 2, *sl 4 sts on cable needle and leave at front of work, K 2, slip the 2 P sts from cable needle to left needle and purl them, K last 2 sts from cable needle, (P 2, K 2) twice, P 2*
Rows 12, 14, 16, 18: *P 2, K 2*, P 2
Row 20: *(P 2, K 2) twice, P 2, sl 4 sts on cable needle and leave at back of work, K 2, slip the 2 P sts from cable needle to left needle and purl them, K last 2 sts from cable needle*, P 2

Crossed ribs with faggoting: Cable combined with openwork: suitable for lightweight or medium-weight yarns.
Multiple of 6 sts plus 2
Rows 1, 3, 5, 7, 9, 11 (wrong side):
K 2, *P 2 tog, yrn, P 2, K 2*
Rows 2, 4, 6, 8, 10: P 2, *ybk, sl 1 K 1, psso, yfwd, K 2, P 2*
Row 12: P 2, *sl 2 sts on cable needle and leave at front of work, ybk, sl 1, K 1, psso, yfwd, K 2 sts from cable needle, P 2*

Crossed cables: Elongated cable ribs in an all-over pattern.
Multiple of 8 sts plus 6
Row 1 and alt rows (wrong side):
K 2, P 2, K 2
Rows 2, 4, 6: *P 2, K 2*, P 2
Row 8: *P 2, sl 3 sts on cable needle and leave at front of work, K 3, K 3 sts from cable needle*, P 2, K 2, P 2
Rows 10, 12, 14: *P 2, K 2*, P 2
Row 16: P 2, K 2, P 2, *sl 3 sts on cable needle and leave at back of work, K 3, K 3 sts from cable needle, P 2*

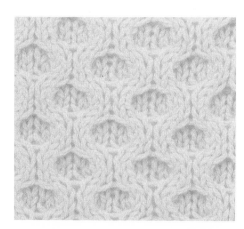

Honeycomb: A popular stitch for Aran knitting.
Multiple of 8 sts
Row 1: *C 4B (sl 2 sts on cable needle and leave at back of work, K 2, K 2 sts from cable needle), C 4F (sl 2 sts on cable needle and leave at front of work, K 2, K 2 sts from cable needle)*
Rows 2, 4, 6, 8: purl
Rows 3 and 7: knit
Row 5: *C 4F, C 4B (see above)*

Trellis stitch: An example of a cable worked with an uneven number of stitches.
Multiple of 6 sts
Rows 1 and 3: *P 2, K 2, P 2*
Row 2 and alt rows: K the P sts and P the K sts of previous row
Row 5: *sl 2 sts on cable needle and leave at back of work, K 1, P 2 sts from cable needle, sl 1 st on cable needle and leave at front of work, P 2, K 1 st from cable needle*
Rows 7 and 9: *K 1, P 4, K 1*
Row 11: *sl 1 st on cable needle and leave at front of work, P 2, K 1 st from cable needle, sl 2 sts on cable needle and leave at back of work, K 1, P 2 from cable needle*

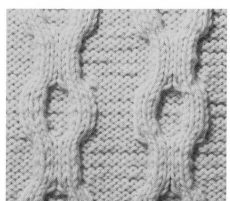

Chain cable: A large and bold stitch.
Multiple of 18 sts plus 6
Rows 1, 3, 5, 7 (wrong side):
K 6, P 3, K 6
Rows 2, 4, 6: *P 6, K 3*, P 6
Row 8: *P 6, sl 3 sts on cable needle and leave at front of work, P 3, K 3 sts from cable needle, sl 3 sts on cable needle and leave at back of work, K 3, P 3 sts from cable needle*, P 6
Rows 9, 11, 13, 15: K 9, *P 6, K 12*, K 9
Rows 10, 12, 14: P 9, *K 6, P 12*, P 9
Row 16: *P 6, sl 3 sts on cable needle and leave at back of work, K 3, P 3 sts from cable needle, sl 3 sts on cable needle and leave at front of work, P 3, K 3 sts from cable needle*, P 6

Knitting stitches

Novelty stitches

Daisy stitch: Elongated petal loops.
Multiple of 10 sts plus 8
Rows 1, 3, 5: knit
Rows 2, 4, 6: purl
Row 7: K 2, make daisy [insert needle in loop 3 rows below the 2nd st on left needle, draw up a loop, K 2, draw 2nd loop through same st, K 2, draw 3rd loop through same st], *K 6, make daisy*, K 2
Row 8: P 2, *(P 2 tog, P 1) twice, P 2 tog, P 5*, (P 2 tog, P 1) twice, P 2 tog, P 1
Rows 9, 11, 13: knit
Rows 10, 12, 14: purl
Row 15: K 7, *make daisy, K 6*, K 1
Row 16: P 2, *P 5, (P 2 tog, P 1) twice, P 2 tog*, P 6

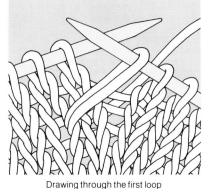

Drawing through the first loop

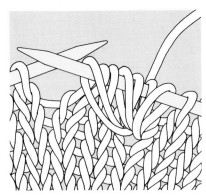

Three loops drawn through the same stitch

Bowknot: Yarn strands carried loosely across the knitted face, caught together at a designated point to form a bow.
Multiple of 10 sts plus 7
Rows 1 and 3 (wrong side): purl
Rows 2, 4, 6, 8: knit
Rows 5, 7, 9: P 6, *ybk, sl 5 sts P-wise, yfwd, P 5*, P 1
Row 10: K 8, *make bowknot [slip right needle under 3 strands, knit next st, pulling the loop through under the strands], K 9*, make bowknot, K 8
Rows 11 and 13: purl
Rows 12, 14, 16, 18: knit
Rows 15, 17, 19: P 1, *ybk, sl 5 sts P-wise, yfwd, P 5*, ybk, sl 5 sts, P 1
Row 20: K 3, *bowknot, K 9*, bowknot, K 3

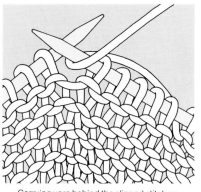

Carrying yarn behind the slipped stitches

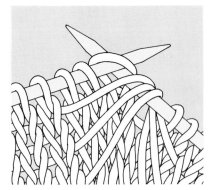

Needle picking up 3 strands to form bowknot

Loop stitch: Shaggy texture suitable for a rug, cushion cover, or trim. The right-handed method is given here since it yields the firmest stitch. If desired, loop length can be adjusted by winding yarn over one or three fingers instead of two. A loop stitch can also be crocheted.
Multiple of 2 sts plus 1
Rows 1 and 3: knit
Row 2: K 1, *make 1 loop [insert needle in next st, wind yarn over needle point, then over two fingers of left hand, then over needle point again; draw 2 loops through the st and place them back on left needle; knit the 2 loops together through the back], K 1*
Row 4: K 2, *make 1 loop, K 1*, K 1

Winding yarn over 2 fingers of left hand

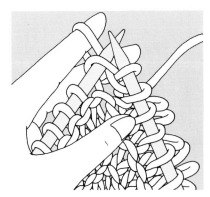

The 2 loops drawn through the stitch

Jacquards worked with stranding

Abstract diamond: A lively pattern, somewhat dramatic; can be equally attractive in subtle or bold colour combinations.

Flower border: Traditional motif in the Fair Isle style; typical use would be along the bottom of a plain jumper.

Geometric border: Fascinating theme of triangles and diamonds; suitable for a man's or a woman's garment.

multiple

multiple

multiple

Knitting stitches

Weaving multicoloured stitches

Weaving is a way of working unused yarn into the fabric back when colours must be carried over more than a five-stitch span. The procedure is similar to stranding (page 474), but the carried yarn is brought alternately above and below each stitch; in effect, weaving it in. The result is a thick fabric, sturdy on both right and wrong sides. (The carried yarns cannot be snagged as they might with stranding.) Weaving is practical for a heavy outer garment or blanket. For general use, however, weaving is not recommended, as the fabric may be too firm and have an uneven surface, and the woven colour may show through the surface of the work.

This method, like stranding, is easier to work using two hands simultaneously. The movements may seem awkward at first, but work will go more smoothly as a rhythm is established. If a pattern has a mixture of long and short spans, weave the longer yarns and strand the short ones.

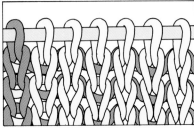
Woven yarns carried above and below stitches

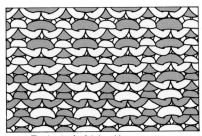
The back of a fabric with woven yarns

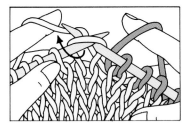

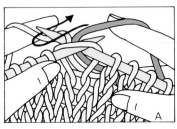

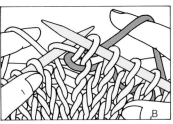

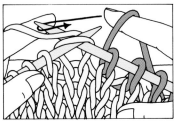

WITH KNIT STITCHES

To weave right yarn above a knit stitch, simply hold yarn away from the work with the right index finger, then knit with the left yarn.

To weave right yarn below a knit stitch, two movements are necessary. (A) Make a knit movement with the right yarn, then a knit movement with the left yarn.

(B) Reverse the right yarn, taking it back around and beneath the right needle, at the same time drawing the left knit stitch through the loop.

To weave left yarn above a knit stitch, bring it over (but not around) the right needle, as shown, then make your knit stitch with the right yarn.

To weave left yarn below a knit stitch, hold it away from the work with the left index finger, then make the knit stitch with the right yarn.

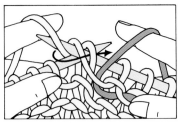

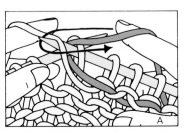

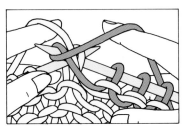

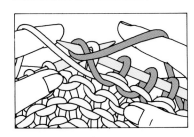

WITH PURL STITCHES

To weave right yarn above a purl stitch, pull it up with the right index finger, then make the purl stitch with the left yarn.

To weave right yarn below a purl stitch, two movements are necessary. (A) Make a purl movement with the right yarn, then a purl movement with the left yarn.

(B) Reverse the right yarn, taking it back around and beneath the stitch made with the left yarn, then draw the purl stitch through the loop.

To weave left yarn above a purl stitch, bring it over (but not around) the right needle, as shown, then make your purl stitch with the right yarn.

To weave left yarn below a purl stitch, hold it taut with the left index finger, as you make the purl stitch with the right yarn.

Stitch charts

Knitting stitches can be represented by symbols which are used to chart a pattern stitch visually. Because a chart resembles the actual look of a pattern, it aids in visualising an unfamiliar stitch and helps keep track of a complex pattern. No adjustment is needed for circular knitting because a chart represents each technique as viewed from the right side.

The knitting symbols presented here are from universal stitch charts. Knitting patterns are increasingly being presented in charted form. Although it may take a little while to get used to patterns presented as graphs, one great advantage is that you will be able to use patterns from foreign-language publications.

Listed are the symbols and their definitions. Usually only a few symbols are used in one pattern, so it is necessary to remember only those for which you have immediate use.

The following information is essential, however, for reading any chart.

1. Each row is represented as it appears on the right side. For example, a dash (−), which stands for reverse stocking stitch, would be purled on a right side row, but knitted on a wrong side row.

2. A chart is read from bottom to top, starting at the lower right corner.

3. To keep track of rows worked, it is helpful to place a ruler on the chart, and move it upwards as you work.

4. The multiple in a chart is enclosed by heavy parallel lines, the equivalent of asterisks in written directions.

5. Rows are numbered to either side of a chart; when the odd numbers appear to the left, they represent wrong side rows, to the right, right side rows.

6. A chart can show as many multiples or repeats as desirable for an accurate picture of the pattern stitch.

Comparison of written and charted directions

Lace and cable pattern:
Multiple of 13 sts
Rows 1 and 5: °K 1, yfwd, sl 1, K 1, psso, K 1, K 2 tog, yfwd, K 1, P 1, K 4, P 1°
Row 2 and alt rows: °K 1, P 4, K 1, P 7°
Row 3: °K 2, yfwd, sl 1, K 2 tog, psso, yfwd, K 2, P 1, C 4F [slip 2 sts on cable needle and leave at front of work, K 2, K 2 from cable needle], P 1°
Rows 7 and 11: °K 2, yfwd, sl 1, K 2 tog, psso, yfwd, K 2, P 1, K 4, P 1°
Row 9: °K 1, yfwd, sl 1, K 1, psso, K 1, K 2 tog, yfwd, K 1, P 1, C4F, P 1°

Small diamond seed stitch:
A smaller version of diamond seed stitch given on page 456.
Multiple of 6 sts plus 1
Row 1: K 3, °P 1, K 5°, P 1, K 3
Rows 2 and 6: P 2, °K 1, P 1, K 1, P 3°, K 1, P 1, K 1, P 2
Rows 3 and 5: K 1, °P 1, K 3, P 1, K 1°
Row 4: K 1, °P 5, K 1°

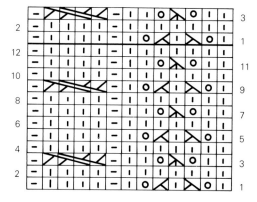

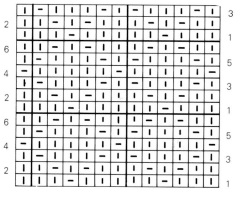

Universal stitch charts

⊞ Selvage or edge stitch.

▯ **St st:** Stocking stitch (knit RS, purl WS).

▯ **rev St st:** Reverse stocking stitch (purl on RS, knit on WS).

▯ **twisted St st:** Knit stitch through back loop on RS; purl stitch through back loop on WS.

▯ **twisted rev St st:** Purl stitch through back loop on RS; knit stitch through back loop on WS.

▯ **sl st K-wise:** With yarn at back, slip stitch knitwise on RS; with yarn in front, slip stitch knitwise on WS.

▯ **sl st P-wise:** With yarn at back, slip stitch purlwise on RS; with yarn in front, slip stitch purlwise on WS.

▯ **sl st P-wise** (to create a float): With yarn in front, slip stitch purlwise on RS; with yarn at back, slip stitch purlwise on WS.

○ **yon:** Yarn over needle.

▯ **K 1-b:** Knit stitch in row below on RS; P 1-b: purl stitch in row below on WS.

▯ **P 1-b:** Purl stitch in row below on RS; K 1-b: knit stitch in row below on WS.

▯ **M1:** Make 1 stitch: on RS, insert left needle from front to back under horizontal strand between stitch just worked and next stitch on left needle. Knit this strand through back loop. On WS, insert left needle from back to front under strand as before and purl it through back loop.

▯ Make 1 stitch to form an eyelet: on RS, insert left needle from front to back under

Knitting stitches

Universal stitch charts (continued)

horizontal strand between stitch just worked and next stitch on left needle. Knit this strand. On WS, insert left needle from back to front under strand as before and purl it.

inc 1 st: Increase 1 stitch: knit in front then in back of stitch on RS; purl in back then in front of stitch on WS.

Increase 1 stitch to the right: with right needle, pick up next stitch on left needle in row below. Place loop on left needle and knit it.

Increase 1 stitch to the left: with left needle, pick up next stitch on right needle one row below and knit it.

Increase 3 stitches in 2: insert right needle knitwise into next two stitches on left needle. Knit 1, purl 1, knit 1. Drop loops off left needle.

K 2 tog: On RS, knit 2 stitches together; P 2 tog: on WS, purl 2 stitches together.

SK, psso: On RS, slip 1 stitch. Knit next stitch and pass slipped stitch over knitted stitch. On WS, slip next 2 stitches knitwise. Slip these 2 stitches back to left needle without twisting them and purl them together through the back loops.

SSK: On RS, slip next 2 stitches knitwise. Insert tip of left needle into fronts of these and knit them together. On WS, slip 1 stitch, purl 1 stitch, then pass slipped stitch over purl stitch.

P 2 tog: On RS, purl 2 stitches together; K 2 tog: on WS, knit 2 stitches together.

P 2 tog tbl: On RS, purl 2 stitches together through the back loops; K 2 tog tbl: on WS, knit 2 stitches together through back loops.

K 3 tog: On RS, knit 3 stitches together; P 3 tog: on WS, purl 3 stitches together.

P 3 tog: On RS, purl 3 stitches together; K 3 tog: on WS, knit 3 stitches together.

SK 2 tog, psso: On RS, slip 1 stitch, knit 2 stitches together. Pass slipped stitch over 2 stitches knitted together. On WS, slip 2 stitches to right needle as if knitting two together. Slip next stitch knitwise. Slip all stitches to left needle without twisting. Purl these 3 stitches together through back of the loops.

K 4 tog: On RS, knit 4 stitches together; P 4 tog: on WS, purl 4 stitches together.

make bobble: [K 1, P 1] twice into next stitch, turn, P 4, turn, K 4, turn [P 2 tog] twice, turn, K 2 tog. Or make bobble as specified in pattern.

2-st right twist: On RS rows, K 2 tog leaving sts on LH needle, knit first st again, slip both sts from needle. On WS rows, wyaf skip next st and purl the 2nd st, then purl skipped st, slip both sts from needle tog.

2-st left twist: With RH needle behind LH needle, skip the first st and knit 2nd st tbl, insert RH needle into backs of both sts, K 2 tog tbl.

2-st right purl twist: Slip one st onto cable needle and hold at back of work, K 1, then P 1 from cable needle.

2-st left purl twist: Slip one st onto cable needle and hold at front of work, P 1, then K 1 from cable needle.

3-st right twist: Slip 2 sts onto cable needle and hold at back of work, K 1, then K 2 from cable needle.

3-st left twist: Slip one st onto cable needle and hold at front of work, K 2, then K 1 from cable needle.

3-st right cable: Slip one st onto cable needle and hold at back of work, K 2, then K 1 from cable needle.

3-st left cable: Slip 2 sts onto cable needle and hold at front of work, K 1, then K 2 from cable needle.

3-st right purl cable: Slip one st onto cable needle and hold at back of work, K 2, then P 1 from cable needle.

3-st left purl cable: Slip 2 sts onto cable needle and hold at front of work, P 1, then K 2 from cable needle.

4-st right cable: Slip 2 sts onto cable needle and hold at back of work, K 2, then K 2 from cable needle.

4-st left cable: Slip 2 sts onto cable needle and hold at front of work, K 2, then K 2 from cable needle.

4-st right purl cable: Slip one st onto cable needle and hold at back of work, P 3, then K 1 from cable needle.

4-st left purl cable: Slip 3 sts onto cable needle and hold at front of work, K 1, then P 3 from cable needle.

4-st right purl cable: Slip one st onto cable needle and hold at back of work, K 3, then P 1 from cable needle.

4-st left purl cable: Slip 3 sts onto cable needle and hold at front of work, P 1, then K 3 from cable needle.

4-st wrap: Wyab slip 4, wyaf slip same 4 sts to LH needle, wyab slip same 4 sts back to RH needle.

5-st right cable: Slip 3 sts onto cable needle and hold at back of work, K 2, slip purl st from cable needle to LH needle and purl it, then K 2 from cable needle.

5-st right purl cable: Slip 2 sts onto cable needle and hold at back of work, K 3, then P 2 from cable needle.

5-st left purl cable: Slip 3 sts onto cable needle and hold at front of work, P 2, then K 3 from cable needle.

tie st: Slip 5 sts onto cable needle and hold at back of work, wrap yarn around these 5 sts three times, return sts to LH needle, then work them as follows: K 1, P 3, K 1.

6-st right cable: Slip 3 sts onto cable needle and hold at back of work, K 3, then K 3 from cable needle.

6-st left cable: Slip 3 sts onto cable needle and hold at front of work, K 3, then K 3 from cable needle.

wrapped sts: K 2, P 2, K 2, slip the last 6 sts worked onto cable needle and wrap yarn four times counterclockwise around these 6 sts; then slip the 6 sts back onto RH needle.

12-st right cable: Slip 6 sts onto cable needle and hold at back of work, K 6; K 6 from cable needle.

12-st left cable: Slip 6 sts onto cable needle and hold at front of work, K 6; K 6 from cable needle.

Once you have learnt the basics of knitting, you will be ready to knit a garment, and this chapter guides you through from start to finish. The first step in knitting a garment is to take your measurements: this is essential, whether you are going to use a commercial pattern or create a design of your own. Instructions for shaping, making pleats, working necklines and collars, sleeves, borders, hems, pockets and buttonholes will help you understand the steps used in patterns or give you the basis for designing for yourself. But the ultimate success of your garment will depend upon careful assembling and finishing. Methods of blocking the knitted pieces, joining them together, finishing off and adjusting fit are all described to help you achieve a professional finish. The decorative possibilities of embroidery are covered, with instructions for knitting stitch, cross stitch and other embroidery stitches. The chapter concludes with an introduction to crochet, with instructions for making crocheted edgings and buttons that would suit any garment.

Knitting a garment

Introduction

It is essential, from the beginning, to familiarise yourself with basic knitting procedures so that you can better understand pattern directions, and if you would like to, design your own garments.

Before knitting a garment, always follow these steps. (1) Compare pattern measurements with those of the person for whom the garment is intended. If measurements are not specified, you can determine them by dividing a stitch or row total by the tension. For example, if the shoulder has 25 stitches, and the tension is 20 stitches to 10 centimetres, the shoulder should measure 12.5 centimetres. (2) Check the tension. Planned garment dimensions can be obtained only by duplicating the tension specified in the pattern.

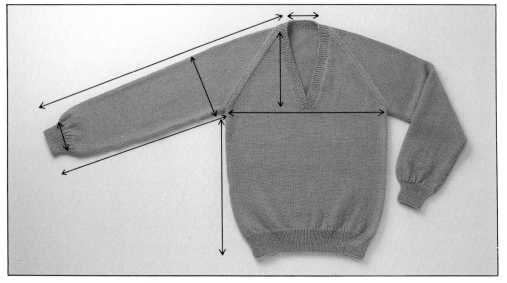

When taking measurements from a garment, lay it flat, and as you measure, pull each seam or area comfortably (that is, without distortion) to its fullest dimension. Take all measurements as indicated by arrows; double the upper arm and wrist measurements for the sleeve width.

Taking and using measurements

Garment dimensions are based on body measurements plus ease. For good fit, you should be aware of what these finished measurements are.

The body measurements described alongside are all the ones you might need, though you will not need all of them for every garment. Waist and hip measurements, for example, are used only for a fitted style; head circumference is needed only for a hat. To be accurate, measurements should be taken over undergarments and with someone's help.

Ease must be added to measurements of circumference, for example, chest and upper arm. Ease allowances range from 1.5 to 10 centimetres and are determined by the following: the garment's purpose—a cardigan, for instance, would have more ease than a pullover; garment style—a dolman sleeve is fitted more loosely than a set-in sleeve; the garment area—more ease is needed for

the bust than the wrist; yarn type—a garment of bulky yarn requires more ease than one of fine yarn; personal preference—a close or a loose fit.

If you do not have body measurements to work with, there are two other ways of sizing a garment. One way is to measure a similar garment, bearing in mind that ease is included. The other is to work from measurement charts, like the ones designers use to plan a garment in a certain size. Such charts are useful as guidelines, especially for determining proportions of a jumper or cardigan. A person's measurements are always more reliable for obtaining perfect fit.

Commercial patterns are for more than one size. The stitch numbers for the smallest size are given first, followed by stitch numbers for larger sizes, in order, in brackets. (See the pattern on page 482.) Circle your chosen size and its stitch numbers throughout the pattern before knitting.

Chest or bust: Straight across back, under the arms, and across fullest part of chest or bust.
Shoulder width: Across back between outside edges of shoulder bones (about 7 cm below neck base on a toddler, 10 cm on a child, 12 cm on a woman, 15 cm on a man).
Shoulder length: From base of neck to tip of shoulder.
Neck: Around the neck just above the collarbone.
Armhole depth: From top of shoulder bone, straight down to desired depth of armhole.
Underarm to waist: From 2.5 cm below armpit to waist indentation.
Sleeve upper arm: Around the top portion of the arm, just below the armpit.
Sleeve seam length: From 2.5 cm below armpit, straight down inside of arm to wristbone.
Wrist: Just above wristbone.
Waist: At natural indentation.
Hip: Around the fullest part (about 10–15cm below waist for a child, 17–22 cm for an adult).
Head: Around the crown at mid-forehead level.

BABIES AND TODDLERS°

Age	3 mths	6 mths	9 mths	1 year	2–3
Chest	35	40	45	50	55
Around neck	20.5	22	23.5	25	27
Back of neck†	6.5	7	7.5	8	8.5
Armhole depth	7.5	8	8.5	9.5	10.5
Sleeve upper arm	14	15	16	17	18.5
Sleeve seam length	11	12.5	15	18	21
Waist	35	40	45	50	54
Head	35	40	45	48	51

CHILDREN°

Approx. age	4–5	6–7	8–9	10 and over
Chest	60	65	70	75–85
Around neck	28.5	30	31.5	33–36
Back of neck†	9	9.5	10	11–12
Armhole depth	12	14	16	18–19.5
Sleeve upper arm	19.5	21	23	25–27
Sleeve seam length	26	31	35	39–43
Waist	57	59	61–63	63–75
Head	52	53	54	55–56

GIRLS AND WOMEN°

Bust	75	80	85	90	95	100	110	120
Shoulder width	30	31	32	33	34	35	38	40
Shoulder length	10	10	10.5	10.5	11	12	14	14
Back of neck†	11	11	11.5	12	12.5	13	14	15
Armhole depth	18	19	19	20	20	21	22	23
Underarm to waist	17.5	18.5	19	19.5	20	21	22	24
Sleeve upper arm	23	24	26	28	29	31	35	38
Sleeve seam length	43	43	43	43	43	43	43	43
Waist	55	60	65	70	75	80	90	100
Hip (18 cm below waist)	80	85	90	95	100	105	115	125
Seat (23 cm below waist)	85	90	95	100	105	110	120	130
Head	56	56	56	56	56	56	56	56

BOYS AND MEN°

Chest	85	90	95	100	105	110	115	120	125
Shoulder width	35	37	38	39	40	41	42	43	44
Shoulder length	11.5	12	13	13.5	14	14.5	15	15.5	16
Back of neck†	12.5	13	13.5	14	14.5	15	15.5	15.5	16
Armhole depth	20	22	22	23	23	24	24	25	25
Shoulder to waist	41	45	45	46	46	47	47	48	48
Sleeve upper arm	28	29	30	31	32	33	35	36	38
Sleeve seam length	48	48	48	48	48	48	48	48	48
Waist	75	80	85	90	95	100	105	110	115
Seat	90	95	100	105	110	115	120	125	130

°All measurements are in centimetres.
†This is a garment, not a body measurement.

Designing a knitted garment

There are two ways of designing a garment. One is to alter an existing pattern to suit your needs; the other is to create a pattern of your own. With either approach you will need:
1. An accurate list of body or garment measurements (see opposite page).
2. A test swatch to determine tension and calculate yarn needs.
3. Familiarity with structuring garment areas (see pages 484–494).
4. Paper to outline or chart a pattern.

First, write down length and width dimensions for each section of the garment you are planning. If your plan is based on body measurements, you must add ease, explained opposite. You also need to add 6 millimetres for seams, and to plan the overall length. Next, choose a yarn and a stitch pattern; knit a swatch, or several if necessary, until you like the appearance of the stitch, then measure tension.

To translate width dimensions into stitches, multiply stitch tension by number of centimetres. For instance, if you are planning a jacket that measures 42.5 centimetres at the bottom edge of the back, and the stitch tension is 20 stitches to 10 centimetres (or 2 sts per cm), you will need to cast on 85 stitches plus 2 stitches for seams.

To translate length dimensions into rows, multiply row tension by centimetres. If the jacket measures 35 centimetres from bottom edge to underarm, and row tension is 28 rows per 10 centimetres (or 2.8 rows per cm), you will need 98 rows from starting point to underarm.

To determine the number and distribution of increases or decreases for shaping, see guidelines on pages 484 to 489. To plan garment details, see pages 490 to 494. Finally, prepare a chart or outline (see pp. 482–483).

Determining yarn needs

To estimate how much yarn you need for your design, you can use the amount specified for a similar pattern, structured of the same yarn and stitch. This quantity may not be precisely what you need, however, so it is advisable to buy extra yarn.

Another approach is to consult a yarn shop. Salespeople usually have the experience or pattern files, or both, from which to make an estimate of your project's yarn needs.

If necessary, you can make your own estimate. Buy a skein or ball and make a tension swatch. Weigh it (kitchen scales will do) and record the weight. It might be, say, 11 grams. Also record the swatch area; for example, 100 square centimetres for a 10 x 10 centimetre swatch.

Next, calculate the approximate area for each garment section by multiplying widest dimension by overall length. Add these figures together, then divide the sum by the swatch area and multiply this number by the swatch weight. Here is an example:

Jumper back
across the chest	45cm
length, neck to bottom	50cm
total area (roughly)	2250cm^2

Jumper front
area, same as the back	2250cm^2

Jumper sleeve
width at upper arm	30cm
overall length	57cm
total area, both sleeves	3420cm^2

Total area for jumper 7920cm^2
Jumper area divided by swatch area (100) 79

The number 79 represents the number of 10 centimetre swatches needed to knit this jumper. Multiply 11 grams (swatch weight) by 79 to determine the approximate yarn that is needed—870 grams. Deduct 10 per cent of 870 to allow for shaping decreases; 783 grams is the estimate.

Written and charted instructions

This boat neck jumper is shown in both written and charted form so that you can compare the two methods. Instructions are given for women's sizes as listed in the chart below.

MEASUREMENTS (in centimetres)

Size	8	10	12	14	16	18
Bust	75	80	85	90	95	100
Length	58	59	59	60	60	61
Sleeve seam	43	43	43	43	43	43
			(or length desired)			
Garment measures	85	90	95	100	105	110
	(This is an easy-fitting garment.)					

Materials 10 (11–11–12–12–13) 50 g balls of Patons 8 ply Totem (or DK), one pair each 4 mm and 3.25 mm needles.
Tension 22½ sts and 30 rows to 10 cm over stocking stitch.
BACK AND FRONT ALIKE:
Using 3.25 mm needles, cast on 97 (**103**-109-**115**-121-**125**) sts.
Row 1: K 2, * P 1, K 1, rep from *to last st, K 1.
Row 2: K 1, * P 1, K 1, rep from * to end.
Rep Rows 1 and 2 eight times (18 rows of rib in all). Change to 4 mm needles.
Work in stocking st until work measures 37 cm from beg, ending with a purl row.
Tie a coloured thread at each end of last row to mark beg of armholes.
Work a further 50 (**52**-52-**56**-56-**58**) rows stocking st.

Work 10 rows rib as before.
Shape shoulders: Keeping rib correct, cast off 6 (**6**-7-**8**-9-**9**) sts at beg of next 6 (**4**-6-**6**-6-**6**) rows, then 5 (**7**-8-**8**-8-**10**) sts at beg of foll 2 (**4**-2-**2**-2-**2**) rows.
Cast off rem 51 sts loosely in rib.
SLEEVES: Using 3.25 mm needles, cast on 49 (**49**-49-**51**-51-**51**) sts.
Work 17 rows rib as for back and front.
Row 18: Rib 6 (**4**-4-**4**-4-**2**), * inc in next st, rib 1, rep from * to last 7 (**5**-5-**3**-3-**1**) st/s, rib to end . . . 67 (**69**-69-**73**-73-**75**) sts.
Change to 4 mm needles.
Work 4 rows stocking st.
Row 5: K 2, M 1, knit to last 2 sts, M 1, K 2.
Cont in stocking st, inc (as before) at each end of foll 10th (**8th**-8th-**8th**-8th-**6th**) row/s until there are 79 (**75**-75-**89**-89-**79**) sts, and then in the foll 12th (**10th**-10th-**10th**-10th-**8th**) rows until there are 85 (**89**-89-**95**-95-**99**) sts.
Cont without shaping until work measures 43 cm (or length desired) from beg, ending with a purl row.
Shape top: Cast off 7 (**7**-7-**8**-8-**8**) sts at beg of next 10 rows.
Cast off rem sts.
MAKE UP: With a slightly damp cloth and warm iron, press lightly. Join shoulder seams. Join sleeve and side seams to coloured threads. Sew in sleeves. Press seams.

Lady's jumper has a boat neck and dropped shoulders

How to make a garment chart

A garment chart is a visual representation of written instructions. There are two different chart forms—**outline** and **graph.**

An outline is a drawing of the exact dimensions of each main garment section, with shaping information written on it. This form gives you a realistic view of garment shape; it can be used later, if desired, for blocking. To make an outline, use sturdy wrapping paper. Draw a straight line on it equal to the widest dimension of the garment back (usually the underarm). Then draw a second line perpendicular to and through the centre of the first. Using these as reference points, measure other areas. Draw the sleeve and any other garment sections in the same way. (If the front differs from the back only in neck shaping, you can draw an alternative line for the front neck on your back pattern, instead of making a second outline.)

A graph is worked on paper that is marked off into squares. Each square represents a stitch, each line of squares a row. To chart this way, the tension must already have been determined. You can graph an entire garment section or just the shaped areas (as shown opposite); only half need be graphed. A graph gives a less realistic view of garment shape than an outline, but it is easier to follow.

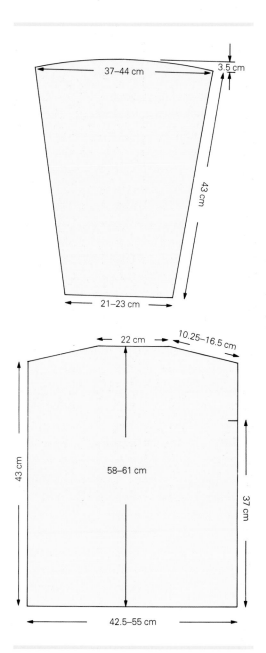

An **outline** is an exact duplicate of garment dimensions

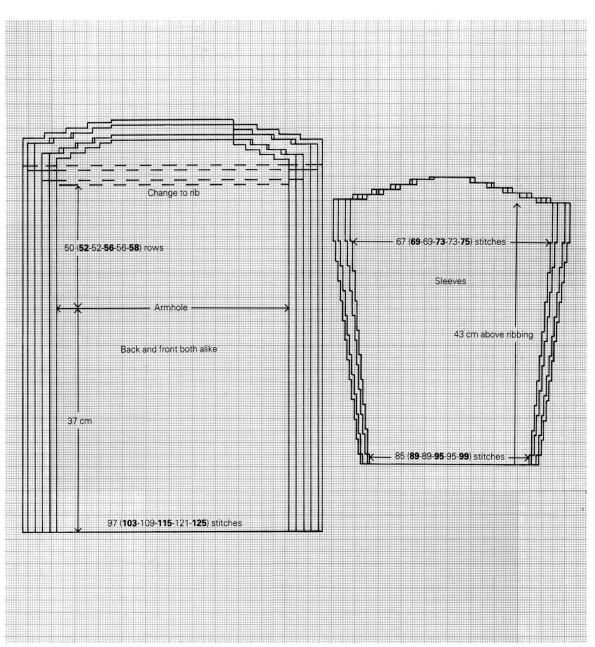

In a **graph,** each square represents a stitch, each line of squares a row. Only half of each area need be represented

Knitting a garment

Shaping

Shaping a knitted garment is a matter of working increases or decreases where the knitted fabric must conform to body contours. There are formulas for shaping major garment areas. This section deals with those for flat pieces (knitted on two needles). For uniformity of concept, every example is shown in stocking stitch. Most flat knits are contoured along the outside edges only. Certain dress or skirt styles may require darts for a closer fit, but such shaping is suited mainly to garments worked in fine yarns and smooth textures.

If this is your first experience with shaping a garment, it may help to think of each piece initially as a rectangle, as wide and long as the widest and longest dimensions of that garment portion. From the wide points, you subtract stitches gradually in order to obtain the narrower and shorter measurements.

These shaping guidelines can be used to design your own garment or alter an existing pattern to suit your needs, keeping these points in mind:
1. After making calculations, chart your design before knitting it.
2. Except for necklines, shapings are usually exactly the same for both the front and the back.
3. Changes in shape are made on the right side of your work and as gradually as possible.

Shaping diagonals

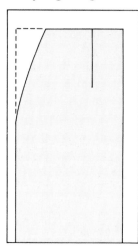

Forming a diagonal by decreasing is the way to shape an A-line; contour a skirt from hipline to waist, a sleeve cap or a hat crown worked from the bottom up.
Side seam decreases are calculated by subtracting the number of stitches required at the waist from the number at the starting point (skirt bottom or hipline), allotting half to each side and distributing them evenly over the rows to be knitted.
Skirt darts are calculated the same way and should end 10–15 cm from the side seam at the waist. Average depth is 20–25 mm, length 13 cm.
Hat darts are distributed evenly around the crown.

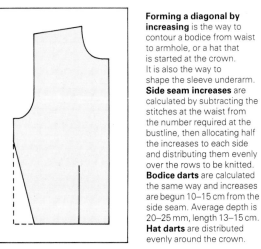

Forming a diagonal by increasing is the way to contour a bodice from waist to armhole, or a hat that is started at the crown. It is also the way to shape the sleeve underarm.
Side seam increases are calculated by subtracting the stitches at the waist from the number required at the bustline, then allocating half the increases to each side and distributing them evenly over the rows to be knitted.
Bodice darts are calculated the same way and increases are begun 10–15 cm from the side seam. Average depth is 20–25 mm, length 13–15 cm.
Hat darts are distributed evenly around the crown.

To shape side seams on a skirt, first calculate the number and distribution of decreases, then work them in pairs. For example, if you are decreasing 30 stitches (15 on each side) over 90 rows, you would decrease at the beginning and end of every sixth row.

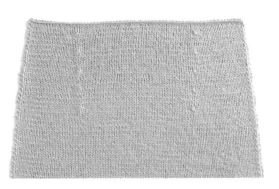

To make paired darts on a skirt, place a marker at the beginning of each dart (approximately 18 cm from each side). For the first dart, knit to the marked stitch and decrease left (sl 1, K 1, psso); for the second dart, decrease right (K 2 tog).

To shape side seams on a bodice, first calculate the number and distribution of increases, then work them in pairs. For example, if you are increasing 20 stitches (10 on each side) over 40 rows, you would increase at the beginning and end of every fourth row.

To make paired vertical darts on a bodice, place a marker at the beginning of each dart. For the first dart, increase right (lifted increase is especially suitable); for the second dart, increase left, using the same type of increase as for the first dart.

Shaping shoulders

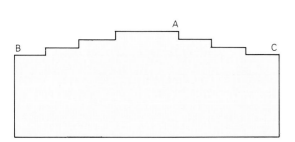

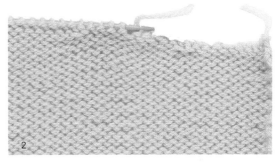

Forming a diagonal by turning is a way to shape a shoulder seam or sock heel by working rows in graduated lengths. The angle is controlled by the number of stitches that are worked in each stage of the procedure.

A shoulder is usually worked in two, three or four steps and the stitches are not cast off immediately.

To shape a pair of shoulders, for a back, work Steps 1 and 2 simultaneously until point A is reached. Turn and work across all

stitches to B; turn and work back to C, taking care to pick up the wraps on the way. The front and back shoulders may then be joined with a three needle cast-off or grafted together. A complete back is shown on p. 495.

To slope to the right, in three steps, for example, on 24 stitches (above), °work to within 6 stitches of the armhole edge, yarn forward, slip 1 stitch, yarn back, return slipped stitch to the left needle, taking care not to twist it. Turn and work to neck edge.

Rep from ° twice, leaving 6 more stitches unworked each time. Work one more row across all stitches, picking up yarn wrapped around slipped stitches and working it together with the stitch. Leave stitches on a scrap of yarn or safety pins.

To slope to the left (above), work as for right shoulder, but start with a wrong side row and, when wrapping slipped stitch, take yarn to back, slip 1, yarn forward, taking care to pick up this wrapped yarn from the right side of the fabric on final row.

Pleats

Pleats add fullness to the bottom of a skirt and, in some cases, additional thickness at the waist. There are two basic pleat types, **regular** and **mock;** examples of each are shown below.

Both look best in finer yarns and are most suited to slender figures.

Regular pleats have a face, turnback and underside. When knitting is complete, pleat tops can be

knitted together by transferring the turnback and underside to spare needles and working three stitches together across pleat width; they can also be sewn.

Mock pleats do not have true folds but their effect is created by knitting in a broad rib pattern, such as K 7, P 4, or in a textured stitch with one stocking stitch rib to suggest a fold.

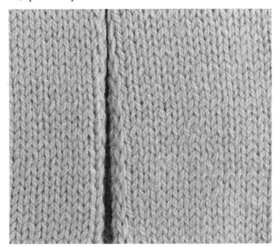

Knife pleats: All folds face in the same direction; face, turnback and underside are the same width. This pattern has a multiple of 26 and is knitted so that the seam can be placed at a backfold. **Right side,** °K 16, sl 1, K 8, P 1. ° **Wrong side,** °K 1, P 25°.

Box pleats: The two outer folds face away from each other and the backfolds meet at the centre. Pattern shown has a multiple of 58 and is worked as follows: **Right side,** °K 9, sl 1, K 18, sl 1, K 9, P 1, K 18, P 1.° **Wrong side,** °K 1, P 18, K 1, P 38°.

Mock pleats: The impression of folds is created in this instance by regularly inserting a stocking stitch rib on the face of garter stitch. This pattern has a multiple of 8 and is knitted as follows: **Right side,** °K 7, P 1.° **Wrong side,** K 3, °P 1, K 7, °P 1, K 4.

Knitting a garment

Shaping necklines and collars

Special care should be taken in knitting a neckline, as this part of a garment is particularly noticeable. In general, the fit should be smooth, with no gaping or wrinkling. In the case of a pullover, the opening must be large enough for the head to pass through comfortably; for a child's jumper, you may need an additional opening, because a child's head is large in proportion to the neck size.

The neck width equals about one-third of the shoulder width or the number of stitches that remain after subtracting both of the shoulder measurements. Front neck depth is calculated in relation to armhole depth, and varies according to style. With few exceptions, the back of a neckline is cast off straight across.

If the front is oval or square, the back may be shaped the same way, but would be less deep. In shaping a neckline, work is usually divided, each half knitted separately, and all decreases made on the right side.

A neckline is finished with a band, a facing, or a collar that is knitted by picking up stitches along the neck edge, or worked as a separate piece and sewn in place. For the first method, a general rule is to pick up 1 stitch for each stitch and 3 stitches for every 4 rows. A more precise approach is to pick up a number of stitches that will yield the required measurement in the tension of your finishing stitch (a test swatch of the border stitch may be needed to determine this).

Square neckline

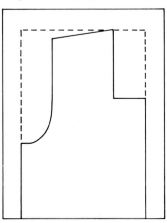

Square neckline shaping is begun 10–15 cm below the the start of shoulder shaping with the casting off of all stitches allotted for the neckline. (The number of stitches for the neck is what remains after subtracting stitches for each shoulder.) There is no decreasing for this style: after casting off the centre, you work straight up the sides. When adding a border, as shown right, you can cast off 2.5 cm more of stitches on each side to maintain the full width after a band is added.

Ribbed band: Pick up stitches across front; work 1 × 1 ribbing for 2.5 cm, decreasing 1 stitch at beginning and end of right side rows. Repeat for other sections; sew sections at corners.

Facing: Pick up and knit each section separately as for a ribbed band, but work in stocking stitch and increase at each corner; fold facing to wrong side; slipstitch it to garment.

V-neckline

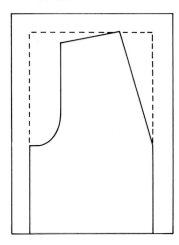

A V-neckline is usually started 17–23 cm below the shoulder, or just after casting off to begin armhole shaping. Work is divided at the centre and each side is knitted separately, with decreases evenly spaced over the number of rows to be worked to the top of the shoulder. Decreases can be made either at the neck edge, or 3–4 stitches from the edge, in which case they must be paired. If you have an odd number of stitches across the front, decrease the centre stitch before dividing the work.

Ribbed band: Pick up stitches on 3 dp needles; knit 1 × 1 ribbing, double decreasing at point each round; or work rows on circular needle, decreasing at each end; sew 'V' edges.

Overlapping band: Work a strip of 1 × 1 ribbing, 2.5 cm wide and long enough to fit around neckline. Sew strip to neck edge with a slipstitch, overlapping two ends at front, as shown.

Round necklines

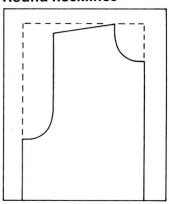

A high round neckline is the classic shaping in the same sense as the set-in sleeve. Shaping is begun 5 cm below the shoulder tip for an adult's garment, 3 cm for a child's. Half the total of stitches to be decreased are either placed on a holder or cast off; the remaining stitches are decreased at each neck edge every other row. The rest of the neckline is then worked over all stitches until the shoulder shaping is complete.

Turtleneck: Pick up stitches on three dp needles; work 1 × 1 ribbing (or another rib pattern if preferred) for 15–23 cm. Cast off loosely. Fold collar to the right side.

Polo collar: Pick up stitches on straight or circular needle and work 1 × 1 ribbing in rows, increasing just inside each edge every other row; work chain selvage on both edges to finish.

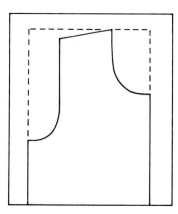

A lower round neckline can vary in depth from 7 to 10 cm below the shoulder. The 7 cm depth is ideal for a crew neck (right); the 10 cm depth is suitable for summer or evening wear. To shape the 7 cm neckline, cast off and decrease just as for a high round neck. To shape a lower neckline, subtract a few stitches from each shoulder and work them into the neckline so that the neck is proportionately wider as well as deeper.

Crew neck: Pick up stitches on three dp needles; work 1 × 1 ribbing for 5–7 cm. Cast off (invisible cast-off recommended). Fold ribbing in half and sew loosely to wrong side of neck edge.

Crocheted edging: Using a hook 1 or 2 sizes smaller than the needles used for garment, work 12 mm of double crochet around neck edge, decreasing as necessary to keep edge flat.

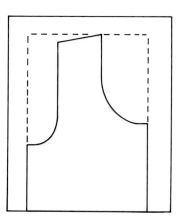

A low oval or U-shaped neckline is begun 15–17 cm below the shoulder; its overall depth is usually greater than its width. When calculating the division for shoulders and neck opening, be sure to include the width of the band, if you are using one. For example, if the finished neckline width is to be 17 cm and the band will measure 2.5 cm, the neck opening should be 23 cm when you shape it.

Ribbed band: Pick up stitches on three dp needles; work 1 × 1 ribbing for 2.5 cm. On the cast-off row, work several decreases along the deep part of the curve at the centre front.

Bias border: Knit a bias strip in stocking stitch, twice desired width and long enough to go around neck. Sew one edge to garment; fold; sew other edge to inside of neck edge.

Knitting a garment

Shaping armholes and sleeves

The armhole and sleeve shapings are an important part of knitting a garment. Five basic styles are described here. The **classic** armhole with a set-in sleeve is suited to any garment. A **saddle yoke** is generally chosen for a sportier style. The **raglan** is a comfortable shaping. The last two can also become a decorative part of the design if the decreases are worked two to three stitches in from the selvage. A **dropped shoulder** is the easiest armhole and sleeve to work, and the most comfortable to wear. A **dolman** is an extension of the garment body and, with its deep armhole, is also very comfortable.

To chart an armhole, you need the measurements for shoulder width, chest or underarm across half the garment, plus standard shoulder length and armhole depth for your garment size and, for a raglan only, the neck circumference. To chart a sleeve, you need wrist, underarm length, and upper-arm measurements.

The usual way of knitting a sleeve is from the bottom edge up, shaping the underarm seam as a diagonal, increasing symmetrically between wrist and underarm. For comfort, you may want to add 2.5 cm of ease at the wrist, and at least 5 cm at the upper-arm area for a fitted sleeve. Armhole and sleeve caps are shaped with decreases, which must be paired, slanting to the left at the beginning of a row and to the right at the end, or vice versa.

There are two ways to shape a standard shoulder seam. The most common is to cast off in steps (see jumper, pp. 482–483), which produces a stepped edge. A better method is to shape by turning (p. 485), which makes a smooth line. The back and front shoulders are then joined with a three-needle cast-off (p. 439).

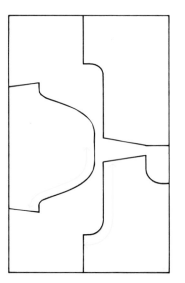

A classic armhole shape is formulated by subtracting the number of stitches for shoulder width from the number at underarm. This figure is then halved and the result is the number of stitches to decrease for each armhole. At start of shaping, cast off half these stitches (the equivalent usually of 25–40 mm); decrease the remainder over the next few rows, then work over all stitches until desired depth is reached. To start sleeve cap, cast off the same number of stitches as at beginning of armhole. Work decreases symmetrically until curve of cap matches that of armhole and measures 5–12 cm across. Cast off remaining stitches.

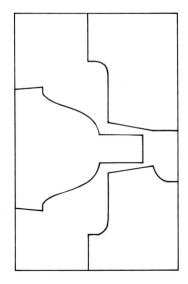

A saddle yoke armhole is shaped just like the classic style but is 25–40 mm shorter to accommodate the yoke width. The set-in sleeve cap is also shaped the same, but instead of casting off the shoulder stitches, you continue to work on them until the yoke section equals the shoulder length. To fit well, the top of the sleeve cap and the yoke should be no less than 5 cm and no more than 7.5 cm across. The cast-off edge of the yoke becomes part of the neckline. Saddle yokes may also be worked with dropped shoulder styles.

A set-in sleeve has a symmetrically curved cap that fits a classic armhole

A saddle yoke sleeve combines a classic sleeve with yoke extension

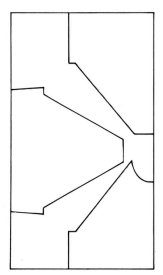

A raglan armhole ends at the neckline and must be planned in relation to it. To calculate decreases, subtract stitches for half the neck circumference from the number of stitches at the underarm. Take off another 5 cm of stitches (these will go at the top of sleeves); this figure is the total of decreases for both armholes. Start raglan shaping with a cast-off of 1–2 cm on each side; distribute remaining decreases symmetrically and evenly over rows to be knitted (armhole depth). Work sleeves with same number of rows and a 5 cm width at neckline.

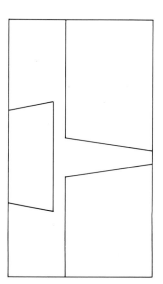

A dropped shoulder is the easiest armhole to design and execute. The shoulder may be sloped or straight and the sleeve may be straight across or have a slight cap. Calculate the depth of the armhole and place a marker on the sides of the back and front. Measure between the markers to calculate the number of stitches required at the top of the sleeve, and then deduct the number of stitches on the needle after ribbing and divide this number into the number of rows to be worked to estimate the rate of increasing.

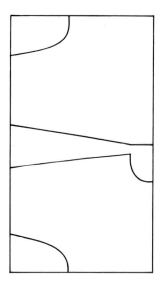

A dolman sleeve is formed by adding stitches to the garment body. Begin shaping at desired armhole depth, gradually increasing stitches at each side to form the underarm curve. For the sleeve, cast on 2–5 cm of stitches at beginning and end of each right side row until you have the total sleeve length. Continue to work over all the stitches until sleeve depth is half the wrist measurement plus 2–5 cm for ease. Shape the top edge by casting off in the same stitch sequence as casting on. Shape shoulder the standard way.

A raglan sleeve is shaped in a continuous slope to the neckline

A dropped shoulder makes the most comfortable armhole

A dolman sleeve is wide at the armhole, narrow at the wrist

Knitting a garment

Long-sleeve finishes

A *ribbed cuff* is the typical finish for a long sleeve on a jumper. It is usually knitted to the wrist size plus 2.5 centimetres so the hand can pass through easily, and is worked on needles a size or two smaller than those used for the sleeves so that it will fit snugly. The usual stitch choices are 1 × 1 or 2 × 2 ribbing because these have good elasticity and trim appearance.

A *bracelet cuff* is the type of sleeve finish that might be used for a blouse, fashion jumper or jacket. It is usually worked in a firmer stitch, such as moss or garter, and so must be combined with a sleeve opening and some kind of closure. Two typical examples are illustrated below.

A *border or hem* is a suitable finish for a full sleeve that is wide at the wrist (a kimono sleeve, for instance), or a straight sleeve where no rib is desired. See pp. 491–492 for these finishes.

Cuff in single ribbing: This neat and inconspicuous style is used more than any other. Average depth is 5–10 cm; the fuller the sleeve, the longer the cuff should be.

Cast on an even number of stitches and work in 1 × 1 ribbing for the desired length. When sewing the cuff, use mattress stitch, taking in one stitch (one knit and one purl) from each side. The join should be nearly invisible.

Cuff in double ribbing: A bolder style than single ribbing, more suitable for sporty garments than tailored ones.

Cast on a multiple of 4 stitches plus 2; work in 2 × 2 ribbing, beginning and ending each right side row with K 2. Sew the cuff seam with mattress stitch, taking in one knit stitch from each side. The finished cuff will appear to have continuous ribbing.

Turn-back cuff in ribbing: Either single or double ribbing can be used; overall length is 10–12 cm. This cuff is a particularly good choice for a child's jumper, as it gives some adjustability to the sleeve length.

Following the directions above for either single or double ribbing, knit cuff to twice the usual length. When joining the cuff seam, sew the lower half with wrong sides together and the upper half with right sides together.

Bracelet cuff with slit opening: Especially suitable for a knitted blouse with full sleeve. The opening should be 5–7 cm long and the cuff 2–3 cm deep in a stitch that does not curl.

To make the opening, divide the bottom of the sleeve into two parts—one-third for the back, two-thirds for the front. Work the parts separately, casting on 2 extra stitches at each opening edge for a facing, casting off these stitches again before joining the sections. When the sleeve is finished, sew the seam, turn the facings to the inside and slipstitch them in place.
To knit the cuff, pick up stitches along the sleeve bottom equal to the wrist measurement plus 12 mm for ease. If the sleeve is exceptionally full, pick up more stitches than you need and decrease along the first row to obtain the wrist measurement. When cuff is finished, make a crocheted button loop on the edge that faces the sleeve back; sew a button on opposite edge.

Bracelet cuff with banded opening: This is appropriate for a jumper, jacket, or coat sleeve fitted snugly at the wrist. It could also be used for decorative styling on a wider sleeve; for this use you would not need buttonholes. Opening should be 7–10 cm long, the cuff 2–3 cm deep.

To make the opening, divide and work the sleeves as directed above for a slit but do not add facing stitches. Instead, make a double selvage along the back edge of the opening; leave the front edge plain. Complete the sleeve and sew the underarm seam.
To knit the band and cuff, pick up stitches along the bottom edge of the sleeve and front edge of the slit. Mark the corner stitch and work a double increase at this point every other row. Make two horizontal buttonholes in the band. When completed, sew top edge of band to sleeve; attach buttons.

Borders

A border or band is an extension of a knitted edge that makes a decorative finish and helps to retain shape. There are two basic types—single, which should be worked in a non-curling pattern, such as moss or garter stitch or ribbing; and double, which is usually done in stocking stitch. Finished width is 5 mm to 3.5 cm. If necessary, work with needles of a different size so tensions match.

Border knitted with garment body: Direction of the garment and border stitch are the same. *For horizontal border,* work bottom of garment in border stitch, then change to garment pattern. *For vertical border,* knit the border stitches alongside the garment pattern. *Combine horizontal and vertical borders* to edge a cardigan. Similar to a mitred border.

Border knitted on picked-up stitches: This band is the easiest to knit, as it needs no seam if you sew garment sections together before picking up the stitches.
For a single straight border, take care to pick up the correct number of stitches for a flat, even edge. When using needles two sizes smaller than those used for body fabric, a good guide is to pick up 3 stitches for every 4 rows.
For a single curved border, follow the same procedure as for straight border. Decreases or increases are not needed, as the ribbing will mould to the curve.
For a double border, work in stocking stitch for 2–5 cm; purl 1 row on the right side for a turning ridge; continue in stocking stitch for 2–5 cm; cast off loosely. Fold border in half and slipstitch free edge to inside of garment.

Border knitted separately and sewn on: This method takes more time than either of the two above, but size and shape are easier to control.
For a vertical button band, add the stitches for the band to the number given for garment fronts, and cast on simultaneously. On completion of ribbing, leave the band stitches on a holder and, casting on an extra selvage stitch, continue with the garment. To work bands, return to stitches left aside and work in rib for required length. Join bands to garment with flat seam.
For a straight border, cast on stitches needed for length of garment edge; knit desired width; cast off loosely. Join border to garment with flat seam.
For a mitred border, cast on stitches needed and mark corner stitch; work a double increase at the marked stitch every other row; cast off and join to garment as for straight border.

Horizontal border

Vertical border

Combined borders

Single straight border

Single curved border

Double border

Vertical band

Straight border, sewn on

Mitred border

Hems and facings

A hem is a turned-up finish for the lower edge of a garment; a facing is a turned-in finish for any other edge. In general, these are functional rather than decorative finishes that help keep an edge from curling or stretching.

To make a flat edge where a facing or hem is to be folded, a turning ridge is usually worked. Depending on the desired effect, this can be a purl ridge on a knit face, or lacy picot edge.

To prevent buckling, a hem or facing allowance is knitted in stocking stitch on needles one or two sizes smaller. Average hem allowance is about 2 cm for an adult; allow more on a child's garment, of course, to provide for growth.

To keep the stitch line inconspicuous, the hem or facing should be sewn with matching yarn, the stitches pulled firmly but not too tight. If yarn is thick, separate one or two plies for use when sewing.

Making a hem

Purl ridge: Suitable for tailored garments in stocking stitch.

On smaller needles (one size smaller) than those used for the garment, cast on the stitches needed for the bottom edge. Work in stocking stitch until the hem is the desired length, ending with a wrong side row. On the next (right side) row, purl to form a ridge. Change to larger needles and continue in stocking stitch. Hem will fold along the purled ridge.

Picot edge: Attractive for babies' and children's clothing and for dressy garments.

With one size smaller needles, cast on a multiple of 2 stitches plus 1. Work in stocking stitch until the hem is the desired length, ending with a wrong side row. On the next (right side) row, ° K 2 tog, yfwd°, K 1. At end of this row, change to larger needles and pattern stitch.

Knitting a hem edge to the garment

Knitted-in hem on stocking stitch: A trim finish for a jacket or jumper for which limited stretch but a moderate fit is desired at the bottom edge. Usually worked without a turning ridge, but you could add one if you preferred. It is very important to use smaller needles for the hem allowance, or the edge will fan outward at the bottom.

Sewing the hem edge

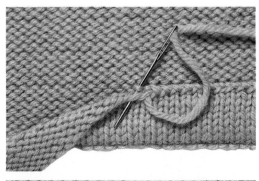

The slipstitch is a neat and firm way to sew the hem on a medium- or lightweight knit.

Using matching yarn, insert needle at a rightangle, taking it through the back of one stitch on the garment and a corresponding stitch on the hem edge. Pull stitches firmly—but not too tight, otherwise the sewing line may pucker.

The stitch-by-stitch sewing method is a better choice for thick knits because the ridge on the edge is eliminated. This technique can be used either when a hem is formed at the end of work or is started with a provisional cast-on.

For hem at end of work, sew each stitch directly from the needle to a corresponding one on the wrong side (as shown). *For provisional cast-on,* sew stitches in place; remove foundation yarn.

A blind-hemming stitch is the best choice for a heavy or bulky knit that has a cast-off edge, because the hem edge is not pressed against the garment. Stitches are taken inside between hem and garment.

Turn hem edge back 6–12 mm. Working from right to left, take 1 stitch in the garment, then 1 stitch in the hem, placing each stitch to the left of the previous one. Do not pull yarn too tight.

Pockets

Pockets are both decorative and functional additions to a knitted garment. The most commonly used pocket is the inside type.

Patch pockets, less commonly used nowadays, are easy to make. Any stitch type is suitable for them, including crochet patterns. If stocking stitch is used, add facings or a non-curling border to make edges neat.

Inside pockets vary in style, but all are basically worked the same way, and each must be lined. A knitted lining is best, but a fabric lining plus knitted extension may be preferable for bulky yarns. The directions below are for a right pocket; reverse shaping for a left pocket.

A general rule for placement is to centre the pocket one-third of the garment width from the side seam. Average size is 10 to 12 centimetres square; 2 to 4 centimetres are allowed for a border.

Horizontal inside pockets

Horizontal pocket with ribbed border: Knit the garment front to within 2.5 cm of the pocket opening. Place a marker at the beginning of the opening and another at the end. Continue up the front, working the stitches between markers in a rib pattern (1 × 1 ribbing shown here). After 2.5 cm of ribbing, cast off the pocket stitches loosely on a right side row and complete the row.

To knit a lining, cast onto a spare needle the same number of stitches as for the pocket opening. Work in stocking stitch for 10–12 cm, ending with a knit row; cut yarn. Work purl stitches across the garment to the pocket opening, purl across the lining then continue with garment on the other side of the opening. The pocket lining is now part of the garment front. Continue to work on all stitches until garment front is complete. Slipstitch the three sides of the pocket lining to the wrong side of the garment.

Vertical inside pockets

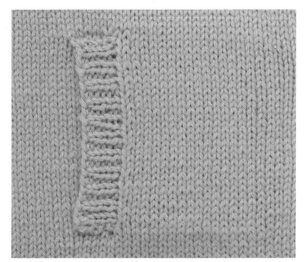

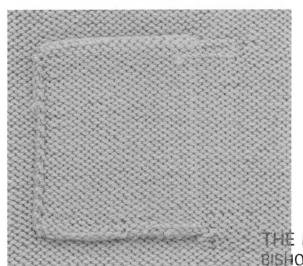

Vertical pocket with picked-up border: Knit the garment front up to the position of pocket openings. Work on the centre stitches only to the depth of the pocket. Return to stitches at side edge, cast on required number of stitches for lining, and work the same number of rows as for the body. Cast off the lining stitches and work straight across all body and side stitches. On completion of garment, return to pocket edge and, picking up stitches as for the border, work 3 cm ribbing. Sew border and lining to garment.

Knitting stitches

Buttonholes

There are three basic buttonhole types —*round*, which is the simplest and used for baby garments and eyelets; *vertical*, usually centred on a vertical band; and *horizontal*, suitable for jackets, coats and cardigans.

Buttonholes are always placed in relation to button placement. A round hole aligns with the button exactly; the top of a vertical style extends 1 row above it; the front end of a horizontal type extends 1 stitch beyond it. Three key placement points are the neck, the fullest part of the bust, and the lower edge just above the hem or border. All other buttonholes are evenly spaced between these points.

Buttonhole finish is optional; you can leave it as formed, or hand-work the edges as shown below. A strand or two of matching yarn is most attractive, but buttonhole twist is suitable too.

Round buttonhole
(also used for eyelet):
Right side row, for
each buttonhole, bring
yarn forward, then
knit 2 together.
Wrong side row, work
all stitches in pattern,
including the made stitch.

Vertical buttonhole:
Divide work at base of
buttonhole and knit
each part separately for
the desired depth, then
re-join the sections.
The last row for both
sections must be worked
in the same direction.
That is, if the first
section ends with
a right side row, so
must the second.

Horizontal buttonhole:
Right side row, cast
off the number of
stitches that equals
the button diameter.
Wrong side row, work
buttonhole opening. Cast
on number of stitches
required by single
cast-on method.
Continue in pattern.

Finishing a buttonhole

Overcast stitch is the
simplest finish for a buttonhole.
It reinforces the edge without
diminishing its flexibility.
To overcast, take diagonal
stitches over the edge of the
buttonhole, spacing them an
even distance apart and at
a uniform depth throughout.

Buttonhole stitch is a firm
finish. It is the better stitch to
use if you have a tape or ribbon
facing, as it covers a cut edge
more effectively than overcasting.
To buttonhole, work right to left
with needle pointed away from the
opening, thread looped as shown.
Space stitches close together.

Cut-in buttonhole

Cut-in buttonhole technique
can be used if you want to add a
buttonhole after work is finished.
To make the buttonhole, mark its
placement by tacking above and
below the row where it is to be
made and at each end of opening.
With small scissors, snip a stitch
at the centre and carefully

pick out the yarn to each end (A),
then tie knots on the wrong side
to prevent further unravelling.
For a simple finish, draw
matching yarn through each loop
of the opening (B); fasten off.
For a crocheted finish, make a slip
knot and place on hook. Working
on wrong side, insert hook in loop

of second stitch at right of
buttonhole, make 1 slipstitch,
then another in next loop; make
1 slipstitch in each open loop of
buttonhole, inserting hook from
right to wrong side, then two
more slipstitches at top left of
opening. Turn work; repeat along
opposite edge (C); fasten off.

Blocking

Blocking is the shaping of knitted pieces to specific dimensions. It can serve, at the same time, to smooth stitch irregularities and flatten out curling edges.

Knitting directions often give blocking measurements. If they do not, or if only some are given, you can calculate the ones you need, using the tension. For example, if there are 28 stitches on the shoulder, and tension is 28 stitches per 10 centimetres, the shoulder should be blocked to 10 centimetres. If an underarm seam has 98 rows, and tension is 32 rows per 10 centimetres, this seam should be blocked to 30.5 centimetres.

There are two basic blocking methods—*steam* and *wet*. The first employs moisture plus heat, and is most suitable for wool and other natural yarns. The second relies on moisture only and is preferred for some synthetic yarns and highly textured stitches in any yarn type. Yarn manufacturers sometimes recommend one particular blocking method. If there are no instructions, or if you have doubts about which procedure to follow, use the wet method to be on the safe side. In this way, the yarn will not be subjected unsuitably to heat.

Note: Some yarn labels say 'do not block' or 'do not press.' Always heed this recommendation, as certain yarns do not respond well to blocking and may be altered unfavourably.

If the garment is a little too close fitting it is possible to alter the size slightly by blocking. The amount of adjustment will depend on the yarn type and the pattern. Natural yarns and open patterns respond to this treatment more favourably than artificial yarns and close, firm patterns. Do not attempt to make a garment smaller by blocking.

How blocking is done

Blocking requires a flat surface large enough to lay out items to their full dimensions. A padded board is ideal for this purpose, or a piece of polystyrene foam, about 60 × 90 cm. A layer of plastic should be laid down to protect the surface from moisture. In addition to a padded surface, you will need a towel and a large cloth for wet blocking, an iron for steam blocking, and rustproof pins.

A garment is usually blocked before sections are joined; they are more easily adjusted in this state, and assembling is easier to do after blocking. To prepare the pieces, weave in all loose yarn ends. Block the back first, then the front(s), matching the armholes, and the shoulder and side seams. Next, block the sleeves, matching them so that the dimensions are the same. **Do not block ribbing,** as it may lose its elasticity.

Steam blocking uses both heat and moisture to shape garment sections. It can be carried out with either an iron or a hand-held steamer. Never place an iron directly on a knitted piece. The iron should be held *above* the knitting, and slowly worked over the whole area, until it is thoroughly dampened. Always use a pressing cloth over the knitting to protect it from the heat. Steam blocking can be done by using a dry press cloth and a steam iron, or a damp cloth and a dry iron. Cotton yarns can be blocked at a higher temperature setting than wool, but artificial yarns are best left unblocked, to avoid damaging the yarns.

Wet blocking is done only with moisture—no heat is applied through steaming or pressing. Once the garment pieces are pinned in place, use a spray bottle to thoroughly dampen them. The pieces should be left to dry completely before removing them from the blocking board.

In steam blocking, a combination of moisture and heat is used to mould a knit to desired shape and dimensions. A steam iron is the best source of steam for this purpose; if unavailable, a dry iron and damp cloth can be substituted. To produce steam, the dry iron should be held lightly against the cloth without applying pressure. *To block a section* as shown here, lay it wrong side up on a padded surface; adjust measurements as described above. Pin the corners, then pin along the edges as needed. Fewer pins are usually better, but not if the edges become scalloped. Apply steam until knit is uniformly damp. Leave section pinned until thoroughly dry.

Washing hand-knits

HAND WASHING
Suitable for any yarn type, but especially recommended for wool.

Wash in lukewarm to cool water, using soap flakes or a mild detergent. Work lather through the fabric by squeezing gently; do not twist or rub it.

Rinse several times, using the same water temperature as for washing. After final rinse, drain water, then lift the article and, supporting it with both hands, gently squeeze out excess water. Roll it in a towel and squeeze again to remove as much moisture as possible.

Dry article on a flat surface, preferably a rack, which allows air to circulate. Mould it into shape and allow to dry completely before moving it.

MACHINE WASHING
Use only when indicated by yarn label. Turn garment wrong side out first.

Wash with setting on 'delicate synthetic' or 'gentle' cycle and warm or cold water.

Rinse with cold water, adding fabric softener to the final rinse if possible.

Dry synthetics in automatic dryer with low setting (no hotter than 50°C), removing article when it is just dry. Check the condition of the garment during the drying process, as the required time may be less than a full machine cycle.

Assembling and finishing a garment

Mattress stitch

The joining of knitted sections edge to edge makes a smooth, bulkless, almost invisible seam. The best way to achieve this is with **mattress stitch,** especially recommended for heavy yarns.

Four mattress stitch methods are illustrated below. All are worked basically the same way, that is, yarn is taken under alternate loops on each edge so that a row of stitches is

formed between the sections. One strand of the knitting yarn is best for this purpose, unless it is nubbly; then a matching smooth yarn might be substituted. A knitter's needle is

advisable because it will not split yarn. Edges to be joined must be neat and have equal numbers of stitches. Yarn must be pulled firmly to ensure the seam is closed.

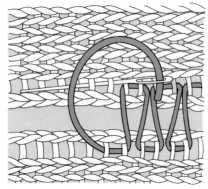

Stocking stitch—side seams: Lay sections right side up, corresponding stitches aligned. Attach yarn at right end. °Insert needle under next horizontal loop adjacent to edge stitch on one section, then under corresponding loop on the other.°

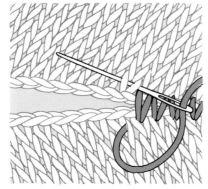

Stocking stitch—shoulder seams: Lay sections right side up, corresponding stitches aligned. Attach yarn at right end. °Take needle under next knit stitch adjacent to cast off on one section, then under next knit stitch on the other.°

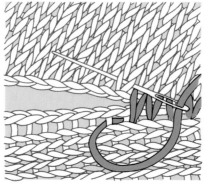

Stocking stitch—sleeves to body: Lay sections right side up, matching underarms and centre sleeve to shoulder. °Take needle under 1½ stitches on sleeve, then under 1½ stitches (or 2 rows) on body.

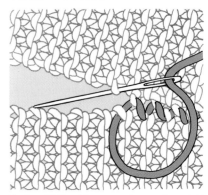

Garter stitch—side seams: Lay sections right side up, corresponding stitches aligned. Attach yarn at right end. °Insert knitter's needle through lower loop on one edge, then through corresponding upper loop on the other edge.°

Grafting

Grafting, also called kitchener stitch, is a way of joining sections horizontally so that the seam is smooth and elastic. Stitches are woven together, directly from the needles.

To graft, both edges must have the same number of stitches. Grafting is used to finish the toe of a sock; or to join shoulders shaped by turning.

There are two ways to position the

work for grafting; use whichever feels more comfortable. Either hold both needles in the left hand with wrong sides of the work facing each other, or lay the two sections face up on a table,

as illustrated below. To graft, use a knitter's needle and one strand of matching yarn, removing each stitch from the needle after the yarn has been pulled through it.

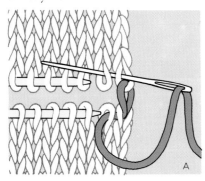

Stocking stitch: Bring needle *purlwise* through bottom and top end stitches; re-insert *knitwise* in bottom stitch, *Purlwise* through next stitch on needle. °Insert needle *Knitwise* in top stitch

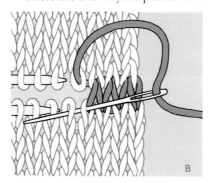

where thread emerges, *purlwise* through next stitch on needle (A). Insert needle *knitwise* through bottom stitch where thread emerges, *purlwise* through next stitch on needle (B).°

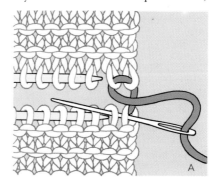

Garter stitch: Bring tapestry needle *purlwise* through bottom and top end stitches, then insert *knitwise* through next top stitch. °Insert needle *knitwise* in bottom stitch where thread emerges.

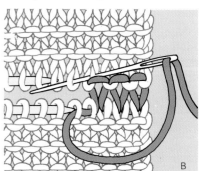

then *purlwise* through next stitch on needle (A). Insert needle *purlwise* through top stitch where thread emerges, then *knitwise* through next stitch on needle (B).°

Joining sections with seam allowances

Joining with seam allowances is ideal for sections with uneven edges, such as a shoulder that has been cast off in steps. It is also suitable for taking in a garment or shaping curved seams, as the stitches can be made any distance from the edge. Both methods below make sturdy and neat joins with any yarn type, but are best suited to fine or medium weights.

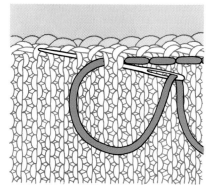

Backstitch: Using knitter's needle and matching yarn, bring needle up 2 stitches ahead of edge. °Insert it 2 stitches back (within row, at the point where thread emerged for previous stitch); bring it out 2 stitches ahead of emerging thread°.

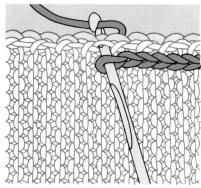

Slipstitch: Using a crochet hook of appropriate size and matching yarn, draw a loop through a corresponding stitch on each section. °Insert hook through next 2 stitches; draw a loop through both stitches and the loop on the hook°.

Setting in a sleeve

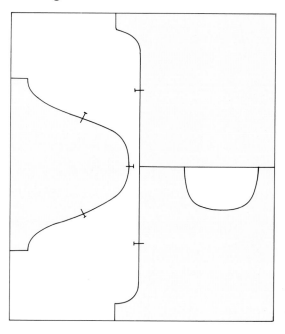

A sleeve cap is curved in a different way from the armhole and is sometimes slightly larger. Follow these steps to ensure a smooth joining. After blocking, join garment shoulder seams. Fold sleeve in half; place a pin in centre of cap. Set two more pins on each side halfway between centre of cap and underarm. On the garment, place pins at shoulder and halfway between shoulder and underarm. With sleeve and garment wrong sides together, pin sleeve to armhole, matching pins and underarm. Sew seam with a mattress stitch. Then sew side and sleeve seams.

Joining an edge to a section

The joining of an edge with a section should be as inconspicuous as possible. Choose a suitable method from those below; as you work, stretch the knit gently to prevent puckering.

Slipstitch A is used for most flat edges; it makes a firm joining and, at the same time, keeps the edge from curling. **Slipstitch B** is suitable only for a folded edge. You would use it, for example, to sew on a patch pocket that has turned-under facings. The **stitch-by-stitch** method is an inconspicuous joining for heavy yarns. It is used primarily when the hem or facing is formed at the end of work, but could be used with a provisional cast-on. Stitches can be sewn in the same way as slipstitch A, or by the technique shown below.

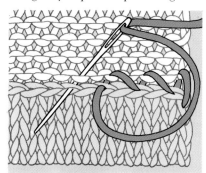

Slipstitch A: °Insert needle at rightangle under 1 loop (purl stitch) on the garment, then under 1 strand of a corresponding stitch on the hem or facing edge; pull yarn through°.

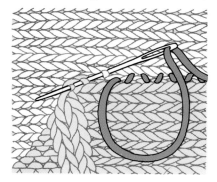

Slipstitch B: °Insert the needle under 1 garment stitch (preferably a purl stitch if the fabric is stocking stitch), then under 1 or 2 stitches of the folded edge; pull yarn through°.

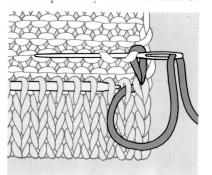

Stitch-by-stitch: To start, insert needle *purlwise* in first stitch on knitting needle, up through first purl stitch on garment and down through next purl stitch. °Insert needle *knitwise* through knit stitch

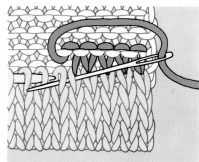

where thread emerges, then *purlwise* through next stitch on knitting needle. Insert needle up through purl stitch where thread emerges, down through next purl stitch°.

Assembling and finishing a garment

Inserting a zipper

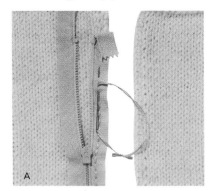

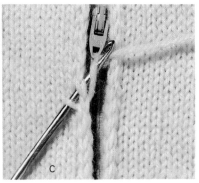

Sewing first half of zipper with backstitch

Second half of zipper sewn in place

Finishing the edge with crocheted slip stitches

For a garment of fine or mediumweight yarn, adding crochet to the edges of the zipper opening makes them flat, neat and firm.
To face the zipper opening, work 1 or 2 rows of double crochet along each side.
To attach zipper, open it and place half of zipper face down against right side of garment, having edge of tape face edge of garment. Sew tape to garment with a backstitch, placing stitches along the line where crochet meets the edge of the knitting (A). Fold garment right sides together with opening edges aligned so that second half of the zipper can be sewn exactly as first half was (B). Close zipper; press zipper opening lightly from right side. Work a row of crocheted slipstitch along both edges of the zipper opening (C).

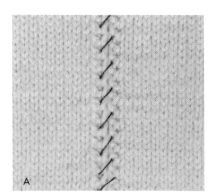

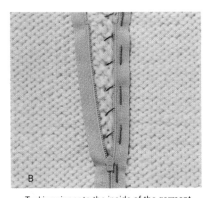

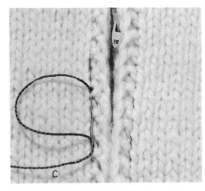

Garment edges tacked

Tacking zipper to the inside of the garment

Backstitching zipper to the garment

For a garment of heavy or tweedy yarn, a two-stitch selvage makes a neat and firm finish for the edge of the zipper opening.
To border the zipper opening, substitute a selvage for 2 stitches of the pattern. Double chain edge or double garter edge is suitable (see p. 440 for the methods). With large overcast stitches, tack the border edges together on the right side (A).
To attach zipper, tack it to wrong side of the garment, teeth aligned with centre of the opening (B). On the right side, sew zipper to garment with a backstitch, placing stitches along the line where border meets edge of the pattern stitch (C). Use a double strand of heavy-duty thread in a matching colour.

Adding tape

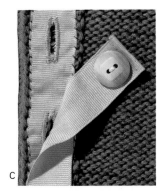

Twill tape added to a seam

Ribbon backing for buttonholes on a cardigan

Tape with buttons inserted in buttonholes

A seam can be taped when extra stability is needed, for example, on a jacket shoulder. Twill tape 12 mm wide is suitable.
To attach tape, centre it over the seam on one section; tack in place. Backstitch seam (A).
Buttonhole and button edges are often backed to prevent sagging; twill tape and petersham ribbon are suitable. Cut two pieces to fit; slipstitch one to edge on which buttons will be sewn; tack other to buttonhole edge and mark buttonhole placements. Remove tape; work buttonholes in it by machine or hand. Re-tack tape, aligning buttonholes; slipstitch edges (B). On right side, finish buttonholes.
Buttons can be sewn to tape to make a child's cardigan suitable for a girl or a boy. Work buttonholes on both sides of cardigan; button the tape onto whichever side is suitable (C).

Adjusting fit

Knit-in elastic knitted with the yarn

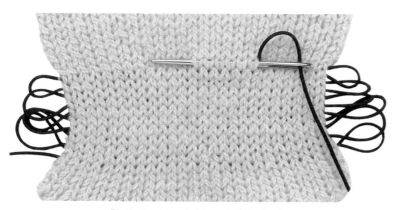

Elastic thread inserted through ribbing back

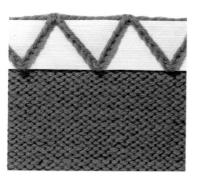

Elastic inserted through a casing stitch

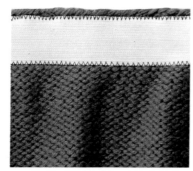

Elastic stitched with machine zigzag

ADDING ELASTIC

For a firmer fit when using yarns with little or no elasticity or to restore stretch to ribbing, the following methods are recommended.
Knit-in elastic is held together with the yarn and used as a double strand for the depth of the rib. It is available in a number of colours, but even when an exact match is impossible, it blends well with the yarn. In this photograph, a contrasting colour has been used to show the elastic clearly.
To restore elasticity use shirring elastic. Thread it through the ribbing using a knitter's needle. Insert it under the vertical knit ribs along each row on the wrong side.

For a close fit at the waist, draw elastic through casing stitch, or stitch it in place.
For casing stitch, use a crochet hook to form zigzag chain that is anchored to garment with slipstitches.
For stitched elastic, cut elastic to fit waist; join ends. With pins, divide elastic and waistline in eight sections; pin them together, matching divisions. With machine zigzag, stitch top and bottom edges of elastic, stretching to fit garment.

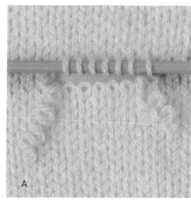

A

B

SHORTENING
OR LENGTHENING

If necessary, a garment can be shortened after it is finished by separating the unwanted length from the garment. This can be done, however, only with a simple pattern, such as stocking stitch or garter stitch. Before beginning, open the seams at least 10 cm past the cut-off point. Snip a yarn in the centre of the row and start to unpick stitch by stitch (A), placing the stitches of the garment section on a smaller needle than was originally used (B). Then re-knit a hem or border.

C

If necessary, a garment can be lengthened after it is finished by first removing the border as described above. Knit on the extra length and graft this to the remaining section of the garment (C).

Decorative finishes/embroidery

Embroidering a knit

Simple knitted patterns, such as garter, moss and stocking stitch, can be enhanced with embroidery.

Embroidery techniques that work well on knitted fabric are chain stitches, in particular lazy daisy; detached filling stitches, especially bullions; and raised needle-weaving, which permits the making of a solid motif without stretching the fabric. (See pp. 501–503). Basic cross stitch and its variations are also suitable, as a knitted structure lends itself to any counted thread technique.

Knitting stitch embroidery, also called Swiss darning or duplicate stitch, is another suitable embroidery form and one that is unique to knitting. It is a way of working over stocking stitches so that they are outlined precisely. Using this technique, you can work a jacquard pattern over plain fabric instead of working in the additional colour(s) as you knit.

Transfer of a design should not be attempted with hand-knitted fabric. It is helpful, however, to mark the area to be embroidered by tacking around it with contrasting yarn. If a design has several parts, you could mark each with a different colour. When working from graph paper, remember that knit stitches are wider than they are tall and adjust proportions, if necessary, making them taller and narrower to compensate for this widening. To preview results, use the charting method below, preferably using knitter's graph paper.

The most appropriate yarn for embroidering on a knit is one that matches the knitting yarn in type and thickness. If yarn is thinner, it tends to sink into the fabric; yarn that is thicker could stretch the knit. If you have no suitable yarn leftovers, buy small skeins of embroidery or canvas work yarns, such as crewel, tapestry, Persian, or embroidery cotton, and use the number of strands that matches the knitting yarn weight.

To start the embroidery, thread yarn in a knitter's needle (this type will not split the stitches) and bring it through from the wrong side, leaving an end long enough to weave into the back later. For the basic cross stitch or the knitting stitch, follow directions on this page; for other stitches, see the following pages. Take special care not to pull stitches too tight. After completion, a light steam blocking may be needed; do not press the embroidered area.

CROSS STITCHING ON STOCKING STITCH

KNITTING STITCH EMBROIDERY

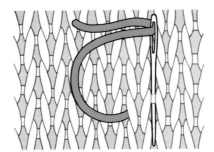

To form a basic cross stitch, bring needle up under a purl strand connecting 2 knit stitches; °cross right, take needle down behind the purl strand that lies between next 2 knit stitches.

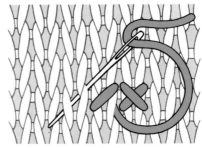

Cross left, insert needle above purl strand between the 2 stitches where thread emerges, then take it diagonally behind next knit stitch, and bring it out again under the next purl stitch°.

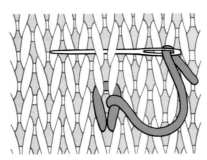

To work knitting stitch embroidery, °bring needle up under the connecting strand at the bottom of a knit stitch (where strands lie close together), then right to left behind knit stitch above.

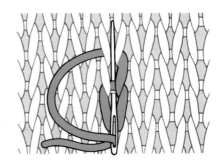

Insert needle bottom to top under same strand where thread emerges for first half of stitch.° As you work, take care to match tension of knitting, otherwise the fabric may pucker.

MAKING A CHART FOR EMBROIDERY

A charted embroidery design is usually represented on a graph in which one square equals one stitch. If you use such a chart to embroider a knit, the design will flatten out because knit stitches are always wider than they are tall. To be sure that a design will work on a knit fabric, you can first adapt it to a rectangular chart like the one shown below. These rectangles are 3 mm tall by 5 mm wide, and nearly duplicate the proportions of most knit stitches. Knitter's graph paper gives an even more precise image.

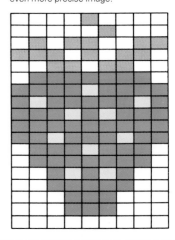

Embroidery stitches

Stem stitch is primarily an outlining stitch, but is often used to work stems in floral designs as well. Working from left to right, bring needle out at 1, insert at 2 and exit a half stitch length back at 3; distances 1–3 and 3–2 should be equal. Repeat sequence. Note that point 3 of previous stitch is now point 1, and the needle emerging at 3 is coming from hole at point 2 of the previous stitch. Keep thread below needle. For a broader stem stitch, angle the needle slightly when entering at 2 and exiting at 3 as in last drawing.

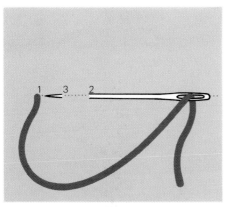

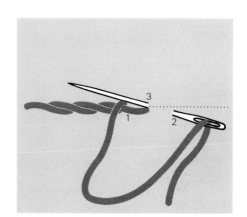

Chain stitch is one of the most popular embroidery stitches for outlining or, if worked in close rows, for filling an area. Bring needle out at 1. Insert back into same hole at point 1 and bring out at 2, carrying thread under needle point, then pull it through. Point 2 is now point 1 of next stitch. Work all stitches the same way, always inserting needle into the hole made by the emerging thread. To end row, take a small stitch over last chain loop to hold it down.

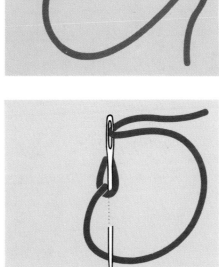
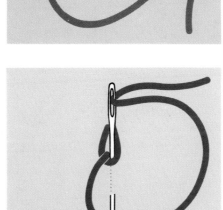
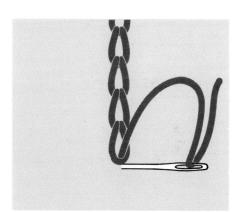

Lazy daisy stitch (or detached chain) is a single unattached stitch worked in a circle to give an impression of petals. Bring needle out at 1. Insert back into same hole at point 1, and exit at 2; carry thread under needle point, then pull through. Insert needle at 3 over chain loop, then bring needle out at point 1 for next chain stitch. Continue this way until all petals are completed. Stitches may be scattered at random over an area provided thread does not have to be carried too far on wrong side.

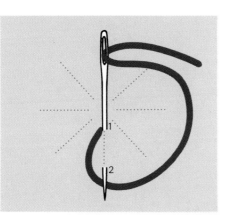
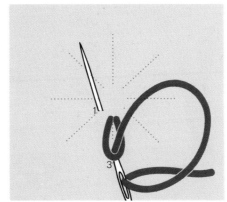
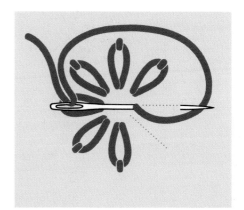

Embroidery stitches (continued)

Feathered chain stitch is a delicate border stitch that resembles a vine. It is worked between double lines. Starting at one side of double line, work a slanted chain stitch in the basic 1 to 2 sequence shown. Insert needle in the same slanting direction at 3, then bring it back up at 4, approximately across from 2. Work subsequent chain stitches the same way, keeping alternating slants of chains consistent on each side.

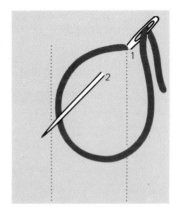 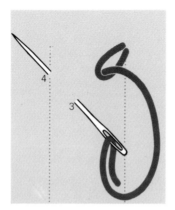  

Sheaf filling stitch resembles a tied bundle of wheat. Stitches can be arranged in alternate rows or set close together, one right below another. Bring needle out at 1. Oversew three stitches, following numbered sequence shown. Bring needle up at point 7, midway between 5 and 6. Pass needle around the stitch bundles twice without piercing fabric and pull thread taut. Insert needle under bundle and through fabric; secure stitch at back. For a different effect, work the tying stitches in a contrasting colour.

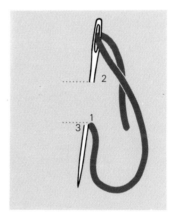 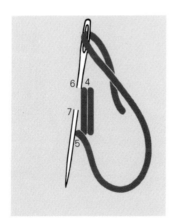  

Fly stitch is a single, looped stitch. When completed it resembles a 'Y'. It can be scattered about as a filling or lined up for a border. Bring needle up at 1. Insert at 2 directly across, then angle needle out at 3. Points 1, 2, and 3 should be equidistant. Carry the thread under the needle point and pull through. Complete stitch by inserting at 4 over loop. Work as many fly stitches as necessary to fill design area.

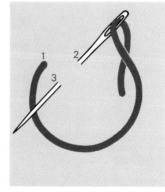 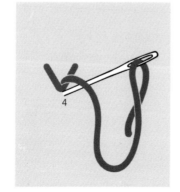  

Bullion knot can be used as a filling or as an outline stitch. Bring needle up at 1. Insert at 2 and exit at 1 again, but do not pull thread through. Twist thread around needle point five to seven times depending on length of stitch (distance from 1 to 2). Then carefully pull needle through both fabric and twists; take care not to distort twists. Pull thread towards point 2 so coil can lie flat. Pull working thread tight and use point of needle to pack threads in coil together evenly. Re-insert needle into point 2.

  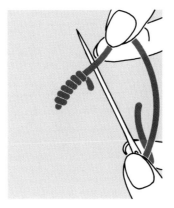 

French knot is a slightly textured and raised stitch. Knots can be worked close together to fill an area completely, producing a knobbly effect, or scattered. Bring needle up at 1. Holding thread taut with left hand, wrap thread around needle twice as shown; gently pull the thread so the twists are tightened against the needle. Carefully insert needle near point 1 and pull through; be sure thread is still held taut. Scatter knots as desired within design area. French knots can be made larger by increasing number of twists of thread around needle.

 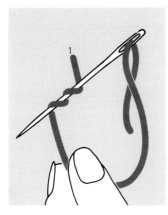 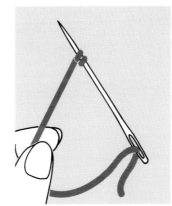 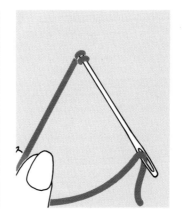 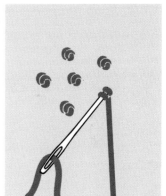

Making a tasselled fringe

The fringe shown here has ten strands of yarn in each group, but the technique is the same for any type.

Cut a piece of cardboard the length of the finished fringe, plus 2 to 3 centimetres. Wind yarn around cardboard as many times as necessary for one group, then cut through yarn at one end. With reverse side of work facing, use a crochet hook to draw folded end through one stitch in the edge of your project. Draw yarn ends through loop and pull to tighten.

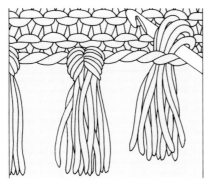

Draw folded end of yarn group into a stitch

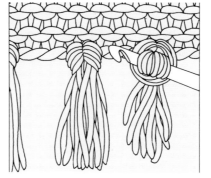

Draw the ends through the loop and tighten it

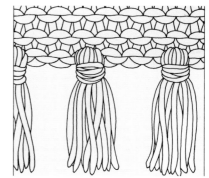

The fringe looks like this on the right side

Decorative finishes/crochet

Crochet

Crochet can be worked with a great variety of yarn types including most knitting yarns. The yarn should suit the purpose and be worked with an appropriate hook (refer to the chart on this page). Crochet can be used for many articles, but is included here to give you a range of edgings to work. Crochet buttons are also included as these can add an attractive highlight. The instructions for the basic stitches are described and illustrated with step-by-step diagrams.

Crochet terminology

There is a special vocabulary for written crochet instructions, much of it expressed in abbreviated or symbolic form. You may encounter slight variations of the terms given here, but these are in common use. Before using a crochet pattern, find out its country of origin, as American terms have different meanings.

ch	chain p.505
dc	double crochet p. 506
htr	half treble crochet p.506
tr	treble crochet p. 506
dtr	double treble crochet
tr tr	triple treble crochet
alt	alternate
beg	begin, beginning
dec	decrease
inc	increase
patt	pattern
rep	repeat
rnd	round
tog	together
sk	skip or miss
sl st	slipstitch p.504
sp	space
yrh	yarn round hook
° °	instructions between asterisks should be repeated as many times as there are stitches to accommodate them.
( )	a series of steps within parentheses should be worked according to instructions that follow the parentheses. Such a series is either worked into one stitch, or repeated a specified number of times.
[ ]	instructions within brackets explain the method for working a particular technique.

Slipstitch

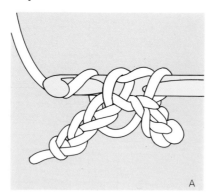

A

B

Slipstitch (sl st): A very short stitch used principally for joining, as in the closing of a ring or motif round, or the seaming of two finished pieces. Though not used to produce fabric, it is sometimes worked along an edge to strengthen it and to minimise stretching. Insert hook in chain (or stitch), catch yarn (A), draw a loop through both the chain and the loop on the hook (B).

BASIC CROCHET RULES

1. The chain on the hook is never counted as part of a foundation row. For example, if directions say chain 18, you should have 18 in addition to the one on the hook.
2. Always insert hook into a chain or stitch from front to back.°
3. Always insert hook under the two top loops of a chain or stitch.°
4. There should be just one loop left on the hook at completion of a stitch or sequence.

°unless directions say otherwise.

CROCHET HOOK SIZES

Metric	Old English	American
0.60 mm		14 steel
0.75 mm		12 steel
1.00 mm		10 steel
1.50 mm		6 steel
1.75 mm		5 steel
2.00 mm	14	B/1
2.50 mm	12	C/2
3.00 mm	10	D/3
3.50 mm	9	E/4
4.00 mm	8	F/5
4.50 mm	7	G/6
5.00 mm	6	H/8
5.50 mm	5	I/9
6.00 mm	4	J/10
6.50 mm	3	
7.00 mm	2	K/10½

TURNING CHAINS

At the beginning of each row (including the first one), a certain number of chains are needed to bring work up to the level that is to be formed. The exact number of chains depends on the height of the stitch (see below), and in the case of tall stitches—treble, double treble and so on—this chain usually replaces the first stitch of each row. When instructions place the turning chain at the end of a row, you should turn work right to left to avoid twisting the chain, then insert the hook in the stitch that is specified.

Double crochet	chain 1 to turn, insert hook in 1st stitch
Half treble crochet	chain 2 to turn, insert hook in 1st stitch
Treble crochet	chain 3 to turn, insert hook in 2nd stitch
Double treble crochet	chain 4 to turn, insert hook in 2nd stitch
Triple treble crochet	chain 5 to turn, insert hook in 2nd stitch
Quadruple treble crochet	chain 6 to turn, insert hook in 2nd stitch

Joining and securing yarns

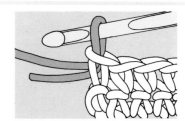

To join a new yarn at the end of a row, work last stitch with first yarn to final 2 loops; draw up last loop with new yarn.

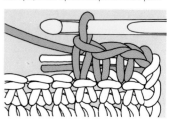

Cut first yarn to 5 cm. Make a chain; turn. Pull up 2 short yarns and lay over previous row; work over them for 4 or 5 stitches.

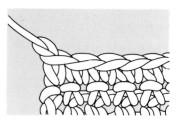

To secure yarn end on a finished piece, cut yarn to a 15 cm length; pull this end through the last loop and tighten it.

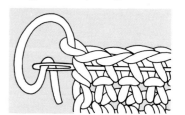

Thread yarn end into knitter's needle; weave into back of work for a few centimetres, below top row. Cut remainder.

Forming crochet stitches

All crochet stitches are formations of interlocking loops, the simplest of which is the chain stitch. The hook is held in one hand and yarn is tensioned in the other, while the hand holding the yarn also supports the work where the hook enters it.

Two common ways to hold a hook with the right hand are shown, right. Use whichever feels more comfortable. There are several methods of holding yarn; one popular technique is illustrated below. The idea is to keep yarn taut so that you can manipulate it easily and with even tension around the hook.

Holding the hook: right-handed method

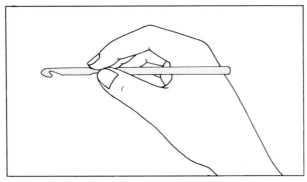

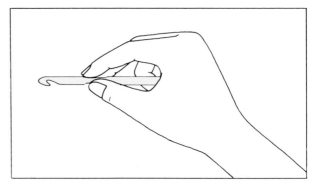

Method 1: With hook facing down, grasp it in the right hand, holding it as you would a pencil, with thumb and index finger on either side of the flat portion, middle finger resting against the thumb.

Method 2: With hook facing down, grasp it in the right hand, holding it almost as you would a knife, with thumb and index finger on either side of the flat portion, middle finger resting against the thumb.

Making the chain stitch: right-handed method

Chain stitch (ch st) is used to form the first row of crochet, and is an integral part of many pattern stitches as well. As the foundation, it should be formed fairly loosely, so that the hook can enter each chain easily, and the edge of the work will not draw in.

1. To start chain, make a slip knot about 15 cm from the yarn end; insert hook right to left.

2. Pulling both yarn ends, draw in the loop until it is close to hook, but not too tight.

3. Wrap ball end of yarn around the finger of left hand, take it under fourth and third fingers, then over top of index finger, leaving about 5 cm of yarn between finger and hook.

4. Holding the slip knot between thumb and middle finger of left hand, and keeping yarn taut over index finger, push hook forward, at the same time twisting it, so yarn passes over it back to front and is caught in the slot.

5. Draw yarn through the loop, thus forming a new loop on the hook. The newly formed loop should be fairly loose, so that the next chain can be drawn through it easily.

6. Holding chain nearest hook with thumb and middle finger, repeat Steps 4 and 5 until you have desired number of chains (loop on hook does not count as part of the total). All chains should be the same size. If they are not, it is best to pull them out and start again.

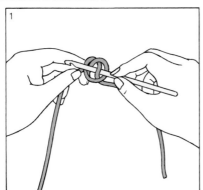

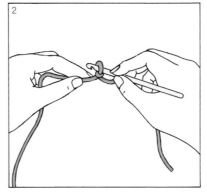

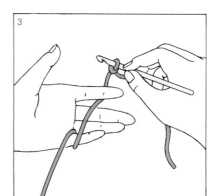

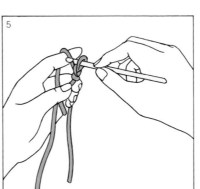

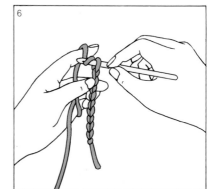

Forming the basic stitches

Double crochet (dc): Shortest of the basic stitches, it makes a firm, flat fabric. Often used to finish edges of other stitch patterns, and sometimes to join two finished sections.

Insert hook in 2nd chain from hook, catch yarn (A), and draw a loop through the chain (2 loops on hook), yarn round hook and draw through 2 loops to complete stitch (B). Make 1 double crochet in each chain across row. After last stitch, chain 1 and turn; insert hook in 1st stitch to start next row (C).

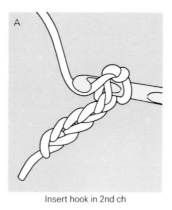

Insert hook in 2nd ch

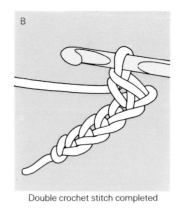

Double crochet stitch completed

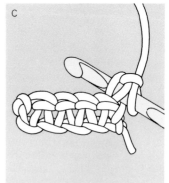

Ch 1 to turn, insert hook in 1st st

Half treble crochet (htr): Slightly taller than double crochet, this stitch has a pronounced ridge in its texture and makes a firm, attractive fabric.

Yarn round hook and insert hook in 3rd chain from hook, catch yarn (A), and draw a loop through the chain (3 loops on hook), yarn round hook and draw a loop through 3 loops to complete stitch (B). Make 1 half treble crochet in each chain across the row. After last stitch, chain 2 and turn; yarn round hook, insert hook in 1st stitch to start next row (C).

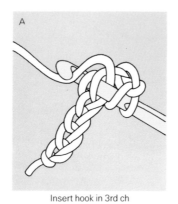

Insert hook in 3rd ch

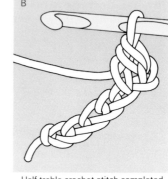

Half treble crochet stitch completed

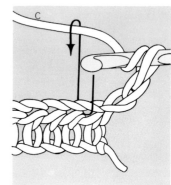

Ch 2 to turn, insert hook in 1st st

Treble crochet (tr): Twice as tall as double crochet and less compact. Forms the basis of many pattern stitches.

Yarn round hook and insert hook in 4th chain from hook, catch yarn (A), and draw a loop through the chain (3 loops on hook), yarn round hook and draw through 2 loops, yarn round hook and draw through last 2 loops to complete stitch (B). Make 1 treble crochet in each chain across the row. After last stitch, chain 3 and turn; yarn round hook, insert hook in 2nd stitch to start next row (C).

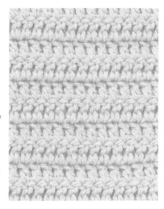

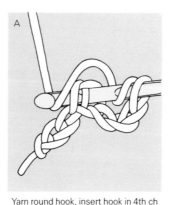

Yarn round hook, insert hook in 4th ch

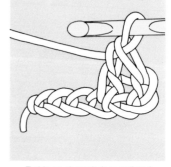

Treble crochet stitch completed

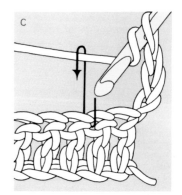

Ch 3 to turn, insert hook in 2nd st

Crocheted edgings

Crochet lends itself so naturally to use as a trim that pattern possibilities are nearly endless. Worked along the edge of crochet or knitting (see below), it serves to make an edge firm, give it a trim look and reinforce its shape with a distinctive outline. When applied to a garment, seams should be joined first and the edge stitch begun at one seam. Worked separately, a trimming can be crocheted horizontally or vertically and sewn to crocheted, knitted or woven fabrics. Any yarn is suitable as long as it is compatible with the fabric to which it is applied.

Double crochet edging: Use one to four rows for sleeveless armholes or a neckline, at least 2.5 cm for front or bottom edges of a garment.

Corded edging: A very firm and neat trimming.
Row 1: double crochet, working right to left.
Row 2: double crochet, working left to right.

Picot edging: Suitable for a child's dress.
One row: °1 sl st in each of next 2 sts, 1 dc in next st, ch 3, 1 dc in same st as last dc°.

Scalloped edging: Suitable for any lacy item.
One row: 1 sl st, °miss 2 sts, 5 tr in next st, miss 2 sts, 1 sl st in next st°.

Buttonholes

Buttonhole, double crochet:
At the beginning of buttonhole placement, make a number of chain stitches that will accommodate the diameter of the button (usually from 1 to 5). Skip the number of stitches for which you have chains, then continue in pattern (A).
Next row: Work over the buttonhole chain in double crochet, making the same number of stitches as there are chains (B).

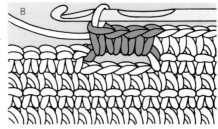

A 4-chain buttonhole completed

Double crochet stitches worked over buttonhole chain

Buttons

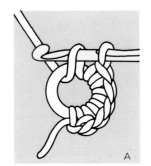

Ring button: Yarn is worked over a plastic ring 3 mm smaller than desired button size. To start, make a slip knot. Inserting hook through ring to form each st, work around it in dc (A) until ring is completely covered; sl st in first st to close; fasten off. Cut yarn, leaving 30 cm; thread the end in a knitter's needle. Make an overcast st in each outside loop (B), then pull stitches toward centre. Tie beginning and end strands together, then sew an 'X' across the button back for attaching it to the garment.

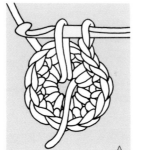
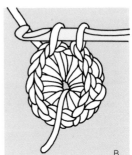

Ball button: Yarn is worked into a 3-dimensional motif; size and thickness depend on yarn weight. *Ch 3 and join in ring with sl st.* **Round 1:** ch 1, 8 dc in ring, sl st to beg ch. **Round 2:** ch 1, (1 dc in next st, 2 dc in next st) 4 times, sl st to beg ch; pull the short yarn end up through centre hole. **Round 3:** ch 1, (insert hook through centre hole, draw up a long loop (A), yrh, draw through 2 loops) 16 times, sl st to beg ch. **Round 4:** 1 dc in every other st (B); fasten off, overcast and finish off as for ring button.

507

Note that instead of the customary overall index covering the entire book, sewing and knitting have been indexed separately. The knitting index starts on page 515. Entries in bold type indicate that a section of the book is devoted to that subject.

Acknowledgments

A large number of individuals and firms, listed below, freely offered their help in the preparation of this book. The publishers wish to express their gratitude to them, and in particular they wish to acknowledge the close cooperation received from Bernina Australia Pty Ltd and Birch Haberdashery.

Aeroslide Fasteners Pty Ltd
Anne's Glory Box
Ascraft Fabrics
Australian Sewings Pty Ltd
Austral Swiss Knitting Pty Ltd
Debra Bauchop
Bernina Australia Pty Ltd
Birch Haberdashery
Birdsall (Leather) Co. Pty Ltd
Bradmill Industries Ltd
Brigdens Pty Ltd
Brother International (Aust.) Pty Ltd
Butterick Company Pty Ltd
Carnaby Dress Material
David Carroll
Monique Claesen
Coats Patons Crafts
Crawshaw Wilcox Pty Ltd
Curtrax Pty Ltd
Sandra Dauncey
Robin Doohan
Edtex Australia Pty Ltd
Elna Sewing Machine Pty Ltd
Freudenberg Pty Ltd
Grace Bros Pty Ltd
Greigs Fabrics
Greta's Handcraft Centre
H. & D. Leather
Hill Textiles
Home Yardage (NSW) Pty Ltd
Husqvarna Sewing Machines
Janome Sewing Machine Co.
  (Australia) Pty Ltd
Ray Joyce
Kirsch-Mello-Lite Drapery Hardware
Korbond Industries Pty Ltd
Laines Anny Blatt
Penny Lee
Lincraft Fabrics
McCalls Pattern Service Pty Ltd
N. Millings & Co Pty Ltd
Paul B. Nelson
Newey Brothers Pty Ltd
Pfaff Australia Pty Ltd
F.H. Price Pty Ltd
Quality Bargain Furnishing Fabrics
Quality Vogues
Rowan Australia Pty Ltd
School of Fabric Science and
  Technology, UNSW

Faye Scott
Selwyn Fabrics Pty Ltd
Anne Schultz
Betty Sinclair
Singer Australia Limited
Tissus Michels International Pty Ltd
Toni Warburton
XLN Fabrics

Revised edition

Publishing Coordinator
Barbara Beckett

Consultants
Rosemary King, Brenda Horne,
Sunny Bidner

Editors
Deborah Conyngham, Meryl Potter

Designers
Barbara Beckett, Amanda McPaul

Researchers
Joanna Collard, Jennifer Powell

Illustrators
Jan Düttmer, Jane O'Connell

Photographer
Ray Jarratt

Sewers and knitters
Diana Saxton, Robyn Potter,
Glennys Jarratt, Rebecca Chapman

Printed and bound by
Dai Nippon Co. Ltd, Hong Kong